KT-448-977

DIRECTORY OF PUBLISHING

2014

Reading Borough Council

3412600075036 7

BLOOMSBURY & THE PUBLISHERS ASSOCIATION

DIRECTORY OF PUBLISHING

2014

UNITED KINGDOM AND THE REPUBLIC OF IRELAND

Bloomsbury Academic

An imprint of Bloomsbury Publishing Plc

50 Bedford Square   1385 Broadway
London   New York
WC1B 3DP   NY 10018
UK   USA

www.bloomsbury.com

© Bloomsbury 2013

38th Edition 2013

All rights reserved. No part of this publication may be
reproduced or transmitted in any form or by any means,
electronic or mechanical, including photocopying, recording
or any information storage or retrieval system,
without prior permission in writing from the publishers.

No responsibility for loss caused to any individual or organization
acting on or refraining from action as a result of the material in this publication
can be accepted by Bloomsbury or the author.

British Library Cataloguing-in-Publication Data
A catalogue record for this book is available from the British Library

ISBN: PB: 978-1-4725-2191-0

Library of Congress Cataloguing-in-Publication Data
A catalogue record for this title is available from the Library of Congress

Editing by Peter B. J. Gill
Text processing and typesetting by John Ainslie Consultancy
Printed and bound in Great Britain

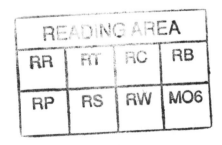

Contents

1 Introduction

FOREWORD

The 38th edition of the *Directory of Publishing*, now published by Bloomsbury in association with The Publishers Association, provides an indispensable guide to book publishing in the United Kingdom and Republic of Ireland and contains details of nearly 900 publishers. In addition to the detailed entries on publishers, the *Directory* offers in depth coverage of the wider UK book trade, and lists over 500 organizations associated with the industry, including packagers, distributors, library suppliers, authors' agents and translation services. An appendix analyses publishers by field of speciality. Indexes include ISBN prefix numbers; names of key personnel and publishers' imprints; and a listing of UK publishers by postcode.

The directory is updated annually. Previous entrants are sent last year's entry and new entrants a questionnaire. We are grateful to all those who have provided information for this edition. We have done all we can to ensure accuracy and completeness, but cannot accept responsibility for errors or omissions that escaped us. New entrants either approached the publisher or were discovered by monitoring various sources – the trade press, publishers' catalogues, exhibitions, book fairs, and the files of the Publishers Association itself.

As in the previous edition we have not excluded all organizations which have failed to reply to our mailings. Instead we have re-run their 2012 entries and marked them with an asterisk. However, such organizations will be deleted from the next edition if they fail to update their entries for the second year running.

Underlined entries are members of the Publishers Association.

We welcome all comments and suggestions from readers for improvements. We are also happy to receive details of possible new entries, but please note these must meet our criteria for inclusion. Publishers should either be a Publishers Association or Foilsiú Éireann member or be of a certain size, publishing at least 5 new titles a year or employing at least 4 people.

All organizations are entered free of charge.

Bloomsbury

HOW TO OBTAIN BRITISH BOOKS

This introduction is particularly intended for booksellers ordering from a British publisher for the first time.

HOW TO ORDER
1   If you have not previously ordered from a publisher, you should write for details on:
   trade discounts;
   credit facilities;
   catalogue mailing.
Please enclose in your letter information including:
   name and address of your bank;
   names and addresses of one or two publishers, preferably British, with whom you already do business. In certain circumstances you may be directed to a local stockist, agent or representative.

2   When the publisher agrees to supply you, your order should include:
   your full name and address;
   order date and order number;
   dispatch instructions: where you want the books to be sent and where you want the invoice sent;
   carriage instructions:
      surface post
      special carrier (e.g. shipper)
      air freight
   invoicing instructions:
      if you want a separate invoice by airmail
      minimum number of copies you require
   full details of the book:
      number of copies you need
      title
      author/editor
      cased/limp/paperback
      international standard book number (ISBN)

3   Orders Clearing, Mardev Ltd, Quadrant House, The Quadrant, Sutton, Surrey SM2 5AS (tel: +44 (0)20 8652 3899, fax: +44 (0)20 8652 4597, email: enquiries@mardev.com, web site: http://www.mardevlists.com) have an Orders Clearing system: by sending all your orders for different publishers to the one address, you can save yourself money. Similarly, Orders Clearing operates a service for the payment of publishers' accounts, the Overseas Booksellers' Clearing House (OBCH). Booksellers may send one cheque for various accounts and OBCH will then distribute the payments to the different publishers.

4   An Orders Clearing Service is also offered by the Booksellers Order Distribution Ltd (BOD). Their address is 49 Victoria Road, Aldershot, Hampshire GU11 1SJ (tel: +44 (0)1252 20697, fax: +44 (0)1252 20697).

5   Nielsen BookNet provides a range of e-commerce services that allow electronic trading between booksellers, distributors, publishers, libraries and other suppliers, regardless of their size and location. Services include BookNet for booksellers and publishers/distributors, TeleOrdering and EDI messaging. Contact Nielsen BookData, 3rd Floor, Midas House, 62 Goldsworth Road, Woking, GU21 6LQ (tel: +44 (0)870 777 8710, fax: +44 (0)870 777 8711, email: sales@nielsenbookdata.co.uk, website: http://www.bookdata.co.uk).

FOR REFERENCE
1   **Nielsen BookData:**
Provides monthly and quarterly content-rich book information for English-language titles published internationally. Available on CD-ROM and online by subscription from Nielsen BookData, 3rd Floor, Midas House, 62 Goldsworth Road, Woking, GU21 6LQ (tel: +44 (0)870 777 8710, fax: +44 (0)870 777 8711, email: sales@nielsenbookdata.co.uk, website: http://www.bookdata.co.uk).

2   **The Bookseller:**
The British book trade journal, published weekly by Bookseller Publications, containing correspondence, articles, trade news, together with a list of books published each week (web site: http://www.theBookseller.com). See also section 6.12 for details of other periodicals and reference books of the trade.

3   **British National Bibliography:**
A subject list of new British books arranged by Dewey classification. Published weekly with interim cumulations and an annual cumulation by the British Library, National Bibliographic Service, Boston Spa, Wetherby, West Yorkshire LS23 7BQ (tel: +44 (0)1937 546585, fax: +44 (0)1937 546586, email: nbs-info@bl.uk, web site: http://www.bl.uk).

4   Individual publishers will normally provide catalogues of their own publications on request.

HOW TO PAY
You can pay by:
   cheque, bank draft or letter of credit
   bill of exchange drawn by the publisher on your giro or postal account
   international money order/postal order

IMPORTANT
Please make sure that:
   the publisher receives the *full amount* of the invoice value, free of all bank charges and transfer fees;
   you pay *promptly*;
   if you have any problems, raise them *promptly*;
   if you have any difficulty in paying, consult your local bank manager, or the British Embassy, Consulate or High Commission.

WHEN YOU HAVE DIFFICULTY IN OBTAINING BRITISH BOOKS
1   If you have a problem of a *general* nature, please write to the Publishers Association, 29b Montague Street, London WC1B 5BH (email: mail@publishers.org.uk, tel: +44 (0)20 7691 9191, fax: +44 (0)20 7691 9199). The Association cannot intervene in problems which may arise between individual booksellers and publishers.

2   British Council
Your nearest office may be able to help you with enquiries about UK publishing. Details of its network of offices are available from: British Council Information Centre, tel: +44 (0)161 957 7755, fax: +44 (0) 161 957 7762, email: general.enquiries@britishcouncil.org, minicom: +44 (0)161 957 7188, web site: http://www.britishcouncil.org.

PUBLISHERS' ABBREVIATED ANSWERS
Most publishers use one of the answers below when books are not available, and give an explanation of their answer codes at the bottom of the invoice.

NK	Not known, not ours, or so far in the future or so long out of print that it is unknown to the trade department
OO/TF	On order, to follow shortly
B8 *or* **BDG8**	Binding, will be available in August
B/ND	Binding (no date)
RP/June *or* **RP/6**	Reprint available in June
RP/2M	Reprint available in 2 months
NYP	Not yet published
NEP	New edition in preparation
RPUC	Reprint under consideration
OP	Out of print
OO/USA	On order, to be supplied by USA
TOP	Temporarily out of print
OS	Out of stock
RP/ND	Reprinting, no date

TECHNICAL TERMS
Firm
Books are normally supplied 'firm'. This means you will accept the books, pay for them, and will not be able to return them.

See-safe or On approval
Some publishers are prepared to supply books on the basis that they are paid for at normal credit terms, but if the books remain unsold they may be returned with the publisher's authorization for crediting against future orders. You will be expected to return the books at your own expense. You should always obtain in writing details from publishers of any such agreements they are prepared to offer to their customers.

Standing Orders
Some publishers operate a scheme which allows a bookseller automatically to receive books in given subjects as they are published. These are normally supplied 'on approval'. You should write to individual publishers for details of their schemes.

Continuation Orders
Continuation Orders can be placed for books published in series and multi-volume works. This means that each new volume that appears will be sent to you automatically.

Pro-forma Invoice
Some publishers may prefer to supply initial orders by means of a pro-forma invoice which has to be paid before the books are sent.

THE PUBLISHERS ASSOCIATION

29b Montague Street, London WC1B 5BW
Telephone: +44 (0)20 7691 9191 **Fax:** +44 (0)20 7691 9199
Email: mail@publishers.org.uk
Web site: http://www.publishers.org.uk

Chief Executive: Richard Mollet
Director of Publisher Relations: Emma House

Making the case for UK publishers
– **The Publishers Association** is the leading organisation working on the behalf of book, journal and electronic publishers based in the UK. We bring publishers together to discuss the critical issues facing the industry and to define the practical policies, which will drive our lobbying and campaigns in the UK and internationally. The aim of The Publishers Association is to ensure a secure future for the UK publishing industry.
– **Acting for the Industry:** The PA's mission is to strengthen the trading environment for UK publishers by ensuring that the needs and concerns of the industry are heard at all levels of Government in the UK, in Europe and internationally. We are actively involved in issues such as: copyright legislation; the adaptation of legislation to digital technology; copyright licensing arrangements for education, business, and public bodies; legislation on VAT, e-commerce and other issues affecting publishers; funding for learning and information resources in schools, colleges and universities; the promotion of books and reading; export promotion of books and journals; anti-piracy campaigns (terrestrial and internet); efficiency in supply and marketing; the protection of freedom to publish.
– **Front Line Information:** PA posts front line information to our website and communicates with members through our regular e-mail bulletins. The Members Only section of the PA website contains detailed information prepared exclusively for members including: the latest market statistics, copyright law updates, comments on current government policy, PA briefs and reports on market concerns, anti-piracy action updates, digital rights information, and updates on EU legislation.

Home and Export Markets
Market development is at the heart of the PA's activities, which include:
– **International trade fairs**, operating with UK Trade & Investment a subsidy scheme for companies wishing to exhibit. Additionally, our TurnKey Exhibition Services offer publishers a complete exhibition service for major fairs.
– **Market intelligence**, including online access to the Global Publishing Information website (http://www.publishers.org.uk/gpi.nsf), and exclusive access to the Aid Digest.
– **Trade delegations and seminars** organised with UK Trade & Investment support, to gain knowledge of and exposure in growth markets such as China, Africa, Asia and Eastern Europe.
– **Home trade initiatives**, such as World Book Day, which result in a significant increase in sales, particularly of children's books, during the period of promotion.

Join the PA now – add your voice, have your say
As a PA member you can add your voice and have your say on the vital issues affecting our industry today. Membership is open to any company registered in the UK engaged in book, journal or electronic publishing as a bona fide and continuing operation. Subscription rates are based on turnover, with special introductory rates for new members and discounted rates for journal publishers.

The International Division
The International Division actively supports the international sales activities of PA members. We act against piracy, and on copyright and trade barrier issues, organise trade missions and UK representation at international trade fairs.

Trade Publishers Council
The Trade Publishers Council determines PA policy on consumer market matters, and acts on specific issues with the objectives of expanding the market and increasing efficiency. Other trade groups include our Children's Book Group, Christian Books Group and Digital Directors' Group.

Academic and Professional Division
The Academic and Professional Division provides a forum for higher education, monograph, journal and reference publishers. We represent publishers' concerns to key stakeholders, conduct market research and run a number of events.

The Educational Publishers Council
The Educational Publishers Council provides a voice for school and college publishers. We campaign for better funding for learning resources and represent the industry in the development of the electronic market, as well as running seminars and compiling market statistics.

2 Publishers

AA PUBLISHING
[trading as AA Media Ltd]
Fanum House, Basingstoke, Hants
RG21 4EA
Telephone: 01256 491578
Fax: 01256 322575
Email: AAPublish@TheAA.com
Website: www.theAA.com

Distribution (UK):
Littlehampton Book Services Ltd,
Faraday Close, Durrington, Worthing,
West Sussex BN13 3RB

Personnel:
D. Watchus (Head of AA Media)
S. Dyos (Sales & Marketing Director)
R. Hennessey (Production)
A. Neale (Finance)
L. Thompson (Human Resources)

Atlases & Maps; Guide Books; Natural
History; Photography; Transport; Travel &
Topography

Imprints, Series & ISBNs:
Automobile Association: 978-0-7495, 978-
0-86145
Travel Series: Citypacks: 978-0-7495
Travel Series: Essentials: 978-0-7495
Travel Series: Key Guides: 978-0-7495
Travel Series: Spiral Guides: 978-0-7495

ACAIR LTD
Unit 7, 7 James Street, Stornoway,
Isle of Lewis HS1 2QN
Telephone: 01851 703020
Fax: 01851 703294
Email: info@acairbooks.com
Website: www.acairbooks.com

Distribution:
BookSource, 50 Cambuslang Road,
Glasgow G32 8NB
Telephone: 0845 370 0067
Fax: 0845 370 0068

Personnel:
Agnes Rennie (Chief Executive)
Donalda Riddell (Office Manager)
Margaret Anne Macleod (Designer)

Children's Books; Educational & Textbooks;
Fiction; History & Antiquarian;
Photography; Poetry

Imprints, Series & ISBNs:
Acair Ltd: 978-0-86152

Book Trade Association Membership:
Publishing Scotland; Booksellers
Association

ACUMEN PUBLISHING LTD
4 Saddler Street, Durham DH1 3NP
Telephone: 0191 383 1889
Fax: 0191 386 2542
Email:
steven.gerrard@acumenpublishing.co.uk
Website: www.acumenpublishing.co.uk

**Warehouse, Trade Enquiries, Orders &
Distribution:**
Macmillan Distribution (MDL), Brunel Road,
Basingstoke RG21 6XS
Telephone: 01256 302692
Fax: 01256 812558
Email: orders@macmillan.co.uk
Website:
www.macmillandistribution.co.uk

Personnel:
Steven Gerrard (Publisher)
Kate Williams (Prepress Manager)
Tristan Palmer (Senior Editor)

Academic & Scholarly; Archaeology;
Biography & Autobiography; Educational &
Textbooks; History & Antiquarian;
Philosophy; Politics & World Affairs;
Reference Books, Directories &
Dictionaries; Religion & Theology; Sociology
& Anthropology

New Titles: 65 (2012) , 60 (2013)

Imprints, Series & ISBNs:
Acumen Publishing Ltd: 978-1-84465, 978-
1-902683

Overseas Representation:
Australia & New Zealand: Palgrave
  Macmillan, South Yarra, Vic, Australia
Austria, Germany & Switzerland: Frauke
  Feldmann, Berlin, Germany
Botswana, Lesotho, Namibia, South Africa,
  Swaziland & Zimbabwe: The African
  Moon Press, Kelvin, South Africa
Brunei, Cambodia, Indonesia, Laos,
  Philippines, Singapore, Thailand &
  Vietnam: APD Singapore Pte Ltd,
  Singapore
Canada: McGill-Queen's University Press,
  Montreal, PQ, Canada
China, Hong Kong & Taiwan: Ian Taylor
  Associates, Beijing, China
Eastern Europe: Laszlo Horvath, Budapest,
  Hungary
France, Italy, Portugal & Spain: Flavio
  Marcello Publishers' Agents &
  Consultants, Padua, Italy
Greece, Cyprus & Malta: Charles Gibbes
  Associates, Louslitges, France
India: Maya Publishers Pvt Ltd, New Delhi,
  India
Japan: Tim Burland, Tokyo, Japan
Middle East: Avicenna Ltd, Oxford, UK

Scandinavia: Colin Flint Ltd, Cambridge, UK
USA: ISD, Bristol, CT, USA

Book Trade Association Membership:
Independent Publishers Guild

*ADAM MATTHEW DIGITAL LTD
Pelham House, London Road,
Marlborough, Wiltshire SN8 2AG
Telephone: 01672 511921
Fax: 01672 511663
Email: david@amdigital.co.uk
Website: www.amdigital.co.uk

Personnel:
William Pidduck (Chairman)
David Tyler (Managing Director)
Khal Rudin (Sales & Marketing Director)

Academic & Scholarly; Electronic
(Educational); Electronic (Professional &
Academic); Gender Studies; History &
Antiquarian; Literature & Criticism; Military
& War

Associated Companies:
USA: Adam Matthew Education Inc.

Overseas Representation:
Italy: Licosa SPA, Florence, Italy
Japan: Maruzen Co Ltd, Tokyo, Japan
Korea: GDI, Seoul, Republic of Korea
Taiwan: Transmission Books & Microforms
  Co Ltd, Taipei, Taiwan

ADAMSON PUBLISHING LTD
8 The Moorings, Norwich NR3 3AX
Telephone: 01603 623336
Fax: 01603 624767
Email: stephen@adamsonbooks.com
Website: www.adamsonbooks.com

Personnel:
Stephen Adamson (Chairman)

Educational & Textbooks; Electronic
(Educational); Reference Books, Directories
& Dictionaries

New Titles: 5 (2012) , 3 (2013)
No of Employees: 1
Annual Turnover: £80,000

Imprints, Series & ISBNs:
Adamson Publishing Ltd: 978-0-948543

ADVANCE MATERIALS LTD
41 East Hatley, Sandy, Bedfordshire
SG19 3JA
Telephone: 01767 652140

Fax: 01767 652937
Email: office@advancematerials.co.uk
Website: www.advancematerials.co.uk

Orders:
Turpin Distribution Services, Pegasus Drive,
Stratton Business Park, Biggleswade
SG18 8TQ
Telephone: 01767 604951
Fax: 01767 601640
Email: custserv@turpin-distribution.com
Website: www.turpin-distribution.com

Personnel:
Mrs Jennifer Ollerenshaw (Director)
Dr Timothy Ollerenshaw (IT Manager)

Educational & Textbooks; Languages &
Linguistics

New Titles: 2 (2012) , 2 (2013)
No of Employees: 4

Imprints, Series & ISBNs:
Advance Materials: 978-0-9532440, 978-0-
  9547695, 978-0-9559265, 978-0-
  9565431, 978-0-9576012

Overseas Representation:
Australia & New Zealand: Foreign Language
  Bookshop Pty Ltd, Melbourne, Vic,
  Australia
North America: IB Source, Chicago, IL, USA

Book Trade Association Membership:
Independent Publishers Guild

AEON BOOKS
118 Finchley Road, London W5 4YX
Telephone: 020 7431 1075
Fax: 020 7435 9076
Email: trade@karnacbooks.com
Website: www.karnacbooks.com

Warehouse, Distribution:
Marston Book Services Ltd,
160 Eastern Avenue, Milton Park,
Abingdon, Oxon OX14 4SB
Telephone: 01235 465500
Fax: 01235 465555
Email: enquiries@marston.co.uk
Website: www.marston.co.uk

Personnel:
Oliver Rathbone (Managing Director)

Magic & the Occult

Imprints, Series & ISBNs:
Aeon Books: 978-1-904658

Overseas Representation:
USA: Stylus Publishing Inc, Sterling, VA, USA

Book Trade Association Membership:
Booksellers Association

2008

AIR-BRITAIN (HISTORIANS) LTD
41 Penshurst Road, Leigh, Tonbridge, Kent
TN11 8HL
Telephone: 01732 835637
Fax: 01732 835637
Email: mike@absales.demon.co.uk
Website: www.air-britain.com

Personnel:
Rod Simpson *(Chairman)*
Howard Nash *(Membership Sec)*
Michael Graham Rice *(Sales Director)*
Mark Simons *(Treasurer)*
Nigel Dingley *(Co Secretary)*
Dr Chris Chatfield *(Director)*

Aviation; Military & War

New Titles: 12 (2012) , 6 (2013)
No of Employees: 4
Annual Turnover: £400,000

Imprints, Series & ISBNs:
Air-Britain (Historians) Ltd: 978-0-85130

2009

ALANNA BOOKS
46 Chalvey Road East, Slough SL1 2LR
Email: info@alanna.demon.co.uk
Website: www.alannabooks.com

Personnel:
Ms Anna McQuinn *(Publisher)*

Children's Books

New Titles: 2 (2012) , 2 (2013)

Imprints, Series & ISBNs:
Alanna Books: 978-0-9551998, 978-1-
907825

2010

ALBAN BOOKS LTD
14 Belford Road, Edinburgh EH4 3BL
Telephone: 0131 226 2217
Fax: 0131 225 5999
Email: sales@albanbooks.com
Website: www.albanbooks.com

**Warehouse, Invoicing, Customer
 Services:**
c/o Marston Book Services Ltd,
160 Milton Park, Abingdon, Oxon
OX14 4SD
Telephone: 01235 465500
Fax: 01235 465555

Personnel:
Jonny Gallant *(Managing Director)*
Nigel Parkinson *(Sales Manager)*
Elaine Reid *(Marketing Manager)*
Margaret Reid *(Accounts & Special Orders)*
Nadia Suchdev *(Sales & Marketing
 Assistant)*

*Academic & Scholarly; Children's Books;
Educational & Textbooks; Fiction;
Philosophy; Reference Books, Directories &
Dictionaries; Religion & Theology*

Distributor for:
Australia: Mosaic Resources
USA: Ave Maria Press; Convivium Press;
 Wm B. Eerdmans Publishing Co;
 Hendrickson Publishers; Kregel
 Academic; Orbis Books

Book Trade Association Membership:
Publishing Scotland

2011

ALBYN PRESS
2 Caversham Street, Chelsea, London
SW3 4AH
Telephone: 020 7351 4995
Fax: 020 7351 4995
Email:
 leonard.holdsworth@btopenworld.com

Personnel:
James Hughes *(Editorial Director)*
Leonard Holdsworth *(Production)*
Margaret Fletcher *(Sales)*

*Fiction; Fine Art & Art History; Geography &
Geology; Guide Books; History &
Antiquarian; Illustrated & Fine Editions;
Literature & Criticism; Poetry; Reference
Books, Directories & Dictionaries; Transport*

Imprints, Series & ISBNs:
Albyn Press: 978-0-284

Parent Company:
UK: Christchurch Publishers Ltd

Associated Companies:
UK: Charles Skilton Publishing Group; Tallis
 Press

Book Trade Association Membership:
Independent Publishers Guild

2012

IAN ALLAN PUBLISHING LTD
Riverdene Business Park, Molesey Road,
Hersham, Surrey KT12 4RG
Telephone: 01932 266600
Fax: 01932 266601
Email: marketing@ianallanpublishing.co.uk
Website: www.ianallanpublishing.com

Trade Distribution:
Littlehampton Book Services,
Faraday Close, Durrington, Worthing,
West Sussex BN13 3RB
Telephone: 01903 828500 (trade orders)
Fax: 01903 828802
Email: orders@lbsltd.co.uk

Representation (UK, Wales & Ireland):
DJ Segrue, 1st Floor, 9 Church Road,
Stanmore, Middlesex HA7 4AR
Telephone: 020 8420 6548
Fax: 020 8420 6548
Email: davids@djsegrueltd.co.uk

Overseas Distributor :
DLS Australia, 12 Phoenix Court, Braeside,
Victoria 3195, Australia
Telephone: 03 9587 5044
Fax: 03 9587 5044
Email: tradesales@dlsbooks.com

Representation (Scotland):
Alan Scollan, Earnockmuir Cottage,
Meikle Earnock Road, Hamilton ML3 8RL
Telephone: 01698 459371

Overseas Distributor:
Bookmaster Distribution Services - Canada
and USA, 30 Amberwood Parkway, Ohio,
44805, USA, USA
Telephone: +1 419 281 5100
Fax: +1 419 281 6883
Email: orders@bookmasters.com

Personnel:
David Allan *(Chairman)*
Nick Lerwill *(Managing Director)*
Kevin Robertson *(Director of Publishing)*
Nick Grant *(Publisher)*
Nigel Passmore *(Sales Manager)*
Sue Frost *(Marketing Manager)*
Christobelle Krishnan *(Assistant Marketing
 Manager)*
Alan Butcher *(Production Manager)*

Atlases & Maps; Aviation; History &
*Antiquarian; Military & War; Nautical;
Reference Books, Directories &
Dictionaries; Sports & Games; Transport*

New Titles: 52 (2012) , 52 (2013)
No of Employees: 15

Imprints, Series & ISBNs:
Ian Allan: 978-0-7110
Classic Publications: 978-1-906537
Lewis Masonic : 978-0-85318
Midland Publishing: 978-1-85780
OPC: 978-0-86093

Parent Company:
UK: Ian Allan Group Ltd

Associated Companies:
UK: Key Publishing; The
 Railwaycentre.com

Distributor for:
UK: KRB (formerly Kestrel Railway Books);
 Millstream; Noodle Books; The
 Railwaycentre.com; Red Kite

Overseas Representation:
*Australia, New Zealand & Papua New
 Guinea:* DLS Australia (Pty) Ltd, Braeside,
 Vic, Australia
*Austria, Belgium, France, Germany,
 Netherlands & Switzerland:* European
 Marketing Services, London, UK
Canada & USA: Bookmasters Distribution
 Services, Ashland, Ohio, USA
Central & Eastern Europe: Tony Moggach,
 InterMedia Americana (IMA) Ltd,
 London, UK
Middle & Far East: Julian Ashton, Ashton
 International Marketing Services,
 Sevenoaks, Kent, UK
Scandinavia: Gill Angell & Stewart Siddall,
 Angell Eurosales, Berwick-upon-Tweed,
 UK
South Africa: Zytek Publishing (pty),
 Johannesburg, South Africa
*Spain, Portugal, Gibraltar, Italy, Malta,
 Greece, Slovenia, Croatia, Bosnia &
 Montenegro:* Bookport Associates,
 Corsico (MI), Italy
USA (Aviation titles only): Specialty Press,
 North Branch, MN, USA
USA (Masonic titles only): Atlas Books (a
 division of BookMasters Inc), Ashland,
 OH, USA
USA (Military titles only): Casemate
 Publishers & Book Distributors LLC,
 Havertown, PA, USA

Book Trade Association Membership:
Booksellers Association; Independent
Publishers Guild

2013

J. A. ALLEN
[an imprint of Robert Hale Ltd]
45–47 Clerkenwell Green, London
EC1R 0HT
Telephone: 020 7251 2661
Fax: 020 7490 4958
Email: allen@halebooks.com
Website: www.allenbooks.co.uk

Warehouse & Shipping:
Combined Book Services Ltd, Unit D,
Paddock Wood Distribution Centre,
Paddock Wood, Tonbridge, Kent TN12 6UU
Telephone: 01892 837171
Fax: 01892 837272
Email: orders@combook.co.uk

Personnel:
Lesley Gowers *(Publisher)*

*Animal Care & Breeding; Sports & Games;
Veterinary Science*

Imprints, Series & ISBNs:
J. A. Allen: 978-0-85131, 978-1-908809

Parent Company:
UK: Robert Hale Ltd

Overseas Representation:
See: Robert Hale Ltd, London, UK

2014

ALLISON & BUSBY
12 Fitzroy Mews, London W1T 6DW
Telephone: 020 7580 1080
Fax: 020 7580 1180
Email: susie@allisonandbusby.com
Website: www.allisonandbusby.com

Warehouse & Distribution:
Turnaround Publisher Services Ltd, Unit 3,
Olympia Trading Estate, Coburg Road,
London N22 6TZ
Telephone: 020 8829 3000
Fax: 020 8881 5088
Email: orders@turnaround-uk.com

Personnel:
Susie Dunlop *(Publishing Director & UK
 Sales)*
Chiara Priorelli *(Publicity & Online
 Marketing Manager)*
Lesley Crooks *(Sales & Digital Manager)*
Sara Magness *(Editorial Administrator)*
Christina Griffiths *(Art Editor)*
Sophie Robinson *(Publishing Assistant)*

*Biography & Autobiography; Children's
Books; Crime; Fiction; Humour; Science
Fiction*

Imprints, Series & ISBNs:
Allison & Busby: 978-0-7490, 978-0-85031

Parent Company:
Spain: Editorial Prensa Iberica SA

Overseas Representation:
Africa, Middle East & Gulf: InterMedia
 Americana (IMA) Ltd, London, UK
Australia: DLS, Australia
Canada: Georgetown Publications Inc,
 Toronto, Ont, Canada
France, Belgium & Netherlands: Michael
 Geoghegan, London, UK
Germany: Gabriele Kern Publishers Services,
 Frankfurt-am-Main, Germany
India: Maya Publishers Pvt Ltd, New Delhi,
 India
Italy: Ted Dougherty, London, UK
Scandinavia: Angell Eurosales, Berwick-on-
 Tweed, UK
*South & South East Europe, Eastern Europe
 & Egypt:* IMA, UK
Spain, Portugal & Malta: Peter Prout Iberian
 Book Services, Madrid, Spain
USA: International Publishers Marketing Inc,
 Sterling, VA, USA

Book Trade Association Membership:
Independent Publishers Guild

2015

ALMA BOOKS LTD
London House,
243–253 Lower Mortlake Road, Richmond,
Surrey TW9 2LL
Telephone: 020 8948 9550
Fax: 020 8948 5599
Email: info@almabooks.com
Website: www.almabooks.com

Personnel:
Alessandro Gallenzi *(Managing Director)*
Elisabetta Minervini *(Sales & Marketing
 Director)*

*Biography & Autobiography; Crime;
Fiction; Humour; Poetry*

Imprints, Series & ISBNs:
Alma Books Ltd: 978-1-84688
Alma Classics

Associated Companies:
UK: Herla Publishing

Overseas Representation:
Australia: Bloomsbury, Australia
South Africa: Jonathan Ball, South Africa
USA & Canada: Trafalgar Square Publishing / IPG, Chicago, IL, USA

Book Trade Association Membership:
Independent Publishers Guild

2016 ▬▬

ALMA CLASSICS
London House,
243–253 Lower Mortlake Road, Richmond, Surrey TW9 2LL
Telephone: 020 8948 9550
Fax: 020 8948 5599
Email: info@almabooks.com
Website: www.almaclassics.com

Personnel:
Alessandro Gallenzi *(Publishing Director)*
Elisabetta Minervini *(Associate Publisher)*

Fiction; Literature & Criticism; Poetry

Imprints, Series & ISBNs:
Alma Classics: 978-1-84749
Calder Publications: 978-0-7145

Associated Companies:
UK: Calder Publications Ltd

Overseas Representation:
Australia: Bloomsbury, Australia
South Africa: Jonathan Ball, South Africa
USA & Canada: Trafalgar Square Publishing / IPG, Chicago, IL, USA

Book Trade Association Membership:
Independent Publishers Guild

2017 ▬▬

ALPHA SCIENCE INTERNATIONAL LTD
7200 The Quorum,
Oxford Business Park North,
Garsington Road, Oxford OX4 2JZ
Telephone: 01865 481433
Email: alphascience@vsnl.net
Website: www.alphasci.com

Academic & Scholarly; Agriculture; Animal Care & Breeding; Biology & Zoology; Chemistry; Computer Science; Educational & Textbooks; Electronic (Educational); Electronic (Professional & Academic); Engineering; Environment & Development Studies; Industry, Business & Management; Mathematics & Statistics; Medical (incl. Self-Help & Alternative Medicine); Physics; Reference Books, Directories & Dictionaries; Scientific & Technical; Veterinary Science

Book Trade Association Membership:
Publishers Association; Independent Publishers Guild

2018 ▬▬

AMBER BOOKS LTD
74–77 White Lion Street, London N1 9PF
Telephone: 020 7520 7600
Email: enquiries@amberbooks.co.uk
Website: www.amberbooks.co.uk

Personnel:
Stasz Gnych *(Managing Director)*
Sara Ballard *(Rights Director)*
Peter Thompson *(Head of Production)*
Charles Catton *(Publishing Manager)*
Mark Batley *(Design Manager)*
Terry Forshaw *(Picture Manager)*

Atlases & Maps; Aviation; Children's Books; Crafts & Hobbies; Crime; Electronic

(Entertainment); Fashion & Costume; Health & Beauty; History & Antiquarian; Illustrated & Fine Editions; Military & War; Natural History; Nautical; Reference Books, Directories & Dictionaries; Sports & Games; Transport

Imprints, Series & ISBNs:
Amber Books Ltd: 978-1-78274, 978-1-904687, 978-1-905704, 978-1-906626, 978-1-907446, 978-1-908273, 978-1-909160

Book Trade Association Membership:
Book Packagers Association

2019 ▬▬

AMERICAN PSYCHIATRIC PUBLISHING
2 Lucas Bridge Business Park,
Old Greens Norton Road, Towcester NN12 8AX
Telephone: 01327 357770
Email: appi@oppuk.co.uk
Website: www.appi.org

Warehouse & Distribution:
NBN International, 10 Thornbury Road, Plymouth PL6 7PP
Telephone: 01752 202301
Fax: 01752 202331
Email: orders@nbninternational.com
Website: www.nbninternational.com

Personnel:
Gary Hall *(Manager)*

Academic & Scholarly; Educational & Textbooks; Medical (incl. Self-Help & Alternative Medicine); Psychology & Psychiatry; Reference Books, Directories & Dictionaries

Imprints, Series & ISBNs:
American Psychiatric Publishing Inc: 978-0-89042, 978-1-58562

Parent Company:
USA: American Psychiatric Publishing

2020 ▬▬

AMMONITE PRESS
166 High Street, Lewes. BN7 1XU
Telephone: 01273 488006
Fax: 01273 472418
Email: richard.wiles@ammonitepress.com
Website: www.ammonitepress.com

Personnel:
Richard Wiles *(Managing Editor)*
Jonathan Phillips *(Joint Managing Director)*
Ms Jennifer Phillips *(Joint Managing Director)*

Humour; Photography; Reference Books, Directories & Dictionaries

New Titles: 35 (2012), 23 (2013)

Associated Companies:
UK: Guild of Master Craftsmen Publications

Overseas Representation:
Australia: Capricorn Link, Windsor, Australia
UK: GMC Distribution, Lewes, UK

2021 ▬▬

AMS EDUCATIONAL
Unit 2, Aston Way, Middlewich CW10 0HS
Telephone: 01606 836699
Email: sales@amseducational.co.uk
Website: www.amseducational.com

Personnel:
Paul Uttley *(Contact)*

Educational & Textbooks

Imprints, Series & ISBNs:
AMS Educational: 978-1-86029
Educational Fun Factory: 978-1-86029
Falconwood Series: 978-1-900899
Leopard Learning: 978-1-899929
New Education Press (N.E.P.): 978-0-946947
Propagator Press: 978-1-86029
Senter Series: 978-1-902751

Book Trade Association Membership:
Independent Publishers Guild

2022 ▬▬

ANDERSEN PRESS LTD
20 Vauxhall Bridge Road, London SW1V 2SA
Telephone: 020 7840 8701
Fax: 020 7233 6263
Email: andersenpublicity@randomhouse.co.uk
Website: www.andersenpress.co.uk

Warehouse, Orders & Payments:
TBS Ltd, Colchester Road, Frating Green, Colchester, Essex CO7 7DW
Telephone: 01206 255678
Fax: 01206 255930

Address for Returns Requests:
Sales Department,
Random House Children's Books,
61–63 Uxbridge Road, London W5 5SA
Telephone: 020 8231 6800
Fax: 020 8231 6767

Personnel:
Klaus Flugge *(Managing Director & Publisher)*
Mark Hendle *(Company Secretary)*
Sarah Pakenham *(Rights & Permissions)*
Rona Selby *(Editorial Director, Picture Books)*
Charlie Sheppard *(Editorial Director, Fiction)*
Eve Warlow *(Publicity & Marketing)*

Children's Books

Imprints, Series & ISBNs:
Andersen Press: 978-0-86264, 978-0-905478, 978-1-78344, 978-1-84270, 978-1-84939

Associated Companies:
UK: Random House

Overseas Representation:
Other overseas markets – see: Random House Group Ltd, London, UK
USA: Lerner Publishing Group, USA; Trafalgar House, USA

2023 ▬▬

CHRIS ANDREWS PUBLICATIONS LTD
15 Curtis Yard, North Hinksey Lane, Oxford OX2 0LX
Telephone: 01865 723404
Fax: 01865 725294
Email: chris.andrews1@btclick.com
Website: www.cap-ox.co.uk

Personnel:
Chris Andrews *(Director)*
Virginia Andrews *(Director)*
Annabel Matthews *(Personal Assistant)*

Travel & Topography

New Titles: 20 (2012), 25 (2013)
No of Employees: 3

Imprints, Series & ISBNs:
Chris Andrews Publications Ltd: 978-0-9509643, 978-0-9540331, 978-1-905385, 978-1-906725, 978-1-909759

Book Trade Association Membership:
Independent Publishers Guild

2024 ▬▬

ANGLO-SAXON BOOKS
Hereward, 11 Black Bank Road,
Little Downham, Ely, Cambs CB6 2UA
Telephone: 07576 452901
Email: tony@asbooks.co.uk
Website: www.asbooks.co.uk

Personnel:
Tony Linsell *(Contact)*

Academic & Scholarly; Educational & Textbooks; History & Antiquarian; Languages & Linguistics; Magic & the Occult; Military & War; Poetry; Reference Books, Directories & Dictionaries

New Titles: 3 (2012), 3 (2013)

Imprints, Series & ISBNs:
Anglo-Saxon Books: 978-1-898281, 978-1-903313
Athelney: 978-1-903313

Overseas Representation:
USA & Canada: The David Brown Book Co, Oakville, CT, USA

2025 ▬▬

ANSHAN LTD
6 Newlands Road, Tunbridge Wells, Kent TN4 9AT
Telephone: 01892 557767
Fax: 01892 530358
Email: info@anshan.co.uk
Website: www.anshan.co.uk

Warehouse:
CBS, Unit D,
Paddock Wood Distribution Centre,
Paddock Wood, Tonbridge, Kent TN12 6UU
Telephone: 01892 837171
Fax: 01892 837272
Email: orders@combook.co.uk
Website: www.combook.co.uk

Representation (UK):
Quantum Publishing Solutions Ltd,
2 Cheviot Road, Paisley PA2 8AN

Personnel:
Shân White *(Managing Director)*
Andrew White *(Sales Director)*

Academic & Scholarly; Biography & Autobiography; Chemistry; Computer Science; Educational & Textbooks; Engineering; Environment & Development Studies; Health & Beauty; Mathematics & Statistics; Medical (incl. Self-Help & Alternative Medicine); Physics; Psychology & Psychiatry; Reference Books, Directories & Dictionaries; Scientific & Technical

Imprints, Series & ISBNs:
Anshan Ltd: 978-1-848290, 978-1-904798, 978-1-905740

Overseas Representation:
Australia & New Zealand: Contact Anshan Direct, UK
Central Europe & Ireland: Contact Anshan Direct, UK
China: China Publishers Services Ltd, Hong Kong
Greece & Eastern Europe: Philip Tyers, UK
Japan (Medical titles): Nankodo Co Ltd, Tokyo, Japan
Japan (Science titles): United Publishers Services Ltd, Tokyo, Japan
Scandinavia: Colin Flint Ltd, Harlow, UK
Taiwan: Unifacmanu Trading Co Ltd, Taipei, Taiwan
USA: Princeton Selling Group Inc, Wayne, PA, USA

2026

ANTHEM PRESS
[an imprint of Wimbledon Publishing Company]
75–76 Blackfriars Road, London SE1 8HA
Telephone: 020 7401 4200
Fax: 020 7401 4225
Email: info@wpcpress.com
Website: www.anthempress.com

Personnel:
Tej Sood (Managing Director)

Academic & Scholarly; Atlases & Maps; Chemistry; Cinema, Video, TV & Radio; Economics; Educational & Textbooks; Electronic (Educational); Electronic (Professional & Academic); Engineering; Environment & Development Studies; Gender Studies; Geography & Geology; Industry, Business & Management; Law; Literature & Criticism; Mathematics & Statistics; Medical (incl. Self-Help & Alternative Medicine); Philosophy; Physics; Poetry; Politics & World Affairs; Reference Books, Directories & Dictionaries; Scientific & Technical; Sociology & Anthropology

Imprints, Series & ISBNs:
Anthem Press: 978-1-84331, 978-1-898855
Anthem Press India: 978-81-905835, 978-81-907570
Wimbledon Publishing Co: 978-1-84331

Book Trade Association Membership:
Publishers Association; Independent Publishers Guild

2027

ANTIQUE COLLECTORS' CLUB LTD
Sandy Lane, Old Martlesham, Woodbridge, Suffolk IP12 4SD
Telephone: 01394 389950
Fax: 01394 389999
Email: sales@antique-acc.com
Website: www.accdistribution.com

Personnel:
Diana Steel (Managing Director)
Sarah Smye (Marketing Director)
Vanessa Shorten (Financial Director)
James Smith (Sales Director)
Marco Jellinek (Business Development Director)
John Brancati (General Manager, USA)

Antiques & Collecting; Architecture & Design; Children's Books; Cookery, Wines & Spirits; Fashion & Costume; Fine Art & Art History; Gardening; Humour; Natural History; Photography; Reference Books, Directories & Dictionaries; Travel & Topography

Imprints, Series & ISBNs:
ACC Editions
Antique Collectors' Club Ltd: 978-0-902028, 978-0-907462, 978-1-85149, 978-1-870673
Garden Art Press

Distributor for:
France: Editions du Chene
Germany: Arnoldsche Verlagsanstalt; Benteli Verlag; Edition Lammerhuber; Scheidegger & Spiess
Italy: 24 Ore Cultura (Motta); Umberto Allemandi; Arsenale Editrice; Centro Di; Congedo Editore; Gambero Rosso
Netherlands: Stichting Kunstboek; Waanders
UK: Acanthus Press; ACR Edition; Art Power; Artmedia Press; Ashmolean Museum Publications; The Azur Corporation Ltd; Bauer & Dean Publishers; Beta Plus; George Braziller; Cannibal/Hannibal; Delius Klasing; Giles; Glitterati Incorporated; Hudson Hills

Press; Images; Lannoo Publishers; Luster; Park Books; PI Global; River Books; Roli Books; Scala; Vivays Publishing

Overseas Representation:
All other territories: Antique Collectors' Club, Woodbridge, Suffolk, UK
Australia: Peribo Pty Ltd, Mount Kuring-Gai, NSW, Australia
Czech Reblic, Slovak Republic, Hungary, Estonia, Latvia, Lithuania: Ewa Ledochowicz, PO Box 8, 05-520 Konstancin, Poland
Far East (including Hong Kong, Taiwan, Philippines & China): Asia Publishers Services Ltd, Hong Kong
France: Interart SARL, Paris, UK
Germany, Austria & Switzerland: Michael Klein, Vilsbiburg, Germany
Holland, Belgium and Luxembourg: Fred Hermans, Academic Book Promotions, Bovenkarspel, Netherlands
India: Roli Books, New Delhi, India
Iran: Vijeh-Nashr Co, Intl. Journals & Books Services, Tehran, Iran
Italy, Spain, Portugal & Greece: Penny Padovani, London, UK
Japan & South Korea: Ralph & Sheila Summers, Woodford Green, Essex, UK
Malaysia: APD Kuala Lumpur Pte Ltd, Selangor, Malaysia
Near & Middle East & Turkey: Avicenna Partnership, Dumfries, UK
New Zealand: Book Reps NZ Ltd, Auckland, New Zealand
Republic of Ireland & Northern Ireland: Robert Towers, Monkstown, Co Dublin, Republic of Ireland
Scandinavia & Iceland: Elisabeth Harder-Kreimann, Hamburg, Germany
South & Central America, Caribbean & Mexico: InterMedia Americana (IMA) Ltd, London, UK
South East Asia (including Singapore, Thailand, Vietnam, Cambodia, Indonesia & Brunei): APD Singapore Pte Ltd, Singapore
USA: Antique Collectors Club, New York, NY, USA
West, Central & East Africa (excluding Sudan): InterMedia Africa Ltd (IMA), London, UK

Book Trade Association Membership:
Independent Publishers Guild

2028

ANVIL PRESS POETRY LTD
Neptune House, 70 Royal Hill, London SE10 8RF
Telephone: 020 8469 3033
Email: anvil@anvilpresspoetry.com
Website: www.anvilpresspoetry.com

Distribution:
NBN International, Thornbury Road, Plymouth, Devon PL6 7PP
Telephone: 01752 20230
Fax: 01752 202333
Email: orders@nbninternational.com
Website: www.nbninternational.com

Personnel:
Peter Jay (Managing Director: Editorial & Production)
Kit Yee Wong (Rights & Administrative Manager)

Poetry

Imprints, Series & ISBNs:
Anvil Editions: 978-0-85646, 978-0-900977
Poetica: 978-0-85646, 978-0-900977

Overseas Representation:
Australia: Eleanor Brasch Enterprises, Artarmon, NSW, Australia

Eastern Europe, Greece & Israel: Tony Moggach, InterMedia Americana (IMA) Ltd, London, UK
France, Benelux, Germany, Austria & Switzerland: Ted Dougherty, London, UK
Republic of Ireland: Robert Towers, Monkstown, Co Dublin, Republic of Ireland
Spain: Peter Prout Iberian Book Services, Madrid, Spain
USA: Consortium Book Sales & Distribution Inc, Minneapolis, MN, USA

Book Trade Association Membership:
Independent Publishers Guild

2029

APPLETREE PRESS LTD
Roycroft House, 164 Malone Road, Belfast BT9 5LL
Telephone: 028 9024 3074
Fax: 028 9024 6756
Email: reception@appletree.ie
Website: www.appletree.ie

Distribution:
Gill and Macmillan, Republic of Ireland
Telephone: +353 (0)1 500 9500
Fax: +353 (0)1 500 9599
Email: sales@gillmacmillan.ie
Website: www.gillmacmillan.ie

Personnel:
John Murphy (Managing Director)
Jean Brown (Editor)
Paul McAvoy (Production Manager)
Mark Elliott (Sales Manager)

Cookery, Wines & Spirits; Guide Books; History & Antiquarian; Humour; Reference Books, Directories & Dictionaries; Sports & Games; Travel & Topography

Imprints, Series & ISBNs:
Appletree Press Ltd: 978-0-86281, 978-0-904651

Overseas Representation:
Australia & New Zealand: Peribo Pty Ltd, Mount Kuring-Gai, NSW, Australia
France, Belgium, Scandinavia, Germany, Austria, Switzerland & Spain: Appletree Press, Belfast, UK
Greece, Cyprus, Israel, Russia, Eastern Europe & the Baltic States: IMA, Greece
Italy: Penguin Italia srl, Milan, Italy
Netherlands: Novelty Books, Weesp, Netherlands
Republic of Ireland: Compass Independent Book Sales Ltd, Naas, Co Kildare, Republic of Ireland
USA & Canada: Independent Publishers Group (IPG), Chicago, IL, USA

Book Trade Association Membership:
Publishing Ireland (Foilsiú Éireann)

2030

ARCADIA BOOKS LTD
139 Highlever Road, London W10 6PH
Telephone: 020 8960 4967
Email: gary@arcadiabooks.co.uk
Website: www.arcadiabooks.co.uk

Distribution:
MDL Brunel Road, Houndmills, Basingstoke, Hants RG21 6XS
Telephone: 01256 329242
Fax: 01256 812558
Email: mdlqueries@macmillan.co.uk
Website: www.macmillandistribution.co.uk

EBook Sales:
Faber Factory, Bloomsbury House, 74–77 Great Russell Street, London WC1B 3DA
Telephone: 020 7927 3913
Email: factory@faber.co.uk
Website: faberfactory.co.uk

Book Sales:
Faber Factory, Bloomsbury House, 74–77 Great Russell Street, London WC1B 3DA
Telephone: 020 7927 3809
Email: bridgetlj@faber.co.uk
Website: faberfactory.co.uk/faber-factory-plus/

Personnel:
Piers Russell-Cobb (Director)
Gary Pulsifer (Publisher)
Karen Sullivan (Managing Editor)
Colin Midson (PR)
Diana Medesan (Executive Assistant)

Biography & Autobiography; Crime; Fiction; Gay & Lesbian Studies; Gender Studies; Photography; Politics & World Affairs; Travel & Topography

New Titles: 24 (2013)
No of Employees: 5

Imprints, Series & ISBNs:
Arcadia Books Ltd: 978-1-909807
EuroCrime

Overseas Representation:
Australia/New Zealand: NewSouth Books, University of New South Wales, Sydney, NSW, Australia
Europe: Anne Bowman, Faber Factory Plus, London, UK
Israel (selected titles only): Steimatzky Ltd, Bnei Brak, Israel
North America: Dufour Editions, Chester Springs, PA, USA
South Africa: Jacana Media (Pty) Ltd, Johannesburg , South Africa

Book Trade Association Membership:
Independent Publishers Guild; English PEN; BTBS (The Book Trade Charity)

2031

ARCHAEOPRESS LTD
Gordon House, 276 Banbury Road, Oxford OX2 7ED
Telephone: 01865 311914
Fax: 01865 512231
Email: bar@archaeopress.com
Website: www.archaeopress.com

Personnel:
Dr David Davison (Director)
Dr Rajka Makjanic (Director)

Archaeology

Imprints, Series & ISBNs:
Archaeopress: 978-1-905739
British Archaeological Reports: 978-1-4073

Overseas Representation:
Worldwide: Hadrian Books Ltd, Oxford, UK

2032

ARCHITECTURAL ASSOCIATION PUBLICATIONS
36 Bedford Square, London WC1B 3ES
Telephone: 020 7887 4021
Fax: 020 7414 0783
Email: publications@aaschool.ac.uk
Website: www.aaschool.ac.uk

Personnel:
Marilyn Sparrow (Sales & Marketing Manager)
Kirsten Morphet (Publications Co-ordinator)
Pamela Johnston (Editor)
Thomas Weaver (Editor)

Architecture & Design

Imprints, Series & ISBNs:
Architectural Association: 978-1-870890, 978-1-902902, 978-1-907414, 978-1-907896
Bedford Press: 978-1-907414

Parent Company:
UK: Architectural Association Inc

Overseas Representation:
Australia: Perimeter Distribution, Thornbury, Vic., Australia
France: Christophe Pourcines, Paris, France
Germany & Austria: Kurt Salchli, Berlin, Germany
Scandinavia: Elisabeth Harder-Kreimann, Germany
Southern Europe: Bookport Associates, Milan, Italy

Book Trade Association Membership:
Publishers Association

2033 ■

ARCHIVE PUBLISHING
West Barn, Wimborne Road, Blandford, Dorset DH11 9HN
Telephone: 01258 450404
Email: orders@archivepublishing.co.uk
Website: www.transpersonalbooks.com

Personnel:
Ian Thorp *(Publisher)*

Children's Books; Fiction; Magic & the Occult; Medical (incl. Self-Help & Alternative Medicine); Music; Psychology & Psychiatry

New Titles: 4 (2012) , 2 (2013)
No of Employees: 1

Imprints, Series & ISBNs:
Archive Publishing: 978-0-9542712, 978-1-906289
Talking Stick

Book Trade Association Membership:
Booksellers Association; Independent Publishers Guild

2034 ■

ARENA BOOKS (PUBLISHERS)
6 Southgate Green, Bury St Edmunds, Suffolk IP33 2BL
Telephone: 01284 754123
Fax: 01284 754123
Email: arenabooks@tiscali.co.uk
Website: www.arenabooks.co.uk

Personnel:
James Farrell *(Managing Director)*
Robert Corfe *(Director)*
Russell Corfe *(Editor)*
June Hardy *(Sales Manager)*

Academic & Scholarly; Biography & Autobiography; Cinema, Video, TV & Radio; Economics; Environment & Development Studies; Fashion & Costume; Fiction; Fine Art & Art History; History & Antiquarian; Industry, Business & Management; Literature & Criticism; Military & War; Philosophy; Politics & World Affairs; Religion & Theology; Science Fiction; Sociology & Anthropology; Travel & Topography

Imprints, Series & ISBNs:
Arena Books (Publishers): 978-0-9538460, 978-0-9543161, 978-0-9556055, 978-1-906791, 978-1-909421

Overseas Representation:
Egypt: Abdul Radder Al-Bakkar, Cairo, Egypt
Poland: Graal Sp, Warsaw, Poland
USA: Ingram Publisher Services, La Vergne, TN, USA

Book Trade Association Membership:
Independent Publishers Guild

2035 ■

THE ARMCHAIR TRAVELLER AT THE BOOKHAUS LTD
70 Cadogan Place, London SW1X 9AH
Telephone: 020 7838 9055
Email: info@hauspublishing.com
Website: www.thearmchairtraveller.com

Personnel:
Dr Barbara Schwepcke *(Publisher)*
Mrs Ilse Schwepcke *(Commissioning Editor)*

Archaeology; Guide Books; Travel & Topography

New Titles: 15 (2012) , 15 (2013)

Associated Companies:
UK: Haus Publishing

Book Trade Association Membership:
Independent Publishers Guild

2036 ■

ASHGATE PUBLISHING LTD
Wey Court East, Union Road, Farnham, Surrey GU9 7PT
Telephone: 01252 736600
Fax: 01252 736736
Email: info@ashgatepublishing.com
Website: www.ashgate.com

Warehouse & Mailing Shop, Orders:
Ashgate Publishing Direct Sales, Bookpoint Ltd, 39 Milton Park, Abingdon, Oxon OX14 4TD
Telephone: 01235 400400
Fax: 01235 400454

Personnel:
Nigel Farrow *(Chairman)*
Dymphna Evans *(Social Sciences Publishing Director)*
Rachel Lynch *(Managing Director)*
Jonathan Norman *(Publisher: Business (Gower))*
Lucy Myers *(Managing Director – Lund Humphries)*
Darren Wise *(Finance/Accounting Director)*
Anne Nolan *(Editorial & Production Director)*
Adrian Shanks *(International Marketing & Digital Publishing Director)*
Richard Dowling *(Sales Director)*
Jo Burges *(Systems Director)*

Academic & Scholarly; Architecture & Design; Aviation; Bibliography & Library Science; Economics; Educational & Textbooks; Electronic (Professional & Academic); Environment & Development Studies; Fine Art & Art History; Gender Studies; Geography & Geology; History & Antiquarian; Illustrated & Fine Editions; Industry, Business & Management; Law; Literature & Criticism; Military & War; Music; Philosophy; Politics & World Affairs; Reference Books, Directories & Dictionaries; Religion & Theology; Sociology & Anthropology; Theatre, Drama & Dance; Transport

Imprints, Series & ISBNs:
Arena: 978-1-85742
Ashgate Publishing: 978-0-7546, 978-1-84014
Avebury: 978-0-291, 978-1-85628, 978-1-85972
Dartmouth: 978-1-85521
Gower Publishing: 978-0-566, 978-1-85904
Gregg International: 978-0-576
Gregg Revivals: 978-0-7512
Lund Humphries: 978-0-85331
Scolar Press: 978-0-85967, 978-1-85928
Variorum: 978-0-86078
Wildwood House: 978-0-7045

Parent Company:
UK: Ashgate Publishing Group

Associated Companies:
UK: Gower Publishing Co Ltd; Lund Humphries; Scolar Fine Art Ltd
USA: Ashgate Publishing Co

Overseas Representation:
Australia, South East Asia, Malaysia, Philippines, China, Hong Kong, Taiwan, Myanmar (Burma) & South Korea: Ashgate Publishing Asia-Pacific, Newport, NSW, Australia
India: Maya Publishers Pvt Ltd, New Delhi, India
Japan: United Publishers Services Ltd, Tokyo, Japan
USA: Ashgate Publishing Co, Burlington, VT, USA

Book Trade Association Membership:
Independent Publishers Guild

2037 ■

ASHGROVE PUBLISHING
27 John Street, London WC1N 2BX
Telephone: 020 7242 4820
Email: ashgrovepublishing@gmail.com

Warehouse & Distribution:
Orca Book Services, Unit 3A, Fleets Corner Industrial Estate, Fleetsbridge, Poole, Dorset BH17 0HL
Telephone: 01202 785714
Fax: 01202 672076
Email: tradeorders@orcabookservices.co.uk
Website: www.orcabookservices.co.uk

Personnel:
Brad Thompson *(Managing Director)*

Audio Books; Biography & Autobiography; Cookery, Wines & Spirits; Fiction; Health & Beauty; Literature & Criticism; Medical (incl. Self-Help & Alternative Medicine); Military & War; Psychology & Psychiatry; Religion & Theology

Imprints, Series & ISBNs:
Ashgrove Publishing: 978-1-85398

Parent Company:
UK: Hollydata Publishers Ltd

Associated Companies:
UK: Childrens Corner Ltd

Overseas Representation:
Worldwide: Star Book Sales, Whimple, Exeter, UK

2038 ■

*ASIAN-E LTD
Ground Floor, Fort Dunlop, Fort Parkway, Birmingham B24 9FE
Telephone: 0121 698 8524
Fax: 0121 698 8593
Website: www.asian-e.co.uk

Book Trade Association Membership:
Publishers Association

2039 ■

ASSOCIATION FOR LEARNING TECHNOLOGY
Gipsy Lane, Headington, Oxford OX3 0BP
Telephone: 01865 484125
Fax: 01865 484165
Email: admin@alt.ac.uk
Website: www.alt.ac.uk

Personnel:
Dr Maren Deepwell *(Chief Executive)*

Academic & Scholarly

Imprints, Series & ISBNs:
Beyond Control (Research Proceeding): 978-0-9545870

2040 ■

ASSOCIATION FOR SCOTTISH LITERARY STUDIES
Scottish Literature, University of Glasgow, 7 University Gardens, Glasgow G12 8QH
Telephone: 0141 330 5309
Fax: 0141 330 5309
Email: office@asls.org.uk
Website: www.asls.org.uk

Trade Enquiries:
BookSource, 50 Cambuslang Road, Glasgow G32 8NB
Telephone: 0845 370 0063
Fax: 0845 370 0064
Email: orders@booksource.net
Website: www.booksource.net

Personnel:
Duncan Jones *(Director)*

Academic & Scholarly; Educational & Textbooks; Fiction; Languages & Linguistics; Literature & Criticism; Poetry; Theatre, Drama & Dance

Imprints, Series & ISBNs:
ASLS Annual Volumes (series)
Association for Scottish Literary Studies: 978-0-948877, 978-1-906841
New Writing Scotland (series)
Occasional Papers (series)
Scotnotes (series)
Scottish Literature International: 978-1-908980

Book Trade Association Membership:
Publishing Scotland

2041 ■

ATLANTIC BOOKS
Ormond House, 26–27 Boswell Street, London WC1N 3JZ
Telephone: 020 7269 1610
Fax: 020 7430 0916
Email: enquiries@atlantic-books.co.uk
Website: www.atlantic-books.co.uk

Distribution:
TBS Ltd, Colchester Road, Frating Green, Colchester, Essex CO7 7DW
Telephone: 01206 255678
Fax: 01206 255930
Email: sales@tbs-ltd.co.uk
Website: www.thebookservice.co.uk

Personnel:
Toby Mundy *(Chief Executive Officer & Publisher)*
Ravi Mirchandani *(Editor-in-Chief)*
Karen Duffy *(Campaigns Director)*
Margaret Stead *(Publishing Director)*
Bunmi Oke *(Sales Director)*
Alan Craig *(Production Director)*
Vanessa Kerr *(Rights Director)*

Aviation; Biography & Autobiography; Crime; Economics; Fiction; History & Antiquarian; Humour; Industry, Business & Management; Law; Literature & Criticism; Mathematics & Statistics; Military & War; Music; Natural History; Philosophy; Poetry; Politics & World Affairs; Psychology & Psychiatry; Reference Books, Directories & Dictionaries; Religion & Theology; Science Fiction; Sports & Games; Transport

New Titles: 140 (2012) , 140 (2013)
No of Employees: 30
Annual Turnover: £6.5M

Imprints, Series & ISBNs:
Atlantic Books: 978-1-78239, 978-1-78239
Corvus

Overseas Representation:
Australia: Allen & Unwin, UK
Europe: Faber & Faber, London, UK

Far East: Julian Ashton, Ashton International Marketing Services, Sevenoaks, Kent, UK
India: Penguin Group, New Delhi, India
New Zealand: Allen & Unwin, UK
Republic of Ireland: Repforce Ireland, Irishtown, Dublin, Republic of Ireland
South Africa: Penguin Group SA, Rosebank, South Africa
United States: Trafalgar, USA

2042

ATLANTIC EUROPE PUBLISHING CO LTD
The Barn, Bottom Lane, Checkendon, Oxon RG8 0NR
Telephone: 01491 684028
Fax: 01491 681795
Email: support@atlanticeurope.com
Website: www.AtlanticEurope.com & www.CurriculumVisions.com

Personnel:
Dr B. J. Knapp *(Director)*

Chemistry; Children's Books; Educational & Textbooks; Electronic (Educational); Environment & Development Studies; Geography & Geology; History & Antiquarian; Mathematics & Statistics; Physics; Reference Books, Directories & Dictionaries; Religion & Theology; Scientific & Technical

Imprints, Series & ISBNs:
Atlantic Europe Publishing Co Ltd: 978-1-78278, 978-1-86214, 978-1-869860

2043

ATTIC PRESS
[an imprint of Cork University Press]
c/o Cork University Press,
Youngline Industrial Estate, Pailaduff Road, Togher, Cork, Republic of Ireland
Telephone: +353 (0)21 490 2980
Fax: +353 (0)21 431 5329
Website: www.corkuniversitypress.com

Representation (Republic of Ireland & Northern Ireland):
Mullet Fitzpatrick, 58 New Vale Cottages, Shankhill, Dublin, Republic of Ireland

Orders & Distribution:
Gill & Macmillan, Hume Avenue, Park West, Dublin 12, Republic of Ireland

Personnel:
Mike Collins *(Publications Director)*

Biography & Autobiography; Cookery, Wines & Spirits; Gender Studies; Music; Politics & World Affairs

Imprints, Series & ISBNs:
Attic Press: 978-0-946211, 978-0-9535353, 978-1-85594

Parent Company:
Republic of Ireland: Cork University Press

Overseas Representation:
UK: Quantum Publishing Solutions Ltd, Paisley, UK
UK (excluding Northern Ireland): Marston Book Services Ltd, Abingdon, UK
USA: Dufour Editions Inc, Chester Springs, PA, USA

Book Trade Association Membership:
Publishing Ireland (Foilsiú Éireann)

2044

AUDIOGO LTD
[The Home of BBC Audiobooks]
St James House, The Square,
Lower Bristol Road, Bath BA2 3BH
Telephone: 01225 878000
Fax: 01225 878003

Email: info@audiogo.co.uk
Website: www.audiogo.co.uk

Personnel:
Mike Bowen *(Managing Director)*
Jan Paterson *(Publishing Director)*
Rachel Josephson *(Sales & Marketing Director)*
Tracy Leeming *(Operations Director)*
Martin Chalmers *(Finance Director)*

Audio Books

Imprints, Series & ISBNs:
Cover to Cover Cassettes (Audio Cassettes & CDs): 978-1-85549
Radio Collection (Audio Cassettes, CDs & MP3 CDs): 978-0-563
Word for Word (Audio Cassettes & CDs)

Overseas Representation:
USA: AudioGO Ltd, USA

Book Trade Association Membership:
Publishers Association

2045

AUDLEY SQUARE LTD
Wanborough House, Stratton Road, Wanborough, Swindon SN4 0AA
Telephone: 01793 790237
Email: info@audleysquare.com
Website: www.audleysquare.com

Book Trade Association Membership:
Publishers Association

2046

AURELIAN INFORMATION LTD
4(A) Alexandra Mansions, West End Lane, London NW6 1LU
Telephone: 020 7794 8609
Fax: 020 7794 8609
Email: paul@aurelian.org.uk
Website: www.dircon.co.uk/aurelian/

Distribution:
Wyvern DM Ltd, Harrier House, Sedgeway Business Park, Witchford, Ely, Cambs CB6 2HY
Telephone: Database enquiries: 01353 667733
Fax: 01353 669030 (Database enquiries)
Website: www.dircon.co.uk/aurelian/

Personnel:
Paul Petzold *(Director)*
Julia Kaufmann OBE *(Company Secretary)*

Industry, Business & Management; Reference Books, Directories & Dictionaries

Imprints, Series & ISBNs:
Aurelian: 978-1-899247
National Charities Database: 978-1-899247

2047

AURORA METRO PUBLICATIONS LTD
67 Grove Avenue, Twickenham, London TW1 4HX
Telephone: 020 3261 0000
Fax: 020 8898 0735
Email: info@aurorametro.com
Website: www.aurorametro.com

Publishers' Distribution:
Central Books, 99 Wallis Road, Hackney, London E9 5LN
Telephone: 020 8986 4854
Fax: 020 8533 5821
Email: info@centralbooks.com & orders@centralbooks.com
Website: www.centralbooks.com

Personnel:
Cheryl Robson *(Publisher)*
Steve Robson *(Sales & Marketing)*

Rebecca Gillieron *(Managing Editor)*
Sumedha Mane *(Administrator)*

Academic & Scholarly; Children's Books; Cinema, Video, TV & Radio; Cookery, Wines & Spirits; Educational & Textbooks; Fiction; Gay & Lesbian Studies; Gender Studies; Humour; Reference Books, Directories & Dictionaries; Theatre, Drama & Dance; Travel & Topography

Imprints, Series & ISBNs:
Aurora Metro Press: 978-0-9515877, 978-0-9536757, 978-0-9542330, 978-0-9546912, 978-0-9551566, 978-1-906582
Supernova Books: 978-0-9566329

Overseas Representation:
Australia: Int Books, 3 Charles St, Coburg North, Victoria, Australia
Canada: Playwrights Press Canada, Toronto, Ont, Canada
USA: TCG/Consortium, St Paul, MN, USA

Book Trade Association Membership:
Independent Publishers Guild

2048

*AUTHENTIC MEDIA
52 Presley Way, Crownhill, Milton Keynes MK8 0ES
Email: info@authenticmedia.co.uk
Website: www.authenticmedia.co.uk

Orders:
Trust Media Distribution (Formerly STL Distribution), PO Box 300, Kingstown Broadway, Carlisle, Cumbria CA3 0HA
Telephone: 01228 512512
Fax: 01228 514949
Website:
www.trustmediadistribution.co.uk

Personnel:
Malcolm Down *(Publisher)*
Sarah Gallagher *(Marketing Co-ordinator, Authentic (General) – Administration)*
Mike Parsons *(Paternoster (Academic) Editorial)*
Liz Williams *(Authentic (General) – Editorial)*
Peter Little *(Production Controller)*
Richard Durham *(Data Administrator)*
Becky Fawcett *(Editorial Administrator)*

Academic & Scholarly; Biography & Autobiography; Children's Books; Religion & Theology

Imprints, Series & ISBNs:
Authentic Bibles: 978-0-85009
Authentic Lifestyle: 978-1-85078, 978-1-86024
Paternoster: 978-1-84227, 978-1-85364

Overseas Representation:
India: OM Book Services, Delhi, India
USA: STL Inc, Waynesboro, GA, USA

Book Trade Association Membership:
Booksellers Association

2049

AUTHORHOUSE UK LLC
c/o AuthorHouse,
1663 Liberty Drive Bloomington, IN, 47403, United States
Telephone: 01908 309250
Fax: 01908 309250
Website: www.authorhouse.co.uk

Personnel:
Tim Davies *(Managing Director)*
Daniel Cooke *(Business Development Director)*

Academic & Scholarly; Biography & Autobiography; Children's Books; Crime; Fiction; Guide Books; History &

Antiquarian; Humour; Poetry; Religion & Theology; Science Fiction

Imprints, Series & ISBNs:
Authorhouse UK Ltd: 978-1-4208, 978-1-4259, 978-1-4343

Parent Company:
USA: Author Solutions Inc

Associated Companies:
USA: Authorhouse (USA); iUniverse; Trafford; Wordclay; Xlibris

2050

AWARD PUBLICATIONS LTD
The Old Riding School, Welbeck Estate, Worksop, Notts S80 3LR
Telephone: 01909 478170
Fax: 01909 484632
Email: info@awardpublications.co.uk
Website: www.awardpublications.co.uk

Personnel:
Anna Wilkinson *(Managing Director)*
Richard Carman *(International Sales Director)*
David Meggs *(UK Sales Director)*
Adam Wilde *(Production Manager)*

Children's Books; Reference Books, Directories & Dictionaries

Imprints, Series & ISBNs:
Award: 978-0-86163, 978-1-78270, 978-1-84135
Horus: 978-1-899762
Picthall and Gunzi: 978-1-90461, 978-1-90550, 978-1-90657, 978-1-90760, 978-1-90976

2051

AXIS EDUCATION
5 Knights Park, Hussey Road, Battlefield Enterprise Park, Shrewsbury SY1 3TE
Telephone: 01743 460021
Fax: 01743 454890
Email: enquiries@axiseducation.co.uk
Website: www.axiseducation.co.uk

Book Trade Association Membership:
Publishers Association

2052

AYEBIA CLARKE PUBLISHING LTD
7 Syringa Walk, Banbury OX16 1FR
Telephone: 01295 709228
Email: info@ayebia.co.uk
Website: www.ayebia.co.uk

Personnel:
Mrs Rebecca Ribiero Clarke MBE *(Director)*
Mrs David Clarke *(Managing Director)*
Mrs Nick K Clarke *(Media Manager)*

Academic & Scholarly; Children's Books; Educational & Textbooks; Fiction; Languages & Linguistics; Literature & Criticism; Philosophy; Politics & World Affairs

Book Trade Association Membership:
Publishers Association

2053

B SMALL PUBLISHING LTD
The Book Shed, 36 Leyborne Park, Kew, Richmond, Surrey TW9 3HA
Telephone: 020 8948 2884
Email: books@bsmall.co.uk
Website: www.bsmall.co.uk

Sales Representation, UK Trade Enquiries & Orders:
Bounce Sales & Marketing Ltd, Quality Court, off Chancery Lane, London WC2A 1HR

Telephone: 020 7138 3650
Fax: 020 7138 3658
Email: sales@bouncemarketing.co.uk
Website: www.bouncemarketing.co.uk

Personnel:
Catherine Bruzzone (Managing Director)
Sam Hutchinson (Director)

Children's Books; Crafts & Hobbies; English as a Foreign Language; Languages & Linguistics

New Titles: 10 (2012) , 14 (2013)
Annual Turnover: £200,000

Imprints, Series & ISBNs:
b small publishing ltd: 978-1-874735, 978-1-902915, 978-1-905710, 978-1-908164, 978-1-909767

Overseas Representation:
Worldwide: Bounce Sales and Marketing, UK

Book Trade Association Membership:
Independent Publishers Guild

2054

BERNARD BABANI (PUBLISHING) LTD
The Grampians, Shepherds Bush Road, London W6 7NF
Telephone: 020 7603 2581/7296
Fax: 020 7603 8203
Email: enquiries@babanibooks.com
Website: www.babanibooks.com

Personnel:
Michael H. Babani (Sales, Production, Managing Director)

Computer Science; Crafts & Hobbies; Educational & Textbooks; Electronic (Educational); Electronic (Entertainment); Electronic (Professional & Academic); Engineering; Mathematics & Statistics; Scientific & Technical

Imprints, Series & ISBNs:
Babani Press: 978-0-85934, 978-0-900162

Associated Companies:
UK: Bernards (Publishers) Ltd

Book Trade Association Membership:
Independent Publishers Guild

2055

*BADGER PUBLISHING LTD
[a division of Haven Books Ltd]
Suite G08, Business & Technology Centre, Bessemer Drive, Stevenage SG1 2DX
Telephone: 01438 791037
Fax: 01438 791036
Email: enquiries@badger-publishing.co.uk
Website: www.badger-publishing.co.uk

Personnel:
Susan Ross (Director & Publisher)
Jean Constantine (Sales & Marketing Manager)
Danny Pearson (Senior Editor)

Children's Books; Educational & Textbooks; Electronic (Educational)

Imprints, Series & ISBNs:
Badger Publishing Ltd: 978-1-84424, 978-1-84691, 978-1-84926, 978-1-85880, 978-1-86509

Parent Company:
UK: Haven Books Ltd

Book Trade Association Membership:
Publishers Association; Educational Publishers Council

2056

BALBERRY PUBLISHING
322 Old Brompton Road, London SW5 9JH
Telephone: 020 7373 7781
Fax: 020 7373 4930

Educational & Textbooks; English as a Foreign Language

Book Trade Association Membership:
Publishers Association

2057

THE BANNER OF TRUTH TRUST
3 Murrayfield Road, Edinburgh EH12 6EL
Telephone: 0131 337 7310
Fax: 0131 346 7484
Email: info@banneroftruth.co.uk
Website: www.banneroftruth.co.uk

Warehouse:
17 Bankhead Drive, Sighthill Industrial Estate, Edinburgh EH11 4DW
Telephone: 0131 442 2945
Fax: 0131 442 2945
Email: info@banneroftruth.co.uk
Website: www.banneroftruth.co.uk

Personnel:
John Rawlinson (General Manager)
Jonathan Watson (Editor)

Religion & Theology

New Titles: 25 (2012) , 25 (2013)

Imprints, Series & ISBNs:
The Banner of Truth Trust: 978-0-85151, 978-1-84871

Associated Companies:
USA: The Banner of Truth

Overseas Representation:
New Zealand: Sovereign Grace Books, Auckland, New Zealand
Nigeria: Amazing Grace Ltd, Kano, Nigeria
Philippines: Evangelical Outreach Inc, Quezon City, Philippines
South Africa: Barnabas Book Room, Durban North, South Africa; Farel Distributors (Pty) Ltd, North Riding, South Africa
USA: The Banner of Truth, Carlisle, PA, USA

2058

BAREFOOT BOOKS
294 Banbury Road, Oxford OX2 7ED
Telephone: 01865 311100
Fax: 01865 514965
Email: info@barefootbooks.com
Website: www.barefootbooks.com

Trade Sales (Orders):
Littlehampton Book Services Ltd, Faraday Close, Durrington, Worthing, West Sussex BN13 3RB
Telephone: 01903 828800
Fax: 01903 828801

Personnel:
Tessa Strickland (Editor-in-Chief)
Nancy Traversy (Managing Director)
Gautam Bhasin (European General Manager)

Audio Books; Children's Books; Educational & Textbooks

Imprints, Series & ISBNs:
Barefoot Books: 978-1-84148, 978-1-84686, 978-1-898000, 978-1-901223, 978-1-902283, 978-1-905236

Overseas Representation:
Australia: Willow Connection Pty Ltd, Brookvale, NSW, Australia
East Africa: A–Z Africa Book Services, Rotterdam, Netherlands
Europe (Trade), Indian Subcontinent & Middle East: Gabriele Kern Publishers Services, Frankfurt-am-Main, Germany; Jenny Padovani, Barcelona, Spain; Penny Padovani, Montanare di Cortona, Italy
Latin America & Caribbean: David Williams, InterMedia Americana (IMA) Ltd, London, UK
New Zealand: Addenda Ltd, Grey Lynn, New Zealand
Republic of Ireland & Northern Ireland: Conor Hackett, Dublin, Republic of Ireland
South Africa: Phambili Agencies CC, Germiston, South Africa; Salmonberry Press, South Africa
South East Asia, Far East, North Asia, Hong Kong, Singapore, Brunei & Malaysia (Libraries), Singapore, Brunei & Malaysia (Trade & Special Sales): Chris Ashdown, Publishers Marketing Services Pte Ltd, Singapore
South East, Far East & North Asia: Publishers International Marketing, London, UK
USA: Barefoot Books Inc, Cambridge, MA, USA

Book Trade Association Membership:
Booksellers Association; Independent Publishers Guild

2059

BARNY BOOKS
11 Millfield Cr, Caythorpe, Grantham NG32 3HG
Telephone: 01400 273469
Email: barnybooks@barnybooks.co.uk
Website: www.barnybooks.co.uk

Orders & Invoices:
76 Cotgrave Lane, Tollerton, Nottingham NG12 4FY
Telephone: 0115 937 5147
Email: info@barnybooks.co.uk
Website: www.barnybooks.co.uk

Personnel:
Molly Burkett (Editor)
Jayne Thompson (Business Manager)

Biography & Autobiography; Children's Books; Cookery, Wines & Spirits; Fiction; Gardening; History & Antiquarian; Humour; Industry, Business & Management; Medical (incl. Self-Help & Alternative Medicine); Military & War; Poetry; Transport

Imprints, Series & ISBNs:
Barny Books: 978-0-948204, 978-1-906542
Events, People to be Remembered (Joseph Banks – Sir John Hawrins)
Once upon a Wartime (Series): 978-1-903172

2060

BATSFORD
[an imprint of Anova Books Group]
10 Southcombe Street, London W14 0RA
Telephone: 020 7605 1400
Fax: 020 7605 1401
Email: reception@anovabooks.com
Website: www.anovabooks.com

Distribution, Warehouse & Enquiries:
HarperCollins Distribution, Campsie View, Westerhill Road, Bishopbriggs, Glasgow G64 2QT
Telephone: 0141 306 3100
Fax: 0141 306 3767

Personnel:
Tina Persaud (Publisher)
Benedicte Lerfald (Senior Marketing Manager)
Sinead Hurley (Head of International Rights)

Archaeology; Architecture & Design; Crafts & Hobbies; Fashion & Costume; Gardening; History & Antiquarian; Poetry

Imprints, Series & ISBNs:
Batsford: 978-0-7134, 978-1-8499

Parent Company:
UK: Anova Books Co Ltd

Overseas Representation:
Australia: Capricorn Link (Australia) Pty Ltd, Windsor, NSW, Australia
Canada: Sterling Publishing Co Inc, New York, NY, USA
Central & Eastern Europe: Adriana Juncu, Romania
Far East: Ashton International Marketing Services, Sevenoaks, Kent, UK
France, Netherlands & Luxembourg: Ted Dougherty, London, UK
Germany, Switzerland & Austria: Gabriele Kern Publishers Services, Frankfurt-am-Main, Germany
India: Maya Publishers Pvt Ltd, New Delhi, India
Mexico & Central America: Christopher Humphrys, Humphrys Roberts Associates, London, UK
Middle East: Richard Ward, London, UK
New Zealand: HarperCollins (NZ) Ltd, Glenfield, Auckland, New Zealand
Russia, Israel, sub-Saharan Africa & Baltic States: Tony Moggach, InterMedia Americana (IMA) Ltd, London, UK
Scandinavia: Melanie Boesen, Mediehuset Rubrik, Copenhagen, Denmark
Singapore: Pansing Distribution Sdn Bhd, Singapore
South Africa: Trinity Books CC, Randburg, South Africa
South America: Terry Roberts, Cotia SP, Brazil
Southern Europe: Penny Padovani, Pergo di Cortona, Italy
USA: Sterling Publishing Co Inc, New York, NY, USA

Book Trade Association Membership:
Independent Publishers Guild

2061

BBH PUBLISHING LTD
[trading as The Francis Frith Collection]
6 Oakley Business Park, Wylye Road, Dinton, Salisbury, Wilts SP3 5EU
Telephone: 01722 716376
Fax: 01722 716881
Email: sales@francisfrith.co.uk
Website: www.francisfrith.com

Personnel:
John Buck (Managing Director)
Jason Buck (Development Director)
Adrian Sanders (Operations Manager)
Julia Skinner (Managing Editor)
Sandra Sanger (Office Sales Manager)
John Brewer (Financial Controller)

History & Antiquarian; Photography; Travel & Topography

New Titles: 48 (2012) , 230 (2013)
No of Employees: 16
Annual Turnover: £800,000

Imprints, Series & ISBNs:
The Francis Frith Collection: 978-1-84589, 978-1-85937

2062

THE BELMONT PRESS
29 Tenby Avenue, Harrow HA3 8RU
Telephone: 020 8907 4700
Fax: 020 8907 7354
Email: belmont@BEL48.org.uk
Website: www.waterways.co.uk & www.belmont1948.co.uk

Personnel:
John Lawes (*Managing Director*)
Mark Lawes (*Technical Director*)

Atlases & Maps; Children's Books; History & Antiquarian; Nautical; Transport; Travel & Topography

Imprints, Series & ISBNs:
Belmont series of books: 978-0-905366
Navigator series of maps: 978-0-905366
Working Waterways series: 978-0-905366

Parent Company:
UK: Belmont (1948) Ltd

Associated Companies:
UK: Belmont Books; Chris Deucher; John Reeve; Waterway Books; Waterways Book Service

Distributor for:
UK: Enigma Publishing; Remus Publishing; W. H. Walker & Bros; Robert Wilson Designs; Working Waterways Series

2063

BENE FACTUM PUBLISHING LTD
PO Box 58122, London SW8 5WZ
Telephone: 020 7720 6767
Email: inquiries@bene-factum.co.uk
Website: www.bene-factum.co.uk

Representation:
Compass DSA, Swan Centre, Fisher's Lane, Chiswick, London W4 1RX
Telephone: 020 8996 5764
Email: sales@compass-dsa.co.uk

Distribution:
Combined Book Services, Unit D, Paddock Wood Distribution Centre, Tonbridge, Kent TN12 6UU
Telephone: 01892 839819
Fax: 01892 837272
Email: orders@combook.co.uk

Personnel:
Anthony Weldon (*Managing Director*)

Antiques & Collecting; Aviation; Biography & Autobiography; Children's Books; Cookery, Wines & Spirits; Fashion & Costume; Fine Art & Art History; Gardening; History & Antiquarian; Humour; Illustrated & Fine Editions; Industry, Business & Management; Law; Medical (incl. Self-Help & Alternative Medicine); Military & War; Poetry; Reference Books, Directories & Dictionaries; Travel & Topography; Vocational Training & Careers

Imprints, Series & ISBNs:
Bene Factum Publishing Ltd: 978-0-9522754, 978-1-903071, 978-1-909657

Overseas Representation:
Australia: Woodslane Pty Ltd, Australia
India: Research Press Pvt Ltd, New Delhi, India
N America: IPG/Trafalgar Square, USA

Book Trade Association Membership:
Independent Publishers Guild

2064

BERGHAHN BOOKS
3 Newtec Place, Magdalen Road, Oxford OX4 1RE
Telephone: 01865 250011
Fax: 01865 250056
Email: publisher@berghahnbooks.com
Website: www.berghahnbooks.com

Warehouse & Orders:
Turpin Distribution, Pegasus Drive, Biggleswade SG18 8TQ
Telephone: +44 (0) 1767 604 976

Email: berghahnbooks@turpin-distribution.com

Also at:
150 Broadway, Suite 812, New York, NY 10038, USA
Telephone: +1 (212) 233 6004
Fax: +1 (212) 233 6007
Website: berghahnbooks.com

Personnel:
Marion Berghahn (*Publisher and Editor-in-Chief*)
Vivian Berghahn (*Managing Director*)
Leigh Waite (*General Manager, UK*)
Rupert Jones-Parry (*International Sales Director*)
Ben Parker (*Publicity/Marketing Executive*)
Charlotte Mosedale (*Production Editor*)

Academic & Scholarly; Biography & Autobiography; Cinema, Video, TV & Radio; Economics; Electronic (Professional & Academic); Environment & Development Studies; Gender Studies; History & Antiquarian; Languages & Linguistics; Literature & Criticism; Military & War; Politics & World Affairs; Religion & Theology; Sociology & Anthropology; Theatre, Drama & Dance; Travel & Topography

Imprints, Series & ISBNs:
Berghahn Books: 978-1-57181, 978-1-84545

Distributor for:
India: Social Science Press
UK: Durkheim Press

Overseas Representation:
Australia & New Zealand: Woodslane Pty Ltd, Warriewood, NSW, Australia
Benelux: Jos de Jong, Belgium
Canada: Renouf Books, Ottawa, Ont, Canada
China & Hong Kong: Inspirees Bowen, Beijing, China
Eastern Europe: László Horváth Publishers Representative, Budapest, Hungary
Europe: Berghahn Books, Oxford, UK
Germany (stockholding): Missing Link International Booksellers, Bremen, Germany
Greece & Cyprus: Charles Gibbes Associates, London, UK
India: Sara Books Pvt Ltd, New Delhi, India
Italy & France: Flavio Marcello Publishers' Agents & Consultants, Padua, Italy
Japan (stockholding): United Publishers Services Ltd, Tokyo; Kinokuniya Ltd, Tokyo, Japan
Latin/Central America: Cranbury International LLC, Montpelier, VT, USA
Middle East & Turkey: Avicenna Partnership, Oxford, UK
Scandinavia: David Towle International, Stockholm, Sweden
South Africa: The African Moon Press, South Africa
Spain & Portugal: Iberian Book Services, Madrid, Spain
Taiwan: Unifacmanu Trading Co Ltd, Taipei, Taiwan

2065

BIBLE READING FELLOWSHIP
15 The Chambers, Vineyard, Abingdon, Oxon OX14 3FE
Telephone: 01865 319700
Fax: 01865 319701
Email: enquiries@brf.org.uk
Website: www.brf.org.uk

Distribution:
Trust Media Distribution, Kingstown, Broadway, Carlisle CA3 0HA
Telephone: 01228 512512
Fax: 01228 514949
Email: info@tmdistribution.co.uk
Website: www.tmdistribution.co.uk

Personnel:
R. Fisher (*Chief Executive Officer*)
Karen Laister (*Deputy Chief Executive*)
Naomi Starkey (*Commissioning Editor*)
Olivia Warburton (*Commissioning Editor & Editorial Services Team Leader*)

Children's Books; Educational & Textbooks; Religion & Theology

New Titles: 81 (2012), 87 (2013)
No of Employees: 30
Annual Turnover: £1,000,000

Imprints, Series & ISBNs:
Barnabas: 978-1-84101
Barnabas for Children: 978-0-85746
Barnabas in Schools: 978-0-85746
Bible Reading Fellowship: 978-0-7459, 978-0-85746, 978-1-84101
Day by Day with God
Foundations21: 978-0-85746
Get Messy
Guidelines
Messy Church: 978-0-85746, 978-0-85746, 978-1-84101
New Daylight
People's Bible Commentary Series
Quiet Spaces
The Upper Room

Overseas Representation:
Australia: Mediacom Education Inc., Australia
New Zealand: Scripture Union Wholesale, Wellington, New Zealand
USA: The Bible Reading Fellowship, Winter Park, FL, USA

Book Trade Association Membership:
Independent Publishers Guild

2066

JOSEPH BIDDULPH PUBLISHER
32 Stryd Ebeneser, Pontypridd CF37 5PB
Telephone: 01443 662559
Email: Joseph.Biddulph@gmail.com

Personnel:
Joseph Biddulph (*Sole Proprietor*)

Academic & Scholarly; Architecture & Design; Languages & Linguistics; Poetry; Reference Books, Directories & Dictionaries; Religion & Theology

New Titles: 2 (2012), 3 (2013)

Imprints, Series & ISBNs:
Joseph Biddulph Publisher: 978-0-948565, 978-1-897999
Languages Information Centre: 978-0-948565

2067

BIRLINN LTD
West Newington House,
10 Newington Road, Edinburgh EH9 1QS
Telephone: 0131 668 4371
Fax: 0131 668 4466
Email: info@birlinn.co.uk
Website: www.birlinn.co.uk

Distribution:
BookSource, 50 Cambuslang Road, Glasgow G32 8NB
Telephone: 0845 370 0067
Fax: 0845 370 0068
Email: info@booksource.net
Website: www.booksource.net

Personnel:
Hugh Andrew (*Managing Director*)
Rona Stewart (*Finance*)
Liz Short (*Production*)
Neville Moir (*Publisher*)
Andrew Simmons (*Editorial*)
Vikki Reily (*Sales*)
Maria White (*Rights*)

Jan Rutherford (*Publicity*)
Laura Poynton (*Sales Director*)

Children's Books; Cookery, Wines & Spirits; Economics; Fiction; Guide Books; History & Antiquarian; Humour; Illustrated & Fine Editions; Military & War; Music; Photography; Poetry; Politics & World Affairs

Imprints, Series & ISBNs:
Birlinn: 978-1-84158, 978-1-874744
Birlinn General (Military & Adventure titles): 978-1-84341
John Donald: 978-0-85976
John Donald (print on demand titles): 978-1-904607
Mercat: 978-1-84183
Polygon: 978-0-7486, 978-0-9544075, 978-1-84697, 978-1-904598

Associated Companies:
UK: John Donald Publishers Ltd; Polygon

Distributor for:
UK: Maclean Press

Overseas Representation:
Australia: UNIREPS University and Reference Publishers' Services, Sydney, NSW, Australia
Austria, Belgium, France, Germany, Greece, Italy, Luxembourg, Netherlands & Switzerland: Ted Dougherty, London, UK
Canada: Vanwell Publishing Ltd, St Catharines, Ont, Canada
Denmark, Finland, Iceland, Norway, Portugal, Spain, Sweden & Eastern Europe: Bill Bailey Publishers Representatives, Newton Abbot, UK
USA (academic): Interlink Publishing Group Inc, Northampton, MA, USA
USA (for military & adventure titles only): Casemate Publishers & Book Distributors LLC, Havertown, PA, USA

Book Trade Association Membership:
Independent Publishers Guild

2068

BITTER LEMON PRESS
37 Arundel Gardens, London W11 2LW
Telephone: 020 7727 7927
Fax: 020 7460 2164
Email: books@bitterlemonpress.com
Website: www.bitterlemonpress.com

Crime; Fiction

Book Trade Association Membership:
Independent Publishers Guild

2069

BLACK DOG PUBLISHING LTD
10A Acton Street, London WC1X 9NG
Telephone: 020 7713 5097
Fax: 020 7713 8682
Website: www.blackdogonline.com

Warehouse & Distribution:
Marston Book Services, PO Box 269, Abingdon, Oxon OX14 4YN
Telephone: 01235 465500
Fax: 01235 465555
Email: direct.orders@marston.co.uk

Architecture & Design; Cinema, Video, TV & Radio; Crafts & Hobbies; Environment & Development Studies; Fashion & Costume; Fine Art & Art History; Gardening; Illustrated & Fine Editions; Music; Photography; Travel & Topography

Imprints, Series & ISBNs:
Architecture & Urbanism (Serial books): 978-1-901033
Artworld
Black Dog Publishing Ltd: 978-1-904772, 978-1-906155, 978-1-907317
-De, -Dis, -Ex: 978-1-901033

Labels Unlimited
Revisions: 978-1-901033
Serial Books Design: 978-1-901033

Associated Companies:
UK: Artifice Books on Architecture

Overseas Representation:
Asia: Asia Publishers Services and APD
 Singapore Ltd, Singapore
Australia & New Zealand: Peribo Pty Ltd,
 Mount Kuring-Gai, NSW, Australia
Canada & USA: Perseus Group, Jackson,
 TN, USA
Europe & New Zealand: Marston Book
 Services Ltd, Abingdon, UK
France: Critiques Livres Distribution,
 Bagnolet, France
UK: Yale Representation Ltd, UK

2070

BLACK SPRING PRESS LTD
Curtain House, 134–146 Curtain Road,
London EC2A 3AR
Telephone: 020 7613 3066
Fax: 020 7613 0028
Email: general@blackspringpress.co.uk
Website: www.blackspringpress.co.uk

Distribution:
Turnaround Publisher Services Ltd, Unit 3,
Olympia Trading Estate, Coburg Road,
London N22 6TZ
Telephone: 020 8829 3000
Fax: 020 8881 5088
Email: orders@turnaround-uk.com
Website: www.turnaround-uk.com

Personnel:
Robert Hastings *(Publisher)*

*Biography & Autobiography; Cinema,
Video, TV & Radio; Fiction; Music*

Imprints, Series & ISBNs:
Black Spring Press Ltd: 978-0-948238

Overseas Representation:
Europe, Middle East & Far East: Turnaround
 Publisher Services Ltd, London, UK

2071

BLACKTHORN PRESS
Blackthorn House, Middleton Road,
Pickering, North Yorks YO18 8AL
Telephone: 01751 474043
Email: blackthornpress@yahoo.com
Website: www.blackthornpress.com

Personnel:
Alan Avery *(Proprietor)*

*Fine Art & Art History; History &
Antiquarian*

New Titles: 7 (2012) , 6 (2013)
Annual Turnover: £30,000

Imprints, Series & ISBNs:
Blackthorn Press: 978-0-9540535, 978-1-
 906259

2072

JOHN BLAKE PUBLISHING LTD
[incorporating Smith Gryphon Publishers
Ltd & Metro Publishing Ltd]
3 Bramber Court, 2 Bramber Road, London
W14 9PB
Telephone: 020 7381 0666
Fax: 020 7381 6868
Email: rosie@blake.co.uk
Website: www.johnblakepublishing.co.uk

Distribution:
Littlehampton Book Services,
Faraday Close, Durrington, Worthing,
West Sussex BN13 3RB
Telephone: 01903 828800
Fax: 01903 828802

Email: orders@lbsltd.co.uk
Website: www.lbsltd.co.uk

Personnel:
John Blake *(Managing Director)*
Rosie Virgo *(Deputy Managing Director)*
Ray Mudie *(Sales Director)*
Joanna Kennedy *(Accounts Executive)*
Clare Tillyer *(Head of Marketing)*
Stuart Finglass *(Head of UK Sales & Digital)*
Moira Ashcroft *(Production)*
Liz Mallett *(Head of Publicity)*

*Audio Books; Biography & Autobiography;
Cookery, Wines & Spirits; Crime; Humour;
Military & War; Music; Sports & Games*

Imprints, Series & ISBNs:
John Blake Publishing Ltd: 978-1-84358,
 978-1-84454, 978-1-85782

Associated Companies:
UK: Metro Books; Smith Gryphon
 Publishers Ltd

Overseas Representation:
Australia: Alpa Books, St Agnes, Australia
Germany: Michael Mellor, Munich,
 Germany
New Zealand: Bookreps, Auckland, New
 Zealand
South Africa: Peter Hyde Associates (Pty)
 Ltd, Cape Town, South Africa
USA: Trafalgar Publishing, Chicago, IL, USA

Book Trade Association Membership:
Booksellers Association; Independent
Publishers Guild

2073

BLOODAXE BOOKS LTD
Highgreen, Tarset, Northumberland
NE48 1RP
Telephone: 01434 240500 (editorial)
 01678 521550 (sales)
Fax: 01434 240505 (editorial) 01678
 521544 (sales)
Email: editor@bloodaxebooks.com
 (editorial), sales@bloodaxebooks.com
Website: www.bloodaxebooks.com

Warehouse, Trade Enquiries & Orders:
Macmillan Distribution Ltd, Houndmills,
Basingstoke Hampshire RG21 6XS
Telephone: 01256 302692
Fax: 01256 812558
Email: orders@macmillan.co.uk

Personnel:
Neil Astley *(Editor & Managing Director)*
Simon Thirsk *(Executive Chair)*
Alison Davis *(Company Secretary)*
Bethan Jones *(Finance Manager)*
Christine Macgregor *(Publicity Manager)*
Suzanne Fairless-Aitken *(Rights Manager)*
Jean Smith *(Finance & Sales Assistant)*
Rebecca Hodkinson *(Prizes &
 Administration)*

Literature & Criticism; Poetry

Imprints, Series & ISBNs:
Bloodaxe Books: 978-0-906427, 978-1-
 78037, 978-1-85224

Associated Companies:
UK: Pandon Press Ltd

Overseas Representation:
Europe: Michael Geoghegan, London, UK
India: Surit Mitra, New Delhi, India
Italy, Spain & Portugal: Penny Padovani,
 London, UK
North America: Dufour Editions Inc, Chester
 Springs, PA, USA
Republic of Ireland: Repforce Ireland,
 Irishtown, Dublin, Republic of Ireland
*South & Central America, Africa (excluding
 South Africa), Eastern Europe, Middle*

East, Turkey, Israel, Greece & Cyprus:
 InterMedia Americana (IMA) Ltd,
 London, UK

2074

**BLOOMSBURY ACADEMIC &
PROFESSIONAL**
50 Bedford Square WC1B 3DP
Telephone: 020 7631 5600
Website: www.bloomsbury.com

Personnel:
Jonathan Glasspool *(Managing Director,
 Bloomsbury Academic & Professional)*
Martin Casimir *(Managing Director,
 Bloomsbury Professional)*
Richard Price *(Sales & Marketing Director,
 Bloomsbury Professional)*
Derek Stordahl *(Head of Sales, Americas,
 Bloomsbury Academic)*
Kathryn Earle *(Head of Academic
 Publishing, Bloomsbury Academic)*

*Academic & Scholarly; Accountancy &
Taxation; Archaeology; Architecture &
Design; Educational & Textbooks; Electronic
(Professional & Academic); Environment &
Development Studies; Fashion & Costume;
Gay & Lesbian Studies; Gender Studies;
History & Antiquarian; Industry, Business &
Management; Languages & Linguistics;
Law; Literature & Criticism; Military & War;
Music; Philosophy; Politics & World Affairs;
Reference Books, Directories &
Dictionaries; Religion & Theology; Sociology
& Anthropology; Theatre, Drama & Dance*

Imprints, Series & ISBNs:
Arden Shakespeare: 978-1-904271
AVA
Berg
Bloomsbury Academic: 978-0-85785
Bloomsbury Professional: 978-1-84766,
 978-1-84930
Fairchild Books
The Herbert Press
Methuen Drama: 978-1-4081
T & T Clark: 978-0-567

Overseas Representation:
Africa (except as under): Tula Publishing
 Ltd, Oxford, UK
Asia Pacific: Taylor & Francis Asia Pacific,
 Singapore
Australasia: Bloomsbury Publishing Pty Ltd,
 Sydney, NSW, Australia
Austria, Greece & Cyprus: Tyers Book Sales
 Ltd, Athens, Greece
*Canada (former Continuum & T. & T. Clark
 titles)*: Codasat Canada Ltd, Vancouver,
 BC, Canada
Canada (other titles): Penguin Group
 (Canada), Toronto, Ont, Canada
Central & Eastern Europe: Jacek Lewinson,
 Warsaw, Poland
Central & South America, Caribbean:
 Bloomsbury USA, New York, NY, USA
*Denmark, Finland, Iceland, Norway &
 Sweden*: Colin Flint Ltd, Cambridge, UK
Indian Subcontinent: Bloomsbury
 Publishing India Pvt, New Delhi, India
*Middle East (excluding Israel), North Africa
 & Malta*: International Publishers
 Services, Dubai, United Arab Emirates
South Korea: Information and Culture
 Korea, Seoul, Republic of Korea
Southern Africa: Book Promotions,
 Roggebaai, South Africa
Spain, Portugal & Gibraltar: Iberian Book
 Services, Madrid, Spain
USA: Bloomsbury USA, New York, NY, USA

2075

BLOOMSBURY PUBLISHING PLC
50 Bedford Square WC1B 3DP
Telephone: 020 7631 5600
Website: www.bloomsbury.com

Personnel:
Nigel Newton *(Chief Executive)*

Richard Charkin *(Executive Director)*
Wendy Pallott *(Finance Director)*
Kathy Rooney *(Managing Director,
 Bloomsbury Information)*
Louise Cameron *(Group Production
 Director)*
Kathleen Farrar *(Group Sales & Marketing
 Director)*
Emma Hopkin *(Managing Director,
 Children's & Education)*
Jonathan Glasspool *(Managing Director,
 Academic & Professional)*

*Archaeology; Architecture & Design;
Biography & Autobiography; Biology &
Zoology; Children's Books; Cinema, Video,
TV & Radio; Cookery, Wines & Spirits;
Crafts & Hobbies; Crime; Educational &
Textbooks; Electronic (Educational); Fashion
& Costume; Fiction; Fine Art & Art History;
Gardening; Geography & Geology; Health
& Beauty; History & Antiquarian; Humour;
Industry, Business & Management;
Languages & Linguistics; Literature &
Criticism; Military & War; Music; Natural
History; Nautical; Philosophy; Politics &
World Affairs; Psychology & Psychiatry;
Reference Books, Directories &
Dictionaries; Religion & Theology; Sports &
Games; Theatre, Drama & Dance*

New Titles: 2000 (2012) , 2100 (2013)
No of Employees: 500
Annual Turnover: £100M

Imprints, Series & ISBNs:
A & C Black: 978-1-4081
A & C Black Music
Absolute Press: 978-1-906650
Adlard Coles Nautical: 978-1-4081
Bloomsbury Children's: 978-1-4088
Bloomsbury Circus
Bloomsbury Continuum
Bloomsbury Press: 978-1-60819
Bloomsbury Reader
Andrew Brodie
Featherstone
T & D Poyser
Thomas Reed
Whitaker's: 978-1-4729
Wisden: 978-1-4081

Associated Companies:
Australia: Bloomsbury Publishing Pty Ltd
India: Bloomsbury Publishing India Pvt Ltd
USA: Bloomsbury Publishing Inc

Overseas Representation:
Australia & New Zealand: Bloomsbury
 Publishing Pty Ltd, Sydney, NSW,
 Australia
Canada: Penguin Group (Canada), Toronto,
 Ont, Canada
Central & Eastern Europe: Penguin Poland,
 Poznan, Poland
France: Penguin Group, Amsterdam,
 Netherlands
Germany & Austria: Penguin Books
 Deutschland GmbH, Frankfurt-am-Main,
 Germany
India: Bloomsbury Publishing India Pvt Ltd,
 New Delhi, India
Italy: Penguin Books SA, Milan, Italy
Latin America & Caribbean: International
 Sales, New York, NY, USA
Middle East & North Africa (excluding UAE):
 Bloomsbury Qatar Foundation
 Publishing, Doha, Qatar
Netherlands, Belgium & Luxembourg:
 Penguin Benelux, Amsterdam,
 Netherlands
Pakistan & Sri Lanka: Bloomsbury
 International Sales, London , UK
*Scandinavia, Switzerland, South-Eastern
 Europe, Malta, Gibraltar, Asia, Africa*:
 Penguin International Sales, London, UK
Singapore & Malaysia: Penguin Books,
 Singapore
South Africa: Book Promotions, Cape Town,
 South Africa
Spain & Portugal: Penguin Books SA,
 Madrid, Spain

United Arab Emirates: Penguin Group (Arabia), Dubai, United Arab Emirates
USA (Bloomsbury USA titles): Bloomsbury Publishing, New York, NY, USA

Book Trade Association Membership:
Publishers Association; Booksellers Association; Educational Publishers Council; Independent Publishers Guild

2076

BLUE SKY PRESS
57 Longfield Avenue, Fareham, Hants
PO14 1BU
Telephone: 07816 411341
Email: blueskypress@BurgessMcCain.com
Website: www.blueskypress.co.uk &
www.thealicefactor.com

Personnel:
Victoria Stone *(Executive Assistant)*
Cfyn Markwick-Day *(Managing Editor)*

Fiction; Music; Poetry

Parent Company:
UK: Burgess McCain Ltd

2077

BLUE OCEAN PUBLISHING
St John's Innovation Centre, Cowley Road,
Cambridge CB4 0WS
Telephone: 01763 208887
Email:
blueoceanpublishing@btconnect.com
Website: www.blueoceanpublishing.biz

Personnel:
Miss Angela Wilde *(Publisher)*

*Academic & Scholarly; Children's Books;
Cookery, Wines & Spirits; Crafts & Hobbies;
Educational & Textbooks; History &
Antiquarian; Industry, Business &
Management; Literature & Criticism;
Poetry; Religion & Theology; Theatre,
Drama & Dance*

Imprints, Series & ISBNs:
Blue Ocean Publishing: 978-0-9556430,
978-1-907527

2078

BLUEBERRY PRESS LTD
Unit 1A, Red House Glass Cone,
High Street, Stourbrige, West Midlands
DY8 4AZ
Telephone: 07795 360294
Email:
andrew.corcoran@blueberrypress.co.uk
Website: www.blueberrypress.co.uk

Personnel:
Andrew Corcoran *(Director)*

*Academic & Scholarly; Children's Books;
Educational & Textbooks; Fiction; Industry,
Business & Management*

Imprints, Series & ISBNs:
Blueberry Press Ltd: 978-0-9564572

2079

BODLEIAN LIBRARY PUBLISHING
Osney One, Osney Mead, Oxford OX2 0EW
Telephone: 01865 283850
Fax: 01865 277620
Email: publishing@bodleian.ox.ac.uk
Website: www.bodleianbookshop.co.uk

Trade Enquiries & Orders:
Turpin Distribution Ltd, Pegasus Drive,
Stratton Business Park, Biggleswade, Beds
SG18 8TQ
Telephone: 01767 604968
Fax: 01767 601640
Email: custserv@turpin-distribution.com
Website: www.turpin-distribution.com

Representation (UK Book Trade):
Yale University Press WC1B 3DP
Telephone: 020 7079 4900
Email: yalerep@yaleup.co.uk

Personnel:
Samuel Fanous *(Publisher)*
Deborah Susman *(Managing Editor)*
Su Wheeler *(Marketing & Sales Co-
ordinator)*

*Academic & Scholarly; Antiques &
Collecting; Architecture & Design;
Biography & Autobiography; Children's
Books; Fine Art & Art History; History &
Antiquarian; Humour; Literature &
Criticism; Military & War; Natural History;
Politics & World Affairs; Reference Books,
Directories & Dictionaries; Sports & Games*

Imprints, Series & ISBNs:
Bodleian Library Publishing: 978-1-85124
Original Rules
Postcards from...
Treasures of the Bodleian Library

Parent Company:
UK: University of Oxford

Overseas Representation:
Australia & New Zealand: Inbooks, Australia
USA & Canada: Chicago University Press,
Chicago, IL, USA

Book Trade Association Membership:
Independent Publishers Guild; Association
of Cultural Enterprises

2080

*BONACIA LTD
Remus House, Coltsfoot Drive, Woodston,
Peterborough PE2 9BF
Telephone: 01733 890099
Fax: 01733 313524
Email: info@bonacia.co.uk
Website: www.Bonacia.co.uk

Personnel:
Morgan Walton *(Director)*
Rosie Walton *(Director)*
Kirsty Ogden *(Accounts Manager)*

Poetry

Imprints, Series & ISBNs:
Bookprinting UK
Forward Poetry
Leavers Books
Need2Know
New Fiction
Poetry Rivals
Proprint
School Artists
School Products
Young Writers

Book Trade Association Membership:
Booksellers Association

2081

BONNIER PUBLISHING LTD
Appledram Barns, Birdham Road,
Chichester PO20 7EQ
Telephone: 01243 531473
Website: www.bonnierpublishing.co.uk

Book Trade Association Membership:
Publishers Association

2082

BORTHWICK PUBLICATIONS
Borthwick Institute, University of York,
Heslington, York YO10 5DD
Telephone: 01904 321166
Website: www.york.ac.uk/borthwick

Personnel:
Christopher Webb *(General Editor)*

*Academic & Scholarly; Archaeology;
Educational & Textbooks; History &
Antiquarian; Law; Religion & Theology*

Imprints, Series & ISBNs:
Borthwick List & Indexes: 978-0-903857
Borthwick Papers: 978-0-903857
Borthwick Publications: 978-1-09
Borthwick Studies in History: 978-0-903857
Borthwick Texts & Calendars: 978-0-
903857
Borthwick Wallets: 978-0-903857
Monastic Research Bulletin: 978-0-903857

Parent Company:
UK: University of York

2083

BOSSINEY BOOKS LTD
33 Queens Drive, Ilkley LS29 9QW
Telephone: 01943 602779
Email: bossineybooks@btinternet.com
Website: www.bossineybooks.com

Distribution:
Tor Mark Press, PO Box 4, Redruth,
Cornwall TR16 5YX
Telephone: 01209 822101
Fax: 01209 822035
Email: office@tormark.co.uk
Website: www.tormark.co.uk

Personnel:
Jane White *(Director)*
Paul White *(Director)*

*Cookery, Wines & Spirits; Guide Books;
History & Antiquarian; Travel & Topography*

Imprints, Series & ISBNs:
Bossiney Books Ltd: 978-1-906474
Tamar Books: 978-1-906474
Whinray Books: 978-0-9571939

2084

**BOWKER MARKET RESEARCH
(FORMERLY BML)**
[a division of Bowker]
St Andrew's House,
18–20 St Andrew Street, London
EC4A 3AG
Telephone: 020 7832 1782
Email: jo.henry@bowker.co.uk
Website: www.bookconsumer.co.uk

Personnel:
Jo Henry *(Global Director)*
Steve Bohme *(Research Director)*
James Howitt *(Director of Client Services)*

*Academic & Scholarly; Antiques &
Collecting; Archaeology; Architecture &
Design; Atlases & Maps; Audio Books;
Biography & Autobiography; Cinema,
Video, TV & Radio; Cookery, Wines &
Spirits; Crafts & Hobbies; Crime;
Economics; Electronic (Entertainment);
Electronic (Professional & Academic);
Fiction; Fine Art & Art History; Guide
Books; Health & Beauty; History &
Antiquarian; Humour; Industry, Business &
Management; Languages & Linguistics;
Law; Magic & the Occult; Military & War;
Music; Natural History; Philosophy;
Photography; Poetry; Politics & World
Affairs; Psychology & Psychiatry; Reference
Books, Directories & Dictionaries; Religion &
Theology; Science Fiction; Scientific &
Technical; Sociology & Anthropology;
Sports & Games; Travel & Topography*

Imprints, Series & ISBNs:
Bowker Market Research

Parent Company:
UK: Bowker

Overseas Representation:
New South Books: Melbourne, Australia

Book Trade Association Membership:
Booksellers Association; Independent
Publishers Guild

2085

BOWKER (UK) LTD
St Andrew's House,
18–20 St Andrew Street, London
EC4A 3AG
Telephone: 020 7832 1770
Fax: 020 7832 1710
Email: sales@bowker.co.uk
Website: www.bowker.co.uk

Personnel:
Doug McMillan *(Managing Director)*
Mrs Jo Grange *(EMEA Field Marketing
Manager)*
Darren Roberts *(Sales Specialist)*
Ian Pattenden *(Sales Specialist)*

*Academic & Scholarly; Bibliography &
Library Science; Electronic (Educational);
Electronic (Professional & Academic)*

Imprints, Series & ISBNs:
Bowker (UK) Ltd: 978-0-8352

Overseas Representation:
All: www.bowker.com/go/findarep, UK

Book Trade Association Membership:
Booksellers Association; CILIP

2086

MARION BOYARS PUBLISHERS LTD
26 Parke Road, London SW13 9NG
Email: catheryn@marionboyars.com
Website: www.marionboyars.co.uk

Distribution:
Central Books, 99 Wallis Road, London
E9 5LN
Telephone: 020 8986 4854
Fax: 020 8533 5821
Email: orders@centralbooks.com

Personnel:
Catheryn Kilgarriff *(Managing Director)*
Rebecca Gillieron *(Editorial Manager)*

*Biography & Autobiography; Children's
Books; Cinema, Video, TV & Radio; Fiction;
Literature & Criticism; Music; Philosophy;
Theatre, Drama & Dance*

Imprints, Series & ISBNs:
Marion Boyars Publishers Ltd: 978-0-7145

Associated Companies:
USA: Marion Boyars Publishers Inc

Overseas Representation:
USA: Consortium Book Sales & Distribution
Inc, MN, USA

Book Trade Association Membership:
Independent Publishers Guild

2087

BOYDELL & BREWER LTD
PO Box 9, Woodbridge, Suffolk IP12 3DF
Telephone: 01394 610600
Fax: 01394 610316
Email: trading@boydell.co.uk
Website: www.boydellandbrewer.com

Personnel:
P. Clifford *(Managing Director)*
M. J. Richards *(Sales Director)*
C. L. Palmer *(Editorial Director)*
W. Ellis *(Accounts Director)*
J. Pearce *(Group Financial Controller)*
M. L. Webb *(Production Manager)*
Dr M. Middeke *(Senior Commissioning
Editor)*
M. Jordan *(Customer Service Manager)*

*Academic & Scholarly; Archaeology;
Architecture & Design; History &
Antiquarian; Literature & Criticism; Military
& War; Music; Philosophy; Reference
Books, Directories & Dictionaries; Travel &
Topography*

Imprints, Series & ISBNs:
Boydell Press: 978-0-85115
D. S. Brewer: 978-0-85991
Camden House: 978-1-57113
Companion Guides: 978-1-900639
James Currey: 978-1-84701
Tamesis: 978-1-85566
York Medieval Press: 978-1-903153

Associated Companies:
USA: Boydell & Brewer Inc; University of
Rochester Press

Distributor for:
UK: Bedfordshire Historical Record Society;
Henry Bradshaw Society; Burke's
Peerage; Canterbury & York Society;
Catholic Record Society; Church of
England Record Society; Early English
Text Society; Ecclesiastical History
Society; King's College London Medieval
Studies; Lincoln Records Society;
Plumbago Books; Royal Historical
Society; Scholarly Digital Editions;
Scottish Text Society; Suffolk Records
Society; Surtees Society; Toccata Press;
Victoria County History; Yorkshire
Archaeological Society
USA: University of Rochester Press

Overseas Representation:
Africa (excluding South Africa): Tony
Moggach, IMA, London, UK
Australia: Inbooks, Brookvale, NSW,
Australia
Belgium, Luxembourg & Netherlands:
Kemper Conseil Publishing,
Leidschendam, Netherlands
Eastern Europe: Marek Lewinson, Warsaw,
Poland
France: Mare Nostrum, Paris, France
Germany, Austria & Switzerland: Frauke
Feldmann, Berlin, Germany
Greece & Cyprus: Charles Gibbes
Associates, Louslitges, France
India & Sri Lanka: Govinda Berry, New Delhi,
India
Italy: David Pickering, Mare Nostrum
Publishing Consultants, Harrogate, UK
Middle East & North Africa: Publishers
International Marketing, Storrington, UK
Pakistan: T.M.L. Publishers' Consultants &
Representatives, Lahore, Pakistan
Philippines: Edwin Makabenta, Quezon
City, Philippines
Republic of Ireland: Global Book Marketing,
London, UK
Scandinavia: Colin Flint Ltd, Publishers
Scandinavian Consultancy, Cambridge,
UK
South East Asia & Korea: Publishers
International Marketing, London, UK
Spain & Portugal: Iberian Book Services,
Madrid, Spain

Book Trade Association Membership:
Independent Publishers Guild

2088 ▬▬▬▬▬▬▬▬▬▬

*BRADT TRAVEL GUIDES LTD
1st Floor, IDC House, The Vale,
Chalfont St Peter, Bucks SL9 9RZ
Telephone: 01753 893444
Fax: 01753 892333
Email: info@bradtguides.com
Website: www.bradtguides.com

Orders to:
NBN International, 10 Thornbury Road,
Plymouth PL6 7PP
Telephone: 01752 202301
Fax: 01752 202331
Email: orders@nbninternational.com

Personnel:
Donald Greig *(Executive Director)*
Peter Jay *(Finance Director)*
Adrian Phillips *(Publishing Director)*

Guide Books; Travel & Topography

Imprints, Series & ISBNs:
Bradt Travel Guides: 978-1-84162

Overseas Representation:
*Africa (excluding South Africa, Namibia, &
Zimbabwe):* A–Z Africa Book Services,
Rotterdam, Netherlands
Australia: Woodslane Pty Ltd, Warriewood,
NSW, Australia
Austria: Freytag & Berndt, Vienna, Austria
Belgium: Craenen bvba, Herent (Winksele),
Belgium
Eastern Europe: CLB Marketing Services,
Budapest, Hungary
France: Cartothèque EGG, Notre Dame
D'Oé, France
Germany & Luxembourg: Durnell
Marketing Ltd, Tunbridge Wells, UK
Israel: Steinhard Katzir, Netanya, Israel
Netherlands: Nilsson & Lamm BV, Weesp,
Netherlands
Portugal: Iberian Book Services, Madrid,
Spain
Scandinavian Europe: Angell Eurosales,
Berwick-on-Tweed, UK
Singapore: Pansing Distribution Pte Ltd,
Singapore
South & Central America: David Williams,
InterMedia Americana (IMA) Ltd,
London, UK
South Africa: Jacana Media, Johannesburg,
South Africa
Spain: Altair, Barcelona, Spain
Switzerland: Distribution OLF SA, Fribourg,
Switzerland
USA & Canada: Globe Pequot Press,
Guilford, CT, USA

Book Trade Association Membership:
Independent Publishers Guild

2089 ▬▬▬▬▬▬▬▬▬▬

BRADWELL BOOKS
9 Orgreave Close Sheffield S13 9NP
Telephone: 0114 288 9522
Fax: 0114 269 1499
Email: info@bradwellbooks.co.uk
Website: www.bradwellbooks.com

Personnel:
Andrew Smith *(MD)*
Bill Noakes *(Sales Director)*
Chris Gilbert *(Publisher)*

*Atlases & Maps; Children's Books; Guide
Books; Humour; Photography; Reference
Books, Directories & Dictionaries; Travel &
Topography*

New Titles: 10 (2012) , 54 (2013)
No of Employees: 2

Imprints, Series & ISBNs:
Bradwell Books

Parent Company:
UK: NMD Trading Company

Distributor for:
UK: Mayfield Books & Gifts

2090 ▬▬▬▬▬▬▬▬▬▬

NICHOLAS BREALEY PUBLISHING
3–5 Spafield Street, London EC1R 4QB
Telephone: 020 7239 0360
Fax: 020 7239 0370
Email: rights@nicholasbrealey.com
Website: www.nicholasbrealey.com

Orders & Warehouse:
TBS Ltd, Colchester Road, Frating Green,
Colchester, Essex CO7 7DW
Telephone: 01206 256000

Fax: 01206 819587

Personnel:
Nicholas Brealey *(Managing Director)*
David Segrue *(Sales Manager)*
Sally Lansdell *(Publishing Manager)*

*Biography & Autobiography; Economics;
Industry, Business & Management;
Psychology & Psychiatry; Travel &
Topography; Vocational Training & Careers*

Imprints, Series & ISBNs:
Nicholas Brealey: 978-1-85788
Nicholas Brealey International
Davies-Black: 978-0-89106
Industrial Society (acquired titles): 978-0-
85290
Intercultural Press

Parent Company:
UK: NB Ltd

Associated Companies:
USA: NB Publishing Inc

Overseas Representation:
Asia (excluding Singapore & Malaysia):
Sales East, Bangkok, Thailand
Australia: Allen & Unwin Pty Ltd, Sydney,
NSW, Australia
*Europe (excluding Scandinavia) &
Switzerland:* Michael Geoghegan,
London, UK
India: Research Press, New Delhi, India
Republic of Ireland: Gill Simpson, Dublin,
Republic of Ireland
Scandinavia: Angell Eurosales, Berwick-
upon-Tweed, UK
Singapore & Malaysia: Horizon Books Pte
Ltd, Singapore
South Africa: Wild Dog Press, Highlands
North, South Africa
USA: National Book Network, Lanham, MD,
USA; Nicholas Brealey Publishing North
America, Boston, MA, USA

Book Trade Association Membership:
Independent Publishers Guild

2091 ▬▬▬▬▬▬▬▬▬▬

BREWIN BOOKS LTD
Doric House, 56 Alcester Road, Studley,
Warwickshire B80 7LG
Telephone: 01527 854228
Fax: 01527 852746
Email: admin@brewinbooks.com
Website: www.brewinbooks.com

Warehouse:
Supaprint Works, Unit 19,
Enfield Industrial Estate, Redditch, Worcs
B97 6BY
Telephone: 01527 62212
Fax: 01527 60451
Email: admin@supaprint.com
Website: www.supaprint.com

Personnel:
Alan Brewin *(Managing Director)*
Alistair Brewin *(Art, Book Design &
Production Director)*
Julie Brewin *(Company Secretary)*

*Biography & Autobiography; Fiction;
History & Antiquarian; Military & War;
Transport*

Imprints, Series & ISBNs:
Alton Douglas Books: 978-1-85858
Brewin Books: 978-0-947731, 978-0-
9505570, 978-1-85858
History-into-Print: 978-1-85858

Distributor for:
UK: City of Birmingham Libraries; Hunt End
Books

2092 ▬▬▬▬▬▬▬▬▬▬

BRIDGE BOOKS
61 Park Avenue, Wrexham LL12 7AW
Telephone: 01978 358661 & 0845 166
2851
Email: enquiries@bridgebooks.co.uk
Website: www.bridgebooks.co.uk

Distribution:
Welsh Books Council,
Glanrafon Industrial Estate, Llanbadarn,
Aberystwyth, Ceredigion SY23 3AQ
Telephone: 01970 624455
Website: www.gwales.com

Personnel:
W. Alister Williams *(Partner)*
Susan A. Williams *(Partner)*

*Aviation; History & Antiquarian; Military &
War; Travel & Topography*

Imprints, Series & ISBNs:
Bridge Books: 978-0-9508285, 978-1-
84494, 978-1-872424

2093 ▬▬▬▬▬▬▬▬▬▬

BRILLIANT PUBLICATIONS
Unit 10, Sparrow Hill Farm, Edlesborough,
Dunstable LU6 2ES
Telephone: 01525 222292
Fax: 01525 222720
Email: info@brilliantpublications.co.uk
Website: www.brilliantpublications.co.uk

Sales & Distribution:
Brilliant Publications,
Mendlesham Industrial Estate,
Norwich Road, Mendlesham, Suffolk
IP14 5ND
Telephone: 01449 766629
Fax: 01449 767122
Email: orders@tradecounter.co.uk

Personnel:
Priscilla Hannaford *(Publisher)*
Richard Dorrance *(Finance Director)*
Alison Marshall *(Marketing)*

*Educational & Textbooks; Languages &
Linguistics*

New Titles: 21 (2012) , 20 (2013)

Imprints, Series & ISBNs:
Brilliant Publications: 978-0-85747, 978-1-
78317, 978-1-897675, 978-1-903853,
978-1-905780

Book Trade Association Membership:
Publishers Association; Educational
Publishers Council; Independent Publishers
Guild

2094 ▬▬▬▬▬▬▬▬▬▬

**BRITISH ASSOCIATION FOR
ADOPTION & FOSTERING**
[BAAF]
Saffron House, 6–10 Kirby Street, London
EC1N 8TS
Telephone: 020 7421 2602
Fax: 020 7421 2601
Email: shaila.shah@baaf.org.uk
Website: www.baaf.org.uk

Trade Enquiries:
Turnaround Distribution, Unit 3,
Olympia Trading Estate, Coburg Road,
London N22 6TZ
Telephone: 020 8829 3000
Fax: 020 8881 5088
Email: orders@turnaround-uk.com

Personnel:
Shan Nicholas *(Interim Chief Executive)*
Shaila Shah *(Publisher)*

*Academic & Scholarly; Children's Books;
Psychology & Psychiatry; Reference Books,*

Directories & Dictionaries; Sociology & Anthropology

New Titles: 35 (2012) , 35 (2013)
No of Employees: 150

Imprints, Series & ISBNs:
British Association for Adoption & Fostering: 978-0-903534, 978-1-873868, 978-1-903699, 978-1-905664, 978-1-907585

Overseas Representation:
Australia (selected titles): Innovative Resources, Bendigo, Vic, Australia

Book Trade Association Membership:
The Publishers Forum for the Voluntary Sector

2095

BRITISH GEOLOGICAL SURVEY
Keyworth, Nottingham NG12 5GG
Telephone: 0115 936 3241 (sales) & 0115 936 3147 (returns)
Fax: 0115 936 3488
Email: sales@bgs.ac.uk & ikp@bgs.ac.uk (returns)
Website: www.bgs.ac.uk & www.geologyshop.com (online shop)

Distribution & Representation:
Cordee Ltd, 11 Jacknell Road, Dodswell Bridge Industrial Estate, Hinckley, Leics LE10 3BS
Telephone: 01455 611185
Fax: 01455 635687
Email: info@cordee.co.uk
Website: www.cordee.co.uk

Personnel:
Prof John Ludden *(Director)*
Jim Rayner *(Science Services Manager)*
Chris Luton *(Copyright & IPR)*
Ivan Page *(Sales Manager)*

Atlases & Maps; Geography & Geology; Guide Books; Scientific & Technical

Imprints, Series & ISBNs:
British Geological Survey (Books & Reports) : 978-0-85272
British Geological Survey (Maps) : 978-0-7518

Parent Company:
UK: Natural Environment Research Council

Distributor for:
UK: Durham County Council

2096

BRITISH LIBRARY
96 Euston Road, London NW1 2DB
Telephone: 0843 208 1144
Fax: 020 7412 7768
Email: publishing_editorial@bl.uk
Website: www.bl.uk

Distribution:
NBN International, 10 Thornbury Road, Plymouth PL6 7PP
Telephone: 01752 202301
Fax: 01752 202333
Email: orders@nbninternational.com
Website: www.nbninternational.com

Personnel:
David Way *(Publisher)*
Lara Speicher *(Commissioning Editor)*
Robert Davies *(Project Editor)*
Martin Oestreicher *(Sales Manager, Publishing & Brand Licensing)*

Academic & Scholarly; Bibliography & Library Science; Biography & Autobiography; Fine Art & Art History; History & Antiquarian; Illustrated & Fine Editions

Imprints, Series & ISBNs:
Bibliography of British Newspapers: 978-0-7123
The British Library: 978-0-7123
British Library Guides: 978-0-7123
British Library Occasional Papers: 978-0-7123
The British Library Studies in Medieval Culture: 978-0-7123
The British Library Studies in the History of the Book: 978-0-7123
Corpus of British Medieval Library Catalogues: 978-0-7123
The Panizzi Lectures: 978-0-7123

Overseas Representation:
Australia: InBooks, Belrose, NSW, Australia
USA & Canada: University of Chicago Press, Chicago, IL, USA

Book Trade Association Membership:
Booksellers Association; Independent Publishers Guild

2097

BRITISH MUSEUM PRESS
38 Russell Square, London WC1B 3QQ
Telephone: 020 7323 1234
Fax: 020 7436 7315
Email: publicity@britishmuseum.co.uk
Website: www.britishmuseum.org/publishing

Trade Distributor:
Littlehampton Book Services, Faraday Close, Durrington, Worthing, West Sussex BN13 3RB
Telephone: 01903 828501
Fax: 01903 828801/2
Email: enquiries@lbsltd.co.uk

Personnel:
Rosemary Bradley *(Publishing Director)*
Coralie Hepburn *(Editorial)*
Susan Walby *(Head of Production)*
Sheila McKenna *(Head of Sales, Marketing & Rights)*
Kate Hilsen *(Marketing/Publicity)*
Victoria Benjamin *(Marketing/Publicity)*

Academic & Scholarly; Antiques & Collecting; Archaeology; Children's Books; Fine Art & Art History; History & Antiquarian; Reference Books, Directories & Dictionaries; Sociology & Anthropology

Imprints, Series & ISBNs:
British Museum Press: 978-0-7141

Parent Company:
UK: The British Museum Co Ltd

Overseas Representation:
USA (Trade orders): British Museum Press, London, UK
Worldwide (excluding USA): Thames & Hudson (Distributors) Ltd, Farnborough, Hants, UK

Book Trade Association Membership:
Publishers Association

2098

BROWN DOG BOOKS
7c Green Park Station, Green Park Road, Bath BA1 1JB
Telephone: 01225 478444
Fax: 01225 478440
Email: sales@manning-partnership.co.uk
Website: www.manning-partnership.co.uk

Personnel:
Garry Manning *(Managing Director)*
Roger Hibbert *(Sales & Marketing Director)*
Heather Morris *(Editorial Director)*
Karen Twissell *(Office Manager)*
James Wheeler *(Sales Manager)*

Children's Books; Cookery, Wines & Spirits; Humour; Sports & Games

Imprints, Series & ISBNs:
Brown Dog Books: 978-1-903056, 978-1-903222
Nightingale: 978-1-903222

Parent Company:
UK: Accent; Arcturus; ATP; Humpty Dumpty; Manning Partnership Ltd; Worth Press; Xcite

Distributor for:
UK: Anness; Carroll & Brown; Hometown World; Interpet Publishing; Nightingale Press; Search Press
USA: Source Books

2099

BROWN, SON & FERGUSON, LTD
4–10 Darnley Street, Glasgow G41 2SD
Telephone: 0141 429 1234
Fax: 0141 420 1694
Email: info@skipper.co.uk
Website: www.skipper.co.uk

Personnel:
T. Nigel Brown *(Chairman & Production Director)*
Richard P. B. Brown *(Director)*

Nautical; Theatre, Drama & Dance

Imprints, Series & ISBNs:
Brown, Son & Ferguson, Ltd: 978-0-85174, 978-1-84927

Associated Companies:
UK: James Munro & Co

Book Trade Association Membership:
Publishing Scotland

2100

BRYNTIRION PRESS
Bryntirion, Bridgend, Mid Glamorgan CF31 4DX
Telephone: 01656 655886

Representation:
Evangelical Press, Faverdale North, Darlington DL3 0PH
Telephone: 01325 380232
Fax: 01325 466153
Email: sales@evangelical-press.org

Personnel:
Sharon Barnes *(Press Officer)*

Religion & Theology

Parent Company:
UK: Evangelical Movement of Wales

Distributor for:
UK: Association of Christian Teachers of Wales

Book Trade Association Membership:
Booksellers Association; Undeb Cyhoeddwyr a Llyfrwerthwyr Cymru (The Union of Welsh Publishers and Booksellers)

2101

BUTTERFINGERS BOOKS
30 Tor View Avenue, Glastonbury, Somerset BA6 8AF
Telephone: 01458 830900
Email: laurie@butterfingersbooks.co.uk
Website: www.butterfingersbooks.co.uk

Personnel:
L. H. R. Collard *(Rights Director)*

Educational & Textbooks; Sports & Games

Imprints, Series & ISBNs:
Butterfingers Books: 978-0-9513240, 978-1-898591

Distributor for:
Switzerland: Jonglerie Diffusion
UK: Circustuff
USA: Brian Dubé Inc; Renegade Juggling

Overseas Representation:
North America: Brian Dube Inc, New York, NY, USA

2102

CABI
Nosworthy Way, Wallingford, Oxon OX10 8DE
Telephone: 01491 832111
Fax: 01491 833508 & 829292 (order fulfilment)
Email: publishing@cabi.org
Website: www.cabi.org/

Personnel:
Ms Caroline McNamara *(Executive & Commercial Director)*
Ms Andrea Powell *(Executive & Publishing Director)*
Shaun Hobbs *(Director, Plantwise Knowledge Bank)*
Elizabeth Dodsworth *(Knowledge for Development Director)*
Nigel Farrar *(Editorial Director)*

Academic & Scholarly; Agriculture; Animal Care & Breeding; Biology & Zoology; Environment & Development Studies; Medical (incl. Self-Help & Alternative Medicine); Scientific & Technical; Veterinary Science

Imprints, Series & ISBNs:
CABI: 978-0-85198, 978-0-85199, 978-1-84593

Parent Company:
UK: CAB International

Distributor for:
UK: International Food Information Service; Royal Society of Edinburgh

Overseas Representation:
Africa: CABI Africa, Nairobi, Kenya
All other areas: Commercial Department, Wallingford, UK
Asia: CABI South East & East Asia, Serdang, Malaysia
Australia, New Zealand & Papua New Guinea: DA Information Services Pty Ltd, Mitcham, Vic, Australia
Canada: CABI North America, Cambridge, MA, USA
Caribbean: CABI Caribbean & Latin America, Curepe, Trinidad
Denmark, Finland, Iceland, Norway & Sweden: Colin Flint Ltd, Harlow, UK
Germany, Austria & Switzerland: Missing Link International Booksellers, Bremen, Germany
India: Book Marketing Services, Chennai, India
Middle East (excluding Iran): James & Lorin Watt Ltd, Publishing Consultants, Oxford, UK
South Africa: Academic Marketing Services (Pty) Ltd, Craighall, South Africa
USA, Central America, Caribbean, Mexico, Puerto Rico & Guam: Oxford University Press, Cary, NC, USA

Book Trade Association Membership:
Booksellers Association

2103

CALYPSO PUBLICATIONS
2 Gatcombe Road, London N19 4PT
Telephone: 020 7281 4948
Fax: 020 7281 4948
Email: Gerald@calypso.org.uk & enquiries@calypso.org.uk
Website: www.calypso.org.uk/ourbooks & www.calypso.org.uk/bookshop

Personnel:
G. H. Jennings *(Proprietor)*

Academic & Scholarly; Animal Care & Breeding; Biology & Zoology; Crafts & Hobbies; Educational & Textbooks; Natural History; Reference Books, Directories & Dictionaries; Scientific & Technical; Travel & Topography; Veterinary Science

Imprints, Series & ISBNs:
Calypso Publications: 978-0-906301, 978-1-902788

Parent Company:
UK: The Calypso Organization

Overseas Representation:
Australia: Andrew Isles Bookshop, Melbourne, Vic, Australia
USA: The Aquatic Bookshop, Placerville, CA, USA

2104 ━━━━━━

CAMBRIDGE UNIVERSITY PRESS
The Edinburgh Building, Shaftesbury Road, Cambridge CB2 8RU
Telephone: 01223 358331
Email: information@cambridge.org
Website: www.cambridge.org

Personnel:
Peter Phillips *(Chief Executive)*
Cathy Armor *(Director for People)*
Andrew Chandler *(Chief Financial Officer)*
Tony Lund *(Managing Director, Asia)*
Mark Maddocks *(Chief Information Officer)*
Richard Fisher *(Managing Director, Academic)*
Michael Peluse *(Managing Director, English Language Teaching and Americas)*
Hanri Pieterse *(Managing Director, Cambridge Education)*
Kevin Taylor *(Director of Syndicate Affairs)*
Sandra Waterhouse *(Director of Operations)*
Simon Ross *(Deputy Managing Director, Academic and Managing Director, Journals)*
William Bowes *(General Counsel and Secretary to the Press Board)*

Academic & Scholarly; Archaeology; Architecture & Design; Biology & Zoology; Chemistry; Computer Science; Economics; Educational & Textbooks; Electronic (Educational); Electronic (Professional & Academic); Engineering; English as a Foreign Language; Environment & Development Studies; Fine Art & Art History; Gender Studies; Geography & Geology; History & Antiquarian; Industry, Business & Management; Languages & Linguistics; Law; Literature & Criticism; Mathematics & Statistics; Medical (incl. Self-Help & Alternative Medicine); Music; Natural History; Philosophy; Physics; Politics & World Affairs; Psychology & Psychiatry; Reference Books, Directories & Dictionaries; Religion & Theology; Scientific & Technical; Sociology & Anthropology; Theatre, Drama & Dance

New Titles: 4000 (2012)
No of Employees: 2000
Annual Turnover: £245M

Imprints, Series & ISBNs:
Cambridge University Press: 978-0-511, 978-0-521, 978-1-107, 978-1-108, 978-1-139

Book Trade Association Membership:
Publishers Association; Booksellers Association; Educational Publishers Council; International Group of Scientific, Medical & Technical Publishers; Independent Publishers Guild; Association of Learned & Professional Society Publishers; BML; IBD

2105 ━━━━━━

CAMRA BOOKS
230 Hatfield Road, St Albans, Herts AL1 4LW
Telephone: 01727 867201
Fax: 01727 867670
Email: books@camra.org.uk
Website: www.camra.org.uk

UK Distribution:
Macmillan Distribution (MDL), Houndmills, Basingstoke, Hampshire RG21 6XS
Telephone: 01256 329242
Fax: 01256 328339

Personnel:
Tony Jerome *(Head of Marketing)*
Simon Hall *(Head of Publishing)*
Chris Lewis *(Marketing Officer)*

Biography & Autobiography; Cookery, Wines & Spirits; Guide Books; Reference Books, Directories & Dictionaries; Travel & Topography

Imprints, Series & ISBNs:
Camra Books: 978-1-85249

Parent Company:
UK: Campaign for Real Ale Ltd

Overseas Representation:
USA: Trafalgar (Independent Publishers Group) Chicago, IL, USA

Book Trade Association Membership:
Independent Publishers Guild

2106 ━━━━━━

CANONGATE BOOKS
14 High Street, Edinburgh EH1 1TE
Telephone: 0131 557 5111
Fax: 0131 557 5211
Email: info@canongate.co.uk
Website: www.canongate.tv

Warehouse & Orders:
The Book Service Ltd, Distribution Centre, Colchester Road, Frating Green, Colchester, Essex CO7 7DW
Telephone: 01206 256000
Fax: 01206 255715
Email: helpdesk@tbs-ltd.co.uk
Website: www.thebookservice.co.uk

Personnel:
Jamie Byng *(Publisher)*
Jenny Todd *(Associate Publisher)*
Francis Bickmore *(Publishing Director)*
Caroline Gorham *(Production Director)*
Katie Moffat *(Campaigns Director)*
Andrea Joyce *(Rights Director)*
Susie Tastard *(Finance Director)*
Sian Gibson *(Head of Sales)*
Lindsey Terrell *(Marketing Executive)*
Anna Frame *(Head of Publicity)*

Audio Books; Biography & Autobiography; Cinema, Video, TV & Radio; Crime; Fiction; Fine Art & Art History; History & Antiquarian; Humour; Illustrated & Fine Editions; Literature & Criticism; Music; Philosophy; Poetry; Politics & World Affairs; Psychology & Psychiatry; Religion & Theology; Travel & Topography

Imprints, Series & ISBNs:
Canongate: 978-0-86241, 978-1-84195
Canongate Classics: 978-0-86241, 978-1-84195
Canons: 978-0-85786, 978-0-86241
Myths: 978-0-86241, 978-1-84195

Associated Companies:
Australia: Text Publishing
USA: Canongate US

Overseas Representation:
Australia: Penguin Books Australia Ltd, Camberwell, Vic, Australia
Canada: Penguin Group Canada, Toronto, Ont, Canada
Eastern Europe: Csaba & Jackie Lengyel de Bagota, Budapest, Hungary
Far East: Julian Ashton, Ashton International Marketing Services, Sevenoaks, Kent, UK
India: Rave Media, Nandan Jha, India
Latin America & Caribbean: InterMedia Americana (IMA) Ltd, London, UK
Netherlands, Africa & Pakistan: Export Sales Department, Canongate Books, Edinburgh, UK
New Zealand: Penguin Books (New Zealand) Ltd, Auckland, New Zealand
Northern Europe: Bridget Lane, Faber & Faber, London, UK
South Africa: Penguin Books South Africa, Gardenview, South Africa
Southern Europe: Melissa Elders, Faber & Faber, London, UK
USA: Publishers Group West, Berkeley, CA, USA

Book Trade Association Membership:
Publishers Association; Publishing Scotland; Independent Publishers Guild

2107 ━━━━━━

CAPALL BANN PUBLISHING LTD
Auton Farm, Milverton, Somerset TA4 1NE
Telephone: 01823 401528
Email: enquiries@capallbann.co.uk
Website: www.capallbann.co.uk

Personnel:
Jon Day *(Sales & Rights Publisher)*
Julia Day *(Administration & Editorial Publisher)*

Animal Care & Breeding; Archaeology; Cookery, Wines & Spirits; Crafts & Hobbies; Educational & Textbooks; Environment & Development Studies; Gardening; Gender Studies; Guide Books; Health & Beauty; History & Antiquarian; Magic & the Occult; Medical (incl. Self-Help & Alternative Medicine); Music; Natural History; Philosophy; Psychology & Psychiatry; Religion & Theology; Theatre, Drama & Dance

Imprints, Series & ISBNs:
Capall Bann Publishing: 978-1-86163, 978-1-898307

Overseas Representation:
Australia (New Age): Brumby Books Holdings Pty Ltd, Kilsyth South, Vic, Australia
South Africa: Bacchus Books, Cresta, South Africa
USA: Holmes Publishing Group, Edmunds, WA, USA; New Leaf Distributing Co, Lithia Springs, GA, USA

2108 ━━━━━━

CAPUCHIN CLASSICS
128 Kensington Church Street, London W8 4BH
Telephone: 020 7221 7166
Fax: 020 7792 9288
Email: info@stacey-international.co.uk
Website: www.stacey-international.co.uk

Personnel:
Hannah Young *(Editor)*
Liz Holmes *(Production Manager)*
Emma Howard *(Editor)*

Academic & Scholarly; Archaeology; Biography & Autobiography; Children's Books; Cookery, Wines & Spirits; Fiction; Gardening; Guide Books; History & Antiquarian; Natural History; Politics & World Affairs; Reference Books, Directories & Dictionaries; Religion & Theology; Travel & Topography

Parent Company:
UK: Stacey Publishing Ltd

Overseas Representation:
Australia: Peribo, NSW, Australia
Europe: Durnell Marketing, Tunbridge Wells, UK
South Africa: Stephan Philips, Cape Town, South Africa
USA: Midpoint, New York, NY, USA

Book Trade Association Membership:
Independent Publishers Guild

2109 ━━━━━━

CAREL PRESS LTD
4 Hewson Street, Carlisle, Cumbria CA2 5AU
Telephone: 01228 538928
Fax: 01228 591816
Email: office@carelpress.co.uk
Website: www.carelpress.com & www.shortershakespeare.com

Personnel:
Chas White *(Publisher)*
Mrs Ann Batey *(Office Manager)*

Atlases & Maps; Educational & Textbooks; Electronic (Educational); Languages & Linguistics; Literature & Criticism; Mathematics & Statistics; Reference Books, Directories & Dictionaries; Sports & Games; Theatre, Drama & Dance

Imprints, Series & ISBNs:
Carel Press Ltd: 978-1-872365, 978-1-905600

Distributor for:
UK: Arc Theatre Co; ODT Inc (Maps); One Page Book Co

Book Trade Association Membership:
Independent Publishers Guild

2110 ━━━━━━

CARNEGIE PUBLISHING LTD
Carnegie House, Chatsworth Road, Lancaster LA1 4SL
Telephone: 01524 840111
Email: anna@carnegiepublishing.com
Website: www.carnegiepublishing.com

Personnel:
Alistair Hodge *(Managing Director)*
Anna Goddard *(Publishing & Marketing Director)*
Lucy Frontani *(Book Design Manager)*

Academic & Scholarly; Archaeology; Cookery, Wines & Spirits; History & Antiquarian; Industry, Business & Management; Magic & the Occult; Military & War; Natural History

New Titles: 15 (2012) , 10 (2013)
No of Employees: 9
Annual Turnover: £450,000

Imprints, Series & ISBNs:
Carnegie Publishing Ltd: 978-1-85936, 978-1-874181, 978-1-904244, 978-1-905472
Crucible Books: 978-1-905472
Palatine Books: 978-1-874181
Scotforth Books: 978-1-904244

Book Trade Association Membership:
Publishers Association

2111 ━━━━━━

JON CARPENTER PUBLISHING
Alder House, Market Street, Charlbury OX7 3PH
Telephone: 01608 819117
Email: jon@joncarpenter.co.uk

Trade Orders:
Central Books, 99 Wallis Road, London
E9 5LN
Telephone: 020 8986 4854
Fax: 020 8533 5821
Email: orders@centralbooks.com

Personnel:
Jon Carpenter (Publisher)

Cookery, Wines & Spirits; Economics;
History & Antiquarian

Imprints, Series & ISBNs:
Jon Carpenter: 978-0-9549727, 978-1-
897766, 978-1-906067
The Wychwood Press: 978-1-902279

Overseas Representation:
Australia: Envirobook, Annandale, NSW,
Australia
USA: Independent Publishers Group (IPG),
Chicago, IL, USA

Book Trade Association Membership:
Booksellers Association

2112

CARROLL & BROWN LTD
259–269 Old Marylebone Road, London
NW1 5RA
Telephone: 020 7025 5300
Email: mail@carrollandbrown.co.uk
Website: www.carrollandbrown.co.uk

Personnel:
Amy Carroll (Managing Director)
Chrissie Lloyd (Art Director)
Simonne Waud (Sales, Rights Director)
Derek Thornhill (Marketing Director)

Animal Care & Breeding; Cookery, Wines &
Spirits; Crafts & Hobbies; Electronic
(Entertainment); Health & Beauty; Medical
(incl. Self-Help & Alternative Medicine)

Imprints, Series & ISBNs:
Carroll & Brown Ltd: 978-1-903258, 978-1-
904760, 978-1-907952

Associated Companies:
UK: Carroll & Brown Publishers Ltd

Overseas Representation:
Worldwide: Derek Thornhill, Carroll &
Brown Ltd, London, UK

Book Trade Association Membership:
Independent Publishers Guild; Book
Packagers Association

2113

THE CATHOLIC TRUTH SOCIETY
[Publishers to the Holy See]
42–46 Harleyford Road, London SE11 5AY
Telephone: 020 7640 0042
Fax: 020 7640 0046
Email: orders@ctsbooks.org
Website: www.ctsbooks.org

Retail Bookshop:
25 Ashley Place, London SW1P 1LT
Telephone: 020 7834 1363
Fax: 020 7821 7398
Email: bookshop@cts-online.org.uk
Website: www.ctsbooks.org

Personnel:
Rt Rev Paul Hendricks (Chairman)
Fergal Martin (General Secretary)
John Dilger (Hon Treasurer & Director)
Stephen Campbell (Production Manager)
Pierpaolo Finaldi (Commissioning Editor)
Christine Parreno (Editorial Assistant)

Biography & Autobiography; Children's
Books; Guide Books; History &
Antiquarian; Reference Books, Directories &
Dictionaries; Religion & Theology

New Titles: 70 (2012) , 35 (2013)
No of Employees: 25

Imprints, Series & ISBNs:
The Catholic Truth Society: 978-0-85183
Catholic Truth Society: 978-1-86082

Distributor for:
Vatican City State: L' Osservatore Romano

Overseas Representation:
Australia & New Zealand: St Pauls
Publications, Strathfield, NSW, Australia
North America: Ignatius Press, CA, USA

Book Trade Association Membership:
Booksellers Association

2114

*CATNIP PUBLISHING
14 Greville Street, London EC1N 8SB
Telephone: 020 7138 3650
Fax: 020 7138 3658
Website: www.catnippublishing.co.uk

Book Trade Association Membership:
Publishers Association

2115

CAXTON PUBLISHING GROUP LTD
20 Bloomsbury Street, London WC1B 3JH
Telephone: 020 7636 7171
Fax: 020 7636 1922
Email: office@caxtonpublishing.com

Personnel:
Finbarr McCabe (Managing Director)
James Birney (Sales Director)

Archaeology; Atlases & Maps; Children's
Books; Cookery, Wines & Spirits;
Gardening; Geography & Geology; Guide
Books; Health & Beauty; History &
Antiquarian; Literature & Criticism; Military
& War; Reference Books, Directories &
Dictionaries

Imprints, Series & ISBNs:
Caxton Publishing Group Ltd: 978-1-84560,
978-1-904668

Parent Company:
UK: Caxton Publishing Group

Overseas Representation:
Australia, USA & Far East: Finbarr McCabe,
UK
Canada: James Birney, UK
South Africa: Peter Matthews Agencies,
Alberton, South Africa

2116

CBD RESEARCH LTD
Chancery House, 15 Wickham Road,
Beckenham, Kent BR3 5JS
Telephone: 020 8650 7745
Fax: 020 8650 0768
Email: cbd@cbdresearch.com
Website: www.cbdresearch.com

Crime; Reference Books, Directories &
Dictionaries

Imprints, Series & ISBNs:
CBD Research: 978-0-900246
CBD Research Ltd: 978-0-9554514
Chancery House Press: 978-0-900246

Book Trade Association Membership:
Independent Publishers Guild; Data
Publishers Association

2117

CENGAGE LEARNING EMEA LTD
Cheriton House, North Way, Andover,
Hants SP10 5BE
Telephone: 01264 332424
Fax: 01264 342745

Website: www.cengage.co.uk

Personnel:
Julian Drinkall (Chief Executive Officer &
President)
Chad Bonney (Chief Financial Officer)
Andrew Robinson (Sales Director)
Carrie Willicome (Customer Service
Director)
Rossella Proscia (Marketing Director)
Linden Harris (Publishing Director)
Pedja Paulicic (Digital Solutions Director)

Academic & Scholarly; Accountancy &
Taxation; Biology & Zoology; Chemistry;
Economics; Educational & Textbooks;
Engineering; English as a Foreign
Language; Health & Beauty; Industry,
Business & Management; Mathematics &
Statistics; Physics; Psychology & Psychiatry;
Reference Books, Directories &
Dictionaries; Vocational Training & Careers

Distributor for:
UK: Brooks/Cole; Cengage Learning;
Course Technology; Delmar Learning;
Gale; Heinle; South Western;
Wadsworth

Book Trade Association Membership:
Publishers Association

2118

**CENTRE FOR ECONOMIC POLICY
RESEARCH**
3rd Floor, 77 Bastwick Street, London
EC1V 3PZ
Telephone: 020 7183 8801
Fax: 020 7183 8820
Email: cepr@cepr.org
Website: www.cepr.org

Personnel:
Stephen Yeo (Chief Executive Officer)
Charlie Anderson (Publications Officer)

Academic & Scholarly; Economics; Industry,
Business & Management; Politics & World
Affairs

Imprints, Series & ISBNs:
Centre for Economic Policy Research: 978-
0-9557009, 978-1-898128, 978-1-
907142

Overseas Representation:
USA & Canada: The Brookings Institution,
Washington, DC, USA
Worldwide: Central Books, London, UK

2119

CENTRE FOR POLICY ON AGEING
28 Great Tower Street, London EC3R 5AT
Telephone: 020 7553 6500
Fax: 020 7553 6501
Email: cpa@cpa.org.uk
Website: www.cpa.org.uk/

Warehouse, Trade Enquiries & Orders:
Central Books, 99 Wallis Road, London
E9 5LN
Telephone: 0845 458 9911
Fax: 0845 458 9912
Email: orders@centralbooks.com
Website: www.centralbooks.co.uk

Personnel:
Gillian Crosby (Director)
Nat Lievesley (Manager)

Academic & Scholarly; Electronic
(Professional & Academic); Sociology &
Anthropology

Imprints, Series & ISBNs:
Centre for Policy on Ageing: 978-0-904139,
978-1-901097

Book Trade Association Membership:
Independent Publishers Guild

2120

CFBT EDUCATION TRUST
60 Queens Road, Reading RG1 4BS
Telephone: 0118 902 1000
Fax: 0118 902 1434
Email: enquiries@cfbt.com
Website: www.cfbt.com

Distribution & Orders:
Central Books Ltd, 99 Wallis Road, London
E9 5LN
Telephone: 0845 458 9910
Fax: 0845 458 9912
Email: mo@centralbooks.com
Website: www.centralbooks.co.uk

Personnel:
Samantha Lacey (Publishing Co-ordinator)

Academic & Scholarly; Educational &
Textbooks; Languages & Linguistics;
Vocational Training & Careers

New Titles: 3 (2012)

Imprints, Series & ISBNs:
Advanced Pathfinder
Classic Pathfinder
Curriculum Guides
Info Tech
New Pathfinder
Pathfinder
Reflections on Practice
Resource File
Young Pathfinder

Book Trade Association Membership:
Educational Publishers Council

2121

CHALKSOFT
PO Box 49, Spalding, Lincs PE11 1NZ
Telephone: 01775 725717
Email: chalksoft@clara.co.uk
Website: www.chalksoft.clara.co.uk

Personnel:
David Baldwin (Publisher)
Mrs Gillian Baldwin (Sales & Rights, Office
Manager)

Academic & Scholarly; Animal Care &
Breeding; Children's Books; Educational &
Textbooks; Electronic (Educational);
Gardening; Geography & Geology;
Mathematics & Statistics; Music; Natural
History; Scientific & Technical

Imprints, Series & ISBNs:
Chalksoft: 978-1-85116

Book Trade Association Membership:
Independent Publishers Guild

2122

CHANNEL VIEW PUBLICATIONS LTD
St Nicholas House, 31–34 High Street,
Bristol BS1 2AW
Telephone: 0117 315 8562
Fax: 0117 315 8563
Email: info@channelviewpublications.com
Website:
www.channelviewpublications.com

Distribution:
Marston Book Services,160 Eastern
Avenue, Abingdon OX14 4SB
Telephone: 01235 465500
Fax: 01235 465555
Email: trade.order@marston.co.uk
Website: www.marston.co.uk

Personnel:
Tommi Grover (Managing Director)
Anna Roderick (Editorial Director)
Elinor Robertson (Marketing Manager)
Sarah Williams (Production Manager)
Laura Longworth (Rights Manager)

Academic & Scholarly; Educational & Textbooks; Environment & Development Studies; Languages & Linguistics; Psychology & Psychiatry; Sociology & Anthropology; Travel & Topography

New Titles: 50 (2012) , 44 (2013)
No of Employees: 6
Annual Turnover: £900,000

Imprints, Series & ISBNs:
Channel View Publications: 978-1-78309
Multilingual Matters: 978-0-905028, 978-1-78309, 978-1-84769, 978-1-85359

Overseas Representation:
Canada: University of Toronto Press, North York, Ont, Canada
China: Sarah Zhao, Meme Media, China
India: Govinda Book House, New Delhi, India
Iran: Kowkab Publishers, Tehran, Iran
Japan: Eureka Press, Kyoto, Japan
Korea: Se-Yung Jun, Seoul, Republic of Korea
Malaysia: Publishers Marketing Services, Selangor, Malaysia
Philippines: Andrew White, Tunbridge Wells, UK
Singapore: Publishers Marketing Services Pte Ltd, Singapore
Taiwan: Andrew White, Tunbridge Wells, UK
USA: UTP, Tonawanda, NY, USA

Book Trade Association Membership:
Independent Publishers Guild; Association of Learned & Professional Society Publishers

2123

CHARTERED INSTITUTE OF PERSONNEL & DEVELOPMENT
151 The Broadway, London SW19 1JQ
Telephone: 020 8612 6564
Fax: 020 8543 4371
Email: publishing@cipd.co.uk
Website: www.cipd.co.uk/bookstore

Distribution:
McGraw-Hill Education,
McGraw-Hill House,
Shoppenhangers Road, Maidenhead, Berks SL6 2QL
Telephone: 01628 502700
Fax: 01628 770224
Website: www.cipd.co.uk/bookstore

Personnel:
Samantha Whittaker *(Head of Publishing)*
Margaret Marriott *(Managing Editor)*
Jeff Wood *(Operations Manager)*
Sinead Burke *(Sales & Marketing Manager)*
Holly Spice *(Senior Online Commissioning Editor)*
Katy Hamilton *(Commissioning Editor)*
Catherine Jeffrey *(Senior Operations Executive)*
Frank Kebbedies *(Operations XML Executive)*
Elizabeth Hall *(Sales & Marketing Executive)*
Phill Thompson *(Journals Executive)*
Pauline Allsop *(Operations Coordinator)*
Heidi Partridge *(Commissioning Coordinator)*

Academic & Scholarly; Educational & Textbooks; Industry, Business & Management

Imprints, Series & ISBNs:
Chartered Institute of Personnel & Development: 978-1-84398

Overseas Representation:
Worldwide: McGraw-Hill Education, Maidenhead, UK

2124

THE CHARTERED INSTITUTE OF PUBLIC FINANCE & ACCOUNTANCY
3 Robert Street, London WC2N 6RL
Telephone: 020 7543 5600
Fax: 020 7543 5607
Email: publications@cipfa.org
Website: www.cipfa.org/publications

Personnel:
Ms Sara Hackwood *(Publications Manager)*

Accountancy & Taxation; Economics

Imprints, Series & ISBNs:
The Chartered Institute of Public Finance & Accountancy: 978-0-85299, 978-1-84508

2125

CHARTRIDGE BOOKS OXFORD
Hexagon House, Avenue 4, Station Lane, Witney, Oxon OX28 4BN
Telephone: 01993 848726
Fax: 01865 884448
Email: editorial@chartridgebooksoxford.com
Website: www.chartridgebooksoxford.com

Personnel:
Dr Glyn Jones *(Managing Director)*
Dr Melinda Taylor *(Finance Director)*

Academic & Scholarly; Chemistry; Industry, Business & Management; Medical (incl. Self-Help & Alternative Medicine); Scientific & Technical

Imprints, Series & ISBNs:
Biohealthcare Publishing (Oxford) Ltd: 978-1-907568

Overseas Representation:
China: Benjamin Pan, CPM, Beijing, China
India: Ravindra Saxena, Sara Books, Delhi, India
Japan: Ben Kato, Tokyo, Japan
Middle East: Avicenna, Oxford, UK
North America: Martin Hill, New York, NY, USA
Republic of Korea: Se-Yung Jun, ICK, Seoul, Republic of Korea
South East Asia: Steven Goh, APAC, Singapore
Southern Europe: Mare Nostrum, Harrogate, UK
Taiwan: Unifacmanu, Taipei, Taiwan

2126

CHATHAM PUBLISHING
3 Barham Avenue, Elstree, Herts WD6 3PW
Telephone: 0208 953 4969
Email: michael@frontline-books.com
Website: www.chathampublishing.com

Trade Enquiries & Orders:
Pen and Sword Books, 57 Church Street, Barnsley, South Yorkshire S70 2AS
Telephone: 01226 734222
Email: trade@pen-and-sword.co.uk

Personnel:
Lionel Leventhal *(Publisher)*

Military & War; Nautical; Transport

Imprints, Series & ISBNs:
Chatham Publishing: 978-1-86176

Parent Company:
UK: Lionel Leventhal Ltd

Overseas Representation:
Australia & New Zealand: Peribo Pty Ltd, Mount Kuring-Gai, NSW, Australia
Austria, Switzerland, Czech & Slovak Republics, Hungary, Poland, Croatia, Slovenia, Spain (including Gibraltar) &

Portugal: Sandro Salucci, Florence, Italy
Canada: Vanwell Publishing Ltd, St Catharines, Ont, Canada
USA: MBI Publishing Co, St Paul, MN, USA

2127

CHEMCORD LTD
16 Inch Keith, St Leonards, East Kilbride, Glasgow G74 2JZ
Telephone: 01355 235447
Fax: 01355 235447
Email: office@chemcord.co.uk
Website: www.chemcord.co.uk

Personnel:
Jim Melrose *(Director)*
Douglas Buchanan *(Director)*
Pat Buchanan *(Sales Manager & Company Secretary)*

Educational & Textbooks

New Titles: 2 (2012) , 4 (2013)
No of Employees: 6
Annual Turnover: £60,000

Imprints, Series & ISBNs:
Chemcord

2128

CHICKEN HOUSE PUBLISHING LTD
2 Palmer Street, Frome, Somerset BA11 1DS
Telephone: 01373 454488
Fax: 01373 454499
Email: chickenhouse@doublecluck.com
Website: www.doublecluck.com

Warehouse, Trade Enquiries & Orders:
HarperCollins Publishers,
Customer Services, 103 Westerhill Road, Bishopbriggs, Glasgow G64 2QT
Telephone: 0844 576 8121
Fax: 0844 576 8131
Email: uk.orders@harpercollins.co.uk

Personnel:
Barry Cunningham *(Managing Director)*
Rachel Hickman *(Deputy Managing Director)*
Elinor Bagenal *(Rights Director)*
Rachel Leyshon *(Senior Editor)*
Imogen Cooper *(Senior Editor)*
Laura Myers *(Publishing Manager)*
Tina Waller *(Marketing & Publicity)*
Becky Davies *(Sales & Marketing Officer)*

Children's Books

New Titles: 16 (2012) , 24 (2013)
No of Employees: 6

Imprints, Series & ISBNs:
Chicken House Publishing Ltd: 978-1-903434, 978-1-904442, 978-1-905294, 978-1-906427, 978-1-908435, 978-1-909489

Parent Company:
USA: Scholastic Inc.

Overseas Representation:
Foreign Territories & Export: Scholastic, UK

2129

CHILD'S PLAY (INTERNATIONAL) LTD
Ashworth Road, Bridgemead, Swindon, Wilts SN5 7YD
Telephone: 01793 616286
Fax: 01793 512795
Email: office@childs-play.com
Website: www.childs-play.com

Personnel:
Neil Burden *(Publisher, Chief Executive)*
Paul Gerrish *(Sales Director)*
Claire Matthews *(Production Manager)*
Adriana Twinn *(Chair)*

Sue Baker *(Editor)*
Annie Kubler *(Artistic Director)*
Nicola Gardner *(Data Processing Manager)*

Children's Books

Imprints, Series & ISBNs:
Child's Play: 978-0-85953, 978-1-84643, 978-1-904550

Overseas Representation:
Australia: Child's Play Australia, Terrey Hills, NSW, Australia
Canada: Monarch Books of Canada Ltd, Downsview, Ont, Canada
New Zealand: Nationwide Book Distributors, Oxford, New Zealand
South Africa: Phambili Agencies CC, Germiston, South Africa
United Arab Emirates: Child's Play Dubai, Dubai, UAE, United Arab Emirates
USA: Child's Play Inc, Auburn, ME, USA

Book Trade Association Membership:
Booksellers Association; Educational Publishers Council; Independent Publishers Guild

2130

CHRISTIAN EDUCATION
1020 Bristol Road, Selly Oak, Birmingham B29 6LB
Telephone: 0121 472 4242
Fax: 0121 472 7575
Email: enquiries@christianeducation.org.uk
Website: www.christianeducation.org.uk

Personnel:
Zoe Keens *(Chief Executive Officer)*
Anstice Hughes *(Managing Editor)*
Gill Neuenhaus *(Finance Officer)*
Diane Horton *(Office, Sales & Administration Manager)*
Rosemary Rivett *(Director of Professional Services)*

Academic & Scholarly; Children's Books; Educational & Textbooks; Electronic (Professional & Academic); Religion & Theology

New Titles: 29 (2012) , 12 (2013)
No of Employees: 13
Annual Turnover: £800,000

Imprints, Series & ISBNs:
Christian Education Publications: 978-1-904024, 978-1-905893
International Bible Reading Association: 978-1-904024
RE Today Services: 978-1-904024

Associated Companies:
UK: Christian Education Publications; RE Today Services

Book Trade Association Membership:
Publishers Association; Educational Publishers Council; Christian Booksellers Convention

2131

CHRISTIAN FOCUS PUBLICATIONS
Geanies House, Fearn, Tain, Ross-shire IV20 1TW
Telephone: 01862 871011
Fax: 01862 871699
Email: info@christianfocus.com
Website: www.christianfocus.com

Distribution:
Trust Media Distribution, PO Box 300, Kingstown Broadway, Carlisle, Cumbria CA3 0QS
Telephone: 0800 282728
Fax: 0800 282530
Email: salesline@tmdistribution.co.uk
Website: www.TMDistribution.co.uk

Personnel:
William MacKenzie (Managing Director)
Donnie Morrison (Sales & Marketing Manager)
Willie Mackenzie (Director of Publishing (Adult Editorial))
Jonathan Dunbar (Production Manager)
Catherine Mackenzie (Children's Editor)
Daniel van Straaten (Design Manager)

Biography & Autobiography; Children's Books; Educational & Textbooks; History & Antiquarian; Religion & Theology; Sports & Games

Imprints, Series & ISBNs:
Christian Focus 4 Kids
Christian Focus Publications: 978-0-906731, 978-1-84550, 978-1-85792, 978-1-871676
Christian Heritage
Mentor

Parent Company:
UK: Balintore Holdings

Overseas Representation:
Australia: Koorong, Blackburn South, Vic, Australia; Reformers Bookshop, Stanmore, Australia; Word, Nunawading, Vic, Australia
Far East: Chris Ashdown, Publishers' International Marketing, Ferndown, Dorset, UK
New Zealand: Soul Distributors, Auckland, New Zealand
South Africa: Struik Christian Books, Cape Town, South Africa
USA & Canada: LG & G Group, LLC, Waxhaw, North Carolina, USA; STL Distribution, Elizabethton, TN, USA

Book Trade Association Membership:
Evangelical Christian Publishers Association (USA); Christian Booksellers Association (USA)

2132 ▄▄▄▄▄▄▄

CHURCH HOUSE PUBLISHING
The Archbishops' Council, Church House, Great Smith Street, London SW1P 3AZ
Telephone: 020 7898 1451
Fax: 020 7898 1449
Email: publishing@churchofengland.org
Website: www.chpublishing.co.uk

Sales, Customer Service & Warehouse:
Norwich Books & Music,
13a Hellesdon Park Road, Norwich NR6 5DR
Telephone: 01603 785923
Fax: 01603 785915
Email: orders@norwichbooksandmusic.co.uk
Website: www.chpublishing.co.uk

See also:
SCM-Canterbury Press

Personnel:
Thomas Allain-Chapman (Publishing Manager)

Reference Books, Directories & Dictionaries; Religion & Theology

Imprints, Series & ISBNs:
Church House Publishing: 978-0-7151
In association with Saint Andrew Press: 978-0-9562821

Parent Company:
UK: The Archbishops' Council

Associated Companies:
UK: Hymns Ancient & Modern Ltd

Overseas Representation:
Australia & New Zealand: Rainbow Book Agencies, Preston, Vic, Australia

Canada: Bayard/Novalis Distribution, Toronto, Ont, Canada
USA: Westminster John Knox Press, Louisville, KY, USA

Book Trade Association Membership:
Independent Publishers Guild; Christian Suppliers' Group

2133 ▄▄▄▄▄▄▄

CICERONE PRESS LTD
2 Police Square, Milnthorpe, Cumbria LA7 7PY
Telephone: 01539 562069
Fax: 01539 563417
Email: info@cicerone.co.uk
Website: www.cicerone.co.uk

Personnel:
Jonathan Williams (Managing Director)
Lesley Williams (Sales & Marketing Director)

Guide Books; Sports & Games; Travel & Topography

Imprints, Series & ISBNs:
Cicerone Press Ltd: 978-0-902363, 978-1-84965, 978-1-85284

Overseas Representation:
Europe: Bill Bailey Publishers Representatives, Newton Abbot, UK
France: Editeur, Vaison la Romaine, France
Netherlands: Nilsson & Lamm BV, Houten, Netherlands
Spain: Map Iberia FeB SL, Avila, Spain
USA: Midpoint Trade Books Inc, New York, USA

Book Trade Association Membership:
Independent Publishers Guild

2134 ▄▄▄▄▄▄▄

CITY & GUILDS
1 Giltspur Street, London EC1A 9DD
Telephone: 020 7294 2540
Website: www.cityandguilds.com

Personnel:
Ms Melody Dawes (Head of Publishing)
Charlie Evans (Publisher)
Ms Fiona McGlade (Commissioning Editor)
Thomas Guy (Commissioning Editor)
Ms Hannah Cooper (Development Manager)
Ms Claire Owen (Development Editor)
Ms Fiona Freel (Production and Manufacturing Manager)
Ms Lauren Heaney (Production Editor)
Ms Naomi Hall (Production Assistant)
Ms Ellie Wheeler (Development Editor)
Ms Frankie Jones (Development Editor)
James Hobbs (Development Editor)

Educational & Textbooks; Electronic (Educational); Vocational Training & Careers

Book Trade Association Membership:
Publishers Association

2135 ▄▄▄▄▄▄▄

CLAIRE PUBLICATIONS
Unit 8, Tey Brook Centre, Great Tey, Colchester, Essex CO6 1JE
Telephone: 01206 211020
Fax: 01206 212755
Email: mail@clairepublications.com
Website: www.clairepublications.com

Personnel:
Noel Graham (Production Managing Director)
Noel Graham (Finance)
Noel Graham (Rights)

Educational & Textbooks; Electronic (Educational); Languages & Linguistics; Mathematics & Statistics

Book Trade Association Membership:
British Educational Supplies Association

2136 ▄▄▄▄▄▄▄

CLAIRVIEW BOOKS LTD
Russet, Sandy Lane, West Hoathly, West Sussex RH19 4QQ
Telephone: 0870 486 3526
Email: office@clairviewbooks.com
Website: www.clairviewbooks.com

Personnel:
Sevak Gulbekian (Chief Editor)

Agriculture; Cookery, Wines & Spirits; Environment & Development Studies; Health & Beauty; Medical (incl. Self-Help & Alternative Medicine); Military & War; Politics & World Affairs; Religion & Theology

Imprints, Series & ISBNs:
Clairview Books Ltd: 978-1-905570

Overseas Representation:
Australia: Footprint Books, Melbourne, Vic, Australia
Canada: Tri-Fold Books, Ont, Canada
New Zealand: Ceres Books, Auckland, New Zealand
South Africa: Stephan Phillips Ltd, Cape Town, South Africa
USA: Steinerbooks, New York, NY, USA

Book Trade Association Membership:
Independent Publishers Guild

2137 ▄▄▄▄▄▄▄

JAMES CLARKE & CO
PO Box 60, Cambridge CB1 2NT
Telephone: 01223 350865
Fax: 01223 366951
Email: publishing@jamesclarke.co.uk & orders@jamesclarke.co.uk
Website: www.james.clarke.co.uk

Personnel:
Adrian Brink (Managing Director)

Academic & Scholarly; Bibliography & Library Science; Biography & Autobiography; History & Antiquarian; Literature & Criticism; Philosophy; Reference Books, Directories & Dictionaries; Religion & Theology

New Titles: 41 (2012) , 18 (2013)
No of Employees: 7

Imprints, Series & ISBNs:
James Clarke & Co: 978-0-227

Associated Companies:
UK: The Lutterworth Press

Overseas Representation:
USA: The David Brown Book Co (DBBC), Oakville, CT, USA

Book Trade Association Membership:
Publishers Association; Independent Publishers Guild

2138 ▄▄▄▄▄▄▄

CLASS PROFESSIONAL
The Exchange, Express Park, Bristol Road, Bridgwater TA6 4RR
Telephone: 01278 427800
Fax: 01278 421077
Email: lorna.downing@class.co.uk
Website: www.classprofessional.co.uk

Warehouse, Trade Enquiries & Orders:
Macmillan Distribution (MDL), Brunel Road, Houndmills, Basingstoke RG21 6XS
Telephone: 01256 329242
Fax: 01256 331413
Email: mdl@macmillan.co.uk
Website: www.macmillan-mdl.co.uk

Personnel:
Richard Warner (Managing Director)
Lorna Downing (European Manager)
Chris Gribble (Sales Manager)

Biology & Zoology; Chemistry; Computer Science; Educational & Textbooks; Geography & Geology; Law; Mathematics & Statistics; Medical (incl. Self-Help & Alternative Medicine); Physics; Psychology & Psychiatry; Scientific & Technical; Sports & Games; Vocational Training & Careers

Imprints, Series & ISBNs:
Class Professional Publishing: 978-0-7637, 978-0-86729, 978-1-2840, 978-1-4496

Associated Companies:
USA: Jones & Bartlett Inc

Book Trade Association Membership:
Independent Publishers Guild

2139 ▄▄▄▄▄▄▄

CLEAR ANSWER MEDICAL PUBLISHING LTD
128a Queens Court, Queensway, London W2 4QS
Telephone: 020 7229 0893
Email: info@camp-books.com

Personnel:
Dr Frank Seibert-Alves (Managing Director)
Mrs Catarina A. Seibert-Alves (Company Secretary)

Academic & Scholarly; Biology & Zoology; Educational & Textbooks; Medical (incl. Self-Help & Alternative Medicine)

Imprints, Series & ISBNs:
Clear Answer Medical Publishing Ltd: 978-1-903573

Book Trade Association Membership:
Independent Publishers Guild

2140 ▄▄▄▄▄▄▄

COASTAL PUBLISHING LTD
The Studio, Puddletown Road, Wareham, Dorset BH20 6AE
Telephone: 01929 554195
Email: orders@coastalpublishing.co.uk
Website: www.coastalpublishing.co.uk

Personnel:
Peter Sills (Managing Director)

Geography & Geology; Guide Books; Photography; Travel & Topography

Imprints, Series & ISBNs:
Jurassic Coast Series: 978-0-9544845, 978-1-907701
South West Coast Path

2141 ▄▄▄▄▄▄▄

COIS LIFE
204 DMG House,
Deansgrange Business Park,
Gráinseach an Déin, An Charraig Dhubh,
Co. Bhaile Átha Cliath, Republic of Ireland
Telephone: +353 (0)1 219 0223
Email: eolas@coislife.ie
Website: www.coislife.ie

Trade - Wholesaler:
Áis, 31 Fenian Street, Dublin 2, Republic of Ireland
Telephone: +353 (0)1 661 6522

Personnel:
C. Nic Pháidín (Company Secretary)
S. Ó Cearnaigh (Chairman)
F. Cloke (Publishing Officer)

Academic & Scholarly; Audio Books; Children's Books; Educational & Textbooks; Fiction; Languages & Linguistics; Literature

& Criticism; Poetry; Theatre, Drama & Dance

Imprints, Series & ISBNs:
Cois Life: 978-1-901176, 978-1-907494

Book Trade Association Membership:
Publishing Ireland (Foilsiú Éireann)

2142 ━━━

*COLLINS GEO
[a division of HarperCollins Publishers]
Westerhill Road, Bishopbriggs, Glasgow
G64 2QT
Telephone: 0141 306 3576
Fax: 020 8237 4209
Email:
elizabeth.mclachlan@harpercollins.co.uk
Website: www.collinsbartholomew.com

Personnel:
Sheena Barclay (Managing Director)
James Graves (Production Director)
Judith House (Marketing Manager)
Tom Fussell (Commercial Director)

Atlases & Maps; Educational & Textbooks;
Electronic (Educational); Environment &
Development Studies; Geography &
Geology; Guide Books; Travel & Topography

Imprints, Series & ISBNs:
Bartholomew: 978-0-7028
Collins Cartographic: 978-0-00
Collins Longman: 978-0-00
Nicholson: 978-0-7028
Times Books: 978-0-7230

Parent Company:
UK: HarperCollins

Overseas Representation:
Australia: HarperCollins Publishers, Pymble,
NSW, Australia
Canada: HarperCollins Publishers, Toronto
& Scarborough, Ont, Canada
Denmark: Scanvik Books ApS,
Copenhagen, Denmark
France: Editions Geographiques Generales,
Paris, France
Germany & Austria: Internationales
Landkartenhaus Geocenter, Stuttgart,
Germany
India: Maya Publishers Pvt Ltd, New Delhi,
India; Rupa, New Delhi, India
Italy: InterOrbis Media Distribution srl Ed,
Corsico (Milan), Italy
Japan: Maruzen Co Ltd, Tokyo, Japan
Netherlands: Nilsson & Lamm BV, Weesp,
Netherlands
New Zealand: HarperCollins (NZ) Ltd,
Glenfield, Auckland, New Zealand
Singapore & Malaysia: MPH Distributors,
Singapore
South Africa: Jonathan Ball, HarperCollins
Publishers, Johannesburg & Jeppestown,
South Africa
Sweden: Lantmateriet Kartbutiken,
Stockholm & Vällingby, Sweden
Thailand: Asia Book Co Ltd, Bangkok,
Thailand
USA: Hammond Inc, Maplewood, NJ, USA

Book Trade Association Membership:
Publishers Association; Publishing Scotland

2143 ━━━

COLOUR HEROES LTD
The Smithy, Hawkhill Estate,Easingwold,
York YO61 3FE
Telephone: 01347 825283
Fax: 01347 822543
Email: info@colourheroes.com
Website: www.colourheroes.com

Personnel:
Lorraine Ives (Sales & Marketing Director)

Archaeology; Architecture & Design;
Educational & Textbooks; Fiction; Fine Art &
Art History; Geography & Geology; Guide
Books; History & Antiquarian; Illustrated &
Fine Editions; Military & War; Natural
History; Religion & Theology; Scientific &
Technical; Sports & Games

2144 ━━━

COLUMBA
55A Spruce Avenue,
Stillorgan Industrial Park, Blackrock,
Co Dublin, Republic of Ireland
Telephone: +353 (0)1 294 2556
Fax: +353 (0)1 294 2564
Email: info@columba.ie
Website: www.columba.ie

Personnel:
Fearghal O Boyle (Managing Director &
Publisher)
Patricia Lowth (Business Manager)
Michael Brennan (Sales Manager)

Academic & Scholarly; History &
Antiquarian; Religion & Theology

Imprints, Series & ISBNs:
The Columba Press: 978-0-948183, 978-1-
78218, 978-1-85607
Currach Press: 978-1-85607

Overseas Representation:
Australia: Rainbow Books, Preston, Vic,
Australia
New Zealand: Pleroma, Central Hawkes Bay,
New Zealand
USA & Canada: Dufour Editions Inc, Chester
Springs, PA, USA

Book Trade Association Membership:
Publishing Ireland (Foilsiú Éireann);
Booksellers Association

2145 ━━━

COMMONWEALTH SECRETARIAT
Marlborough House, Pall Mall, London
SW1Y 5HX
Telephone: 020 7747 6342
Fax: 020 7839 9081
Email: publications@commonwealth.int
Website: www.thecommonwealth.org/
publications

Distributor:
Turpin Distribution, Pegasus Drive,
Stratton Business Park, Biggleswade
SG18 8TQ
Telephone: +44 (0) 1767 604800
Fax: +44 (0) 1767 601640
Email: custserv@turpin-distribution.com
Website: www.turpin-distribution.com

Personnel:
Sherry Dixon (Publications Manager)
Nicola Perou (Publications Assistant)

Academic & Scholarly; Economics;
Environment & Development Studies;
Gender Studies; Industry, Business &
Management; Law; Politics & World
Affairs; Reference Books, Directories &
Dictionaries; Scientific & Technical

New Titles: 20 (2012) , 20 (2013)
No of Employees: 2

Imprints, Series & ISBNs:
Commonwealth Secretariat: 978-0-85092,
978-1-84859, 978-1-84929

Associated Companies:
UK: Nexus Strategic Partnerships

Distributor for:
UK: Commonwealth Association of Tax
Administrators; Commonwealth
Foundation; Commonwealth Local
Government Forum

Overseas Representation:
Canada: Renouf Publishing Co Ltd, Ottawa,
Ont, Canada
Iberia: Iberian Book Services, Madrid, Spain
India: Parrot Reads Publishers, New Delhi,
India
USA: Stylus Publishing Inc, Sterling, VA, USA

Book Trade Association Membership:
Publishers Association; Independent
Publishers Guild

2146 ━━━

CONRAN OCTOPUS
[a division of Octopus Publishing Group]
Endeavour House,
189 Shaftesbury Avenue, London
WC2H 8JY
Telephone: 020 7632 5400
Email: info@octopusbooks.co.uk
Website: www.octopusbooks.co.uk

Distribution:
Littlehampton Book Services Ltd,
Faraday Close, Durrington, Worthing,
West Sussex BN13 3TG
Telephone: 01903 828500
Fax: 01903 828802

Personnel:
Denise Bates (Group Publishing Director)
Jonathan Christie (Art Director)

Architecture & Design; Cookery, Wines &
Spirits; Crafts & Hobbies; Gardening

Imprints, Series & ISBNs:
Conran: 978-1-84091

Parent Company:
UK: Hachette UK

Overseas Representation:
See: Octopus Publishing Group, London, UK

2147 ━━━

CONSTABLE & ROBINSON LTD
55-56 Russell Square, London, WC1B 4HP
Telephone: 020 7268 9700
Email: general@constablerobinson.com
Website: www.constablerobinson.com

Warehouse & Distribution:
TBS Ltd, Colchester Road, Frating Green,
Colchester, Essex CO7 7DW
Telephone: 01206 256000
Fax: 01206 819587

Personnel:
Nick Robinson (Publisher)
Pete Duncan (Managing Director)
Nova Jayne Robinson (Online-Publishing
Director)
Adrian Andrews (Finance Director)
Martin Palmer (Group Sales Director)
Eryl Humphrey Jones (Rights Director)
Sam Evans (Publicity Director)
Rob Nichols (Digital and Communicatons
Director)
Krystyna Green (Editorial Director Crime
Fiction)
Duncan Proudfoot (Non-Fiction Editor)
James Gurbutt (Publisher, Corsair imprint)
Andreas Campomar (Editorial Director, Non-
Fiction)
Fritha Saunders (Editor, Psychology)
Hugh Barker (Special Sales Manager)

Biography & Autobiography; Cookery,
Wines & Spirits; Crafts & Hobbies; Crime;
Electronic (Entertainment); Fiction;
Gardening; Health & Beauty; Humour;
Illustrated & Fine Editions; Medical (incl.
Self-Help & Alternative Medicine); Military
& War; Politics & World Affairs; Psychology
& Psychiatry; Reference Books, Directories &
Dictionaries; Science Fiction; Sports &
Games

Imprints, Series & ISBNs:
C&R Crime
Canvas
Constable: 978-1-84119, 978-1-84529,
978-1-84901, 978-1-85487
Corsair: 978-1-84901
How to Books
Magpie Books: 978-1-84119, 978-1-
84901, 978-1-85487
Much-in-Little
Right Way: 978-0-7160
Robinson: 978-1-84119, 978-1-84529,
978-1-84901, 978-1-85487

Parent Company:
Australia: Someone else

Associated Companies:
UK: One more

Distributor for:
UK: Anyone

Overseas Representation:
Australia and New Zealand (Constable &
Robinson – Library Supplies): Allen and
Unwin, Australia
Australia and New Zealand (Constable &
Robinson – Retail): Allen and Unwin, UK
Europe, Russia, CIS, Middle East, France,
Italy & Greece: Walker Books, UK
Far East : Walker Books, UK
India: Penguin, India
Japan: Tim Burland, UK
Republic of Ireland: Vivienne Lavery,
Blackrock, Co Dublin, Republic of Ireland
South Africa: Book Promotions, Cape Town,
South Africa
West Indies : Chris Humphrys and Lynda
Hopkins, London, UK

Book Trade Association Membership:
Publishers Association; Independent
Publishers Guild

2148 ━━━

DAVID C. COOK (UK)
Lottbridge Drove, Eastbourne, East Sussex
BN23 6NT
Telephone: 01323 437700
Fax: 01323 411970
Email: tradeorders@kingsway.co.uk
Website: www.kingsway.co.uk

Trade Orders:
Kingsway, 26–28 Lottbridge Drove,
Eastbourne, East Sussex BN23 6NT
Telephone: 01323 437700
Fax: 01323 411970
Email: tradeorders@kingsway.co.uk
Website: www.kingsway.co.uk

Personnel:
Jonathan Brown (Business Development
Director)
Bill Owen (Finance & Administration
Manager)

Biography & Autobiography; Religion &
Theology

Imprints, Series & ISBNs:
David C. Cook: 978-0-78140, 978-0-
78143, 978-0-78144, 978-0-78145,
978-1-43470, 978-1-55513, 978-1-
56292, 978-1-58919
Kingsway: 978-0-85476, 978-0-85491,
978-0-86065, 978-0-86239, 978-0-
902088, 978-1-84291

Distributor for:
UK: 22 Media; Barbour Publishing Inc.;
Beacon Hill Press; Charisma House;
Dernier Publishers; Faithwords; Freeman
Smith; Gospel Light & Regal Books;
Guideposts/Ideals; Influence; Kregal;
Lifeway, Broadman & Holmon; Moody;
NavPress; New Leaf Publishing Group;
Standard Publishing; Worthy Publishing

Overseas Representation:
Australia: Kennedy International, NSW, Australia
Canada: David C. Cook Distribution Canada, Paris, Ont, Canada
South Africa: Struik Christian Books Pty Ltd, Maitland, Cape Town, South Africa

2149

COORDINATION GROUP PUBLICATIONS LTD (CGP LTD)
Broughton-in-Furness, Cumbria LA20 6BN
Telephone: 01229 715700
Fax: 01229 716958
Email: customerservices@cgpbooks.co.uk
Website: www.cgpbooks.co.uk

Personnel:
Graham Servante *(Managing Director)*
Jane Barnes *(Publishing Director)*

Educational & Textbooks

Imprints, Series & ISBNs:
Coordination Group Publications Ltd (CGP Ltd): 978-1-84146, 978-1-84762

Associated Companies:
USA: CGP Study; Coordination Group Publications Inc (trading as CGP Education)

2150

*COPPER BEECH PUBLISHING LTD
PO Box 159, East Grinstead, Sussex RH19 4FS
Telephone: 01342 314734
Fax: 01342 312196
Email: sales@copperbeechpublishing.co.uk
Website:
www.copperbeechpublishing.co.uk

Personnel:
Jan Barnes *(Rights)*
Julie Hird *(Editorial)*
Elizabeth Moreira *(Finance)*

Cookery, Wines & Spirits; Fashion & Costume; Gardening; History & Antiquarian; Sports & Games; Transport

Imprints, Series & ISBNs:
Copper Beech Publishing Ltd: 978-0-9516295, 978-1-898617
English Eccentricities
The Etiquette Collection

Book Trade Association Membership:
Independent Publishers Guild

2151

CORK UNIVERSITY PRESS
Youngline Industrial Estate, Pailaduff Road, Togher, Cork, Republic of Ireland
Telephone: +353 (0)21 490 2980
Fax: +353 (0)21 431 5329
Email: corkuniversitypress@ucc.ie
Website: www.corkuniversitypress.com

Orders & Distribution (Republic of Ireland, Northern Ireland & Europe):
Gill & Macmillan Distribution, Hume Avenue, Park West, Dublin 12, Republic of Ireland
Telephone: +353 (0)1 500 9500
Fax: +353 (0)1 500 9596

Representation (Republic of Ireland & Northern Ireland):
Robert Towers, 2 The Crescent, Monkstown, Co Dublin, Republic of Ireland
Telephone: +353 (0)1 280 6532
Fax: +353 (0)1 280 6020

Personnel:
Mike Collins *(Publications Director)*
Maria O'Donovan *(Production Editor)*

Academic & Scholarly; Archaeology; Architecture & Design; Atlases & Maps; Biography & Autobiography; Cinema, Video, TV & Radio; Cookery, Wines & Spirits; Economics; Environment & Development Studies; Fine Art & Art History; Gardening; Gay & Lesbian Studies; Gender Studies; Geography & Geology; History & Antiquarian; Literature & Criticism; Military & War; Music; Natural History; Philosophy; Photography; Psychology & Psychiatry; Sports & Games; Theatre, Drama & Dance

Imprints, Series & ISBNs:
Atrium
Attic Press
Field Day Essays: 978-0-902561, 978-1-85918
Irish Narratives: 978-0-902561, 978-1-85918
Undercurrents: 978-0-902561, 978-1-85918

Overseas Representation:
North America: Stylus Publishing LLC, Herndon, VA, USA
UK & Europe: Quantum Publishing Solutions Ltd, Paisley, UK
UK (excluding Northern Ireland) (Distribution): Marston Book Services Ltd, Abingdon, UK

Book Trade Association Membership:
Publishing Ireland (Foilsiú Éireann)

2152

CORNWALL EDITIONS LTD
8 Langurtho Road, Fowey, Cornwall PL23 1EQ
Telephone: 01726 832483
Fax: 01726 832483
Email: info@cornwalleditions.co.uk
Website: www.cornwalleditions.co.uk

Personnel:
Ian Grant *(Publisher)*
Judy Martin *(Customer Services Manager)*

Archaeology; Children's Books; Fiction; History & Antiquarian; Natural History

Imprints, Series & ISBNs:
Cornwall Editions: 978-1-904880
Ian Grant Publishers: 978-1-904880

Book Trade Association Membership:
Independent Publishers Guild

2153

COUNCIL FOR BRITISH ARCHAEOLOGY
St Mary's House, 66 Bootham, York YO30 7BZ
Telephone: 01904 671417
Fax: 01904 671384
Email: books@archaeologyUK.org
Website: www.archaeologyUK.org

Distribution:
Central Books Ltd, 99 Wallis Road, London E9 5LN
Telephone: 0845 458 9910
Fax: 0845 458 9912
Email: mo@centralbooks.com
Website: www.centralbooks.com

Personnel:
Michael Heyworth *(Director)*
Peter Olver *(Finance Director)*
Siona Mackelworth *(Marketing and Communications Director)*
Catrina Appleby *(Publications Officer)*
Mike Feider *(Information Officer)*
Mike Pitts *(British Archaeology Magazine Editor)*
Nicky Milsted *(Young Archaeologists' Club Magazine Editor)*
Tara-Jane Sutcliffe *(Training Co-ordinator)*

Archaeology

Imprints, Series & ISBNs:
Archaeology of York
British and Irish Archaeological Bibliography
British Archaeology
CBA Research Reports: 978-1-902771
Practical Handbooks in Archaeology: 978-1-902771

Book Trade Association Membership:
Association of Learned & Professional Society Publishers

2154

COUNTRYSIDE BOOKS
2 Highfield Avenue, Newbury, Berks RG14 5DS
Telephone: 01635 43816
Fax: 01635 551004
Email: info@countrysidebooks.co.uk
Website: www.countrysidebooks.co.uk

Personnel:
Nicholas Battle *(Publisher)*
Suzanne Battle *(Publicity Manager)*
Jackie Arrowsmith *(Sales Manager)*

Architecture & Design; Aviation; Guide Books; History & Antiquarian; Humour; Military & War; Reference Books, Directories & Dictionaries; Sociology & Anthropology; Transport; Travel & Topography

Imprints, Series & ISBNs:
Countryside Books: 978-0-86368, 978-0-905392, 978-1-84674, 978-1-85306, 978-1-85455

Parent Company:
UK: Countryside Books UK

Distributor for:
UK: The Dovecote Press; Historical Publications Ltd; Kent County Council; Power Publications

Overseas Representation:
USA & Canada: The David Brown Book Co, Oakville, CT, USA

Book Trade Association Membership:
Independent Publishers Guild

2155

COUNTYVISE LTD
14 Appin Road, Birkenhead CH41 9HH
Telephone: 0151 647 3333
Email: admin@birkenheadpress.co.uk
Website: www.countyvise.co.uk

Personnel:
Jean Emmerson *(Managing Director)*

Academic & Scholarly; Biography & Autobiography; Children's Books; Crime; Fiction; History & Antiquarian; Humour; Military & War; Natural History; Nautical; Poetry; Religion & Theology; Sports & Games; Transport

Imprints, Series & ISBNs:
Appin Press: 978-1-906205
Countyvise Ltd: 978-0-907768, 978-1-901231, 978-1-906823
Liver Press: 978-1-871201
Merseyside Port Folios: 978-0-9516129
Picton Press (Liverpool): 978-1-873245

2156

CREATIVE CONTENT LTD
Roxburge House, 273–287 Regent Street, London W1B2HA
Telephone: 07771 766838
Website: www.creativecontentdigital.com

Personnel:
Lorelei King *(Company Director)*
Alison Muirden *(Company Director)*

Audio Books; Crime; Fiction; Languages & Linguistics; Military & War; Vocational Training & Careers

New Titles: 6 (2012) , 13 (2013)

Imprints, Series & ISBNs:
The Lifestyle Lowdown Creative Content
The Lowdown Creative Content

Book Trade Association Membership:
Publishers Association

2157

CRÉCY PUBLISHING LTD
Unit 1A, Ringway Trading Estate, Shadowmoss Road, Manchester M22 5LH
Telephone: 0161 499 0024
Fax: 0161 499 0298
Email: sales@crecy.co.uk
Website: www.crecy.co.uk

Personnel:
Jeremy M. Pratt *(Managing Director)*
Gill Richardson *(Customer Services and Editorial Manager)*
Chris Tordoff *(Marketing Manager)*

Aviation; History & Antiquarian; Military & War; Nautical; Transport

Imprints, Series & ISBNs:
Airdata Publications: 978-0-85979
Airplan Flight Equipment Ltd: 978-1-874783, 978-1-906559
Crécy: 978-0-947554
Flight Recorder Publications: 978-0-95542
Goodall Publications: 978-0-907579
Hikoki Publications: 978-1-902109
Nostalgia Road: 978-1-903016

Distributor for:
UK: Aerospace Masterbooks; Air Research Publications; Airplan Flight Equipment Ltd; Aviation Publications Inc; Camber Publications Ltd; Independent Books; Leandoer + Ekholm; Pacific Century; Specialty Press

Overseas Representation:
Australia: J. B. Wholesalers, Bibra Lake, WA, Australia
Canada: Vanwell Publishing Ltd, St Catharines, Ont, Canada
Eastern Europe: Tony Moggach, UK
Europe: Bookport Associates, Corsico (MI), Italy
New Zealand: South Pacific Books (Imports) Ltd, Auckland, New Zealand
USA: Specialty Press, North Branch, MN, USA
Western Europe: Anselm Robinson, UK

2158

CRESSRELLES PUBLISHING CO LTD
10 Station Road Industrial Estate, Colwall, Malvern WR13 6RN
Telephone: 01684 540154
Email: simon@cressrelles.co.uk
Website: www.cressrelles.co.uk

Personnel:
Simon Smith *(Sales Director)*
Leslie Smith *(Director)*

Theatre, Drama & Dance

Imprints, Series & ISBNs:
Actinic Press
Cressrelles: 978-0-85956
J. Garnet Miller: 978-0-85343
Kenyon-Deane: 978-0-7155
New Playwrights' Network: 978-0-86319, 978-0-903653, 978-0-906660

Distributor for:
USA: Anchorage Press Inc

Overseas Representation:
Australia: Origin Theatrical, Sydney, NSW, Australia
New Zealand: Play Bureau of New Zealand Ltd, New Plymouth, New Zealand
Republic of Ireland: Drama League of Ireland, Dublin, Republic of Ireland
South Africa: Dalro (Pty) Ltd, Braamfontein, South Africa
USA: Bakers Plays, Quincy, MA, USA

2159 ▬▬▬

CRIMSON PUBLISHING
2nd Floor, Westminster House, Kew Road, Richmond, Surrey TW9 2ND
Telephone: 020 8334 1600
Fax: 020 8334 1601
Email: info@crimsonpublishing.co.uk
Website: www.crimsonbooks.co.uk

Bookshop Orders:
Faber Factory Plus, Bloomsbury House, 74-77 Great Russell St, London WC1B 3DA
Telephone: 020 7927 3809
Email: factory@faber.co.uk
Website: www.faberfactory.co.uk

Personnel:
David Lester *(Managing Director)*
Hugh Brune *(Publishing Director)*
Jo Jacomb *(Production Manager)*

Atlases & Maps; Crafts & Hobbies; Educational & Textbooks; Electronic (Educational); Guide Books; Health & Beauty; Industry, Business & Management; Travel & Topography; Vocational Training & Careers

Imprints, Series & ISBNs:
Crimson: 978-1-85458
Pathfinder
Pocket Bibles
Trotman: 978-1-84455
White Ladder Press

Overseas Representation:
Australia: Woodslane Pty Ltd, Warriewood, NSW, Australia
South Africa: Phambili Agency, Sunnyrock, Germiston, South Africa
USA: Letter Soup Rights Agency, Woodbury, MN, USA

2160 ▬▬▬

CROWN HOUSE PUBLISHING LTD
Crown Buildings, Bancyfelin, Carmarthenshire SA33 5ND
Telephone: 01267 211345
Fax: 01267 211882
Email: books@crownhouse.co.uk
Website: www.crownhouse.co.uk

Distribution:
Grantham Book Services, Trent Road, Grantham, Lincolnshire NG31 7XQ
Telephone: 01476 541 080
Fax: 01476 541 061
Email: orders@gbs.tbs-ltd.co.uk

Personnel:
David Bowman *(Managing Director)*
Caroline Lenton *(Sales & Marketing Director)*

Academic & Scholarly; Medical (incl. Self-Help & Alternative Medicine); Psychology & Psychiatry

Distributor for:
UK: The Developing Co; The Quest Institute
USA: Free Spirit; Kagan Professional Development; Kendall Hunt Publishing; Meta Publications; Science & Behaviour Books; Westwood Publishing

Overseas Representation:
Australasia: Footprint Books Pty Ltd, NSW, Australia
Central & Eastern Europe: IMA Publishers' Sales Representation, London, UK
Hong Kong & Macau: Transglobal Publishers Services Ltd, Hong Kong
India: Research Press, New Delhi, India
Israel: Probook Ltd, Israel
Malaysia: Publishers Marketing Services Pte Ltd, Malaysia
Philippines, Korea & Taiwan: I. J. Sagun Enterprises Inc, Philippines
Singapore: Publishers Marketing Services Pte Ltd, Singapore
South Africa: Juta & Co, Claremont, South Africa
Spain, Portugal & Gibraltar: Iberian Book Services, Spain

Book Trade Association Membership:
Booksellers Association; Independent Publishers Guild

2161 ▬▬▬

THE CROWOOD PRESS LTD
The Stable Block, Crowood Lane, Ramsbury, Marlborough, Wiltshire SN8 2HR
Telephone: 01672 520320
Fax: 01672 520280
Email: enquiries@crowood.com
Website: www.crowood.com

Distribution:
Grantham Book Services, Trent Road, Grantham, Lincs NG31 7XQ
Telephone: 01476 541000
Fax: 01476 541060
Email: orders@gbs.tbs-ltd.co.uk
Website: www.crowood.com

Personnel:
John Dennis *(Chairman)*
Ken Hathaway *(Managing Director)*
Julie Sankey *(Sales & Marketing)*

Agriculture; Animal Care & Breeding; Antiques & Collecting; Architecture & Design; Aviation; Crafts & Hobbies; Do-It-Yourself; Gardening; Military & War; Natural History; Nautical; Sports & Games; Theatre, Drama & Dance; Transport

Imprints, Series & ISBNs:
The Crowood Press Ltd: 978-0-946284, 978-1-84797, 978-1-85223, 978-1-86126

Overseas Representation:
Australia: Peribo Pty Ltd, Mount Kuring-Gai, NSW, Australia
Scandinavia: Angell Eurosales, Berwick-upon-Tweed, UK
Singapore, Malaysia & Brunei: Publishers Marketing Services Pte Ltd, Singapore
South Africa: Peter Hyde Associates (Pty) Ltd, Cape Town, South Africa
Southern Europe: Bookport Associates, Corsico (MI), Italy
USA: Motorbooks International, Minneapolis, MN, USA; Trafalgar Square Publishing, North Pomfret, VT, USA
Western Europe: Anselm Robinson, London, UK

2162 ▬▬▬

G. L. CROWTHER
224 South Meadow Lane, Preston PR1 8JP
Telephone: 01772 257126

Personnel:
G. L. Crowther *(Sole Proprietor/Executive)*

Atlases & Maps; Geography & Geology; Transport

New Titles: 38 (2012) , 15 (2013)
No of Employees: 1

Imprints, Series & ISBNs:
National Series of Waterway Tramway and Railway Atlases: 978-1-85615

2163 ▬▬▬

CRW PUBLISHING LTD
6 Turville Barns, Eastleach, Cirencester, Glos GL7 3QB
Telephone: 01367 850448
Email: clive.reynard@btinternet.com
Website: www.collectors-library.com

Trade Orders:
Macmillan Distribution (MDL), Brunel Road, Basingstoke, Hants RG21 6XS
Telephone: 01256 302692 & 0845 070 5656 (automated line – orders & availability)
Fax: 01256 812558
Email: orders@macmillan.co.uk

Personnel:
Cameron Brown *(Chairman, Director)*
Clive Reynard *(Sales Director)*
Marcus Clapham *(Editorial Director)*
Ken Webb *(Production Director)*

Children's Books; Fiction; Humour

Imprints, Series & ISBNs:
Collector's Library: 978-1-904633, 978-1-904919, 978-1-905716, 978-1-907360, 978-1-909621
Collector's Library Editions/Cases: 978-1-904633, 978-1-904919, 978-1-905716

Overseas Representation:
Australia: NewSouth Books, NSW, Australia
Far East: Sales East, Thailand
Germany, Eastern Europe, Russia, Benelux, Austria & Switzerland: Clive Reynard, CRW Publishing, UK
Greece: Bookport Associates, Italy
New Zealand: David Bateman Ltd, Auckland, New Zealand
Scandinavia: Anglo-Nordic Books Ltd, UK
Spain, Portugal & Italy: Penguin Books SA, Madrid, Spain

2164 ▬▬▬

CYHOEDDIADAU'R GAIR
Ael y Bryn, Chwilog, Pwllheli, Gwynedd LL53 6SH
Telephone: 01766 819120
Fax: 01766 819120
Email: aled@ysgolsul.com
Website: www.ysgolsul.com

Personnel:
Aled Davies *(Director)*

Children's Books; Religion & Theology

Imprints, Series & ISBNs:
Cyhoeddiadau'r Gair: 978-1-85994

Parent Company:
UK: Welsh Sunday School Council

Overseas Representation:
Worldwide: Welsh Books Council, Aberystwyth, UK

Book Trade Association Membership:
Independent Publishers Guild

2165 ▬▬▬

DANCE BOOKS LTD
Southwold House, Isington Road, Binsted, Hampshire GU34 4PH
Telephone: 01420 525299
Email: dwl@dancebooks.co.uk
Website: www.dancebooks.co.uk

Warehouse, Trade Enquiries & Orders:
Vine House Distribution,
The Old Mill House, Mill Lane, Uckfield, East Sussex TN22 5AA
Telephone: 01825 767396

Fax: 01825 765649
Email: sales@vinehouseuk.co.uk
Website: www.vinehouseuk.co.uk

Personnel:
John O'Brien *(Chairman)*
David Leonard *(Managing, Editorial & Production Director)*
Richard Holland *(Sales Director)*

Academic & Scholarly; Music; Theatre, Drama & Dance

Imprints, Series & ISBNs:
Dance Books Ltd: 978-0-903102, 978-1-85273

Distributor for:
USA: Dance Horizons; Princeton Book Co

Overseas Representation:
Australia: Footprint Books Pty Ltd, Warriewood, NSW, Australia
USA: Princeton Book Co, Hightstown, NJ, USA

2166 ▬▬▬

THE DAVENANT PRESS
The Cottage, Priory Lane, Burford OX18 4SG
Telephone: 01865 292148
Fax: 01993 824129
Email: judithdavenant@googlemail.com
Website: www.davenantpress.co.uk

Personnel:
Judith Ann Loades *(Proprietor)*

Academic & Scholarly; Archaeology; Biography & Autobiography; Educational & Textbooks; History & Antiquarian; Literature & Criticism; Politics & World Affairs; Religion & Theology

New Titles: 4 (2012) , 16 (2013)
No of Employees: 1

Imprints, Series & ISBNs:
Davenant Press (General Academic Titles): 978-1-85944
Notes on English Literature: 978-1-85944
Notes on History: 978-1-85944
Notes on Politics: 978-1-85944

Book Trade Association Membership:
Independent Publishers Guild

2167 ▬▬▬

DELANCEY PRESS LTD
23 Berkeley Square, London W1J 6HE
Telephone: 020 7665 6605
Email: delanceypress@aol.com
Website: www.delanceypress.co.uk & www.peoplesbookprize.com

Personnel:
Tatiana Wilson *(Managing Director: Marketing)*
Jackie Crouch *(Finance)*
Rupert Jones-Parry *(Rights Manager)*
Alexandra Shelly *(Editor)*

Children's Books; Fiction; Humour; Nautical; Psychology & Psychiatry

Imprints, Series & ISBNs:
Delancey Press Ltd: 978-0-9539119, 978-1-907205

Book Trade Association Membership:
Publishers Association; Booksellers Association

2168 ▬▬▬

DELTA ALPHA PUBLISHING LTD
19H John Spencer Square, London N1 2LZ
Telephone: 020 7359 1822
Fax: 020 7359 1822
Email: dap@deltaalpha.com

Website: www.deltaalpha.com

Personnel:
Damien Abbott *(Director)*
Deborah Lloyd *(Marketing Manager)*
John Knox *(Marketing Manager)*

Economics; Law; Photography; Reference Books, Directories & Dictionaries

Imprints, Series & ISBNs:
Delta Alpha Publishing Ltd: 978-0-9668946

Associated Companies:
USA: Delta Alpha Publishing

Overseas Representation:
Australia: Delta Alpha, Scarborough, Qld, Australia
USA: Port City Fulfilment, Kimball, MI, USA

Book Trade Association Membership:
Independent Publishers Guild; Publisher Marketing Association, USA; Australian PA

2169 ▬▬▬

DELTA ELT PUBLISHING LTD
Hoe Lane, Peaslake, Surrey GU5 9SW
Telephone: 01306 731770
Email: info@deltapublishing.co.uk
Website: www.deltapublishing.co.uk

Educational & Textbooks; English as a Foreign Language; Languages & Linguistics

Imprints, Series & ISBNs:
Delta ELT Publishing Ltd: 978-1-900783, 978-1-905085

2170 ▬▬▬

RICHARD DENNIS PUBLICATIONS
The New Chapel, Shepton Beauchamp, Ilminster, Somerset TA19 0JT
Telephone: 01460 240044
Email:
books@richarddennispublications.com
Website:
www.richarddennispublications.com

Personnel:
Richard Dennis *(Production)*
Sharon Pearce *(Administration)*
Tracie Welch *(Accounts)*
Magnus Dennis *(Photographer)*
Buchan Dennis *(Marketing)*

Academic & Scholarly; Antiques & Collecting; Architecture & Design; Biography & Autobiography; Fine Art & Art History; History & Antiquarian; Illustrated & Fine Editions

Imprints, Series & ISBNs:
Richard Dennis Publications: 978-0-903685, 978-0-9553741

Overseas Representation:
USA: Antique Collectors Club Ltd, Easthampton, MA, USA

2171 ▬▬▬

DENOR PRESS LTD
3 Hillcourt Avenue London N12 8EY
Telephone: 07768 855995
Fax: 020 8446 4504
Email: denorgroup@gmail.com
Website: www.denorpress.com

Personnel:
Lucille Leader *(Production & Editorial Director)*
Dr Geoffrey Leader *(Director)*
Philip Woolfson *(Consultant/Accountant)*

Academic & Scholarly; Biography & Autobiography; Children's Books; Educational & Textbooks; Fiction; Medical (incl. Self-Help & Alternative Medicine); Music

Imprints, Series & ISBNs:
Denor Press Ltd: 978-0-9526056, 978-0-9561722

Distributor for:
UK: Leading Note Productions

Overseas Representation:
USA: Lightning Source Inc (US), Lavergne, TN, USA

2172 ▬▬▬

J. M. DENT
Orion House, 5 Upper St Martins Lane, London WC2H 9EA
Telephone: 020 7240 3444
Fax: 020 7240 4822

Trade Counter & Warehouse:
Littlehampton Book Services Ltd, Faraday Close, Durrington, Worthing, West Sussex BN13 3RB
Telephone: 01903 828500
Fax: 01903 828625

Academic & Scholarly; Biography & Autobiography; Children's Books; Economics; Fiction; Gardening; History & Antiquarian; Law; Literature & Criticism; Music; Reference Books, Directories & Dictionaries; Scientific & Technical

Imprints, Series & ISBNs:
J M Dent: 978-0-460
Everyman Paperbacks: 978-0-460

Parent Company:
UK: The Orion Publishing Group Ltd

Overseas Representation:
see: The Orion Publishing Group Ltd, London, UK

2173 ▬▬▬

DISCOVERY WALKING GUIDES LTD
10 Tennyson Close, Dallington, Northampton NN5 7HJ
Website: www.walking.demon.co.uk

Personnel:
David Brawn *(Company Secretary)*
Ros Brawn *(Director)*

Atlases & Maps; Guide Books; Travel & Topography

New Titles: 8 (2012) , 45 (2013)

Imprints, Series & ISBNs:
Bus & Touring Maps: 978-1-904946
Tour & Trail Maps: 978-1-904946
Walk! Guide Books: 978-1-904946

2174 ▬▬▬

DJØF
5 Victoria House, 138 Watling Street East, Towcester NN12 6BT
Telephone: 01327 357770
Fax: 01327 359572

Warehouse & Distribution:
Marston Book Services, 160 Milton Park, PO Box 269, Abingdon OX14 4YN
Telephone: 01235 465577
Fax: 01235 465555
Website: www.djoef-forlag.dk

Personnel:
Gary Hall *(Manager)*

Economics; Industry, Business & Management; Law

Parent Company:
Denmark: DJØF Publishing

2175 ▬▬▬

THE DOVECOTE PRESS
Stanbridge, Wimborne Minster, Dorset BH21 4JD
Telephone: 01258 840549
Fax: 01258 840958
Email: online@dovecotepress.com
Website: www.dovecotepress.com

Personnel:
David Burnett *(Managing Director)*

Archaeology; Biography & Autobiography; Geography & Geology; Guide Books; History & Antiquarian; Military & War; Natural History; Transport; Travel & Topography

Imprints, Series & ISBNs:
The Dovecote Press: 978-0-946159, 978-1-874336, 978-1-904349

2176 ▬▬▬

ASHLEY DRAKE PUBLISHING LTD
PO Box 733, Cardiff CF14 7ZY
Telephone: 029 2021 8187
Email: post@ashleydrake.com
Website: www.ashleydrake.com

Distribution:
NBN International, Estover Road, Plymouth PL6 7PY
Website: www.nbninternational.com

Personnel:
Ashley Drake *(Managing Director)*
Siwan Wyn *(Company Secretary)*

Academic & Scholarly; Biography & Autobiography; Children's Books; Educational & Textbooks; History & Antiquarian; Industry, Business & Management; Literature & Criticism; Military & War; Politics & World Affairs; Religion & Theology; Sports & Games; Travel & Topography

Imprints, Series & ISBNs:
Y Ddraig Fach: 978-1-899877
Gwasg Addysgol Cymru: 978-1-899869
Hisarlik Press: 978-1-874312
Morgan Publishing: 978-1-903532
Scandinavian Academic Press: 978-1-904609
St David's Press (formerly Ashley Drake Publishing): 978-1-902719
Welsh Academic Press: 978-1-86057

Overseas Representation:
North America: ISBS, Portland, OR, USA

2177 ▬▬▬

DRAMATIC LINES
PO Box 201, Twickenham TW2 5RQ
Telephone: 020 8296 9502
Fax: 020 8296 9503
Email: mail@dramaticlinespublishers.co.uk
Website: www.dramaticlines.co.uk

Personnel:
John Nicholas *(Managing Editor)*
Heather Stephens *(Sales, Marketing & Production)*
Irene Palko *(Development)*

Children's Books; Educational & Textbooks; History & Antiquarian; Theatre, Drama & Dance

2178 ▬▬▬

GERALD DUCKWORTH & CO LTD
30 Calvin Street, London E1 6NW
Telephone: 020 7490 7300
Fax: 020 7490 0080
Email: info@duckworth-publishers.co.uk
Website: www.ducknet.co.uk

Distribution:
Grantham Book Services, Trent Road, Grantham, Lincs NG31 7XQ

Personnel:
Peter Mayer *(Owner & Managing Director)*
Ray Davies *(Production Director)*
Matt Nieman Simms *(Sales & Marketing Executive)*
Jamie-Lee Nardone *(Publicity Manager)*

Architecture & Design; Biography & Autobiography; Children's Books; Cinema, Video, TV & Radio; Crime; Economics; Fashion & Costume; Fiction; Fine Art & Art History; History & Antiquarian; Humour; Illustrated & Fine Editions; Literature & Criticism; Magic & the Occult; Military & War; Music; Natural History; Philosophy; Physics; Politics & World Affairs; Reference Books, Directories & Dictionaries; Religion & Theology; Science Fiction; Sports & Games; Theatre, Drama & Dance; Travel & Topography

Imprints, Series & ISBNs:
Duckworth: 978-0-7156

Overseas Representation:
Australia & New Zealand: Bloomsbury, Sydney, Australia
Central & Eastern Europe: Penguin Poland, Poznan-Baranowo, Poland
France, Morocco, Algeria & Tunisia: Penguin Group, Amsterdam, Netherlands
Germany & Austria: Uli Hoernemann, Belin Verlag, Berlin, Germany
Holland, Belgium & Luxembourg: Penguin Benelux, Amsterdam, Netherlands
India: Penguin Books India, New Delhi, India
Italy: Penguin Italia, Milano, Italy
Middle East: Penguin Group (Arabia), Dubai, UAE, United Arab Emirates
Scandinavia & Switzerland: Penguin International Sales, London, UK
Singapore & Malaysia: Penguin Books Singapore, Singapore
South Africa: Book Promotions Pty Ltd, Diep River, South Africa
Spain & Portugal: Penguin Books S.A., Madrid, Spain

Book Trade Association Membership:
Independent Publishers Guild

2179 ▬▬▬

DUNEDIN ACADEMIC PRESS
Hudson House, 8 Albany Street, Edinburgh EH1 3QB
Telephone: 0131 473 2397
Fax: 01250 870920
Email: mail@dunedinacademicpress.co.uk
Website:
www.dunedinacademicpress.co.uk

Representation (UK):
Compass Academic Ltd,
The Barley Mow Centre,
10 Barley Mow Passage, Chiswick, London W4 4PH
Telephone: 020 8994 6477
Fax: 020 8400 6132
Email: AS@compass-academic.co.uk

Distribution (excluding North America & Australasia):
Dunedin Academic Press, c/o Turpin Distribution, Pegasus Drive, Stratton Business Park, Biggleswade, Beds SG18 8TQ
Telephone: 01767 604951
Fax: 01767 601640
Email: custserv@turpin-distribution.com

Personnel:
Anthony Kinahan *(Director)*
Robert McKay *(Director)*
Norman Steven *(Director)*

Academic & Scholarly; Geography & Geology; History & Antiquarian; Medical

*(incl. Self-Help & Alternative Medicine);
Sociology & Anthropology*

New Titles: 18 (2012) , 15 (2013)

Imprints, Series & ISBNs:
Dunedin Academic Press: 978-1-78046,
978-1-903765, 978-1-906716
Terra Publishing: 978-1-903544

Overseas Representation:
Arab World & Iran: Dar Kreidieh, Beirut,
Lebanon
Australasia: Inbooks, c/o James Bennett Pty
Ltd, Belrose, NSW, Australia
China & Taiwan: China Publishing Services,
Hong Kong
Hong Kong & Macau: Transglobal
Publishers Services Ltd, Hong Kong
*India, Bangladesh, Indonesia, Sri Lanka,
Singapore, Pakistan, Thailand:* The White
Partnership, Tunbridge Wells, Kent, UK
North America: International Specialized
Book Services Inc, Portland, OR, USA
Republic of Ireland & Northern Ireland:
Brookside Publishing Services, Dublin,
Republic of Ireland
Spain & Portugal: Chris Humphrys, Gaucin,
Spain
Taiwan & Philippines: Edwin Makabenta,
Quezon City, Philippines

Book Trade Association Membership:
Publishing Scotland

2180

DYNASTY PRESS
36 Ravensdon Street, London SE11 4AQ
Telephone: 020 7735 0506
Email: admin@dynastypress.co.uk
Website: www.dynastypress.co.uk

Personnel:
Roger Day *(Manager)*

*Biography & Autobiography; Crime;
Fashion & Costume; Gay & Lesbian Studies;
Gender Studies; History & Antiquarian;
Humour; Law; Philosophy; Politics & World
Affairs; Psychology & Psychiatry; Religion &
Theology*

2181

ECO-LOGIC BOOKS
Mulberry House, 19 Maple Grove, Bath
BA2 3AF
Telephone: 01225 484472
Fax: 0871 522 7054
Email: info@eco-logicbooks.com
Website: www.eco-logicbooks.com

Personnel:
Peter Andrews *(Publisher)*

*Agriculture; Architecture & Design; Crafts &
Hobbies; Environment & Development
Studies; Gardening; Politics & World Affairs*

New Titles: 1 (2012) , 3 (2013)

Imprints, Series & ISBNs:
Eco-logic Books: 978-1-899233

Distributor for:
Australia: Holmgren Design Services
UK: Common Ground; Tagari
USA: Alan C. Hood & Co Inc; Mole
Publishing Co; Oasis Design; Trucking
Turtle Publishing

Book Trade Association Membership:
Allaince of Radical Booksellers

2182

EDINBURGH UNIVERSITY PRESS
22 George Square, Edinburgh EH8 9LF
Telephone: 0131 650 4218
Fax: 0131 650 3286
Email: marketing@eup.ed.ac.uk

Website: www.euppublishing.com

Personnel:
Timothy Wright *(Chief Executive)*
Ian Davidson *(Head of Production)*
Jan Thompson *(Head of Finance)*
Nicola Ramsey *(Head of Editorial)*
Sarah Edwards *(Head of Journals)*
Anna Glazier *(Head of Sales & Marketing)*

*Academic & Scholarly; Educational &
Textbooks; History & Antiquarian;
Languages & Linguistics; Law; Literature &
Criticism; Philosophy; Politics & World
Affairs; Religion & Theology*

New Titles: 109 (2012) , 146 (2013)
No of Employees: 29

Imprints, Series & ISBNs:
Edinburgh University Press: 978-0-7486

Overseas Representation:
North and South America: Oxford
University Press USA, New York, USA

Book Trade Association Membership:
Publishing Scotland; Independent
Publishers Guild

2183

EDWARD ELGAR PUBLISHING LTD
The Lypiatts, 15 Lansdown Road,
Cheltenham GL50 2JA
Telephone: 01242 226934
Fax: 01242 262111
Email: info@e-elgar.co.uk
Website: www.e-elgar.com

Distribution:
Marston Book Services Ltd,
160 Eastern Avenue, Milton Park,
Abingdon, Oxon OX14 4SB
Telephone: 01235 465500
Fax: 01235 465555
Email: direct.enq@marston.co.uk
Website: www.marston.co.uk

Personnel:
Edward Elgar *(Chairman)*
Tim Williams *(Managing Director)*
Alex Pettifer *(Editorial Director)*
Julie Leppard *(Head of Editorial &
Production Services)*
Hilary Quinn *(Sales & Marketing Manager)*

*Academic & Scholarly; Agriculture;
Economics; Educational & Textbooks;
Electronic (Professional & Academic);
Environment & Development Studies;
Gender Studies; Industry, Business &
Management; Law; Politics & World
Affairs; Reference Books, Directories &
Dictionaries; Transport*

New Titles: 350 (2012) , 350 (2013)

Imprints, Series & ISBNs:
Edward Elgar Publishing Ltd: 978-0-85793,
978-1-78100, 978-1-78195, 978-1-
78254, 978-1-78347, 978-1-84064,
978-1-84376, 978-1-84542, 978-1-
84720, 978-1-84844, 978-1-84980,
978-1-85278, 978-1-85898

Associated Companies:
USA: Edward Elgar Publishing Inc

Overseas Representation:
Japan: United Publishers Services Ltd,
Tokyo, Japan
North & South America: Edward Elgar
Publishing Inc, Northampton, MA, USA
*Singapore, Malaysia, Thailand, Indonesia,
Philippines, Brunei, Vietnam, Myanmar,
Laos & Cambodia:* Taylor & Francis Asia
Pacific, Singapore

Book Trade Association Membership:
Independent Publishers Guild

2184

EGON PUBLISHERS LTD
618 Leeds Road, Outwood, Wakefield
WF1 2LT
Telephone: 01924 871697
Fax: 01924 871697
Email: information@egon.co.uk
Website: www.egon.co.uk

Personnel:
Colin Redman *(Managing Director)*
Mrs Rachel Redman *(Company Secretary)*

Educational & Textbooks

Imprints, Series & ISBNs:
Egon Publishers Ltd: 978-0-905858, 978-1-
899998, 978-1-904160, 978-1-907656

Associated Companies:
UK: SEN Marketing

Overseas Representation:
Australia: Auspeld Bookstore, Perth,
Australia; Silvereye Publications, Avalon,
NSW, Australia
New Zealand: Aquila Enterprises, Auckland,
New Zealand
Singapore: September 21, Braddell Tech,
Singapore

2185

ELAND PUBLISHING LTD
3rd Floor, 61 Exmouth Market, London
EC1R 4QL
Telephone: 020 7833 0762
Email: info@travelbooks.co.uk
Website: www.travelbooks.co.uk

Trade Distribution:
Grantham Book Services, Trent Road,
Grantham, Lincs NG31 7XG
Telephone: 01476 541080
Fax: 01476 541061
Email: orders@gbs.tbs-ltd.co.uk

Personnel:
Barnaby Rogerson *(Publisher)*
Rose Baring *(Production Director)*
Stephanie Allen *(Publicity Director)*
Lucy Underhill *(Financial Director)*

Travel & Topography

Imprints, Series & ISBNs:
Eland Publishing Ltd: 978-0-907871

Associated Companies:
UK: Baring & Rogerson; Sickle Moon Books

Overseas Representation:
Australia & New Zealand: New South
Books, NSW, Australia
*Eastern Europe, Russia & Sub-Saharan
Africa:* Tony Moggach, London, UK
*France, Benelux, Germany, Austria &
Switzerland:* Ted Dougherty, London, UK
Italy, Spain, Portugal, Greece & Gibraltar:
Jenny & Penny Padovani, London, UK
Mexico, Central & Southern America: David
Williams, InterMedia Americana (IMA)
Ltd, London, UK
Middle East, North Africa, Turkey & Iran:
Peter Ward Book Exports, London, UK
Thailand, Burma, Laos & Vietnam: Orchid
Press, Bangkok, Thailand
USA & Canada: Dufour Editions Inc, Chester
Springs, PA, USA

Book Trade Association Membership:
Independent Publishers Guild

2186

ELLIOTT & THOMPSON
27 John Street, London WC1N 2BX
Telephone: 020 7831 5013
Email: info@eandtbooks.com
Website: www.eandtbooks.com

Personnel:
Lorne Forsyth *(Chairman)*
Olivia Bays *(Publisher)*
Pippa Crane *(Senior Editor)*

*Biography & Autobiography; Economics;
History & Antiquarian; Industry, Business &
Management; Military & War; Music;
Natural History; Politics & World Affairs;
Sports & Games*

Imprints, Series & ISBNs:
Elliott & Thompson: 978-1-904027, 978-1-
907642, 978-1-908739, 978-1-909653

Overseas Representation:
German-language European territories:
Gabriele Kern, UK
*Middle East & Far East (ex. Singapore &
Malaysia):* Faber & Faber, UK
Singapore and Malaysia: Penguin Group,
UK
South Africa: Penguin Group, UK
*South America, Central America &
Caribbean:* David Williams, UK
USA: Trafalgar Square, USA

Book Trade Association Membership:
Independent Publishers Guild

2187

ELSEVIER LTD
The Boulevard, Langford Lane, Kidlington,
Oxford OX5 1GB
Telephone: 01865 843000
Fax: 01865 853010
Email: initial.surname@elsevier.com
Website: www.elsevier.com

Also at:
32 Jamestown Road, London NW1 7BY
Telephone: 020 7424 4200
Fax: 020 7424 4431

Also at:
20–22 East Street, Edinburgh EH7 4BQ
Telephone: 0131 524 1700
Fax: 0131 524 1800

*Academic & Scholarly; Agriculture; Biology
& Zoology; Chemistry; Computer Science;
Economics; Educational & Textbooks;
Electronic (Professional & Academic);
Engineering; Industry, Business &
Management; Languages & Linguistics;
Mathematics & Statistics; Medical (incl. Self-
Help & Alternative Medicine); Physics;
Psychology & Psychiatry; Scientific &
Technical; Veterinary Science*

Imprints, Series & ISBNs:
Academic Press: 978-0-12
Churchill-Livingstone: 978-0-443
Elsevier Advanced Technology: 978-0-08
Elsevier Applied Science: 978-0-08
Elsevier Trends Journals: 978-0-08
Harcourt Health Sciences
Harcourt Publishers Ltd
Mosby: 978-0-7243
Pergamon: 978-0-08
W. B. Saunders: 978-0-7020
Scutari Press

Parent Company:
Netherlands: Elsevier BV

Associated Companies:
USA: Elsevier Inc

Overseas Representation:
Australia: Elsevier Australia, Marrickville,
NSW, Australia
Brazil: Editora Campus Ltda, Rio de Janeiro,
Brazil
India: Elsevier India, New Delhi, India
Japan: Elsevier Japan, Tokyo, Japan
Korea: Elsevier, Seoul, Republic of Korea
Pakistan: Rae & Sons Publishers
Representatives, Lahore, Pakistan

Book Trade Association Membership:
Publishers Association; International Group of Scientific, Medical & Technical Publishers; STM

2188

ENCYCLOPAEDIA BRITANNICA (UK) LTD
2nd Floor, Unity Wharf, 13 Mill Street, London SE1 2BH
Telephone: 020 7500 7800
Fax: 020 7500 7578
Email: enquiries@britannica.co.uk
Website: www.britannica.co.uk

Distributors:
Encyclopaedia Britannica (UK) Ltd, Unit Y, Paddock Wood Distribution Centre, Paddock Wood, Tonbridge, Kent TN12 6UU
Telephone: 01892 839814
Fax: 01892 837272
Email: britannica@combook.co.uk

Personnel:
Ian Grant (Managing Director)
Jane Helps (Operations Vice-President)
Caroline Kennard (International Schools Director EMEA)
Mark Simes (UK Schools Director)

Academic & Scholarly; Electronic (Educational); Reference Books, Directories & Dictionaries

Imprints, Series & ISBNs:
Encyclopaedia Britannica (UK) Ltd

Parent Company:
USA: Encyclopaedia Britannica Inc

Distributor for:
France: Encyclopaedia Universalis

Overseas Representation:
Germany, Austria, Switzerland & Netherlands: Ted Dougherty, London, UK
Italy: Mare Nostrum Publishing Consultants, Rome, Italy
Scandinavia: Colin Flint Ltd, Harlow, UK
South-East Europe, North Africa & Middle East (excluding GCC): Avicenna Partnership, Oxford, UK
Spain & Portgual: Iberian Book Services, Madrid, Spain
Sub-Saharan Africa (excluding South Africa), Eastern Europe (excluding Russia): InterMedia Americana (IMA) Ltd, London, UK

Book Trade Association Membership:
Independent Publishers Guild

2189

ENERGY INSTITUTE
61 New Cavendish Street, London W1G 7AR
Telephone: 020 7467 7100
Fax: 020 7255 1472
Website: www.energypublishing.org

Personnel:
Erica Sciolti (Publishing Manager)

Academic & Scholarly; Aviation; Chemistry; Electronic (Professional & Academic); Engineering; Environment & Development Studies; Industry, Business & Management; Reference Books, Directories & Dictionaries; Scientific & Technical

Imprints, Series & ISBNs:
Energy Institute: 978-0-85293

Book Trade Association Membership:
Association of Learned & Professional Society Publishers

2190

ENGLISH HERITAGE
The Engine House, Fire Fly Avenue, Swindon SN2 2EH
Telephone: 01793 414619
Email: robin.taylor@english-heritage.org.uk
Website: www.english-heritage.org.uk

Distribution:
Orca Book Services, Unit A3, Fleets Corner Industrial Estate, Poole BH17 0HL
Telephone: 01235 465577
Fax: 01235 465556
Email: direct.orders@marston.co.uk

Personnel:
John Hudson (Head of Publishing)
Robin Taylor (Managing Editor)
Clare Blick (Sales & Publicity Manager)

Academic & Scholarly; Archaeology; Architecture & Design; Educational & Textbooks; Guide Books; History & Antiquarian; Military & War; Travel & Topography

Imprints, Series & ISBNs:
English Heritage: 978-1-84802, 978-1-85074, 978-1-873592, 978-1-905624

Overseas Representation:
Australia: Inbooks, Brookvale, NSW, Australia
Benelux: Roy de Boo, Hooge Mierde, Netherlands
Scandinavia: Jan Norbye, Olstykke, Denmark
Spain and Portugal: Peter Prout, Iberian Book Services, Madrid, Spain
USA: The David Brown Book Co, Oakville, CT, USA

Book Trade Association Membership:
Association of Learned & Professional Society Publishers

2191

ENITHARMON PRESS
10 Bury Place, London WC1A 2JL
Email: info@enitharmon.co.uk
Website: www.enitharmon.co.uk

Warehouse:
Central Books, 99 Wallis Road, London E9 5LN
Telephone: 020 8986 4854
Fax: 020 8533 5821

Personnel:
Stephen Stuart-Smith (Managing Director)
Isabel Brittain (Director)
Natalie Ferris (Sales and Administration)
Peter Target (Publicity)
Anne Stewart (Finance)

Fiction; Illustrated & Fine Editions; Literature & Criticism; Poetry

Imprints, Series & ISBNs:
Enitharmon Press: 978-1-870612, 978-1-900564, 978-1-904634, 978-1-907587

Associated Companies:
UK: Enitharmon Editions Ltd; London Magazine Editions

Overseas Representation:
USA & Canada: Dufour Editions Inc, Chester Springs, PA, USA

2192

EQUINOX PUBLISHING LTD
Unit S3, Kelham House, 3 Lancaster Street, Sheffield, South Yorkshire S3 8AF
Telephone: 0114 272 5957
Fax: 0560 345 9046

Email: jjoyce@equinoxpub.com
Website: www.equinoxpub.com

Distribution:
Macmillan Distribution, Brunel Road, Houndmills, Basingstoke RG21 6XS
Telephone: 01256 302692
Fax: 01256 812558
Email: orders@macmillan.co.uk

Personnel:
Janet Joyce (Publisher)
Valerie Hall (Editorial & Rights)
Yvonne Nazareth (Journals)
Sarah Hussell (Journal Customer Services)

Academic & Scholarly; Archaeology; Biography & Autobiography; Cookery, Wines & Spirits; Educational & Textbooks; Electronic (Professional & Academic); Gender Studies; History & Antiquarian; Languages & Linguistics; Music; Reference Books, Directories & Dictionaries; Religion & Theology; Sociology & Anthropology

Imprints, Series & ISBNs:
Equinox: 978-1-78179, 978-1-84553, 978-1-904768, 978-1-908049
Southover Press

Distributor for:
UK: J. R. Collis Publications; Contact Pastoral Trust; Vanias Editions

Overseas Representation:
Australia & New Zealand: Eleanor Brasch Enterprises, Artarmon, NSW, Australia
China, Hong Kong & Taiwan: Ian Taylor & Associates, Beijing, China
Europe: various, UK
India: Maya Publishers Pvt Ltd, New Delhi, India
Japan: United Publishers Services Ltd and Tim Burland, Tokyo, Japan
Middle East: Avicenna Partnership Ltd, Oxford, UK
North America: ISD, USA
Singapore, Malaysia & Brunei: Publishers Marketing Services Pte Ltd, Singapore
South Africa, Botswana, Lesotho, Namibia, Swaziland & Zimbabwe: Chris Reinders, The African Moon Press, Kelvin, South Africa

Book Trade Association Membership:
Independent Publishers Guild; Association of Learned & Professional Society Publishers (UK Serials Interest Group)

2193

THE ERSKINE PRESS
The White House, Sandfield Lane, Eccles, Norwich, Norfolk NR16 2PB
Telephone: 01953 887277
Fax: 01953 888361
Email: erskpres@aol.com
Website: www.erskine-press.com

Personnel:
Crispin de Boos (Director)
Lesley de Boos (Commissioning Editor)

Academic & Scholarly; Biography & Autobiography; Crime; Health & Beauty; History & Antiquarian; Illustrated & Fine Editions; Medical (incl. Self-Help & Alternative Medicine); Military & War; Natural History; Travel & Topography

New Titles: 4 (2012) , 2 (2013)
No of Employees: 2

Imprints, Series & ISBNs:
Archival Facsimiles: 978-0-948285, 978-1-85297
Erskine Press: 978-0-948285, 978-1-85297

Parent Company:
UK: jack afrika Publishing Ltd

Email: jjoyce@equinoxpub.com
Website: www.equinoxpub.com

2194

ESPRESSO EDUCATION
200 Shepherds Bush Road, Hammersmith, London W6 7NL
Telephone: 020 7870 4500
Fax: 020 7870 4501
Email: info@espresso.co.uk
Website: www.espresso.co.uk

Educational & Textbooks; Electronic (Educational)

Book Trade Association Membership:
Publishers Association

2195

ETHICS INTERNATIONAL PRESS LTD
[publishes for Centre for Business & Public Sector Ethics]
St Andrews Castle, St Andrews Street South, Bury St Edmunds, Suffolk IP33 3PH
Telephone: 01954 710086
Fax: 01954 710103
Email: info@ethicspress.com
Website: www.ethicspress.com

Personnel:
Dr Rosamund Thomas (Director)
Robert Willis (Marketing Manager)
Christopher Thomas (General Manager)

Academic & Scholarly; Educational & Textbooks; Electronic (Educational); Electronic (Professional & Academic); Environment & Development Studies; Industry, Business & Management; Law; Politics & World Affairs; Vocational Training & Careers

New Titles: 2 (2012) , 2 (2013)
No of Employees: 9

Imprints, Series & ISBNs:
Ethics International Press Ltd: 978-1-871891
Teaching Ethics (Book series)

Associated Companies:
UK: Ethics International MultiMedia Ltd

Book Trade Association Membership:
Publishers Association

2196

EVERYMAN'S LIBRARY
Northburgh House, 10 Northburgh Street, London EC1V 0AT
Telephone: 020 7566 6350
Fax: 020 7490 3708
Email: books@everyman.uk.com
Website: www.everymanslibrary.co.uk

Trade Orders & Enquiries:
Grantham Book Services, Trent Road, Grantham, Lincs NG31 7XQ
Telephone: 01476 541000
Fax: 01476 541061
Website:
www.granthambookservices.co.uk

Personnel:
David Campbell (Managing Director)
Jane Holloway (Editorial (Classics))

Academic & Scholarly; Children's Books; Fiction; Guide Books; Illustrated & Fine Editions; Literature & Criticism; Philosophy; Poetry; Science Fiction; Travel & Topography

Imprints, Series & ISBNs:
Everyman Children's Classics
Everyman Classics
Everyman Guides
Everyman Pocket Classics
Everyman Pocket Poets
Everyman Wodehouse

Parent Company:
USA: Alfred A. Knopf

Overseas Representation:
Worldwide (excluding North America):
Random House International (Everyman's
Library), UK

2197 ▬▬▬▬

EX LIBRIS PRESS
11 Regents Place, Bradford on Avon,
Wiltshire BA15 1ED
Telephone: 01225 865191
Email: roger.jones@ex-librisbooks.co.uk
Website: www.ex-librisbooks.co.uk

Distributor:
Gardners Books Ltd, 1 Whittle Drive,
Eastbourne, East Sussex BN23 6QH
Telephone: 01323 521555
Fax: 01323 521666
Email: sales@gardners.com
Website: www.gardners.com

Personnel:
Roger Jones *(Proprietor)*

*Archaeology; Biography & Autobiography;
Cookery, Wines & Spirits; Gardening;
Geography & Geology; Guide Books;
History & Antiquarian; Natural History;
Nautical; Poetry; Transport; Travel &
Topography*

Imprints, Series & ISBNs:
ELSP (Ex Libris Self Publishing)
Ex Libris Press: 978-1-906641
Seaflower Books: 978-0-948578, 978-0-
9506563, 978-1-903341

2198 ▬▬▬▬

***EXECUTIVE GRAPEVINE
INTERNATIONAL LTD**
Rosanne House, Parkway,
Welwyn Garden City AL8 6HG
Telephone: 01707 351451
Fax: 01707 390143
Email: info@askgrapevine.com
Website: www.askgrapevine.com

Personnel:
Helen Barrett *(Chief Executive Officer)*
Anna Weston *(Managing Director)*
Sabrina Ponte *(Director, Sales & Marketing)*
Sally Griffin *(Chief Operating Officer)*

*Industry, Business & Management;
Reference Books, Directories & Dictionaries*

Imprints, Series & ISBNs:
Executive Grapevine International Ltd: 978-
1-903530, 978-1-903550

Book Trade Association Membership:
Data Publishers Association

2199 ▬▬▬▬

*EXPRESS PUBLISHING
Liberty House, New Greenham Park,
Newbury, Berks RG19 6HW
Telephone: 01635 817363
Fax: 01635 817463
Email: inquiries@expresspublishing.co.uk
Website: www.expresspublishing.co.uk

Book Trade Association Membership:
Publishers Association

2200 ▬▬▬▬

FABER & FABER LTD
Bloomsbury House,
74–77 Great Russell Street, London
WC1B 3DA
Telephone: 020 7927 3800
Fax: 020 7927 3801
Email: gasales@faber.co.uk
Website: www.faber.co.uk

Accounts:
16 Burnt Mill, Elizabeth Way, Harlow, Essex
CM20 2HX
Fax: 01279 417366
Website: www.faber.co.uk

Orders:
Telephone: 020 7927 3800
Fax: 020 7927 3805
Email: gasales@faber.co.uk/
gaexport@faber.co.uk
Website: www.faber.co.uk

Distribution:
TBS Ltd, Colchester Road, Frating Green,
Colchester CO7 7DW
Telephone: 01206 255678
Fax: 01206 255930
Email: sales@tbs-ltd.co.uk/export@tbs-
ltd.co.uk

Personnel:
Will Atkinson *(Sales & Marketing Director)*
Neal Price *(UK Sales Director)*
David Woodhouse *(Head of UK Key
Accounts)*

*Biography & Autobiography; Children's
Books; Cinema, Video, TV & Radio;
Cookery, Wines & Spirits; Fiction; Literature
& Criticism; Music; Poetry; Politics & World
Affairs; Theatre, Drama & Dance*

Imprints, Series & ISBNs:
Faber & Faber Ltd: 978-0-571, 978-0-857,
978-1-782, 978-1-846

Overseas Representation:
Africa: InterMedia Americana (IMA) Ltd,
London, UK
*Asia (including Japan, Korea, Taiwan, Hong
Kong, Thailand, Cambodia, Laos,
Vietnam & Myanmar):* Faber and Faber,
London, UK
Australia: Allen & Unwin Pty Ltd, Crows
Nest, NSW, Australia
Canada: Penguin Books Canada Ltd,
Toronto, Ont, Canada
*Eastern Europe (including Russia & Baltic
States):* Adriana Juncu, Jud. Ilfov,
Romania
India & Sri Lanka: Penguin Books India Pvt
Ltd, New Delhi, India
Italy: Penguin Italia SRL, Milan, Italy
Latin America & Caribbean: InterMedia
Americana (IMA) Ltd, London, UK
Malaysia: Penguin Books Malaysia, c/o
Pearson Malaysia Sdn Bhd, Petaling Jaya,
Malaysia
*Middle East (including Israel & Iran), North
Africa, Malta & Turkey:* Faber and Faber,
London, UK
New Zealand: Allen & Unwin Pty Ltd,
Auckland, New Zealand
*Northern Europe (Norway, Sweden, Finland,
Iceland, Denmark, Belgium, Netherlands,
Switzerland):* Faber and Faber, London,
UK
Republic of Ireland: Gill Hess Ltd, Skerries,
Co Dublin, Republic of Ireland
Singapore: Penguin Singapore, Jurong,
Singapore
Southern Africa: Book Promotions, Cape
Town, South Africa
*Southern Europe (Germany, France, Italy,
Spain, Malta, Portugal, Austria, Greece &
Cyprus):* Faber and Faber, London, UK
Spain & Portugal: Penguin España, Madrid,
Spain
USA: Faber & Faber Inc (a division of Farrar,
Straus & Giroux), New York, USA

Book Trade Association Membership:
Publishers Association

2201 ▬▬▬▬

FABIAN SOCIETY
61 Petty France, London SW1H 9EU
Telephone: 020 7227 4900
Fax: 020 7976 7153
Email: info@fabian-society.org.uk

Website: www.fabians.org.uk

Personnel:
Andrew Harrop *(General Secretary)*
Phil Mutero *(Sales)*
Ed Wallis *(Editorial Director)*

*Academic & Scholarly; Economics;
Environment & Development Studies;
Philosophy; Politics & World Affairs*

Imprints, Series & ISBNs:
Fabian Pamphlet: 978-0-7163

Associated Companies:
UK: NCLC Publishers Ltd

Book Trade Association Membership:
Booksellers Association

2202 ▬▬▬▬

A. & A. FARMAR
78 Ranelagh Village, Dublin 6,
Republic of Ireland
Telephone: +353 (0)1 496 3625
Fax: +353 (0)1 497 0107
Email: afarmar@iol.ie
Website: www.aafarmar.ie

Trade Orders (Republic of Ireland):
Gill and Macmillan, Hume Avenue,
Park West, Dublin 12, Republic of Ireland
Telephone: +353 (0)1 500 9500
Fax: +353 (0)1 500 9599
Email: sales@gillmacmillan.ie

Personnel:
Anna Farmar *(Editorial)*
Tony Farmar *(Production)*

*Academic & Scholarly; History &
Antiquarian*

Imprints, Series & ISBNs:
A. & A. Farmar: 978-1-899047, 978-1-
906353

Overseas Representation:
UK (Trade Orders): Central Books Ltd,
London, UK

Book Trade Association Membership:
Publishing Ireland (Foilsiú Éireann)

2203 ▬▬▬▬

*FIFTH DIMENSION LTD
[t/a Dimensional Entertainment]
Marston House, 28 Marston Road,
Blakenhall, Wolverhampton, West Midlands
WV2 4NL
Telephone: 0788 874 2758
Email: hello@fifthdimension.com

Book Trade Association Membership:
Publishers Association

2204 ▬▬▬▬

FILAMENT PUBLISHING LTD
16 Croydon Road, Waddon, Croydon,
Surrey CR0 4PA
Telephone: 020 8688 2598
Fax: 020 7183 7186
Email: info@filamentpublishing.com
Website: www.filamentpublishing.com

Personnel:
Christopher Day *(Director)*
Bernard Marchant *(Finance)*
Zara Thatcher *(Editor)*
Catriona Cotton *(Bookkeeper)*

*Academic & Scholarly; Accountancy &
Taxation; Audio Books; Biography &
Autobiography; Crafts & Hobbies;
Educational & Textbooks; Electronic
(Professional & Academic); Industry,
Business & Management; Medical (incl.
Self-Help & Alternative Medicine); Military*

*& War; Philosophy; Religion & Theology;
Sports & Games; Theatre, Drama & Dance;
Vocational Training & Careers*

Imprints, Series & ISBNs:
Filament Publishing Ltd: 978-1-905493

Book Trade Association Membership:
Independent Publishers Guild

2205 ▬▬▬▬

FINDHORN PRESS LTD
Delft Cottage, Dyke, Forres, Moray
IV36 2TF
Telephone: 01309 690582
Fax: 0131 777 2711
Email: info@findhornpress.com
Website: www.findhornpress/

Personnel:
Thierry Bogliolo *(Publisher)*
Carol Shaw *(Marketing & Publicity
Manager)*
Sabine Weeke *(Rights, Editorial Manager)*

*Animal Care & Breeding; Guide Books;
Health & Beauty; Medical (incl. Self-Help &
Alternative Medicine); Religion & Theology*

Imprints, Series & ISBNs:
Findhorn Press Ltd: 978-0-905249, 978-1-
84409, 978-1-899171

Overseas Representation:
Australia: Brumby Books Holdings Pty Ltd,
Kilsyth South, Vic, Australia
New Zealand: Ceres Books, Ellerslie, New
Zealand
North America: Independent Publishers
Group (IPG), Chicago, IL, USA
Republic of Ireland & Europe: Deep Books
Ltd, London, UK
Singapore: Pen International Ltd, Singapore
South Africa: Faradawn CC, Saxonwold,
South Africa
USA: New Leaf Distributing Co, Lithia
Springs, GA, USA

Book Trade Association Membership:
Independent Publishers Guild

2206 ▬▬▬▬

FIRCONE BOOKS LTD
44 Wales Street, King's Sutton, Banbury
OX17 3RR
Telephone: 01295 811113
Email: info@firconebooks.com
Website: www.firconebooks.com

Personnel:
Richard Wheeler *(Publisher)*
Su Wheeler *(Director)*

*Architecture & Design; Children's Books;
Fine Art & Art History; Guide Books*

New Titles: 1 (2012)
No of Employees: 2

Imprints, Series & ISBNs:
Fircone Books: 978-1-907700

2207 ▬▬▬▬

FIRST & BEST IN EDUCATION
Earlstrees Court, Earlstrees Road, Corby,
Northants NN17 4HH
Telephone: 01536 399011 (Orders &
Accounts), 399004 (Editorial)
Fax: 01536 399012
Email: sales@firstandbest.co.uk
Website: www.shop.firstandbest.co.uk

Personnel:
Jane Edmonds *(Finance Manager)*
Tony Attwood *(Managing Director)*
Anne Cockburn *(Senior Editor)*

Academic & Scholarly; Educational &

Textbooks; Electronic (Educational); Sports & Games

New Titles: 20 (2012) , 20 (2013)
No of Employees: 20
Annual Turnover: £250,000

Imprints, Series & ISBNs:
First & Best in Education: 978-1-86083

Parent Company:
UK: Hamilton House Mailings Ltd

Book Trade Association Membership:
Educational Publishers Council

2208 ▬▬▬▬▬▬

FIVE LEAVES PUBLICATIONS
PO Box 8786, Nottingham NG1 9AW
Telephone: 0115 989 5465
Email: info@fiveleaves.co.uk
Website: www.fiveleaves.co.uk

Personnel:
Ross Bradshaw (Publisher)
Pippa Hennessy (Marketing)

Academic & Scholarly; Children's Books; Crime; Fiction; History & Antiquarian; Poetry; Politics & World Affairs

New Titles: 16 (2012) , 8 (2013)
No of Employees: 2

Imprints, Series & ISBNs:
Bromley House Editions: 978-1-905512
Crime Express: 978-1-905512
Five Leaves Publications: 978-0-907123, 978-1-905512
New London Editions: 978-1-905512
Richard Hollis: 978-1-905512

Overseas Representation:
Iberia: Iberian Book Representation, Spain

2209 ▬▬▬▬▬▬

FLORIS BOOKS TRUST LTD
15 Harrison Gardens, Edinburgh EH11 1SH
Telephone: 0131 337 2372
Fax: 0131 347 9919
Email: floris@florisbooks.co.uk
Website: www.florisbooks.co.uk

Warehouse & Orders:
BookSource, 50 Cambuslang Road, Glasgow G32 8NB
Telephone: 0845 370 0067
Fax: 0845 370 0068
Email: orders@booksource.net

Personnel:
Katy Lockwood-Holmes (Publisher)
Eleanor Collins (Editorial)
Sally Polson (Editorial)

Children's Books; Crafts & Hobbies; Gardening; Health & Beauty; Medical (incl. Self-Help & Alternative Medicine); Philosophy; Religion & Theology

Imprints, Series & ISBNs:
Floris Books Trust Ltd: 978-0-86315, 978-1-78250

Distributor for:
UK: Steiner Waldorf Schools Fellowship
USA: Adonis Press; AWSNA (Association of Waldorf Schools of North America); Biodynamic Farming & Gardening Association; Lindisfarne Books; Macromedia Press; WECAN (Waldorf Early Childhood Association of North America)

Overseas Representation:
Australia: Footprint Books Pty Ltd, Warriewood, NSW, Australia
New Zealand: Ceres Books, Ellerslie, New Zealand

USA (all titles): Steiner Books Inc, Herndon, VA, USA

Book Trade Association Membership:
Publishing Scotland

2210 ▬▬▬▬▬▬

FOOD TRADE PRESS LTD
Normandie Lodge, 2 Chatsfield, Ewell, Epsom KT17 1QS
Telephone: 020 8394 0238
Email: info@foodtradereview.com
Website: www.foodtradereview.com

Personnel:
Adrian Binsted (Publishing Director)

Agriculture; Chemistry; Reference Books, Directories & Dictionaries; Scientific & Technical

Imprints, Series & ISBNs:
Food Trade Press Ltd: 978-0-900379, 978-0-903962

Associated Companies:
UK: Attwood & Binsted Ltd

Distributor for:
Denmark: Mercantila Publishing AS
Italy: Chiriotti Editori Srl
Spain: Montagud Editores SA
Switzerland: Binsted Frères SA
UK: Campden BRI; Leatherhead Food International
USA: American Association of Cereal Chemists; American Institute of Baking; Chemical Publishing Co Inc; CTI Publications Inc; Food & Nutrition Press Inc; Food Processors Institute; Edward E. Judge & Sons

2211 ▬▬▬▬▬▬

FOOTPRINT TRAVEL GUIDES
6 Riverside Court, Lower Bristol Road, Bath BA2 3DZ
Telephone: 01225 469141
Fax: 01225 469461
Email: contactus@footprintbooks.com
Website: www.footprinttravelguides.com

Personnel:
Patrick Dawson (Commercial Director)

Guide Books; Sports & Games; Travel & Topography

Imprints, Series & ISBNs:
Footprint Handbooks: 978-1-904777, 978-1-906098, 978-1-907263, 978-1-908206, 978-1-909268
Footprint Travel Guides: 978-0-900751

Parent Company:
USA: Morris Communications LLC

Associated Companies:
UK: Compass Maps Ltd
USA: Globe Pequot Press

Distributor for:
UK: Wexas International
USA: Globe Pequot Press; Insiders' Guides

Overseas Representation:
Australia & New Zealand: Woodslane Pty Ltd, Warriewood, NSW, Australia
Belgium: Craenen BVBA, Herent (Winksele), Belgium
Canada: Manda Group, Toronto, Ont, Canada
Europe: Bill Bailey Publishers Representatives, Newton Abbot, UK
Israel: SKP, Tel Aviv, Israel
Latin America: InterMedia Americana (IMA) Ltd, London, UK
Middle East: Peter Ward Book Exports, UK
Netherlands: Nilsson & Lamm BV, Weesp, Netherlands

Singapore & Malaysia: Pansing Distribution Pte Ltd, Singapore
South Africa: Faradawn CC, Saxonwold, South Africa
South East Asia: DDP, Paris, France
USA: Globe Pequot Press, Guilford, CT, USA

2212 ▬▬▬▬▬▬

FORENSIC SCIENCE SOCIETY
Clarke House, 18A Mount Parade, Harrogate HG1 1BX
Telephone: 01423 506068
Fax: 01423 566391
Email: journal@forensic-science-society.org.uk
Website: www.forensic-science-society.org.uk

Personnel:
Dr Leon Barron (Hon Editor)

Scientific & Technical

2213 ▬▬▬▬▬▬

THE FOSTERING NETWORK
87 Blackfriars Road, London SE1 8HA
Telephone: 020 7620 6400
Fax: 020 7620 6401
Email: info@fostering.net
Website: www.fostering.net

Personnel:
Lucy Peake (Head of External Affairs)
Gill Cronin (Head of Marketing & Membership)

Educational & Textbooks; Psychology & Psychiatry; Vocational Training & Careers

New Titles: 5 (2012) , 5 (2013)
No of Employees: 3
Annual Turnover: £500,000

Imprints, Series & ISBNs:
The Fostering Network: 978-0-946015

2214 ▬▬▬▬▬▬

W. FOULSHAM & CO LTD
33 Bath Road, The Oriel, Slough, Berks SL1 3UF
Telephone: 01753 526769
Fax: 01753 535003
Email: marketing@foulsham.com
Website: www.foulsham.com

Distribution:
Macmillan Distribution (MDL), Houndmills, Basingstoke RG21 2XS
Telephone: 01256 329242
Fax: 01256 812558
Email: mdl@macmillan.co.uk
Website: www.mdl.macmillan.co.uk

Personnel:
Barry Belasco (Managing Director)
Graham Darlow (Production Manager)

Antiques & Collecting; Cookery, Wines & Spirits; Crafts & Hobbies; Do-It-Yourself; Educational & Textbooks; Fashion & Costume; Gardening; Gender Studies; Guide Books; Health & Beauty; Humour; Industry, Business & Management; Magic & the Occult; Mathematics & Statistics; Medical (incl. Self-Help & Alternative Medicine); Military & War; Nautical; Poetry; Psychology & Psychiatry; Reference Books, Directories & Dictionaries; Sports & Games; Travel & Topography

Imprints, Series & ISBNs:
Foulsham: 978-0-572
Quantum: 978-0-572

Overseas Representation:
Australia: Capricorn Link (Australia) Pty Ltd, Windsor, NSW, Australia
Belgium, Germany, Luxembourg,

Netherlands, Switzerland & Austria: Robbert J. Pleysier, Heerde, Netherlands
Cambodia, Laos, Myanmar, Thailand, Philippines & Vietnam: Ashton International Marketing Services, Sevenoaks, Kent, UK
Canada: Codasat, Vancouver, BC, Canada
Caribbean: Macmillan Caribbean Ltd, Oxford, UK
Central & Eastern Europe: Dr László Horváth Publishers Representative, Budapest, Hungary
Central & South America: InterMedia Americana (IMA) Ltd, London, UK
Far East, Singapore & Malaysia: Ashton International Marketing Services, Sevenoaks, Kent, UK
India: Maya Publishers Pvt Ltd, New Delhi, India
Middle East: Richard Carman Associates, Northwich, UK
New Zealand: Southern Publishers Group, Auckland, New Zealand
South Africa: Trinity Books, PO Box 242, Randburgh 2125, South Africa
Sub-Saharan Africa: InterMedia Africa Ltd (IMA), London, UK
USA: Associated Publishers Group, Nashville, TN, USA

2215 ▬▬▬▬▬▬

FOUR COURTS PRESS
7 Malpas Street, Dublin 8, Republic of Ireland
Telephone: +353 (0)1 453 4668
Fax: +353 (0)1 453 4672
Email: info@fourcourtspress.ie
Website: www.fourcourtspress.ie

Distribution:
Gill & Macmillan, Hume Avenue, Park West, Dublin 12, Republic of Ireland
Telephone: +353 (0)1 500 9555
Fax: +353 (0)1 500 9599
Email: info@fourcourtspress.ie
Website: www.fourcourtspress.ie

Personnel:
Martin Healy (Managing Director)
Anthony Tierney (Marketing)
Martin Fanning (Editorial)
Michael Potterton (Editorial)
Meghan Donaldson (Marketing)

Academic & Scholarly; Archaeology; Fine Art & Art History; History & Antiquarian; Law; Literature & Criticism; Military & War; Music; Philosophy; Reference Books, Directories & Dictionaries; Religion & Theology

New Titles: 46 (2012) , 48 (2013)
No of Employees: 5

Imprints, Series & ISBNs:
Four Courts Press: 978-0-906127, 978-1-84682, 978-1-85182
Open Air

Overseas Representation:
USA: International Specialized Book Services Inc, Portland, OR, USA

2216 ▬▬▬▬▬▬

SAMUEL FRENCH LTD
52 Fitzroy Street, London W1T 5JR
Telephone: 020 7387 9373
Fax: 020 7387 2161
Email: theatre@samuelfrench-london.co.uk
Website: www.samuelfrench-london.co.uk

Personnel:
David Webster (UK Operations Director)
Nathan Collins (Chairman)

Theatre, Drama & Dance

Imprints, Series & ISBNs:
Acting Editions: 978-0-573

Parent Company:
UK: Samuel French Inc

Distributor for:
USA: Samuel French Inc

Book Trade Association Membership:
Publishers Association; Booksellers
Association

2217 ▬▬▬▬

FRIENDS OF THE EARTH
26–28 Underwood Street, London N1 7JQ
Telephone: 020 7490 1555
Fax: 020 7490 0881
Email: info@foe.co.uk
Website: www.foe.co.uk

Personnel:
Adam Bradbury *(Publications Manager)*

*Academic & Scholarly; Educational &
Textbooks; Environment & Development
Studies; Gardening; Reference Books,
Directories & Dictionaries; Transport*

Imprints, Series & ISBNs:
Friends of the Earth: 978-1-85750

2218 ▬▬▬▬

F&W MEDIA INTERNATIONAL LTD
[formerly David & Charles]
Brunel House, Forde Close, Newton Abbot,
Devon TQ12 4PU
Telephone: 01626 323200
Fax: 01626 323317
Website: www.fwmedia.co.uk

Trade Orders & Enquiries:
Customer Services, Trade Department, GBS,
Trent Road, Grantham, Lincolnshire
NG31 7QX
Telephone: 01476 541080
Fax: 0117 654 1061
Email: orders@gbs.tbs-ltd.co.uk

Personnel:
James Woollam *(Managing Director)*
Ali Myer *(Craft Community Leader)*
Brian O'Donnell *(eCommerce Director)*
Sam Vallance *(Head of International Sales)*
Annabel Youldon *(Head of UK Sales)*

*Cookery, Wines & Spirits; Crafts & Hobbies;
History & Antiquarian; Humour;
Photography; Transport*

Imprints, Series & ISBNs:
David & Charles: 978-0-7153

Parent Company:
USA: F+W Media, Inc.

Distributor for:
Italy: White Star Edizione
USA: Adams Media; Dover Publications;
  F+W Media (North Light Books, Writer's
  Digest Books, Betterway Books); Krause
  Publications

Overseas Representation:
Asia: Andrew White, Tunbridge Wells, Kent,
  UK
Australia: Capricorn Link (Australia) Pty Ltd,
  Windsor, NSW, Australia
Belgium, France & Netherlands: Ted
  Dougherty, London, UK
Cyprus, Gibraltar, Spain and Portugal:
  Penny & Jenny Padovani Frias, Barcelona,
  Spain
*Denmark, Finland, Norway, Sweden &
  Netherlands (Foreign Rights Agent):*
  Candida Buckley, Leeds, Kent, UK
Denmark, Sweden, Norway & Finland:
  Angell Eurosales, Berwick-on-Tweed, UK
Eastern Europe: Bill Bailey Publishers
  Representatives, Newton Abbot, UK
Germany, Austria & Switzerland: Gabriele
  Kern Publishers Services, Frankfurt-am-
  Main, Germany

India: Penguin India, India
Italy & Greece: Penny Padovani, London, UK
Latin America & Caribbean: David Williams,
  London, UK
*Mauritius, Kenya, Gambia, Botswana &
  Zimbabwe:* Export Sales Manager, ;
  David & Charles Ltd, Newton Abbot, UK
Middle East: IPR agency, Cyprus
New Zealand: David Bateman Ltd,
  Auckland, New Zealand
South Africa: Trinity Books CC, Randburg,
  South Africa
USA & Canada: F + W Media Inc, Cincinnati,
  USA

Book Trade Association Membership:
Independent Publishers Guild

2219 ▬▬▬▬

GALACTIC CENTRAL PUBLICATIONS
25a Copgrove Road, Leeds, West Yorkshire
LS8 2SP
Telephone: 0113 248 8124
Email: philsp@philsp.com
Website: www.philsp.com

Personnel:
Phil Stephensen-Payne *(Publisher)*

Bibliography & Library Science

Imprints, Series & ISBNs:
Galactic Central Publications: 978-1-
871133

Overseas Representation:
USA: Chris Drumm, Polk City, IA, USA

2220 ▬▬▬▬

THE GALLERY PRESS
Loughcrew, Oldcastle, Co Meath,
Republic of Ireland
Telephone: +353 (0)49 854 1779
Fax: +353 (0)49 854 1779
Email: gallery@indigo.ie
Website: www.gallerypress.com

Personnel:
Peter Fallon *(Editorial, Production Director)*
Jean Barry *(Administration)*
Suella Wynne *(Administration)*
Anne Duggan *(Sales & Accounts)*

Poetry; Theatre, Drama & Dance

New Titles: 12 (2012) , 10 (2013)
No of Employees: 4

Imprints, Series & ISBNs:
The Gallery Press: 978-0-902996, 978-0-
904011, 978-1-85235

Book Trade Association Membership:
Publishing Ireland (Foilsiú Éireann)

2221 ▬▬▬▬

GALORE PARK PUBLISHING LTD
338 Euston Road NW1 3BH
Telephone: 020 7873 6405
Fax: 01580 764142
Email: info@galorepark.co.uk
Website: www.galorepark.co.uk

Personnel:
Caroline Edwards *(Marketing Manager)*
Tammy Poggo *(Publisher)*
Eruke Ideh-Ichofu *(Project Manager)*

*Children's Books; Educational & Textbooks;
Electronic (Educational)*

Imprints, Series & ISBNs:
Galore Park Publishing: 978-1-902984
Iseb Publications: 978-1-902984

Parent Company:
UK: Galore Park (Holdings) Ltd

Distributor for:
UK: Learning Together; ZimZamZoum

Book Trade Association Membership:
Publishers Association; Booksellers
Association; Educational Publishers
Council; Independent Publishers Guild

2222 ▬▬▬▬

GARNET PUBLISHING LTD
8 Southern Court, South Street, Reading
RG1 4QS
Telephone: 0118 959 7847
Fax: 0118 959 7356 (Trade Enquiries &
  Orders)
Email: enquiries@garnetpublishingltd.com
Website: www.garnetpublishing.co.uk

Personnel:
Nadia Khayat *(Managing Director)*
Arash Hejazi *(Publisher)*

*Architecture & Design; Cookery, Wines &
Spirits; Crime; Fiction; Fine Art & Art
History; Guide Books; History &
Antiquarian; Literature & Criticism;
Photography; Politics & World Affairs;
Religion & Theology; Sociology &
Anthropology; Travel & Topography*

Imprints, Series & ISBNs:
Garnet Publishing: 978-1-85964, 978-1-
85964
Ithaca Press: 978-0-86372, 978-0-86372,
978-1-902932
South Street Press: 978-1-85964, 978-1-
873938, 978-1-902932

Associated Companies:
UK: Garnet Education; Ithaca Press; South
  Street Press

Overseas Representation:
USA (Trade): IPM, Dulles, VA, USA
Worldwide: Salt Way Publishing Ltd,
  Cirencester, Glos, UK

Book Trade Association Membership:
Publishers Association; Independent
Publishers Guild

2223 ▬▬▬▬

GATEHOUSE MEDIA LTD
PO Box 965, Warrington, Cheshire
WA4 9DE
Telephone: 01925 267778
Fax: 01925 267778
Email: info@gatehousebooks.com
Website: www.gatehousebooks.com

Personnel:
Catherine White *(Managing Director)*

*Audio Books; Educational & Textbooks;
English as a Foreign Language*

Imprints, Series & ISBNs:
Gatehouse Books: 978-1-84231

Overseas Representation:
Canada: Grass Roots Press, Edmonton, Alb,
  Canada
USA: Peppercorn Books & Press, Hartford,
  MI, USA

Book Trade Association Membership:
Publishers Association

2224 ▬▬▬▬

THE GEOGRAPHICAL ASSOCIATION
160 Solly Street, Sheffield S1 4BF
Telephone: 0114 296 0088
Fax: 0114 296 7176
Email: info@geography.org.uk
Website: www.geography.org.uk

Personnel:
David Lambert *(Chief Executive)*
John Lyon *(Programme Director)*

Richard Gill *(Business Manager)*
Ruth Totterdell *(Publications Manager)*
Dorcas Turner *(Assistant Editor)*
Anna Grandfield *(Senior Production Editor)*

*Atlases & Maps; Educational & Textbooks;
Electronic (Educational); Geography &
Geology; Guide Books; Travel & Topography*

New Titles: 7 (2012) , 4 (2013)
No of Employees: 15

Imprints, Series & ISBNs:
The Geographical Association: 978-1-
84377

2225 ▬▬▬▬

GEOGRAPHY PUBLICATIONS
24 Kennington Road, Templeogue,
Dublin 6W, Republic of Ireland
Telephone: +353 (0)1 456 6085
Fax: +353 (0)1 456 6085
Email: books@geographypublications.com
Website:
  www.geographypublications.com

Personnel:
William Nolan *(Contact)*

*Academic & Scholarly; Archaeology; Atlases
& Maps; Biography & Autobiography;
Educational & Textbooks; Geography &
Geology; History & Antiquarian; Languages
& Linguistics; Reference Books, Directories
& Dictionaries*

Imprints, Series & ISBNs:
History & Society Series: 978-0-906602

2226 ▬▬▬▬

THE GEOLOGICAL SOCIETY
Unit 7, Brassmill Enterprise Centre,
Brassmill Lane, Bath BA1 3JN
Telephone: 01225 445046
Fax: 01225 442836
Email: sales@geolsoc.org.uk
Website: www.geolsoc.org.uk/bookshop

Personnel:
Neal Marriott *(Director of Publishing)*
Anne Davenport *(Head of Sales, Marketing
  and Distribution)*
Emily Milroy *(Marketing Co-ordinator)*
Angharad Hills *(Commissioning Editor)*
Sarah Gibbs *(Senior Production Editor)*
Dawn Angel *(Sales & Customer Services
  Supervisor)*

*Academic & Scholarly; Engineering;
Environment & Development Studies;
Geography & Geology; Scientific &
Technical*

Imprints, Series & ISBNs:
Geological Society: 978-0-903317, 978-1-
86239, 978-1-897799

Distributor for:
USA: American Association of Petroleum
  Geologists; SEPM

Overseas Representation:
India: EWP, New Delhi, India
South East Asian Territories: The White
  Partnership, Singapore
Spain & Portugal: Iberian Book Services,
  Madrid, Spain
USA: AAPG, Tulsa, USA; Princeton Selling
  Group Inc, Wayne, PA, USA

Book Trade Association Membership:
Association of Learned & Professional
Society Publishers

2227 ▬▬▬▬

STANLEY GIBBONS
399 Strand, London WC2R 0LX
Telephone: 020 7836 8444
Fax: 020 7836 8444

Email: enquiries@stanleygibbons.co.uk
Website: www.stanleygibbons.com

Publishing, Mail Order:
7 Parkside, Christchurch Road, Ringwood,
Hants BH24 3SH
Telephone: 01425 472363
Fax: 01425 470247
Email: rswain@stanleygibbons.co.uk
Website: www.stanleygibbons.com

Personnel:
Michael Hall (Chief Executive)
Donal Duff (Chief Operating Officer)
Richard Purkis (Company Secretary)
Keith Heddle (Sales & Marketing Director)
Robert Swain (Publisher)

Crafts & Hobbies; Reference Books,
Directories & Dictionaries

New Titles: 46 (2012) , 48 (2013)
No of Employees: 150

Imprints, Series & ISBNs:
Stanley Gibbons: 978-0-85259

Parent Company:
UK: Stanley Gibbons

Associated Companies:
UK: Benham; Fraser's

Overseas Representation:
Australia: Renniks Publications Pty Ltd,
Banksmeadow, NSW, Australia
Belgium: N. V. deZittere (DZT)/Davo, Tielt
(Brabant), Belgium
Canada: Unitrade Associates, Toronto, Ont,
Canada
Denmark: Samlerforum/Davo, Karup,
Denmark
Finland: Davo C/o Kapylan, Helsinki, Finland
France: ARPHI/Davo, Viroflay, France
Germany: Schaubek Verlag Leipzig,
Markranstaedt, Germany
Italy: Ernesto Marini SRL, Genoa, Italy
Japan: Japan Philatelic, Tokyo, Japan
Netherlands: Uitgeverij Davo BV, Deventer,
Netherlands
New Zealand: House of Stamps,
Paraparaumu, New Zealand; Philatelic
Distributors, New Plymouth, New
Zealand
Norway: Skanfil A/S, Haugesund, Norway
Saudi Arabia: Arabian Stamp Centre,
Riyadh, Saudi Arabia
Singapore: C S Philatelic Agency, Singapore
Sweden: Chr Winther Sorensen AB,
Knaered, Sweden
USA: Filatco, Appleton, WI, USA

Book Trade Association Membership:
Publishers Association

2228 ▬▬▬▬

GIBSON SQUARE
See website
Telephone: 020 7096 1100
Fax: 020 7993 2214
Email: info@gibsonsquare.com
Website: www.gibsonsquare.com

Warehouse:
Macmillan Distribution (MDL), Units 5–8,
Lye Industrial Estate, Pontarddulais,
Swansea SA4 8QD
Telephone: 01256 329242
Email: mdlqueries@macmillan.co.uk
Website: www.macmillan.co.uk

Personnel:
Camille Pandian

Archaeology; Architecture & Design;
Biography & Autobiography; Cinema,
Video, TV & Radio; Crime; Economics; Fine
Art & Art History; Gay & Lesbian Studies;
Health & Beauty; History & Antiquarian;
Humour; Medical (incl. Self-Help &
Alternative Medicine); Philosophy; Politics &

World Affairs; Psychology & Psychiatry;
Sociology & Anthropology; Theatre, Drama
& Dance; Travel & Topography

Imprints, Series & ISBNs:
Gibson Square: 978-1-78334

Overseas Representation:
Australia, New Zealand: NewSouthBooks,
Coogee, NSW 2034, Australia

Book Trade Association Membership:
Independent Publishers Guild

2229 ▬▬▬▬

GILL & MACMILLAN
Hume Avenue, Park West, Dublin 12,
Republic of Ireland
Telephone: +353 (0)1 500 9500
Fax: +353 (0)1 500 9599
Email: nhoward@gillmacmillan.ie
Website: www.gillmacmillan.ie

Personnel:
M. H. Gill (Chairman)
M. D. O'Dwyer (Managing Director)
A. Murray (Educational Publishing Director)
P. A. Thew (Marketing & Sales Director)
B. D. Curtin (Company Secretary/Financial
Director)
M. O'Keeffe (Production Director)
F. M. Tobin (General Publishing Director)
J. Manning (Distribution Director)

Academic & Scholarly; Biography &
Autobiography; Cookery, Wines & Spirits;
Economics; Educational & Textbooks; Guide
Books; History & Antiquarian; Humour;
Politics & World Affairs; Psychology &
Psychiatry; Reference Books, Directories &
Dictionaries

Imprints, Series & ISBNs:
Gill & Macmillan: 978-0-7171
RíRá: 978-0-7171

Overseas Representation:
Australia: Brumby Books Holdings Pty Ltd,
Kilsyth South, Vic, Australia
India, Pakistan & Sri Lanka: Pan Macmillan,
New Delhi, India
Middle East, South East & North Asia: Pan
Macmillan Asia, Hong Kong
New Zealand: New Holland Publishers (NZ)
Ltd, Auckland, New Zealand
South Africa: Pan Macmillan SA Pty Ltd,
Johannesburg, South Africa
UK: Bounce! Sales & Marketing Ltd,
London, UK

Book Trade Association Membership:
Publishing Ireland (Foilsiú Éireann)

2230 ▬▬▬▬

GL ASSESSMENT LTD
The Chiswick Centre,
414 Chiswick High Road, London W4 5TF
Telephone: 020 8996 3363
Email: info@gl-education.com
Website: www.gl-assessment.co.uk

Book Trade Association Membership:
Publishers Association

2231 ▬▬▬▬

GLOWWORM BOOKS & GIFTS LTD
Unit 2, 5 Youngs Road,
East Mains Industrial Estate, Broxburn,
West Lothian EH52 5LY
Telephone: 01506 857570
Fax: 01506 858100
Website: www.glowwormbooks.co.uk

Personnel:
Katrena Allan (Managing Director)
Gordon Allan (Production Director)

Children's Books

New Titles: 1 (2012) , 1 (2013)
No of Employees: 5
Annual Turnover: £250,000

Imprints, Series & ISBNs:
Glowworm Books & Gifts Ltd: 978-0-
9557559, 978-1-871512

2232 ▬▬▬▬

GNAEUS JULIUS COMICS
Digital World Centre, 1 Lowry Plaza,
Salford Quays, Manchester M50 3UB
Telephone: 0161 246 9883
Email: info@gnaeusjulius.com
Website: www.gnaeusjulius.com

Book Trade Association Membership:
Publishers Association

2233 ▬▬▬▬

*ALAN GODFREY MAPS
Prospect Business Park, Leadgate, Consett
DH8 7PW
Telephone: 01207 583388
Fax: 01207 583399
Email: godfreyedition@btinternet.com
Website: www.alangodfreymaps.co.uk

Personnel:
Alan Godfrey (Contact)

Atlases & Maps; History & Antiquarian

Imprints, Series & ISBNs:
Alan Godfrey Maps: 978-0-85054, 978-0-
907554, 978-1-84151, 978-1-84784

Overseas Representation:
Australia: Mapworks, North Essendon, Vic,
Australia
Germany: GeoCenter Touristik
Medienservice GmbH, Stuttgart,
Germany

Book Trade Association Membership:
British Cartographic Society

2234 ▬▬▬▬

GODSFIELD PRESS LTD
Endeavour House,
189 Shaftesbury Avenue, London
WC2H 8JY
Telephone: 020 7632 5400
Email: info@octopusbooks.co.uk
Website: www.octopusbooks.co.uk

Personnel:
Denise Bates (Group Publishing Director)
Clare Churly (Senior Managing Editor)
John Saunders-Griffiths (Foreign Rights
Director)

Magic & the Occult; Medical (incl. Self-Help
& Alternative Medicine); Religion &
Theology

Imprints, Series & ISBNs:
Godsfield Press Ltd: 978-1-85675

Parent Company:
UK: Hachette UK

Overseas Representation:
see:: Octopus Publishing Group, London,
UK

2235 ▬▬▬▬

VICTOR GOLLANCZ LTD
Orion House, 5 Upper St Martins Lane,
London WC2H 9EA
Telephone: 020 7240 3444
Fax: 020 7240 4822
Website: www.gollancz.co.uk

Warehouse, Trade Enquiries & Orders:
see The Orion Publishing Group Ltd

Personnel:
Gillian Redfearn (Deputy Publishing
Director)
Simon Spanton (Associate Publisher)
Marcus Gipps (Editor)
Charlie Panayiotou (Editorial Manager)

Fiction; Science Fiction

Imprints, Series & ISBNs:
Victor Gollancz Ltd: 978-0-575, 978-1-473
VGSF: 978-0-575

Parent Company:
UK: The Orion Publishing Group Ltd

Overseas Representation:
see: The Orion Publishing Group Ltd,
London, UK

2236 ▬▬▬▬

GOMER
Llandysul, Ceredigion SA44 4JL
Telephone: 01559 363090
Fax: 01559 363758
Email: gwasg@gomer.co.uk
Website: www.gomer.co.uk

Personnel:
J. H. Lewis (Director)
Jonathan Lewis (Managing Director)
Roderic Lewis (Director)
Meinir James (Head of Marketing)

Biography & Autobiography; Children's
Books; History & Antiquarian; Languages &
Linguistics; Literature & Criticism;
Photography; Poetry; Reference Books,
Directories & Dictionaries; Sports & Games;
Transport; Travel & Topography

Imprints, Series & ISBNs:
Gomer: 978-1-84323, 978-1-84851, 978-
1-85902

Parent Company:
UK: J. D. Lewis & Sons Ltd

Associated Companies:
UK: Lewis Printers

Book Trade Association Membership:
Booksellers Association; Independent
Publishers Guild; Cwlwm Cyhoeddwyr
Cymru (Welsh Publishers)

2237 ▬▬▬▬

GOTHIC IMAGE PUBLICATIONS
7 High Street, Glastonbury, Somerset
BA6 9DP
Telephone: 01458 831281
Fax: 01458 833385
Email: publications@gothicimage.co.uk
Website: www.gothicimage.co.uk

Trade Orders:
Deep Books Ltd, Unit 3,
Goose Green Trading Estate,
47 East Dulwich Road, London SE22 9BN
Telephone: 020 8693 0234
Fax: 020 8693 1400
Email: sales@deep-books.co.uk

Personnel:
Frances Howard-Gordon (Editorial &
Commissioning Director)
Jamie George (Export Sales Director)
Diana Macleash (Financial Controller)

Biography & Autobiography; Fiction; Fine
Art & Art History; Guide Books; Humour;
Magic & the Occult; Philosophy; Politics &
World Affairs; Psychology & Psychiatry;
Religion & Theology; Travel & Topography

New Titles: 2 (2012) , 1 (2013)
No of Employees: 3

Imprints, Series & ISBNs:
Traveller's Guide Series: 978-0-906362

Associated Companies:
UK: Gothic Image Ltd (Retail Shop); Gothic Image Tours (Tour Operator)

Overseas Representation:
Europe: Deep Books Ltd, London, UK
USA: SCB Distributors, Gardena, CA, USA

2238 ▬▬▬▬▬▬

GOWER PUBLISHING CO LTD
Wey Court East, Union Road, Farnham, Surrey GU9 7PT
Telephone: 01252 736600
Fax: 01252 736736
Email: info@gowerpublishing.com
Website: www.gowerpublishing.com

Customer Service Department/World Distribution:
Bookpoint Ltd, 130 Park Drive, Abingdon, Oxon OX14 4SE
Telephone: 01235 400400
Fax: 01235 400454
Email: gower@bookpoint.co.uk
Website: www.gowerpublishing.com

Personnel:
N. A. E. Farrow *(Chairman)*
Rachel Lynch *(Managing Director)*
Darren Wise *(Finance and IT Director)*
Richard Dowling *(Sales Director)*
Josephine Burgess *(Systems Director)*
Jonathan Norman *(Publishing Director)*
Adrian Shanks *(International Marketing & Digital Publishing Director)*
Susan White *(Marketing Manager)*
Keith Towndrow *(Foreign Rights)*
Lilly Chesterman *(E-Books Manager)*

Accountancy & Taxation; Architecture & Design; Economics; Educational & Textbooks; Electronic (Educational); Electronic (Professional & Academic); Engineering; Industry, Business & Management; Vocational Training & Careers

Imprints, Series & ISBNs:
Ashgate: 978-0-7546
Gower: 978-0-566, 978-0-7546
Lund Humphries: 978-0-85331

Parent Company:
UK: Ashgate Publishing Co Ltd

Associated Companies:
USA: Ashgate Publishing Co

Overseas Representation:
Africa (excluding South Africa & North Africa): InterMedia Africa Ltd (IMA), London, UK
Central & Eastern Europe: Dr László Horváth Publishers Representative, Budapest, Hungary
India: Maya Publishers Pvt Ltd, New Delhi, India
Iran: Kowkab Publishers, Tehran, Iran
Japan: United Publishers Services Ltd, Tokyo, Japan
Korea: Information & Culture Korea (ICK), Seoul, Republic of Korea
Middle East: Publishers International Marketing, Burmarsh, UK
North & South America: Ashgate Publishing Co, Burlington, VT, USA
Pakistan: Book Bird Publishers Representatives, Lahore, Pakistan
South East Asia, Myanmar (Burma), China, Hong Kong, South Korea, Australia & New Zealand: Ashgate Publishing Asia-Pacific, Newport, NSW, Australia

Book Trade Association Membership:
Independent Publishers Guild

2239 ▬▬▬▬▬▬

GRACEWING PUBLISHING
Gracewing House, 2 Southern Avenue, Leominster, Herefordshire HR6 0QF
Telephone: 01568 616835

Fax: 01568 613289
Email: gracewingx@aol.com
Website: www.gracewing.co.uk

Personnel:
Tom Longford *(Managing Director)*
Rev'd Dr Paul Haffner *(Theological and Editorial Director)*
Adrian Hodnett *(Customer Service Manager)*
Mary Clewer *(Accounts Manager)*
Monica Manwaring *(Publicity Manager)*

Academic & Scholarly; Architecture & Design; Biography & Autobiography; Guide Books; History & Antiquarian; Philosophy; Religion & Theology

Imprints, Series & ISBNs:
Gracewing Publishing: 978-0-85244

Distributor for:
Republic of Ireland: Mercier University Press
UK: Newman House; OSV; Smyth & Helwys; St Bedes; Templegate
USA: Ignatius Press

Overseas Representation:
Australia: Freedom Publishing, North Melbourne, Vic, Australia
USA: Liturgy Training Publications, Chicago, IL, USA

2240 ▬▬▬▬▬▬

GRAFFEG LIMITED
[Imprint of Gill Advertising]
16 Neptune Court, Vanguard Way, Cardiff Bay CF24 5PJ
Telephone: 029 2043 6560
Fax: 029 2043 6556
Email: info@graffeg.com
Website: www.graffeg.com

Personnel:
Peter Gill *(Managing Director)*
Matthew Howard *(Publisher)*
Chris Williams *(Publishing Assistant)*

Architecture & Design; Cookery, Wines & Spirits; Fine Art & Art History; Gardening; Geography & Geology; Guide Books; Natural History; Photography; Sports & Games; Travel & Topography

Imprints, Series & ISBNs:
Graffeg: 978-0-9544334, 978-1-905582, 978-1-909823

Parent Company:
UK: Gill Advertising

Overseas Representation:
USA & Canada: Antique Collectors' Club, Woodbridge, Suffolk, UK

Book Trade Association Membership:
Booksellers Association; Independent Publishers Guild

2241 ▬▬▬▬▬▬

GRANTA BOOKS
12 Addison Avenue, London W11 4QR
Telephone: 020 7605 1360
Fax: 020 7605 1361
Email: rights@granta.com
Website: www.granta.com

Trade Orders:
TBS Ltd, Distribution Centre, Colchester Road, Frating Green, Colchester, Essex CO7 7DW
Telephone: 01206 255678
Fax: 01206 255930
Email: mdl@macmillan.co.uk

Personnel:
Sigrid Rausing *(Publisher)*
Laura Barber *(Editorial Director)*
Bella Lacey *(Editorial Director)*
Pru Rowlandson *(Publicity)*

Sarah Wasley *(Production)*
Angela Rose *(Rights)*
Iain Chapple *(Sales and Marketing)*

Biography & Autobiography; Fiction; Politics & World Affairs; Travel & Topography

Imprints, Series & ISBNs:
Granta Books: 978-1-78378, 978-1-86207, 978-1-909889
Granta Magazine
Portobello Books: 978-1-84627

Parent Company:
UK: Granta Publications; Portobello Books

Associated Companies:
UK: Granta Magazine

Overseas Representation:
Australia & New Zealand: Allen & Unwin Pty Ltd, Sydney, NSW, Australia
Canada: House of Anansi, Toronto, Ont, Canada
Europe: International Sales Director, Miles Poynton, Faber & Faber, London, UK
Indian Subcontinent: Penguin Books India, New Delhi, India
Northern Europe: Faber & Faber, London, UK
Republic of Ireland: Faber & Faber, Republic of Ireland
South Africa: Penguin Books South Africa (Pty) Ltd, Johannesburg, South Africa
Southern Europe: Melissa Elders, Faber & Faber, London, UK
USA, Middle East, Eastern Europe, Africa (excluding South Africa), Latin America & Caribbean: sales@granta.com, UK

2242 ▬▬▬▬▬▬

W. GREEN THE SCOTTISH LAW PUBLISHER
[a Thomson Reuters Company]
21 Alva Street, Edinburgh EH2 4PS
Telephone: 0131 225 4879
Fax: 0131 225 2104
Email: alan.bett@thomsonreuters.com
Website: www.wgreen.co.uk

Personnel:
Mrs Gilly Grant *(Director)*
Alan Bett *(Marketing Manager)*
Janet Campbell *(Publisher)*

Law

Imprints, Series & ISBNs:
W. Green The Scottish Law Publisher: 978-0-414

Parent Company:
UK: Thomson Reuters

Book Trade Association Membership:
Publishing Scotland

2243 ▬▬▬▬▬▬

GREENHILL BOOKS / LIONEL LEVENTHAL LTD
3 Barham Avenue, Elstree WD6 3PW
Telephone: 0208 953 2969
Email: michael@frontline-books.com
Website: www.greenhillbooks.com

Warehouse:
Pen and Sword Books, 57 Church Street, Barnsley, South Yorkshire S70 2AS
Telephone: 01226 734222
Email: trade@pen-and-sword.co.uk

Personnel:
Michael Leventhal *(Director)*

Aviation; History & Antiquarian; Military & War

Parent Company:
UK: Lionel Leventhal Ltd

Associated Companies:
UK: Chatham Publishing

Overseas Representation:
Australia & New Zealand: Peribo Pty Ltd, Mount Kuring-Gai, NSW, Australia
Austria, Switzerland, Czech & Slovak Republics, Hungary, Poland, Croatia, Slovenia, Spain (including Gibraltar) & Portugal: Sandro Salucci, Florence, Italy
Canada: Vanwell Publishing Ltd, St Catharines, Ont, Canada
USA: MBI Publishing Co, St Paul, MN, USA

2244 ▬▬▬▬▬▬

GREENLEAF PUBLISHING
Aizlewood's Mill, Nursery Street, Sheffield S3 8GG
Telephone: 0114 282 3475
Fax: 0114 282 3476
Email: sales@greenleaf-publishing.com
Website: www.greenleaf-publishing.com

Personnel:
John Stuart *(Publishing Director)*
Dean Bargh *(Managing Production Editor)*
Amanda Briggs *(Director)*
Tom Harryman *(Sales Manager)*
Jayney Needham *(Marketing Executive)*

Academic & Scholarly; Educational & Textbooks; Environment & Development Studies; Industry, Business & Management; Scientific & Technical

Imprints, Series & ISBNs:
Greenleaf Publishing: 978-0-9554505, 978-1-78353, 978-1-874719, 978-1-906093, 978-1-907643, 978-1-909493

Associated Companies:
UK: GSE Research Limited

Overseas Representation:
Australia: DA Information Services Pty Ltd, Mitcham, Vic, Australia
India: Viva Books, New Delhi, India
Japan: United Publisher Services Ltd, Tokyo, Japan
Taiwan: Unifacmanu Trading Co Ltd, Taipei, Taiwan
USA & Canada: Renouf Publishing Co Ltd, Ottawa, Ont, Canada

2245 ▬▬▬▬▬▬

GRESHAM BOOKS LTD
Milroy House, Tenterden, Kent TN30 6BW
Telephone: 0844 257 9200
Fax: 0844 257 9212
Email: info@gresham-books.co.uk
Website: www.gresham-books.co.uk

Personnel:
Nicholas Oulton *(Managing Director)*

Educational & Textbooks; History & Antiquarian; Music; Religion & Theology

Imprints, Series & ISBNs:
Gresham Books Ltd: 978-0-905418, 978-0-946095, 978-0-9502121

Book Trade Association Membership:
Booksellers Association; Educational Publishers Council; Independent Publishers Guild

2246 ▬▬▬▬▬▬

GRUB STREET
4 Rainham Close, London SW11 6SS
Telephone: 020 7924 3966 & 7738 1008
Fax: 020 7738 1009
Email: post@grubstreet.co.uk
Website: www.grubstreet.co.uk

Distribution:
Littlehampton Book Services Ltd, Faraday Close, Durrington, Worthing, West Sussex BN13 3RB

Telephone: 01903 828500
Fax: 01903 828802
Email: ...@lbsltd.co.uk
Website: www.lbsltd.co.uk

Personnel:
John Davies *(Director)*
Anne Dolamore *(Sales & Marketing)*

Aviation; Cookery, Wines & Spirits; Military & War

Imprints, Series & ISBNs:
Grub Street: 978-0-948817, 978-1-898697, 978-1-902304, 978-1-904010, 978-1-904943, 978-1-906502, 978-1-908117, 978-1-909166

Overseas Representation:
Australia: Capricorn Link (Australia) Pty Ltd, Windsor, NSW, Australia
Canada: Fitzhenry and Whiteside Limited, Markham, Canada
France, Germany, Switzerland & Austria: EMS (Anselm Robinson), London, UK
India: Research Press, New Delhi, India
Middle and Near East, Turkey, Greece, Caribbean, Netherlands & Belgium: John Edgeler, Worthing, UK
New Zealand: Nationwide Book Distributors, New Zealand
Republic of Ireland: Vivienne Lavery, Blackrock, Co Dublin, Republic of Ireland
Scandinavia: Angell Eurosales, Berwick-upon-Tweed, UK
Singapore & the Far East: PMS, Singapore
South Africa: Trinity Books, Johannesburg, South Africa
Spain & Portugal: Humphrys Roberts Associates, Marbella Area, Spain
USA: Casemate Publishers & Book Distributors LLC, Havertown, PA, USA

Book Trade Association Membership:
Independent Publishers Guild; BA (Associate Member)

2247 ■

GUILDHALL PRESS
Unit 15, Rath Mor Centre, Bligh's Lane, Derry BT48 0LZ
Telephone: 028 7136 4413
Fax: 028 7137 2949
Email: info@ghpress.com
Website: www.ghpress.com

Personnel:
Paul Hippsley *(Project & Managing Editor, Marketing Manager)*

Academic & Scholarly; Biography & Autobiography; Children's Books; Crime; Educational & Textbooks; Fiction; Gay & Lesbian Studies; Guide Books; History & Antiquarian; Humour; Literature & Criticism; Music; Photography; Poetry; Politics & World Affairs; Theatre, Drama & Dance

Imprints, Series & ISBNs:
Guildhall Press: 978-0-946451

Overseas Representation:
Australia: Irish Book Centre, Melbourne, Australia
USA: Irish Books & Media Inc, Minneapolis, MN, USA

Book Trade Association Membership:
Publishing Ireland (Foilsiú Éireann)

2248 ■

*GULLANE CHILDREN'S BOOKS
See: Meadowside Children's Books

2249 ■

GWASG GWYNEDD
Hafryn, Llwyn Hudol, Pwllheli, Gwynedd LL53 5YE

Email: cyhoeddi@gwasggwynedd.com

Personnel:
Alwyn Elis *(Managing Director)*
Nan Elis *(Editor)*

Biography & Autobiography; Children's Books

Imprints, Series & ISBNs:
Gwasg Gwynedd: 978-0-86074

2250 ■

HACHETTE CHILDREN'S BOOKS
338 Euston Road, London NW1 3BH
Telephone: 020 7873 6000
Fax: 020 7873 6024
Email: ad@hachettechildrens.co.uk

Personnel:
Marlene Johnson *(Managing Director)*
Clare Somerville *(Deputy Managing Director)*
Susan Barry *(Group Marketing Director)*
Les Phipps *(Group Sales Director)*
Charmian Allwright *(Group Production Director)*
Andrew Sharp *(Group Rights Director)*
Joyce Bentley *(Publishing Director, Wayland)*
Rachel Cooke *(Publishing Director, Franklin Watts)*
Megan Larkin *(Publishing Director, Orchard)*
Anne McNeil *(Publishing Director, Hodder Children's Books)*
Anne Marimuthu *(Finance Director)*

Audio Books; Children's Books; Educational & Textbooks; Fiction; Fine Art & Art History; Poetry; Reference Books, Directories & Dictionaries

Imprints, Series & ISBNs:
Franklin Watts
Hodder Children's Books: 978-0-340
Orchard Books
Wayland

Parent Company:
UK: Hachette UK

Overseas Representation:
Africa, West Indies, South & Central America: Tony Moggach, InterMedia Americana (IMA) Ltd, London, UK
Australia: Hachette Livre Australia, Sydney, NSW, Australia
Australia & New Zealand: Watts ANZ, Sydney, NSW, Australia
Brazil (paperbacks): Agencia Siciliano de Livros, São Paulo, Brazil
Canada (trade & paperbacks): McArthur & Co Publishers Ltd, Toronto, Ont, Canada
Eastern Europe: David Williams, InterMedia Americana (IMA) Ltd, London, UK
Germany, Switzerland & Austria: Gabriele Kern Publishers Services, Frankfurt-am-Main, Germany
Southern Africa (trade): Jonathan Ball Publishers (Pty) Ltd, Johannesburg, South Africa

Book Trade Association Membership:
Publishers Association; Educational Publishers Council

2251 ■

HACHETTE UK
338 Euston Road, London NW1 3BH
Telephone: 020 7873 6000
Email: communication@hachette.co.uk
Website: www.hachette.co.uk

Personnel:
Tim Hely Hutchinson *(Group Chief Executive)*
Chris Emerson *(Chief Operating Officer)*
Richard Kitson *(Commercial Director)*
David Young *(Deputy CEO, Hachette UK and CEO, Orion Publishing Group)*

Clare Harington *(Group Communications Director)*
Dominic Mahony *(Group HR Director)*
Pierre de Cacqueray *(Group Finance Director)*

Parent Company:
France: Hachette Livre

Associated Companies:
UK: Bookpoint; Hachette Australia; Hachette Children's Books; Hachette India; Hachette Ireland; Hachette New Zealand; Headline Publishing Group; Hodder & Stoughton; Hodder Education; LBS (Littlehampton Book Services); Little, Brown Book Group; Octopus Publishing Group; Orion Publishing Group

Book Trade Association Membership:
Publishers Association

2252 ■

*HALBAN PUBLISHERS
22 Golden Square, Piccadilly, London W1F 9JW
Telephone: 020 7437 9300
Fax: 020 7437 9512
Email: books@halbanpublishers.com
Website: www.halbanpublishers.com

Distribution:
Littlehampton Book Services,
Faraday Close, Durrington, Worthing, West Sussex BN13 3RB
Telephone: 01903 828842
Fax: 01903 828621
Email: sales@lbsltd.co.uk

Personnel:
Peter Halban *(Director)*
Martine Halban *(Director)*

Biography & Autobiography; Fiction; History & Antiquarian; Literature & Criticism; Philosophy; Politics & World Affairs; Religion & Theology

Imprints, Series & ISBNs:
Halban Publishers: 978-1-870015, 978-1-905559

Overseas Representation:
Australia: Allen & Unwin Pty Ltd, Crows Nest, NSW, Australia
Canada: McArthur & Co Publishers Ltd, Toronto, Ont, Canada
Caribbean: Humphrys Roberts Associates, London, UK
East & West Africa: Richard Carman Associates, Northwich, UK
Eastern Europe: Csaba & Jackie Lengyel de Bagota, Budapest, Hungary
Europe (excluding Scandinavia & Netherlands): c/o Florence Chatelain, The Orion Publishing Group Ltd, London, UK
India, Sri Lanka & Bangladesh: Maya Publishers Pvt Ltd, New Delhi, India
Japan, South East Asia, Far East & Pakistan: Ralph & Sheila Summers, Woodford Green, Essex, UK
Middle East & North Africa: Peter Ward Book Exports, London, UK
Netherlands: Consul Books, Blaricum, Netherlands
New Zealand: Hodder Moa Beckett Publishers (NZ) Ltd, Auckland, New Zealand
Republic of Ireland: Gill Hess Ltd, Skerries, Co Dublin, Republic of Ireland
Russia, Baltic States & former USSR: Tony Moggach, IMA, London, UK
Scandinavia: Pernille Larsen (Books for Europe), Roskilde, Denmark
South Africa: Jonathan Ball Publishers (Pty) Ltd, Johannesburg, South Africa
South America: Humphrys Roberts Associates, Cotia SP, Brazil

USA & other territories: Export Department, The Orion Publishing Group Ltd, London, UK

Book Trade Association Membership:
Independent Publishers Guild

2253 ■

HALDANE MASON LTD
PO Box 34196, London NW10 3YB
Telephone: 020 8459 2131
Fax: 020 8728 1216
Email: info@haldanemason.com
Website: www.haldanemason.com

Warehouse, Trade Enquiries & Orders:
Vine House Distribution Ltd,
The Old Mill House, Mill Lane, Uckfield, East Sussex TN22 5AA
Telephone: 01825 767396
Fax: 01825 765649
Email: sales@vinehouseuk.co.uk

Personnel:
Ron Samuel *(Director)*
Ms Sydney Francis *(Director)*

Children's Books; Cookery, Wines & Spirits; Crafts & Hobbies; Educational & Textbooks; Health & Beauty; Medical (incl. Self-Help & Alternative Medicine); Natural History; Sports & Games

Imprints, Series & ISBNs:
Haldane Mason Ltd: 978-1-902463, 978-1-905339
Red Kite Books

Book Trade Association Membership:
Independent Publishers Guild

2254 ■

ROBERT HALE LTD
Clerkenwell House,
45–47 Clerkenwell Green, London EC1R 0HT
Telephone: 020 7251 2661
Fax: 020 7490 4958
Email: enquire@halebooks.com
Website: www.halebooks.com

Warehouse & Returns:
Combined Book Services, Unit D, Paddock Wood Distribution Centre, Paddock Wood, Tonbridge, Kent TN12 6UU
Telephone: 01892 837171
Fax: 01892 837272
Email: orders@combook.co.uk

Personnel:
John Hale *(Chairman)*
Gill Jackson *(Managing Director)*
Robert Hale *(Production Director)*
Nick Chaytor *(Rights Manager)*
Mrs Amanda Alabaster *(Financial Controller)*

Animal Care & Breeding; Antiques & Collecting; Biography & Autobiography; Cinema, Video, TV & Radio; Crafts & Hobbies; Crime; Electronic (Entertainment); Fiction; Fine Art & Art History; Gardening; History & Antiquarian; Humour; Magic & the Occult; Military & War; Music; Natural History; Photography; Politics & World Affairs; Reference Books, Directories & Dictionaries; Sports & Games; Transport; Travel & Topography

Imprints, Series & ISBNs:
J. A. Allen: 978-0-85131
Robert Hale: 978-0-7090, 978-0-7091, 978-0-7198
NAG: 978-0-7198

Distributor for:
UK: Phoenix

Overseas Representation:
Australia: DLS Australia (Pty) Ltd, Braeside, Vic, Australia

France, Germany, Netherlands, Austria & Switzerland: Ted Dougherty, London, UK
Ireland: Andrew Russell, Holywell, Dromore, Bantry, Republic of Ireland
Italy, Spain, Portugal, Greece & Gibraltar: Penny Padovani, London, UK
New Zealand: South Pacific Books (Imports) Ltd, Auckland, New Zealand
South Africa: Trinity Books CC, Randburg, South Africa
USA: Independent Publishers Group, 814 N Franklin St, Chicago, ILL 60610, USA

Book Trade Association Membership:
Independent Publishers Guild; Faber Factory

2255

HARLEQUIN MILLS & BOON LTD
Eton House, 18–24 Paradise Road, Richmond, Surrey TW9 1SR
Telephone: 020 8288 2800
Fax: 020 8288 2899
Email: customer.relations@hmb.co.uk
Website: www.millsandboon.co.uk

Personnel:
Mandy Ferguson (*Managing Director*)
Stuart Barber (*Finance & IS Director, Company Secretary*)
Tim Cooper (*Commerical Director*)
Jackie McGee (*Human Resources Director*)
Angela Barnatt (*Retail Operations & Production Director*)
Donna Condon (*UK Editorial Director*)
Jason McKenzie (*Head of Retail Sales*)
Tara Benson (*Head of Marketing*)
Nick Bates (*Senior Manager of Digital Commerce*)

Fiction

Imprints, Series & ISBNs:
Carina UK
Mills & Boon
Mira: 978-0-373
Mira Ink: 978-0-373

Book Trade Association Membership:
Publishers Association

2256

JOHN HARPER PUBLISHING LTD
27 Palace Gates Road, London N22 7BW
Telephone: 020 8881 4774
Email: orders@johnharperpublishing.co.uk
Website: www.johnharperpublishing.co.uk

Book Orders:
Turpin Distribution Services Ltd, Stratton Business Park, Pegasus Drive, Biggleswade SG18 8QB
Telephone: 01767 604951
Email: custserv@turpin-distribution.com

Academic & Scholarly; Educational & Textbooks; Politics & World Affairs

Imprints, Series & ISBNs:
John Harper Publishing Ltd: 978-0-9543811, 978-0-9551144, 978-0-9556202, 978-0-9564508, 978-0-9571501

Book Trade Association Membership:
Independent Publishers Guild

2257

HARPERCOLLINS PUBLISHERS LTD
77–85 Fulham Palace Road, London W6 8JB
Telephone: 020 8741 7070
Fax: 020 8307 4440
Email: enquiries@harpercollins.co.uk
Website: www.harpercollins.co.uk

Registered Office (Warehouse, Trade Orders & Distribution, Finance):
Westerhill Road, Bishopbriggs, Glasgow G64 2QR
Telephone: 0141 772 3200
Fax: 0141 772 3200 x3119

Personnel:
Victoria Barnsley (*Chief Executive Officer*)
Simon Johnson (*Group Managing Director*)
Colin Hughes (*Managing Director, Collins Learning*)
Sheena Barclay (*Managing Director, Collins Geo*)
Oliver Wright (*Group Sales Director*)
Tom Fussell (*Group Commercial Director*)
Ed Kielbasiewicz (*Finance Director*)
Simon Dowson-Collins (*Director of Legal Services*)
Siobhan Kenny (*Group Communications Director*)
David Roth-Ey (*Executive Publisher, 4th Estate & William Collins*)
John Athanasiou (*Director of People*)
Barnaby Dawe (*Chief Marketing Officer*)
Laura Meyer (*Chief Information Officer*)
Kate Elton (*Publisher, HarperFiction*)
Ann-Janine Murtagh (*Publisher, Children's Books*)
Carole Tonkinson (*Publisher, Harper NonFiction*)

Academic & Scholarly; Animal Care & Breeding; Antiques & Collecting; Architecture & Design; Atlases & Maps; Audio Books; Biography & Autobiography; Biology & Zoology; Chemistry; Children's Books; Cinema, Video, TV & Radio; Cookery, Wines & Spirits; Crafts & Hobbies; Crime; Do-It-Yourself; Economics; Educational & Textbooks; Electronic (Educational); Electronic (Entertainment); Electronic (Professional & Academic); English as a Foreign Language; Environment & Development Studies; Fiction; Fine Art & Art History; Gardening; Gender Studies; Geography & Geology; Guide Books; Health & Beauty; History & Antiquarian; Humour; Illustrated & Fine Editions; Industry, Business & Management; Languages & Linguistics; Literature & Criticism; Magic & the Occult; Medical (incl. Self-Help & Alternative Medicine); Military & War; Music; Natural History; Photography; Physics; Poetry; Politics & World Affairs; Psychology & Psychiatry; Reference Books, Directories & Dictionaries; Religion & Theology; Science Fiction; Scientific & Technical; Sports & Games; Transport; Travel & Topography

New Titles: 1000 (2013)
No of Employees: 900

Imprints, Series & ISBNs:
Avon
Blue Door
Collins Learning
Collins New Naturalists
Fourth Estate
Harper NonFiction
Harper Voyager
HarperAudio
HarperCollins Children's Books
HarperFiction
The Friday Project
Tolkien
William Collins

Parent Company:
UK: News Corporation

Overseas Representation:
Australia: HarperCollins Publishers, Sydney, NSW, Australia
Canada: HarperCollins Publishers, Toronto & Scarborough, Ont, Canada
India: HarperCollins Publishers India, New Delhi, India
New Zealand: HarperCollins (NZ) Ltd, Glenfield, Auckland, New Zealand

USA: HarperCollins Publishers, New York, NY, USA
Worldwide (except countries listed): HarperCollins Publishers Ltd, Glasgow & London, UK

Book Trade Association Membership:
Publishers Association; Publishing Scotland

2258

HARRIMAN HOUSE
3A Penns Road, Petersfield, Hants GU32 2EW
Telephone: 01730 233870
Fax: 01730 233880
Email: info@harriman-house.com
Website: www.harriman-house.com

Personnel:
Myles Hunt (*Managing Director*)
Suzanne Anderson (*Rights*)
Rebecca Blackman (*Publicity & Marketing*)
Nick Read (*Head of Production*)
Craig Pearce (*Editor*)
Chris Parker (*Sales & New Media*)

Accountancy & Taxation; Economics; Industry, Business & Management

Imprints, Series & ISBNs:
Harriman House: 978-0-85719, 978-1-897597, 978-1-905641, 978-1-906659

Overseas Representation:
Central & Eastern Europe: Tony Moggach, Publishers Sales Representation, London, UK
Spain, Portugal & Gibraltar: Peter Prout, Iberian Book Services, Madrid, Spain
West Africa: Joseph Makope, InterMedia Americana (IMA) Ltd, London, UK
Western Europe (including Austria, Belgium, France, Germany, Greece, Italy, Luxembourg, Malta, Netherlands & Switzerland): Ted Dougherty, London, UK

2259

HART PUBLISHING
16C Worcester Place, Oxford OX1 2JW
Telephone: 01865 517530
Fax: 01865 510710
Email: mail@hartpub.co.uk
Website: www.hartpub.co.uk

Personnel:
Richard Hart (*Joint Owner & Managing Director*)
Jane Parker (*Joint Owner, Sales & Marketing Director*)

Academic & Scholarly; Law

New Titles: 150 (2012) , 150 (2013)
No of Employees: 13

Imprints, Series & ISBNs:
Hart Publishing: 978-1-84113, 978-1-84946, 978-1-901362

Overseas Representation:
Africa: Tula Publishing Ltd, UK
Benelux: Intersentia, Antwerp, Belgium
Canada: Codasat, c/o University of Toronto Press Distribution, Downsview, Ont, Canada
Central & Eastern Europe: Jacek Lewinson, Poland
Greece, Turkey, Arab Middle East & North Africa: Avicenna Partnership Ltd, UK
Italy & France: Mare Nostrum Publishing Consultants, Rome, Italy
Scandinavia: Colin Flint Ltd, Harlow, UK
South East Asia: STM Publisher Services Pte Ltd, Singapore
Spain & Portugal: Peter Prout Iberian Book Services, Madrid, Spain
USA: International Specialized Book Services Inc, Portland, OR, USA

Book Trade Association Membership:
Independent Publishers Guild

2260

HARVARD UNIVERSITY PRESS
Vernon House, 23 Sicilian Avenue, London WC1A 2QS
Telephone: 020 3463 2350
Fax: 020 7831 9261
Email: info@harvardup.co.uk
Website: www.hup.harvard.edu

Orders & Warehouse:
c/o John Wiley & Sons, European Distribution Centre, Bognor Regis, West Sussex PO22 9NQ
Telephone: 01243 779777
Fax: 01243 829121
Email: cs-books@wiley.co.uk

Personnel:
Richard Howells (*Sales Director*)
Rebekah White (*Publicity & Promotion Manager*)

Academic & Scholarly; Biography & Autobiography; Biology & Zoology; Cinema, Video, TV & Radio; Economics; Fine Art & Art History; Gender Studies; Health & Beauty; History & Antiquarian; Law; Literature & Criticism; Military & War; Music; Natural History; Philosophy; Politics & World Affairs; Psychology & Psychiatry; Reference Books, Directories & Dictionaries; Religion & Theology; Sociology & Anthropology

Imprints, Series & ISBNs:
Belknap: 978-0-674
Harvard University Press: 978-0-674
Loeb Classical Library: 978-0-674

Parent Company:
USA: Harvard University Press

Overseas Representation:
China: Everest International Publishing Services, Beijing, China
Germany, Austria, Switzerland, Italy, Spain & Portugal: Uwe Lüdemann, Berlin, Germany
Hong Kong: Jane Lam, Aromix Books, Hong Kong
Japan: Rockbook, Tokyo, Japan
Malaysia: Simon Tay, Apex Knowledge, Selangor, Malaysia
Middle East (excluding Greece & Israel): Avicenna Partnership, Oxford, UK
North America, Mexico & Central America: Harvard University Press, Cambridge, MA, USA
Poland, Hungary, Croatia, Slovenia, Slovakia, Czech Republic, Russia, Lithuania, Latvia, Estonia, Romania, Serbia, Albania & Bosnia Herzegovina: Ewa Ledóchowicz, Konstancin-Jeziorna, Poland
Scandinavia, Netherlands, Luxembourg, Belgium & France: Fred Hermans, Bovenkarspel, Netherlands
South Africa: Cory Voigt Associates, Johannesburg, South Africa
South East Asia: Joseph Goh, IGP Services, Singapore
South Korea: Se-Yung Jun & Min-Hwa Yoo, Seoul, Republic of Korea
Taiwan: B. K. Norton, Taipei, Taiwan

Book Trade Association Membership:
Independent Publishers Guild

2261

HARVEY MAP SERVICES LTD
12–22 Main Street, Doune, Perthshire FK16 6BJ
Telephone: 01786 841202
Fax: 01786 841098
Email: sh@harveymaps.co.uk
Website: www.harveymaps.co.uk

Personnel:
Susan Harvey (Managing Director)
Jacci Cameron (Office Manager)

Atlases & Maps; Sports & Games; Travel &
Topography

New Titles: 6 (2012) , 8 (2013)
No of Employees: 8
Annual Turnover: £600,000

Imprints, Series & ISBNs:
Harvey Map Services Ltd: 978-1-85137

Distributor for:
Canada: Chrismar Inc
Denmark: Compukort

Book Trade Association Membership:
International Map Industry Association

2262 ▬

HAUS PUBLISHING LTD
70 Cadogan Place, London SW1X 9AH
Telephone: 0207 838 9055
Email: info@hauspublishing.com
Website: www.hauspublishing.com

Personnel:
Dr Barbara Schwepcke (Publisher)
Harry Hall (Associate Publisher)

Biography & Autobiography; Crime;
Environment & Development Studies;
Fiction; History & Antiquarian; Literature &
Criticism; Military & War; Politics & World
Affairs

New Titles: 20 (2012) , 20 (2013)

Associated Companies:
UK: The Armchair Traveller at the bookHaus
Ltd

Book Trade Association Membership:
Independent Publishers Guild

2263 ▬

HAWKER PUBLICATIONS
Culvert House, Culvert Road, London
SW11 5DH
Telephone: 020 7720 2108
Fax: 020 7498 3023
Email: info@hawkerpublications.com
Website: www.careinfo.org

Distribution:
NBN Plymbridge Ltd, Estover Road,
Plymouth, Devon PL6 7PZ
Telephone: 01752 202300

Personnel:
Dr R. Hawkins (Managing Director)
P. Petker (Sales Director)

Health & Beauty; Medical (incl. Self-Help &
Alternative Medicine); Vocational Training &
Careers

Imprints, Series & ISBNs:
Better Care Guides: 978-1-874790
Hawker Publications: 978-1-874790

Overseas Representation:
Australia: Basing House Books,
Hammondville, NSW, Australia

2264 ▬

HAWTHORN PRESS
Hawthorn House, 1 Lansdown Lane,
Stroud, Glos GL5 1BJ
Telephone: 01453 757040
Fax: 01453 751138
Email: info@hawthornpress.com
Website: www.hawthornpress.com

Distribution & Sales:
BookSource, 50 Cambuslang Road,
Glasgow G32 8NB

Telephone: 0845 370 0063
Fax: 0845 370 0064
Email: orders@booksource.net

Personnel:
Martin Large (Director)
Judy Large (Director)
Farimah Englefield (Finance Manager)
Claire Percival (Administrator)

Academic & Scholarly; Children's Books;
Crafts & Hobbies; Educational & Textbooks;
Gardening; Gender Studies; Industry,
Business & Management; Medical (incl.
Self-Help & Alternative Medicine); Music;
Politics & World Affairs; Psychology &
Psychiatry; Religion & Theology; Sociology
& Anthropology

Imprints, Series & ISBNs:
Early Years Education: 978-1-869890, 978-
1-903458, 978-1-907359
Family Activities & Crafts: 978-1-869890
Hawthorn Press: 978-1-869890, 978-1-
903458, 978-1-907359
Parenting & Child Health: 978-1-869890
Psychology & Self Help: 978-1-869890
Rudolf Steiner Education: 978-1-869890

Overseas Representation:
Australia: Footprint Books Pty Ltd,
Warriewood, NSW, Australia
Canada: Tri-fold Books, Guelph, Ont,
Canada
New Zealand: Ceres Books, Ellerslie, New
Zealand
South Africa: Peter Hyde Associates (Pty)
Ltd, Cape Town, South Africa; Rudolf
Steiner Publications, Bryanston, South
Africa
USA (all titles): Steiner Books Inc, Herndon,
VA, USA

Book Trade Association Membership:
Independent Publishers Guild

2265 ▬

HAYNES PUBLISHING
Sparkford, Nr Yeovil, Somerset BA22 7JJ
Telephone: 01963 440635
Fax: 01963 440825
Email: sales@haynes.co.uk
Website: www.haynes.co.uk

Customer Services (Trade):
Telephone: 01963 442080
Fax: 01963 440001
Email: sales@haynes.co.uk
Website: www.haynes.co.uk

Personnel:
Eric Oakley (Chief Executive Officer)
J. Haynes (Chairman)
Jeremy Yates-Round (Managing Director –
UK & Europe; Sales & Marketing Director)
James Bunkum (Finance Director & Group
Company Secretary)
Nigel Clements (Production Director)
Graham Cook (Overseas Sales & Rights
Director)
Mark Hughes (Book Trade Division, Editorial
Director)
Matthew Minter (Motor Trade Division,
Editorial Director)

Animal Care & Breeding; Architecture &
Design; Atlases & Maps; Aviation;
Biography & Autobiography; Children's
Books; Computer Science; Cookery, Wines
& Spirits; Crafts & Hobbies; Crime; Do-It-
Yourself; Electronic (Entertainment);
Electronic (Professional & Academic);
Gardening; Guide Books; Health & Beauty;
History & Antiquarian; Humour; Medical
(incl. Self-Help & Alternative Medicine);
Military & War; Music; Nautical;
Photography; Reference Books, Directories ;
& Dictionaries; Scientific & Technical; Sports
& Games; Transport; Travel & Topography

New Titles: 83 (2012) , 84 (2013)

No of Employees: 70
Annual Turnover: £30M

Imprints, Series & ISBNs:
G. T. Foulis: 978-0-85429
Haynes: 978-0-85733, 978-1-84425, 978-
1-85010, 978-1-85960
J. H. Haynes & Co Ltd: 978-0-85696, 978-0-
900550
Oxford Illustrated Press: 978-0-902280,
978-0-946609, 978-1-85509
Patrick Stephens Ltd: 978-0-85059, 978-1-
85260

Parent Company:
UK: Haynes Publishing Group P.L.C.

Overseas Representation:
Australia: Haynes Manuals Inc, Padstow,
NSW, Australia
Sweden: Haynes Publishing Nordiska AB,
Uppsala, Sweden
USA: Haynes Manuals Inc, Newbury Park,
CA, USA
USA (non-Manual titles only): Quayside
Distribution Services, Minneapolis, USA

Book Trade Association Membership:
Booksellers Association

2266 ▬

HAYWARD PUBLISHING
Southbank Centre, Belvedere Road, London
SE1 8XX
Telephone: 020 7921 0826
Fax: 020 7921 0700
Email: alex.glen@southbankcentre.co.uk
Website: www.southbankcentre.co.uk

Personnel:
Ben Fergusson (Acting Art Publisher)
Alex Glen (Sales Officer)
Ms Faye Robson (Editor)
Ms Diana Adell (Press & Marketing Co-
Ordinator)

Architecture & Design; Fine Art & Art
History; Illustrated & Fine Editions;
Photography

Imprints, Series & ISBNs:
Hayward Publishing: 978-1-85332

Overseas Representation:
UK: Cornerhouse, UK
USA: DAP / Artbook, USA

Book Trade Association Membership:
Booksellers Association; Association of
Cultural Enterprises

2267 ▬

HB PUBLICATIONS
PO Box 21660, London SW16 1WJ
Telephone: 020 8769 1585
Fax: 020 8769 2320
Website: www.hbpublications.com

Personnel:
Lascelles Hussey (Director)
Ms Jennifer Bean (Director)

Accountancy & Taxation; Educational &
Textbooks; Industry, Business &
Management; Mathematics & Statistics

Imprints, Series & ISBNs:
HB Publications L Hussey: 978-1-
899448524, 978-1-899448579, 978-1-
899448623, 978-1-899448678, 978-1-
899448722, 978-1-899448777, 978-1-
899448821, 978-1-899448876, 978-1-
899448920

Book Trade Association Membership:
Publishers Association

2268 ▬

HEADLINE BOOK PUBLISHING LTD
338 Euston Road, London NW1 3BH
Telephone: 020 7873 6000
Email: enquiries@headline.co.uk
Website: www.headline.co.uk

Audio Books; Biography & Autobiography;
Crime; Fiction; Humour; Science Fiction

Imprints, Series & ISBNs:
Business Plus
Eternal Romance
Headline Review
Tinder Press

Parent Company:
UK: Hachette UK

Book Trade Association Membership:
Publishers Association

2269 ▬

HEART OF ALBION PRESS
113 High Street, Avebury, Marlborough
SN8 1RF
Telephone: 01672 539077
Email: albion@indigogroup.co.uk
Website: www.hoap.co.uk

Personnel:
R. N. Trubshaw (Owner)

Archaeology; Guide Books; History &
Antiquarian; Magic & the Occult;
Philosophy; Psychology & Psychiatry;
Religion & Theology; Sociology &
Anthropology

Imprints, Series & ISBNs:
Alternative Albion: 978-1-872883, 978-1-
905646
Explore Books: 978-1-872883, 978-1-
905646
Heart of Albion: 978-1-872883, 978-1-
905646

2270 ▬

ROGER HEAVENS
125 Keddington Road, Louth, Lincolnshire
LN11 0BL
Telephone: 01507 606102
Email: roger.heavens@btinternet.com
Website: www.booksoncricket.net

Personnel:
Roger Heavens (Proprietor)
Sally Heavens (Editor)
Roger Packham (Editor)

Academic & Scholarly; Sports & Games

Imprints, Series & ISBNs:
Roger Heavens: 978-1-900592, 978-1-
900592
RH Business Books: 978-1-900592

Overseas Representation:
Australia: Roger Page, Yallambe, Vic,
Australia

2271 ▬

HELION & CO LTD
26 Willow Road, Solihull, West Midlands
B91 1UE
Telephone: 0121 705 3393
Fax: 0121 711 4075
Email: info@helion.co.uk
Website: www.helion.co.uk

Personnel:
Duncan Rogers (Managing Director)
Wilfrid Rogers (General Manager)

Academic & Scholarly; History &
Antiquarian; Military & War

Imprints, Series & ISBNs:
Helion & Co Ltd: 978-1-874622, 978-1-906033, 978-1-907677

Distributor for:
UK: Aegis Consulting/Aberjona Press; Eagle Editions; Reid Air Publishing; Vanwell Publishing

Overseas Representation:
Australia & New Zealand: Crusader Trading Pty Ltd, Weston, ACT, Australia
Austria, France, Switzerland, Benelux, Germany, Eastern Europe, Greece, Italy, Portugal, Spain, Gibraltar, Slovenia & Croatia: Casemate Publishing UK, Newbury, UK
Canada: Vanwell Publishing Ltd, St Catharines, Ont, Canada
USA: Casemate Publishers & Book Distributors LLC, Havertown, PA, USA

2272

HELTER SKELTER PUBLISHING LTD
PO Box 50497, London W8 9FA
Telephone: 0794 1206045
Email: sales@helterskelterpublishing.com
Website:
www.helterskelterpublishing.com

Personnel:
Graeme Milton *(Director)*
Michael O'Connell *(Company Secretary)*

Music

Imprints, Series & ISBNs:
Helter Skelter Publishing Ltd: 978-1-900924, 978-1-905139

2273

HEMMING INFORMATION SERVICES
32 Vauxhall Bridge Road, London
SW1V 2SS
Telephone: 020 7973 6604
Fax: 020 7973 4686
Website: www.hgluk.com

Also at:
8 The Old Yarn Mills, Sherborne, Dorset
DT9 3RQ
Telephone: 01935 816030
Fax: 01935 817200
Email: info@hisdorset.com

Personnel:
Graham Bond *(Managing Director)*
Mike Burton *(Editorial Director)*
Emma Sabin *(Sales Director)*
Phaedra Rees *(Head of Marketing)*
Matt Hobley *(Head of Digital)*
Dean Wanless *(Senior Editor)*

Engineering; Politics & World Affairs; Reference Books, Directories & Dictionaries; Scientific & Technical; Transport

New Titles: 15 (2012) , 15 (2013)
No of Employees: 100

Imprints, Series & ISBNs:
Hemming Information Services: 978-0-7079

Parent Company:
UK: Hemming Group Ltd

Book Trade Association Membership:
Data Publishers Association; European Directory Publishers Association; PPA

2274

IAN HENRY PUBLICATIONS LTD
20 Park Drive, Romford, Essex RM1 4LH
Telephone: 01708 749119
Fax: 01708 736213
Email: info@ian-henry.com
Website: www.ian-henry.com

Personnel:
Ian Wilkes *(Publisher & Managing Director)*

Cookery, Wines & Spirits; Educational & Textbooks; Fiction; History & Antiquarian; Humour; Medical (incl. Self-Help & Alternative Medicine); Theatre, Drama & Dance; Transport

Imprints, Series & ISBNs:
Ian Henry Publications Ltd: 978-0-86025

Distributor for:
UK: Havering Museum

2275

NICK HERN BOOKS
The Glasshouse, 49a Goldhawk Road,
London W12 8QP
Telephone: 020 8749 4953
Fax: 020 8735 0250
Email: info@nickhernbooks.co.uk
Website: www.nickhernbooks.co.uk

Distribution:
Grantham Book Services Ltd, Trent Road,
Grantham, Lincs NG31 7XQ
Telephone: 01476 541000
Fax: 01476 541060
Email: orders@gbs.tbs-ltd.co.uk

Personnel:
Nick Hern *(Publisher)*
Matt Applewhite *(Managing Director)*
Robin Booth *(Marketing & Publicity Manager)*
Ian Higham *(Sales Manager)*

Theatre, Drama & Dance

Imprints, Series & ISBNs:
Nick Hern Books: 978-1-84842, 978-1-85459

Distributor for:
Canada: Playwrights Press Canada
USA: Drama Book Publishers; Theatre Communications Group

Overseas Representation:
Australia: Currency Press, Sydney, Australia
Canada: Playwrights Press Canada, Toronto, Ont, Canada
USA: Theatre Communications Group, New York, USA

Book Trade Association Membership:
Independent Publishers Guild

2276

HIGHLAND BOOKS
Two High Pines, Knoll Road, Godalming,
Surrey GU7 2EP
Telephone: 01483 424560
Fax: 01483 424388
Email: info@highlandbks.com
Website: www.highlandbks.com

Distribution / Trade Orders:
Trust Media Distribution, PO Box 300,
Kingstown Broadway, Carlisle, Cumbria
CA3 0QS
Telephone: 01228 611511
Fax: 01228 514949
Email: info@highlandbks.com
Website: www.stldistribution.co.uk

Personnel:
Philip Ralli *(Director)*

Biography & Autobiography; Children's Books; Fiction; Religion & Theology

Imprints, Series & ISBNs:
Highland: 978-0-946616, 978-1-897913
Usharp: 978-1-905496

Overseas Representation:
South Africa: Methodist Wholesale, Cape Town, South Africa

2277

HINTON HOUSE PUBLISHERS LTD
Newman House, 4 High Street,
Buckingham MK18 1NT
Telephone: 01280 822557
Fax: 0560 313 5274
Email: info@hintonpublishers.com
Website: www.hintonpublishers.com

Personnel:
Sarah Miles *(Publisher)*

Educational & Textbooks; Languages & Linguistics; Medical (incl. Self-Help & Alternative Medicine); Psychology & Psychiatry; Theatre, Drama & Dance

Imprints, Series & ISBNs:
Hinton House Publishers Ltd: 978-1-906531

Overseas Representation:
Malaysia: Publishers Marketing Services Pte Ltd, Kuala Lumpur, Malaysia
Singapore: SpEd LLP, Singapore

Book Trade Association Membership:
Publishers Association

2278

HIPPOPOTAMUS PRESS
22 Whitewell Road, Frome, Somerset
BA11 4EL
Telephone: 01373 466653
Fax: 01373 466653
Email: rjhippopress@aol.com

Personnel:
R. John *(Publisher)*
M. Pargitter *(Editor)*
Anna Martin *(Editorial Assistant)*

Literature & Criticism; Poetry

Imprints, Series & ISBNs:
Hippopotamus Press: 978-0-904179

Distributor for:
Austria: University of Salzburg Press
USA: Ramparts Inc

2279

HISTORICAL PUBLICATIONS LTD
14 Saddleton Road, Whitstable CT54JD
Telephone: 01227 272605
Fax: none
Email:
richardson@historicalpublications.co.uk
Website: www.historicalpublications.co.uk

Distribution:
Countryside Books, 2 Highfield Avenue,
Newbury, Berks RG14 5DS
Telephone: 01635 43816
Fax: 01635 551004
Email: info@countrysidebooks.co.uk
Website: www.countrysidebooks.co.uk

Personnel:
John Richardson *(Managing Director)*
Helen English *(Secretary)*

Academic & Scholarly; Architecture & Design; History & Antiquarian; Travel & Topography

New Titles: 4 (2012) , 22 (2013)
No of Employees: 2
Annual Turnover: £80,000

Imprints, Series & ISBNs:
Historical Publications Ltd: 978-0-948667, 978-1-905286

2280

HOBNOB PRESS
30c Deverill Road Trading Estate,
Sutton Veny, Warminster BA12 7BZ
Telephone: 07715 620790

Email: john@hobnobpress.co.uk
Website: www.hobnobpress.co.uk

Editorial:
15 Castle Court, Castle Street, Stroud
GL5 2JD
Telephone: 07715 620790
Email: john@hobnobpress.co.uk
Website: www.hobnobpress.co.uk

Personnel:
John Chandler *(Sole Trader)*

Academic & Scholarly; Archaeology; Guide Books; History & Antiquarian; Literature & Criticism; Travel & Topography

New Titles: 6 (2012) , 4 (2013)

Imprints, Series & ISBNs:
Hobnob Press: 978-0-946418, 978-1-906978

Distributor for:
UK: Wiltshire Buildings Record; Wiltshire Record Society

2281

HODDER GIBSON
[An imprint of Hodder Education]
2A Christie Street, Paisley PA1 1NB
Telephone: 0141 848 1609
Fax: 0141 889 6315
Email: hoddergibson@hodder.co.uk
Website: www.hoddereducation.co.uk

Distribution:
Bookpoint, 130 Park Drive, Abingdon,
Oxon OX14 4SE
Telephone: 01235 400400
Fax: 01235 400454
Email: education@bookpoint.co.uk

Personnel:
John Mitchell *(Managing Director)*
Ian MacLean *(Sales Representative)*
Elizabeth Fletcher *(Project Editor (Scotland))*
Ella Austin *(Desk Editor)*

Academic & Scholarly; Educational & Textbooks; Electronic (Educational)

Imprints, Series & ISBNs:
formerly Robert Gibson & Sons: 978-0-7169
Hodder Gibson: 978-0-340

Parent Company:
UK: Hachette UK

Book Trade Association Membership:
Publishers Association; Publishing Scotland; Educational Publishers Council

2282

HODDER EDUCATION
338 Euston Road, London NW1 3BH
Telephone: 020 7873 6000
Website: www.hoddereducation.co.uk

Distribution Centre:
Bookpoint Ltd, 130 Milton Park, Abingdon,
Oxon OX14 4SB
Telephone: 01235 400400
Fax: 01235 400445

Personnel:
Elisabeth Tribe *(Managing Director)*
Alyssum Ross *(Business Operations Director)*
John Mitchell *(Scotland – Hodder Gibson Director)*
Robert Sulley *(International Director)*
Steve Connolly *(Digital Director)*
Alex Jones *(Finance Director)*
Victoria Goodall *(Marketing Director)*
Paul Cherry *(Philip Allan Director)*
Janice Holdcroft *(Director of Sales and Online Services)*
Rebecca Duprey *(Head of International Sales)*

Academic & Scholarly; Accountancy & Taxation; Atlases & Maps; Audio Books; Biology & Zoology; Chemistry; Computer Science; Cookery, Wines & Spirits; Economics; Educational & Textbooks; Electronic (Educational); English as a Foreign Language; Environment & Development Studies; Geography & Geology; Health & Beauty; History & Antiquarian; Industry, Business & Management; Languages & Linguistics; Law; Literature & Criticism; Mathematics & Statistics; Natural History; Philosophy; Physics; Politics & World Affairs; Psychology & Psychiatry; Reference Books, Directories & Dictionaries; Religion & Theology; Scientific & Technical; Sociology & Anthropology; Sports & Games; Vocational Training & Careers

Imprints, Series & ISBNs:
Galore Park
Hodder Gibson: 978-0-7169
Philip Allan: 978-0-86003, 978-1-84489

Parent Company:
UK: Hodder Headline Plc/Hachette Livre

Associated Companies:
UK: Headline Book Publishing Ltd; Hodder & Stoughton

Overseas Representation:
All other international queries: Rebecca Duprey, Head of International Sales, Hodder Education, London, UK
Antigua: The Best of Books, St John's, Antigua
Argentina: Kel Ediciones SA (Agents), Buenos Aires, Argentina
Australia: Cengage (Australia), NSW, Australia
Bangladesh: Cambridge University Press, India
Barbados: Julian Atherley, Educational Consultant, Barbados
Cameroon: Kelvin Van Hasselt, Cameroon
Canada: Bacon & Hughes Ltd, Ottawa, Ont, Canada
China: Ian Taylor Associates Ltd, London, UK
Colombia: English Language Services, Colombia; Grup Ktdra Ltda, Colombia
Eastern Europe (Further Education): Jacek Lewinson, Warsaw, Poland
Egypt: Macmillan Publishers Egypt Ltd, Cairo, Egypt
Ethiopia: Etcon Ltd, Ethiopia
Europe: Gill Dee, International Schools Sales Manager, Hodder, London, UK; Jo Arnold, International Schools Consultant, Hodder, London, UK
Ghana: EPP Book Services Ltd, Accra, Ghana
Hong Kong & Macau: Transglobal Publishers Services Ltd, Hong Kong
India: Viva Group, New Delhi, India
Indonesia: P.T. Mentari Books, Indonesia
Jamaica: Kingston Bookshop, Kingston, Jamaica
Japan & South Korea: Tim Burland, Japan
Kenya: Educate Yourself Ltd, Kenya
Malawi: Bookland International, Malawi
Malaysia: APD Malaysia, Malaysia
Maldives: Asrafee Bookshop, Maldives
Malta, Greece, Cyprus, Turkey and Italy: Taran Arrigo, Educational Consultant, Hodder Education, Malta
Mauritius: Editions le Printemps, Vacoas, Mauritius
Middle East: George Savage, Hodder, London, UK; Gill Dee, Hodder, London, UK
Middle East (Further Education): IPR, Cyprus
Namibia, Swaziland, Botswana, Lesotho & South Africa: Macmillan South Africa Publishers (Pty) Ltd, Braamfontein, South Africa
New Zealand: Cengage Learning, New Zealand
Nigeria: Bounty Press Ltd, Ibadan, Nigeria
Pakistan: Paramount Books Pvt Ltd, Pakistan
Rwanda: School Book Distributors, Rwanda

Scandinavia, Estonia, Latvia, Lithuania & Russia: Witra Publishing Group, Sweden
Singapore, Brunei, Malaysia, Thailand, Vientam & Cambodia: APD, Singapore
Sri Lanka: Jeya Agency (Pvt) Ltd, Sri Lanka; Zubair Makeen Sons, Sri Lanka
St Lucia: Nathaniel's Books, St Lucia
Tanzania: Aidan Publishers, Dar es Salaam, Tanzania
Trinidad & Tobago: Penny Roodal-Mohammed, Education Consultant, Trinidad
Uganda: Moran Publishers Uganda Ltd, Kampala, Uganda
Uruguay: EQ Opciones Education, Uruguay
USA: Jennifer Smith, Hodder Education, Educational Consultant, USA
USA (Further Education): Oxford University Press Inc USA, New York, NY, USA
Zambia: Macmillan Zambia, Lusaka, Zambia

Book Trade Association Membership:
Publishers Association; Educational Publishers Council

2283

HODDER FAITH
338 Euston Road, London NW1 3BH
Telephone: 020 7873 6000
Fax: 020 7873 6059
Email: hodderfaith-sales@hodder.co.uk
Website: www.hodderfaith.com

Distribution:
Bookpoint Ltd, 130 Milton Park, Abingdon, Oxon OX14 4SB
Telephone: 01235 400400
Fax: 01235 400445

Personnel:
Jamie Hodder-Williams (CEO)
Ian Metcalfe (Publishing Director)
Lucy Hale (Sales Director)

Biography & Autobiography; Fiction; History & Antiquarian; Philosophy; Religion & Theology

Imprints, Series & ISBNs:
Hodder & Stoughton: 978-0-340, 978-1-444
Hodder Windblown: 978-0-340

Parent Company:
UK: Hachette UK Ltd

Associated Companies:
UK: Hachette UK; Headline Book Publishing Ltd

Distributor for:
USA: FaithWords

Overseas Representation:
Australia: Hachette Australia, Sydney, NSW, Australia
Canada: Hachette Canada, New York, USA
India: Hachette India, Mumbai, India
New Zealand: Hachette New Zealand, Auckland, New Zealand
Singapore: Pansing Distribution Sdn Bhd, Singapore
Southern Africa: Jonathan Ball Publishers (Pty) Ltd, Johannesburg, South Africa
USA: Trafalgar Square Publishing, North Pomfret, VT, USA

Book Trade Association Membership:
Publishers Association; Booksellers Association; ECPA

2284

HODDER & STOUGHTON
338 Euston Road, London NW1 3BH
Telephone: 020 7873 6000

Distribution Centre:
Bookpoint Ltd, 130 Milton Park, Abingdon, Oxon OX14 4SB
Telephone: 01235 400400

Fax: 01235 400445

Personnel:
Jamie Hodder-Williams (CEO)
Lisa Highton (Publisher)
Kerry Hood (Publicity Director)
Auriol Bishop (Creative Director)
Lucy Hale (Sales and Marketing Director)
Nick Davies (Managing Director, John Murray Press)
Carolyn Mays (Managing Director)
Karen Geary (Publicity Director)
Rowena Webb (Non-Fiction Director)
Rupert Lancaster (Audio Director)
Carole Welch (Sceptre Director)
Jason Bartholomew (Rights Director)
Roland Philipps (Managing Director, John Murray)

Audio Books; Biography & Autobiography; Cinema, Video, TV & Radio; Cookery, Wines & Spirits; Crime; Fiction; History & Antiquarian; Humour; Military & War; Politics & World Affairs; Science Fiction; Sports & Games

Imprints, Series & ISBNs:
Consumer Learning
Coronet
Hodder & Stoughton: 978-0-340
John Murray
Mulholland
Saltyard
Sceptre: 978-0-340
Two Roads

Parent Company:
UK: Hachette UK Ltd

Associated Companies:
France: Hachette Livre
UK: Headline Book Publishing Ltd

Overseas Representation:
Australia: Hachette Australia, Sydney, NSW, Australia
Canada (trade & paperbacks): Hachette Canada, Toronto, Ont, Canada
Caribbean: Humphreys Roberts Associates, London, UK
Eastern Europe: CLB, Budapest, Hungary
India: Hachette India, New Delhi, India
New Zealand: Hachette New Zealand, Auckland, New Zealand
Singapore: Pansing Distribution Sdn Bhd, Singapore
South America: InterMedia Americana (IMA) Ltd, London, UK
Southern Africa (trade): Jonathan Ball Publishers (Pty) Ltd, Johannesburg, South Africa
USA: Trafalgar Square, Chicago, IL, USA

Book Trade Association Membership:
Publishers Association

2285

ALISON HODGE PUBLISHERS
2 Clarence Place, Penzance, Cornwall TR20 8XA
Telephone: 01736 368093
Email: info@alison-hodge.co.uk
Website:
www.alisonhodgepublishers.co.uk

Distribution:
Tormark, Redruth, Cornwall TR16 5HY
Telephone: 01209 822101
Fax: 01209 822035
Email: sales@tormark.co.uk

Personnel:
Alison Hodge (Publisher)

Biography & Autobiography; Cookery, Wines & Spirits; Fine Art & Art History; Gardening; Geography & Geology; Guide Books; History & Antiquarian; Natural History; Photography; Sports & Games; Travel & Topography

Imprints, Series & ISBNs:
The County Gardens Guides Inspirations Series
Alison Hodge Publishers: 978-0-906720
Pocket Cornwall

Overseas Representation:
Australia and New Zealand (surfing titles only): Woodslane, Warriewood, NSW, Australia
Europe: Bill Bailey Publishers Representatives, Newton Abbot, UK

2286

HOLO BOOKS
Clarendon House, 52 Cornmarket, Oxford OX1 3HJ
Telephone: 01865 513681
Fax: 01865 554199
Email: holobooks@yahoo.co.uk
Website: www.holobooks.co.uk

Orders:
Central Books, 99 Wallis Road, London E9 5LN
Telephone: 020 8986 4854
Fax: 020 8533 5821
Email: orders@centralbooks.com
Website: www.centralbooks.co.uk

Personnel:
Susanna Hoe (Partner)
Derek Roebuck (Partner)
Leonie Harries (Manager)

Academic & Scholarly; Archaeology; Biography & Autobiography; Gender Studies; Guide Books; History & Antiquarian; Humour; Law; Travel & Topography

Imprints, Series & ISBNs:
The Arbitration Press: 978-0-9544056
Of Islands and Women Series
The Women's History Press

Distributor for:
Hong Kong: Roundhouse Publications (Asia)
USA: Bear Creek Books

Overseas Representation:
Hong Kong: Far East Media, Hong Kong
USA: Wm. W. Gaunt & Sons Inc, Holmes Beach, FL, USA

2287

HONNO (WELSH WOMEN'S PRESS)
Unit 14, Creative Units,
Aberystwyth Arts Centre, Penglais Campus, Aberystwyth, Ceredigion SY23 3GL
Telephone: 01970 623150
Fax: 01970 623150
Email: post@honno.co.uk
Website: www.honno.co.uk

Personnel:
Helena Earnshaw (Marketing Manager)
Caroline Oakley (Editor)
Lesley Rice (Production & Administration)
Alison Greeley (Finance)

Biography & Autobiography; Crime; Fiction

New Titles: 7 (2012) , 7 (2013)
No of Employees: 4

Imprints, Series & ISBNs:
Honno Classic Fiction: 978-1-870206, 978-1-906784
Honno Modern Fiction: 978-1-870206, 978-1-906784
Honno Voices: 978-1-870206, 978-1-906784

Overseas Representation:
United States: IPG, USA

Book Trade Association Membership:
Independent Publishers Guild

2288

HOPSCOTCH
[a division of MA Education]
St Jude's Church, Dulwich Road, Herne Hill,
London SE24 0PB
Telephone: 020 7738 5454
Fax: 020 7778 8317
Email: angela.s@markallengroup.com
Website: www.hopscotchbooks.com

Sales & Distribution:
Mark Allen Distribution, Unit A,
1–5 Dinton Business Park,
Catherine Ford Road, Dinton, Salisbury
SP3 5HZ
Telephone: 01722 716935
Fax: 01722 716812
Email: sales@hopscotchbooks.com
Website: www.hopscotchbooks.com

Personnel:
Angela Shaw (Associate Publisher)

Educational & Textbooks; Electronic
(Educational)

Imprints, Series & ISBNs:
Hopscotch: 978-1-902239, 978-1-904307,
978-1-905390, 978-1-90933, 978-1-
90986

Parent Company:
UK: Mark Allen Group

2289

HOUSE OF STRATUS
Lisandra House, Fore Street, Looe, Cornwall
PL13 1AD
Telephone: 01503 220131
Fax: 0870 3836922
Email: cust@houseofstratus.com
Website: www.houseofstratus.com

Personnel:
David Lane (Managing Director)

Biography & Autobiography; Crime;
Fiction; Humour; Literature & Criticism;
Philosophy; Politics & World Affairs; Science
Fiction

Book Trade Association Membership:
Publishers Association

2290

HOW TO BOOKS LTD
Spring Hill House, Spring Hill Road,
Begbroke, Oxford OX5 1RX
Telephone: 01865 375794
Email: info@howtobooks.co.uk
Website: www.howtobooks.co.uk

Customer Services:
The Book Service, Colchester Road,
Frating Green, Colchester CO7 7DW
Telephone: 01206 256000
Fax: 01206 255930
Email: info@tbs-ltd.co.uk
Website: www.howtobooks.co.uk

Sales Representation:
Constable & Robinson Ltd,
55–56 Russell Square, London WC1B 4HP
Telephone: 020 7268 9700
Fax: 020 7255 1674
Email: sales@constablerobinson.co.uk
Website: www.constablerobinson.co.uk

Personnel:
Giles Lewis (Publisher)
Nikki Read (Editorial Director)

Animal Care & Breeding; Antiques &
Collecting; Cookery, Wines & Spirits; Do-It-
Yourself; Educational & Textbooks;
Gardening; Guide Books; Health & Beauty;
Industry, Business & Management;
Literature & Criticism; Medical (incl. Self-
Help & Alternative Medicine); Reference

Books, Directories & Dictionaries; Travel &
Topography; Vocational Training & Careers

Imprints, Series & ISBNs:
How To Books: 978-1-84528, 978-1-85703,
978-1-905862

Parent Company:
UK: Constable & Robinson Ltd.

Overseas Representation:
World: Constable & Robinson Ltd, UK

Book Trade Association Membership:
Independent Publishers Guild

2291

H & S MEDIA
No 1, 4 Town Meadow, Brentford TW8 0BX
Telephone: 020 3589 4060
Email: info@handsmedia.com
Website: www.handsmedia.com

Audio Books; Fine Art & Art History;
Literature & Criticism; Music; Poetry; Politics
& World Affairs; Religion & Theology;
Theatre, Drama & Dance

Book Trade Association Membership:
Publishers Association

2292

HUMAN KINETICS EUROPE LTD
107 Bradford Road, Stanningley, Leeds
LS28 6AT
Telephone: 0113 255 5665
Fax: 0113 255 5885
Email: hk@hkeurope.com
Website: www.humankinetics.com/

Personnel:
Sara Cooper (Managing Director)
Sian Partridge (Sales Director)
Helen Ackroyd (Finance Manager)
Claire Davey (Customer Services Manager)
Rory Aspell (Marketing Manager)
Chris Wright (Editorial Manager)

Academic & Scholarly; Educational &
Textbooks; Electronic (Educational);
Electronic (Professional & Academic);
Health & Beauty; Medical (incl. Self-Help &
Alternative Medicine); Psychology &
Psychiatry; Scientific & Technical; Sports &
Games; Theatre, Drama & Dance

Imprints, Series & ISBNs:
Human Kinetics Europe Ltd: 978-0-7360,
978-0-87322, 978-0-88011, 978-0-
918438, 978-0-931250

Parent Company:
USA: Human Kinetics Inc

Associated Companies:
Australia: Human Kinetics
Canada: Human Kinetics
New Zealand: Human Kinetics

Overseas Representation:
Australia: Human Kinetics (Australia),
Torrens Park, SA, Australia
Brazil (academic): Tecmedd, São Paulo,
Brazil
Canada: Human Kinetics (Canada),
Windsor, Ont, Canada
China (including Hong Kong): AA Media
Services, Shanghai, China
India: Disvan Enterprises, New Delhi, India
Iran: Kowkab Publishers, Tehran, Iran
Japan: Eureka Press, Kyoto, Japan
Korea: Daehan Media Co Ltd, Seoul,
Republic of Korea
New Zealand: Human Kinetics (New
Zealand), Auckland, New Zealand
Singapore & Malaysia: Icon Books
Singapore Pte Ltd, Singapore
South Africa (academic): Academic &
Professional Book Distributor,
Johannesburg, South Africa

South Africa (trade): Real Books CC,
Johannesburg, South Africa
Taiwan: Unifacmanu Trading Co Ltd, Taipei,
Taiwan
Thailand, Indonesia, Bangladesh, Brunei &
Philippines: Alkem Co (S) Pte Ltd,
Singapore
USA: Human Kinetics, Champaign, IL, USA

Book Trade Association Membership:
Independent Publishers Guild

2293

JOHN HUNT PUBLISHING LTD
Laurel House, Jacklyns Lane, Alresford,
Hants SO24 9JH
Telephone: 01962 735802
Email: office1@o-books.net
Website: www.johnhuntpublishing.com

Personnel:
John Hunt (Owner Publisher)
Jed Rose (Managing Director)
Catherine Harris (Manager)

Architecture & Design; Children's Books;
Fiction; Fine Art & Art History; Gay &
Lesbian Studies; Industry, Business &
Management; Literature & Criticism; Magic
& the Occult; Medical (incl. Self-Help &
Alternative Medicine); Philosophy; Politics &
World Affairs; Psychology & Psychiatry;
Religion & Theology; Sociology &
Anthropology

Imprints, Series & ISBNs:
Circle Books
John Hunt: 978-1-84298
O-Books: 978-1-903816
Zero Books

Overseas Representation:
Australia: Brumby Books Holdings Pty Ltd,
Kilsyth South, Vic, Australia
New Zealand: Peaceful Living Publications,
Auckland, New Zealand
Singapore: STP Distributors Pte Ltd,
Singapore
South Africa: Alternative Books CC,
Ferndale, South Africa
USA & Canada: NBN, Blue Ridge Summit,
PA, USA

Book Trade Association Membership:
Independent Publishers Guild

2294

C. HURST & CO (PUBLISHERS) LTD
41 Great Russell Street, London WC1B 3PL
Telephone: 020 7255 2201
Email: michael@hurstpub.co.uk
Website: www.hurstpublishers.com

Distribution:
Macmillan Distribution (MDL)
Telephone: 08450705656
Fax: 01256812558
Email: orders@macmillan.co.uk

Personnel:
Michael Dwyer (Managing Director &
Publisher)
Kathleen May (Marketing Director)
Daisy Leitch (Managing Editor)
Jonathan de Peyer (Senior Editor)
Rob Pinney (Assistant Editor)
Georgie Williams (Assistant Editor &
Publicist)

Academic & Scholarly; Gender Studies;
Military & War; Politics & World Affairs;
Religion & Theology; Sociology &
Anthropology

Imprints, Series & ISBNs:
C. Hurst & Co (Publishers) Ltd: 978-0-
903983, 978-0-905838, 978-1-84904,
978-1-85065

Distributor for:
UK: Signal Books

Overseas Representation:
Australia & New Zealand: InBooks, Australia
Austria, Belgium, Bulgaria, Croatia, Czech
Republic, France, Germany, Hungary,
Poland, Netherlands, Romania, Serbia,
Slovakia, Slovenia, Switzerland: Michael
Geoghegan, London, UK
Britain: Kathleen May, UK
Denmark, Finland, Iceland, Norway
Sweden: Ben Greig, UK
Eire & Northern Ireland: Geoff Bryan, UK
Greece & Cyprus: Charles Gibbes
Associates, Louslitges, France
Italy & Malta: Flavio Marcello, Italy
Japan: Tim Burland, Japan
Middle East: Avicenna Partnership, Oxford,
UK
North & South America: Oxford University
Press, USA
Republic of Ireland: Geoff Bryan, Dublin,
Republic of Ireland
Rest of Africa: Inter Media Africa Ltd., UK
Russia & CIS: Tony Moggach, UK
South Africa: Bacchus Books,
Johannesburg, South Africa
South East Asia: Andrew White, Singapore
Spain & Portugal: Peter Prout, Spain
Taiwan: Unifacmanu Trading Co. Ltd.,
Taiwan

Book Trade Association Membership:
Independent Publishers Guild

2295

HYMNS ANCIENT & MODERN LTD
Third Floor, Invicta House,
108-114 Golden Lane, London EC1Y 0TG
Telephone: 020 7776 7551
Fax: 020 7776 7556
Website: www.hymnsam.co.uk

Warehouse & Distribution:
Norwich Books & Music,
13a Hellesdon Park Road, Norwich, Norfolk
NR6 5DR
Telephone: 01603 785925
Fax: 01603 785915
Email: info@norwichbooksandmusic.co.uk
Website:
www.norwichbooksandmusic.co.uk

Personnel:
Dominic Vaughan (Group Chief Executive
Officer)
Michael Addison (Sales & Marketing
Director)
Christine Smith (Publishing Director)
Stephen Rogers (Production Manager)
Sue Stapleford (Financial Director)
Aude Pasquier (UK Sales Manager)
Rebecca Goldsmith (Rights Administrator)
Natalie Watson (SCM Press Commissioning
Editor)

Academic & Scholarly; Biography &
Autobiography; Educational & Textbooks;
Music; Philosophy; Reference Books,
Directories & Dictionaries; Religion &
Theology

New Titles: 90 (2012) , 80 (2013)
No of Employees: 25

Imprints, Series & ISBNs:
Canterbury Press, Norwich: 978-1-85311
Church House Publishing: 978-0-7151
Hymns Ancient & Modern: 978-0-907547
Religious and Moral Education Press: 978-0-
900274, 978-1-85175
SCM Press: 978-0-334
St Andrew Press

Distributor for:
UK: Acora; Cairns; Canterbury Press;
Church House Publishing; Churches
Together in Britain & Ireland; Concilium;
Darton, Longman & Todd; HarperCollins
Religious; Joint Liturgical Studies; Royal

School of Church Music (RSCM); SCM Press; SLG Press; Westminster John Knox Press
USA: Church Publishing Inc

Overseas Representation:
Australia (all imprints): Rainbow Books, Fairfield, Vic, Australia
Canada (all imprints): Novalis Inc, Toronto, Ont, Canada
New Zealand (Canterbury Press): Church Book Stores, Auckland, New Zealand
Republic of Ireland (all imprints): Columba Book Service, Blackrock, Co Dublin, Republic of Ireland
South Africa (all imprints): Methodist Publishing House, South Africa
USA (all imprints): Westminster John Knox Press, Louisville, KY, USA

Book Trade Association Membership:
Publishers Association; Publishing Scotland; Independent Publishers Guild

2296

HYPATIA PUBLICATIONS
[including Patten Press & Jamieson Library imprints]
Jamieson Library, Old Post Office, Newmill, Penzance, Cornwall TR20 8XN
Telephone: 01736 360549
Fax: 01736 333307
Email: info@hypatia-trust.org.uk
Website: www.hypatia-trust.org.uk

Warehouse:
Jamieson Library, Old Post Office, Newmill, Penzance, Cornwall TR20 8XN
Telephone: 01736 360549
Email: info@hypatia-trust.org.uk
Website: www.hypatia-trust.org.uk

Personnel:
Ms Polly Attwood *(Director)*
Tom Goskar *(IT Director)*

Academic & Scholarly; Bibliography & Library Science; Biography & Autobiography; Educational & Textbooks; Fine Art & Art History; History & Antiquarian; Reference Books, Directories & Dictionaries

New Titles: 2 (2012) , 2 (2013)
No of Employees: 3
Annual Turnover: £2000

Imprints, Series & ISBNs:
Hypatia Publications: 978-1-872229

Parent Company:
UK: The Hypatia Trust

Associated Companies:
UK: Jamieson Library; Patten Press

2297

ICON BOOKS LTD.
Omnibus Business Centre, 39–41 North Road, London N7 9DP
Telephone: 020 7697 9695
Fax: 020 7697 9501
Email: info@iconbooks.net
Website: www.iconbooks.net

Sales Representation (UK):
Faber & Faber, Bloomsbury House, 74–77 Great Russell Street, London WC1B 3DA
Telephone: 020 7465 0045
Fax: 020 7465 0034
Email: sales@faber.co.uk

Distribution:
TBS Distribution Centre, Colchester Road, Frating Green, Colchester, Essex CO7 7DW
Telephone: 01206 255678 (UK trade) & 255644 (Export)
Fax: 01206 255930 (UK trade) & 255916 (Export)

Email: sales@tbs-ltd.co.uk & export@tbs-ltd.co.uk
Website: http://tbs-ltd.co.uk

Translation Rights:
The Marsh Agency, 50 Albemarle Street, London W1S 4BD
Telephone: 020 7493 4361
Fax: 020 7495 8961
Email: camilla@marsh-agency.co.uk
Website: http://marsh-agency.co.uk

Personnel:
Peter Pugh *(Chairman)*
Philip Cotterell *(Managing Director)*
Duncan Heath *(Editorial Director)*
Andrew Furlow *(Sales & Marketing Director)*
Henry Lord *(Publicity Manager)*

Antiques & Collecting; Biography & Autobiography; Biology & Zoology; Chemistry; Cookery, Wines & Spirits; Economics; Educational & Textbooks; Gender Studies; Geography & Geology; Health & Beauty; History & Antiquarian; Humour; Languages & Linguistics; Literature & Criticism; Mathematics & Statistics; Military & War; Music; Natural History; Philosophy; Physics; Politics & World Affairs; Psychology & Psychiatry; Reference Books, Directories & Dictionaries; Religion & Theology; Science Fiction; Scientific & Technical; Sociology & Anthropology; Sports & Games

New Titles: 51 (2012) , 50 (2013)
No of Employees: 13
Annual Turnover: £2.5M

Imprints, Series & ISBNs:
Icon Books Ltd: 978-1-84046, 978-1-84831, 978-1-90685

Overseas Representation:
Australasia: Allen & Unwin Pty Ltd, Sydney, NSW, Australia
Canada: Penguin Group Canada, Toronto, Ont, Canada
India: Penguin India, New Delhi, India
Singapore & Malaysia: Penguin Books Singapore, Jurong, Singapore
South Africa: Book Promotions Ltd, Johannesburg, South Africa
USA (Distribution): Consortium, Minneapolis, MN, USA
USA (Rights): Carol Mann Agency, New York, NY, USA

Book Trade Association Membership:
Independent Publishers Guild

2298

ICSA INFORMATION & TRAINING LTD
16 Park Crescent, London W1B 1AH
Telephone: 020 7612 7020
Fax: 020 7323 1132
Email: publishing@icsa.co.uk
Website: www.icsabookshop.co.uk

Personnel:
Clare Grist Taylor *(Joint Managing Director)*
Kate Murphy *(Marketing Manager)*
Emma Reitano *(Commissioning Editor)*
Kelly Jones *(Production Editor)*
Henry Kerr *(Publishing Assistant)*
Valerie Phillip *(Customer Services Executive)*

Educational & Textbooks; Industry, Business & Management

Imprints, Series & ISBNs:
ICSA Information & Training Ltd: 978-0-902197, 978-1-85418, 978-1-86072

Book Trade Association Membership:
Independent Publishers Guild

2299

THE ILEX PRESS LTD
210 High Street, Lewes, East Sussex BN7 2NS
Telephone: 01273 403124
Fax: 01273 487441
Website: www.ilexpress.com

Sales & Distribution, Trade Enquiries & Orders:
Thames & Hudson Distribution, 181A High Holborn, London WC1V 7QX
Telephone: 020 7845 5000
Fax: 020 7845 5055
Email:
customerservices@thameshudson.co.uk

Personnel:
Alastair Campbell *(Publisher)*
Stephen Paul *(Director)*
Roly Allen *(Executive Publisher)*

Architecture & Design; Atlases & Maps; Cinema, Video, TV & Radio; Computer Science; Crafts & Hobbies; Educational & Textbooks; Electronic (Entertainment); Fashion & Costume; Fine Art & Art History; Photography; Reference Books, Directories & Dictionaries

Imprints, Series & ISBNs:
The Ilex Press Ltd: 978-1-904705

Associated Companies:
UK: The Ivy Press Ltd

2300

IMPERIAL COLLEGE PRESS
57 Shelton Street, Covent Garden, London WC2H 9HE
Telephone: 020 7836 0888
Fax: 020 7836 2020
Email: edit@icpress.co.uk
Website: www.icpress.co.uk

Trade Enquiries & Orders:
World Scientific Publishing, 57 Shelton Street, Covent Garden, London WC2H 9HE
Telephone: 020 7836 0888
Fax: 020 7836 2020
Email: sales@wspc.co.uk
Website: www.wspc.co.uk

Personnel:
Prof K. K. Phua *(Chairman)*
Jackie Downs *(Editorial Manager)*

Academic & Scholarly; Biology & Zoology; Chemistry; Computer Science; Economics; Electronic (Educational); Electronic (Professional & Academic); Engineering; Environment & Development Studies; Industry, Business & Management; Mathematics & Statistics; Medical (incl. Self-Help & Alternative Medicine); Physics; Scientific & Technical; Sociology & Anthropology

Imprints, Series & ISBNs:
Imperial College Press: 978-1-86094

Parent Company:
Singapore: World Scientific

Overseas Representation:
Hong Kong: World Scientific Publishing (HK) Co Ltd, Hong Kong
India: World Scientific Publishing Co Pte Ltd, Bangalore, India
Singapore: World Scientific Publishing Co Pte Ltd, Singapore
Taiwan: World Scientific Publishing Co Pte Ltd, Taipei, Taiwan
USA: World Scientific Publishing Co Inc, River Edge, NJ, USA

2301

IMPRINT ACADEMIC LTD
PO Box 200, Exeter, Devon EX5 5HY
Telephone: 01392 851550
Fax: 01392 851178
Email: sandra@imprint.co.uk
Website: www.imprint.co.uk

Personnel:
J. K. B. Sutherland *(Managing Director)*
K. A. Sutherland *(Director)*
S. Good *(Company Secretary)*
A. Roppert *(Print Manager)*
J. Pomroy *(Packaging)*
D. Pomroy *(Binder)*
Jamie Rand *(Print Processor)*
Alex Carvill *(Binder)*

Academic & Scholarly; Philosophy; Politics & World Affairs; Psychology & Psychiatry; Religion & Theology; Scientific & Technical; Sociology & Anthropology

Imprints, Series & ISBNs:
Idealist Studies: 978-0-907845, 978-1-84540
Imprint Art: 978-0-907845, 978-1-84540
Societas: 978-0-907845, 978-1-84540

Overseas Representation:
USA: Ingram Publisher Services Inc, Chambersburg, PA, USA

2302

IMRAY LAURIE NORIE & WILSON LTD
Wych House, The Broadway, St Ives, Huntingdon PE27 5BT
Telephone: 01480 462114
Fax: 01480 496109
Email: enquiries@imray.com
Website: www.imray.com

Personnel:
William Wilson *(Managing Director)*
Ms Pip Wilson *(Director)*
Ian Rippington *(Sales Director)*
Mrs Emma Woodfield *(Accountant)*

Geography & Geology; Nautical; Sports & Games; Transport; Travel & Topography

Imprints, Series & ISBNs:
Imray Laurie Norie & Wilson Ltd: 978-0-85288, 978-1-84623

Distributor for:
France: Editions du Briel; Editions Vagnon; Euromapping; Fluviacarte
Netherlands: ANWB; Hydrographic Office
Norway: Hydrographic Office
Republic of Ireland: Irish Cruising Club
UK: Clyde Cruising Club; Ordnance Survey; J. M. Pearson & Sons; RCC Pilotage Foundation; Royal Yachting Association; RYA Royal Yachting Association; United Kingdom Hydrographic Office
USA: Cruising Guide Publications; Seaworthy Publications; University of Hawaii Press

Overseas Representation:
Australia: Boat Books (Australia) Pty Ltd, Melbourne, Vic, Australia; Boat Books (Australia) Pty Ltd, Sydney, NSW, Australia
Belgium: The Boathouse, Nieuwpoort, Belgium
France: Editions Vagnon, France
Germany: Edition Maritim GmbH, Hamburg, Germany
Greece: AP Marine, Thessaloniki, Greece; Contract Yacht Services, Levkas, Greece; Lalizas, Piraeus PC, Greece; Tecrep Marine SA, Piraeus, Greece
Italy: Edizioni Il Frangente, Verona, Italy
Netherlands: Vrolijk Watersport BV, Scheveningen, Netherlands
New Zealand: Trans-Pacific Marine Ltd, Auckland, New Zealand

Russia: My Planet Publishing, Moscow, Russia
Spain: Flint Suministros SL, Barcelona, Spain
USA: Bluewater Books and Charts, Fort Lauderdale, FL, USA; Paradise Cay, Arcata, CA, USA

Book Trade Association Membership:
International Map Trade Association; British Cartographic Society

2303

IN EASY STEPS LIMITED
16 Hamilton Terrace, Holly walk, Leamington Spa, Warks CV32 4LY
Telephone: 01926 831557
Fax: 01926 422775
Email: info@ineasysteps.com
Website: www.ineasysteps.com

Distribution:
Bookpoint Ltd, 130 Milton Park, Abingdon, Oxon OX14 4SB
Telephone: 01235 400400
Fax: 01235 832068

Personnel:
Sevanti Kotecha *(Director)*

Accountancy & Taxation; Computer Science; Crafts & Hobbies; Educational & Textbooks; Electronic (Educational); Electronic (Professional & Academic); Industry, Business & Management; Photography; Reference Books, Directories & Dictionaries; Scientific & Technical; Vocational Training & Careers

New Titles: 36 (2012) , 45 (2013)

Imprints, Series & ISBNs:
Complete Guides: 978-1-874029
In Easy Steps: 978-1-84078, 978-1-874029

Overseas Representation:
Australia & New Zealand: Woodslane Pty Ltd, Warriewood, NSW, Australia
India: Tata McGraw-Hill, Utar Paradesh, India
South Africa: Intersoft Simon (Pty) Ltd, Johannesburg, South Africa
South East Asia: McGraw-Hill Education, Singapore
USA: Publishers Group West, Berkeley, CA, USA

Book Trade Association Membership:
Independent Publishers Guild

2304

INCORPORATED COUNCIL OF LAW REPORTING FOR ENGLAND AND WALES
Megarry House, 119 Chancery Lane, London WC2A 1PP
Telephone: 020 7242 6471
Fax: 020 7831 5247
Email: enquiries@iclr.co.uk
Website: www.iclr.co.uk

Personnel:
Kevin Laws *(CEO)*
Clive Scowen *(Editor)*
Rebecca Herle *(Head of Marketing & Operations)*
Paul Magrath *(Head of Product Development and Online Content)*

Law

Overseas Representation:
Australia: Thomson Legal & Regulatory, Rozelle, NSW, Australia
Canada: Carswell (a Thomson Reuters company), Scarborough, Ont, Canada
Online sales in Australia, New Zealand and Hong Kong: TimeBase Pty Ltd, Sydney , Australia

2305

INDEPENDENT MUSIC PRESS
PO Box 69, Church Stretton, Shropshire SY6 6WZ
Email: info@impbooks.com
Website: www.impbooks.com

Biography & Autobiography; Music

2306

INDEPENPRESS PUBLISHING LTD
25 Eastern Place, Brighton BN2 1GJ
Telephone: 01273 272758
Fax: 01273 261434
Email: info@penpress.co.uk
Website: www.penpress.co.uk & www.indepenpress.co.uk

Personnel:
Lynn Ashman *(Director)*
Grace Rafael *(Director)*

Biography & Autobiography; Children's Books; Cookery, Wines & Spirits; Crafts & Hobbies; Crime; Do-It-Yourself; Educational & Textbooks; Fiction; Gay & Lesbian Studies; Health & Beauty; Humour; Industry, Business & Management; Literature & Criticism; Magic & the Occult; Medical (incl. Self-Help & Alternative Medicine); Military & War; Music; Philosophy; Poetry; Politics & World Affairs; Reference Books, Directories & Dictionaries; Religion & Theology; Science Fiction; Sports & Games; Theatre, Drama & Dance; Travel & Topography

Imprints, Series & ISBNs:
Indepenpress Publishing Ltd: 978-1-900796, 978-1-904018, 978-1-904754, 978-1-905203, 978-1-906206, 978-1-906710, 978-1-907172, 978-1-907499
Pen Press
Pink Press

Book Trade Association Membership:
Booksellers Association; Independent Publishers Guild

2307

INDIGO DREAMS PUBLISHING LTD
24 Forest Houses, Cookworthy Moor, Beaworthy EX21 5UU
Email: publishing@indigodreams.co.uk
Website: www.indigodreams.co.uk

Personnel:
Ronnie Goodyer *(Director)*
Ms Dawn Bauling *(Director)*

Biography & Autobiography; Crime; Fiction; Guide Books; Humour; Music; Poetry; Travel & Topography

New Titles: 40 (2012) , 50 (2013)
No of Employees: 5

Imprints, Series & ISBNs:
Indigo Dreams Publishing: 978-0-9574742, 978-1-909357
Tamar Books

Parent Company:
UK: Indigo Dreams Publishing Ltd

2308

*INSTANT-BOOKS UK LTD
10 Tennyson Close, Dallington, Northampton NN5 7HJ
Email: instant.books@ntlworld.com
Website: www.instant-books.org

Personnel:
David Brawn *(Company Secretary, Director)*
Ros Brawn *(Director)*
P. Tomlinson *(Director)*
J. Cawley *(Director)*

N. Robbins-Cherry *(Director)*
G. Robbins-Cherry *(Director)*

Atlases & Maps; Crafts & Hobbies; Environment & Development Studies; Guide Books; Travel & Topography

Imprints, Series & ISBNs:
Instant-Book Editions: 978-1-84834
Tour & Trail Maps: 978-1-84834
Walk! Guidebooks: 978-1-84834

2309

INSTITUTE FOR EMPLOYMENT STUDIES
Sovereign House, Church Street, Brighton BN1 1UJ
Telephone: 01273 763400
Fax: 01273 763401
Email: iesbooks@employment-studies.co.uk
Website: www.employment-studies.co.uk

Distributors:
Gardners Books Ltd, 1 Whittle Drive, Eastbourne BN23 6QH
Telephone: 01323 521555
Fax: 01323 521666
Email: sales@gardners.com
Website: www.gardners.com

Personnel:
Lorna Hardy *(Information Manager)*

Academic & Scholarly; Industry, Business & Management

New Titles: 5 (2012) , 1 (2013)
No of Employees: 40

Imprints, Series & ISBNs:
IES Report Series: 978-1-85184

2310

INSTITUTE OF ACOUSTICS
St Peter's House, 45-49 Victoria Street, St Albans, Herts AL1 3WZ
Telephone: 01727 848195
Fax: 01727 850553
Email: ioa@ioa.org.uk
Website: www.ioa.org.uk

Personnel:
Allan Chesney *(Chief Executive)*
Charles Ellis *(Editor)*
Dennis Baylis *(Advertising Manager)*

Academic & Scholarly; Engineering; Scientific & Technical

2311

INSTITUTE OF EDUCATION PRESS
20 Bedford Way, London WC1H 0AL
Telephone: 020 7911 5538
Email: ioepress@ioe.ac.uk
Website: www.ioe.ac.uk/ioepress

Trade Enquiries, Orders & Distribution:
Central Books Ltd, 99 Wallis Road, London E9 5LN
Telephone: 0845 458 9911
Fax: 0845 458 9912
Email: info@centralbooks.com
Website: www.centralbooks.com

Personnel:
Jim Collins *(Publishing Director)*
Dr Gillian Klein *(Publisher, Trentham Books)*
Sally Sigmund *(Marketing Manager)*
Jonathan Dore *(Production Editor, Team Leader)*
Dr Nicole Edmondson *(Production Editor)*
Chandrima Ghosh *(Editorial and Marketing Assistant)*

Academic & Scholarly; Educational & Textbooks; Sociology & Anthropology; Vocational Training & Careers

New Titles: 12 (2012) , 30 (2013)
No of Employees: 6

Imprints, Series & ISBNs:
IOE Press: 978-1-78277, 978-1-85473, 978-1-85856
IOE Press, Bedford Way Papers (series): 978-0-85473
IOE Press, Inaugural Professorial Lectures (series): 978-0-85473
IOE Press, Issues in Practice (series): 978-0-85473
IOE Press, Viewpoints (series): 978-0-85473
Trentham Books

Overseas Representation:
North America: Stylus Publishing Inc, Sterling, VA, USA

Book Trade Association Membership:
Independent Publishers Guild

2312

INSTITUTE OF EMPLOYMENT RIGHTS
4th Floor, Jack Jones House, 1 Islington, Liverpool L3 8EG
Telephone: 0151 207 5265
Fax: 0151 207 5264
Email: office@ier.org.uk
Website: www.ier.org.uk

Personnel:
Carolyn Jones *(Director)*
Treena Johnson *(Administration Officer)*
Carolyn Starr *(Events Officer)*
Sarah Glenister *(IT Development & Communications Officer)*

Academic & Scholarly; Economics; Law; Politics & World Affairs

Imprints, Series & ISBNs:
Workers in Cuba: unions and labour relations: 978-1-906703

2313

INSTITUTE OF FOOD SCIENCE & TECHNOLOGY
5 Cambridge Court, 210 Shepherds Bush Road, London W6 7NJ
Telephone: 020 7603 6316
Email: info@ifst.org
Website: www.ifst.org

Personnel:
Jon Poole *(Chief Executive)*
Angela Winchester *(Communications Officer)*
Miss Sophia Griffiths *(Digital Content Editor)*

Scientific & Technical

Imprints, Series & ISBNs:
Institute of Food Science & Technology: 978-0-905367

Book Trade Association Membership:
Association of Learned Society Publishers

2314

INSTITUTE OF MATHEMATICS AND ITS APPLICATIONS
Catherine Richards House, 16 Nelson Street, Southend-on-Sea, Essex SS1 1EF
Telephone: 01702 354020
Fax: 01702 354111
Email: post@ima.org.uk
Website: www.ima.org.uk

Personnel:
David Youdan *(Executive Director)*
John Meeson *(Assistant Director)*

Mathematics & Statistics

Imprints, Series & ISBNs:
Institute of Mathematics and its
Applications: 978-0-905091

Book Trade Association Membership:
Association of Learned & Professional
Society Publishers

2315

INSTITUTE OF PHYSICS & ENGINEERING IN MEDICINE
Fairmount House, 230 Tadcaster Road, York
YO24 1ES
Telephone: 01904 610821
Fax: 01904 612279
Email: office@ipem.ac.uk
Website: www.ipem.ac.uk

Personnel:
Ms R. G. Cook CBE *(Chief Executive)*
Miss M. Goodall *(Publications Co-ordinator)*

*Engineering; Medical (incl. Self-Help &
Alternative Medicine); Physics; Scientific &
Technical*

Imprints, Series & ISBNs:
IPEM Report Series: 978-1-903613

Book Trade Association Membership:
Association of Learned & Professional
Society Publishers

2316

INSTITUTION OF ENGINEERING AND TECHNOLOGY (IET)
Michael Faraday House, Six Hills Way,
Stevenage, Herts SG1 2AY
Telephone: 01438 767328
Fax: 01438 765515
Email: books@theiet.org
Website: www.theiet.org

Trade Enquiries & Orders:
PO Box 96, Stevenage, Herts SG1 2SD
Telephone: 01438 767328
Fax: 01438 767375
Email: sales@theiet.org
Website: www.theiet.org

Warehouse:
7 Fulton Close, Argyle Way, Stevenage,
Herts
Telephone: 01438 355029
Fax: 01438 355034

Personnel:
Daniel Smith *(Head of Academic Publishing)*
Amanda Weaver *(Head of Practitioner
Publishing)*
Chris Grandy *(Head of Sales)*

*Academic & Scholarly; Computer Science;
Educational & Textbooks; Electronic
(Professional & Academic); Engineering;
Industry, Business & Management;
Scientific & Technical*

Imprints, Series & ISBNs:
Institution of Engineering and Technology
(IET): 978-0-85296, 978-0-86341, 978-
0-901223, 978-0-906048, 978-1-84919
SciTech Publishing: 978-1-61353, 978-1-
89112

Associated Companies:
USA: IET USA

Overseas Representation:
USA & Canada: Stylus Publishing LLC, USA

Book Trade Association Membership:
Booksellers Association; International
Group of Scientific, Medical & Technical
Publishers; Association of Learned &
Professional Society Publishers

2317

INTELLECT LTD
The Mill, Parnall Road, Fishponds, Bristol
BS16 3JG
Telephone: 0117 958 9910
Fax: 0117 958 9911
Email: info@intellectbooks.com
Website: www.intellectbooks.com/

Distribution:
The University of Chicago Press,
c/o John Wiley & Sons Ltd,
European Distribution Centre,
New Era Estate, Oldlands Way,
Bognor Regis, West Sussex PO22 9NQ
Telephone: 01243 779777
Fax: 01243 820250
Email: cs-books@wiley.co.uk
Website: www.press.uchicago.edu

Personnel:
Masoud Yazdani *(Chairman & Editor-in-
Chief)*
May Yao *(Operations Director)*

*Academic & Scholarly; Architecture &
Design; Cinema, Video, TV & Radio;
Computer Science; Educational &
Textbooks; Electronic (Educational);
Electronic (Professional & Academic);
Environment & Development Studies;
Fashion & Costume; Gender Studies;
History & Antiquarian; Languages &
Linguistics; Literature & Criticism;
Philosophy; Scientific & Technical; Sociology
& Anthropology; Theatre, Drama & Dance*

Imprints, Series & ISBNs:
Advances in Art & Urban Futures
Advances in Human Computer Interaction
Bahá'í Books (series)
Changing Media, Changing Europe (series)
Computers and the History of Art (series)
Decode Books (series)
Directory of World Cinema
ECREA (series)
Elm Bank Publications
European Studies Series
Fan Phenomena
Intellect Live
Intellect Ltd: 978-0-89391, 978-1-56750,
978-1-84150, 978-1-871516
Intellect Play Series
Progress in Neural Networks
Readings in Art and Design Education
(series)
Studies in Popular Culture (series)
Theatre & Consciousness (series)
Theatre in Education
Trends in Functional Programming
Venton
Who's Who in Research
World Film Locations

Overseas Representation:
Footprint Books: Footprint Books Pty Ltd,
Warriewood, NSW, Australia
North America and Rest of World:
University of Chicago Press, Chicago, IL,
USA
*UK, Europe, Middle East, India, Pakistan and
Africa:* The University of Chicago Press, c/
o John Wiley & Sons Ltd, Bognor Regis,
UK

Book Trade Association Membership:
Independent Publishers Guild

2318

INTER-VARSITY PRESS
IVP Book Centre, Norton Street,
Nottingham NG7 3HR
Telephone: 0115 978 1054
Fax: 0115 942 2694
Email: ivp@ivpbooks.com
Website: www.thinkivp.com

Personnel:
Brian Wilson *(Chief Executive Officer)*
George Russell *(Finance & Operations)*

*Academic & Scholarly; Biography &
Autobiography; Reference Books,
Directories & Dictionaries; Religion &
Theology*

Imprints, Series & ISBNs:
Apollos: 978-0-85110, 978-0-85111, 978-
1-84474
IVP: 978-0-85110, 978-0-85111, 978-1-
84474

Distributor for:
Australia: Matthias Media
Denmark: Scandinavia Publishing House
UK: Bible Society; CWR; Dorling Kindersley
Religious; EP; Good Book Company;
HarperCollins Religious; Hodder Faith;
Piquant
USA: Crossway; IVP-USA; NavPress; P&R;
Youthworks; Zondervan

Overseas Representation:
East Africa: Keswick Book Society, Nairobi,
Kenya
Netherlands: ASAF Import 3, Westervoort,
Netherlands
New Zealand: Soul Distributors, Auckland,
New Zealand
Philippines: Evangelical Outreach Inc,
Quezon City, Philippines; Overseas
Missionary Fellowship, Manila,
Philippines
Singapore: Bethesda Book Centre,
Singapore
South Africa: Protestant Book Centre, Cape
Town, South Africa
Sweden: Din Bok –
Formsamlingsbokhandeln, Goteborg,
Sweden
USA: InterVarsity Press, Downers Grove, IL,
USA

Book Trade Association Membership:
Christian Suppliers' Group; Evangelical
Christian Publishers Association

2319

*INTERNATIONAL MEDICAL PRESS
2–4 Idol Lane, London EC3R 5DD
Telephone: 020 7398 0500
Fax: 020 7398 0701
Email: info@intmedpress.com
Website: www.intmedpress.com

*Academic & Scholarly; Electronic
(Professional & Academic); Medical (incl.
Self-Help & Alternative Medicine)*

Imprints, Series & ISBNs:
International Medical Press: 978-1-901769

Book Trade Association Membership:
Publishers Association

2320

IPS EDUCATIONAL PUBLISHING
Unit 19, Edison Road, Aylesbury, Bucks
HP19 8TE
Telephone: 01296 395777
Email: enquiries@ipspublishing.co.uk
Website: www.elevenplus.com

Personnel:
Geoff Walters *(Sales Manager)*

Educational & Textbooks

Book Trade Association Membership:
Publishers Association

2321

IRISH ACADEMIC PRESS
8 Chapel Lane, Sallins, Co. Kildare,
Republic of Ireland
Telephone: +353 45 895562
Fax: +353 45 895563
Email: info@iap.ie
Website: www.iap.ie

Personnel:
Conor Graham *(Publisher and Managing
Director)*
Colin Eustace *(Marketing and Publicity
Executive)*
Lisa Hyde *(Commissioning Editor and
Production Manager)*

*Academic & Scholarly; Biography &
Autobiography; Gender Studies; History &
Antiquarian; Literature & Criticism; Military
& War; Politics & World Affairs; Religion &
Theology; Sociology & Anthropology;
Theatre, Drama & Dance*

Imprints, Series & ISBNs:
Irish Academic Press: 978-0-7165, 978-190-
089
Merrion

Overseas Representation:
North America: ISBS, Republic of Ireland

Book Trade Association Membership:
Publishing Ireland (Foilsiú Éireann)

2322

IRWELL PRESS LTD
59A High Street, Clophill, Beds MK45 4BE
Telephone: 01525 861888
Fax: 01525 862044
Email: George@irwellpress.co.uk
Website: www.irwellpress.co.uk

Personnel:
George Reeve *(Director)*
Chris Hawkins *(Director)*

Transport

Imprints, Series & ISBNs:
Irwell Press Ltd: 978-1-871608, 978-1-
903266, 978-1-906919

Overseas Representation:
Australia: Train World Property, East
Brighton, Vic, Australia

2323

ISIS PUBLISHING LTD
Unit 7, Centremead, Osney Mead, Oxford
OX2 0ES
Telephone: 01865 250333
Fax: 01865 790358
Email: pauline.horne@isis-publishing.co.uk
Website: www.isis-publishing.co.uk

Distribution:
Ulverscroft Large Print Books Ltd,
The Green, Bradgate Road, Anstey,
Leicester LE7 7FU
Telephone: 0116 236 4325
Fax: 0116 234 0205
Email: sales@ulverscroft.co.uk
Website: www.ulverscroft.co.uk

Sales:
Soundings, Isis House, Kings Drive,
Whitley Bay NE26 2JT
Telephone: 0191 253 4155
Fax: 0191 251 0662

Personnel:
Robert Thirlby *(Chief Executive Director)*
Pauline Horne *(Distribution, General, Sales
& Marketing Manager)*
Lorna Dubose *(Finance Manager)*
Becky Curtis *(Editorial – General Books
Manager)*
Catherine Thompson *(Studio/Post
Production Manager)*

*Audio Books; Biography & Autobiography;
Crime; Fiction; Humour; Military & War;
Poetry; Science Fiction*

New Titles: 480 (2012)

Imprints, Series & ISBNs:
ISIS Publishing Ltd: 978-0-7531, 978-1-4450, 978-1-84559, 978-1-85089, 978-1-85695

Parent Company:
UK: Ulverscroft Group Ltd

Overseas Representation:
Australia: Ulverscroft Large Print Books (Australia) Pty Ltd, Crows Nest, NSW, Australia
Canada: Stricker Books, Toronto, Ont, Canada
Denmark: Bierman & Bierman A/S, Grindsted, Denmark
Japan: PIC, Tokyo, Japan
New Zealand: Ulverscroft Large Print Books Ltd, Fielding, New Zealand
Norway: Lydlitteratur, Nesoya, Norway
Republic of Ireland: Ulverscroft Large Print Books Ltd, Dublin, Republic of Ireland
South Africa (Audio): Book Talk Pty Ltd, Parkhurst, South Africa
Sweden: Bibliotekstjanst AB, Lund, Sweden
USA (Audio & Large print): Ulverscroft Large Print Books (USA) Inc, West Seneca, NY, USA

2324

THE ISLAMIC TEXTS SOCIETY
Miller's House, Kings Mill Lane, Great Shelford, Cambridge CB22 5EN
Telephone: 01223 842425
Fax: 01223 842425
Email: mail@its.org.uk
Website: www.its.org.uk

Distribution:
Orca Book Services Ltd, Unit A3, Fleets Corner, Poole, Dorset BH17 0HL
Telephone: 01202 665432
Fax: 01202 666219
Email: orders@orcabookservices.co.uk

Personnel:
Fatima Azzam (Managing Director)
Mohamed Eldakrouri (General Manager)

Academic & Scholarly; Law; Religion & Theology

Imprints, Series & ISBNs:
The Islamic Texts Society: 978-0-946621, 978-1-903682

Overseas Representation:
USA: Independent Publishers Group (IPG), Chicago, IL, USA

Book Trade Association Membership:
Publishers Association

2325

IT GOVERNANCE PUBLISHING
Unit 3, Clive Court, Bartholomew's Walk, Cambridgeshire Business Park, Ely CB7 4EH
Telephone: 0845 070 1750
Fax: 01353 662667
Email: hperrett@itgovernance.co.uk
Website: www.itgovernance.co.uk

Electronic (Professional & Academic); Industry, Business & Management; Scientific & Technical

Parent Company:
UK: IT Governance Ltd

Book Trade Association Membership:
Publishers Association; Independent Publishers Guild

2326

ITHACA PRESS
8 Southern Court, South Street, Reading RG1 4QS
Telephone: 0118 959 7847

Fax: 0118 959 7356 (Trade Enquiries & Orders)
Email: info@garnetpublishing.co.uk
Website: www.ithacapress.co.uk

Representation (UK):
Compass Academic,
The Barley Mow Centre,
10 Barley Mow Passage, Chiswick, London W4 4PH
Telephone: 020 8994 6477

Personnel:
Nadia Khayat (Managing Director)
Stephen Grantham (Sales & Marketing)
Sam Barden (Project Manager)
Sarah Church (Operations Manager)

Academic & Scholarly; Architecture & Design; Cookery, Wines & Spirits; Economics; Fiction; Fine Art & Art History; Gender Studies; History & Antiquarian; Languages & Linguistics; Law; Literature & Criticism; Poetry; Politics & World Affairs; Religion & Theology; Sociology & Anthropology

Imprints, Series & ISBNs:
Ithaca Press: 978-0-86372, 978-0-903729

Parent Company:
UK: Garnet Publishing Ltd

Overseas Representation:
USA (academic): International Specialized Book Services Inc, Portland, OR, USA
Worldwide: Salt Way Publishing Ltd, Cirencester, Glos, UK

Book Trade Association Membership:
Independent Publishers Guild

2327

IWA PUBLISHING
[Wholly owned subsidiary of the International Water Association (IWA)]
Alliance House, 12 Caxton Street, London SW1H 0QS
Telephone: 020 7654 5500
Fax: 020 7654 5555
Email: publications@iwap.co.uk
Website: www.iwapublishing.com

Orders:
Portland Customer Services,
Commerce Way, Whitehall Industrial Estate, Colchester CO2 8HP
Telephone: 01206 796351
Fax: 01206 799331
Email: sales@portland-services.com

Personnel:
Michael Dunn (Managing Director)
Ian Morgan (Marketing Manager)
Margarita Lygizou (Digital Marketing Manager)
Emma Gulseven (Journals Manager)
Maggie Smith (Books Editor)
Michelle Jones (Production Manager)
Chloe Parker (WaterWiki Community Manager)
Keith Hayward (Water21 Editor)
Catherine Fitzpatrick (Publishing Assistant)

Academic & Scholarly; Electronic (Professional & Academic); Engineering; Industry, Business & Management; Reference Books, Directories & Dictionaries; Scientific & Technical

New Titles: 53 (2012) , 49 (2013)

Imprints, Series & ISBNs:
IWA Publishing: 978-1-78040, 978-1-84339, 978-1-900222

Parent Company:
UK: International Water Association

Overseas Representation:
Australia & New Zealand: Australian Water

Association, PO Box 222, St Leonards, NSW 1590, Australia; DA Information Services Pty Ltd, Mitcham, Vic, Australia
China, Korea, Vietnam, Thailand, Malaysia, Philippines, Singapore: Tony Poh, STM Publisher Services Pte Ltd, Singapore
India: Kailash Balani, Aditya Books Pvt Ltd, New Delhi, India
Japan: iGroup Japan, Tokyo, Japan
Middle East: Zoe Kaviani, International Publishing Services Ltd, Dubai, UAE, United Arab Emirates
North America: Martin P. Hill Consulting, New York, NY, USA
Taiwan: Ta Tong Book Co Ltd, Taipei, Taiwan

Book Trade Association Membership:
Association of Learned & Professional Society Publishers

2328

JAMES & JAMES (PUBLISHERS) LTD
[an imprint of Third Millennium Information Group]
2–5 Benjamin Street, London EC1M 5QL
Telephone: 020 7336 0144
Fax: 020 7608 1188
Email: info@tmiltd.com
Website: www.tmiltd.com

Personnel:
Hamish MacGibbon (Chairman)

Academic & Scholarly; History & Antiquarian; Industry, Business & Management

Imprints, Series & ISBNs:
James & James (Publishers) Ltd: 978-1-906507

Parent Company:
UK: Third Millennium Information Ltd

2329

*JANUS PUBLISHING CO LTD
105–107 Gloucester Place, London W1U 6BY
Telephone: 020 7486 6633
Fax: 020 7486 6090
Email: publisher@januspublishing.co.uk
Website: www.januspublishing.co.uk

Distribution/Sales:
25 Winnock Road, Colchester, Essex CO1 2BG
Telephone: 01206 578856
Fax: 01206 573221
Email: sales@januspublishing.co.uk
Website: www.januspublishing.co.uk

Personnel:
Jeannie Leung (Managing, Rights & Permissions Director)
Tina Brand (Sales Director)

Academic & Scholarly; Biography & Autobiography; Children's Books; Crime; Do-It-Yourself; Economics; Educational & Textbooks; Fiction; Fine Art & Art History; History & Antiquarian; Humour; Literature & Criticism; Magic & the Occult; Medical (incl. Self-Help & Alternative Medicine); Military & War; Nautical; Philosophy; Poetry; Politics & World Affairs; Religion & Theology; Science Fiction; Sociology & Anthropology; Sports & Games; Theatre, Drama & Dance

Imprints, Series & ISBNs:
Empiricus Books: 978-1-902835
Janus Books: 978-1-85756

Parent Company:
UK: Junction Books Ltd

Overseas Representation:
India: Ane Books Pvt Ltd, New Delhi, India
Malaysia, Singapore & Brunei: Proof Line (M) Sdn Bhd, Petaling Jaya, Malaysia

Philippines: IJ Sagun Enterprises Inc, Philippines
South Africa: Vuga Booksellers, Durban, South Africa

Book Trade Association Membership:
Booksellers Association; Independent Publishers Guild

2330

JARNDYCE BOOKSELLERS
46 Great Russell Street, London WC1B 3PA
Telephone: 020 7631 4220
Fax: 020 7631 1882
Email: books@jarndyce.co.uk
Website: www.jarndyce.co.uk

Personnel:
Brian Lake (Partner)
Janet Nassau (Partner)

Academic & Scholarly; Bibliography & Library Science; Economics; Fiction; Languages & Linguistics; Literature & Criticism; Poetry; Reference Books, Directories & Dictionaries; Sociology & Anthropology

Imprints, Series & ISBNs:
Jarndyce Booksellers: 978-1-900718

Book Trade Association Membership:
Antiquarian Booksellers' Association; Provincial Booksellers' Fairs Association

2331

JOLLY LEARNING LTD
Tailours House, High Road, Chigwell, Essex IG7 6DL
Telephone: 020 8501 0405
Fax: 020 8500 1696
Email: chris@jollylearning.co.uk
Website: www.jollylearning.co.uk

Personnel:
Christopher Jolly (Managing Director)
Diane Harding (Accounts Manager)
Androula Stratton (Marketing Manager)
Angela Hockley (Editorial Manager)

Educational & Textbooks; Electronic (Educational)

Imprints, Series & ISBNs:
Jolly Learning Ltd: 978-1-84414, 978-1-870946, 978-1-903619

Overseas Representation:
USA: Jolly Learning Ltd, c/o American International Distribution Corporation, Williston, VT, USA

Book Trade Association Membership:
Independent Publishers Guild

2332

JORDAN PUBLISHING LTD
21 St Thomas Street, Bristol BS1 6JS
Telephone: 0117 918 1530
Fax: 0117 925 0486
Website: www.jordanpublishing.co.uk

Personnel:
Will Ricketts (Managing Director)
Stuart Harrison (Head of Marketing & Sales)
Achim Bosse (Editorial Manager)

Accountancy & Taxation; Crime; Electronic (Professional & Academic); Industry, Business & Management; Law

Imprints, Series & ISBNs:
Family Law: 978-0-85308, 978-1-84661
Jordans: 978-0-85308, 978-1-84661

Parent Company:
UK: West of England Trust

2333 ■

RICHARD JOSEPH PUBLISHERS LTD
PO Box 15, Torrington, Devon EX38 8ZJ
Telephone: 01805 625750
Fax: 01805 625376
Email: office@sheppardsconfidential.com
Website: www.sheppardsconfidential.com

Personnel:
Richard Joseph *(Managing Director)*
(to be appointed) *(Compiler)*
Claire Hudson *(Production Manager)*

Reference Books, Directories & Dictionaries

Imprints, Series & ISBNs:
Sheppard: 978-1-872699

2334 ■

S. KARGER AG
c/o London Liaison Office, 4 Rickett Street,
London SW6 1RU
Telephone: 020 7386 0500
Fax: 020 7610 3337
Email: uk@karger.com
Website: www.karger.com

Personnel:
Dr Thomas Karger *(President)*
Gabriella Karger *(Chief Executive Officer)*
Moritz Thommen *(Sales & Marketing)*
Hermann Vonlanthen *(Production)*
Thomas Nold *(Editor)*

*Academic & Scholarly; Chemistry; Medical
(incl. Self-Help & Alternative Medicine);
Psychology & Psychiatry*

No of Employees: 200

Imprints, Series & ISBNs:
S. Karger AG: 978-3-318, 978-3-8055

Parent Company:
Switzerland: S. Karger AG

Overseas Representation:
Australia: DA Information Services Pty Ltd,
Mitcham, Vic, Australia
Baltic States: Bookshop Krisostomus, Tartu,
Estonia
Brazil, Argentina, Chile, Uruguay: dot.lib,
São Paulo, Brazil
France: Librairie Médi-Sciences SARL, Paris,
France
Germany: S. Karger GmbH, Freiburg,
Germany
India, Bangladesh & Sri Lanka: Medscience
India, New Delhi, India
Japan: Karger Japan Inc, Tokyo, Japan
Pakistan: Tahir M. Lodhi, Lahore, Pakistan
Republic of Ireland: S. Karger AG, London,
UK
*South Africa, Botswana, Namibia,
Zimbabwe:* Medical Book Marketing,
Craighall, South Africa
South East Asia, China, Taiwan: Karger
Regional Office, Malaysia
Sub-Saharan Africa (w/o South Africa): Guy
Simpson, UK
Switzerland (Head Office): S. Karger AG,
Basel, Switzerland
Thailand: S. Karger AG / Karger Libri,
Bangkok, Thailand
USA: S. Karger Publishers Inc, Unionville,
USA

2335 ■

KARNAC BOOKS LTD
118 Finchley Road, London NW3 5HT
Telephone: 020 7431 1075
Fax: 020 7435 9076
Email: shop@karnacbooks.com
Website: www.karnacbooks.com

Personnel:
Oliver Rathbone *(Managing Director)*
Alex Massey *(Sales Director)*

Psychology & Psychiatry

New Titles: 90 (2012) , 54 (2013)
No of Employees: 11

Imprints, Series & ISBNs:
Aeon Books: 978-1-904658
Clunie Press: 978-0-902965, 978-0-
946439, 978-1-78049, 978-1-85575
Harris Meltzer Trust: 978-1-78049, 978-1-
85575
Institute of Psycho-Analysis, London: 978-0-
946439, 978-1-85575
International Psychoanalytical Association:
978-1-78049, 978-1-85575
Karnac Books: 978-0-946439, 978-1-
78049, 978-1-85575
Library of Analytical Psychology: 978-0-
946439, 978-1-85575
Maresfield Library: 978-0-946439, 978-1-
85575
Systemic Thinking Theory & Practice Series:
978-0-946439, 978-1-85575
Tavistock Clinic Series: 978-1-85575
Tavistock Institute of Marital Studies (TIMS):
978-0-946439, 978-1-85575
UKCP Series: 978-1-85575
Winnicott Studies (Series): 978-0-946439,
978-1-85575

Distributor for:
UK: Zeig Tucker & Co

Book Trade Association Membership:
Booksellers Association; Independent
Publishers Guild

2336 ■

KENYON-DEANE
10 Station Road Industrial Estate, Colwall,
Malvern, Worcs WR13 6RN
Telephone: 01684 540154
Email: simon@cressrelles.co.uk
Website: www.cressrelles.co.uk

Personnel:
Leslie Smith *(Finance, Production, Editorial
& Rights Manager)*
Simon Smith *(Sales & Marketing Manager)*

Theatre, Drama & Dance

Imprints, Series & ISBNs:
Kenyon-Deane: 978-0-7155

Parent Company:
UK: Cressrelles Publishing Co Ltd

Distributor for:
USA: Anchorage Press

Overseas Representation:
Australia: Origin Theatrical, Sydney, NSW,
Australia
New Zealand: Play Bureau of New Zealand
Ltd, New Plymouth, New Zealand
Republic of Ireland: Drama League of
Ireland, Dublin, Republic of Ireland
South Africa: Dalro (Pty) Ltd, Braamfontein,
South Africa
USA: Bakers Plays, Quincy, MA, USA

2337 ■

KEW PUBLISHING
[Royal Botanic Gardens, Kew]
Herbarium, 3rd Floor Wing E,
Royal Botanic Gardens, Kew, Richmond,
Surrey TW9 3AE
Telephone: 020 8332 5751
Fax: 020 8332 5646
Email: publishing@kew.org
Website: www.kew.org &
www.kewbooks.com

Personnel:
Gina Fullerlove *(Head of Publishing)*
Lydia White *(Sales & Marketing)*
Georgie Smith *(Production Controller)*

*Academic & Scholarly; Biology & Zoology;
Children's Books; Fine Art & Art History;
Gardening; Natural History; Reference
Books, Directories & Dictionaries; Scientific
& Technical*

Imprints, Series & ISBNs:
Kew Publishing: 978-1-84246

Parent Company:
UK: Royal Botanic Gardens, Kew

Overseas Representation:
*All territories (excluding USA, Canada &
Mexico):* Marston Book Services Ltd,
Abingdon, Oxon, UK
USA, Canada & Mexico: University of
Chicago Press, Chicago, IL, USA

Book Trade Association Membership:
Independent Publishers Guild; Association
of Cultural Enterprises

2338 ■

LAURENCE KING PUBLISHING LTD
4th Floor, 361–373 City Road, London
EC1V 1LR
Telephone: 020 7841 6900
Fax: 020 7841 6939
Email: enquiries@laurenceking.com
Website: www.laurenceking.com

Personnel:
Nick Perren *(Chairman)*
Laurence King *(Managing Director)*
Maria Treacy-Lord *(Finance Director)*
Philip Cooper *(Editorial Director)*
Jo Lightfoot *(Editorial Director)*
Felicity Awdry *(Production Manager)*
Kara Hattersley-Smith *(Editorial – College &
Fine Art Director)*
Janet Pilch *(Rights Manager)*
Lewis Gill *(Publicity Manager)*
Sarah Mitchell *(Rights Manager)*
Eleanor Muir *(Marketing Manager)*

*Architecture & Design; Fashion & Costume;
Fine Art & Art History*

New Titles: 90 (2012)

Imprints, Series & ISBNs:
Laurence King Publishing: 978-1-78067
Portfolio (series)
Portfolio Skills (series)

Book Trade Association Membership:
Publishers Association

2339 ■

THE KING'S ENGLAND PRESS
111 Meltham Road, Lockwood,
Huddersfield HD4 7BG
Telephone: 01484 663790
Email: steve@kingsengland.com
Website: www.kingsengland.com &
www.pottypoets.com

Personnel:
Steve Rudd *(Managing Director)*
Debbie Nunn *(Company Secretary)*

*Archaeology; Biography & Autobiography;
Children's Books; Fiction; History &
Antiquarian; Humour; Military & War;
Poetry; Transport; Travel & Topography*

Imprints, Series & ISBNs:
The King's England Press
The King's England Press: 978-1-872438,
978-1-909548

2340 ■

JESSICA KINGSLEY PUBLISHERS
73 Collier Street, London N1 9BE
Telephone: 020 7833 2307
Fax: 020 7837 2917
Email: post@jkp.com

Website: www.jkp.com

Trade Enquiries & Orders:
Macmillan Distribution (MDL), Brunel Road,
Houndmills, Basingstoke, Hants RG21 6XS
Telephone: 01256 302985
Fax: 01256 841426
Email: trade@macmillan.co.uk
Website:
www.macmillandistribution.co.uk

Personnel:
Jessica Kingsley *(Managing Director)*
Frank Roney *(Finance Director)*
Jemima Kingsley *(Sales Director)*
Octavia Kingsley *(Production Director)*

*Academic & Scholarly; Children's Books;
Educational & Textbooks; Electronic
(Educational); Electronic (Professional &
Academic); Health & Beauty; Law; Medical
(incl. Self-Help & Alternative Medicine);
Psychology & Psychiatry; Religion &
Theology; Sociology & Anthropology;
Sports & Games; Vocational Training &
Careers*

New Titles: 170 (2012) , 180 (2013)
No of Employees: 35

Imprints, Series & ISBNs:
Children in Charge: 978-1-85302
Community, Culture and Change: 978-1-
84310
Forensic Focus: 978-1-85302
Jessica Kingsley Publishers: 978-1-84310,
978-1-85302
Research Highlights in Social Work: 978-1-
85302
Singing Dragon: 978-1-84819

Associated Companies:
USA: Jessica Kingsley Publishers Inc

Overseas Representation:
Australia & New Zealand: Footprint Books
Pty, Warriewood, NSW, Australia
Canada: UBC Press, Toronto, Ontario,
Canada
Europe: Durnell Marketing Ltd, Tunbridge
Wells, UK
*Singapore, Malaysia, Hong Kong, Taiwan,
China, Philippines & Korea:* Taylor and
Francis, Singapore
USA: Jessica Kingsley Publishers Inc,
Philadelphia, USA

Book Trade Association Membership:
Publishers Association; Educational
Publishers Council

2341 ■

SEAN KINGSTON PUBLISHING
2 Hermitage Cottages. Canon Pyon,
Hereford HR4 8NN
Telephone: 01432 769517
Email: mail@seankinston.co.uk
Website: www.seankinston.co.uk/
publishing.html

Personnel:
Dr Sean Kingston *(Publisher)*
Selina Kingston *(Marketing)*

*Academic & Scholarly; Archaeology; Fine
Art & Art History; Sociology &
Anthropology*

Imprints, Series & ISBNs:
Sean Kingston Publishing: 978-0-9545572,
978-0-9556400, 978-1-907774

2342 ■

KOGAN PAGE LTD
2nd Floor, 45 Gee Street, London EC1V 3RS
Telephone: 020 7278 0433
Fax: 020 7837 6348
Email: kpinfo@koganpage.com
Website: www.koganpage.com

Distribution Centre:
The Book Service Ltd, Colchester Road,
Frating Green, Colchester, Essex CO7 7DW
Telephone: +44 (0)1206 256000
Fax: +44 (0)1206 255715
Website: www.thebookservice.co.uk

Personnel:
Philip Kogan (*Chairman*)
Helen Kogan (*Managing Director*)
Mark Briars (*Financial Director*)
Martin Klopstock (*Digital & Operations
Director*)
Matthew Smith (*Publishing Director*)
John Sadler (*Commercial Director*)
Shereen Muhyeddeen (*Marketing Manager*)
Helena Taylor (*Head of International Sales*)
Taryn Sachs (*Sales Manager, UK & Ireland*)
Jane Davies (*Business Development
Manager*)

*Academic & Scholarly; Accountancy &
Taxation; Educational & Textbooks;
Electronic (Educational); Electronic
(Professional & Academic); Industry,
Business & Management; Reference Books,
Directories & Dictionaries; Transport;
Vocational Training & Careers*

Imprints, Series & ISBNs:
Kogan Page Ltd: 978-0-7494

Overseas Representation:
Australia & NZ: Woodslane, Australia
China: China Publisher Services, China
Europe: Durnell, UK
Ghana: EPP, Ghana
Japan, Taiwan & Philippines: The White
Partnership, UK
Middle East: IPS, United Arab Emirates
Nigeria: Rombic, Nigeria
Singapore & Malaysia: Pansing, Singapore
South Africa: Book Promotions, South
Africa
UK: Compass Academic, UK
USA & Canada: Kogan Page USA,
Philadelphia, USA

Book Trade Association Membership:
Publishers Association; Independent
Publishers Guild; Data Publishers
Association

2343

KUBE PUBLISHING LTD
Markfield Conference Centre, Ratby Lane,
Markfield, Leicestershire LE67 9SY
Telephone: 01530 249230
Fax: 01530 249656
Email: info@kubepublishing.com
Website: www.kubepublishing.com

Personnel:
Haris Ahmad (*Director*)
Anwar Cara (*Production Executive*)
Manzoor Khalid (*UK Sales Manager*)
Miss Rufeedah Cara (*Administration*)
Yahya Birt (*Commissioning Editor*)
Yosef Smyth (*Childrens Editor & BDM*)
Yasser Tariq (*International & UK Sales
Manager*)

*Academic & Scholarly; Audio Books;
Children's Books; Economics; Educational &
Textbooks; Fiction; Law; Religion &
Theology*

Imprints, Series & ISBNs:
The Islamic Foundation: 978-0-86037
Kube Publishing: 978-1-84774
Revival: 978-0-9536768

Parent Company:
UK: The Islamic Foundation

Distributor for:
Pakistan: Institute of Policy Studies; Islamic
Book Publishers
USA: Foundation for Islamic Knowledge;
International Institute of Islamic Thought

Overseas Representation:
Middle East: CIEL S.a.r.l, Beirut, Lebanon
Pakistan: Paradise Books & Distribution,
Karachi, Pakistan
USA & Canada: Consortium Sales &
Distribution, Minneapolis, MN, USA

2344

KYLE BOOKS
67–69 Whitfield Street, London W1T 4HF
Telephone: 020 7692 7215
Fax: 020 7692 7260
Email: general.enquiries@kylebooks.com
Website: www.kylebooks.com

Distribution:
Littlehampton Book Services Ltd,
Faraday Close, Durrington, West Sussex
BN13 3RB
Telephone: 01903 828800
Fax: 01903 828801
Email: orders@lbsltd.co.uk
Website: www.lbsltd.co.uk

Personnel:
Kyle Cathie (*Managing Director*)
Julia Barder (*Sales & Marketing Director*)
Catherine Heygate (*Rights Director*)
Judith Hannam (*Senior Commissioning
Editor*)

*Cookery, Wines & Spirits; Crafts & Hobbies;
Gardening; Health & Beauty; Reference
Books, Directories & Dictionaries; Sports &
Games*

Imprints, Series & ISBNs:
Kyle Books: 978-0-85783, 978-1-85626

Distributor for:
UK: Duncan Petersen Publishing Ltd

Overseas Representation:
Australia: Simon & Schuster (Australia) Pty
Ltd, Pymble, NSW, Australia
India: Penguin Books India, New Delhi, India
New Zealand: New Holland Publishers (NZ)
Ltd, Auckland, New Zealand
Singapore: Pansing Distribution, Singapore
South Africa: Penguin Books South Africa
(Pty) Ltd, Johannesburg, South Africa
USA & Canada: National Book Network,
Lanham, MD, USA

2345

PETER LANG LTD
52 St Giles, Oxford OX1 3LU
Telephone: 01865 514160
Fax: 01865 604028
Email: oxford@peterlang.com
Website: www.peterlang.com

Personnel:
Lucy Melville (*Publishing Director*)
Hannah Godfrey (*Senior Editor*)
Christabel Scaife (*Senior Commissioning
Editor*)
Mette Bundgaard (*Production Manager*)
Laurel Plapp (*Commissioning Editor*)

Academic & Scholarly

New Titles: 117 (2012) , 150 (2013)
No of Employees: 7

Imprints, Series & ISBNs:
Peter Lang Ltd: 978-3-03911

Parent Company:
Switzerland: Peter Lang

Associated Companies:
Belgium: P. I. E. – Peter Lang SA
Germany: Peter Lang GmbH
USA: Peter Lang Publishing Inc

Overseas Representation:
Worldwide: Peter Lang, Pieterlen,
Switzerland

Book Trade Association Membership:
Independent Publishers Guild

2346

LAPWING PUBLICATIONS
1 Ballysillan Drive, Belfast BT14 8HQ
Telephone: 028 9050 0796
Email: lapwing.poetry@ntlworld.com
Website: www.lapwingpoetry.com.

Personnel:
Dennis Greig (*Editor & Production
Management*)
Rene Greig (*Editor*)
Adam Rudden (*Editor & Internet Services
Management*)

Poetry

New Titles: 25 (2012) , 29 (2013)
Annual Turnover: £10,000

Imprints, Series & ISBNs:
Lapwing Publications: 978-1-898472, 978-
1-905425, 978-1-907276, 978-1-
909252

2347

LAVENDER AND WHITE PUBLISHING
Rosudgeon Farm, Prussia Cove Road,
Rosudgeon, Cornwall TR20 9AX
Email: info@lavenderandwhite.co.uk
Website: www.lavenderandwhite.co.uk

Personnel:
Jacqueline Smalley (*Editorial Director*)

*Animal Care & Breeding; Fiction; Sports &
Games*

2348

LAW REPORTS INTERNATIONAL LTD
Eden House, 2 St Aldate's Courtyard,
Oxford OX1 1BN
Telephone: 01865 794638
Fax: 01865 794628
Email: lawreports@clara.co.uk
Website: www.lawreports.com

Personnel:
Mrs Sarah Smith (*Production Editor*)
Mrs Sarah Snell (*Senior Editor*)
Dr Alan Milner (*Editor-in-Chief & Director*)
Mrs Patricia Milner (*Company Secretary &
Director*)

Law

Imprints, Series & ISBNs:
Law Reports International Ltd: 978-1-
870584, 978-1-902907, 978-1-906585

Distributor for:
Zambia: The Zambia Law Journal

2349

LAW SOCIETY PUBLISHING
113 Chancery Lane, London WC2A 1PL
Telephone: 0207 242 1222
Fax: 0207 831 0344
Email: publishing@lawsociety.org.uk
Website: www.lawsociety.org.uk/
bookshop

Distribution:
Prolog, PO Box 99, Sudbury, Suffolk
CO10 2SN
Telephone: 0870 850 1422
Fax: 01787 313995
Email: lawsociety@prolog.uk.com
Website: www.lawsociety.org.uk/
bookshop

Personnel:
Stephen Honey (*Publishing and E-Learning
Manager*)
Sarah Foulkes (*Production Manager*)

Millie Patel (*Marketing Manager*)
Janet Noble (*Senior Commissioning Editor*)
Ben Mullane (*Commissioning Editor*)
Simon Blackett (*Commissioning Editor*)

Law

New Titles: 23 (2012) , 26 (2013)

Imprints, Series & ISBNs:
The Law Society: 978-1-85328, 978-1-
90769

Parent Company:
UK: The Law Society

Book Trade Association Membership:
Data Publishers Association

2350

LEARNING MATTERS
1 Oliver's Yard, 55 City Road, London
EC1Y 1SP
Telephone: 020 7324 8500
Fax: 020 7324 8600
Website: www.sagepub.co.uk/
learningmatters

Distribution:
1 Oliver's Yard, 55 City Road, London
EC1Y1SP
Telephone: 020 7324 8500
Fax: 020 7324 8600

Personnel:
Stephen Barr (*Managing Director*)
Marianne Lagrange (*Publisher*)

*Academic & Scholarly; Educational &
Textbooks; Electronic (Professional &
Academic); Psychology & Psychiatry;
Sociology & Anthropology; Vocational
Training & Careers*

Imprints, Series & ISBNs:
Learning Matters: 978-0-85725, 978-1-
4462

Parent Company:
UK: SAGE Publications

Overseas Representation:
Australia and New Zealand: Footprint,
Australia

Book Trade Association Membership:
Independent Publishers Guild

2351

LEARNING TOGETHER
18 Shandon Park, Belfast BT5 6NW
Telephone: 028 9040 2086
Fax: 028 9040 2086
Website: www.learningtogether.co.uk

Distribution:
Orca Book Services, Unit A3, Fleets Corner,
Poole, Dorset BH17 0HL
Telephone: 01202 665432
Fax: 01202 666219
Email: mail@orcabookservices.co.uk

Representation:
c/o Alan Goodworth, Roundhouse Group,
Millstone, Limers Lane, Northam,
North Devon EX39 2RG
Telephone: 01237 474474
Fax: 01237 474774
Email: roundhouse.group@ukgateway.net

Personnel:
Janet McConkey (*Managing Director*)
Stephen McConkey (*Author/Publisher*)

Educational & Textbooks

Imprints, Series & ISBNs:
Practice Tests In Series: 978-1-873385

Book Trade Association Membership:
Publishers Association; Educational
Publishers Council

2352

*LEGAL ACTION GROUP
242 Pentonville Road, London N1 9UN
Telephone: 020 7833 2931
Fax: 020 7837 6094
Email: lag@lag.org.uk
Website: www.lag.org.uk

Personnel:
Steve Hynes (Director)
Esther Pilger (Publisher)
Nim Moorthy (Marketing Manager)
Adam Wilson (Customer Services Executive)
Andrew Troszok (Customer Services
Executive)

Law

Imprints, Series & ISBNs:
Legal Action Group: 978-0-905099, 978-1-
903307

Book Trade Association Membership:
Independent Publishers Guild

2353

THE LETTERMEN
54 South Parade, Northallerton DL7 8SL
Telephone: 0160 977 7433
Website: www.thelettermen.co.uk

Personnel:
Roger Knights (Managing Director)

Children's Books

Book Trade Association Membership:
Publishers Association

2354

DEWI LEWIS PUBLISHING
8 Broomfield Road, Heaton Moor,
Stockport SK4 4ND
Telephone: 0161 442 9450
Fax: 0161 442 9450
Email: mail@dewilewispublishing.com
Website: www.dewilewispublishing.com

Trade Enquiries & Orders:
Turnaround, Unit 3, Olympia Trading Estate,
Coburg Road, London N22 6TZ
Telephone: 020 8829 3000
Fax: 020 8881 5088
Email: orders@turnaround-uk.com
Website: www.turnaround-uk.com

Personnel:
Dewi Lewis (Publisher)
Caroline Warhurst (Sales & Marketing
Director)

Architecture & Design; Fine Art & Art
History; Illustrated & Fine Editions;
Photography; Reference Books, Directories
& Dictionaries; Sports & Games

New Titles: 17 (2012) , 22 (2013)
No of Employees: 2
Annual Turnover: £400,000

Imprints, Series & ISBNs:
Dewi Lewis Publishing: 978-1-899235, 978-
1-904587, 978-1-907893

Overseas Representation:
Germany: Visual Books Sales Agency, Berlin,
Germany
North America: Consortium Book Sales &
Distribution Inc, St Paul, MN, USA

2355

LEXUS LTD
60 Brook Street, Glasgow G40 2AB
Telephone: 0141 556 0440

Fax: 0141 556 2202
Email:
peterterrell@lexusforlanguages.co.uk
Website: www.lexusforlanguages.co.uk

Personnel:
Peter Terrell (Publisher)
Elfreda Crehan (Production Editor)

Children's Books; Educational & Textbooks;
Languages & Linguistics; Reference Books,
Directories & Dictionaries

New Titles: 2 (2012) , 4 (2013)
No of Employees: 2

Imprints, Series & ISBNs:
Lexus Bridge: 978-1-904737
Lexus Ltd: 978-1-904737

2356

LIBERTIES PRESS
140 Terenure Road North, Terenure,
Dublin 6W, Republic of Ireland
Telephone: +353 (0)1 905 6073
Email: sean@libertiespress.com
Website: www.libertiespress.com

Personnel:
Sean O'Keeffe (Director)

Architecture & Design; Cookery, Wines &
Spirits; Crafts & Hobbies; Crime;
Economics; Fiction; Fine Art & Art History;
Gardening; Guide Books; Health & Beauty;
History & Antiquarian; Humour; Illustrated
& Fine Editions; Literature & Criticism;
Music; Poetry; Politics & World Affairs;
Psychology & Psychiatry; Religion &
Theology; Sports & Games

Imprints, Series & ISBNs:
Liberties Press: 978-0-9545335, 978-1-
905483

Parent Company:
Republic of Ireland: Liberties Media Ltd

Book Trade Association Membership:
Publishing Ireland (Foilsiú Éireann)

2357

*LIBRARIO PUBLISHERS LTD
Brough House, Kinloss, Moray IV36 2UA
Telephone: 01343 850178
Email: amlawson@librario.com
Website: www.librario.com

Personnel:
Mark Lawson (Managing Director)
Mrs Rosemary Lawson (Sales Director)
Mrs Janet Barcis (Bookkeeper)

Crime; Fiction; History & Antiquarian;
Medical (incl. Self-Help & Alternative
Medicine); Military & War; Natural History;
Nautical

Imprints, Series & ISBNs:
Librario Publishers Ltd: 978-0-9542960,
978-1-904440, 978-1-906775

Overseas Representation:
UDSA / Canada: Creative Books
International, USA

2358

THE LILLIPUT PRESS LTD
62–63 Sitric Road, Arbour Hill, Dublin 7,
Republic of Ireland
Telephone: +353 (0)1 671 1647
Fax: +353 (0)1 671 1233
Email: info@lilliputpress.ie
Website: www.lilliputpress.ie

Distributors (Trade Orders):
Gill & Macmillan, Hume Avenue,
Park West, Dublin 12, Republic of Ireland
Telephone: +353 (0)1 500 9500

Fax: +353 (0)1 500 9599

Personnel:
Antony Farrell (Managing Director &
Publisher)
David Dickson (Director)
Vincent Hurley (Director)
Terence Brown (Director)
Vivienne Guinness (Director)
Kathy Gilfillan (Director)
Daniel Caffrey (Director)
Fiona Dunne (Editor)
Kitty Lyddon (Office Manager)

Academic & Scholarly; Architecture &
Design; Biography & Autobiography;
Fiction; Fine Art & Art History; History &
Antiquarian; Illustrated & Fine Editions;
Literature & Criticism; Music; Photography;
Reference Books, Directories & Dictionaries

New Titles: 14 (2012) , 20 (2013)
No of Employees: 3

Imprints, Series & ISBNs:
The Lilliput Press Ltd: 978-0-946640, 978-1-
84351, 978-1-874675, 978-1-901866

Distributor for:
UK: The Houyhnhnm Press

Overseas Representation:
UK: Central Books Ltd, London, UK

Book Trade Association Membership:
Publishing Ireland (Foilsiú Éireann)

2359

LIMEHOUSE BOOKS
Flat 30, 58 Glasshouse Fields, London
E1W 3AB
Telephone: 020 7001 1177
Website: www.limehousebooks.co.uk

Book Trade Association Membership:
Publishers Association

2360

*LION HUDSON PLC
Wilkinson House, Jordan Hill Road, Oxford
OX2 7DR
Telephone: 01865 302750
Fax: 01865 302757
Email: info@lionhudson.com
Website: www.lionhudson.com

Personnel:
Alice Lawhead (Non-Executive Director)
Paul Clifford (Managing Director)
Nicholas Jones (Deputy Managing Director)
Suzanne Wilson-Higgins (UK Sales &
Marketing Director)
Roy McCloughry (Chairman)
Jonathan Carr (Production Manager)
Robert Wendover (Export Sales Manager)
Paul Whitton (International & Subsidiary
Rights)
Caroline Gregory (Financial Controller)

Biography & Autobiography; Children's
Books; Educational & Textbooks; Fiction;
Religion & Theology

Imprints, Series & ISBNs:
Aslan: 978-0-7459, 978-0-85648
Candle: 978-1-85985
Lion: 978-0-7459, 978-0-85648
Lion Children's: 978-0-7459, 978-0-85648
Monarch: 978-1-85424

Overseas Representation:
Australia: New Book Distributors, Sydney,
Australia
New Zealand: New Holland Publishers (NZ)
Ltd, Auckland, New Zealand
South Africa: Pearson Education, Cape
Town, South Africa

Book Trade Association Membership:
Independent Publishers Guild

2361

LISU
Loughborough University, Loughborough,
Leics LE11 3TU
Telephone: 01509 635680
Fax: 01509 635699
Email: lisu@lboro.ac.uk
Website: www.lboro.ac.uk/microsites/
infosci/lisu/

Personnel:
Claire Creaser (Director)

Bibliography & Library Science; Reference
Books, Directories & Dictionaries

Imprints, Series & ISBNs:
LISU: 978-0-948848, 978-1-905499
LISU Reports: 978-1-901786

Parent Company:
UK: Loughborough University

2362

LITTLE, BROWN BOOK GROUP
100 Victoria Embankment, London
EC4Y 0DY
Telephone: 020 7911 8000
Fax: 020 7911 8100
Email: info@littlebrown.co.uk
Website: www.littlebrown.co.uk,
www.orbitbooks.co.uk &
www.virago.co.uk

Distribution Centre:
Littlehampton Book Services Ltd,
Faraday Close, Durrington, West Sussex
BN13 3RB
Telephone: 01903 828511
Fax: 01903 828801
Email: orders@lbsltd.co.uk

Personnel:
Ursula Mackenzie (Chief Executive Officer)
Diane Spivey (Rights Director)
Duncan Spilling (Design Director)
Robert Manser (Group Sales, Marketing &
Publishing Director)
Richard Beswick (Managing Director – Little
Brown & Abacus)
Tim Holman (Publisher – Orbit)
Lennie Goodings (Publisher – Virago)
Antonia Hodgson (Editor-in-Chief)
Nick Ross (Production Director)
Maddie Mogford (Legal Director)
Emily-Jane Taylor (Finance Director)
Rebecca Saunders (Editorial Director –
Sphere Fiction)
Emma Beswetherick (Editorial Director –
Piatkus Fiction)
Tim Whiting (Publishing Director – LB/
Abacus & Piatkus non-fiction)

Audio Books; Biography & Autobiography;
Crime; Fiction; History & Antiquarian;
Humour; Literature & Criticism; Military &
War; Music; Politics & World Affairs;
Psychology & Psychiatry; Science Fiction;
Sports & Games; Travel & Topography

Imprints, Series & ISBNs:
Abacus: 978-0-349
Atom: 978-1-904233, 978-1-905654
Audio Books: 978-1-4055
Little, Brown: 978-0-316, 978-1-4087
Orbit: 978-1-84149, 978-1-85723
Piatkus: 978-0-7499
Sphere: 978-1-84744
Virago: 978-1-84408, 978-1-85381, 978-1-
86049

Parent Company:
UK: Hachette UK

Overseas Representation:
Africa: A–Z Africa Book Services,
Rotterdam, Netherlands
Australia: Hachette Livre Australia, Sydney,
NSW, Australia

Canada: Hachette Canada, New York, NY, USA
Caribbean, Central & South America: Jerry Carrillo Inc, USA
China: Wei Zhao, New York, NY, USA
France & Scandinavia: Melanie Boesen, Hachette US, Denmark
Germany, Sweden & Middle East: Simon McArt, Little, Brown Book Group, London, UK
India: Hachette India, Gurgaon, India
Italy: Penguin Italia SRL, Milan, Italy
Japan, Thailand, Indonesia, Hong Kong, Korea & Taiwan: Gilles Fauveau, Japan
New Zealand: Hachette Livre New Zealand, Auckland, New Zealand
Singapore & Malaysia: Penguin Books Singapore, Jurong, Singapore
South Africa: Penguin Books SA (Pty) Ltd, Denver Ext 4, South Africa
Spain & Portugal: Penguin Books SA, Madrid, Spain
Switzerland, Belgium, Netherlands, Gibraltar, Malta & Cyprus: Rachel Hurn, Little, Brown Book Group, London, UK

Book Trade Association Membership:
Publishers Association; Booksellers Association; Book Marketing Ltd

2363

LITTLE TIGER PRESS
1 The Coda Centre, 189 Munster Road, London SW6 6AW
Telephone: 020 7385 6333
Fax: 020 7385 7333
Email: info@littletiger.co.uk
Website: www.littletiger.co.uk

Distribution:
Macmillan Distribution (MDL), Brunel Road, Houndmills, Basingstoke, Hants RG21 6XS
Telephone: 01256 302692
Fax: 01256 812558
Email: mdl@macmillan.co.uk

Personnel:
Monty Bhatia *(Proprietor)*
Jill Coleman *(Managing Director)*
David Bucknor *(Sales Director)*
Aude Lavielle *(Rights Director)*
Yolande Denny *(Production Director)*
Jude Evans *(Publisher)*

Children's Books

New Titles: 130 (2012) , 130 (2013)
No of Employees: 55

Imprints, Series & ISBNs:
Caterpillar Books: 978-1-84857
Little Tiger Kids: 978-1-84895
Little Tiger Press: 978-1-84506, 978-1-84895, 978-1-85430
Stripes Publishing: 978-1-84715

Overseas Representation:
Malaysia, Singapore & Brunei: Penguin Singapore, Jurong, Singapore
Southern Africa: Phambili, Johannesburg, South Africa

Book Trade Association Membership:
Independent Publishers Guild

2364

THE LITTMAN LIBRARY OF JEWISH CIVILIZATION
PO Box 645, Oxford OX2 0UJ
Telephone: 01865 790740
Email: info@littman.co.uk
Website: www.littman.co.uk

Distribution:
NBN International, 10 Thornbury Road, Plymouth PL6 7PY
Telephone: 01752 202300
Fax: 01752 202333
Email: orders@nbninternational.com

Website: www.nbninternational.com

Personnel:
Ludo Craddock *(Chief Executive Officer)*
Connie Webber *(Managing Editor)*
Colette Littman *(Director)*
Robert Littman *(Director)*

Academic & Scholarly; Biography & Autobiography; Educational & Textbooks; Fine Art & Art History; History & Antiquarian; Literature & Criticism; Music; Philosophy; Politics & World Affairs; Religion & Theology; Sociology & Anthropology; Theatre, Drama & Dance

Imprints, Series & ISBNs:
The Littman Library of Jewish Civilization: 978-1-874774, 978-1-904113, 978-1-906764

Overseas Representation:
Australia & New Zealand: DA Information Services, Mitcham, Vic, Australia
Israel: The Hebrew University Magnes Press, Jerusalem, Israel
USA & Canada: International Specialized Book Services Inc, Portland, OR, USA

Book Trade Association Membership:
Independent Publishers Guild

2365

LIVERPOOL UNIVERSITY PRESS
4 Cambridge Street, Liverpool L69 7ZU
Telephone: 0151 794 2233
Fax: 0151 794 2235
Email: lup@liv.ac.uk
Website: http://www.liverpooluniversitypress.co.uk

Sales & Distribution:
Turpin Distribution, Stratton Business Park, Pegasus Drive, Biggleswade, Bedfordshire SG18 8TQ
Telephone: 01767 604977
Fax: 01767 601640
Email: liverpool@turpin-distribution.com
Website: www.turpin-distribution.com

Personnel:
Anthony Cond *(Managing Director)*
Jennifer Howard *(Sales & Marketing Director)*
Justine Greig *(Finance Director)*
Patrick Brereton *(Production Manager)*
Clare Hooper *(Journals Publishing Manager)*
Janet McDermott *(Sales & Marketing Co-ordinator)*
Alison Welsby *(Editorial Director and Commissioning Editor)*
Charly Paige *(Marketing Executive)*
Karen Phair *(Finance Assistant)*

Academic & Scholarly; Architecture & Design; Educational & Textbooks; Fine Art & Art History; History & Antiquarian; Languages & Linguistics; Literature & Criticism; Poetry; Politics & World Affairs; Science Fiction; Sociology & Anthropology

Imprints, Series & ISBNs:
Liverpool University Press: 978-0-85323, 978-1-84631

Overseas Representation:
Australia and New Zealand: InBooks, Frenchs Forest, NSW 2086, Australia
Benelux & Germany: Roy de Boo, Hooge Mierde, Netherlands
Central & Latin America: InterMedia. Americana (IMA) Ltd, London, UK
Eastern and Central Europe and the ex-Soviet Republics: Laszlo Horvath, Budapest, Hungary
India: Viva Group, New Delhi, India
Malaysia: Yuha Associates, Selangor Darul Ehsan, Malaysia
North America and Mexico: University of Chicago Press, Chicago, USA

South East Asia, Korea, Taiwan, China and Hong Kong: Tony Poh, STM Publisher Services Pte Ltd, Yew Mei Green, Singapore
Spain & Portugal: Iberian Book Services, Madrid, Spain
Taiwan: Ta Tong Book Company Ltd, Taipei, Taiwan
The Middle East, North Africa and Turkey: Avicenna Partnership Ltd, Oxford, UK
UK and Ireland: Quantum Publishing Ltd, London, UK

Book Trade Association Membership:
Independent Publishers Guild

2366

LOGASTON PRESS
Little Logaston, Woonton, Almeley, Herefordshire HR3 6QH
Telephone: 01544 327344
Email: logastonpress@btinternet.com
Website: www.logastonpress.co.uk

Personnel:
Andy Johnson *(Proprietor)*
Karen Johnson *(Proprietor)*

Archaeology; Architecture & Design; Fine Art & Art History; Geography & Geology; Guide Books; History & Antiquarian; Natural History; Reference Books, Directories & Dictionaries

New Titles: 9 (2012) , 11 (2013)

Imprints, Series & ISBNs:
Monuments in the Landscape Series: 978-0-9510242, 978-1-873827, 978-1-904396, 978-1-906663

2367

LOMOND BOOKS LTD
14 Freskyn Place, East Mains Industrial Estate, Broxburn EH52 5NF
Telephone: 01506 855955
Fax: 01506 855965
Email: sales@lomondbooks.co.uk
Website: www.lomondbooks.com

Personnel:
Crawford Goodwin *(Commercial Director)*
Duncan Baxter *(Sales Director)*
Jackie Brown *(Managing Director)*
Arthur Robertson *(Buyer)*

Children's Books; Cookery, Wines & Spirits; Crafts & Hobbies; Guide Books; History & Antiquarian; Humour; Illustrated & Fine Editions; Natural History; Reference Books, Directories & Dictionaries; Sports & Games

Imprints, Series & ISBNs:
Lomond Books Ltd: 978-1-84204, 978-1-90568
Lyrical Scotland

Book Trade Association Membership:
Booksellers Association

2368

LONDUBH BOOKS
18 Casimir Avenue, Harold's Cross, Dublin 6W, Republic of Ireland
Email: info@londubh.ie
Website: www.londubh.ie

Distribution:
Gill and Macmillan Distribution, Park West, Dublin 12, Republic of Ireland
Email: sales@gillmacmillan.ie
Website: www.gillmacmillan.ie

Personnel:
Jo O'Donoghue *(Publisher)*
David Parfrey *(Production)*

Academic & Scholarly; Biography & Autobiography; Cookery, Wines & Spirits; Guide Books; Health & Beauty; History & Antiquarian; Medical (incl. Self-Help & Alternative Medicine); Psychology & Psychiatry; Travel & Topography

Imprints, Series & ISBNs:
Londubh Books: 978-1-907535

Book Trade Association Membership:
Publishing Ireland (Foilsiú Éireann)

2369

LUATH PRESS LTD
543/2 Castlehill, The Royal Mile, Edinburgh EH1 2ND
Telephone: 0131 225 4326
Fax: 0131 225 4324
Email: gavin.macdougall@luath.co.uk
Website: www.luath.co.uk

Distribution:
HarperCollins, Westerhill Road, Bishopbriggs, Glasgow G64 2QR
Telephone: 0870 787 1722
Fax: 0870 787 1723
Email: enquiries@harpercollins.co.uk
Website: b2b.harpercollins.co.uk

Personnel:
Gavin MacDougall *(Director, Rights & Overseas Distribution)*
Kirsten Graham *(Production, Sales & Marketing)*
Louise Hutcheson *(Press, Events, Editorial)*
Jennie Renton *(Press & Events)*

Biography & Autobiography; Children's Books; Cinema, Video, TV & Radio; Cookery, Wines & Spirits; Crime; Economics; Fiction; Gardening; Geography & Geology; Guide Books; History & Antiquarian; Humour; Languages & Linguistics; Literature & Criticism; Magic & the Occult; Medical (incl. Self-Help & Alternative Medicine); Military & War; Music; Natural History; Photography; Poetry; Politics & World Affairs; Sports & Games; Theatre, Drama & Dance; Travel & Topography; Veterinary Science

Imprints, Series & ISBNs:
Let's Explore: 978-0-946487, 978-1-84282
Luath: 978-0-946487, 978-1-84282, 978-1-905222, 978-1-906307, 978-1-906817, 978-1-908373
Luath Guides to Scotland: 978-0-946487
Luath Storyteller: 978-1-84282, 978-1-905222
On the Trail of: 978-0-946487, 978-1-84282
The Quest for: 978-0-946487, 978-1-84282
Scots in
Viewpoints
Walk with Luath: 978-0-946487
Wild Lives: 978-0-946487

Overseas Representation:
Australia & New Zealand: Luath Press Ltd, Edinburgh, UK
Canada: McArthur & Co, Toronto, Canada
USA: Midpoint Book Sales & Distribution, New York, USA

Book Trade Association Membership:
Publishing Scotland; Independent Publishers Guild

2370

LUND HUMPHRIES
Ashgate Publishing Group, Wey Court East, Union Road, Farnham, Surrey GU9 7PT
Telephone: 01252 736600
Fax: 01252 736736
Email: info@lundhumphries.com
Website: www.lundhumphries.com

Trade Distribution:
Bookpoint Ltd, 130 Park Drive, Milton Park, Abingdon, Oxon OX14 4SE
Telephone: 01235 400400
Fax: 01235 400413
Email: orders@bookpoint.co.uk

Personnel:
Nigel Farrow (Chairman, Ashgate Publishing)
Lucy Myers (Managing Director)

Academic & Scholarly; Antiques & Collecting; Architecture & Design; Fine Art & Art History; Illustrated & Fine Editions; Military & War; Photography

Imprints, Series & ISBNs:
Lund Humphries: 978-1-84822

Parent Company:
UK: Ashgate Publishing

Overseas Representation:
Africa (excluding South Africa): Tony Moggach, IMA, London, UK
Australia, China, Southeast Asia and Taiwan: Ashgate-Gower Asia-Pacific, Warriewood, NSW, Australia
Central & Eastern Europe: Dr László Horváth, Budapest, Hungary
Central and South America: Davud Williams, IMA, London, UK
France : Jean-Marc Evans, Casemate UK Ltd, Oxford, UK
Germany, Austria, Switzerland, Italy, Greece, Luxembourg, Belgium and Netherlands: Ted Dougherty, London, UK
India: Surit Mitra, Maya Publishers Pvt Ltd, New Delhi, India
Ireland (incl. N. Ireland) and Scandinavia: Andrew Durnell, Durnell Marketing, Tunbridge Wells, UK
New Zealand: Liza Raybould, South Pacific Books, Auckland, New Zealand
North America: Ashgate Publishing Company, Williston, VT, UK
South Africa: Peter Hyde Associates, Cape Town, South Africa
South America & Africa (excluding South Africa): InterMedia Americana (IMA) Ltd, London, UK
Spain & Portugal: Jenny Padovani, Barcelona, Spain
USA & Canada: Lund Humphries, Burlington, VT, USA

THE LUTTERWORTH PRESS
PO Box 60, Cambridge CB1 2NT
Telephone: 01223 350865
Fax: 01223 366951
Email: publishing@lutterworth.com
Website: www.lutterworth.com

Trade Enquiries & Orders:
James Clarke & Co, PO Box 60, Cambridge CB1 2NT
Telephone: 01223 350865
Fax: 01223 366951
Email: orders@jamesclarke.co.uk
Website: www.lutterworth.com

Personnel:
Adrian Brink (Managing Director)

Academic & Scholarly; Antiques & Collecting; Architecture & Design; Biography & Autobiography; Children's Books; Crafts & Hobbies; Educational & Textbooks; Fine Art & Art History; History & Antiquarian; Illustrated & Fine Editions; Literature & Criticism; Military & War; Natural History; Philosophy; Politics & World Affairs; Reference Books, Directories & Dictionaries; Religion & Theology; Sports & Games

New Titles: 22 (2012) , 11 (2013)
No of Employees: 7

Imprints, Series & ISBNs:
Acorn Editions: 978-0-906554
Patrick Hardy: 978-0-7444
The Lutterworth Press: 978-0-7188

Parent Company:
UK: James Clarke & Co Ltd

Overseas Representation:
USA: The David Brown Book Co (DBBC), Oakville, CT, USA

Book Trade Association Membership:
Publishers Association; Independent Publishers Guild

McCRIMMON PUBLISHING CO LTD
10–12 High Street, Great Wakering, Essex SS3 0EQ
Telephone: 01702 218956
Fax: 01702 216082
Email: info@mccrimmons.com
Website: www.mccrimmons.com

Personnel:
Joan McCrimmon (Secretary)
Don McCrimmon (Sales Director)
Nick Snode (Graphic Designer)
Sue Anderson (Accounts)
Louise Madden (Sales)
Caroline Lee (Sales Ledger)
Robert Mossop (Warehouse)

Children's Books; Educational & Textbooks; Electronic (Educational); Music; Religion & Theology

Imprints, Series & ISBNs:
McCrimmon Publishing Co Ltd: 978-0-85597

Distributor for:
USA: LTP Publications; Printery House Inc

Overseas Representation:
Australia: John Garrett Publishing, Mulgrave, Vic, Australia
Hong Kong: Catholic Truth Society, Hong Kong
New Zealand: Pleroma Christian Supplies, Otane, Central Hawkes Bay, New Zealand
South Africa: The Catholic Bookshop, Cape Town, South Africa

McGRAW-HILL EDUCATION
Shoppenhangers Road, Maidenhead, Berks SL6 2QL
Telephone: 01628 502500
Fax: 01628 770224
Email:
firstname.lastname@mheducation.com
Website: www.mcgraw-hill.co.uk

Personnel:
John Donovan (Managing Director Europe)
Alice Duijser (Director, Higher Education, UK/N. Europe/South Africa)
Jim Voute (Director, Professional, Medical & OpenUp – NECE/South Africa)
Thanos Blintzios (MEA Managing Director)
Lefteris Souris (Sales & Marketing Director, MEA)
Katie Donnison (Senior Sales & Marketing Manager – Schools)

Academic & Scholarly; Accountancy & Taxation; Architecture & Design; Aviation; Biology & Zoology; Chemistry; Computer Science; Economics; Educational & Textbooks; Electronic (Educational); Electronic (Professional & Academic); Engineering; English as a Foreign Language; Geography & Geology; Industry, Business & Management; Law; Mathematics & Statistics; Medical (incl. Self-Help & Alternative Medicine); Philosophy; Physics; Politics & World Affairs; Psychology

& Psychiatry; Reference Books, Directories & Dictionaries; Scientific & Technical; Sociology & Anthropology; Transport; Vocational Training & Careers

Imprints, Series & ISBNs:
McGraw-Hill Education: 978-0-07

Parent Company:
USA: McGraw-Hill Inc

Associated Companies:
Australia: McGraw-Hill Education
Canada: McGraw-Hill Ryerson Ltd
India: McGraw-Hill Education (India) Pvt Ltd
Italy: McGraw-Hill Education Italy SRL
Mexico: Libros McGraw-Hill de Mexico SA de CV
Singapore: McGraw-Hill International Book Co
Spain: McGraw-Hill Interamericana de España SAU
UK: Open University Press
USA: Wm. C. Brown; Brown & Benchmark; Irwin; Irwin Professional; Osborne/McGraw-Hill
Venezuela: McGraw-Hill/InterAmericana (Venezuela) SA

Distributor for:
USA: Amacom; Berrett-Koehler; R & D Books

Book Trade Association Membership:
Publishers Association; Booksellers Association

MACMILLAN CHILDREN'S BOOKS LTD
20 New Wharf Road, London N1 9RR
Telephone: 020 7014 6000
Fax: 020 7014 6001
Website: www.panmacmillan.com

Trade Enquiries:
Macmillan Distribution (MDL), Houndmills, Basingstoke, Hants RG21 6XS
Telephone: 01256 329242
Fax: 01256 840154
Email: mdl@macmillan.co.uk

Personnel:
Belinda Rasmussen (Publisher, MCB)
Ian Mitchell (Production Director)
Michele Young (Rights Director)
Chris Inns (Art Director)
Venetia Gosling (Publishing Director, Fiction)
Suzanne Carnell (Editorial, Picture & Gift Books Director)
Gaby Morgan (Editorial, Poetry & Non-Fiction Director)
Catherine Brereton (Publishing Director, Kingfisher)
Sarah Clarke (Sales Director)

Audio Books; Children's Books; Poetry

Imprints, Series & ISBNs:
Campbell Books: 978-0-330, 978-0-333
Kingfisher: 978-0-7534
Macmillan Children's Books: 978-0-330, 978-0-333
Young Picador: 978-0-330, 978-0-333

Parent Company:
UK: Macmillan Ltd

Associated Companies:
UK: Macmillan Education Ltd; Macmillan Publishers Ltd; Palgrave Macmillan Ltd; Pan Macmillan Ltd

Book Trade Association Membership:
Publishers Association; Children's Book Circle; PA Children's Book Group

MACMILLAN SCIENCE AND EDUCATION
The Macmillan Campus, 4 Crinan Street, London N1 9XW
Telephone: 020 7833 4000
Website: www.macmillan.com

Personnel:
Simon Allen (Chief Executive Macmillan Education)
Jeremy Dieguez (Managing Director, Europe)
Mark Chalmers (Group Finance Director, Mac Ed)
Paul Emmett (Finance Director ELT)
Kate Melliss (Publisher, Spain)
Flavio Centofanti (Regional Director, Middle East)
Jo Greig (International Marketing Director)
Steven Maginn (Regional Director, East Asia)
Karen Hadley (Business Systems Director)
Anne Young (Production Director)
Sharon Jervis (Publisher, Latin America)
Martin Powter (Company Secretary)
Nick Evans (Commercial Director, Africa)
Dan Wilson (Regional Director – Latin America)

Atlases & Maps; Biology & Zoology; Chemistry; Children's Books; Educational & Textbooks; English as a Foreign Language; Environment & Development Studies; Geography & Geology; History & Antiquarian; Languages & Linguistics; Mathematics & Statistics; Physics; Reference Books, Directories & Dictionaries; Vocational Training & Careers

Book Trade Association Membership:
Publishers Association

McNIDDER & GRACE
Bridge Innovation Centre, Pembrokeshire Science & Technology Park, Pembroke Dock SA72 6UN
Telephone: 01646 689239
Email: andy@mcnidderandgrace.co.uk
Website: www.mcnidderandgrace.co.uk

Orders::
Orca Book Services, c/o 160 Milton Park, Abingdon, Oxfordshire OX14 4SD
Telephone: 01235 465521
Fax: 01235 465555
Email:
tradeorders@orcabookservices.co.uk
Website: www.orcabookservices.co.uk

Personnel:
Andrew Peden Smith (Publisher)
Linda MacFadyen (Publicity & Events Manager)

Biography & Autobiography; Cookery, Wines & Spirits; Fiction; Fine Art & Art History; Guide Books; History & Antiquarian; Music; Photography; Politics & World Affairs; Reference Books, Directories & Dictionaries; Theatre, Drama & Dance

New Titles: 9 (2012) , 10 (2013)
No of Employees: 2

Imprints, Series & ISBNs:
McNidder & Grace: 978-0-85716

Overseas Representation:
Europe: Bill Bailey Publishers' Representatives, UK
North America: David Wightman, Global Book Sales, USA

Book Trade Association Membership:
Publishers Association; Independent Publishers Guild

2377 ▬▬▬▬▬

*MAGNA LARGE PRINT BOOKS
Magna House, Long Preston, Skipton,
North Yorks BD23 4ND
Telephone: 01729 840225 & 840526
Fax: 01729 840683
Email: dallen@magnaprint.co.uk
Website: www.ulverscroft.co.uk

Personnel:
Robert Thirlby (Chairman)
Diane Allen (General Manager)
David Mellin (Accounts)

Audio Books; Fiction

Imprints, Series & ISBNs:
Audio: 978-1-85903
Large Print: 978-0-7505, 978-1-84262

Parent Company:
UK: Ulverscroft Large Print Books

Distributor for:
UK: Mills & Boon Large Print

Overseas Representation:
Worldwide: Ulverscroft Large Print Books,
UK

2378 ▬▬▬▬▬

**MAINSTREAM PUBLISHING CO
(EDINBURGH) LTD**
7 Albany Street, Edinburgh EH1 3UG
Telephone: 0131 557 2959
Fax: 0131 556 8720
Email:
seonaid.macleod@mainstreampublishing
.com
Website: www.mainstreampublishing.com

Distribution, Trade Enquiries & Orders:
TBS Ltd, Colchester Road, Frating Green,
Colchester, Essex CO7 7DW
Telephone: 01206 256000
Fax: 01206 255930

Personnel:
Bill Campbell (Joint Managing Director,
Editorial)
Peter MacKenzie (Joint Managing Director,
Sales)
Fiona Brownlee (Marketing & Rights,
Publicity Director)
Ailsa Bathgate (Editorial Director)
Douglas Nicoll (Company Accountant)
Neil Graham (Production Manager)
Fiona Atherton (Publicity Manager)

Biography & Autobiography; Cinema,
Video, TV & Radio; Cookery, Wines &
Spirits; Crime; Fine Art & Art History; Guide
Books; Health & Beauty; History &
Antiquarian; Humour; Illustrated & Fine
Editions; Literature & Criticism; Medical
(incl. Self-Help & Alternative Medicine);
Military & War; Music; Photography;
Politics & World Affairs; Psychology &
Psychiatry; Sports & Games; Travel &
Topography

Imprints, Series & ISBNs:
Mainstream Digital: 978-1-78057, 978-1-
845968, 978-1-845969, 978-1-907195
Mainstream Publishing Co (Edinburgh) Ltd:
978-0-906391, 978-1-84018, 978-1-
84596, 978-1-85158

Associated Companies:
UK: Random House UK

Overseas Representation:
Australia: Random House Australia Pty Ltd,
Sydney, NSW, Australia
Canada: Random House of Canada Ltd,
Mississauga, Ont, Canada
Caribbean & Latin America: Random House
Inc, New York, NY, USA
Germany, Switzerland, Austria, Belgium,

Denmark, Finland & Luxembourg: Jörg
Riekenbrauk, Cologne, Germany
Hong Kong, Taiwan, South Korea & China:
Stanson Yeung, Random House of
Canada Ltd, Toronto, Ont, Canada
India, Sri Lanka & Bangladesh: Nandan Jha,
Random House Publishers India Pte Ltd,
New Delhi, India
New Zealand: Random House New Zealand
Ltd, Auckland, New Zealand
South Africa: Random House (SA) Pty Ltd,
Parktown, South Africa
Sweden, Iceland, Spain, France, Italy,
Portugal, Cyprus, Greece, Malta, Middle
East, Pakistan & Africa (excluding South
Africa): Random House Group Ltd,
London, UK
USA: Trafalgar Square Publishing / IPG,
Chicago, IL, USA

Book Trade Association Membership:
Publishing Scotland; Booksellers
Association

2379 ▬▬▬▬▬

MANCHESTER UNIVERSITY PRESS
Oxford Road, Manchester M13 9NR
Telephone: 0161 275 2310
Fax: 0161 274 3346
Email: mup@manchester.ac.uk
Website: manchesteruniversitypress.co.uk

**Distribution (Trade Enquiries, Orders &
Warehouse):**
NBN International, Plymbridge House,
Estover Road, Plymouth, Devon PL6 7PY
Telephone: 01752 202301
Fax: 01752 202333
Email: enquiries@nbninternational.com
Website: www.nbninternational.com

Sales Representation (UK):
Yale University Press, 47 Bedford Square,
London WC1B 3DP
Telephone: 020 7079 4900
Fax: 020 7079 4901
Email: sales@yaleup.co.uk

Personnel:
David Rodgers (Chief Executive)
Emma Brennan (Editorial Director)
Simon Bell (Director of Sales & Marketing)

Academic & Scholarly; Architecture &
Design; Cinema, Video, TV & Radio;
Economics; Educational & Textbooks; Gay &
Lesbian Studies; Gender Studies; History &
Antiquarian; Illustrated & Fine Editions;
Languages & Linguistics; Law; Literature &
Criticism; Politics & World Affairs;
Reference Books, Directories &
Dictionaries; Sociology & Anthropology;
Theatre, Drama & Dance; Transport

Imprints, Series & ISBNs:
Manchester University Press: 978-0-7190
Mandolin: 978-1-901341

Parent Company:
UK: The University of Manchester

Overseas Representation:
Asia & Middle East: Publishers International
Marketing, Sutton St Nicholas,
Herefordshire, UK
Australia & New Zealand: Footprint Books
Pty Ltd, Warriewood, NSW, Australia
Canada: University of British Columbia
Press, Vancouver, BC, Canada
Canada (Orders & Customer Service): UPT
Distribution, Toronto, Ont, Canada
Europe: Andrew Durnell Marketing Ltd,
Tunbridge Wells, UK
India (Representation): Andrew White, The
White Partnership, Tunbridge Wells, UK
India (Sales): Viva Books, New Delhi, India
Japan: United Publishers Services Ltd,
Tokyo, Japan
Malaysia: Publishers Marketing Services,
Petaling Jaya, Malaysia

Republic of Ireland: Robert Towers,
Monkstown, Co Dublin, Republic of
Ireland
Singapore: Publishers Marketing Services
Pte Ltd, Singapore
USA: Palgrave, New York, NY, USA

Book Trade Association Membership:
Independent Publishers Guild; Association
of Learned & Professional Society Publishers

2380 ▬▬▬▬▬

MANDRAKE OF OXFORD
PO Box 250, Oxford OX1 1AP
Telephone: 01865 243671
Fax: 01865 432929
Email: mandrake@mandrake.uk.net
Website: www.mandrake.uk.net

Personnel:
Mogg Morgan (Director)
Kim Morgan (Director)

Children's Books; Crime; Fiction; Fine Art &
Art History; Literature & Criticism; Magic &
the Occult; Medical (incl. Self-Help &
Alternative Medicine); Philosophy; Poetry;
Religion & Theology; Sociology &
Anthropology

Imprints, Series & ISBNs:
Golden Dawn: 978-1-869928
Mandrake of Oxford: 978-1-869928, 978-
1-906958

Overseas Representation:
USA: Ingram Publisher Services, Nashville,
TN, USA; New Leaf Distributing Co, Lithia
Springs, GA, USA

Book Trade Association Membership:
Independent Publishers Guild

2381 ▬▬▬▬▬

MANEY PUBLISHING
Suite 1C, Joseph's Well, Hanover Walk,
Leeds LS3 1AB
Telephone: 0113 243 2800
Fax: 0113 386 8178
Email: maney@maneypublishing.com
Website: www.maneypublishing.com

Also at:
1 Carlton House Terrace, London
SW1Y 5AF
Telephone: 020 7451 7300
Fax: 020 7451 7307
Email: maney@maneypublishing.com
Website: www.maneypublishing.com

Personnel:
Michael Gallico (Managing Director)
Mark Simon (Publishing Director)
Shelly Turner (Sales & Marketing Director)
Liz Rosindale (Publishing Manager)
Mark Hull (Publishing Manager)
Emily Simpson (Head of Marketing)
Gaynor Redvers-Mutton (Business
Development Manager)
Kim Martin (US Executive Publisher)
Lucy McIvor (Business Development
Manager)
Kathy Rutz (US Executive Publisher)
Rachel Young (Executive Publisher)

Academic & Scholarly; Archaeology;
Architecture & Design; Atlases & Maps;
Bibliography & Library Science; Biography &
Autobiography; Electronic (Professional &
Academic); Engineering; Environment &
Development Studies; Fashion & Costume;
Fine Art & Art History; Geography &
Geology; History & Antiquarian; Illustrated
& Fine Editions; Languages & Linguistics;
Literature & Criticism; Medical (incl. Self-
Help & Alternative Medicine); Military &
War; Philosophy; Religion & Theology;
Scientific & Technical; Transport; Travel &
Topography

Imprints, Series & ISBNs:
Legenda
Maney Publishing: 978-0-901286, 978-1-
902653

Distributor for:
UK: Pasold Research Fund; Society for
Italian Studies; Society for Medieval
Archaeology

Book Trade Association Membership:
International Group of Scientific, Medical &
Technical Publishers; Association of Learned
& Professional Society Publishers

2382 ▬▬▬▬▬

MARITIME BOOKS
Lodge Hill, Liskeard, Cornwall PL14 4EL
Telephone: 01579 343663
Fax: 01579 346747
Email: sales@navybooks.com
Website: www.navybooks.com

Personnel:
M. Critchley (Managing Director)
S. Bush (Editor)
P. Garnett (Manager)

Military & War; Transport

Imprints, Series & ISBNs:
Maritime Books: 978-0-907771, 978-1-
904459

2383 ▬▬▬▬▬

***MEADOWSIDE CHILDREN'S
BOOKS & GULLANE CHILDREN'S
BOOKS**
185 Fleet Street, London EC4A 2HS
Telephone: 020 7400 1092
Fax: 020 7400 1037
Email: info@meadowsidebooks.com &
info@gullanebooks.com
Website: www.meadowsidebooks.com &
www.gullanebooks.com

Personnel:
Simon Rosenheim (Publisher)
Rupert Harbour (Sales Director)
Katherine Judge (Rights Director)

Children's Books

Imprints, Series & ISBNs:
Gullane: 978-1-86233
Meadowside: 978-1-84539

Parent Company:
UK: D. C. Thomson

2384 ▬▬▬▬▬

MELISENDE UK LTD
G8 Allen House, The Maltings,
Station Road, Sawbridgeworth, Herts
CM21 9JX
Telephone: 01279 721398
Email: info.melisende@btinternet.com
Website: www.melisende.com

Personnel:
Leonard Harrow (Editorial)
Alan Ball (Sales & Marketing)
Vicki Coombs (Office Manager)

Academic & Scholarly; Antiques &
Collecting; Archaeology; Architecture &
Design; Crafts & Hobbies; Fine Art & Art
History; History & Antiquarian; Illustrated &
Fine Editions; Politics & World Affairs;
Religion & Theology; Travel & Topography

Imprints, Series & ISBNs:
Atelier: 978-1-901360, 978-1-901764
Melisende: 978-1-901764

Distributor for:
India: Orientblackswan/Universities Press;
Sangam Books Ltd; Social Science Press;
Visva-Bharati

Overseas Representation:
Middle East: Rimal Publications, Cyprus

2385

MERCIER PRESS LTD
Unit 3b, Oak House, Bessboro Road,
Blackrock, Cork, Republic of Ireland
Telephone: +353 (0)21 461 4700
Fax: +353 (0)21 461 4802
Email: info@mercierpress.ie
Website: www.mercierpress.ie

Personnel:
Mary Feehan *(Managing Director/
Commissioning Editor)*
Sharon O'Donovan *(Rights & Permissions)*
Wendy Logue *(Managing Editor)*
Niamh Hatton *(Sales Executive)*
Patrick Dunphy *(Marketing Co-ordinator)*
Sarah O' Flaherty *(Design)*

*Academic & Scholarly; Biography &
Autobiography; Children's Books; Cookery,
Wines & Spirits; Crafts & Hobbies; Crime;
Fiction; History & Antiquarian; Humour;
Literature & Criticism; Military & War;
Poetry; Politics & World Affairs; Religion &
Theology; Sports & Games; Theatre, Drama
& Dance*

New Titles: 29 (2012) , 28 (2013)
No of Employees: 7

Imprints, Series & ISBNs:
Marino Books: 978-1-86023
Mercier Press: 978-0-85342, 978-1-85635

Overseas Representation:
USA: Dufour, Chester Springs, PA, USA;
James Trading Group, Nanuet, NY, USA

Book Trade Association Membership:
Publishing Ireland (Foilsiú Éireann);
Independent Publishers Guild

2386

THE MERLIN PRESS LTD
99b Wallis Road, London E9 5LN
Telephone: 020 8533 5800
Email: info@merlinpress.co.uk
Website: www.merlinpress.co.uk

Distribution:
Central Books Ltd, 99 Wallis Road, London
E9 5LN
Telephone: 020 8986 4854
Fax: 020 8533 5821
Email: orders@centralbooks.com

Personnel:
Anthony Zurbrugg *(Managing Director)*
Adrian Howe *(Manager)*

*Academic & Scholarly; Biography &
Autobiography; Economics; Gender
Studies; History & Antiquarian; Politics &
World Affairs; Sociology & Anthropology*

Imprints, Series & ISBNs:
Green Print: 978-1-85284
The Merlin Press Ltd: 978-0-85036

Overseas Representation:
Australia: Eleanor Brasch Enterprises,
Artarmon, NSW, Australia
Canada: Brunswick Books, Toronto, Ont,
Canada
South Africa: Blue Weaver Marketing,
Tokai, South Africa
USA: River North Editions, c/o Independent
Publishers Group (IPG), Chicago, IL, USA

2387

MERRELL PUBLISHERS LTD
81 Southwark Street, London SE1 0HX
Telephone: 020 7928 8880
Website: www.merrellpublishers.com

Trade & Credit Orders, Returns:
Marston Book Services, PO Box 269,
Abingdon, Oxon OX14 4YN
Telephone: 01235 465500
Fax: 01235 465555
Email: trade.order@marston.co.uk
Website: www.marston.co.uk

Personnel:
Hugh Merrell *(Publisher)*
Claire Chandler *(Head of Editorial)*
Nicola Bailey *(Creative Director)*

*Architecture & Design; Cookery, Wines &
Spirits; Crafts & Hobbies; Fashion &
Costume; Fine Art & Art History;
Gardening; History & Antiquarian;
Illustrated & Fine Editions; Natural History;
Photography; Transport*

Imprints, Series & ISBNs:
Merrell Publishers Ltd: 978-1-85894

Overseas Representation:
All other territories: Mark Scott, Merrell
Publishers, London, UK
Australasia: Peribo Pty Ltd, Mt Kuring-Gai,
NSW, Australia
Canada: Canadian Manda Group, Toronto,
Ont, Canada
Central America & Caribbean: Chris
Humphrys, Humphrys Roberts
Associates, London, UK
Eastern Europe: Adriana Juncu, Voluntari,
Jud. Ilfov, Romania
Estonia, Latvia, Lithuania & Ukraine: Tony
Moggach, InterMedia Americana (IMA)
Ltd, London, UK
France: Critiques Livres Distribution,
Bagnolet, France
Germany, Austria & Switzerland: Gabriele
Kern Publishers Services, Frankfurt-am-
Main, Germany
*Hong Kong, Taiwan, China, Korea, Japan,
Indonesia, Philippines & Thailand:* Julian
Ashton, Ashton International Marketing
Services, Sevenoaks, Kent, UK
*India, Bangladesh, Nepal, Bhutan & Sri
Lanka:* Surit Mitra, Maya Publishers Pvt
Ltd, New Delhi, India
Italy, Greece, Spain & Portugal: Padovani
Books Ltd, Montanare di Cortona, Italy
Malaysia, Singapore & Brunei: Pansing
Distribution Pte Ltd, Singapore
Middle East, Turkey, Israel, Cyprus & Malta:
Peter Ward Book Exports, London, UK
Netherlands, Belgium & Luxembourg: Van
Ditmar Boekenimport B.V., Amsterdam,
The, Netherlands
Republic of Ireland & Northern Ireland:
Robert Towers, Monkstown, Co Dublin,
Republic of Ireland
Scandinavia: Elisabeth Harder-Kreimann,
Hamburg, Germany
South America: David Williams, InterMedia
Americana (IMA) Ltd, London, UK
Southern Africa: Giulietta Campanelli, SG
Distributors, Johannesburg, South Africa
Sub-Saharan Africa & Russian Federation:
Tony Moggach, InterMedia Africa,
London, UK
USA: Perseus Distribution, Jackson, TN, USA

2388

MERTON PRIORY PRESS LTD
9 Owen Falls Avenue, Chesterfield S41 0FR
Telephone: 01246 554026
Email: mertonpriory@btinternet.com
Website: www.mertonpriory.co.uk

Personnel:
Philip Riden *(Controlling Director)*

*Academic & Scholarly; Archaeology;
Biography & Autobiography; History &
Antiquarian; Transport*

New Titles: 2 (2012) , 2 (2013)
Annual Turnover: £5000

Imprints, Series & ISBNs:
Merton Priory Press Ltd: 978-1-898937

2389

MICHELIN TRAVEL PARTNER
Hannay House, 39 Clarendon Road,
Watford WD17 1JA
Telephone: 01923 205240
Fax: 01923 205241
Website: www.michelinonline.co.uk/travel

Warehouse/Returns:
Michelin Tyre Plc, Maps & Guides,
Building 82, Campbell Road,
Stoke-on-Trent, Staffs ST4 4EY
Telephone: 01923 205242
Fax: 01923 205241

Personnel:
I. Murray *(Commercial Director, Head of
Travel Publications)*
C. Lemonnier *(Trade Marketing Manager)*

*Atlases & Maps; Children's Books; Guide
Books; Travel & Topography*

Imprints, Series & ISBNs:
The Green Guide Series
I-Spy Series
Local Map Series: 978-2-06
National Map Series: 978-2-06
The Red Guide Series: 978-2-06
Regional Map Series: 978-2-06
Zoom Map Series: 978-2-06

Parent Company:
France: Manufacture Française des
Pneumatiques Michelin

Overseas Representation:
Belgium & Luxembourg: Michelin Belux,
Brussels, Belgium
Italy: Michelin Italiana SPA, Milan, Italy
Spain: Michelin Espana Portugal SA,
Madrid, Spain
USA: Michelin Travel Publications,
Greenville, SC, USA

Book Trade Association Membership:
Booksellers Association

2390

**MICROFORM ACADEMIC
PUBLISHERS**
Main Street, East Ardsley, Wakefield,
West Yorkshire WF3 2AP
Telephone: 01924 825700
Fax: 01924 871005
Email: map@microform.co.uk
Website: www.britishonlinearchives.co.uk

Personnel:
Nigel Le Page *(Managing Director)*
David Sarsfield *(Head of Publishing)*

*Academic & Scholarly; Biography &
Autobiography; Economics; Electronic
(Professional & Academic); History &
Antiquarian; Literature & Criticism; Military
& War; Politics & World Affairs; Religion &
Theology; Sociology & Anthropology*

Imprints, Series & ISBNs:
British Broadcasting Corporation (online
series): 978-1-85117
British Records on the Atlantic World,
1700–1900 (online series): 978-1-85117
British Records Relating to America in
Microform (BRRAM) (series): 978-1-
85117
Colonial & missionary records (online series):
978-1-85117
Communist Party of Great Britain (online
edition): 978-1-85117
People & Protest in Britain and Abroad,
1800-2000 (online series): 978-1-85117
Records of the Raj (series): 978-1-85117
Twentieth century political history (series):
978-1-85117

Associated Companies:
UK: Microform Imaging Ltd

Overseas Representation:
*Asia Pacific (excluding Japan, Australia &
New Zealand):* Micrographics Data Pte
Ltd, Singapore
*Australia, Europe, Israel, New Zealand &
South Africa:* Publishers Communication
Group, Cambridge, MA, USA
Japan: Far Eastern Booksellers, Tokyo, Japan
USA & Canada: Bludeau Partners
International, New York, NY, USA;
PraXess, New York, NY, USA

2391

*MIDDLETON PRESS
Easebourne Lane, Midhurst, West Sussex
GU29 9AZ
Telephone: 01730 813169
Fax: 01730 812601
Email: sales@middletonpress.co.uk
Website: www.middletonpress.co.uk

Personnel:
Dr J. C. V. Mitchell *(Author & Proprietor)*
Mrs B Mitchell *(Partner)*
Mrs D Esher *(Partner)*

Military & War; Nautical; Transport

Imprints, Series & ISBNs:
Middleton Press: 978-0-906520, 978-1-
873793, 978-1-901706, 978-1-904474,
978-1-906008, 978-1-908174

2392

*MILESTONE PUBLICATIONS
62 Murray Road, Horndean, Waterlooville,
Hants PO8 9JL
Telephone: 023 9259 7440
Fax: 023 9259 1975
Email: info@gosschinaclub.co.uk
Website: www.gosschinaclub.co.uk

Personnel:
Lynda Pine *(Managing Director)*
Debbie Webb *(Manageress)*

Antiques & Collecting

Imprints, Series & ISBNs:
Milestone Publications: 978-1-85265, 978-
1-903852

Parent Company:
UK: Goss & Crested China Ltd

2393

J. GARNET MILLER
10 Station Road Industrial Estate, Colwall,
Malvern, Worcs WR13 6RN
Telephone: 01684 540154
Email: simon@cressrelles.co.uk
Website: www.cressrelles.co.uk

Personnel:
Leslie Smith *(Manager)*
Simon Smith *(Manager)*

Theatre, Drama & Dance

Imprints, Series & ISBNs:
Garnet Miller: 978-0-85343

Parent Company:
UK: Cressrelles Publishing Co Ltd

Overseas Representation:
Australia: Origin Theatrical, Sydney, NSW,
Australia
New Zealand: Play Bureau of New Zealand
Ltd, New Plymouth, New Zealand
Republic of Ireland: Drama League of
Ireland, Dublin, Republic of Ireland
South Africa: Dalro (Pty) Ltd, Braamfontein,
South Africa
USA: Bakers Plays, Quincy, MA, USA

2394

MILLER'S
Endeavour House,
189 Shaftesbury Avenue, London
WC2H 8JY
Telephone: 020 7632 5400
Email: info@octopusbooks.co.uk
Website: www.octopusbooks.co.uk

Distribution:
Littlehampton Book Services Ltd,
Faraday Close, Durrington, Worthing,
West Sussex BN13 3RB
Telephone: 01903 828500
Fax: 01903 828625

Personnel:
Judith Miller *(Author)*

Antiques & Collecting

Parent Company:
UK: Hachette UK

Overseas Representation:
See: Octopus Publishing Group, London, UK

Book Trade Association Membership:
Booksellers Association

2395

THE MIT PRESS LTD
Suite 2, 1 Duchess Street, London
W1W 6AN
Telephone: 020 7306 0603
Email: info@mitpress.org.uk
Website: www.mitpress.mit.edu

Trade & Warehouse:
Wiley Distribution Services, New Era Estate,
Oldlands Way, Bognor Regis, West Sussex
PO22 9NQ
Telephone: 01243 779777
Fax: 01243 843296
Email: cs-books@wiley.com

European Sales Office:
University Press Group, 1st Floor Office,
New Era Estate, Oldlands Way,
Bognor Regis PO22 9NQ
Telephone: 01243 842165
Fax: 01243 842167
Email: lois@upguk.com

Personnel:
Judith Bullent *(Promotion Manager)*
Ann Twiselton *(Publicity Manager)*

Academic & Scholarly; Architecture & Design; Bibliography & Library Science; Biography & Autobiography; Biology & Zoology; Computer Science; Economics; Educational & Textbooks; Electronic (Professional & Academic); Engineering; Environment & Development Studies; Fine Art & Art History; Gay & Lesbian Studies; Gender Studies; Industry, Business & Management; Languages & Linguistics; Music; Natural History; Philosophy; Photography; Politics & World Affairs; Psychology & Psychiatry; Reference Books, Directories & Dictionaries; Scientific & Technical

Parent Company:
USA: MIT Press

Distributor for:
UK: Afterall Books
USA: Semiotext(e); Zone Books

Overseas Representation:
Africa: Cameroon, Ethiopia, Gambia, Ghana, Kenya, Malawi, Mauritius, Nigeria, Rwanda, Tanzania, Uganda, Zambia: Tony Moggach (IMA), London, UK
Australia & New Zealand: Footprint Books Pty Ltd, , Australia

Brazil: Renata Reichmann, Cranbury International LLC, Sao Paulo, Brazil
Canada: John Eklund, Milwaukee, WI, USA
Caribbean: John Atkin, Norwalk, CT, USA
Central America, Northern South America, Mexico: Jose Rios, Guatemala
China: Wei Zhao, Everest International Publishing Services, Beijing, China
France, Belgium, Scandinavia, Switzerland, Italy, Poland: Peter Jacques, University Press Group,London, UK
Hong Kong: Jane Lam, Aromix Books Company, Hong Kong
India, Bangladesh, Sri Lanka: S. Janakiraman, Book Marketing Services, Chennai, India
Israel: Rodney Franklin Agency, Tel Aviv, Israel
Japan: Akiko Iwamoto, Tokyo, Japan
Middle East (excluding Greece & Israel): Avicenna Partnership, Oxford, UK
Netherlands, Germany, Austria, Spain, Portugal, Greece, Hungary, Czech Republic, Croatia, Slovenia: Dominique Bartshukoff, Paris, France
Puerto Rico: David Rivera, San Juan, Puerto Rico
Republic of Ireland: Ben Mitchell, London, UK
SE Asia: Brunei, Cambodia, Indonesia, Laos, Malysia, Myanmar, Philippines, Singapore, Thailand, Vietnam: Ian Pringle, APD Singapore Pte Ltd, Singapore
South Africa: Cory Voigt, Palgrave, Johanesburg, South Africa
South Korea: Se-Yung Jun & Min-Hwa Yoo, Seoul, Republic of Korea
Taiwan: Chiafeng Peng, Taipei, Taiwan
Thailand: Suphaluck Sattabuz, Booknet Co., Bangkok, Thailand
Trinidad: Patrice Ammon-Jagdeo, Trinidad

2396

MITCHELL BEAZLEY
Endeavour House,
189 Shaftesbury Avenue, London
WC2H 8JY
Telephone: 020 7632 5400
Email: info@octopusbooks.co.uk
Website: www.octopusbooks.co.uk

Distribution:
Littlehampton Book Services,
Faraday Close, Durrington, Worthing,
West Sussex BN13 3RB
Telephone: 01903 828801
Fax: 01903 828802
Website: www.pubeasy.books.lbsltd.co.uk

Personnel:
Denise Bates *(Group Publishing Director)*
Tracey Smith *(Head of Editorial)*

Antiques & Collecting; Archaeology; Architecture & Design; Cookery, Wines & Spirits; Crafts & Hobbies; Fashion & Costume; Fine Art & Art History; Gardening; Health & Beauty; History & Antiquarian; Illustrated & Fine Editions; Medical (incl. Self-Help & Alternative Medicine); Music; Natural History; Photography; Reference Books, Directories & Dictionaries; Sports & Games; Travel & Topography

Imprints, Series & ISBNs:
Mitchell Beazley: 978-1-84533

Parent Company:
UK: Hachette UK

Overseas Representation:
See: Octopus Publishing Group, London, UK

Book Trade Association Membership:
Booksellers Association

2397

MOORLEY'S PRINT & PUBLISHING LTD
23 Park Road, Ilkeston, Derbyshire DE7 5DA
Telephone: 0115 932 0643
Fax: 0115 932 0643
Email: sales@moorleys.co.uk
Website: www.moorleys.co.uk

Personnel:
Peter R. Newberry *(Joint Managing, Financial)*
Patrick Mancini *(Joint Managing, Production)*

History & Antiquarian; Music; Poetry; Religion & Theology; Theatre, Drama & Dance

New Titles: 10 (2012) , 8 (2013)
No of Employees: 6
Annual Turnover: £390,000

Imprints, Series & ISBNs:
Moorley's Print & Publishing Ltd: 978-0-86071, 978-0-901495

Distributor for:
Malaysia: Pustaka Sufes Sdn Bhd
UK: Cliff College Publishing; Darby Publications; Met Specials; Nimbus Press; Social Work Christian Fellowship; Wesley Fellowship Publications

Book Trade Association Membership:
Publishing Licensing Society

2398

*MOTOR RACING PUBLICATIONS LTD
PO Box 1318, Croydon, Surrey CR9 5YP
Telephone: 020 8654 2711
Fax: 020 8407 0339
Email: john@mrpbooks.co.uk
Website: www.mrpbooks.co.uk

Orders:
Vine House Distribution Ltd,
The Old Mill House, Mill Lane, Uckfield,
East Sussex TN22 5AA
Telephone: 01825 767396
Fax: 01825 765649
Email: sales@vinehouseuk.co.uk
Website: www.vinehouseuk.co.uk

Personnel:
John Blunsden *(Managing Director)*

Biography & Autobiography; Sports & Games; Transport

New Titles: 3 (2012)

Imprints, Series & ISBNs:
The Fitzjames Press: 978-0-948358
Motor Racing Publications: 978-0-900549, 978-0-947981, 978-1-899870
MRP Publishing: 978-0-900549, 978-0-947981, 978-1-899870

Overseas Representation:
All territories (excluding Australia, New Zealand, USA, Canada & Republic of Ireland): Gunnar Lie Associates, London, UK
USA & Canada: MBI Distribution Services, Osceola, WI, USA

2399

*MPOWR LTD
Suite 11352, 2nd floor,
145–157 St John Street, London EC1V 4PY
Telephone: 020 8133 9783
Email: info@mpowrpublishing.com
Website: www.mpowrpublishing.com

Personnel:
Richard Hagen *(Contact)*

Children's Books

Book Trade Association Membership:
Publishers Association

2400

MURDOCH BOOKS
6th Floor, Erico House,
93–99 Upper Richmond Road, London
SW15 2TG
Telephone: 020 8785 5995
Fax: 020 8785 5985
Email: info@murdochbooks.co.uk
Website: www.murdochbooks.co.uk

Distribution & Invoicing:
Macmillan Distribution Ltd, Brunel Road,
Houndmills, Basingstoke, Hants RG21 2XS
Telephone: 01256 329242
Fax: 01256 327961

Personnel:
Christine Jones *(UK Managing Director)*
John Sprinks *(UK Finance Director)*
Cathy Slater *(Foreign Rights Director)*

Biography & Autobiography; Cookery, Wines & Spirits; Crafts & Hobbies; Do-It-Yourself; Gardening; Health & Beauty; History & Antiquarian; Travel & Topography

Imprints, Series & ISBNs:
Murdoch Books: 978-1-74045, 978-1-74196, 978-1-74266

Parent Company:
Australia: Allen and Unwin Pty Ltd

Overseas Representation:
Africa: A–Z Africa Book Services, Rotterdam, Netherlands
Asia: Pan Macmillan Asia, Hong Kong
Australia, New Zealand & USA: Murdoch Books Pty Ltd, Sydney, NSW, Australia
Europe: Angell Eurosales, Berwick-on-Tweed, UK; Gabriele Kern Publishers' Services, Frankfurt-am-Main, Germany; Penny Padovani, London, UK
Middle East: Peter Ward Book Exports, London, UK

Book Trade Association Membership:
Independent Publishers Guild

2401

JOHN MURRAY PUBLISHERS
[a division of Hachette UK]
338 Euston Road, London NW1 3BH
Telephone: 020 7873 6000
Fax: 020 7873 6446
Website: www.johnmurray.co.uk

UK Orders & Invoicing, Payments & Credit Control & Warehouse:
Bookpoint, 130 Milton Park, Abingdon,
Oxon OX14 4SB
Telephone: 01235 400400
Fax: 01235 821511

Personnel:
Roland Philipps *(Managing Director)*
Nick Davies *(Managing Director: John Murray Press)*
Ben Gutcher *(Sales Director: John Murray Press)*
Rosie Gailer *(Communications Director)*
Jason Bartholomew *(Rights Director)*
Eleanor Birne *(Publishing Director)*

Biography & Autobiography; Fiction; Fine Art & Art History; History & Antiquarian; Humour; Languages & Linguistics; Military & War; Travel & Topography

Imprints, Series & ISBNs:
John Murray Publishers: 978-0-7195, 978-1-84854

Parent Company:
UK: Hachette UK

Overseas Representation:
Australia: Alliance Distribution Services Pty Ltd, Tuggerah, NSW, Australia; Hachette Livre Australia, Sydney, NSW, Australia
Canada: McArthur & Co Publishers Ltd, Toronto, Ont, Canada
Hong Kong: Asia Publishers Services Ltd, Hong Kong
India: Hachette Book Publishing India Pvt Ltd, Gurgaon, India
Netherlands (Hardbacks and Trade Paperbacks): Nilsson & Lamm BV, Weesp, Netherlands
Netherlands (Paperbacks): Van Ditmar BV, Amsterdam, Netherlands
New Zealand: Hachette Livre New Zealand, Auckland, New Zealand
Pakistan: Oxford University Press Pakistan Branch, Karachi, Pakistan
Singapore & Malaysia: Pansing Distribution Sdn Bhd, Singapore
South Africa: Jonathan Ball Publishers (Pty) Ltd, Johannesburg, South Africa
USA: Trafalgar Square Publishing, North Pomfret, VT, USA

Book Trade Association Membership:
Publishers Association; Independent Publishers Guild

2402 ▬▬▬▬▬▬▬

MW EDUCATIONAL
1391 London Road, Leigh-on-Sea, Essex SS9 2SA
Telephone: 07907 609962
Email: mweducational@yahoo.co.uk
Website: www.mweducational.co.uk

Distribution:
Gardners Books Ltd, 1 Whittle Drive, Eastbourne, East Sussex BN23 6QH
Telephone: 01323 521555

Personnel:
Mark Chatterton (*Proprietor*)

Children's Books; Educational & Textbooks; English as a Foreign Language; Mathematics & Statistics

Imprints, Series & ISBNs:
The A Plus Series of 11+ Practice Papers: 978-0-953863, 978-1-901146, 978-1-901146
The Advantage Series of SATs Practice Papers: 978-1-901146
Need To Know Books

2403 ▬▬▬▬▬▬▬

MYRIAD EDITIONS
59 Lansdowne Place, Brighton BN3 1FL
Telephone: 01273 720000
Email: info@MyriadEditions.com
Website: www.MyriadEditions.com

Personnel:
Candida Lacey (*Managing Director*)
Robert Benewick (*Director*)
Judith Mackay (*Director*)
Corinne Pearlman (*Creative Director*)
Isabelle Lewis (*Designer*)
Jannet King (*Editor*)
Vicky Blunden (*Fiction Editor*)
Emma Dowson (*Publicist*)
Adrian Weston (*Rights*)
Holly Ainley (*Editor*)

Academic & Scholarly; Atlases & Maps; Crime; Electronic (Professional & Academic); Environment & Development Studies; Fiction; Gender Studies; Military & War; Politics & World Affairs

New Titles: 9 (2012) , 9 (2013)

Imprints, Series & ISBNs:
Myriad Editions: 978-0-9549309, 978-0-9565599, 978-0-9567926, 978-1-908434

Overseas Representation:
China & Taiwan: Big Apple Tuttle-Mori Agency Inc, Taipei, Taiwan
France: Anna Jarota Agency, Paris, France
Greece: Iris Literary Agency, Greece
Hungary: Torus-Books Agency, Hungary
Israel: The Book Publishers Association of, Israel
Italy: Il Caduceo Literary Agency, Milan, Italy
Japan: Tuttle-Mori Agency Inc, Tokyo, Japan
Korea: EYA Literary Agency, Seoul, Democratic People's Republic of Korea
Romania: Kessler Agency, Romania
Russia: Andrew Nurnberg Literary Agency, Moscow, Russia
Serbia & Croatia: Plima Literary Agency, Belgrade, Serbia
Spain, Portugal & South America: Ilustrata Empresariale SL, Barcelona, Spain
Turkey: Nurcihan Kesim Literary Agency, Istanbul , Turkey

Book Trade Association Membership:
Independent Publishers Guild

2404 ▬▬▬▬▬▬▬

MYRMIDON BOOKS LTD
Rotterdam House, 116 Quayside, Newcastle upon Tyne NE1 3DY
Telephone: 0191 206 4005
Email: ed@myrmidonbooks.com
Website: www.myrmidonbooks.com

Distribution:
Littlehampton Book Services, Faraday Close, Durrington, Worthing, West Sussex TN13 3RB
Telephone: 01903 828500
Fax: 01903 828625
Email: enquiries@lbsltd.co.uk
Website: www.lbsltd.co.uk

Personnel:
Edward Handyside (*Publishing Director*)
Kate Nash (*Marketing Director*)

Fiction

Imprints, Series & ISBNs:
Myrmidon : 978-1-905802

Overseas Representation:
China, Japan, Korea & neighbouring territories: Julian Ashton, UK
Singapore, Malaysia & neighbouring territories: Pansing Distribution Pte Ltd, Singapore
South Africa & neighbouring territories: Penguin Books, South Africa
Spain Portugal and Gibraltar: Iberia Books, Spain
USA and Canada: IPG Trafalgar Square, USA

Book Trade Association Membership:
Publishers Association; Independent Publishers Guild

2405 ▬▬▬▬▬▬▬

THE MYRTLE PRESS
Billing Wharf, Station Road, Cogenhoe, Northamptonshire NN7 1NH
Telephone: 01604 890208
Email: PA@themyrtlepress.com
Website: www.themyrtlepress.com

Biography & Autobiography; Sports & Games

Imprints, Series & ISBNs:
The Myrtle Pres: 978-0-9565656

Book Trade Association Membership:
Publishers Association

2406 ▬▬▬▬▬▬▬

THE NATIONAL ACADEMIES PRESS
5 Victoria House, 138 Watling Street East, Towcester NN12 6BT
Telephone: 01327 357770

Fax: 01327 359572
Email: nap@oppuk.co.uk
Website: www.nap.edu

Warehouse & Distribution:
Marston Book Services, 160 Milton Park, PO Box 169, Abingdon, Oxon OX14 4YN
Telephone: 01235 465521
Email: direct.orders@marston.co.uk
Website: www.marston.co.uk

Personnel:
Gary Hall (*Marketing Manager*)

Academic & Scholarly; Agriculture; Animal Care & Breeding; Biology & Zoology; Chemistry; Educational & Textbooks; Engineering; Environment & Development Studies; Geography & Geology; Industry, Business & Management; Mathematics & Statistics; Medical (incl. Self-Help & Alternative Medicine); Natural History; Nautical; Physics; Psychology & Psychiatry; Scientific & Technical; Veterinary Science

Imprints, Series & ISBNs:
National Academies Press: 978-0-309

Parent Company:
USA: National Academies Press

2407 ▬▬▬▬▬▬▬

*NATIONAL CHILDREN'S BUREAU
NCB Publications, 8 Wakley Street, London EC1V 7QE
Telephone: 020 7843 6317
Fax: 020 7843 6087
Email: publications@ncb.org.uk
Website: www.ncb.org.uk/books

Distributor:
Central Books, 99 Wallis Road, London E9 5LN
Telephone: 0845 458 9912
Fax: 0845 458 9910
Email: ncb@centralbooks.com
Website: www.centralbooks.com

Personnel:
Paula McMahon (*Publishing Manager*)
Agnes Niciejewska (*Publishing Officer*)
Judith Sabah (*Marketing Officer*)

Academic & Scholarly; Educational & Textbooks; Electronic (Professional & Academic); Vocational Training & Careers

Imprints, Series & ISBNs:
National Children's Bureau: 978-0-902817, 978-1-870985, 978-1-874579, 978-1-900990, 978-1-904787, 978-1-905818, 978-1-907969

Book Trade Association Membership:
Independent Publishers Guild

2408 ▬▬▬▬▬▬▬

NATIONAL HOUSING FEDERATION
Lion Court, 25 Procter Street, Holborn, London WC1V 6NY
Telephone: 020 7067 1010
Fax: 020 7067 1011
Email: info@housing.org.uk
Website: www.housing.co.uk

Personnel:
Rick Lloyd (*Communications Officer – Publications*)

Academic & Scholarly; Educational & Textbooks; Industry, Business & Management; Reference Books, Directories & Dictionaries; Vocational Training & Careers

Imprints, Series & ISBNs:
National Housing Federation: 978-0-86297

2409 ▬▬▬▬▬▬▬

THE NATIONAL TRUST
Heelis, Kemble Drive, Swindon, Wilts SN2 2NA
Telephone: 01793 817400
Fax: 01793 817401
Email: grant.berry@nationaltrust.org.uk
Website: www.nationaltrust.org.uk

Also at:
Anova Books, 10 Southcombe Street, London W14 0RA
Telephone: 020 7605 1400
Website: www.anovabooks.com

Personnel:
John Stachiewicz (*Publisher & Commercial Manager*)
Grant Berry (*Publishing Manager*)
Oliver Garrett (*Property Publisher*)
Claire Masset (*Editor*)
Claire Forbes (*Assistant Editor*)

Academic & Scholarly; Agriculture; Antiques & Collecting; Archaeology; Architecture & Design; Biography & Autobiography; Children's Books; Cookery, Wines & Spirits; Fashion & Costume; Fine Art & Art History; Gardening; Guide Books; History & Antiquarian; Humour; Natural History; Reference Books, Directories & Dictionaries; Travel & Topography

Imprints, Series & ISBNs:
The National Trust: 978-0-7078, 978-1-8435

Associated Companies:
UK: Anova Books; The History Press

2410 ▬▬▬▬▬▬▬

THE NATIONAL AUTISTIC SOCIETY (NAS)
393 City Road, London EC1V 1NG
Telephone: 020 7833 2299
Fax: 020 7833 9666
Email: nas@nas.org.uk
Website: www.autism.org.uk

Trade Enquiries & Orders:
Central Books, 99 Wallis Road, London E9 5LN
Telephone: 0845 458 9911
Fax: 0845 458 9912
Email: nas@centralbooks.com
Website: www.autism.org.uk/shop

Personnel:
Bonnie Molins (*Communications*)
David Mason (*Publications Sales Officer*)

Children's Books; Educational & Textbooks; Psychology & Psychiatry

Imprints, Series & ISBNs:
The National Autistic Society (NAS): 978-1-899280, 978-1-905722

Book Trade Association Membership:
Publishers Form, NCVO

2411 ▬▬▬▬▬▬▬

NATIONAL GALLERIES OF SCOTLAND
75 Belford Road, Edinburgh EH4 3DR
Telephone: 0131 624 6261 & 6257
Fax: 0131 623 7135
Email: publishing@nationalgalleries.org
Website: www.nationalgalleries.org

Personnel:
Christine Thompson (*Publisher*)
Sarah Worrall (*Publishing Project Manager*)
Mairi Lafferty (*Publishing Assistant*)

Academic & Scholarly; Architecture & Design; Fine Art & Art History; Guide Books; Illustrated & Fine Editions; Photography

New Titles: 12 (2012) , 10 (2013)
No of Employees: 3
Annual Turnover: £250,000

Imprints, Series & ISBNs:
National Galleries of Scotland: 978-0-903148, 978-0-903598, 978-1-903278, 978-1-906270

Overseas Representation:
North America: ACC, Easthampton, MA, USA

Book Trade Association Membership:
Publishing Scotland

2412 ▬▬▬▬▬

NATIONAL PORTRAIT GALLERY PUBLICATIONS
National Portrait Gallery, St Martin's Place, London WC2H 0HE
Telephone: 020 7306 0055 ext 266 & 020 7312 2482 (direct line)
Fax: 020 7321 6657
Email: publications@npg.org.uk
Website: www.npg.org.uk/publications

Distribution:
Littlehampton Book Services, Faraday Close, Durrington, Worthing, West Sussex BN13 3RB
Telephone: 01903 828501
Fax: 01903 828801
Email: customerservices@lbsltd.co.uk
Website: http://www.lbsltd.co.uk/

Representation (UK):
Thames & Hudson Ltd, Head Office, 181a High Holborn, London WC1V 7QX
Telephone: 020 7845 5000
Fax: 020 7845 5050
Email: sales@thameshudson.co.uk
Website: http://www.thamesandhudson.com/

Personnel:
Robert Carr-Archer *(Head of Trading)*
Nicola Saunders *(Head of Business Development)*
Ruth Müller-Wirth *(Production Manager)*
Christopher Tinker *(Managing Editor)*
Sarah Ruddick *(Editor)*
Andrew Roff *(Assistant Editor)*
Jess Kim *(Marketing Co-ordinator)*

Academic & Scholarly; Biography & Autobiography; Fashion & Costume; Fine Art & Art History; Guide Books; History & Antiquarian; Illustrated & Fine Editions; Photography; Reference Books, Directories & Dictionaries

No of Employees: 10

Imprints, Series & ISBNs:
National Portrait Gallery Publications: 978-0-904017, 978-1-85514

Book Trade Association Membership:
Booksellers Association; Independent Publishers Guild

2413 ▬▬▬▬▬

NATIONAL RECORDS OF SCOTLAND
HM General Register House, Edinburgh EH1 3YY
Telephone: 0131 535 1314
Fax: 0131 535 1360
Email: enquiries@nas.gov.uk
Website: www.nrscotland.gov.uk

Also at:
Ladywell House, Ladywell Road, Edinburgh EH12 7TF
Telephone: 0131 314 4299
Fax: 0131 314 4696
Email: customer@gro-scotland.gsi.gov.uk
Website: www.gro-scotland.gov.uk

Personnel:
Tim Ellis *(Chief Executive, National Records of Scotland)*

Academic & Scholarly; Electronic (Professional & Academic); History & Antiquarian; Mathematics & Statistics

New Titles: 2 (2012) , 2 (2013)
No of Employees: 400

Imprints, Series & ISBNs:
National Records of Scotland: 978-1-870874, 978-1-874451

Book Trade Association Membership:
Publishing Scotland

2414 ▬▬▬▬▬

NATIONAL THEATRE
Upper Ground, South Bank, London SE1 9PX
Telephone: 020 7452 3333
Email: info@nationaltheatre.org.uk
Website: www.nationaltheatre.org.uk

Personnel:
Sir Nicholas Hytner *(Director)*
Nick Starr *(Executive Director)*
Ms Lisa Burger *(Chief Operating Officer)*

Book Trade Association Membership:
Publishers Association

2415 ▬▬▬▬▬

NATURAL HISTORY MUSEUM PUBLISHING
The Natural History Museum, Cromwell Road, London SW7 5BD
Telephone: 020 7942 5060
Fax: 020 7942 5291
Email: publishing@nhm.ac.uk
Website: www.nhm.ac.uk/publishing

Warehouse & Distribution:
Littlehampton Book Services, Faraday Close, Durrington, Worthing, West Sussex BN13 3RB
Telephone: 01903 828500
Fax: 01903 828625
Email: pubeasy@lbsltd.co.uk
Website: www.lbsltd.co.uk

Personnel:
Lynn Millhouse *(Production Manager)*
Trudy Brannan *(Editorial Manager)*
Colin Ziegler *(Head of Publishing)*
Howard Trent *(Sales & Marketing Executive)*

Academic & Scholarly; Biology & Zoology; Children's Books; Educational & Textbooks; Fine Art & Art History; Geography & Geology; Illustrated & Fine Editions; Natural History

Imprints, Series & ISBNs:
Natural History Museum Publishing: 978-0-565

2416 ▬▬▬▬▬

NELSON THORNES LTD
Delta Place, 27 Bath Road, Cheltenham GL53 7TH
Telephone: 01242 267100
Fax: 01242 221914 (General) & 253695 (Orders)
Email: csupport@nelsonthornes.com
Website: www.nelsonthornes.com

Personnel:
Richard Hodson *(Managing Director)*
Wendy Rimmington *(Sales & Marketing Director, UK & International)*
Claire Varlet-Baker *(Publishing Director)*
Neil McQuillan *(Operations Director)*
Adrian Wheaton *(Publishing Strategy Director)*

Margot van de Weijer *(Head of Customer Services & Distribution)*
Caroline Blackburn *(Head of Finance)*

Accountancy & Taxation; Biology & Zoology; Chemistry; Children's Books; Computer Science; Economics; Educational & Textbooks; Electronic (Educational); Engineering; Environment & Development Studies; Fashion & Costume; Geography & Geology; Health & Beauty; History & Antiquarian; Industry, Business & Management; Languages & Linguistics; Law; Literature & Criticism; Mathematics & Statistics; Medical (incl. Self-Help & Alternative Medicine); Music; Philosophy; Physics; Poetry; Politics & World Affairs; Psychology & Psychiatry; Religion & Theology; Scientific & Technical; Sociology & Anthropology; Sports & Games; Theatre, Drama & Dance; Vocational Training & Careers

Imprints, Series & ISBNs:
Nelson Thornes Ltd: 978-0-17, 978-0-7487, 978-1-4085

Parent Company:
UK: Oxford University Press

Distributor for:
Australia: Cengage; Macmillan Library

Overseas Representation:
Argentina: Kel Ediciones SA (Agents), Buenos Aires, Argentina
Australia: Cengage (Australia), NSW, Australia
Barbados: Days Bookstore, Bridgetown, Barbados
Botswana, South Africa, Lesotho, Swaziland, Mozambique & Namibia: Macmillan Education Ltd, Oxford, UK
Egypt: Galaxy Trade, Giza, Egypt
Gulf States, Iran, Syria, Libya, Jordan, Lebanon, Cyprus, Yemen, Tunis, Turkey, Morocco & Algeria (Further & Higher Education only): International Publishing Services (IPS) Middle East Ltd, Dubai, United Arab Emirates
Guyana: Austin's Book Services, Georgetown, Guyana
Hong Kong & Macao: Transglobal Publishers Services Ltd, Hong Kong
India, Bangladesh, Sri Lanka, Nepal & Bhutan: Overleaf, New Delhi, India
Jamaica: Kingston Bookshop, Kingston, Jamaica
Kenya: Educate Yourself, Kenya
Malaysia: APD Kuala Lumpur Pte Ltd, Selangor, Malaysia
Malta: Miller Distributors Ltd, Luqa, Malta
Mauritius: Editions le Printemps, Vacoas, Mauritius
New Zealand: Cengage, New Zealand
Nigeria: Chelis Bookazine, Lagos, Nigeria
Pakistan: Publishers Marketing Associates, Karachi, Pakistan
Republic of Ireland (Primary, Secondary & Further Education): Carrol Educational Supplies, Dublin, Republic of Ireland
Singapore & Brunei: APD Singapore Pte Ltd, Singapore
St Vincent & The Grenadines: Gaymes Book Centre, St Vincent
Sweden, Denmark, Norway, Finland, Iceland, Estonia, Latvia & Lithuania (Health Science & Science & Engineering titles only): David Towle International, Stockholm, Sweden
Tajikistan, Uzbekistan, Kazakhstan, Kyrgyzstan & Turkmenistan: Silk Road Media, London, UK
Trinidad & Tobago: Books Etc, San Fernando, Trinidad
Uruguay: Opiciones en Educacion, Uruguay

Book Trade Association Membership:
Publishers Association; Educational Publishers Council

2417 ▬▬▬▬▬

NEW CARAMEL LONDON LTD
12–13 Ship Street, Brighton BN1 1AD
Website: www.caramel.eu

Children's Books

Book Trade Association Membership:
Publishers Association

2418 ▬▬▬▬▬

NEW ISLAND BOOKS LTD
2 Brookside, Dundrum Road, Dublin 14, Republic of Ireland
Telephone: +353 (0)1 298 3411
Fax: +353 (0)1 298 2783
Email: sales@newisland.ie
Website: www.newisland.ie

Distribution:
Gill & Macmillan, Hume Avenue, Park West, Dublin 12, Republic of Ireland
Telephone: +353 (0)1 500 9555
Fax: +353 (0)1 500 9599
Email: sales@gillmacmillan.ie

Representation (Republic of Ireland & Northern Ireland):
Brookside Publishing Svs, Dundrum, Republic of Ireland
Telephone: +353 (0)1 2989937
Fax: +353 (0)1 2982783
Email: michael.darcy@brookside.ie

Personnel:
Edwin Higel *(Publisher)*
Eoin Purcell *(Commissioning Editor)*
Aisling Glynn *(Accounts Manager)*
Ms Mariel Deegan *(Marketing and Publicity)*
Dr Justin Corfield *(Editorial Assistant)*
Maria White *(Rights Agent)*

Biography & Autobiography; Children's Books; English as a Foreign Language; Fiction; Gender Studies; Guide Books; History & Antiquarian; Humour; Literature & Criticism; Poetry; Politics & World Affairs; Theatre, Drama & Dance

Imprints, Series & ISBNs:
New Island: 978-1-84840, 978-1-874597, 978-1-902602, 978-1-904301, 978-1-905494

Overseas Representation:
UK: Compass DSA, Slough, UK
USA & Canada: Dufour Editions Inc, Chester Springs, PA, USA; ISBS, Portland, OR, USA

Book Trade Association Membership:
Publishing Ireland (Foilsiú Éireann)

2419 ▬▬▬▬▬

NEW PLAYWRIGHTS' NETWORK
10 Station Road Industrial Estate, Colwall, Malvern, Worcs WR13 6RN
Telephone: 01684 540154
Email: simon@cressrelles.co.uk
Website: www.cressrelles.co.uk

Personnel:
L. G. Smith *(Managing Director)*
S. R. Smith *(Sales Director)*

Theatre, Drama & Dance

Imprints, Series & ISBNs:
New Playwrights' Network: 978-0-86319, 978-0-903653, 978-0-906660

Parent Company:
UK: Cressrelles Publishing Co Ltd

Overseas Representation:
Australia: Origin Theatrical, Sydney, NSW, Australia

New Zealand: Play Bureau of New Zealand Ltd, New Plymouth, New Zealand
Republic of Ireland: Drama League of Ireland, Dublin, Republic of Ireland
South Africa: Dalro (Pty) Ltd, Braamfontein, South Africa
USA: Bakers Plays, Quincy, MA, USA

2420 ▬▬▬

NIELSEN
3rd Floor, Midas House,
62 Goldsworth Road, Woking, Surrey
GU21 6LQ
Telephone: 01483 712200
Fax: 01483 712201
Email: info.book@nielsen.com
Website: www.nielsenbook.co.uk

Editorial:
89–95 Queensway, Stevenage, Herts
SG1 1EA
Telephone: 01483 712200
Fax: 01438 745578
Email: newtitles.book@nielsen.com &
pubhelp.book@nielsen.com
Website: www.nielsenbook.co.uk

Personnel:
Jonathan Nowell *(President)*
Ann Betts *(Commercial Director)*
Jon Windus *(Operations Director)*
Andrew Sugden *(Financial Director)*
Simon Skinner *(Sales Director)*
Mo Siewcharran *(Head of Marketing)*
Peter Mathews *(Senior Manager, Publishing Services)*
Howard Willows *(Senior Manager, Data Development)*
Gwyneth Morgan *(Editorial Systems, Senior Manager)*
Samantha Watson *(Quality Assurance, Senior Manager)*
Vesna Nall *(Publisher Subscriptions Manager)*
Paul Dibble *(Head of Data Sales)*
Stephen Long *(Head of BookNet)*
Christine Broadbent *(HRBP)*

Bibliography & Library Science

Parent Company:
Netherlands: Nielsen Holdings NV (NYSE: NLSN)

Associated Companies:
Singapore: Nielsen BookData Asia Pacific
UK: BDS; ISTC Agency; Nielsen BookData; Nielsen BookNet; Nielsen BookScan; UK ISBN Agency; UK SAN Agency

Overseas Representation:
Germany & Western Balkans: Missing Link, Germany
South Africa: Publications Network (Pty) Ltd (trading as SAPNet), South Africa

Book Trade Association Membership:
Publishing Scotland; Publishing Ireland (Foilsiú Éireann); Booksellers Association; Independent Publishers Guild

2421 ▬▬▬

NMS ENTERPRISES LIMITED - PUBLISHING
National Museums Scotland,
Chambers Street, Edinburgh EH1 1JF
Telephone: 0131 247 4026
Fax: 0131 247 4012
Email: publishing@nms.ac.uk
Website: www.nms.ac.uk/books

Representation:
CPR, SPCK Head Office, 36 Causton Street, London SW1P 4ST
Telephone: 020 7592 3900
Email: sales@spck.org.uk

Distribution (UK):
BookSource, 50 Cambuslang Road, Glasgow G32 8NB

Telephone: 0845 370 0067
Fax: 0845 370 0068
Email: orders@booksource.net

Personnel:
Lesley A. Taylor *(Director of Publishing)*
Kate Blackadder *(Marketing Manager)*
Maggie Wilson *(Administration & Sales)*

Academic & Scholarly; Antiques & Collecting; Archaeology; Architecture & Design; Biography & Autobiography; Biology & Zoology; Children's Books; Cookery, Wines & Spirits; Educational & Textbooks; Fine Art & Art History; Geography & Geology; Guide Books; History & Antiquarian; Military & War; Natural History; Poetry; Scientific & Technical; Sociology & Anthropology; Transport

Imprints, Series & ISBNs:
NMS Enterprises Limited - Publishing: 978-0-948636, 978-1-901663, 978-1-905267

Parent Company:
UK: National Museums Scotland

Overseas Representation:
USA: ACC Distributions, New York, NY, USA

Book Trade Association Membership:
Publishing Scotland

2422 ▬▬▬

NORTH YORK MOORS NATIONAL PARK AUTHORITY
The Old Vicarage, Bondgate, Helmsley, Yorks YO62 5BP
Telephone: 01439 772700
Fax: 01439 772700
Email: J.Renney@northyorkmoors.org.uk
Website: www.northyorkmoors.org.uk

Personnel:
Richard Gunton *(Director of Park Management)*
Catherine Raistrick *(Finance Officer)*
Jill Renney *(Information & Interpretation Manager)*
Julian Brown *(Interpretation Officer)*

Archaeology; Biology & Zoology; Children's Books; Educational & Textbooks; Environment & Development Studies; Geography & Geology; Guide Books; History & Antiquarian; Natural History; Travel & Topography

New Titles: 1 (2012)

Imprints, Series & ISBNs:
North York Moors National Park Authority: 978-0-907480, 978-1-904622

2423 ▬▬▬

NORTHCOTE HOUSE PUBLISHERS LTD
Horndon House, Horndon, Tavistock, Devon
PL19 9NQ
Telephone: 01822 810066
Fax: 01822 810034
Email: northcote.house@virgin.net
Website: www.northcotehouse.co.uk

Distributors:
Combined Book Services, Unit D, Paddock Wood Distribution Centre, Paddock Wood, Tonbridge, Kent TN12 6UU
Telephone: 01892 837171
Fax: 01892 837372
Email: orders@combook.co.uk
Website: www.combook.co.uk

Personnel:
Brian Hulme *(Managing Director & Publisher)*
Sarah Piper *(Marketing Manager)*

Academic & Scholarly; Educational & Textbooks; Literature & Criticism; Theatre, Drama & Dance

Imprints, Series & ISBNs:
Northcote House: 978-0-7463
Resources in Education: 978-0-7463
Starting Out...: 978-0-7463
Writers and their Work: 978-0-7463

Overseas Representation:
Africa (excluding South Africa) & Eastern Europe: Tony Moggach, IMA, London, UK
Australia & New Zealand: Book & Volume, Birregurra, Vic, Australia
Germany, Austria, Switzerland, France, Japan, Italy & Benelux: Ted Dougherty, London, UK
India: Maya Publishers Pvt Ltd, New Delhi, India
Japan: Koro Komori, Eureka Press, Kyoto, Japan
Middle East: Hani Kreidieh, Beirut, Lebanon
Pakistan: Book Bird Publishers Representatives, Lahore, Pakistan
Scandinavia: David Towle International, Stockholm, Sweden
Spain & Portugal: Peter Prout Iberian Book Services, Madrid, Spain
USA, Canada & Mexico: David Brown Book Co, Oakville, CT, USA

Book Trade Association Membership:
Independent Publishers Guild

2424 ▬▬▬

W. W. NORTON & COMPANY LTD
Castle House, 75–76 Wells Street, London
W1T 3QT
Telephone: 020 7323 1579
Fax: 020 7436 4553
Email: office@wwnorton.co.uk
Website: www.wwnorton.co.uk

Distribution:
John Wiley & Sons Ltd, 1 Oldlands Way, Shripney, Bognor Regis, West Sussex
PO22 9SA
Telephone: 01243 779777
Fax: 01243 820250
Email: cs-books@wiley.com

Personnel:
Edward Crutchley *(Managing Director)*
R. A. Cameron *(Chairman)*
W. D. McFeely *(USA Director)*
S. King *(Director)*
G. Luciano *(USA Director)*
R. Harrington *(USA Director)*
J. Reidhead *(Director)*
P. Wright *(Director)*
A. J. Llewellyn *(Director)*

Academic & Scholarly; Architecture & Design; Biology & Zoology; Chemistry; Cinema, Video, TV & Radio; Computer Science; Cookery, Wines & Spirits; Economics; Educational & Textbooks; Fiction; Fine Art & Art History; Gardening; Gender Studies; Geography & Geology; History & Antiquarian; Literature & Criticism; Mathematics & Statistics; Military & War; Music; Natural History; Nautical; Philosophy; Physics; Poetry; Politics & World Affairs; Psychology & Psychiatry; Religion & Theology; Sociology & Anthropology; Sports & Games; Theatre, Drama & Dance

Imprints, Series & ISBNs:
C.I.R.C
The Countryman Press: 978-0-393
Dalkey Archives
Liveright: 978-0-87140
New Directions
W.W. Norton: 978-0-393
Peacehill Press
Pegasus
Quantuck Lane

Parent Company:
USA: W. W. Norton & Company

Distributor for:
USA: Dalkey Archive Press; New Directions Publishing Corporation

Overseas Representation:
Africa & Caribbean: Kelvin van Hasselt Publishing Services, Briningham, Norfolk, UK
India & Sri Lanka: Viva Group, New Delhi, India
Middle East & North Africa: International Publishers Representatives (IPR) Ltd, Nicosia, Cyprus
Pakistan: World Press, Lahore, Pakistan
Republic of Ireland: Andrew Russell Book Representation, Co Cork, Republic of Ireland
South Africa: Chris Reinders, The African Moon Press, Kelvin, South Africa
Spain & Portugal: Cristina de Lara Ruiz, Madrid, Spain

Book Trade Association Membership:
Independent Publishers Guild

2425 ▬▬▬

THE NOSTALGIA COLLECTION
Silver Link Publishing Ltd, The Trundle, Ringstead Road, Great Addington, Kettering, Northants NN14 4BW
Telephone: 01536 330543 & 330588
Fax: 01536 330588
Email: sales@nostalgiacollection.com
Website: www.nostalgiacollection.com

Personnel:
Peter Townsend *(Managing Director, Publisher)*
Frances Townsend *(Company Secretary)*
David Walshaw *(Distribtion, Mail Order & Advertising Manager)*

Aviation; Crafts & Hobbies; Guide Books; History & Antiquarian; Military & War; Nautical; Transport

Imprints, Series & ISBNs:
Past & Present Publishing Ltd: 978-1-85895
Silver Link Publishing Ltd: 978-0-947971, 978-1-85794

Associated Companies:
UK: Past & Present Publishing Ltd; Silver Link Publishing Ltd

Distributor for:
UK: Past & Present Publishing Ltd; Silver Link Publishing Ltd

Book Trade Association Membership:
Booksellers Association

2426 ▬▬▬

NOSY CROW
The Crow's Nest, 10a Lant Street, London
SE1 1QR
Telephone: 020 7089 7575
Email: hello@nosycrow.com
Website: www.nosycrow.com

Personnel:
Kate Wilson *(Managing Director)*

Children's Books

Book Trade Association Membership:
Publishers Association; Independent Publishers Guild

2427 ▬▬▬

OAK TREE PRESS
19 Rutland Street, Cork, Republic of Ireland
Telephone: +353 (0)21 431 3855
Fax: +353 (0)21 431 3496
Email: info@oaktreepress.com
Website: www.oaktreepress.com

49

Personnel:
Brian O'Kane (Managing Director)
Rita O'Kane (Sales Director)
Anne Kennedy (Office Manager)

Academic & Scholarly; Accountancy &
Taxation; Economics; Educational &
Textbooks; Electronic (Professional &
Academic); Industry, Business &
Management; Law

Imprints, Series & ISBNs:
NuBooks: 978-1-84621
Oak Tree Press: 978-1-86076, 978-1-
872853, 978-1-904887

Parent Company:
Republic of Ireland: Cork Publishing Ltd

Book Trade Association Membership:
Publishing Ireland (Foilsiú Éireann)

2428

OAKLEY BOOKS LTD
Advantage Business Centre,
132–134 Great Ancoats Street, Manchester
M4 6DE
Telephone: 020 3286 9179
Email: oakleybooks@gmail.com

Book Trade Association Membership:
Publishers Association

2429

THE O'BRIEN PRESS LTD
12 Terenure Road East, Rathgar, Dublin 6,
Republic of Ireland
Telephone: +353 (0)1 492 3333
Fax: +353 (0)1 492 2777
Email: books@obrien.ie
Website: www.obrien.ie

Personnel:
Michael O'Brien (Publisher)
Ivan O'Brien (Managing Director)
Íde ní Laoghaire (Director)
Mary Webb (Director & Editorial Director)
Kunak McGann (Rights Manager)
Erika McGann (Production Manager)
Ruth Heneghan (Marketing Manager)

Architecture & Design; Biography &
Autobiography; Children's Books; Cookery,
Wines & Spirits; Crime; Fiction; Gardening;
Guide Books; Humour; Photography;
Politics & World Affairs; Sports & Games;
Travel & Topography

New Titles: 40 (2012) , 40 (2013)

Imprints, Series & ISBNs:
Brandon : 978-0-86322, 978-1-84717
The O'Brien Press Ltd: 978-0-86278, 978-0-
905140, 978-1-84717

Associated Companies:
Republic of Ireland: O'Brien Educational

Overseas Representation:
U.K.: Turnaround (represents only Brandon),
London, UK
USA & Canada: Dufour Editions, Chester
Springs, PA, USA

Book Trade Association Membership:
Independent Publishers Guild

2430

OCTOPUS PUBLISHING GROUP
Endeavour House,
189 Shaftesbury Avenue, London
WC2H 8JY
Telephone: 020 7632 5400
Email: info@octopusbooks.co.uk
Website: www.octopusbooks.co.uk

Distribution:
Littlehampton Book Services Ltd,
Faraday Close, Durrington, Worthing,
West Sussex BN13 3PB
Telephone: 01903 828500
Fax: 01903 828625
Email: orders@lbsltd.co.uk
Website: www.lbsltd.co.uk

Personnel:
Alison Goff (Chief Executive)
Andrew Welham (Deputy Chief Executive
Officer; Sales & Marketing Director)
Angela Luxton (Commercial Director)
Caroline Brown (Head of Publicity)
Frances Johnson (Group Operations
Director)
Henri Masurel (Group Finance Director)
Denise Bates (Group Publishing Director)

Animal Care & Breeding; Antiques &
Collecting; Architecture & Design; Atlases &
Maps; Cookery, Wines & Spirits; Crafts &
Hobbies; Do-It-Yourself; Fine Art & Art
History; Gardening; Health & Beauty;
History & Antiquarian; Natural History;
Sports & Games

Imprints, Series & ISBNs:
AWW AUS: 978-1-74245, 978-1-86396
AWW UK
Bounty: 978-0-7537
Cassell: 978-1-84403
Conran: 978-1-84091
Gaia: 978-1-84181
Godsfield Press: 978-1-85675
Hamlyn: 978-0-600
Mitchell Beazley: 978-1-84533
Philips: 978-1-84907
Spruce: 978-1-84601
Ticktock: 978-1-84898

Parent Company:
UK: Hachette UK

Overseas Representation:
All Other Territories: Octopus Export Sales,
Octopus Publishing Group, London, UK
Australia: Hachette Livre Australia, Sydney,
NSW, Australia
Canada: Canadian Manda Group, Toronto,
Ontario, Canada
Caribbean: Chris Humphrys & Linda
Hopkins, London, UK
Caribbean (for Philip's): David Williams,
InterMedia Americana (IMA) Ltd,
London, UK
Central America: Arturo Gutierrez
Hernandez, Mexico
China, Hong Kong & Taiwan: Edward
Summerson, Asia Publishers Services Ltd,
Aberdeen, Hong Kong
France, Belgium, Netherlands, Scandinavia,
Iceland, Baltics, Eastern Europe, Russia,
Cyprus, Germany, Austria, Switzerland &
Malta: Bill Bailey Publishers
Representatives, Newton Abbot, UK
India, Bangladesh & Sri Lanka: Kapil
Agrawal, Hachette Book Publishing India
Pvt Ltd, Gurgaon, India
Italy & Greece: Penny Padovani, Padovani
Books, Italy
Malaysia: Lilian Koe, APD Kuala Lumpur Pte
Ltd, Selangor, Malaysia
Middle East, North Africa & Israel: Matt
Cowdery, Hachette UK Ltd, Dubai,
United Arab Emirates
New Zealand: Hachette Livre New Zealand,
Auckland, New Zealand
Singapore: Ian Pringle, APD Singapore PTE
Ltd, Singapore
South Africa: Jonathan Ball Publishers,
Johannesburg, South Africa
South America: JCC Enterprises Inc, New
Mexico, USA
Spain, Portugal & Gibraltar: Jenny
Padovani, Barcelona, Spain
Sub-Saharan Africa: Anita Zih-De Haan,
Rotterdam, Netherlands
USA: Octopus Books USA, c/o Hachette
Book Group USA, Boston, MA, USA

2431

THE OLD STILE PRESS
Catchmays Court, Llandogo,
Monmouthshire NP25 4TN
Telephone: 01291 689226
Email: frances@oldstilepress.com
Website: www.oldstilepress.com

Personnel:
Nicolas McDowall (Partner)
Frances McDowall (Partner)

Biography & Autobiography; Illustrated &
Fine Editions; Literature & Criticism; Poetry;
Theatre, Drama & Dance

Imprints, Series & ISBNs:
The Old Stile Press: 978-0-907664

Book Trade Association Membership:
Fine Press Book Association

2432

OMNIBUS PRESS
14–15 Berners Street, London W1T 3LJ
Telephone: 020 7612 7400
Fax: 020 7612 7545
Email: music@musicsales.co.uk
Website: www.omnibuspress.co.uk

Warehouse:
Book Sales Ltd, Newmarket Road,
Bury St Edmunds, Suffolk IP33 3YB
Telephone: 01284 702600
Fax: 01284 768301
Email: music@musicsales.co.uk
Website: www.musicroom.com

Personnel:
Robert Wise (Managing Director)
Tony Latham (Financial Director)
Richard Hudson (Sales Director)
Mark Pickard (Production Manager)
Chris Charlesworth (Editor)
David Barraclough (Commissioning Editor)

Biography & Autobiography; Music

Imprints, Series & ISBNs:
Omnibus Press: 978-0-7119, 978-1-78038,
978-1-78305, 978-1-84449, 978-1-
84609, 978-1-84772, 978-1-84938
Wise Publications: 978-0-7119, 978-1-
78038, 978-1-84938

Parent Company:
UK: Music Sales Ltd

Associated Companies:
Australia: Music Sales (Pty) Ltd
USA: Music Sales Corp

Distributor for:
UK: Bobcat Books; Dover Books;
Haymarket Publishing (Gramophone
Guide); Rogan House; Sanctuary;
Schirmer Books; Vision On

Overseas Representation:
Portugal, Gibraltar & Italy: Penny Padovani,
London, UK, Italy
Australia: Macmillan Distribution, South
Yarra, Vic, Australia
Australia (for Music Shops): Music Sales
(Australia), Rosebery, NSW, Australia
Belgium: Exhibitions International, Leuven,
Belgium
Belgium & Luxembourg: Marleen Geukens,
Belgium
Canada: Login Canada, Winnipeg,
Manitoba, Canada
Central America, Mexico & Caribbean:
Humphrys Roberts Associates, London,
UK
Eastern Europe: Tony Moggach, InterMedia
Americana (IMA) Ltd, London, UK
France, Netherlands: Ted Dougherty,
London, UK

Germany, Austria & Switzerland: Gabriele
Kern Publishers Services, Frankfurt-am-
Main, Germany
Greece, Turkey, Cyprus, Malta & Middle
East: Peter Ward Book Exports, London,
UK
Indian Subcontinent: Publishers
International Marketing, Storrington, UK
New Zealand: Macmillan Publishers New
Zealand Ltd, Auckland, New Zealand
Scandinavia: Angell Eurosales, Berwick-
upon-Tweed, UK
South Africa: Trinity Books CC, Randburg,
South Africa
South America: InterMedia Americana
(IMA) Ltd, London, UK
South East & North Asia: Chris Ashdown
Publishers International Marketing,
London, UK
Spain: Jenny Padovani Frias, Barcelona,
Spain

Book Trade Association Membership:
BA (Associate Member)

2433

THE OPEN BIBLE TRUST
Fordland Mount, Upper Basildon, Reading
RG8 8LU
Telephone: 01491 671357
Email: admin@obt.org.uk
Website: www.obt.org.uk

Personnel:
Michael Penny (Administrator, Editor)
Sylvia Penny (Treasurer)

Religion & Theology

New Titles: 9 (2012) , 8 (2013)

Imprints, Series & ISBNs:
The Open Bible Trust: 978-0-947778, 978-
1-78364, 978-1-902859, 978-1-908994

Associated Companies:
USA: Bible Search Publications Inc

Overseas Representation:
Australia: Berean Bible Fellowship of
Australia, Glendale, NSW, Australia
Canada: Ron Moore, Bowmanville, Ont,
Canada
New Zealand: Graeme Abbott, Hamilton,
New Zealand
USA: Bible Search Publications, Brookfield,
WI, USA

2434

OPEN UNIVERSITY WORLDWIDE
Open University, Walton Hall,
Milton Keynes, Bucks MK7 6AA
Fax: 01908 858787
Website: www.ouw.co.uk

Academic & Scholarly; Architecture &
Design; Biology & Zoology; Chemistry;
Computer Science; Crime; Economics;
Educational & Textbooks; Electronic
(Educational); Engineering; English as a
Foreign Language; Environment &
Development Studies; Fine Art & Art
History; Geography & Geology; History &
Antiquarian; Industry, Business &
Management; Languages & Linguistics;
Literature & Criticism; Mathematics &
Statistics; Medical (incl. Self-Help &
Alternative Medicine); Natural History;
Physics; Politics & World Affairs; Psychology
& Psychiatry; Religion & Theology; Scientific
& Technical; Sociology & Anthropology;
Theatre, Drama & Dance

Imprints, Series & ISBNs:
Open University Worldwide: 978-0-7492,
978-1-78007, 978-1-84873

Book Trade Association Membership:
Independent Publishers Guild

2435

OPTIMUS PROFESSIONAL PUBLISHING
[A division of Electric Word Plc]
33–41 Dallington Street, London EC1V 0BB
Telephone: 0845 450 6400
Fax: 0845 450 6410
Email: info@optimus-education.com
Website: www.optimus-education.com

Personnel:
Russell Lawson (Managing Director)
Jenny Lee (Content Manager)

Academic & Scholarly; Educational & Textbooks; Electronic (Educational); Geography & Geology; Vocational Training & Careers

Imprints, Series & ISBNs:
Kington Publishing: 978-1-899857
Optimus Education: 978-1-905538, 978-1-907927, 978-1-908294
Teach to Inspire: 978-1-906517

Parent Company:
UK: Electric Word PLC

Associated Companies:
UK: IGaming Business; Incentive Plus; Peak Performance; Radcliffe Publishing; Speechmark Ltd; SportBusiness Group

Book Trade Association Membership:
Publishers Association; Educational Publishers Council

2436

OPTIMUS EDUCATION
33–41 Dallington Street, London EC1V 0BB
Telephone: 020 7954 3420
Fax: 0845 450 6140
Website: www.optimus-education.com

Personnel:
Russell Lawson (Managing Director - Optimus Education)

Academic & Scholarly; Educational & Textbooks

Imprints, Series & ISBNs:
Chris Kington Publishing: 978-1-8
Optimus Education Books: 978-1-9, 978-1-9, 978-1-9
Optimus Education eBooks
Optimus Education Training

Book Trade Association Membership:
Publishers Association

2437

O'REILLY UK LTD
Gostrey House, Union Road, Farnham, Surrey GU9 7PT
Telephone: 01252 721284
Fax: 01252 722337
Email: information@oreilly.co.uk
Website: www.oreilly.com

Distributors:
John Wiley, 1 Oldlands Way, Bognor Regis PO22 9SA
Telephone: 01243 779777
Fax: 01243 843303
Email: cs-books@wiley.co.uk

Personnel:
Graham Cameron (Managing Director)
Josette Garcia (Public Relations Manager)
Simon Chappell (Sales Director)

Computer Science

Parent Company:
USA: O'Reilly Media Inc

Distributor for:
UK: microsoft press; pragmatic bookshelf; rocky nook

Book Trade Association Membership:
Independent Publishers Guild

2438

ORION BOOKS LTD
[Hachette UK]
Orion House, 5 Upper St Martins Lane, London WC2H 9EA
Telephone: 020 7240 3444
Fax: 020 7240 4822

Trade Counter & Warehouse:
Littlehampton Book Services Ltd, Faraday Close, Durrington, Worthing, West Sussex BN13 3RB
Telephone: 01903 828500
Fax: 01903 828625
Website: www.orionbooks.co.uk

Personnel:
Lisa Milton (Trade Managing Director)
Susan Lamb (Managing Director Paperback Division)
Jon Wood (Deputy Group Publisher)
Fiona Kennedy (Children's Publisher & Rights Director)

Biography & Autobiography; Children's Books; Fiction; Science Fiction

Imprints, Series & ISBNs:
Gollancz: 978-1-85798
Orion: 978-1-85797
Orion Children's: 978-1-84255, 978-1-85881
Orion Paperbacks: 978-1-85797
Phoenix: 978-1-85799
Phoenix House

Parent Company:
UK: The Orion Publishing Group Ltd

Overseas Representation:
see: The Orion Publishing Group Ltd, London, UK

2439

THE ORION PUBLISHING GROUP LTD
[Hachette UK]
Orion House, 5 Upper St Martins Lane, London WC2H 9EA
Telephone: 020 7240 3444
Fax: 020 7240 4822
Email: publishingstaff@orionbooks.co.uk
Website: www.orionbooks.co.uk

Trade Counter & Warehouse:
Littlehampton Book Services Ltd, Faraday Close, Durrington, Worthing, West Sussex BN13 3RB
Telephone: 01903 828500
Fax: 01903 828625
Email: ...@lbsltd.co.uk
Website: www.lbsltd.co.uk

Personnel:
Arnaud Nourry (Chairman)
David Young (Chief Executive)
Malcolm Edwards (Deputy Chief Executive & Publisher)
Susan Lamb (Managing Director – Mass Market)
Lisa Milton (Managing Director – Orion Books)
Dallas Manderson (Group Sales Director)
Dominic Smith (Home Sales Director)
Mark Streatfeild (Export Sales Director)
Fiona McIntosh (Production Director)
Clare Jarvis (Finance Director)
Chris Emerson (Director)
Lord George Weidenfeld (Director)
Susan Howe (Group Rights Director)
Tim Hely Hutchinson (Director)
Pierre de Cacqueray (Director)
Richard Kitson (Director)

Antiques & Collecting; Archaeology; Audio Books; Biography & Autobiography; Children's Books; Cinema, Video, TV & Radio; Cookery, Wines & Spirits; Crafts & Hobbies; Crime; Fashion & Costume; Fiction; Fine Art & Art History; Gardening; Guide Books; Health & Beauty; History & Antiquarian; Humour; Illustrated & Fine Editions; Military & War; Natural History; Nautical; Philosophy; Politics & World Affairs; Reference Books, Directories & Dictionaries; Science Fiction; Sports & Games; Travel & Topography

Imprints, Series & ISBNs:
Cassell: 978-0-304
J. M. Dent: 978-0-460
Everyman Paperbacks: 978-0-460
First Time Authors Fiction
Gollancz: 978-0-575, 978-1-85797, 978-1-85798
Oriel
Orion: 978-1-85797
Orion Children's: 978-1-84255, 978-1-85881
Orion Fiction: 978-0-7528
Orion Media: 978-0-7528
Orion Paperbacks: 978-0-460, 978-0-7528, 978-1-85797
Phoenix House
Phoenix Mass Market: 978-0-7538
Phoenix Press: 978-1-84212
W & N Illustrated: 978-0-297
Weidenfeld & Nicolson: 978-0-297

Parent Company:
France: Hachette Livre

Associated Companies:
UK: Cassell plc; J. M. Dent Ltd; Victor Gollancz; Littlehampton Book Services Ltd; Orion Books Ltd; George Weidenfeld & Nicolson Ltd

Distributor for:
UK: Peter Halban Publishers

Overseas Representation:
Australia: Hachette Livre Australia (Orion Division), Sydney, NSW, Australia
Austria, Belgium, Cyprus, France, Germany, Greece, Italy, Luxembourg, Netherlands, Portugal, Spain & Switzerland: Kim Else, The Orion Publishing Group Ltd, London, UK
Canada: Hachette Book Group, Toronto, Ont, Canada
Caribbean: Chris Humphrys, Humphrys Roberts Associates, London, UK
Eastern Europe: Csaba & Jackie Lengyel de Bagota, Budapest, Hungary
India: Hachette India, New Delhi, India
India, Pakistan, South America, Singapore, Hong Kong, Thailand, Japan, Indonesia & Malaysia: Michael Goff, The Orion Publishing Group Ltd, London, UK
New Zealand: Hachette New Zealand (Orion Division), Auckland, New Zealand
Philippines, Korea & Taiwan: Ralph & Sheila Summers, Woodford Green, Essex, UK
Scandinavia, Middle East, Turkey, Malta, Russia, North Africa & Baltic States: Suzie Jenner, The Orion Publishing Group Ltd, London, UK
South Africa: Jonathan Ball Publishers (Pty) Ltd, Johannesburg, South Africa

2440

ORPEN PRESS
Lonsdale House, Avoca Avenue, Blackrock, Co Dublin, Republic of Ireland
Telephone: +353 (0)1 278 5090
Fax: +353 (0)1 278 4800
Email: info@orpenpress.com
Website: www.orpenpress.com

Send trade orders to::
Gill & Macmillan, Hume Avenue, Park West, Dublin 12, Republic of Ireland
Telephone: +353 (0)1 500 9500
Fax: +353 (0)1 500 9599

Email: sales@gillmacmillan.ie
Website: www.gillmacmillan.ie

Personnel:
Gerard O'Connor (Managing Director)
Conor O'Mahony (Financial Controller)
Eileen O'Brien (Editor)
Benil Shah (Typesetting Manager)
Ciaran MacGlinchey (Online Editor)
Ailbhe O'Reilly (Commissioning Editor)
Jenny Thompson (Editor)

Academic & Scholarly; Accountancy & Taxation; Economics; Industry, Business & Management; Law; Medical (incl. Self-Help & Alternative Medicine); Politics & World Affairs; Psychology & Psychiatry; Sociology & Anthropology

Imprints, Series & ISBNs:
Blackhall Publishing: 978-1-84218, 978-1-901657
Kite Books: 978-1-84218
Lonsdale Law Publishing: 978-1-907325
Orpen Press: 978-1-871305

Associated Companies:
UK: Blackhall Publishing; Kite Books; Lonsdale Law Publishing

Overseas Representation:
UK: Gill & Macmillan, Dublin, Republic of Ireland

Book Trade Association Membership:
Publishing Ireland (Foilsiú Éireann)

2441

OSPREY PUBLISHING LTD
Midland House, West Way, Botley, Oxford OX2 0PH
Telephone: 01865 727022
Fax: 01865 727017
Email: info@ospreypublishing.com
Website: www.ospreypublishing.com

Distribution:
Grantham Book Services, Trent Road, Grantham, Lincs NG31 7XQ
Telephone: 01476 541080
Fax: 01476 541061
Email: orders@gbs-tbs-ltd.co.uk

Personnel:
Rebecca Smart (CEO)
John Bowman (Chief Financial & Operations Officer)
Joanna Sharland (Rights Director)
Kate Moore (Publisher)
Richard Sullivan (Managing Director)

Aviation; History & Antiquarian; Military & War

New Titles: 120 (2012) , 120 (2013)
No of Employees: 45
Annual Turnover: £6M

Imprints, Series & ISBNs:
Osprey Publishing Ltd: 978-0-85045, 978-1-84176, 978-1-84603, 978-1-84908, 978-1-85532

Overseas Representation:
Australia: Capricorn Link (Australia) Pty Ltd, Windsor, NSW, Australia
Belgium, Netherlands & Switzerland: Robbert J. Pleysier, Heerde, Netherlands
Central & Eastern Europe: Tony Moggach, London, UK
Far East: Ashton International Marketing Services, Sevenoaks, Kent, UK
France: Ted Dougherty, London, UK
Germany & Austria: Gabriele Kern, PS Publishers Services, Frankfurt, Germany
Greece & Italy: Sandro Salucci, Florence, Italy
Middle East: Peter Ward Book Exports, London, UK
New Zealand: Nationwide Book Distributors, New Zealand

Scandinavia: Katie McNeish, East Sussex, UK
Spain, Portugal & Gibraltar: Peter Prout, Iberian Book Services, Madrid, Spain
Turkey: Ayse Lale Colakoglu, Istanbul, Turkey
USA, Caribbean & Latin America: Random House Publishing Services, New York, NY, USA

Book Trade Association Membership:
Independent Publishers Guild

2442

OXFAM PUBLISHING
Oxfam House, John Smith Drive, Cowley, Oxford OX4 2JY
Telephone: 01865 472188
Fax: 01865 472393
Email: policyandpractice@oxfam.org.uk
Website: www.oxfam.org.uk/policyandpractice

Personnel:
Robert Cornford *(Marketing and Promotion Manager)*
Helen Moreno *(Digital Communications Lead: Policy, Practice & Research)*
Claire Harvey *(Communications Manager: Content Creation)*
Sarah Totterdell *(Policy and Practice Team Leader)*

Academic & Scholarly; Agriculture; Economics; Environment & Development Studies; Gender Studies; Politics & World Affairs

New Titles: 60 (2012) , 60 (2013)
No of Employees: 9

Imprints, Series & ISBNs:
Oxfam Online: 978-1-78077, 978-1-81814
Oxfam Publications: 978-0-85598

Distributor for:
UK: Practical Action Publishing

Overseas Representation:
Rest of World: Practical Action Publishing Rugby, UK

Book Trade Association Membership:
Independent Publishers Guild; Association of Learned & Professional Society Publishers

2443

OXFORD UNIVERSITY PRESS
Great Clarendon Street, Oxford OX2 6DP
Telephone: 01865 556767
Fax: 01865 556646
Email: web.enquiry@oup.com
Website: www.oup.com

Personnel:
Nigel Portwood *(Chief Executive)*
Kate Harris *(Managing Director: Educational Division)*
Peter Marshall *(Managing Director: ELT)*
Tim Barton *(Managing Director: Academic & Journals and President OUP USA)*
Jesus Lezcano *(Director General: OUP Spain)*
Adrian Mellor *(Managing Director, Asia Education)*

Academic & Scholarly; Architecture & Design; Biology & Zoology; Chemistry; Children's Books; Economics; Educational & Textbooks; Electronic (Professional & Academic); English as a Foreign Language; Fine Art & Art History; Geography & Geology; History & Antiquarian; Industry, Business & Management; Languages & Linguistics; Law; Literature & Criticism; Mathematics & Statistics; Medical (incl. Self-Help & Alternative Medicine); Military & War; Music; Philosophy; Physics; Politics & World Affairs; Psychology & Psychiatry; Reference Books, Directories &

Dictionaries; Religion & Theology; Scientific & Technical; Theatre, Drama & Dance

Book Trade Association Membership:
Publishers Association

2444

PACKARD PUBLISHING LTD
Forum House, Stirling Road, Chichester, West Sussex PO19 7DN
Telephone: 01243 537977
Fax: 01243 537977
Email: packardpublishing@googlemail.com
Website: www.packardpublishing.com

Personnel:
Michael Packard *(Managing Director, Sales, Rights & Permissions)*

Academic & Scholarly; Agriculture; Architecture & Design; Educational & Textbooks; Gardening; Geography & Geology; Languages & Linguistics; Scientific & Technical

New Titles: 2 (2012) , 5 (2013)
No of Employees: 1
Annual Turnover: £20,000

Imprints, Series & ISBNs:
Packard Publishing Ltd: 978-0-906527, 978-1-85341

Overseas Representation:
North America: Stipes Publishing LLC, Champaign, IL, USA

2445

PAGODA TREE PRESS
4 Malvern Buildings, Fairfield Park, Bath BA1 6JX
Telephone: 01225 463552
Fax: 01225 463552
Email: enquiries@pagodatreepress.com
Website: www.pagodatreepress.com

Personnel:
Hugh Rayner *(Managing Director)*
Jane Murphy *(Creative Director)*

Academic & Scholarly; Atlases & Maps; Geography & Geology; Guide Books; Photography; Politics & World Affairs; Reference Books, Directories & Dictionaries; Travel & Topography

New Titles: 2 (2012) , 2 (2013)

Imprints, Series & ISBNs:
Pagoda Tree Press: 978-0-9529782, 978-1-904289

Distributor for:
India: Library of Numismatic Studies
USA: Amur Maple Books
Zimbabwe: CBC Publishing

2446

PALAZZO EDITIONS LTD
2 Wood Street, Bath BA1 2JQ
Telephone: 01225 326444
Fax: 01225 330209
Email: info@palazzoeditions.com
Website: www.palazzoeditions.com

Send orders to:
Orca Book Services, Unit A3, Fleets Corner, Poole BH17 OHL
Telephone: 01202 665432
Email: orders@orcabookservices.co.uk

Personnel:
Colin Webb *(Publisher)*
Mrs Pamela Webb *(Director)*
Mrs Victoria Walters *(Managing Editor)*
Miss Chloe Pew Latter *(PR & Marketing Assistant)*

Architecture & Design; Children's Books; Cinema, Video, TV & Radio; Illustrated & Fine Editions; Music; Photography

2447

*PALGRAVE MACMILLAN
Houndmills, Basingstoke, Hants RG21 6XS
Telephone: 01256 329242
Fax: 01256 479476
Website: www.palgrave.com

Warehouse, Trade Enquiries & Orders:
Macmillan Distribution (MDL), Brunel Road, Houndmills, Basingstoke, Hants RG21 6XS
Telephone: 01256 329242 & 302692
Email: mdl@macmillan.co.uk

Personnel:
Annette Thomas *(Chief Executive Officer)*
D. J. G. Knight *(Managing Director)*
S. Burridge *(Publishing Director, Scholarly & Reference)*
M. Hewinson *(Publishing Director, College)*
D. Bull *(Publishing Director, Journals)*
L. Keelan *(Sales Director)*
V. Capstick *(Marketing Director)*
A. J. Jones *(Digital Development Director)*
R. A. Mathias *(Finance Director)*
A. Williams *(Operations Director)*

Academic & Scholarly; Accountancy & Taxation; Biology & Zoology; Chemistry; Computer Science; Economics; Educational & Textbooks; Electronic (Educational); Engineering; Environment & Development Studies; Gender Studies; Geography & Geology; History & Antiquarian; Industry, Business & Management; Languages & Linguistics; Law; Literature & Criticism; Mathematics & Statistics; Medical (incl. Self-Help & Alternative Medicine); Philosophy; Physics; Politics & World Affairs; Psychology & Psychiatry; Reference Books, Directories & Dictionaries; Religion & Theology; Scientific & Technical; Sociology & Anthropology; Theatre, Drama & Dance; Vocational Training & Careers

Imprints, Series & ISBNs:
Palgrave Macmillan: 978-0-333, 978-1-4039

Parent Company:
UK: Macmillan Ltd

Associated Companies:
UK: Macmillan Children's Books; Macmillan Education; Macmillan Publishers Ltd; Pan Macmillan Ltd; Stockton Press Ltd
USA: Stockton Press Inc

Distributor for:
UK: Bedford; W. H. Freeman; Sinauer Associates; Spectrum; University Science Books; Worth Publishers

Overseas Representation:
Africa (excluding areas listed): Africa Dept, Palgrave Macmillan Ltd, Basingstoke, Hants, UK
Australia: Palgrave Macmillan, South Yarra, Vic, Australia
Austria & Germany: Dan Timmermanns, Frankfurt-am-Main, Germany
Central & Eastern Europe: Jacek Lewinson, Warsaw, Poland
China: Macmillan Publishers China Ltd, Kowloon, China
Colombia: Grupo K-T-Dra Ltda, Santa Fe de Bogota, Colombia
Denmark, Norway, Finland, Sweden & Iceland: Ben Greig, Cambridge, UK
East Asia (including Hong Kong, Philippines, Thailand, Vietnam & Indonesia): Palgrave Macmillan, Hong Kong
Europe (excluding areas listed): Jo Waller, Palgrave Macmillan Ltd, Basingstoke, Hants, UK
Greece & Cyprus: Zitsa Seraphimidi, P. Faliro, Greece

India: Ajit De, Calcutta, India; Anand Vithalkar, Mumbai, India; Kalpana Shukla, Sunil Sharma, Jagat Bahadur, Palgrave Macmillan, New Delhi, India; V. Ravi, Palgrave Macmillan, Chennai, India
Iran: Sepehr Bookshop, Tehran, Iran
Italy & France: David Pickering, Mare Nostrum Publishing Consultants, Rome, Italy
Japan: Palgrave Macmillan Ltd, Basingstoke, Hants, UK
Korea: Macmillan Publishers, Jongro-Gu, Seoul, Republic of Korea
Latin America & Caribbean: Palgrave Macmillan Ltd, Basingstoke, Hants, UK
Malaysia: UBSD Distribution Sdn Bhd, Selangor, Malaysia
Middle East (all areas not listed): Jan Rylewicz, Middle Eastern Dept, Palgrave Macmillan Ltd, Basingstoke, Hants, UK
Netherlands, Belgium, Luxembourg, France & Switzerland: Daan Timmermans, Amsterdam, Netherlands
New Zealand: Macmillan Publishers New Zealand Ltd, Auckland, New Zealand

Book Trade Association Membership:
Publishers Association; BDPA; STM

2448

PAN MACMILLAN
20 New Wharf Road, London N1 9RR
Telephone: 020 7014 6000
Fax: 020 7014 6001
Email: books@macmillan.co.uk
Website: www.panmacmillan.com

Warehouse, Trade Enquiries & Orders:
Macmillan Distribution (MDL), Houndmills, Basingstoke, Hants RG21 6XS
Telephone: 01256 329242
Fax: 01256 840154
Email: mdl@macmillan.co.uk

Personnel:
Anthony Forbes Watson *(Managing Director)*
Lara Borlenghi *(Finance Director)*
Anna Bond *(UK Sales Director)*
Jonathan Atkins *(International Sales Director)*
Ian Mitchell *(Publishing Operations Director)*
Geoff Duffield *(Creative Director)*
Paul Baggaley *(Publisher – Picador)*
Maria Rejt *(Publisher – Mantle)*
Jeremy Trevathan *(Publisher, Fiction – Macmillan, Pan)*
Georgina Morley *(Editorial Director, Non-Fiction)*
Harriet Sanders *(Rights Director)*
Jon Butler *(Publisher, Non-Fiction)*
Sara Lloyd *(Digital & Communications Director)*

Audio Books; Biography & Autobiography; Children's Books; Cinema, Video, TV & Radio; Crime; Fiction; Gardening; Health & Beauty; History & Antiquarian; Literature & Criticism; Poetry; Science Fiction; Sports & Games; Travel & Topography

Imprints, Series & ISBNs:
Boxtree
Campbell: 978-0-333
Macmillan: 978-0-230
Macmillan Children's Books: 978-0-230
Mantle
Pan: 978-0-330
Picador: 978-0-330
Sidgwick & Jackson: 978-0-283
Tor: 978-0-230

Parent Company:
UK: Macmillan Ltd

Associated Companies:
UK: Boxtree Ltd; Macmillan Children's Books; Macmillan Education; Macmillan Publishers Ltd; Palgrave Macmillan; Pan Books Ltd; Sidgwick & Jackson Ltd

Overseas Representation:
All other areas – send orders to:
International Department, Pan
Macmillan, Basingstoke, UK
Australia: Pan Macmillan (Australia) Pty Ltd,
Sydney, NSW, Australia
Hong Kong: Publishers' Associates Ltd,
Hong Kong
India: Pan Macmillan, New Delhi, India
Japan: Shino Yasuda, Tokyo, Japan
New Zealand: Macmillan Publishers New
Zealand Ltd, Auckland, New Zealand
Republic of Ireland: David Adamson,
Dublin, Republic of Ireland
*South Africa, Botswana, Lesotho,
Swaziland, Namibia & Zimbabwe:* Pan
Macmillan SA Pty Ltd, Hyde Park, South
Africa
South East Asia: Pansing Distribution Sdn
Bhd, Singapore
West Indies & Caribbean: Macmillan
Education Ltd, Oxford, UK

Book Trade Association Membership:
Publishers Association

2449

PAPADAKIS PUBLISHER
[a member of New Architecture Group Ltd]
Kimber Studio, Winterbourne, Newbury,
Berkshire RG20 8AN
Telephone: 01635 248833
Email: info@papadakis.net
Website: www.papadakis.net

Personnel:
Alexandra Papadakis *(Publishing Director)*

*Architecture & Design; Fashion & Costume;
Fine Art & Art History; Illustrated & Fine
Editions; Natural History; Photography;
Scientific & Technical*

Imprints, Series & ISBNs:
Papadakis [new ISBN]: 978-1-906506
Papadakis [old ISBN]: 978-1-901092

Parent Company:
UK: New Architecture Group Ltd

Book Trade Association Membership:
Publishers Association

2450

PARRAGON BOOKS LTD
Chartist House, 15–17 Trim Street, Bath
BA1 1HA
Telephone: 01225 478888
Fax: 01225 443681
Email: uk_info@parragon.com
Website: www.parragon.com/uk

2451

PATRICKGEORGE
46 Vale Square, Ramsgate, Kent CT11 9DA
Telephone: 07773 096080
Email: ann@patrickgeorge.biz
Website: www.patrickgeorge.biz

Personnel:
Mrs Ann Scott *(Company director)*
Peter Scott *(Company director)*

New Titles: 11 (2012) , 2 (2013)
No of Employees: 2
Annual Turnover: £170,000

Imprints, Series & ISBNs:
PatrickGeorge: 978-0-9562558, 978-1-
908473

Book Trade Association Membership:
Publishers Association

2452

PAUPERS' PRESS
37 Quayside Close, Trent Bridge,
Nottingham NG2 3BP

Telephone: 0115 986 3334
Fax: 0115 986 3334
Email: books@pauperspress.com
Website: www.pauperspress.com

Personnel:
Colin Stanley *(Managing Editor)*

*Academic & Scholarly; Literature &
Criticism; Philosophy*

New Titles: 3 (2012) , 2 (2013)

Imprints, Series & ISBNs:
Paupers' Press: 978-0-946650, 978-0-
9568663

2453

PCCS BOOKS LTD
2 Cropper Row, Alton Road, Ross-on-Wye
HR9 5LA
Telephone: 01989 763900
Fax: 01989 763901
Email: contact@pccs-books.co.uk
Website: www.pccs-books.co.uk

Personnel:
Maggie Taylor-Sanders *(Director)*
Peter J. Sanders *(Director)*
Heather Allan *(Director)*

*Academic & Scholarly; Gender Studies;
Medical (incl. Self-Help & Alternative
Medicine); Psychology & Psychiatry;
Religion & Theology*

Imprints, Series & ISBNs:
Critical Examinations series
Critical Psychology Division (Series): 978-1-
898059, 978-1-906254
PCCS Books: 978-1-898059
Person-Centred Approach & Client-Centred
Therapy Essential Readers (Series): 978-1-
898059
Primers Series: 978-1-898059
Rogers' Therapeutic Conditions Series (Vols
1–4): 978-1-898059
Steps in Counselling Series: 978-1-898059
Straight Talking Introductions Series: 978-1-
906254

Overseas Representation:
Australasia: Footprint Books, Sydney,
Australia
USA and Canada: Consortium Academic,
USA

Book Trade Association Membership:
Independent Publishers Guild

2454

PENGUIN RANDOM HOUSE UK LTD
20 Vauxhall Bridge Road, London
SW1V 2SA
Telephone: 020 7840 8400
Website: www.penguinrandomhouse.com

Penguin & Dorling Kindersley:
80 Strand, London WC2R 0RL
Telephone: 020 7010 3000
Website: www.penguinrandomhouse.com

**Transworld Publishers & Random House
Children's Publishers:**
61–63 Uxbridge Road, London W5 5SA
Telephone: 020 8579 2652 & 020 8231
6800
Website: www.penguinrandomhouse.com

Personnel:
Gail Rebuck *(Chair)*
Tom Weldon *(Chief Executive Officer)*
Ian Hudson *(Deputy Chief Executive Officer)*
John Duhigg *(CEO, Dorling Kindersley)*

*Academic & Scholarly; Antiques &
Collecting; Archaeology; Architecture &
Design; Atlases & Maps; Audio Books;
Biography & Autobiography; Children's*

*Books; Cinema, Video, TV & Radio;
Cookery, Wines & Spirits; Crafts & Hobbies;
Crime; Do-It-Yourself; Economics;
Electronic (Entertainment); Fashion &
Costume; Fiction; Fine Art & Art History;
Gardening; Guide Books; Health & Beauty;
History & Antiquarian; Humour; Illustrated
& Fine Editions; Industry, Business &
Management; Literature & Criticism;
Medical (incl. Self-Help & Alternative
Medicine); Military & War; Music; Natural
History; Philosophy; Photography; Poetry;
Politics & World Affairs; Psychology &
Psychiatry; Reference Books, Directories &
Dictionaries; Religion & Theology; Science
Fiction; Sports & Games; Transport; Travel &
Topography*

Imprints, Series & ISBNs:
Penguin: 978-0-14

Parent Company:
USA: Penguin Random House

Associated Companies:
Australia: Penguin Random House
India: Penguin Random House
New Zealand: Penguin Random House
South Africa: Penguin Random House
Spain: Random House Mondadori
UK: Arrow; BBC Books; Black Lace; Bodley
Head; Jonathan Cape; Century; Chatto
& Windus; Dorling Kindersley; Ebury;
Everyman; Fodor; Hamish Hamilton;
Harvill Secker; William Heinemann;
Hutchinson; Michael Joseph; Ladybird
Books; Mainstream; Pimlico; Preface;
Random House Books; Rider; Rough
Guides; Time Out; Ventura Publishing;
Vermilion; Viking; Vintage; Virgin Books;
Frederick Warne; Yellow Jersey

Book Trade Association Membership:
Publishers Association

2455

PERCY PUBLISHING
Field House, 93 Theydon Park Road,
Theydon Bois, Essex CM16 7LS
Telephone: 020 7821 6430
Email: enquiries@percy-publishing.com
Website: http://www.percy-
publishing.com

Personnel:
Clifford Marker *(Director)*

*Children's Books; Crime; Fiction; Humour;
Military & War; Science Fiction*

New Titles: 1 (2012) , 3 (2013)
No of Employees: 4
Annual Turnover: £250,000

Imprints, Series & ISBNs:
Percy Publishing: 978-0-9571568

2456

PETAL PEOPLE PUBLISHING LTD
151 Salwarpe Road, Bromsgrove, Worcs
B60 3HS
Telephone: 01527 579377
Email: thepetalpeople@yahoo.co.uk
Website: www.thepetalpeople.co.uk

Personnel:
Ms Pauline Earles *(Managing Director)*

Book Trade Association Membership:
Publishers Association

2457

PHAIDON PRESS LTD
18 Regent's Wharf, All Saints Street,
London N1 9PA
Telephone: 020 7843 1000
Fax: 020 7843 1010
Website: www.phaidon.com

Orders:
Phaidon Customer Services
Telephone: 020 7843 1234
Fax: 020 7843 1111
Email: sales@phaidon.com
Website: www.phaidon.com

Warehouse:
Grove Lane, Marston Trading Estate, Frome,
Somerset BA11 4AT
Telephone: 01373 474710
Fax: 01373 474711
Website: www.phaidon.com

Personnel:
David Davies *(CEO)*
Andrew Price *(Chairman)*
Amanda Renshaw *(Editorial Director)*
Emilia Terragni *(Editorial Director)*
Elaine Ward *(Production Director)*
Peter Goodwin *(Financial Director)*

*Academic & Scholarly; Architecture &
Design; Children's Books; Cinema, Video,
TV & Radio; Cookery, Wines & Spirits;
Fashion & Costume; Fine Art & Art History;
Illustrated & Fine Editions; Music;
Photography*

Imprints, Series & ISBNs:
Phaidon Press Ltd: 978-0-7148

Associated Companies:
France: Phaidon Sarl
Germany: Phaidon Verlag
Japan: Phaidon KK
USA: Phaidon Press Inc

Overseas Representation:
Australia: United Book Distributors,
Scoresby, Vic, Australia
France: Phaidon SARL, Paris, France
Germany: Phaidon Verlag GmbH, Berlin,
Germany
Italy: Phaidon Srl, Milan, Italy
Other Territories: Phaidon Press Ltd,
London, UK
South Africa: Book Promotions Pty Ltd,
Cape Town, South Africa
Spain: Phaidon Press, Barcelona, Spain
USA: Phaidon Press Inc, New York, NY, USA

Book Trade Association Membership:
Independent Publishers Guild

2458

PHILIP'S
Endeavour House,
189 Shaftesbury Avenue, London
WC2H 8JY
Telephone: 020 7632 5400
Email: info@octopusbooks.co.uk
Website: www.octopusbooks.co.uk

Distribution:
Littlehampton Book Services,
Faraday Close, Durrington, West Sussex
BN13 3RP
Telephone: 01903 828500
Fax: 01903 828625
Email: orders@lbsltd.co.uk
Website: www.lbsltd.co.uk

Personnel:
Stephen Mesquita *(Publisher)*

*Atlases & Maps; Educational & Textbooks;
Natural History; Reference Books,
Directories & Dictionaries*

Imprints, Series & ISBNs:
Philip's: 978-1-84907

Parent Company:
UK: Octopus Publishing Group

Overseas Representation:
See: Octopus Publishing Group, London, UK

Book Trade Association Membership:
International Map Traders Association

2459

PHOENIX YARD BOOKS
65 King's Cross Road WC1X 9LW
Telephone: 020 7239 4968
Email: hello@phoenixyardbooks.com
Website: www.phoenixyardbooks.com

Personnel:
Ms Emma Langley *(Publisher)*

Children's Books

New Titles: 12 (2012) , 10 (2013)

Overseas Representation:
Australia: Peribo, Australia
New Zealand: South Pacific Books, New Zealand
North America: Trafalgar Square Publishing, USA
UK and Ireland: Bounce Sales and Marketing, UK

Book Trade Association Membership:
Independent Publishers Guild

2460

PIATKUS BOOKS
[a division of Little, Brown Book Group]
Little, Brown Book Group,
100 Victoria Embankment, London
EC4Y 0DY
Telephone: 020 7911 8030
Fax: 020 7911 8100
Website: www.littlebrown.co.uk & www.piatkus.co.uk

Distribution:
Littlehampton Book Services,
Faraday Close, Durrington, Worthing,
West Sussex BN13 3RB
Telephone: 01903 828511
Fax: 01903 828801
Email: orders@lbsltd.co.uk
Website: www.lbsltd.co.uk

Personnel:
Ursula Mackenzie *(Chief Executive Officer)*
Robert Manser *(UK Sales, Marketing & Publicity Director)*
Nick Ross *(Production Director)*
Emma Beswetherick *(Editorial Director)*
Emily-Jane Taylor *(Finance Director)*
Diane Spivey *(Rights Director)*

Biography & Autobiography; Cookery, Wines & Spirits; Crime; Fiction; Gender Studies; Health & Beauty; History & Antiquarian; Humour; Industry, Business & Management; Magic & the Occult; Medical (incl. Self-Help & Alternative Medicine); Military & War; Music; Psychology & Psychiatry; Sociology & Anthropology

Imprints, Series & ISBNs:
Piatkus Books: 978-0-349, 978-0-7499

Parent Company:
France: Hachette Livre

Overseas Representation:
Australia: Hachette Livre Australia, Sydney, NSW, Australia
Canada: Hachette, Montreal, Canada
New Zealand: Hachette Livre New Zealand, Auckland, New Zealand
Singapore & Malaysia: Pansing Distribution Sdn Bhd, Singapore
South Africa: Penguin Books SA (Pty) Ltd, Denver, South Africa

Book Trade Association Membership:
Booksellers Association

2461

PICCADILLY PRESS
Deepdene Lodge RH5 4AT
Telephone: 01306 876 361
Email: books@piccadillypress.co.uk

Website: www.piccadillypress.co.uk

Warehouse & Distribution:
Grantham Book Services, Trent Road,
Grantham, Lincs NG31 7XQ
Telephone: 01476 541080
Fax: 01476 541061

Personnel:
Mike McGrath *(Managing Director)*
Brenda Gardner *(Publisher and Commissioning Editor)*
Shane Hegarty *(Publishing Manager)*
Melissa Hyder *(Senior Editor)*
Ruth Williams *(Editor)*
Margot Edwards *(Foreign Rights Consultant)*
David Inman *(Sales Manager)*
Laura Smyth *(Publicity Manager)*
Emma O' Donovan *(Marketing Manager)*

Children's Books

Imprints, Series & ISBNs:
Piccadilly Press: 978-1-84812, 978-1-85340

Overseas Representation:
All other countries: Daniel Galagher, UK
Australia: Helen Binns, UK

2462

PICKERING & CHATTO (PUBLISHERS) LTD
21 Bloomsbury Way, London WC1A 2TH
Telephone: 020 7405 1005
Fax: 020 7405 6216
Email: info@pickeringchatto.co.uk
Website: www.pickeringchatto.com

Distribution & Orders:
Turpin Distribution Ltd,
Stratton Business Park, Pegasus Drive,
Biggleswade, Beds SG18 8QT
Telephone: 01767 604800
Fax: 01767 601640
Website: www.turpin-distribution.com

Personnel:
James Powell *(Director)*
Lady Rees-Mogg *(Chairman)*
Mark Pollard *(Editorial, Rights & Production)*
Stephen Warren *(Finance)*

Academic & Scholarly; Economics; History & Antiquarian; Literature & Criticism; Philosophy; Religion & Theology; Scientific & Technical

Imprints, Series & ISBNs:
Pickering & Chatto (Publishers) Ltd: 978-1-78144, 978-1-84893, 978-1-85196

Overseas Representation:
China: China Publisher Services, Beijing, China
India and Pakistan: Sara Books, India
Japan: Japan Book Associates, Kyoto, Japan
Korea: Wise Book Solutions, Seoul, Republic of Korea
Spain & Portugal: Iberian Book Services, Madrid, Spain
Taiwan: Unifacmanu Trading Co Ltd, Taipei, Taiwan
USA: Ashgate Publishing Co, Burlington, VT, USA

Book Trade Association Membership:
Independent Publishers Guild

2463

THE PLAYWRIGHTS PUBLISHING CO
70 Nottingham Road, Burton Joyce, Notts
NG14 5AL
Email:
playwrightspublishingco@yahoo.com
Website: www.playwrightspublishing.com

Personnel:
Tony Breeze *(Partner)*
Liz Breeze *(Partner)*

Theatre, Drama & Dance

New Titles: 10 (2012) , 10 (2013)
No of Employees: 2

Imprints, Series & ISBNs:
Playwrights Publishing Co: 978-1-873130
Ventus Books: 978-1-872758, 978-1-872758

Associated Companies:
UK: Ventus Books

Distributor for:
UK: The Playwrights Publishing Co

2464

POLICY PRESS
University of Bristol, 6th Floor,
Howard House, Queen's Road, Bristol
BS8 1SD
Telephone: 0117 331 5020
Fax: 0117 331 4093
Email: tpp-info@bris.ac.uk
Website: www.policypress.co.uk

Distribution:
Marston Book Services, PO Box 269,
Abingdon, Oxon OX14 4YN
Telephone: 01235 465500
Fax: 01235 465556
Email: direct.orders@marston.co.uk
Website: www.marston.co.uk/

UK Representation:
Compass Academic Ltd,
13 Progress Business Centre,
Whittle Parkway, Slough SL1 6DQ
Telephone: 01628 559500
Fax: 01628 663876
Email: ca@compass-academic.co.uk
Website: www.academic.compass-booksales.co.uk

Personnel:
Alison Shaw *(Director)*
Julia Mortimer *(Assistant Director)*

Academic & Scholarly; Educational & Textbooks; Gender Studies; Politics & World Affairs; Sociology & Anthropology

Imprints, Series & ISBNs:
The Policy Press: 978-1-84742, 978-1-86134

Parent Company:
UK: University of Bristol

Overseas Representation:
Australia, New Zealand & Papua New Guinea: DA Information Services Pty Ltd, Mitcham, Vic, Australia
Europe (excluding UK): Durnell Marketing Ltd, Tunbridge Wells, UK
India, Sri Lanka, Nepal, Bangladesh & Bhutan: Surit Mitra, Maya Publishers Pvt Ltd, New Delhi, India
Japan: Kinokuniya Co Ltd, Tokyo, Japan; Maruzen Co Ltd, Tokyo, Japan
Malaysia & Brunei: UBSD Distribution Sdn Bhd, Selangor, Malaysia
Middle East & North Africa: Dar Kreidieh, Beirut, Lebanon
Pakistan: Tahir M. Lodhi, Lahore, Pakistan
South Africa: Blue Weaver Marketing, Tokai, South Africa
Taiwan: Unifacmanu Trading Co Ltd, Taipei, Taiwan
Thailand, Taiwan, Hong Kong, Korea, China, Singapore, Malaysia, Philippines & Vietnam: Tony Poh Leong Wah, Singapore
USA & Canada: University of Chicago Press, Chicago IL, USA

Book Trade Association Membership:
Independent Publishers Guild

2465

POLPERRO HERITAGE PRESS
Clifton-upon-Teme, Worcestershire
WR6 6EN
Telephone: 01886 812304
Email: polperro.press@virgin.net
Website: www.polperropress.co.uk

Personnel:
Jerry Johns *(Managing Editor)*

Biography & Autobiography; Cinema, Video, TV & Radio; History & Antiquarian; Military & War; Natural History; Nautical; Photography

New Titles: 3 (2012) , 1 (2013)
No of Employees: 2
Annual Turnover: £35,000

Imprints, Series & ISBNs:
The Polperro Heritage Press

Book Trade Association Membership:
Independent Publishers Guild

2466

PORTER HOUSE OF PUBLISHING LTD
Dexter & Sharpe, Rollestone House,
Bridge Street, Horncastle, Lincs LN9 5HZ
Telephone: 0750 410 2225
Website:
www.porterhouseofpublishing.co.uk

Personnel:
Mrs Sheila Clarke *(Director)*

Audio Books; Children's Books; Music; Poetry; Religion & Theology

New Titles: 2 (2013)
No of Employees: 1

Book Trade Association Membership:
Publishers Association

2467

PP PUBLISHING
Suite 74, 17 Holywell Hill, St Albans, Herts
AL1 1DT
Telephone: 01727 833866
Fax: 0845 456 6385
Email: sales@xplpublishing.com
Website: www.peerpractice.co.uk

Personnel:
Andrew Griffin *(Managing Director)*

Academic & Scholarly; Accountancy & Taxation; Industry, Business & Management; Law; Medical (incl. Self-Help & Alternative Medicine)

Imprints, Series & ISBNs:
PP Publishing: 978-1-85811

Parent Company:
UK: Richard Griffin (1820) Ltd

Overseas Representation:
Hong Kong: Bloomsbury Books Ltd, Hong Kong

Book Trade Association Membership:
Independent Publishers Guild

2468

PRACTICAL PRE-SCHOOL BOOKS
[a division of MA Education Ltd]
St Jude's Church, Dulwich Road, Herne Hill,
London SE24 0PB
Telephone: 020 7738 5454
Fax: 020 7733 2325
Email:
orders@practicalpreschoolbooks.com
Website:
www.practicalpreschoolbooks.com

Distributors:
Mark Allen Group, Jesses Farm, Snowhill,
Dinton, Wilts SP3 5HN
Telephone: 01722 716935
Fax: 01722 716812
Email:
orders@practicalpreschoolbooks.com
Website:
www.practicalpreschoolbooks.com

Personnel:
Rebecca Linssen *(Group Editorial Director)*
Matt Govett *(Managing Director)*
Angela Shaw *(Associate Publisher)*
Tracey Mills *(Customer Services Manager)*

*Educational & Textbooks; Vocational
Training & Careers*

Imprints, Series & ISBNs:
Practical Pre-School Books: 978-1-902438,
978-1-904575, 978-1-907241, 978-1-
909101, 978-1-909280

Parent Company:
UK: MA Education Ltd

Associated Companies:
UK: Mark Allen Group

Overseas Representation:
Hong Kong, Macau: Transglobal Publishers
Service Ltd, Tsuen Wan, NT, Hong Kong
India: Overleaf, New Delhi, India
Malaysia: Extrazeal (M) Sdn Bhd, Petaling
Jaya Selangor, Malaysia
Singapore, Brunei, Thailand: The Learning
Needs Centre, Singapore
*South Africa, Namibia, Lesotha, Botswana,
Zimbabwe:* Everybody's Books, South
Africa
*United Arab Emirates, Saudi Arabia, Oman,
Qatar, Kuwait, Bahrain, Egypt and
Lebanon:* Arif Books Distribution LLC,
Dubai, UAE, United Arab Emirates

Book Trade Association Membership:
British Educational Suppliers Association
(BESA)

2469 ■■■■■

PRESTEL PUBLISHING LTD
14-17 Wells Street W1T 3PD
Telephone: 020 7323 5004
Fax: 020 7636 8004
Email: sales@prestel-uk.co.uk
Website: www.prestel.com

Warehouse, Trade Enquiries & Orders:
Granthem Book Services (GBS) ,
Trent Road, Grantham, Lincolnshire
NG31 7ZQ
Telephone: 01476 541052
Fax: 01476 541069
Email: orders@gbs.tbs-ltd.co.uk
Website: http://
www.granthambookservices.co.uk

Personnel:
Andrew Hansen *(Managing Director)*
Ali Gitlow *(Commissioning Editor (London))*
tbc tbc *(Marketing & Publicity Executive)*
Oliver Barter *(Sales Manager)*
Emma Cook *(Office and Sales Executive)*

*Archaeology; Architecture & Design;
Children's Books; Fashion & Costume; Fine
Art & Art History; Photography; Travel &
Topography*

Imprints, Series & ISBNs:
13 Children Should Know: 978-3-7913
50 You Should Know: 978-3-7913
Adventures in Art Series: 978-3-7913
The Colouring Book Series

Parent Company:
Germany: Verlagsgruppe Random House
Bertelsmann

Associated Companies:
USA: Prestel Publishing

Distributor for:
Australia: Think
Canada: Douglas & McIntyre Publishers
Spain: Poligrafa
Switzerland: Lars Müller Publishers
USA: Periscope Publishing Ltd

Overseas Representation:
Africa (excluding South Africa): Tony
Moggach, InterMedia Americana (IMA)
Ltd, London, UK
*Asia (including China, Hong Kong, Korea,
Philippines & Taiwan):* Ed Summerson,
Asia Publishers Services Ltd, Hong Kong
Australia: Peribo Pty Ltd, Mount Kuring-Gai,
NSW, Australia
Canada: Canadian Manda Group, Toronto,
Ont, Canada
Eastern Europe exc Russia: Ewa
Ledochowicz, Germany
France: Interart SARL, Paris, France
India: Tapas Dutta, India
Italy & Greece: Sandro Salucci, Italy
Japan: Andrew Hansen, Prestel, London, UK
*Malta, Cyprus, Turkey, Middle East & North
Africa:* Peter Ward Book Exports, London,
UK
Netherlands : Jan Smit Boeken, The,
Netherlands
Scandinavia: Elisabeth Harder-Kreimann,
Hamburg, Germany
South & Central America: David Williams,
InterMedia Americana (IMA) Ltd,
London, UK
South Africa: Zytek Publishing, Germiston,
South Africa
South East Asia: Peter Couzens, Sales East,
Bangkok, Thailand
Spain & Portugal: Christopher Humphrys,
UK
Switzerland: Buchzentrum AG, Hägendorf,
Switzerland
USA: Prestel Publishing, New York, NY, USA

2470 ■■■■■

PRINCETON UNIVERSITY PRESS
6 Oxford Street, Woodstock, Oxon
OX20 1TR
Telephone: 01993 814500
Fax: 01993 814504
Email: admin@pupress.co.uk
Website: press.princeton.edu

Personnel:
Al Bertrand *(Publishing Director, Europe)*
Caroline Priday *(European Director of
Publicity)*
Benjamin Tate *(Editor and Director of
Foreign Rights)*
Kimberley Williams *(International Rights
Manager)*

*Academic & Scholarly; Biology & Zoology;
Economics; Educational & Textbooks;
Electronic (Professional & Academic);
Environment & Development Studies;
History & Antiquarian; Industry, Business &
Management; Law; Mathematics &
Statistics; Natural History; Philosophy;
Politics & World Affairs; Reference Books,
Directories & Dictionaries; Scientific &
Technical; Sociology & Anthropology*

Imprints, Series & ISBNs:
Princeton University Press: 978-0-691

Parent Company:
USA: Princeton University Press

Overseas Representation:
All other countries: CPFS, Ewing, NJ, USA
EMEA: University Press Group, UK

Book Trade Association Membership:
Independent Publishers Guild

2471 ■■■■■

**THE PROFESSIONAL AND HIGHER
PARTNERSHIP LTD**
4 The Links, Cambridge Road, Newmarket,
Suffolk CB8 0TG
Telephone: 01638 663456
Email:
partners@professionalandhigher.com
Website: http://pandhp.com

Personnel:
Anthony Haynes *(Creative Director)*
Ms Karen Haynes *(Managing Director)*

*Academic & Scholarly; Electronic
(Professional & Academic); Engineering;
Scientific & Technical*

New Titles: 4 (2012) , 6 (2013)

Imprints, Series & ISBNs:
Creative Writing Studies: 978-1-907076
The Professional and Higher Partnership

2472 ■■■■■

PROFILE BOOKS
3A Exmouth House, Pine Street, London
EC1R 0JH
Telephone: 020 7841 6300
Fax: 020 7841 3969
Email: info@profilebooks.com
Website: www.profilebooks.com

Personnel:
Andrew Franklin *(Managing Director)*
Stephen Brough *(Commercial Director)*
Diana Broccardo *(Sales and Marketing
Director)*
Hannah Ross *(Publicity Director)*
Claire Beaumont *(Sales Director)*
Hannah Westland *(Publisher, Serpent's Tail)*
Daniel Crewe *(Publisher)*
Mark Ellingham *(Publisher)*
Rebecca Gray *(Publicity Director, Serpent's
Tail)*
Penny Daniel *(Rights Director)*
Michael Bhaskar *(Digital Publishing Director)*
Geoff Mulligan *(Publisher, The Clerkenwell
Press)*
Niamh Murray *(Marketing Director)*

*Biography & Autobiography; Crime;
Economics; Fiction; History & Antiquarian;
Industry, Business & Management; Politics
& World Affairs*

New Titles: 141 (2012) , 139 (2013)
No of Employees: 35

Imprints, Series & ISBNs:
The Clerkenwell Press: 978-184-668
The Economist Books: 978-178-125
Profile Books: 978-178-125
Serpent's Tail: 978-184-668
Tindal Street Press: 978-190-699

Overseas Representation:
Australia & New Zealand: Allen & Unwin Pty
Ltd, Sydney, NSW, Australia
*Europe, Hong Kong, China, Japan, Korea,
Taiwan, Middle East, North Africa &
Turkey:* Faber & Faber, London, UK
India, Pakistan & Sri Lanka: Hachette, India
Philippines: Sarah Ward, Profile Books, UK
Singapore, Malaysia, Thailand & Vietnam:
APD Singapore Pte Ltd, Singapore
South Africa: Book Promotions Pty Ltd,
Cape Town, South Africa
USA & Canada: Consortium Book Sales &
Distribution, Minneapolis, MN, USA

Book Trade Association Membership:
Publishers Association; Independent
Publishers Guild

2473 ■■■■■

PROQUEST
The Quorum, Barnwell Road, Cambridge
CB5 8SW

Telephone: 01223 215512
Fax: 01223 215513
Email: marketing@proquest.co.uk
Website: www.proquest.com

Personnel:
S. Airley *(Head of Sales UKI)*
Katy Ward *(Head of Field Marketing EMEA)*

*Academic & Scholarly; Accountancy &
Taxation; Agriculture; Architecture &
Design; Bibliography & Library Science;
Biology & Zoology; Cinema, Video, TV &
Radio; Computer Science; Economics;
Electronic (Educational); Electronic
(Professional & Academic); Engineering;
Fashion & Costume; Fine Art & Art History;
History & Antiquarian; Industry, Business &
Management; Literature & Criticism;
Mathematics & Statistics; Medical (incl. Self-
Help & Alternative Medicine); Music;
Natural History; Physics; Poetry; Politics &
World Affairs; Psychology & Psychiatry;
Reference Books, Directories &
Dictionaries; Religion & Theology; Scientific
& Technical; Sociology & Anthropology;
Theatre, Drama & Dance*

Imprints, Series & ISBNs:
ProQuest: 978-0-85964

Parent Company:
USA: ProQuest

Overseas Representation:
Australia & New Zealand: ProQuest,
Melbourne, Vic, Australia
Canada: ProQuest, Toronto, Ont, Canada
China: ProQuest, Beijing, China
Europe: ProQuest, Cambridge, UK
Germany: ProQuest, Berlin, Germany
Hong Kong, Macau & Taiwan: ProQuest,
Wanchai, Hong Kong
Japan: ProQuest, Kanagawa, Japan
Korea: ProQuest, Seoul, Republic of Korea
Latin America: ProQuest, Rio de Janeiro,
Brazil
North America: ProQuest, Ann Arbor, MI,
USA
South East Asia & Far East: ProQuest,
Petaling Jaya, Malaysia
Spain: ProQuest España, Madrid, Spain
United Arab Emirates: ProQuest, Dubai
Media City, UAE, United Arab Emirates

2474 ■■■■■

PROSPECT BOOKS
Allaleigh House, Blackawton, Totnes, Devon
TQ9 7DL
Telephone: 01803 712269
Fax: 01803 712311
Email: tom.jaine@prospectbooks.co.uk
Website: www.prospectbooks.co.uk

Distribution:
Central Books, 99 Wallis Road, London
E9 5LN
Telephone: 020 8986 4854

Personnel:
Tom Jaine *(Owner)*

Cookery, Wines & Spirits

2475 ■■■■■

PROSPERA PUBLISHING
Longreach, 36 Ashley Road, Berkhamsted,
Herts HP4 3BL
Telephone: 020 7935 7750
Fax: 020 7935 7793
Email: suzybrownlee@prospera.co.uk
Website: www.prosperapublishing.co.uk

*Children's Books; Fiction; Travel &
Topography*

Associated Companies:
UK: Impera Books Ltd

2476

PUSHKIN PRESS
71–75 Shelton Street, London WC2H 9JQ
Telephone: 020 7470 8830
Email: books@pushkinpress.com
Website: www.pushkinpress.com

Personnel:
Adam Freudenheim *(Publisher)*
Stephanie Seegmuller *(Associate Publisher)*

Children's Books; Crime; Fiction; History & Antiquarian; Literature & Criticism

New Titles: 15 (2012) , 50 (2013)
No of Employees: 5
Annual Turnover: £240,000

Imprints, Series & ISBNs:
ONE: 978-0-9575488
Pushkin Children's Books: 978-1-782690, 978-1-782691, 978-1-782692, 978-1-782693, 978-1-782694, 978-1-782695, 978-1-782696, 978-1-782697, 978-1-782698, 978-1-782699
Pushkin Press: 978-1-782270, 978-1-782271, 978-1-782272, 978-1-782273, 978-1-782274, 978-1-782275, 978-1-782276, 978-1-782277, 978-1-782278, 978-1-782279, 978-1-901285, 978-1-906548, 978-1-908968

Overseas Representation:
Eastern Europe: Adriana Juncu, UK
Far East (Adult): The White Partnership, UK
Middle East & Africa: Richard Ward, UK
Southern Europe: Penny Padovani, UK
UK & Commonwealth (Adult): Faber Factory Plus, UK
USA & Canada: Consortium Book Sales and Distribution, USA
Western Europe: Michael Gheogegan, UK
Worldwide except Europe and North America (Children): Bounce Sales & Marketing, UK

Book Trade Association Membership:
Publishers Association; Independent Publishers Guild

2477

QUADRILLE PUBLISHING LTD
5th Floor, Alhambra House,
27–31 Charing Cross Road, London
WC2H 0LS
Telephone: 020 7839 7117
Fax: 020 7839 7118
Email: enquiries@quadrille.co.uk
Website: www.quadrille.co.uk

Personnel:
Alison Cathie *(Managing Director)*
Jane O'Shea *(Publishing Director)*
Vincent Smith *(Deputy Managing Director)*
Helen Lewis *(Creative Director)*
Melanie Gray *(Sales Director)*
Margaux Durigon *(International Sales Director)*
Ed Griffiths *(Head of Publicity)*

Architecture & Design; Biography & Autobiography; Cookery, Wines & Spirits; Crafts & Hobbies; Do-It-Yourself; Fashion & Costume; Gardening; Health & Beauty; Humour; Magic & the Occult; Medical (incl. Self-Help & Alternative Medicine); Photography; Travel & Topography

Imprints, Series & ISBNs:
Quadrille Publishing Ltd: 978-1-84400, 978-1-84949, 978-1-899988, 978-1-902757, 978-1-903845

Book Trade Association Membership:
Booksellers Association

2478

QUARTET BOOKS
27 Goodge Street, London W1T 2LD

Telephone: 020 7636 3992
Fax: 020 7637 1866
Email: info@quartetbooks.co.uk
Website: www.quartetbooks.co.uk

Warehouse:
NBN International, Estover Road, Plymouth
PL6 7PZ
Telephone: 01752 202300
Fax: 01752 202330
Website: www.nbninternational.com

Personnel:
Gavin Bower *(Editorial Director)*
Grace Pilkington *(Publicity)*
Bea Watson *(Rights)*

Biography & Autobiography; Fashion & Costume; Fiction; Fine Art & Art History; History & Antiquarian; Illustrated & Fine Editions; Literature & Criticism; Music; Politics & World Affairs; Theatre, Drama & Dance

Imprints, Series & ISBNs:
Robin Clark: 978-0-86072

Parent Company:
UK: Namara Group

Associated Companies:
UK: Robin Clark; The Women's Press

Overseas Representation:
France, Belgium, Germany, Austria, Switzerland, Italy & Greece: Ted Dougherty, London, UK
India, Denmark, Finland, Norway & Sweden: Quartet Books Ltd, London, UK
USA: Interlink Publishing Group Inc, Northampton, MA, USA

2479

THE QUARTO GROUP
230 City Road, London EC1V 2TT
Telephone: 020 7700 6200
Email: info@quarto.com
Website: www.quarto.com

Book Trade Association Membership:
Publishers Association

2480

QUILLER PUBLISHING LTD
Wykey House, Wykey, Shrewsbury SY4 1JA
Telephone: 01939 261616
Fax: 01939 261606
Email: admin@quillerbooks.com
Website: www.countrybooksdirect.com

Warehouse, Distribution, Orders & Sales Enquiries:
Grantham Book Services, Trent Road, Grantham, Lincolnshire NG31 7XQ
Telephone: 01476 541080
Fax: 01476 541061
Email: orders@gbs.tbs-ltd.co.uk

Personnel:
Andrew Johnston *(Managing Director)*
John Beaton *(Editorial Director)*
Jonathan Heath *(Sales Manager)*

Animal Care & Breeding; Antiques & Collecting; Biography & Autobiography; Cookery, Wines & Spirits; Crafts & Hobbies; Fine Art & Art History; Gardening; Guide Books; Humour; Illustrated & Fine Editions; Military & War; Natural History; Nautical; Sports & Games; Veterinary Science

Imprints, Series & ISBNs:
Excellent Press: 978-1-900318
Kenilworth Press: 978-0-901366, 978-1-872082, 978-1-872119, 978-1-905693
Quiller: 978-0-907621, 978-1-84689, 978-1-904057
The Sportsman's Press: 978-0-948253
Swan Hill Press: 978-1-84037, 978-1-85310

Distributor for:
South Africa: Rowland Ward
UK: Greenwood Guides; JJG Publishing; The Pony Club
USA: Safari Press; Stackpole Books; Stonefly Press; Trafalgar Square

Overseas Representation:
Australia: DLS Distribution Services (Equestrian), DLS Australia Pty Ltd, Braeside, Vic, Australia; Peribo Pty Ltd, Mount Kuring-Gai, NSW, Australia
Canada: Can-Pro Horse Equipment Ltd, Hornby, Ont, Canada
Europe: Jonathan Heath, Quiller Publishing Ltd, Shrewsbury, UK
Ireland: Darragh Equestrian Solutions, Shankill, Co Dublin, Republic of Ireland
South Africa: Trinity Books, Randburg, South Africa
USA: Trafalgar Square Books, North Pomfret, VT, USA
USA & Canada: Stackpole Books Inc, Mechanicsburg, PA, USA

Book Trade Association Membership:
Independent Publishers Guild

2481

THE RADCLIFFE PRESS
6 Salem Road, London W2 4BU
Telephone: 020 7243 1225
Fax: 020 7243 1226

Distributor:
Macmillan Distribution Ltd, Brunel Road, Houndmills, Basingstoke, Hants RG21 6XS

Personnel:
Dr Lester Crook *(Publisher)*
Liz Stuckey *(Finance Manager)*
Stuart Weir *(Production Director)*
Alice Orton *(Rights Manager)*
Paul Davighi *(Sales & Marketing Director)*
Antonia Leslie *(Publicity Officer)*

Academic & Scholarly; Biography & Autobiography; History & Antiquarian; Military & War; Politics & World Affairs; Travel & Topography

Imprints, Series & ISBNs:
The Radcliffe Press: 978-1-78076, 978-1-84511, 978-1-84885, 978-1-85043, 978-1-86064

Overseas Representation:
USA: Palgrave Macmillan, New York, NY, USA

2482

RANSOM PUBLISHING LTD
Radley House, 8 St Cross Road, Winchester, Hampshire SO23 9HX
Telephone: 01962 862307
Fax: 05601 148881
Email: ransom@ransom.co.uk
Website: www.ransom.co.uk

Personnel:
Jenny Ertle *(Managing Director/Marketing)*
Stephen Rickard *(Creative Director)*

Audio Books; Children's Books; Educational & Textbooks

Imprints, Series & ISBNs:
321 Go!: 978-1-78127, 978-1-84167, 978-1-900127
Boffin Boy: 978-1-84167, 978-1-900127
Cold Fusion
Cutting Edge: 978-1-84167, 978-1-900127
Dark Man: 978-1-84167, 978-1-900127
GirlfriendZ: 978-1-78127
Goal!: 978-1-84167, 978-1-900127
PIG: 978-1-84167
Professional Development in Literacy: 978-1-84167
Results in English: 978-1-78127
Shades 2.0: 978-1-87127

Siti's Sisters: 978-1-84167, 978-1-900127
Spook Squad: 978-1-84167
Starchasers: 978-1-84167, 978-1-900127
Starstruck: 978-1-84167
Steve Sharp: 978-1-84167
Streetwise: 978-1-84167
Thunderbolts
Trailblazers: 978-1-84167, 978-1-900127
Vampire Dawn: 978-1-84167
Zone 13: 978-1-84167, 978-1-900127

Book Trade Association Membership:
Independent Publishers Guild

2483

RAVEN'S QUILL LTD
63 High Street, Billingshurst, West Sussex
RH14 9QP
Telephone: 01403 782489
Email: info@ravensquill.com
Website: www.ravensquill.com

Personnel:
Mrs Emily Henderson *(Director)*
Alan Gilliland *(Director)*

Children's Books; Fiction

New Titles: 1 (2012)

Imprints, Series & ISBNs:
Raven's Quill Ltd: 978-0-9555486
Shabby Tattler Press: 978-0-9555486

Overseas Representation:
Far East: Big Apple Tuttle-Mori, Shanghai, China
Korea: Amo Agency, Seoul, Republic of Korea
Spain, Portugal & Latin America: Ilustrata, Barcelona, Spain

Book Trade Association Membership:
Publishers Association; Independent Publishers Guild

2484

RAVETTE PUBLISHING LTD
PO Box 876, Horsham, West Sussex
RH12 9GH
Telephone: 01403 711443
Fax: 01403 711554
Email: ravettepub@aol.com
Website: www.ravettepublishing.tel

Warehouse, Invoicing & Accounts:
Orca Book Services, 160 Milton Park, Abingdon, Oxon OX14 4SD
Telephone: 01202 665432
Fax: 01235 465555
Email: tradeorders@orcabookservices.co.uk
Website: www.orcabookservices.co.uk

Personnel:
Mrs M. Lamb *(Managing Director)*
Miss I. Parris *(Company Secretary)*

Children's Books; Humour

Imprints, Series & ISBNs:
Bamforth
Born to Shop: 978-1-84161
Fizzy Moon
Garfield: 978-1-84161
Hackman: 978-1-84161
Juicy Lucy: 978-1-84161
The Odd Squad: 978-1-84161, 978-1-85304
Silvey Jex Humour
Their Finest Hour: 978-1-84161
Yoga Pets: 978-1-84161

Overseas Representation:
Australia: Peribo Pty Ltd, Mount Kuring-Gai, NSW, Australia
Denmark, Sweden, Norway, Finland, Iceland: Angell Eurosales, UK
Eastern Europe, East & West Africa: InterMedia Americana, UK

France, Belgium, Germany, Switzerland &
Austria: Anselm Robinson, UK
Japan: Yasmy International Marketing,
Ageo, Japan
Malaysia, Indonesia, Hong Kong, Taiwan,
China, Philippines, Thailand: Ashton
International Marketing Services,
Sevenoaks, Kent, UK
Middle East: Peter Ward Book Exports,
London, UK
Singapore & Brunei: Pansing Distribution
Sdn Bhd, Singapore
Spain, Portugal, Italy & Malta: Bookport
Associates, Italy

Book Trade Association Membership:
Independent Publishers Guild

2485 ▬▬▬▬▬

REDCLIFFE PRESS LTD
81g Pembroke Road, Bristol BS8 3EA
Telephone: 0117 973 7207
Fax: 0117 923 8991
Email: info@redcliffepress.co.uk
Website: www.redcliffepress.co.uk

Trade Orders:
Orca Book Services Ltd, Unit A3,
Fleets Corner, Poole, Dorset BH17 0HL
Telephone: 01202 665432
Fax: 01202 666219
Email: orders@orcabookservices.co.uk

Personnel:
A. N. Sansom *(Sales Director)*
John Sansom *(Publishing Director)*
Clara Sansom *(Production Director)*

Architecture & Design; Fine Art & Art
History; History & Antiquarian; Literature &
Criticism; Poetry

Imprints, Series & ISBNs:
Redcliffe Press Ltd: 978-1-900178, 978-1-
904537, 978-1-906593, 978-1-908326

Associated Companies:
UK: Art Dictionaries Ltd; Sansom & Co Ltd;
Westcliffe Books

Overseas Representation:
USA: Antique Collectors Club Ltd,
Easthampton, MA, USA

2486 ▬▬▬▬▬

REDEMPTORIST PUBLICATIONS
Alphonsus House, Chawton, Hants
GU34 3HQ
Telephone: 01420 88222
Fax: 01420 88805
Email: rp@rpbooks.co.uk
Website: www.rpbooks.co.uk

Personnel:
Rev Denis McBride *(Publishing Director)*
Christine Thirkell *(Assistant Director)*
Michael Roberts *(Sales & Service Manager)*
Patricia Wilson *(Marketing Manager)*
Lisa Gregoire *(Editorial Manager)*

Religion & Theology

Imprints, Series & ISBNs:
Redemptorist Publications: 978-0-85231

2487 ▬▬▬▬▬

*REFLECTIONS OF A BYGONE AGE
15 Debdale Lane, Keyworth, Notts
NG12 5HT
Telephone: 0115 937 4079
Fax: 0115 937 6197
Email:
reflections@postcardcollecting.co.uk

Personnel:
Brian Lund *(Contact)*
F. Mary Lund *(Contact)*

History & Antiquarian; Sports & Games;
Transport

Imprints, Series & ISBNs:
Reflections of a Bygone Age: 978-0-
946245, 978-1-900138, 978-1-905408

2488 ▬▬▬▬▬

REVENGE INK
Unit 13 Newby Road, Hazel Grove,
Stockport, Cheshire SK7 5DA
Website: www.revengeink.com

Personnel:
Amita Mukerjee *(Managing Director)*

Fiction

2489 ▬▬▬▬▬

RIPLEY PUBLISHING LTD
22 The Causeway, Bishop's Stortford, Herts
CM23 2EJ
Telephone: 01279 502910
Website: www.ripleybooks.com

Personnel:
Anne Marshall *(Publisher)*
Becky Miles *(Editorial Director)*
Amanda Dula *(Foreign Rights Manager)*

Children's Books; Electronic (Educational);
Electronic (Entertainment); Fiction;
Reference Books, Directories & Dictionaries

Parent Company:
Canada: The Jim Pattison Group

2490 ▬▬▬▬▬

RNIB
105 Judd Street, London WC1H 9NE
Telephone: 020 7388 1266
Fax: 020 7388 2034
Website: www.rnib.org.uk

Book Trade Association Membership:
Publishers Association

2491 ▬▬▬▬▬

ROADMASTER PUBLISHING
105 High Street, Rochester, Kent ME1 1JS
Telephone: 01634 862843
Fax: 01634 862843
Email:
roadmasterpublishing@blueyonder.co.uk

Personnel:
Malcolm Wright *(Sales Director)*

Geography & Geology; Guide Books;
Nautical; Transport; Travel & Topography

Imprints, Series & ISBNs:
Roadmaster Publishing: 978-1-871814

2492 ▬▬▬▬▬

VANESSA ROBERTSON
[Director]
27 Bell Place EH3 5HT
Email: info@fidrabooks.com
Website: www.fidrabooks.com

Personnel:
Vanessa Robertson *(Director)*

Children's Books

New Titles: 3 (2012) , 4 (2013)

2493 ▬▬▬▬▬

ROBINSWOOD PRESS LTD
30 South Avenue, Stourbridge,
West Midlands DY8 3XY
Telephone: 01384 397475
Fax: 01384 440443
Email: ops@robinswoodpress.com
Website: www.robinswoodpress.com

Personnel:
Christopher Marshall *(Managing Director)*
Marta Salvado *(Operations Manager)*
Henry Marshall *(Non-Executive and*
Technical Director)
Susan Marshall *(Director / Author)*
George Marshall *(Company Secretary)*

Children's Books; Educational & Textbooks;
Electronic (Educational); English as a
Foreign Language; Fiction; Poetry

New Titles: 1 (2012) , 12 (2013)
No of Employees: 5

Imprints, Series & ISBNs:
High Interest Series: 978-1-906053
Left Hand Writing Skills: 978-1-86981
The Lifeboat Read and Spell Scheme: 978-1-
86981
Robinswood Press Ltd: 978-1-86981, 978-
1-906053
The Spotlight Series: 978-1-86981

Overseas Representation:
Singapore: Knowledge Tree Resources,
Singapore

2494 ▬▬▬▬▬

ALAN ROGERS GUIDES LTD
[part of The Caravan Club]
Spelmonden Old Oast, Goudhurst,
Cranbrook, Kent TN17 1HE
Telephone: 01580 214000
Email: russell@alanrogers.com
Website: www.alanrogers.com

Personnel:
Russell Wheldon *(Marketing Director)*

Travel & Topography

Book Trade Association Membership:
Booksellers Association

2495 ▬▬▬▬▬

ROTOVISION SA
Sheridan House, 114 Western Road, Hove,
East Sussex BN3 1DD
Telephone: 01273 727268
Fax: 01273 727269
Website: www.rotovision.com

Personnel:
David Breuer *(Managing Director)*
April Sankey *(Publisher)*
Nicole Kemble *(Rights Director)*
Andrew Clayden *(Financial Controller)*

Architecture & Design; Cinema, Video, TV &
Radio; Cookery, Wines & Spirits; Crafts &
Hobbies; Fashion & Costume; Fine Art & Art
History; Health & Beauty; Photography;
Reference Books, Directories &
Dictionaries; Theatre, Drama & Dance

Imprints, Series & ISBNs:
RotoVision SA: 978-2-88046

Parent Company:
UK: Quarto Group

Overseas Representation:
France: Interart SARL, Paris, France
Middle East: International Publishing
Services (IPS) Middle East Ltd, Dubai,
UAE, United Arab Emirates
South East Asia: APD Singapore Pte Ltd,
Singapore

Book Trade Association Membership:
Booksellers Association

2496 ▬▬▬▬▬

*ROUND HALL
43 Fitzwilliam Place, Dublin 2,
Republic of Ireland
Telephone: +353 (0)1 662 5301
Fax: +353 (0)1 662 5302

Email: rinfo@thomson.com
Website: www.roundhall.ie

Distribution:
Gill & Macmillan, Hume Avenue,
Park West, Dublin 12, Republic of Ireland
Telephone: +353 (0)1 500 9500

Personnel:
Catherine Dolan *(Director)*
Martin McCann *(Editorial & Content*
Manager)
Terri McDonnell *(Production Manager)*
Martin McCann *(Editorial Manager)*
Maura Smyth *(Marketing & Publishing*
Manager)
Aengus McMorrow *(Online Account*
Manager)
Pauline Ward *(Print Account Manager)*

Academic & Scholarly; Accountancy &
Taxation; Educational & Textbooks;
Electronic (Professional & Academic);
Industry, Business & Management; Law;
Medical (incl. Self-Help & Alternative
Medicine); Reference Books, Directories &
Dictionaries

Imprints, Series & ISBNs:
Round Hall: 978-1-85800, 978-1-899738
Round Hall Professional: 978-1-86089

Parent Company:
USA: Thomson Reuters Corp

Associated Companies:
Australia: LBC
Canada: Carswell
New Zealand: Brookers
UK: Sweet & Maxwell
USA: West Group

2497 ▬▬▬▬▬

ROUNDHOUSE PUBLISHING LTD
Roundhouse Group, Unit B,
18 Marine Gardens, Brighton BN2 1AH
Telephone: 01273 603717
Fax: 01273 697494
Email: sales@roundhousegroup.co.uk
Website: www.roundhousegroup.co.uk

Warehouse & Distribution:
Orca Book Services, Unit A3, Fleets Corner,
Poole BH17 0HL
Telephone: 01235 465521
Fax: 01235 465555
Email: orders@orca-book-services.co.uk
Website: www.orcabookservices.co.uk

Personnel:
Alan Goodworth *(Managing Director)*
Matt Goodworth *(Marketing Manager)*

Animal Care & Breeding; Archaeology;
Architecture & Design; Atlases & Maps;
Biography & Autobiography; Children's
Books; Cinema, Video, TV & Radio;
Cookery, Wines & Spirits; Crafts & Hobbies;
Educational & Textbooks; Fine Art & Art
History; Guide Books; Health & Beauty;
History & Antiquarian; Industry, Business &
Management; Literature & Criticism;
Medical (incl. Self-Help & Alternative
Medicine); Military & War; Philosophy;
Photography; Politics & World Affairs;
Psychology & Psychiatry; Reference Books,
Directories & Dictionaries; Religion &
Theology; Travel & Topography

Imprints, Series & ISBNs:
Roundabout: 978-1-85710, 978-1-85710
Roundhouse Publishing: 978-1-85710

Associated Companies:
UK: Roundabout Books; Roundhouse Arts;
Roundtrip Travel

Distributor for:
Australia: National Library of Australia;
University of Queensland Press
Canada: Crabtree Publishing; National

Gallery of Canada; Rennie Collection; Riverside Architectural Press
Italy: Charta Art Books; Giunti Editore
Netherlands: About Pets
Spain: Santana Books
UK: Cameron & Hollis; Fil Rouge Press; Northern Bee Books; WRTH (World Radio & TV Handbook); Yan Lei Press
USA: Capstone Press; Free Spirit Publishing; Getty Publications; Getty Publications; David Godine Publishers; Gryphon House Publishers; Landauer Books; Martingale; Martingale; Martingale & Co; Panache Partners; Paragon House Publishers; Pelican Publishing Co; Quality Medical Publishing; REA (Research & Education Associates); J. Ross Publishing; Star Bright Books; University Press of Mississippi

Overseas Representation:
Europe (East) & Scandinavia: Bill Bailey Publishers Representatives, Totnes, UK
Europe (South): Bookport Associates, Milan, Italy
Europe (Spain & Portugal only): Iberian Book Services, Madrid, Spain
Europe (West) (excluding Scandinavia): Ted Dougherty, London, UK

2498 ▬▬▬

JOSEPH ROWNTREE FOUNDATION
The Homestead, 40 Water End, York YO30 6WP
Telephone: 01904 629241
Fax: 01904 620072
Email: maria.beech@jrf.org.uk
Website: www.jrf.org.uk

Personnel:
Julia Unwin CBE *(Chief Executive)*
Paul Dack *(Finance Director)*

Academic & Scholarly; Architecture & Design; Economics; Politics & World Affairs; Sociology & Anthropology

2499 ▬▬▬

ROYAL COLLECTION TRUST
Stable Yard House, St James's Palace, London SW1A 1JR
Telephone: 020 7024 5584
Fax: 020 7839 8168
Email: publishing@royalcollection.org.uk
Website: www.royalcollection.org.uk

Distribution:
Thames & Hudson Ltd, 181a High Holborn, London WC1V 7QX
Telephone: 020 7845 5000
Fax: 020 7845 5055
Email: sales@thamesandhudson.co.uk
Website: www.thamesandhudson.com

Personnel:
Jacky Colliss Harvey *(Publisher)*
Kate Owen *(Commissioning Editor)*
Elizabeth Simpson *(Publishing & New Media Project Coordinator)*
Nina Chang *(Project Editor)*

Academic & Scholarly; Antiques & Collecting; Architecture & Design; Biography & Autobiography; Children's Books; Fashion & Costume; Fine Art & Art History; Guide Books; History & Antiquarian; Illustrated & Fine Editions; Natural History; Photography

Imprints, Series & ISBNs:
Royal Collection Trust: 978-1-905686

Overseas Representation:
Rest of World: Thames & Hudson Ltd, London, UK
USA & Canada: University of Chicago Press, Chicago, IL, USA

2500 ▬▬▬

ROYAL COLLEGE OF GENERAL PRACTITIONERS
30 Euston Square, London NW1 2FB
Telephone: 020 3188 7400
Fax: 020 3188 7401
Website: www.rcgp.org.uk

Personnel:
Ms Helen Farrelly *(Publishing Manager)*

Academic & Scholarly; Medical (incl. Self-Help & Alternative Medicine)

Imprints, Series & ISBNs:
Royal College of General Practitioners: 978-0-85084

Book Trade Association Membership:
Association of Learned & Professional Society Publishers

2501 ▬▬▬

THE ROYAL COLLEGE OF PSYCHIATRISTS
17 Belgrave Square, London SW1X 8PG
Telephone: 020 7235 2351
Fax: 020 7259 6507
Email: publications@rcpsych.ac.uk
Website: www.rcpsych.ac.uk

Warehouse:
Turpin Distribution, Customer Services, Pegasus Drive, Stratton Business Park, Biggleswade, Beds SG18 8TQ
Telephone: 01767 604951
Fax: 01767 601640
Email: custserv@turpin-distribution.com
Website: www.turpin-distribution.com

Personnel:
Dave Jago *(Director of Publications and Website)*
Daniel Tomkins *(Sales & Marketing Manager)*

Academic & Scholarly; Electronic (Professional & Academic); Medical (incl. Self-Help & Alternative Medicine); Psychology & Psychiatry

Imprints, Series & ISBNs:
Gaskell: 978-0-902241, 978-1-901242
RCPsych Publications: 978-0-902241, 978-1-901242

Overseas Representation:
Australia & New Zealand: Footprint, Warriewood, NSW, Australia
Republic of Ireland: Compass Academic, London, UK
Scandinavia (including Iceland & Estonia): David Towle International, Stockholm, Sweden
USA & Canada: Princeton Selling Group Inc, Wayne, PA, USA

Book Trade Association Membership:
Independent Publishers Guild; Association of Learned & Professional Society Publishers

2502 ▬▬▬

ROYAL GEOGRAPHICAL SOCIETY
[with Institute of British Geographers]
1 Kensington Gore, London SW7 2AR
Telephone: 020 7591 3019
Fax: 020 7591 3001
Email: admin@rgs.org
Website: www.rgs.org

Personnel:
David Riviere *(Head of Finance & Services)*
Madeleine Hatfield *(Managing Editor: Journal)*

Academic & Scholarly; Electronic (Educational); Electronic (Professional & Academic); Environment & Development Studies; Geography & Geology

Imprints, Series & ISBNs:
RGS-IBG Book Series (academic/scholarly texts only)

2503 ▬▬▬

ROYAL IRISH ACADEMY
Academy House, 19 Dawson Street, Dublin 2, Republic of Ireland
Telephone: +353 (0)1 676 2570 & 676 4222
Fax: +353 (0)1 676 2346
Email: publications@ria.ie
Website: www.ria.ie/Publications

Trade Orders:
Gill & Macmillan Distribution, Hume Avenue, Park West Industrial Park, Dublin 12, Republic of Ireland
Telephone: +353 (0)1 500 9500
Fax: +353 (0)1 500 9599
Email: sales@gillmacmillan.ie
Website: www.gillmacmillan.ie

Personnel:
Ruth Hegarty *(Production & Sales, Managing Editor)*

Academic & Scholarly; Archaeology; Atlases & Maps; Biology & Zoology; History & Antiquarian; Languages & Linguistics; Mathematics & Statistics; Politics & World Affairs; Reference Books, Directories & Dictionaries

Imprints, Series & ISBNs:
Prism
Royal Irish Academy: 978-0-901714, 978-0-9543855, 978-1-874045, 978-1-904890

Overseas Representation:
North America: International Specialized Book Services Inc, Portland, OR, USA

Book Trade Association Membership:
Publishing Ireland (Foilsiú Éireann); Association of Learned & Professional Society Publishers; Cle is now called Publishing Ireland

2504 ▬▬▬

ROYAL SOCIETY OF CHEMISTRY
[RSC Publishing]
Customer Care and Sales, Thomas Graham House, Science Park, Milton Road, Cambridge CB4 0WF
Telephone: 01223 420066
Fax: 01223 423429
Email: sales@rsc.org
Website: www.rsc.org/publishing

Americas Sales Office, Royal Society of Chemistry:
University City Science Centre, 3711 Market Street, Suite 800, Philadelphia, PA 19104, USA
Telephone: +1 215 966 6206
Email: americas@rsc.org
Website: www.rsc.org/publishing

East Asia Pacific Sales Office, Royal Society of Chemistry:
Room 406, Building 2, No 345, Lingling Road, Shanghai 200032, P. R. of China
Telephone: +86 21 64047330
Email: sales@rsc.org
Website: www.rsc.org/publishing

Personnel:
Stephen Hawthorne *(Director - Sales, Marketing & Strategic Partnerships)*
Ms Nadene Sayer *(Head of Marketing)*
Mrs Jennifer Paterson *(Marketing Manager, Publishing)*
Dan Dyer *(Head of Sales - International)*
Matt Straiges *(Sales Manager, Americas)*

Academic & Scholarly; Chemistry; Educational & Textbooks; Electronic (Educational); Electronic (Professional & Academic); Reference Books, Directories & Dictionaries; Scientific & Technical

Imprints, Series & ISBNs:
RSC Publishing: 978-0-85186, 978-0-85404, 978-1-84973

Parent Company:
UK: The Royal Society of Chemistry

Overseas Representation:
Brazil: EBSCO Brazil, Rio de Janeiro, Brazil
Brunei, Indonesia, Malaysia, Philippines, Singapore: Rosalinda Mohammed Razi, Singapore
Cambodia, Laos, Myanmar, Thailand and Vietnam: Wim Van der Putten, Bangkok, Thailand
Egypt: LIMS, Cairo, Egypt
India and Sri Lanka: Book Marketing Services, Chennai, India
Iran: Jahan Adib Publishing, Tehran, Iran
Israel: Inter View Information Resources, Ramat-Gan, Israel
Japan: Bureau Hosoya, Tokyo, Japan
Korea: EBSCO Korea, Seoul, Republic of Korea
Latin America (except Brazil): Accucoms, Lansdale, USA
Lebanon: Levant, Beirut, Lebanon
Middle East: Techknowledge, Dubai, UAE, United Arab Emirates
Taiwan: Flysheet Information Services Co. Ltd, Taipei, Taiwan

Book Trade Association Membership:
Association of Learned Society Publishers; STM (European Group)

2505 ▬▬▬

SAINT ALBERT'S PRESS
[British Province of Carmelites (Carmelite Charitable Trust)]
Carmelite Projects & Publications Office, More House, Heslington, York YO10 5DX
Telephone: 01904 411521
Email: projects@carmelites.org.uk
Website: www.carmelite.org

Orders & Book Deposit:
Saint Albert's Press Book Distribution, Carmelite Friars, 34 Tanners Street, Faversham, Kent ME13 7JN
Telephone: 01795 537038
Fax: 01795 539511
Email: saintalbertspress@carmelites.org.uk
Website: www.carmelite.org

Personnel:
Johan Bergström-Allen *(Director)*
Kevin Bellman *(Sales)*
Father Wilfrid McGreal *(Chair of Carmelite Charitable Trust)*
Father Antony Lester *(Chair of Publications Commission)*
Brother Paul de Groot *(Bursar)*

Academic & Scholarly; History & Antiquarian; Poetry; Religion & Theology

New Titles: 2 (2012)
No of Employees: 2

Imprints, Series & ISBNs:
Saint Albert's Press: 978-0-904849

Parent Company:
UK: The Carmelite Charitable Trust

Associated Companies:
UK: The Carmelite Press; Whitefriars Press

Distributor for:
Italy: Edizioni Carmelitane
USA: Carmelite Institute Washington D.C.

2506 ▬▬▬

ST JEROME PUBLISHING LTD
2 Maple Road West, Brooklands, Manchester M23 9HH

Telephone: 0161 973 9856
Fax: 0161 905 3498
Email: ken@stjeromepublishing.com
Website: www.stjerome.co.uk

Personnel:
Ken Baker (Managing Director)

Academic & Scholarly; Educational & Textbooks; Electronic (Professional & Academic); Gay & Lesbian Studies; Gender Studies; Languages & Linguistics; Reference Books, Directories & Dictionaries

Imprints, Series & ISBNs:
St Jerome Publishing Ltd: 978-1-900650, 978-1-905763

Overseas Representation:
Worldwide: St Jerome Publishing Ltd , UK

Book Trade Association Membership:
Publishers Association; Independent Publishers Guild

2507

SALT PUBLISHING LTD
12 Norwich Road, Cromer, Norfolk
NR27 0AX
Telephone: 01263 511011
Website: www.saltpublishing.com

Book Trade Association Membership:
Publishers Association

2508

*SANDSTONE PRESS LTD
PO Box 5725, 1 High Street, Dingwall,
Ross-shire IV15 9WJ
Telephone: 01349 862583
Fax: 01349 862583
Email: info@sandstonepress.com
Website: www.sandstonepress.com

Personnel:
Robert Davidson (Managing Director)
Iain Gordon (Company Secretary)
Moira Forsyth (Director)

Academic & Scholarly; Biography & Autobiography; Crime; English as a Foreign Language; Environment & Development Studies; Fiction; Humour; Illustrated & Fine Editions; Literature & Criticism; Politics & World Affairs; Science Fiction; Sports & Games

Imprints, Series & ISBNs:
Sandstone Meanmnach Series: 978-1-905207
Sandstone Vista Series: 978-1-905207

Overseas Representation:
USA & Canada: Silvermibe International Books Inc, USA

Book Trade Association Membership:
Publishing Scotland

2509

SANSOM & CO LTD
81g Pembroke Road, Clifton, Bristol
BS8 3EA
Telephone: 0117 973 7207
Fax: 0117 923 8991
Email: johnsansom@aol.com &
info@sansomandcompany.co.uk
Website: www.sansomandcompany.co.uk

Trade Orders:
Orca Book Services, Unit A3, Fleets Corner,
Poole, Dorset BH17 0HL
Telephone: 01202 665432
Fax: 01202 666219
Email: orders@orcabookservices.co.uk
Website: www.orcabookservices.co.uk

Personnel:
A. N. Sansom (Sales Director)

John Sansom (Publishing Director)
Clara Sansom (Production Director)

Architecture & Design; Fine Art & Art History; Literature & Criticism

Imprints, Series & ISBNs:
Sansom & Co Ltd: 978-1-900178, 978-1-904537, 978-1-906593, 978-1-908326

Associated Companies:
UK: Art Dictionaries Ltd; Redcliffe Press Ltd

Overseas Representation:
USA: Antique Collectors' Club,
Woodbridge, Suffolk, UK

2510

SAQI BOOKS
26 Westbourne Grove, London W2 5RH
Telephone: 020 7221 9347
Fax: 020 7229 7492
Website: www.saqibooks.co.uk

Distribution:
Marston Book Services, 160 Milton Park,
Abingdon, Oxon OX14 4SD
Telephone: 01235 465500
Fax: 01235 465555
Email: client.orders@marston.co.uk
Website: www.marston.co.uk

Personnel:
Lynn Gaspard (Publisher)
Ashley Biles (Sales and Marketing Manager)
Ms Rukhsana Yasmin (Commissioning Editor)
Ms Sarah Cleave (Editorial Assistant)
James Nunn (Art Director)
Ms Ailah Ahmed (Publicity Manager)

Academic & Scholarly; Architecture & Design; Biography & Autobiography; Cookery, Wines & Spirits; Economics; Educational & Textbooks; Environment & Development Studies; Fashion & Costume; Fiction; Fine Art & Art History; Gay & Lesbian Studies; Gender Studies; History & Antiquarian; Humour; Illustrated & Fine Editions; Languages & Linguistics; Law; Literature & Criticism; Mathematics & Statistics; Music; Philosophy; Photography; Poetry; Politics & World Affairs; Religion & Theology; Sociology & Anthropology

Imprints, Series & ISBNs:
Saqi Books: 978-0-86356
Saqi Essentials
Telegram Books: 978-1-84659
The Westbourne Press: 978-1-908906

Associated Companies:
Lebanon: Dar Al Saqi Sarl

Overseas Representation:
Australia: Palgrave Macmillan, South Yarra, Vic, Australia
USA: Consortium Publishers, St Paul, MN, USA

Book Trade Association Membership:
Booksellers Association; Independent Publishers Guild

2511

*S. B. PUBLICATIONS
14 Bishopstone Road, Seaford, East Sussex
BN25 2UB
Telephone: 01323 893498
Fax: 01323 893860
Email: sbpublications@tiscali.co.uk
Website: www.sbpublications.co.uk

Personnel:
Mrs L. S. Woods (Owner/Manager)
Mrs D. Quick (Finance)
C. Howden (Proofreader)
Miss C. Gillett (Sales & Administration)

Guide Books; History & Antiquarian; Natural History; Travel & Topography

Imprints, Series & ISBNs:
S. B. Publications: 978-1-85770

2512

SCALA ARTS & HERITAGE PUBLISHERS LTD
21 Queen Anne's Gate, London SW1H 9BU
Telephone: 020 7808 1550
Email: jmckinley@scalapublishers.com
Website: www.scalapublishers.com

All orders:
ACC Distribution, Sandy Lane,
Old Marlesham, Woodbridge, Suffolk
IP12 4SD
Telephone: 01394 389950
Fax: 01394 389999
Email: sales@antique-acc.com
Website: www.antiquecollectorsclub.com

Personnel:
Jenny McKinley (Managing Director)
Jennifer Wright (Head of Museum Publications USA)
Oliver Craske (Editorial Director)
Tim Clarke (Production Director)
Craig McMillan (Finance Manager)

Antiques & Collecting; Architecture & Design; Fashion & Costume; Fine Art & Art History; Guide Books; History & Antiquarian; Illustrated & Fine Editions

Imprints, Series & ISBNs:
Scala Arts & Heritage Publishers Ltd: 978-1-85759

Overseas Representation:
Worldwide: ACC Distribution, Woodbridge, Suffolk, UK

2513

*SCHOFIELD & SIMS
Dogley Mills, Penistone Road, Fenay Bridge,
Huddersfield, West Yorkshire HD8 0NQ
Telephone: 01484 607080
Email: post@schofieldandsims.co.uk
Website: www.schofieldandsims.co.uk

Book Trade Association Membership:
Publishers Association

2514

SCHOLASTIC UK LTD
Euston House, 24 Eversholt Street, London
NW1 1DB
Telephone: 020 7756 7756
Fax: 020 7756 7795
Email: enquiries@scholastic.co.uk
Website: www.scholastic.co.uk

Scholastic Book Clubs:
(as above)

Scholastic Children's Books:
(as above)

Scholastic Book Fairs:
(as above)

Scholastic Education:
Book End, Range Road, Witney, Oxon
OX29 0YD
Fax: 01993 893222

Personnel:
Catherine Bell (Co Group Managing Director)
Steve Thompson (Co Group Managing Director)
Hilary Murray Hill (Scholastic Children's Books – Managing Director)
Nicola Dixon (Finance Director)

Children's Books; Educational & Textbooks

Parent Company:
USA: Scholastic Inc

Associated Companies:
Australia: Scholastic Australia Pty Ltd
Canada: Scholastic Canada Ltd
New Zealand: Scholastic New Zealand Ltd
UK: Chicken House Publishing

Overseas Representation:
Australia: Scholastic Australia Ltd, Gosford, NSW, Australia
Canada: Scholastic Canada Ltd, Markham, Ont, Canada
Far East (excluding Singapore, Malaysia & Indonesia): Scholastic Hong Kong, Hong Kong
New Zealand: Scholastic NZ, Auckland, New Zealand

Book Trade Association Membership:
Publishers Association; Educational Publishers Council; Periodical Publishers Association

2515

SCHOOLPLAY PRODUCTIONS LTD
15 Inglis Road, Colchester, Essex CO3 3HU
Telephone: 01206 540111
Fax: 01206 766944
Email:
chrissie@schoolplayproductions.co.uk
Website:
www.schoolplayproductions.co.uk

Personnel:
J. R. Lucas (Managing Director)
W. Baker (Director)
Mrs C. S. Wenden (Administrator)

Educational & Textbooks; Electronic (Educational); Electronic (Entertainment); Music; Theatre, Drama & Dance

No of Employees: 2

Imprints, Series & ISBNs:
SchoolPlay Productions Ltd: 978-1-872475, 978-1-902472

Book Trade Association Membership:
Publishers Association

2516

SCHOTT MUSIC LTD
48 Great Marlborough Street, London
W1F 7BB
Telephone: 020 7534 0700
Fax: 020 7534 0719
Email: info@schott-music.com
Website: www.schott-music.com

Trade Enquiries & Orders:
MDS Service Centre,
5–6 Raywood Office Complex,
Leacon Lane, Charing, Ashford, Kent
TN27 0EN
Telephone: 01233 712233
Fax: 01233 714948
Email: order@mds-partner.com
Website: www.mds-partner.com

Personnel:
Judith Webb (Joint Managing Director)
Roberto Garcia (Sales & Marketing Director)
Guy Thomas (Buying Manager)
Wendy Lampa (Head of International Publishing)

Academic & Scholarly; Music

Imprints, Series & ISBNs:
Apollo-Verlag Paul Lincke GmbH: 978-3-920030
Ars-Viva-Verlag: 978-3-920045
Atlantis Musikbuch-Verlag AG: 978-3-254
Anton J. Benjamin GmbH: 978-3-923051
Boosey & Hawkes Music Publishers Ltd: 978-0-85162

Bote & Bock GmbH & Co KG: 978-3-7931, 978-3-87090
Cranz GmbH: 978-3-920201
Matth. Hohner AG: 978-3-920468, 978-3-937315
Schott London: 978-0-901938, 978-0-946535, 978-1-902455
Schott Music & Media GmbH (Intuition): 978-3-932398
Schott Music GmbH & Co KG: 978-3-7957
Schott USA: 978-0-930448
Richard Strauss GmbH & Co KG: 978-3-901974

Parent Company:
Germany: Schott Music GmbH & Co KG

Associated Companies:
UK: Ernst Eulenburg Ltd

Distributor for:
Austria: Amadeus; Apollo-Verlag Paul Lincke GmbH; Ars-Viva-Verlag; Atlantis-Musikbuch-Verlag; Anton J. Benjamin GmbH; Boosey & Hawkes GmbH; Bote & Bock GmbH & Co KG; Cranz GmbH; G. Henle Verlag; Matth. Hohner AG
UK: A piacere; Advance Music GmbH; Ars viva; Bardic Edition; Boosey & Hawkes Music Publishers Ltd; Delius Trust; Edition HH; Finzi Trust; Hyperion; Itchy Fingers Publications; Universal Edition Ltd

Overseas Representation:
Europe: Schott Music GmbH & Co KG, Mainz, Germany
Japan: Schott Japan Co Ltd, Tokyo, Japan
USA: Hal Leonard Corporation, Milwaukee, WI, USA

2517

SCION PUBLISHING LTD
The Old Hayloft, Vantage Business Park, Bloxham Road, Banbury, Oxon OX16 9UX
Telephone: 01295 258577
Fax: 01295 275624
Website: www.scionpublishing.com

Distribution:
NBN International, 10 Thornbury Road, Plymouth PL6 7PP
Telephone: 01752 202301

Personnel:
Dr Jonathan Ray *(Managing Director)*
Simon Watkins *(Sales & Marketing Director)*

Academic & Scholarly; Biology & Zoology; Chemistry; Medical (incl. Self-Help & Alternative Medicine); Scientific & Technical

Imprints, Series & ISBNs:
Scion Publishing Ltd: 978-1-904842, 978-1-907904

Distributor for:
Brazil: Artes Medicas
UK: Acheron Press; The Ray Society

Overseas Representation:
Australia & New Zealand: Macmillan Education Australia, South Yarra, Vic, Australia
Europe: Andrew Durnell Marketing Ltd, Tunbridge Wells, UK
Far East: The White Partnership, Tunbridge Wells, UK
South Africa: Mike Brightmore, Academic Marketing Services, Johannesburg, South Africa

Book Trade Association Membership:
International Group of Scientific, Medical & Technical Publishers

2518

SCOTTISH TEXT SOCIETY
School of English Studies, University of Nottingham, Nottingham NG7 2RD

Telephone: 0115 951 5922
Fax: 0115 951 5924
Email: president@scottishtextsociety.org
Website: www.scottishtextsociety.org

Registered Office:
25 Buccleuch Place, Edinburgh EH8 9LN

Personnel:
Nicola Royan *(President)*
John Archer *(Administrative Secretary)*
Dr Rhiannon Purdie *(Editorial Secretary)*
Dr Joanna Martin *(Reviews Secretary)*
Dr Sebastiaan Verweij *(Digital Secretary)*

Academic & Scholarly; History & Antiquarian; Literature & Criticism; Poetry

New Titles: 2 (2012) , 1 (2013)
Annual Turnover: £3000

Imprints, Series & ISBNs:
Scottish Text Society: 978-1-897976

Overseas Representation:
Worldwide: Boydell & Brewer Ltd, Woodbridge, Suffolk, UK

Book Trade Association Membership:
Publishing Scotland

2519

SCRIPTURE UNION PUBLISHING
Scripture Union, 207–209 Queensway, Bletchley, Milton Keynes, Bucks MK2 2EB
Telephone: 01908 856000
Fax: 01908 856111
Email: info@scriptureunion.org.uk
Website: www.scripture.org.uk/

Warehouse & trade orders:
Marston Book Services Ltd, 160 Eastern Avenue, Milton Park, Abingdon, Oxon OX14 4SB
Telephone: 01235 465579
Fax: 01235 465518
Email: christian.orders@marston.co.uk

Mail Order:
PO Box 5148, Milton Keynes MLO MK2 2YX
Telephone: 01908 856006
Fax: 01908 856020
Email: subs@scriptureunion.org.uk

Personnel:
Terry Clutterham *(Ministry Development Director)*
Clive Cornelius *(Publishing Operations Manager)*
Dave Parsons *(Lead Accountant)*
Mrs Rosemary North *(Rights Manager)*
Mrs Esther Price *(Publishing Administration Manager)*

Children's Books; Educational & Textbooks; Music; Religion & Theology

New Titles: 37 (2012) , 9 (2013)

Imprints, Series & ISBNs:
Scripture Union Publishing: 978-0-85421, 978-0-86201, 978-1-84427, 978-1-85999

Overseas Representation:
Australasia, East Asia & Pacific: Resources for Ministry, Gosford, NSW, Australia
Canada: Scripture Union, Pickering, Canada
New Zealand: Scripture Union Wholesale, Wellington, New Zealand
USA: Scripture Union, Wayne, PA, USA

Book Trade Association Membership:
Booksellers Association; Educational Publishers Council

2520

SEREN
57 Nolton Street, Bridgend CF31 3AE

Telephone: 01656 663018
Website: www.serenbooks.com

Distribution:
Central Books, 99 Wallis Road, London E9 5LN
Telephone: 020 8986 4854
Fax: 020 8533 5821
Email: orders@centralbooks.com
Website: www.centralbooks.com

Personnel:
Mick Felton *(Managing Director)*
Simon Hicks *(Sales and Marketing Manager)*
Sarah Davies *(Marketing Officer)*
Amy Wack *(Poetry Editor)*
Penny Thomas *(Fiction Editor)*

Biography & Autobiography; Fiction; Fine Art & Art History; Literature & Criticism; Photography; Poetry

Imprints, Series & ISBNs:
Seren: 978-0-907476, 978-1-85411

Parent Company:
UK: Poetry Wales Press Ltd

Overseas Representation:
Australia: Eleanor Brasch Enterprises, Artarmon, NSW, Australia
USA & Canada: Independent Publishers Group (IPG), Chicago, IL, USA

Book Trade Association Membership:
Independent Publishers Guild

2521

SHELDON PRESS
36 Causton Street, London SW1P 4ST
Telephone: 020 7592 3900
Fax: 020 7592 3939
Email: director@sheldonpress.co.uk
Website: www.sheldonpress.co.uk

Warehouse & Distribution:
Macmillan Distribution Lrd, Brunel Road, Basingstoke RG21 6XS
Telephone: 01256 329242
Email: mdlqueries@macmillan.co.uk

Personnel:
Joanna Moriarty *(Publishing Director)*
Alan Mordue *(Sales & Marketing Director)*
Fiona Marshall *(Editor)*
Alexandra MacDonald *(Rights Manager)*

Gender Studies; Health & Beauty; Medical (incl. Self-Help & Alternative Medicine); Psychology & Psychiatry

New Titles: 22 (2012) , 22 (2013)

Imprints, Series & ISBNs:
Sheldon Press: 978-0-85969, 978-1-84709

Parent Company:
UK: The Society for Promoting Christian Knowledge (SPCK)

Overseas Representation:
Australia & New Zealand: Exisle Publishing, Australia
USA & Canada: Princeton Selling Group, USA

Book Trade Association Membership:
Independent Publishers Guild

2522

SHELDRAKE PRESS
188 Cavendish Road, London SW12 0DA
Telephone: 020 8675 1767
Fax: 020 8675 7736
Email: enquiries@sheldrakepress.co.uk
Website: www.sheldrakepress.co.uk

Distribution:
NBN International Ltd, 10 Thornbury Road, Plymouth PL6 7PP

Telephone: 01752 202300
Fax: 01752 202330
Email: enquiries@nbninternational.com
Website: www.nbninternational.com

Personnel:
Simon Rigge *(Publisher Director)*
Roger Rigge *(Company Secretary)*

Architecture & Design; Children's Books; Cookery, Wines & Spirits; Guide Books; History & Antiquarian; Humour; Music; Natural History; Photography; Transport; Travel & Topography

Imprints, Series & ISBNs:
Sheldrake Press: 978-1-873329

Parent Company:
UK: Sheldrake Holdings Ltd

Overseas Representation:
Australia: John Reed Book Distribution, Tea Gardens, NSW, Australia
USA: Interlink Publishing Group Inc, Northampton, MA, USA

2523

SHEPHEARD-WALWYN (PUBLISHERS) LTD
107 Parkway House, Sheen Lane, London SW14 8LS
Telephone: 020 8241 5927
Email: books@shepheard-walwyn.co.uk
Website: www.shepheard-walwyn.co.uk

Orders:
Central Books, 99 Wallis Road, London E9 5LN
Telephone: 0845 458 9911
Fax: 0845 458 9912
Email: orders@centralbooks.com
Website: www.centralbooks.com

Personnel:
Anthony R. A. Werner *(Managing Director)*

Academic & Scholarly; Biography & Autobiography; Economics; History & Antiquarian; Illustrated & Fine Editions; Philosophy; Politics & World Affairs; Religion & Theology

New Titles: 5 (2012) , 6 (2013)
No of Employees: 1
Annual Turnover: £75,000

Imprints, Series & ISBNs:
The Letters of Marsilio Ficino
Marsilio Ficino's Commentaries on Plato's Writings
Shepheard-Walwyn (Publishers) Ltd: 978-0-85683
Who's Who in British History series

Overseas Representation:
Australia & New Zealand: John Reed Book Distribution, Brookvale, NSW, Australia
USA & Canada: Independent Publishers Group (IPG), Chicago, IL, USA

2524

*SHERWOOD PUBLISHING
Wildhill, Broadoak End, Hertford SG14 2JA
Telephone: 01992 550246
Fax: 01992 535283
Email: sherwood@adinternational.com
Website: www.sherwoodpublishing.com

Personnel:
Mrs Julie Hay *(Chief Executive)*

Industry, Business & Management; Psychology & Psychiatry

Imprints, Series & ISBNs:
Sherwood Publishing: 978-0-9521964, 978-0-9539852

Parent Company:
UK: Psychological Intelligence Ltd

Book Trade Association Membership:
Independent Publishers Guild

2525 ▬

THE SHETLAND TIMES LTD
Gremista, Lerwick, Shetland ZE1 0PX
Telephone: 01595 693622
Fax: 01595 694637
Email: publishing@shetlandtimes.co.uk
Website: www.shetlandtimes.co.uk/shop

Scottish Agent:
BookSource, 50 Cambuslang Road,
Glasgow G32 8NB

Personnel:
Charlotte Black *(Publications Manager)*

Biography & Autobiography; Gardening;
Guide Books; History & Antiquarian;
Music; Natural History

Imprints, Series & ISBNs:
The Shetland Times Ltd: 978-0-900662,
978-1-898852, 978-1-904746

Book Trade Association Membership:
Booksellers Association

2526 ▬

SHIRE PUBLICATIONS LTD
[a division of the Osprey Group]
Kemp House, Chawley Park, Cumnor Hill,
Oxford OX2 9PH
Telephone: 01865 727022
Fax: 01865 727017
Email: shire@shirebooks.co.uk
Website: www.shirebooks.co.uk

Personnel:
Rebecca Smart *(CEO)*
Sue Ross *(Sales Manager)*
Nicholas Wright *(Managing Director & Publisher)*

Academic & Scholarly; Antiques &
Collecting; Archaeology; Architecture &
Design; Atlases & Maps; Biography &
Autobiography; Cookery, Wines & Spirits;
Crafts & Hobbies; Fashion & Costume;
Gardening; Guide Books; History &
Antiquarian; Humour; Illustrated & Fine
Editions; Military & War; Natural History;
Sociology & Anthropology; Sports &
Games; Transport; Travel & Topography

Imprints, Series & ISBNs:
Old House Books & Maps
Shire Publications Ltd: 978-0-7478, 978-0-85263

Parent Company:
UK: Osprey Group

2527 ▬

SHORT BOOKS LTD
3A Exmouth House, Pine Street, London
EC1R 0JH
Telephone: 020 7833 9429
Fax: 020 7833 9500
Email: info@shortbooks.co.uk
Website: www.shortbooks.co.uk

Distribution:
TBS, Colchester Road, Frating Green,
Colchester CO7 7DW
Telephone: 01206 255678
Fax: 01206 255930

Personnel:
Rebecca Nicolson *(Publisher)*
Catherine Gibbs *(Managing Director)*
Aurea Carpenter *(Publisher/Editor)*

Biography & Autobiography; Children's
Books; Fiction; Health & Beauty; History &

Antiquarian; Humour; Natural History;
Philosophy; Sports & Games

Imprints, Series & ISBNs:
Short Books Ltd: 978-0-904095, 978-0-904977, 978-0-906021, 978-0-907595, 978-1-78072

Overseas Representation:
Australasia: Allen & Unwin, Sydney, NSW, Australia
Rest of World: Intercontinental Literature Agency, London, UK
USA: Inkwell Management, New York, NY, USA

Book Trade Association Membership:
Independent Publishers Guild

2528 ▬

SIGEL PRESS
51A Victoria Road, Cambridge CB4 3BW
Telephone: 01223 303303
Fax: 01223 303303
Website: www.sigelpress.com

Also at:
4403 Belmont Court, Medina, OH 44256, USA
Telephone: +1 (330) 722 2541
Fax: +1 (330) 722 2541
Email: info@sigelpress.com
Website: www.sigelpress.com

Personnel:
Thomas Sigel *(Managing & Publisher Director)*
Andrew Hogbin *(Operations Director)*

Academic & Scholarly; Accountancy &
Taxation; Audio Books; Children's Books;
Educational & Textbooks; Engineering;
Environment & Development Studies;
Fiction; Industry, Business & Management;
Military & War; Photography; Psychology &
Psychiatry; Science Fiction; Scientific &
Technical

Imprints, Series & ISBNs:
Sigel Press: 978-1-905941

Associated Companies:
USA: Sigel Press

Book Trade Association Membership:
Independent Publishers Guild

2529 ▬

SIGMA PRESS
Stobart House, Pontyclerc, Penybanc Road,
Ammanford, Carmarthenshire SA18 3HP
Telephone: 01269 593100
Fax: 01269 596116
Email: info@sigmapress.co.uk
Website: www.sigmapress.co.uk

Personnel:
Nigel Evans *(Managing Director)*
Jane Evans *(Managing Editor)*

Cookery, Wines & Spirits; Crafts & Hobbies;
Guide Books; Sports & Games; Travel &
Topography

Imprints, Series & ISBNs:
Sigma Leisure: 978-0-905104, 978-1-85058
Sigma Press: 978-0-905104, 978-1-85058

Parent Company:
UK: Stobart Davies Ltd

Overseas Representation:
Australia & New Zealand: Footprint Books Pty Ltd, Warriwood, NSW, Australia
USA: David Brown Book Co, Oakville, CT, USA

Book Trade Association Membership:
Booksellers Association; Independent
Publishers Guild

2530 ▬

SILVER MOON BOOKS
108c Goldhurst Terrace, London NW6 3HR
Telephone: 020 7625 7592

Trade Enquiries & Orders:
Turnaround Publisher Services, Unit 3,
Olympia Trading Estate, Coburg Road,
London N22 6TZ
Telephone: 020 8829 3000
Fax: 020 8881 5088

Personnel:
Jane Cholmeley *(Director)*

Crime; Fiction; Gay & Lesbian Studies

Imprints, Series & ISBNs:
Silver Moon Books: 978-1-872642

2531 ▬

SIMON & SCHUSTER (UK) LTD
1st Floor, 222 Gray's Inn Road, London
WC1X 8HB
Telephone: 020 7316 1900
Fax: 020 7316 0331
Email: enquiries@sinmonandschuster.co.uk
Website: www.simonandschuster.co.uk

**Customer Services & Distribution
Centre:**
HarperCollins, Customer Service Centre,
Westerhill Road, Bishopbriggs, Glasgow
G64 2QT
Telephone: 0141 306 3100
Fax: 0141 306 3767

Personnel:
Ian Stewart Chapman *(Managing Director)*
Suzanne Baboneau *(Adult Publishing Director)*
Kerr MacRae *(Executive Director)*
Russell Evans *(Commercial Director)*
Mike Jones *(Editorial – Non-Fiction Director)*
Mark Ollard *(Finance Director)*
Ingrid Selberg *(Children's Publishing Director)*
Maxine Hitchcock *(Editorial – Fiction Director)*
Hannah Corbett *(Publicity – Adult Trade Director)*
Sarah Birdsey *(Rights Director)*
Dawn Burnett *(Marketing Director)*
James Horobin *(Group Sales & Marketing Director)*

Audio Books; Biography & Autobiography;
Children's Books; Cinema, Video, TV &
Radio; Cookery, Wines & Spirits; Crime;
Fiction; Gardening; Guide Books; Health &
Beauty; Humour; Industry, Business &
Management; Medical (incl. Self-Help &
Alternative Medicine); Military & War;
Music; Politics & World Affairs; Religion &
Theology; Science Fiction; Sports & Games;
Travel & Topography

Imprints, Series & ISBNs:
Free Press: 978-0-671, 978-0-684, 978-0-7432, 978-0-85720, 978-1-4165, 978-1-4711, 978-1-84983
Pocket: 978-0-671, 978-0-7434, 978-1-4165, 978-1-84739, 978-1-84983
Scribner: 978-0-671, 978-0-684, 978-0-7432, 978-1-4165
Simon & Schuster: 978-0-671, 978-0-684, 978-0-7432, 978-0-85720, 978-1-4165, 978-1-84737
Simon & Schuster Audio: 978-0-7435, 978-0-85720
Simon & Schuster Children's: 978-0-689, 978-0-85707, 978-1-4169, 978-1-84738

Parent Company:
USA: Simon & Schuster Inc

Distributor for:
UK: Duncan Baird; BL Publishing
USA: Andrews McMeel; Atria; Fireside; Free
Press; Gallery; Pocket; Scribner; Simon &
Schuster Audio; Simon & Schuster Inc;
Touchstone; VIZ Media

Overseas Representation:
Australia: Simon & Schuster (Australia) Pty
Ltd, Cammeray, NSW, Australia
Canada: Simon & Schuster (Canada),
Markham, Ont, Canada
India: Simon & Schuster Publishers India Pvt
Ltd, New Delhi, India
New Zealand: HarperCollins (NZ) Ltd,
Glenfield, Auckland, New Zealand
Singapore: Penguin Books Singapore,
Jurong, Singapore
South Africa: Jonathan Ball Publishers (Pty)
Ltd, Johannesburg, South Africa
USA: Trafalgar Square Publishing / IPG,
Chicago, IL, USA

Book Trade Association Membership:
Publishers Association

2532 ▬

CHARLES SKILTON LTD
2 Caversham Street, London SW3 4AH
Telephone: 020 7351 4995
Fax: 020 7351 4995
Email: leonard.holdsworth@btinternet.com

Personnel:
James Hughes *(Managing Director)*
Margaret Fletcher *(Sales Director)*
Leonard Holdsworth *(Editor)*

Cinema, Video, TV & Radio; Cookery, Wines
& Spirits; Fashion & Costume; Fiction; Fine
Art & Art History; Gay & Lesbian Studies;
Guide Books; Illustrated & Fine Editions;
Literature & Criticism; Military & War;
Poetry; Theatre, Drama & Dance;
Transport; Travel & Topography

Imprints, Series & ISBNs:
Christchurch: 978-1-901846
Skilton: 978-0-284

Parent Company:
UK: Christchurch Publishers Ltd

Associated Companies:
UK: Caversham Communications Ltd;
Christchurch Publishers Ltd; Luxor Press

Book Trade Association Membership:
Independent Publishers Guild

2533 ▬

SLIGHTLY FOXED
53 Hoxton Square, London N1 6PB
Telephone: 020 7033 0258
Fax: 0870 199 1245
Email: all@foxedquarterly.com
Website: www.foxedquarterly.com

Personnel:
Gail Pirkis *(Managing Director and Editor)*
Hazel Wood *(Co-Editor)*
Stephanie Allen *(Marketing and Bookshops)*
Jennie Paterson *(Online Manager)*
Anna Kirk *(Subscriptions)*
Faith McAllister *(Subscriptions)*

Academic & Scholarly; Biography &
Autobiography; Children's Books; Fiction;
Gardening; History & Antiquarian;
Illustrated & Fine Editions; Travel &
Topography

Imprints, Series & ISBNs:
Slightly Foxed: 978-1-906562

2534 ▬

SLP EDUCATION
23 West View, Chirk, Wrexham LL14 5HL
Telephone: 01691 774778

Fax: 01691 774849
Email: sales@slpeducation.co.uk
Website: www.slpeducation.co.uk

Personnel:
Phil Roberts *(Marketing Director)*

*Educational & Textbooks; English as a
Foreign Language; Geography & Geology;
History & Antiquarian; Humour;
Mathematics & Statistics; Sports & Games;
Theatre, Drama & Dance*

Imprints, Series & ISBNs:
SLP Education: 978-1-871585

Book Trade Association Membership:
Educational Publishers Council

2535 ▬▬▬

*SMALLFISH BOOKS
5 Thalia Close, Greenwich, London
SE10 9NA
Telephone: 07810 310375
Email: mail@smallfishbooks.com
Website: www.smallfishbooks.com

Children's Books

Book Trade Association Membership:
Publishers Association

2536 ▬▬▬

SMELLESSENCE (AUTUMN GROUP)
Appledram Barns, Birdham Road,
Chichester PO20 7EQ
Telephone: 01243 531660
Website: www.smellessence.co.uk

Personnel:
Mrs Perminder Mann *(Managing Director)*
Ms Helen Wicks *(Publisher)*

2537 ▬▬▬

**SMITH SETTLE PRINTING &
BOOKBINDING LTD**
Gateway Drive, Yeadon, West Yorkshire
LS19 7XY
Telephone: 0113 250 9201
Fax: 0113 250 9223
Email: sales@smithsettle.com
Website: www.smithsettle.com

Personnel:
Donald Walters *(Managing Director)*
Tracey Thorne *(Finance Director)*

*Academic & Scholarly; Agriculture;
Archaeology; Biography & Autobiography;
History & Antiquarian; Illustrated & Fine
Editions; Poetry; Sports & Games; Travel &
Topography*

Imprints, Series & ISBNs:
Smith Settle Printing & Bookbinding Ltd:
978-1-84103

Associated Companies:
UK: Westbury

Distributor for:
UK: Woodstock Books Ltd

Book Trade Association Membership:
Independent Publishers Guild

2538 ▬▬▬

COLIN SMYTHE LTD
38 Mill Lane, Gerrards Cross, Bucks
SL9 8BA
Telephone: 01753 886000
Fax: 01753 886469
Email: sales@colinsmythe.co.uk
Website: www.colinsmythe.co.uk

Warehouse & Dispatch only:
Print on Demand, 9 Culley Court,
Bakewell Road, Orton Southgate,
Peterborough PE2 6WA
Telephone: 01733 237867
Fax: 01733 234309

Personnel:
Colin Smythe *(Managing Director)*
Leslie Hayward *(Director)*

*Academic & Scholarly; Biography &
Autobiography; Literature & Criticism;
Theatre, Drama & Dance*

Imprints, Series & ISBNs:
Dolmen Press: 978-0-85105
Colin Smythe Ltd: 978-0-86140, 978-0-
900675, 978-0-901072
Van Duren: 978-0-905715

Distributor for:
Republic of Ireland: Tir Eolas
USA: ELT Press

Overseas Representation:
USA & Canada: Dufour Editions Inc, Chester
Springs, PA, USA
USA & Canada (recent academic titles):
Oxford University Press Inc USA, New
York, NY, USA

Book Trade Association Membership:
Publishers Association; Booksellers
Association; Independent Publishers Guild

2539 ▬▬▬

SNOWFLAKE BOOKS LTD
28a Old Marston Road, Marston, Oxford
OX3 0JP
Telephone: 07981 666006
Email: info@snowflakebooks.co.uk
Website: www.snowflakebooks.co.uk

Personnel:
Miss Su Yen Hu *(Director)*

Children's Books; Fiction

Imprints, Series & ISBNs:
Snowflake Books : 978-1-908350

Book Trade Association Membership:
Publishers Association

2540 ▬▬▬

SOCCER BOOKS LTD
72 St Peter's Avenue, Cleethorpes, Lincs
DN35 8HU
Telephone: 01472 696226
Fax: 01472 698546
Email: info@soccer-books.co.uk
Website: www.soccer-books.co.uk

Personnel:
John Robinson *(Managing Director)*
Michael Robinson *(Director)*
Petra Askew *(Director)*

Sports & Games; Transport

New Titles: 29 (2012) , 32 (2013)
No of Employees: 5

Imprints, Series & ISBNs:
Complete Results & Line-ups (Series): 978-
1-86223
Football In (Series): 978-1-86223
Marksman Publications
Supporters' Guide (Series): 978-1-86223

2541 ▬▬▬

SOCIAL AFFAIRS UNIT
10/11 Morley House,
314–322 Regent Street, London W1B 5SA
Telephone: 020 7637 4356
Fax: 020 7436 8530
Email: mosbacher@socialaffairsunit.org.uk
Website: www.socialaffairsunit.org.uk

Personnel:
Michael Mosbacher *(Director)*

*Academic & Scholarly; Crime; Economics;
Educational & Textbooks; Environment &
Development Studies; Industry, Business &
Management; Medical (incl. Self-Help &
Alternative Medicine); Politics & World
Affairs; Reference Books, Directories &
Dictionaries; Sociology & Anthropology*

Imprints, Series & ISBNs:
Social Affairs Unit: 978-0-907631, 978-1-
904863

2542 ▬▬▬

**THE SOCIETY FOR PROMOTING
CHRISTIAN KNOWLEDGE (SPCK)**
36 Causton Street, London SW1P 4ST
Telephone: 020 7592 3900
Fax: 020 7592 3939
Website: www.spckpublishing.co.uk

Warehouse & Distribution:
Macmillan Distribution Ltd, Brunel Road,
Houndmills, Basingstoke, Hants RG21 6XS
Telephone: 01256 329242
Email: mdlqueries@macmillan.co.uk
Website: www.macmillan.co.uk

Personnel:
Simon Kingston *(Chief Executive Officer)*
Joanna Moriarty *(Publishing Director)*
Alan Mordue *(Sales Director)*
Barry Finch *(Production Director)*
Alison Barr *(Editor)*
Fiona Marshall *(Editor)*
Ruth McCurry *(Editor)*
Alexandra McDonald *(Rights Manager)*
Cynthia Hamilton *(Senior Marketing &
Publicity Manager)*

Academic & Scholarly; Religion & Theology

Imprints, Series & ISBNs:
Sheldon Press: 978-0-85969, 978-1-84709
SPCK: 978-0-281

Associated Companies:
UK: Sheldon Press

Distributor for:
USA: Baker Academic Publishing; Brazos
Press

Overseas Representation:
Australia: Garratt Publishing, Australia
Far East: Chris Ashdown, UK
South Africa: Methodist Publishing House,
South Africa
USA & Canada: Princeton Selling Group,
USA

Book Trade Association Membership:
Independent Publishers Guild; Christian
Suppliers Group

2543 ▬▬▬

**SOCIETY OF GENEALOGISTS
ENTERPRISES LTD**
14 Charterhouse Buildings, London
EC1M 7BA
Telephone: 020 7702 5483
Fax: 020 7250 1800
Email: sales@sog.org.uk
Website: www.sog.org.uk/

Personnel:
June Perrin *(Chief Executive)*
Anthony Mortimer *(Retail Manager)*

History & Antiquarian

New Titles: 4 (2012)
No of Employees: 3

Imprints, Series & ISBNs:
Society of Genealogists Enterprises Ltd:
978-1-903462

Parent Company:
UK: Society of Genealogists

Book Trade Association Membership:
Booksellers Association

2544 ▬▬▬

***THE SOCIETY OF
METAPHYSICIANS LTD**
Archers' Court, Stonestile Lane, Hastings,
East Sussex TN35 4PG
Telephone: 01424 751577
Fax: 01424 751577
Email: newmeta@btinternet.com
Website: www.metaphysicians.org.uk

Personnel:
Dr J. J. Williamson *(Managing Director)*
Ms C. Yuen *(Secretary)*
D. Cumberland *(Scientific & Literary
Research)*
Miss D. Harris *(Paranormal Research)*
Mervin Gould *(Tutor)*
David Servera-Williamon *(Web)*

*Academic & Scholarly; Educational &
Textbooks; Electronic (Educational);
Environment & Development Studies;
Magic & the Occult; Medical (incl. Self-Help
& Alternative Medicine); Philosophy;
Scientific & Technical*

Imprints, Series & ISBNs:
The Society of Metaphysicians Ltd: 978-0-
900680, 978-1-85228, 978-1-85810

Associated Companies:
Nigeria: Society of Metaphysicians (Nigeria)
Ltd
UK: Metaphysical Research Group

Distributor for:
USA: Ars Obscura; Health Research

Overseas Representation:
Australia: Magic Circle Bookshop, Perth,
Australia
Belgium: Ignoramus, As, Belgium; L' Univers
Particulier, Brussels, Belgium
Netherlands: Boekhandel Synthese, 's
Gravenhage, Netherlands
New Zealand: Bennet's Bookshop,
Palmerston North, New Zealand
Spain: Eyras Editorial, Madrid, Spain
Tenerife: Soluciones, Spain
USA: H.R., Pomeroy, WA, USA

2545 ▬▬▬

SOUTHGATE PUBLISHERS
The Square, Sandford, Crediton, Devon
EX17 4LW
Telephone: 01363 776888
Fax: 01363 776889
Email: info@southgatepublishers.co.uk
Website: www.southgatepublishers.co.uk

Personnel:
Drummond Johnstone *(Managing Director)*
Rachel Johnstone *(Director)*

*Educational & Textbooks; Environment &
Development Studies; Health & Beauty*

Imprints, Series & ISBNs:
Southgate Publishers: 978-1-85741

Distributor for:
UK: Campaign for Learning; Learning
Through Landscapes Trust

Book Trade Association Membership:
Independent Publishers Guild

2546 ▬▬▬

SOUVENIR PRESS LTD
43 Great Russell Street, London WC1B 3PD
Telephone: 020 7580 9307 & 020 7637
5711
Fax: 020 7580 5064

Email: souvenirpress@souvenirpress.co.uk
Website: www.souvenirpress.co.uk

Distribution & Warehouse:
Bookpoint Ltd, 130 Milton Park Drive,
Abingdon, Oxon OX14 4SE
Telephone: 01235 400400
Fax: 01235 400413

Personnel:
Ernest Hecht (Managing Director &
Chairman)

Academic & Scholarly; Animal Care &
Breeding; Antiques & Collecting;
Archaeology; Aviation; Biography &
Autobiography; Cinema, Video, TV &
Radio; Cookery, Wines & Spirits; Crafts &
Hobbies; Electronic (Educational); Electronic
(Entertainment); Fiction; Gardening; Gay &
Lesbian Studies; Gender Studies; Health &
Beauty; Humour; Industry, Business &
Management; Literature & Criticism; Magic
& the Occult; Mathematics & Statistics;
Medical (incl. Self-Help & Alternative
Medicine); Military & War; Music; Natural
History; Nautical; Philosophy; Psychology &
Psychiatry; Religion & Theology; Sociology
& Anthropology; Sports & Games; Theatre,
Drama & Dance; Travel & Topography;
Veterinary Science; Vocational Training &
Careers

Imprints, Series & ISBNs:
Condor Books: 978-0-285
Human Horizons: 978-0-285
Souvenir Press (Educational & Academic)
Ltd: 978-0-285
Souvenir Press Ltd: 978-0-285

Associated Companies:
UK: Souvenir Press (Educational &
Academic) Ltd

Overseas Representation:
Australia & New Zealand : New South
Books, Sydney, NSW, Australia
Austria, Benelux, France, Germany,
Switzerland, Greece & Italy: Ted
Dougherty, London, UK
Middle East: Peter Ward Book Exports,
London, UK
Scandinavia: John Edgeler, London, UK
South Africa: Trinity Books CC, Randburg,
South Africa

Book Trade Association Membership:
Independent Publishers Guild

2547 ▇

**SPARTAN PRESS MUSIC
PUBLISHERS LTD**
Strathmashie House, Laggan,
Inverness-shire PH20 1BU
Telephone: 01528 544770
Fax: 01528 544771
Email: sales@spartanpress.co.uk
Website: www.spartanpress.co.uk

Personnel:
Mark Goddard (Managing Director)
Pat Goddard (Director)

Music

Imprints, Series & ISBNs:
ISMN: 57 999

Distributor for:
Netherlands: European Music Centre
UK: Camden Music; CelloLid; Colne
Edition; G. S. Music; Hunt Edition;
Múzicas Editions; Nova Music; Pan
Educational Music; Queen's Temple
Publications; Sunshine Music Co; Useful
Music; Waveney Music Publishing Ltd;
Yorke Edition

Overseas Representation:
Netherlands: European Music Centre,
Huizen, Netherlands

USA & Canada: Theodore Presser Co, King
of Prussia, PA, USA

2548 ▇

**SPECIAL INTEREST MODEL BOOKS
LTD**
7 Churchfield Crescent, Poole, Dorset
BH15 2QS
Telephone: 01202 649930
Fax: 01202 649950
Email: chrlloyd@globalnet.co.uk
Website:
www.specialinterestmodelbooks.co.uk

Personnel:
Chris Lloyd (Managing Director)

Aviation; Cookery, Wines & Spirits; Crafts &
Hobbies; Engineering; Nautical; Transport

Imprints, Series & ISBNs:
Amateur Winemaker Books: 978-0-900841
formerly Argus Books: 978-1-85486
formerly MAP (Model & Allied Publications):
978-1-85486
formerly Nexus Special Interest Books: 978-
1-85486
Workshop Practice Series: 978-0-85242

Associated Companies:
UK: Amateur Winemaker Books Ltd

Overseas Representation:
Australia: Capricorn Link (Australia) Pty Ltd,
Windsor, NSW, Australia
Eastern Europe, East & West Africa:
Anthony Moggach, InterMedia
Americana (IMA) Ltd, London, UK
New Zealand: South Pacific Books (Imports)
Ltd, Auckland, New Zealand
Scandinavia (including Denmark, Sweden,
Norway, Finland & Iceland) &
Netherlands: Angell Eurosales, Berwick-
on-Tweed, UK
South Africa: Everybody's Books, Kwa Zulu
Natal, South Africa
South & Central America & Caribbean:
David Williams, InterMedia Americana
(IMA) Ltd, London, UK
South East Asia (including Singapore,
Malaysia, Brunei, Indonesia, Hong Kong,
Taiwan, China, Philippines, Thailand &
Japan): Ashton International Marketing
Services, Sevenoaks, Kent, UK
Southern Europe (including Spain, Portugal,
Italy, Malta & Greece): Joe Portelli,
Bookport Associates, Corsico (MI), Italy
Western Europe (including France, Belgium,
Germany, Switzerland & Austria):
Anselm Robinson, European Marketing
Services, London, UK

Book Trade Association Membership:
Publishers Association

2549 ▇

SPOKESMAN
Russell House, Bulwell Lane, Nottingham
NG6 0BT
Telephone: 0115 978 4504 & 970 8318
Fax: 0115 942 0433
Email: elfeuro@compuserve.com
Website: www.spokesmanbooks.com

Personnel:
Ken Fleet (General Manager)
Tony Simpson (Publisher)
Abi Rhodes (Publishing Executive)

Economics; Fiction; History & Antiquarian;
Military & War; Philosophy; Poetry; Politics
& World Affairs; Sociology &
Anthropology; Theatre, Drama & Dance

Imprints, Series & ISBNs:
Socialist Renewal: 978-0-85124
The Spokesman: 978-0-85124

Associated Companies:
UK: Bertrand Russell Peace Foundation Ltd

2550 ▇

SPORTSBOOKS LTD
1 Evelyn Court, Malvern Road, Cheltenham
GL50 2JR
Telephone: 01242 256755
Email: randall@sportsbooks.ltd.uk
Website: www.sportsbooks.ltd.uk

Distribution:
Turnaround Publisher Services Ltd, Unit 3,
Olympia Industrial Estate, Coburg Road,
London N22 6TZ
Telephone: 020 8829 3000
Fax: 020 8881 5088
Email: orders@turnaround-uk.com
Website: www.turnaround-psl.com

Personnel:
Randall Northam (Chairman)
Veronica Northam (Director)

Fiction; History & Antiquarian; Sports &
Games

New Titles: 10 (2012) , 4 (2013)
No of Employees: 2
Annual Turnover: £200,000

Imprints, Series & ISBNs:
BMM: 978-0-9541544
Sportsbooks: 978-1-899807, 978-1-
907524

Overseas Representation:
South Africa: Blue Weaver, South Africa

2551 ▇

STACEY PUBLISHING LIMITED
128 Kensington Church Street, London
W8 4BH
Telephone: 020 7221 7166
Fax: 020 7792 9288
Email: info@stacey-international.co.uk
Website: www.stacey-international.co.uk

Distribution:
NBN International, 10 Thornbury Road,
Plymouth PL6 7PP
Telephone: 01752 202301
Fax: 01752 202331
Email: cservs@nbninternational.com
Website: www.nbninternational.com

Personnel:
T. C. G. Stacey (Chairman)
Hannah Young (Editor)

Archaeology; Biography & Autobiography;
Children's Books; Cookery, Wines & Spirits;
Educational & Textbooks; Environment &
Development Studies; Fiction; Fine Art & Art
History; Gardening; Geography & Geology;
History & Antiquarian; Illustrated & Fine
Editions; Languages & Linguistics; Military &
War; Natural History; Photography; Politics
& World Affairs; Travel & Topography

Imprints, Series & ISBNs:
Capuchin Classics
Stacey International

Parent Company:
UK: Stacey Publishing Ltd

Associated Companies:
UK: Capuchin Classics

Overseas Representation:
Australia: Peribo Pty Ltd, Mount Kuring-Gai,
NSW, Australia
Europe: Durnell Marketing Ltd, Tunbridge
Wells, UK
UK: Signature Books, UK
USA: The David Brown Book Co, Oakville,
CT, USA

Book Trade Association Membership:
Independent Publishers Guild

2552 ▇

STAINER & BELL LTD
PO Box 110, 23 Gruneisen Road, London
N3 1DZ
Telephone: 020 8343 3303
Fax: 020 8343 3024
Email: post@stainer.co.uk
Website: www.stainer.co.uk

Personnel:
Keith Wakefield (Joint Managing Director,
Marketing, Permissions, Accounts &
Distribution)
Carol Wakefield (Joint Managing Director)
Antony Kearns (Deputy Managing Director)
Nicholas Williams (Publishing Director)
Amanda Aknai (Production Director)

Academic & Scholarly; Biography &
Autobiography; History & Antiquarian;
Music; Reference Books, Directories &
Dictionaries; Religion & Theology; Theatre,
Drama & Dance

Imprints, Series & ISBNs:
Augener: 978-0-85249
Early English Church Music: 978-0-85249
Galliard: 978-0-85249
Music for London Entertainment: 978-0-
85249
Musica Britannica: 978-0-85249
Purcell Society Edition: 978-0-85249
Stainer & Bell: 978-0-85249
Weekes: 978-0-85249
Joseph Williams: 978-0-85249

Distributor for:
USA: ECS Publishing Co (Rental Library only)

Overseas Representation:
USA (hymn copyrights & selected titles):
Hope Publishing, Carol Stream, IL, USA
USA (Rental Library): ECS Publishing Co,
Boston, MA, USA

Book Trade Association Membership:
The Music Publishers Association Ltd

2553 ▇

RUDOLF STEINER PRESS LTD
Hillside House, The Square, Forest Row,
East Sussex RH18 5ES
Telephone: 01342 824433
Fax: 01342 826437
Email: office@rudolfsteinerpress.com
Website: www.rudolfsteinerpress.com

Trade Enquiries & Orders:
BookSource, 50 Cambuslang Road,
Glasgow G32 8NB
Telephone: 0845 370 0063
Fax: 0845 370 0064
Email: orders@booksource.net
Website: www.booksource.net

Personnel:
Sevak Gulbekian (Chief Editor)

Audio Books; Biography & Autobiography;
Educational & Textbooks; Fine Art & Art
History; Magic & the Occult; Medical (incl.
Self-Help & Alternative Medicine); Music;
Philosophy; Politics & World Affairs;
Religion & Theology; Sociology &
Anthropology; Theatre, Drama & Dance

Imprints, Series & ISBNs:
Anthroposophic Press: 978-0-88010
Sophia Books: 978-0-85440, 978-1-85584
Steiner Books: 978-0-09, 978-0-88010
Rudolf Steiner Press: 978-0-85440, 978-1-
85584

Distributor for:
USA: Steinerbooks

Overseas Representation:
Australia: Rudolf Steiner Book Centre,
Sydney, NSW, Australia

Canada: Tri-fold Books, Guelph, Ont, Canada
New Zealand: Ceres Books, Auckland, New Zealand
South Africa: Rudolf Steiner Publications, Johannesburg, South Africa
USA: Steiner Books Inc, Herndon, VA, USA

Book Trade Association Membership:
Independent Publishers Guild

2554

STELLIUM LTD
22 Second Avenue, Camels Head, Plymouth, Devon PL2 2EQ
Telephone: 01752 367 300
Fax: 01752 350 453
Email: info@stellium.co.uk
Website: www.stellium.co.uk

Mailing Address:
P.O. Box 221, Plymouth, Devon PL2 2YJ

Personnel:
Jan Budkowski *(Joint MD)*
Mrs Sasha Fenton *(Joint MD)*

Fiction; Poetry

New Titles: 5 (2013)

Imprints, Series & ISBNs:
Stellium: 978-0-9575783

Associated Companies:
UK: Zambezi Publishing Ltd

2555

STENLAKE PUBLISHING LTD
54–58 Mill Square, Catrine, Ayrshire KA5 6RD
Telephone: 01290 551122
Fax: 01290 551122
Email: enquiries@stenlake.co.uk
Website: www.stenlake.co.uk

Personnel:
David Pettigrew *(Editorial)*
Richard Stenlake *(Managing Director)*
Alex F. Young *(Sales)*

Aviation; Crafts & Hobbies; History & Antiquarian; Literature & Criticism; Nautical; Poetry; Transport

Imprints, Series & ISBNs:
Alloway Publishing: 978-0-907526
Stenlake Publishing: 978-1-84033, 978-1-872074

2556

STILLWATER PUBLISHING LTD
Bloxham Mill Business Centre, Barford Road, Bloxham, Banbury OX15 4FF
Telephone: 01295 724193
Email: enquiries@swp.co
Website: www.stillwaterpublishing.co.uk

Personnel:
Alison Campbell *(Publishing Director)*

Audio Books; Computer Science; Cookery, Wines & Spirits; Crafts & Hobbies; Crime; Electronic (Professional & Academic); Engineering; Guide Books; Industry, Business & Management; Philosophy; Psychology & Psychiatry; Religion & Theology; Scientific & Technical; Sociology & Anthropology; Vocational Training & Careers

No of Employees: 5

Imprints, Series & ISBNs:
Stillwater Publishing: 978-0-9554428

Book Trade Association Membership:
Publishers Association

2557

STOBART DAVIES LTD
Stobart House, Pontyclerc, Penybanc Road, Ammanford, Carmarthenshire SA18 3HP
Telephone: 01269 593100
Fax: 01269 596116
Email: sales@stobartdavies.com
Website: www.stobartdavies.com

Personnel:
Jane Evans *(Director)*
Nigel Evans *(Director)*

Archaeology; Cookery, Wines & Spirits; Crafts & Hobbies; Do-It-Yourself; Guide Books; Natural History; Scientific & Technical; Travel & Topography

Imprints, Series & ISBNs:
Sigma Leisure / Sigma Press: 978-1-85058
Stobart Davies Ltd: 978-0-85442

Parent Company:
UK: Stobart Davis (2002) Ltd

Overseas Representation:
Australia & New Zealand: Footprint Books Pty Ltd, Warriewood, NSW, Australia
South Africa: Peter Hyde Associates (Pty) Ltd, Cape Town, South Africa
USA: David Brown Book Co, Oakville, CT, USA

Book Trade Association Membership:
Booksellers Association; Independent Publishers Guild

2558

SUBBUTEO NATURAL HISTORY BOOKS
[a division of CJ Wild Bird Foods Ltd]
The Rea, Upton Magna, Shrewsbury SY4 4UR
Telephone: 01743 709420
Fax: 01743 709504
Email: joy.enston@birdfood.co.uk
Website: www.wildlifebooks.com

Personnel:
Tony Cordery *(Senior Executive)*
Paul Humber *(Finance)*
Claire Smith *(Marketing Manager)*

Natural History

Parent Company:
UK: CJ Wild Bird Foods Ltd

Distributor for:
South Africa: Avian Demography Unit
Spain: Arts Grafiques Delmau; Nayade Editorial
UK: Arlequin Press; Dizzy Daisy Books; Hobby Publications; Osmia Publications; Wings Plants & Paws
USA: American Birding Association

Book Trade Association Membership:
Booksellers Association

2559

SUMMERSDALE PUBLISHERS LTD
46 West Street, Chichester, West Sussex PO19 1RP
Telephone: 01243 771107
Fax: 01243 786300
Email: enquiries@summersdale.com
Website: www.summersdale.com

Warehouse, Trade Enquiries & Orders:
Littlehampton Book Services, Faraday Close, Durrington, Worthing, West Sussex BN13 3RB
Telephone: 01903 828500
Fax: 01903 828625
Email: orders@lbsltd.co.uk
Website: www.lbsltd.co.uk

Personnel:
Alastair Williams *(Managing Director)*
Nicky Douglas *(Sales & Marketing Director)*
Claire Plimmer *(Editorial Director)*
Abbie Headon *(Managing Editor)*
Lizzie Curtin *(Senior Publicist)*

Audio Books; Biography & Autobiography; Cookery, Wines & Spirits; Crafts & Hobbies; Crime; Electronic (Educational); Electronic (Entertainment); Electronic (Professional & Academic); Guide Books; Health & Beauty; History & Antiquarian; Humour; Sports & Games; Travel & Topography

New Titles: 100 (2012) , 120 (2013)
No of Employees: 17

Imprints, Series & ISBNs:
Summersdale Publishers Ltd: 978-1-84024, 978-1-84953, 978-1-873475

Distributor for:
UK: Protection Publications

Overseas Representation:
Australia & New Zealand: Peribo Pty Ltd, Mount Kuring-Gai, NSW, Australia
New Zealand: Andrew Tizzard, Nationwide Book Distribution Ltd, Oxford, New Zealand   , New Zealand
Northern Europe: Michael Geoghegan, London, UK
Scandinavia: Melanie Boeson, Copenhagen, Denmark
South East & North East Asia, Middle East & Africa: Chris Ashdown, Publishers International Marketing, Ferndown, Dorset, UK
Southern Africa: A G Distribution, South Africa
Southern Europe: Bookport Associates, Milan, Italy
US and Canada: Independent Publishers Group, Chicago, IL, USA

Book Trade Association Membership:
Independent Publishers Guild

2560

SUSSEX ACADEMIC PRESS
PO Box 139, Eastbourne, East Sussex BN24 9BP
Telephone: 01323 479220
Fax: 01323 478185
Email: edit@sussex-academic.co.uk
Website: www.sussex-academic.co.uk

Warehouse, Trade Enquiries & Orders:
Gazelle Book Services, White Cross Mills, Hightown, Lancaster LA1 4XS
Telephone: 01524 68765
Fax: 01524 63232

Personnel:
Anthony Grahame *(Editorial Director)*
Anita Grahame *(Finance Director)*

Academic & Scholarly; Archaeology; Bibliography & Library Science; Biography & Autobiography; Economics; Educational & Textbooks; Environment & Development Studies; Fine Art & Art History; Gender Studies; Geography & Geology; History & Antiquarian; Industry, Business & Management; Law; Literature & Criticism; Military & War; Music; Philosophy; Politics & World Affairs; Psychology & Psychiatry; Religion & Theology; Sociology & Anthropology; Sports & Games; Theatre, Drama & Dance

Imprints, Series & ISBNs:
The Alpha Press: 978-1-898595
Sussex Academic: 978-1-84519, 978-1-898723, 978-1-902210, 978-1-903900

Parent Company:
UK: The Alpha Press

Associated Companies:
Canada: Sussex Academic Press (Canada)

Overseas Representation:
Canada: University of Toronto Distribution, Canada
Rest of the World (excluding USA & Canada): Gazelle Book Services Ltd, Lancaster, UK
USA: International Specialized Book Services Inc, Portland, OR, USA

2561

THE SWEDENBORG SOCIETY
20–21 Bloomsbury Way, London WC1A 2TH
Telephone: 020 7405 7986
Fax: 020 7831 5848
Email: stephen@swedenborg.org.uk
Website: www.swedenborg.org.uk

Personnel:
Richard Lines *(Company Secretary)*
Stephen McNeilly *(Publications Manager)*
Nora Foster *(Sales & Marketing Representative)*
Eoin McMahon *(Property Manager)*
James Wilson *(Assistant Editor & Librarian)*

Academic & Scholarly; Literature & Criticism; Religion & Theology

New Titles: 6 (2012) , 5 (2013)
No of Employees: 5

Imprints, Series & ISBNs:
The Swedenborg Society: 978-0-85448

2562

SWEET CHERRY PUBLISHING
Unit E, Vulcan Business Complex, Vulcan Road, Leicester LE5 3EB
Telephone: 0116 212 9780
Fax: 08455190786
Email: info@sweetcherrypublishing.com
Website: www.sweetcherrypublishing.com

Personnel:
A Thadha *(Managing Director)*

Children's Books; Fiction

New Titles: 21 (2012) , 30 (2013)

Imprints, Series & ISBNs:
Sweet Cherry Publishing: 978-1-78226

Book Trade Association Membership:
Publishers Association

2563

SYMPOSIUM PUBLICATIONS LITERARY & ART
193 Church Lane Central Park Manchester M9 4LY
Telephone: 0044 161 205 3967
Email: sympo@sympo.fsworld.co.uk
Website: www.sympo.co.uk

Personnel:
Mrs L. A. Melech *(Director)*

Academic & Scholarly; Children's Books; Educational & Textbooks; English as a Foreign Language; Fine Art & Art History; Literature & Criticism; Poetry

New Titles: 1 (2012)

Imprints, Series & ISBNs:
Sympo Sunrise (Children's Stories)
Symposium Brush-Up Shakespeare Series: 978-0-9524749
Symposium Gem Art Series: 978-0-9524749

Overseas Representation:
Spain: Débora Vázquez Padín, Pontevedra, Spain

2564

TA HA PUBLISHERS LTD
Unit 4, The Windsor Centre,
Windsor Grove, West Norwood, London
SE27 9NT
Telephone: 020 8670 1888
Fax: 020 8670 1998
Email: sales@taha.co.uk
Website: www.tahapublishers.com/

Personnel:
A. Siddiqui *(Director)*
Dr Abia A. Siddiqui *(Editor & Director)*
Affan Aziz

*Children's Books; Languages & Linguistics;
Religion & Theology*

Imprints, Series & ISBNs:
Ta Ha Publishers Ltd: 978-0-907461, 978-1-
84200, 978-1-897940

Overseas Representation:
USA: IB Publishers Ltd, USA

2565

TABB HOUSE
7 Church Street, Padstow, Cornwall
PL28 8BG
Telephone: 01841 532316
Email: tabbhouse.books@btinternet.com
Website: tabbhousebooks.com

**Distributor (for West Country titles in
Cornwall, Devon & Somerset):**
Tor Mark Press, PO Box 4, Redruth,
Cornwall TR16 5YX
Telephone: 01209 822101
Fax: 01209 822035
Email: sales@tormarkpress.prestel.co.uk
Website: www.willowbooks.co.uk

Wholesaler:
Gardners Books Ltd, 1 Whittle Drive,
Willingdon Drove, Eastbourne, East Sussex
BN23 6QH
Telephone: 01323 521555
Fax: 01323 521666
Email: sales@gardners.com
Website: www.gardners.com

Personnel:
Caroline White *(Editorial Director)*
Katharine Bickmore *(Promotion & Sales
Assistant)*

*Biography & Autobiography; Children's
Books; Fiction; Literature & Criticism;
Medical (incl. Self-Help & Alternative
Medicine); Poetry; Religion & Theology*

New Titles: 1 (2012)
No of Employees: 1

Imprints, Series & ISBNs:
Tabb House
Tabb House: 978-0-907018, 978-1-873951

Book Trade Association Membership:
Independent Publishers Guild

2566

TAIGH NA TEUD MUSIC PUBLISHERS
13 Upper Breakish, Isle of Skye IV42 8PY
Telephone: 01471 822528
Fax: 01471 822811
Email: sales@scotlandsmusic.com
Website: www.scotlandsmusic.com &
www.playscottishmusic.com

Personnel:
Alasdair Martin *(Sales Manager)*
Christine Martin *(Music Editor)*

Languages & Linguistics; Music

Imprints, Series & ISBNs:
Taigh na Teud Music Publishers: 978-1-
871931, 978-1-906804

Overseas Representation:
North America: Music Sales Corporation,
Chester, NY, USA

2567

TANGO BOOKS LTD
PO Box 32595, London W4 5YD
Telephone: 020 8996 9970
Fax: 020 8996 9977
Email: info@tangobooks.co.uk
Website: www.tangobooks.co.uk

Sales & Marketing:
Bounce! Quality Court off Chancery Lane,
London WC2A 1HR
Telephone: 020 7138 3650
Email: sales@bouncemarketing.co.uk

Personnel:
Sheri Safran *(Director/Publisher)*
David Fielder *(Director/Publisher)*

*Children's Books; Educational & Textbooks;
Environment & Development Studies;
Natural History*

New Titles: 20 (2012) , 20 (2013)

Imprints, Series & ISBNs:
Tango Books: 978-1-85707, 978-1-909142
Tango Paper

Overseas Representation:
USA & Canada: Trafalgar Square/IPG, USA

2568

TARQUIN PUBLICATIONS
Suite 74, 17 Holywell Hill, St Albans, Herts
AL1 1DT
Telephone: 01727 833866
Fax: 0845 456 6385
Email: sales@tarquinbooks.com
Website: www.tarquingroup.com

Personnel:
Andrew Griffin *(Editorial)*
Peter Watson *(Sales & Promotion)*

*Atlases & Maps; Children's Books; Crafts &
Hobbies; Educational & Textbooks;
Mathematics & Statistics; Scientific &
Technical*

Imprints, Series & ISBNs:
Tarquin Publications: 978-0-906212, 978-1-
899618, 978-1-907550

Parent Company:
UK: Richard Griffin (1820) Ltd

Distributor for:
Australia: Dr Paul Brown
UK: The Maths Press
USA: Tessellations

Overseas Representation:
Australia: H. E. Wootton & Sons, Toorak,
Vic, Australia; W & G Education Pty Ltd,
Berwick, Vic, Australia
New Zealand: Eton Press (Auckland) Ltd,
Auckland, New Zealand
Portugal: Editôra Replicação, Lisbon,
Portugal
Singapore: Nature Craft Pte Ltd, Singapore
South Africa: Creative Learning Systems,
South Africa
USA: Parkwest Publications Inc, Jersey City,
NJ, USA

Book Trade Association Membership:
Independent Publishers Guild

2569

TATE PUBLISHING
[a division of Tate Enterprises Ltd]
Millbank, London SW1P 4RG
Telephone: 020 7887 8869
Fax: 020 7887 8878
Email: tgpl@tate.org.uk

Website: www.tate.org.uk/publishing

Trade Orders and Enquiries:
Tate Enterprises Ltd, Millbank, London
SW1P 4RG
Telephone: 020 7887 8869
Fax: 020 7887 8878
Email: orders@tate.org.uk
Website: www.tate.org.uk/publishing

Warehouse:
Unit 8, Apol Silva Industrial Park,
Dagenham, Essex RM8 1RX
Telephone: 020 8597 8897

Personnel:
Laura Wright *(Chief Executive)*
Roger Thorp *(Publishing Director)*
Robert Read *(Operations Director)*
Rosey Blackmore *(Merchandise Director)*
Sarah Rogers *(Head of Finance)*
Bill Jones *(Production Manager)*
Maxx Lundie *(Sales & Customer Services
Manager)*

*Academic & Scholarly; Architecture &
Design; Children's Books; Electronic
(Educational); Electronic (Professional &
Academic); Fine Art & Art History; Guide
Books; Illustrated & Fine Editions;
Photography*

New Titles: 60 (2012) , 70 (2013)

Imprints, Series & ISBNs:
British Artists
Essential Artists: 978-0-905005, 978-0-
946590, 978-1-85437
Modern Artists: 978-1-85437
Movements in Modern Art
St Ives Artists
Tate Introductions

Parent Company:
UK: Tate Enterprises Ltd

Overseas Representation:
*Asia (including Japan, Hong Kong, Taiwan,
China, South Korea, Malaysia &
Philippines):* Julian Ashton, Sevenoaks,
Kent, UK
Australia and New Zealand: Thames &
Hudson (Australia) Pty Ltd, Fishermans
Bend, Vic, Australia
*Austria, Belgium, Germany, Netherlands &
Switzerland:* Exhibitions International,
Leuven, Belgium
*Caribbean, Bermuda, Mexico, Central
America:* Humphrys Roberts Associates,
London, UK
*Denmark, Finland, Iceland, Norway &
Sweden:* Elisabeth Harder-Kreimann,
Hamburg, Germany
Eastern Europe: Phil Tyers, Athens, Greece
France: Interart SARL, Paris, France
Greece, Italy: Penny Padovani, Cortona,
Italy
*India, Pakistan, Sri Lanki, Bhutan,
Bangladesh:* Roli Books, New Delhi, India
Ireland: Conor Hackett, Balbriggan,
Republic of Ireland
North & South America & Canada: Harry N.
Abrams Inc, New York, NY, USA
Portugal, Spain: Jenny Padovani Frias,
Barcelona, Spain
South Africa: David Krut Publishing,
Johannesburg, South Africa
South America: David Williams, InterMedia
Americana (IMA) Ltd, London, UK

Book Trade Association Membership:
Booksellers Association; Independent
Publishers Guild

2570

I. B. TAURIS & CO LTD
6 Salem Road, London W2 4BU
Telephone: 020 7243 1225
Fax: 020 7243 1226
Email: mail@ibtauris.com
Website: www.ibtauris.com

Distribution:
Macmillan Distribution Ltd, Brunel Road,
Houndmills, Basingstoke, Hants RG21 6XS

Personnel:
Iradj Bagherzade *(Chairman & Publisher)*
Jonathan McDonnell *(Managing Director)*
Stuart Weir *(Production Director)*
Liz Stuckey *(Company Secretary)*
Paul Davighi *(Sales & Marketing Director)*
Antonia Leslie *(Publicity Officer)*

*Academic & Scholarly; Archaeology;
Architecture & Design; Biography &
Autobiography; Cinema, Video, TV &
Radio; Fine Art & Art History; Gender
Studies; Geography & Geology; Guide
Books; History & Antiquarian; Military &
War; Philosophy; Politics & World Affairs;
Reference Books, Directories &
Dictionaries; Religion & Theology; Sociology
& Anthropology; Travel & Topography*

Imprints, Series & ISBNs:
International Library of African Studies:
978-1-78076, 978-1-84511, 978-1-
84885, 978-1-85043, 978-1-86064
International Library of Historical Studies:
978-1-84511, 978-1-85043, 978-1-
86064
International Library of Human Geography:
978-1-84511, 978-1-85043, 978-1-
86064
International Library of Political Studies:
978-1-84511, 978-1-85043, 978-1-
86064
Isma'ili Heritage Series: 978-1-84511, 978-
1-85043, 978-1-86064
Library of International Relations: 978-1-
84511, 978-1-85043, 978-1-86064
Library of Middle East History: 978-1-
84511, 978-1-85043, 978-1-86064
Library of Modern Middle East Studies: 978-
1-84511, 978-1-85043, 978-1-86064
Library of Ottoman Studies: 978-1-84511,
978-1-85043, 978-1-86064
I. B. Tauris & Co Ltd: 978-1-78076, 978-1-
84511, 978-1-84885, 978-1-85043,
978-1-86064
Tauris Parke Paperbacks: 978-1-84511,
978-1-85043, 978-1-86064

Associated Companies:
UK: The Radcliffe Press; Philip Wilson
Publishers Ltd

Distributor for:
Egypt: The American University in Cairo
Press
United Arab Emirates: The Emirates Center
for Strategic Studies & Research

Overseas Representation:
*Africa (excluding South Africa &
Zimbabwe):* InterMedia Americana (IMA)
Ltd, London, UK
Continental Europe & Russia: Andrew
Durnell Marketing Ltd, Tunbridge Wells,
UK
India: Viva Group, New Delhi, India
Iran: Behruz Neirami, Tehran, Iran
Japan: United Publishers Services Ltd,
Tokyo, Japan
South America & Caribbean: Palgrave
Macmillan, London, UK
Southeast Asia and East Asia: Taylor &
Francis Asia Pacific, Singapore
USA & Canada: Palgrave Macmillan, New
York, NY, USA

2571

TAYLOR & FRANCIS
[a divison of Informa]
2–4 Park Square, Milton Park, Abingdon,
Oxford OX14 4RN
Telephone: 020 7017 6000
Fax: 020 7017 6336
Email: info@tandf.co.uk
Website: www.taylorandfrancis.com

Warehouse, Trade Enquiries & Orders:
Bookpoint, 130 Milton Park, Abingdon,
Oxon OX14 4SB
Telephone: 01235 400400

Personnel:
Roger Horton *(Chief Executive)*
Stuart Dawson *(Finance Director)*
Jeremy North *(Managing Director – Books)*
Ian Bannerman *(Managing Director – Journals)*
Christoph Chesher *(Group Sales Director)*
Mark Majurey *(Commercial Director – Digital Publishing)*
David Green *(Publishing Director – Journals)*
Catriona Hauer *(Global Marketing & Customer Services Director – Journals)*
Genevieve Early *(Production Director – Journals)*
Alan Jarvis *(Publishing Director – Books)*
Nigel Eyre *(Director: Production – Books)*
Jackie Harbor *(Global Marketing Director – Books)*
Adele Parker *(Rights Manager – Books)*
Paulette Dooler *(Rights Manager – Journals)*

Academic & Scholarly; Archaeology; Architecture & Design; Biology & Zoology; Chemistry; Economics; Educational & Textbooks; Electronic (Professional & Academic); Engineering; Environment & Development Studies; Gay & Lesbian Studies; Gender Studies; Geography & Geology; History & Antiquarian; Industry, Business & Management; Languages & Linguistics; Law; Literature & Criticism; Mathematics & Statistics; Medical (incl. Self-Help & Alternative Medicine); Military & War; Music; Philosophy; Photography; Physics; Politics & World Affairs; Psychology & Psychiatry; Reference Books, Directories & Dictionaries; Religion & Theology; Scientific & Technical; Sociology & Anthropology; Sports & Games; Theatre, Drama & Dance; Veterinary Science

New Titles: 3889 (2012) , 4105 (2013)
No of Employees: 800

Imprints, Series & ISBNs:
CRC: 978-0-8493
Donhead Publishing: 978-1-873394
Earthscan: 978-1-84407
Garland: 978-0-8153
Manson Publishing: 978-1-84076
Psychology Press: 978-0-415
Routledge: 978-0-415
Taylor & Francis: 978-0-415

Parent Company:
UK: Informa Plc

Associated Companies:
China: Taylor & Francis Beijing
India: Routledge India Office
Norway: Taylor & Francis AS
Singapore: Taylor & Francis Asia Pacific
Sweden: Taylor & Francis AB
USA: Taylor & Francis Group LLC

Distributor for:
UK: Guilford Press; Schlütersche; Swedish Pharmaceutical Press; Teton NewMedia

Overseas Representation:
Australia: Palgrave Macmillan, South Yarra, Vic, Australia
Austria, Switzerland & Germany: Gabriela Mauch, Area Sales Manager, Central Europe, Stuttgart, Germany
Belgium, Netherlands, France & Luxembourg: Liza Walraven, Area Sales Manager, Amsterdam, Netherlands
Botswana: Arthur Oageng, Book Promotions/Horizon Books, Botswana
China: Taylor & Francis, Beijing, China
Eastern Europe: Marek Lewinson, Warsaw, Poland
India: Taylor & Francis Books India Pvt Ltd, New Delhi, India

Ireland & Northern Ireland: Nick Pepper, Sales representative, UK
Israel: Franklins International, Tel Aviv, Israel
Japan: International Sales Department Taylor & Francis Group , UK
Korea: Information & Culture Korea (ICK), Seoul, Republic of Korea
Malaysia & Brunei: David Yeong, General Manager, Petaling Jaya, Malaysia
Mexico, Central & South America: Cranbury International LLC, Montpelier, VT, USA
Middle East & North Africa: International Publishing Services (IPS) Middle East Ltd, Dubai, UAE, United Arab Emirates
New Zealand: Victoria Johnson, Macmillan Publishers New Zealand Ltd, Auckland, New Zealand
Nigeria: Tula Publishing, UK
Nordic Countries: Eva Nyika, Sales Representative, Stockholm, Sweden
North America: Taylor & Francis Group LLC, Boca Raton, FL, USA
Pakistan: M. Anwer Iqbal, Book Bird Publishers Representatives, Lahore, Pakistan
Singapore, Hong Kong, Vietnam, Philippines, Indonesia, Taiwan & Thailand: Taylor & Francis Asia Pacific, Singapore
South Africa, Namibia, Lesotho & Swaziland: Book Promotions Pty Ltd, Diep River, South Africa
Spain, Portugal, Italy & Greece: Philip Veysey, Area Sales Manager, Madrid, Spain
West Indies & Caribbean: Jasmina Basic, Taylor & Francis Group, Abingdon, UK

Book Trade Association Membership:
Publishers Association; International Group of Scientific, Medical & Technical Publishers

2572 ▬▬▬▬

TEACHIT (UK) LTD
11 Charlotte Street, Bath BA1 2NE
Telephone: 01225 788850
Fax: 01225 430233
Email: membership@teachit.co.uk
Website: www.teachit.co.uk

Educational & Textbooks; Electronic (Educational); Electronic (Professional & Academic)

Parent Company:
UK: AQA

Book Trade Association Membership:
Publishers Association; Educational Publishers Council

2573 ▬▬▬▬

TEE PUBLISHING LTD
The Fosse, Fosse Way, Leamington Spa, Warks CV31 1XN
Telephone: 01926 614101
Email: info@teepublishing.co.uk
Website: www.teepublishing.co.uk

Engineering

2574 ▬▬▬▬

TELEGRAM BOOKS
26 Westbourne Grove, London W2 5RH
Telephone: 020 7221 9347
Fax: 020 7229 7492
Email: lynn@telegrambooks.com
Website: www.telegrambooks.com

Distribution (UK):
Marston Book Services Ltd,
160 Milton Park, Abingdon, Oxon OX14 4SD
Telephone: 01235 465500
Fax: 01235 465555
Website: www.marston.co.uk

Sales (UK):
Compass, The Barley Mow Centre,
10 Barley Mow Passage, Chiswick, London W4 4PH
Telephone: 020 8994 6477
Fax: 020 8400 6132
Website: www.compass-booksales.co.uk

Personnel:
Lynn Gaspard *(Publisher)*
Ashley Biles *(Sales Manager)*
Ms Sarah Cleave *(Editorial Assistant)*
James Nunn *(Art Director)*
Ms Ailah Ahmed *(Publicity Manager)*
Ms Rukhsana Yasmin *(Commissioning Editor)*

Fiction

Imprints, Series & ISBNs:
Telegram Books: 978-1-84659

Parent Company:
UK: Saqi Books

Overseas Representation:
Europe: Andrew Durnell, Andrew Durnell Marketing Ltd, Tunbridge Wells, UK
India: Pradeep Kumar, Viva Marketing, New Delhi, India
Middle East: Dar al Saqi SARL, Beirut, Lebanon
Pakistan: Mohammad Eusoph, Mr Books, Islamabad, Pakistan
Singapore: Nelson Koh, Horizon Books Pte Ltd, Singapore
South Africa: Stephan Phillips (Pty) Ltd, Cape Town, South Africa
Spain, Portugal & Germany: Anna Soler-Pont, Pontas Literary & Film Agency, Barcelona, Spain
USA & Canada: Consortium Publishers, St Paul, MN, USA

Book Trade Association Membership:
Independent Publishers Guild

2575 ▬▬▬▬

TELOS PUBLISHING LTD
17 Pendre Avenue, Prestatyn, Denbighshire LL19 9SH
Telephone: 07905 311733
Email: david@telos.co.uk
Website: www.telos.co.uk

Business/Accounts:
5a Church Road, Shortlands, Bromley, Kent BR2 0HP
Telephone: 020 8466 1115
Email: stephen@telos.co.uk

Personnel:
David J. Howe *(Publisher)*
Stephen James Walker *(Publisher)*

Cinema, Video, TV & Radio; Crime; Fiction

New Titles: 13 (2012) , 13 (2013)

Imprints, Series & ISBNs:
Telos Publishing Ltd: 978-1-84583, 978-1-903889

Overseas Representation:
USA & Canada: Fitzhenry & Whiteside Ltd, Markham, Ont, Canada

2576 ▬▬▬▬

TEMPLAR PUBLISHING
Deepdene Lodge, Deepdene Avenue, Dorking, Surrey RH5 4AT
Telephone: 01306 876361
Fax: 01306 889097
Website: www.templarco.co.uk

Distribution:
Grantham Book Services, Trent Road, Grantham, Lincs NG31 7XG

Personnel:
Mike McGrath *(Managing Director)*
David Inman *(Sales and Marketing Director)*
Amanda Wood *(Creative Director)*
Karen Ellison *(Production Director)*

Children's Books; Fiction

Imprints, Series & ISBNs:
Amazing Baby: 978-1-904513
Big Picture Press
Pippbrook Books
Templar Publishing: 978-1-84011, 978-1-898784

Parent Company:
UK: Bonnier Publishing Ltd

Book Trade Association Membership:
Booksellers Association; Independent Publishers Guild

2577 ▬▬▬▬

TEMPLE LODGE PUBLISHING
Hillside House, The Square, Forest Row, East Sussex RH18 5ES
Telephone: 01342 824000
Fax: 01342 826437
Email: office@templelodge.com
Website: www.templelodge.com

Distribution:
BookSource, 50 Cambuslang Road, Glasgow G32 8NB
Telephone: 0141 643 3955
Fax: 0845 370 0068
Email: orders@booksource.net
Website: www.booksource.net

Personnel:
S. E. Gulbekian *(Chief Editor)*

Health & Beauty; Magic & the Occult; Medical (incl. Self-Help & Alternative Medicine); Philosophy; Politics & World Affairs; Religion & Theology

Imprints, Series & ISBNs:
Temple Lodge Publishing: 978-0-904693, 978-1-902636, 978-1-906999

Overseas Representation:
Australia: Rudolf Steiner Book Centre, Sydney, NSW, Australia
Canada: Tri-fold Books, Guelph, Ont, Canada
New Zealand: Steinerbooks, Auckland, New Zealand
South Africa: Rudolf Steiner Publications, Bryanston, South Africa
USA: Steiner Books Inc, Herndon, VA, USA

Book Trade Association Membership:
Independent Publishers Guild

2578 ▬▬▬▬

TENEUES PUBLISHING UK LTD
Unit D, Paddock Wood Distribution Centre, Paddock Wood, Tonbridge, Kent TN12 6UU
Telephone: 0203 542 8997
Email: ctrigger@teneues.co.uk
Website: www.teneues.com

Trade Enquiries & Orders:
Combined Book Services, Unit D, Paddock Wood Distribution Centre, Tonbridge, Kent TN12 6UU
Telephone: 01892 835599
Fax: 01892 837272
Email: orders@combook.co.uk

Personnel:
Hendrik teNeues *(Chairman)*
Claire Trigger *(UK Sales Manager)*

Architecture & Design; Fashion & Costume; Illustrated & Fine Editions; Photography; Travel & Topography

Imprints, Series & ISBNs:
Stern Portfolios: 978-3-570
teNeues: 978-1-60160, 978-3-8238, 978-3-8327

Book Trade Association Membership:
Booksellers Association

2579

TFM PUBLISHING LTD
Castle Hill Barns, Harley, Shrewsbury,
Shropshire SY5 6LX
Telephone: 01952 510061
Fax: 01952 510192
Email: nikki@tfmpublishing.com
Website: www.tfmpublishing.com

Representation (UK):
Gazelle, Lancaster

Personnel:
Nikki Bramhill (Director)
Paul Lawrence (Director)

Academic & Scholarly; Medical (incl. Self-Help & Alternative Medicine)

Imprints, Series & ISBNs:
tfm publishing Ltd: 978-1-903378

Overseas Representation:
Europe: Gazelle, Lancaster, UK
Hong Kong: McBarron Book Co, Kowloon,
Hong Kong
Japan: Igaku-Shoin Ltd, Tokyo, Japan;
Nankodo Co Ltd, Tokyo, Japan
Middle East & North Africa: International
Publishing Services, Dubai, UAE, United
Arab Emirates
South Africa: Academic Marketing Services
(Pty) Ltd, Johannesburg, South Africa
Taiwan: Unifacmanu Trading Co Ltd, Taipei,
Taiwan
USA, Canada & South America: Martin P
Hill Consulting, New York, NY, USA

Book Trade Association Membership:
Booksellers Association

2580

THAMES & HUDSON LTD
181A High Holborn, London WC1V 7QX
Telephone: 020 7845 5000
Fax: 020 7845 5050
Email: l.willis@thameshudson.co.uk
Website: www.thamesandhudson.com

Warehouse, Accounts & Returns:
Littlehampton Book Services,
Faraday Close, Worthing BN13 3RB
Telephone: 01903 828511
Fax: 01903 828801
Email: enquiries@lbsltd.co.uk

Personnel:
Tim Evans (Chairman)
Susanna Reisz Neurath (Deputy Chairman)
Rolf Griseback (CEO)
Sarah Forster (Financial Director)
Christopher Ferguson (Operations Director)
Neil Palfreyman (Production Director)
Johanna Neurath (Design Director)
Lucas Dietrich (Director, Editorial)
Julian Horner (Director, Editorial)
Christian Frederking (Sales & Marketing
Director)
Stephen Embrey (Export Area Manager)
Natasha Ffrench (Export Area Manager)
Scipio Stringer (Export Area Manager)
Laura Willis (Head of Marketing)
Collette Hutchinson (Senior Publicist)
Andrew Stanley (Deputy Sales & Marketing
Director)
Ian Bartley (Export Sales)
Christian Gotsch (Head of Foreign Rights)

Academic & Scholarly; Antiques &
Collecting; Archaeology; Architecture &

Design; Biography & Autobiography;
Children's Books; Crafts & Hobbies;
Educational & Textbooks; Environment &
Development Studies; Fashion & Costume;
Fine Art & Art History; Gardening; Gay &
Lesbian Studies; Guide Books; History &
Antiquarian; Illustrated & Fine Editions;
Literature & Criticism; Magic & the Occult;
Military & War; Music; Natural History;
Philosophy; Photography; Reference Books,
Directories & Dictionaries; Religion &
Theology; Sociology & Anthropology;
Theatre, Drama & Dance; Travel &
Topography

Imprints, Series & ISBNs:
Aperture: 978-0-89381, 978-1-59711,
978-1-931788
Chris Boot: 978-0-9542813, 978-0-
9546894, 978-1-905712
Braun Verlagshaus: 978-3-938780
British Museum Press: 978-0-7141
Contrasto: 978-88-6965
Flammarion SA, France: 978-2-08
Guggenheim Museum Publications: 978-0-
89207
Ilex Press: 978-1-904705
Ivy Press: 978-1-78240
Laurence King: 978-1-85669
Museum of Modern Art, New York: 978-0-
87070
National Portrait Gallery: 978-1-85574
Oscar Riera Ojeda: 978-988-12249
The Royal Academy of Arts: 978-0-900946,
978-1-903973
Royal Collection: 978-1-902163
Scriptum: 978-1-900826, 978-1-902686
Skira Editore: 978-3-87624, 978-88-8118,
978-88-8491
Steidl: 978-3-86521, 978-3-88243, 978-3-
905509, 978-3-931141
Thames & Hudson: 978-0-500
Vendome: 978-0-865565
Violette: 978-1-900828

Parent Company:
UK: T & H Holdings Ltd

Associated Companies:
Australia: Thames & Hudson (Australia) Pty
Ltd
China: Thames & Hudson China Ltd
Singapore: Thames & Hudson (S) Pte Ltd
UK: Thames & Hudson (Distributors) Ltd
USA: Thames & Hudson Inc

Overseas Representation:
Africa, Caribbean, Central America, Eastern
Europe, Eastern Mediterranean,
Germany (South), Italy, Japan, Mexico,
Middle East, Portugal & Spain: Export
Sales Department, Thames & Hudson
Ltd, London, UK
Australia, New Zealand, Papua New Guinea
& Pacific Islands: Thames & Hudson
(Australia) Pty Ltd, Fishermans Bend, Vic,
Australia
Austria, Switzerland & Germany (excluding
South): Michael Klein, Vilsbiburg,
Germany
Bangladesh: Zeenat Book Supply Ltd,
Dhaka, Bangladesh
Brazil & South America: Terry Roberts, Cotia
SP, Brazil
China, Hong Kong & Macau: Thames &
Hudson China Ltd, Aberdeen, Hong
Kong
France: Interart SARL, Paris, France
Korea & Taiwan: Asia Publishers Services
Ltd, Hong Kong
Lebanon: Levant Distributors, Beirut,
Lebanon
Malaysia: Thames & Hudson (S) Pte Ltd,
Petaling Jaya, Malaysia
Netherlands: Sebastian van der Zee,
Amsterdam, Netherlands
Republic of Ireland: UK Sales Department,
Thames & Hudson Ltd, London, UK
Scandinavia & Baltic States: Per Burell,
Stockholm, Sweden
Singapore & South East Asia: Thames &
Hudson (S) Pte Ltd, Singapore

Thailand: Asia Book Co Ltd, Bangkok,
Thailand

Book Trade Association Membership:
Publishers Association; Booksellers
Association; Independent Publishers Guild

2581

THARPA PUBLICATIONS
Conishead Priory, Ulverston, Cumbria
LA12 9QQ
Telephone: 01229 588599
Email: info.uk@tharpa.com
Website: www.tharpa.com/uk

Personnel:
Murdo McNab (Distribution Manager)
Manuel Rivero-De Martine (Production
Manager)
Steph Atkinson (Finance Director; Sales &
Marketing Manager)
Jim Bliether (Editorial)

Philosophy; Religion & Theology

Imprints, Series & ISBNs:
Tharpa Publications: 978-0-948006, 978-0-
9548790

Parent Company:
UK: New Kadampa Tradition

Overseas Representation:
Australia: Gary Allen Pty Ltd, Smithfield,
NSW, Australia
Canada: Tharpa Canada, Toronto, Ont,
Canada
Singapore & Malaysia: Tharpa Asia, Hong
Kong
South Africa: Bacchus Books, Gauteng,
South Africa
USA (Office): Tharpa Publications, New
York, NY, USA

Book Trade Association Membership:
Booksellers Association; Independent
Publishers Guild

2582

**THIRD MILLENNIUM PUBLISHING
LTD**
2–5 Benjamin Street, London EC1M 5QL
Telephone: 020 7336 0144
Fax: 020 7608 1188
Email: info@tmiltd.com
Website: www.tmiltd.com

Personnel:
Julian Platt (Chairman)
Dr Joel Burden (Managing Director)
Dr Neil Titman (Publishing Director)
David Burt (Director)
Bonnie Murray (Production Manager)
Sarah Yeatman (Marketing Manager)

Antiques & Collecting; Educational &
Textbooks; Fine Art & Art History; Guide
Books; Illustrated & Fine Editions; Law;
Military & War; Photography

Imprints, Series & ISBNs:
James & James Publishers
Third Millennium Publishing Ltd: 978-1-
906507

Overseas Representation:
USA & Canada: John Brancati, Antique
Collectors Club Ltd, Easthampton, MA,
USA

2583

***THOMSON REUTERS –
PROFESSIONAL DIVISION**
100 Avenue Road, Swiss Cottage, London
NW3 3PF
Telephone: 020 7393 7000
Fax: 020 7393 7010
Email:
sweetandmaxwell.orders@thomson.com

Website: www.sweetandmaxwell.co.uk

Law

Parent Company:
UK: Thomson Reuters

Associated Companies:
Republic of Ireland: Roundhall
UK: Current Law Publishers; Flosuite; W.
Green & Son; IDS; Lawtel; Localaw;
Solcara; Sweet & Maxwell; Westlaw UK

2584

THOROGOOD PUBLISHING LTD
10–12 Rivington Street, London EC2A 3DU
Telephone: 020 7729 6677
Email: info@thorogoodpublishing.co.uk
Website: www.thorogoodpublishing.co.uk

Trade Orders:
Marston Book Services, 160 Milton Park,
Abingdon, Oxon OX14 4SD
Telephone: 01235 465500
Fax: 01235 465655
Email: trade.enq@marston.co.uk
Website: www.marston.co.uk

Personnel:
Neil Thomas (Chairman)
Nina Rossey (Finance Director)
Angela Spall (General, Editorial, Production
Manager)
Matthew Harris (Marketing Manager)
Martin Thomas (Marketing Executive)

Accountancy & Taxation; Audio Books;
Biography & Autobiography; Crime;
Electronic (Entertainment); Electronic
(Professional & Academic); Fiction; Industry,
Business & Management; Law; Military &
War; Travel & Topography

Imprints, Series & ISBNs:
Thorogood Publishing Ltd: 978-1-85418

Associated Companies:
UK: Falconbury Ltd

Overseas Representation:
Australia & New Zealand: Woodslane Pty
Ltd, Warriewood, NSW, Australia
Hong Kong, Taiwan, China & Korea: Asia
Publishers Services Ltd, Hong Kong
India: Viva Group, New Delhi, India
Latin America: InterMedia Americana (IMA)
Ltd, London, UK
Middle East, Greece & Cyprus: Ray Potts,
Publishers International Marketing,
Polfages, France
Singapore, Malaysia & South East Asia: APD
Singapore Pte Ltd, Singapore

2585

F. A. THORPE PUBLISHING
The Green, Bradgate Road, Anstey,
Leicester LE7 7FU
Telephone: 0116 236 4325
Fax: 0116 234 0205
Email: enquiries@ulverscroft.co.uk
Website: www.ulverscroft.com

Personnel:
Robert Thirlby (Chief Executive)

Biography & Autobiography; Crime;
Fiction; Travel & Topography

Imprints, Series & ISBNs:
Charnwood Series: 978-0-7089, 978-1-
84395, 978-1-84617, 978-1-84782
Charnwood/Ulverscroft/Linford: 978-1-
4448
Linford Softcover Series: 978-0-7089, 978-
1-84395, 978-1-84617, 978-1-84782
Ulverscroft Series: 978-0-7089, 978-1-
84395, 978-1-84617, 978-1-84782

Parent Company:
UK: Ulverscroft Large Print Books Ltd

Associated Companies:
UK: Isis Publishing; Magna Large Print
Books

Overseas Representation:
Australia: Sandra Lavender, Crows Nest,
NSW, Australia
Canada: Charlene Kessel, Ulverscroft, West
Seneca, NY, USA
New Zealand: John Gregory, Feilding, New
Zealand
USA: Jan McGowan, Ulverscroft Large Print
(USA) Inc, West Seneca, NY, USA

2586

THOTH PUBLICATIONS
64 Leopold Street, Loughborough, Leics
LE11 5DN
Telephone: 01509 210626
Fax: 01509 210626
Email: sales@thoth.co.uk
Website: www.thoth.co.uk

Personnel:
Tom Clarke *(Senior Partner)*
Susan Attwood *(Partner)*

*Biography & Autobiography; Magic & the
Occult; Religion & Theology*

Imprints, Series & ISBNs:
Thoth Publications: 978-1-870450

Book Trade Association Membership:
Booksellers Association

2587

THRASS (UK) LTD
The Willows, 18 Long Lane, Upton, Chester
CH2 2PD
Telephone: 01244 373079
Fax: 0872 111 4327
Email: office@thrass.co.uk
Website: www.thrass.co.uk

Personnel:
Alan Davies *(Director)*
Hilary Davies *(Company Secretary)*

*Educational & Textbooks; Electronic
(Educational)*

New Titles: 7 (2012) , 7 (2013)

Imprints, Series & ISBNs:
THRASS (UK) Ltd: 978-1-904912, 978-1-
906295

2588

TINY ISLAND PRESS
1 Bromley Lane, Chislehurst, Kent BR7 6LH
Telephone: 020 3397 2173
Fax: 020 3397 2593
Email: info@tinyislandpress.com
Website: www.tinyislandpress.com

Personnel:
Ms Iris Josiah *(Publisher)*

Children's Books

New Titles: 5 (2012) , 5 (2013)

Imprints, Series & ISBNs:
Tiny Island Stories

Book Trade Association Membership:
Publishers Association

2589

TOP THAT! PUBLISHING LTD
Marine House, Tide Mill Way, Woodbridge,
Suffolk IP12 1AP
Telephone: 01394 386651
Fax: 01394 386011
Email: info@topthatpublishing.com
Website: www.topthatpublishing.com

Personnel:
David Henderson *(Managing Director)*
Dave Greggor *(Sales Director)*
Simon Couchman *(Creative Director)*
Douglas Eadie *(Finance Director)*
Daniel Graham *(Editorial Director)*
Stuart Buck *(Production Director)*
Barrie Henderson *(Chairman)*

*Children's Books; Crafts & Hobbies; Fiction;
Humour; Natural History; Reference Books,
Directories & Dictionaries; Sports & Games*

New Titles: 250 (2012) , 350 (2013)
No of Employees: 42
Annual Turnover: £10M

Imprints, Series & ISBNs:
Imagine That
Kudos: 978-1-84229
Pocket Money Press: 978-1-84956
Top That Publishing

Parent Company:
UK: Tide Mill Media

Book Trade Association Membership:
Independent Publishers Guild

2590

TOPICAL RESOURCES
PO Box 329, Broughton, Preston, Lancs
PR3 5LT
Telephone: 01772 863158
Fax: 01772 866153
Email: sales@topical-resources.co.uk
Website: www.topical-resources.co.uk

Personnel:
Peter Bell *(Partner)*
Heather Bell *(Partner)*
Stewart Bell *(Sales Manager)*
Kath Cope *(Office Manager)*
Lisa Bell *(Office Assistant)*

*Audio Books; Children's Books; Educational
& Textbooks*

Imprints, Series & ISBNs:
Topical Resources: 978-1-872977, 978-1-
905509, 978-1-907269

Overseas Representation:
Australia: Ian Harding, Farr Books, Wilston,
Qld, Australia
Republic of Ireland: Martin Pender, Primary
Educational Resources, Enniscorthy, Co
Wexford, Republic of Ireland

2591

TOTAL-E-NTWINED LTD
Think Tank, Ruston Way, Lincoln LN6 7FL
Telephone: 01522 668916
Email: nicki@totalebound.com
Website: www.total-e-bound.com

Personnel:
Mrs Claire Siemaszkiewicz *(CEO)*
Marek Siemaszkiewicz *(Technical Director)*
Mrs Nicki Richards *(Publisher)*

Fiction

New Titles: 312 (2012) , 390 (2013)
No of Employees: 19

Imprints, Series & ISBNs:
Total-E-Bound Publishing

Book Trade Association Membership:
Publishers Association

2592

TRANSWORLD PUBLISHERS LTD
[a company of the Penguin Random House
Group Ltd]
61–63 Uxbridge Road, London W5 5SA
Telephone: 020 8579 2652
Fax: 020 8579 5479

Email: info@transworld-publishers.co.uk
Website: www.booksattransworld.co.uk

Personnel:
Larry Finlay *(Managing Director)*
Bill Scott-Kerr *(Publisher & Director)*
Sally Gaminara *(Publishing Director –
Bantam Press)*
Marianne Velmans *(Publishing Director –
Doubleday)*
Leon Romero Montalvo *(Head of
Commercial Affairs)*
Ed Christie *(Sales & Marketing Director)*
Martin Higgins *(UK Sales Director)*
Janine Giovanni *(UK Marketing Director)*
Eleanor Wood *(International Sales Director)*
Alison Martin *(Production Director)*
Patsy Irwin *(Publicity Director)*
Claire Ward *(Art Director)*
Helen Edwards *(Rights Director)*

*Audio Books; Biography & Autobiography;
Cinema, Video, TV & Radio; Cookery, Wines
& Spirits; Crime; Fiction; Gardening; History
& Antiquarian; Humour; Military & War;
Music; Politics & World Affairs; Science
Fiction; Sports & Games; Travel &
Topography*

Imprints, Series & ISBNs:
Bantam: 978-0-553
Bantam Press: 978-0-593
Black Swan: 978-0-552
Channel 4 Books
Corgi: 978-0-552
Doubleday: 978-0-385
Eden Project: 978-0-593
Expert Gardening Books
Transworld Ireland

Parent Company:
USA: Random House Inc

Associated Companies:
Australia: Random House Australia Pty Ltd
Canada: Random House of Canada Ltd
New Zealand: Random House New Zealand
Ltd
South Africa: Random House (Pty) Ltd
UK: Random House Children's Books;
Random House UK Ltd

Overseas Representation:
Australia: Random House Australia Pty Ltd,
Sydney, NSW, Australia
Canada: Random House of Canada Ltd,
Toronto, Ont, Canada
New Zealand: Random House New Zealand
Ltd, Auckland, New Zealand
South Africa: Random House Struik Pty Ltd,
Parktown, South Africa

Book Trade Association Membership:
Publishers Association; BA (Associate
Member)

2593

TRENTHAM BOOKS
IOE Press, 20 Bedford Way, London
WC1H 0AL
Telephone: 020 7763 2157
Fax: 020 7763 2411
Email: trenthambooks@ioe.ac.uk
Website: www.trentham-books.co.uk

Editorial:
28 Hillside Gardens, Highgate, London
N6 5ST
Telephone: 020 8348 2174
Email: g.klein@ioe.ac.uk

Personnel:
Gillian Klein *(Publisher, Trentham Books)*
Jim Collins *(Publishing Director)*
Sally Sigmund *(Sales and Marketing
Executive)*
Jonathan Dore *(Production Editor Team
Leader)*
Nicole Edmondson *(Production Editor)*
Chandrima Ghosh *(Editorial and Marketing
Assistant)*

*Academic & Scholarly; Educational &
Textbooks; Gender Studies; Law; Politics &
World Affairs; Theatre, Drama & Dance*

New Titles: 13 (2012) , 14 (2013)
No of Employees: 6

Imprints, Series & ISBNs:
Trentham Books: 978-0-948080, 978-0-
95077, 978-1-85856

Distributor for:
France: European Institute of Education &
Social Policy; UNESCO Institute for
Educational Planning
UK: Commission for Racial Equality; Design
and Technology Association; Open
University

Overseas Representation:
Australia, New Zealand & South East Asia:
DA Information Services Pty Ltd,
Mitcham, Vic, Australia
Canada: Bacon & Hughes Ltd, Ottawa, Ont,
Canada
*China, Taiwan, Hong Kong & South East
Asia*: Tony Poh Leong Wah, Singapore
Malaysia: UBSD Distribution Sdn Bhd,
Selangor, Malaysia
Philippines: Megatexts Phil Inc, Cebu City,
Philippines
Spain & Portugal: Iberian Book Services,
Madrid, Spain
Taiwan: Unifacmanu Trading Co Ltd, Taipei,
Taiwan
USA: Stylus Publishing Inc, Sterling, VA, USA

Book Trade Association Membership:
Independent Publishers Guild

2594

TRINITARIAN BIBLE SOCIETY
Tyndale House, Dorset Road, London
SW19 3NN
Telephone: 020 8543 7857
Fax: 020 8540 7777
Email: contact@tbsbibles.org
Website: www.tbsbibles.org

Personnel:
D. P. Rowland *(General Secretary)*
D. Larlham *(Operations Director)*
D. J. Broome *(Resources Director)*
J. M. Wilson *(Finance & Supporter Manager)*
P. J. D. Hopkins *(Editorial Director)*

Religion & Theology

Imprints, Series & ISBNs:
Trinitarian Bible Society: 978-0-907861,
978-1-86228

Overseas Representation:
Australia: Trinitarian Bible Society
(Australia), Grafton, NSW, Australia
Brazil: Sociedade Bíblica Trinitariana do
Brasil, São Paulo, Brazil
Canada: Trinitarian Bible Society, Chilliwack,
BC, Canada
New Zealand: Trinitarian Bible Society (New
Zealand), Gisborne, New Zealand
USA: Trinitarian Bible Society (USA), Grand
Rapids, MI, USA

2595

*TROG ASSOCIATES LTD
PO Box 243, South Croydon, Surrey
CR2 6NZ
Telephone: 020 8681 3301
Fax: 020 8681 3301
Email:
ericsutherland@writerofbooks.plus.com
Website: www.trogassatesltd.biz

Personnel:
Eric Sutherland *(Contact)*

*Accountancy & Taxation; Health & Beauty;
Industry, Business & Management;
Literature & Criticism; Scientific & Technical*

Imprints, Series & ISBNs:
Trog Associates Ltd: 978-1-906440

Associated Companies:
UK: www.lulu.com/uk

2596 ▬▬▬▬▬

*TROTMAN PUBLISHING
[an imprint of Crimson Publishing Ltd]
Crimson Publishing Ltd,
Westminster House, Kew Road, Richmond
TW9 2ND
Telephone: 020 8334 1788
Fax: 020 8334 1601
Email: GemmaS@crimsonpublishing.co.uk
Website: www.trotman.co.uk

Warehouse:
Grantham Book Services (GBS) Trent Road
Grantham Lincolnshire NG31 7XQ
Telephone: 01476 541080
Fax: 01476 541061

Personnel:
David Lester *(Managing Director)*
Beth Bishop *(Commissioning Editor)*
Holly Ivins *(Commissioning Editor)*

Educational & Textbooks; Industry, Business & Management; Reference Books, Directories & Dictionaries; Vocational Training & Careers

Imprints, Series & ISBNs:
Trotman: 978-0-85660, 978-1-84455
Trotman Education: 978-0-85660, 978-1-84455

Parent Company:
UK: Crimson Publishing Ltd

Book Trade Association Membership:
Independent Publishers Guild; Data Publishers Association

2597 ▬▬▬▬▬

TROUBADOR PUBLISHING LTD
9 Priory Business Park, Wistow Road,
Kibworth Beauchamp, Leics LE8 0RX
Telephone: 0116 279 2299
Fax: 0116 279 2277
Email: books@troubador.co.uk
Website: www.troubador.co.uk

Personnel:
Jeremy Thompson *(Managing Director)*
Jane Rowland *(Marketing Director)*
Terry Compton *(Production Manager)*
Lauren Lewis *(Editorial Manager)*
Sam Copson *(Distribution Manager)*
Rachel Gregory *(Ebook Programme Manager)*

Academic & Scholarly; Accountancy & Taxation; Biography & Autobiography; Children's Books; Cookery, Wines & Spirits; Crime; Economics; Fiction; Guide Books; History & Antiquarian; Humour; Industry, Business & Management; Languages & Linguistics; Literature & Criticism; Magic & the Occult; Medical (incl. Self-Help & Alternative Medicine); Military & War; Music; Natural History; Philosophy; Poetry; Politics & World Affairs; Psychology & Psychiatry; Science Fiction; Sociology & Anthropology; Sports & Games; Theatre, Drama & Dance; Transport; Travel & Topography

New Titles: 300 (2012) , 350 (2013)
No of Employees: 14
Annual Turnover: £1.5M

Imprints, Series & ISBNs:
Italian Studies: 978-1-905237
Matador: 978-1-84876, 978-1-899293, 978-1-905886, 978-1-906221, 978-1-906510

T2: 978-1-904744

Book Trade Association Membership:
Independent Publishers Guild

2598 ▬▬▬▬▬

TWELVEHEADS PRESS
PO Box 59, Chacewater, Truro, Cornwall
TR4 8ZJ
Email: enquiries@twelveheads.com
Website: www.twelveheads.com

Personnel:
Alan Kittridge *(Partner)*
Michael Messenger *(Partner)*
John Stengelhofen *(Partner)*

Archaeology; Guide Books; History & Antiquarian; Nautical; Transport

Imprints, Series & ISBNs:
Twelveheads Press: 978-0-906294

2599 ▬▬▬▬▬

TYNE BRIDGE PUBLISHING
Newcastle Libraries, PO Box 88,
Newcastle upon Tyne NE99 1DX
Telephone: 0191 277 4174
Fax: 0191 277 4137
Email: anna.flowers@newcastle.gov.uk
Website: www.newcastle.gov.uk/tynebridgepublishing

Personnel:
Anna Flowers *(Publications Manager)*
Vanessa Histon *(Marketing Officer)*

Archaeology; Biography & Autobiography; History & Antiquarian

Imprints, Series & ISBNs:
Newcastle City Libraries: 978-0-902653, 978-1-85795
Newcastle Libraries and Information Service: 978-1-85795
Tyne Bridge Publishing: 978-1-85795

Parent Company:
UK: City & Council of Newcastle upon Tyne

2600 ▬▬▬▬▬

UCAS
Rosehill, New Barn Lane, Cheltenham, Glos
GL52 3LZ
Website: www.ucas.com

Trade Enquiries & Orders:
Publication Services, UCAS, PO Box 130,
Cheltenham, Glos GL52 3ZF
Telephone: 01242 544610
Fax: 01242 544806
Email: publicationservices@ucas.ac.uk
Website: www.ucasbooks.com

Personnel:
Graham Bond *(Head of Publishing)*
Sona Waddy *(Publications Officer)*
Amruta Hiremath *(Senior Management Accountant)*
Paul Bird *(Publications Logistics Manager)*

Academic & Scholarly; Educational & Textbooks; Reference Books, Directories & Dictionaries; Vocational Training & Careers

Imprints, Series & ISBNs:
UCAS: 978-1-84361, 978-1-908077

2601 ▬▬▬▬▬

UIT CAMBRIDGE LTD
PO Box 145, Cambridge CB4 1GQ
Telephone: 01223 302041
Website: www.uit.co.uk

Book Trade Association Membership:
Publishers Association

2602 ▬▬▬▬▬

UNICORN PRESS LTD
66 Charlotte Street,. London W1T 4QE
Telephone: 07836 633377
Email: ian@unicornpress.org
Website: www.unicornpress.org

Trade Distributor:
Marston Book Services, 160 Milton Park,
PO Box 269, Abingdon, Oxford OX14 4YN
Telephone: 01235 465604
Fax: 01235 465655
Email: tammy.belcher@marston.co.uk

Personnel:
Lord Ian Strathcarron *(Director)*
Hugh Tempest-Radford *(Director)*
Simon Perks *(Sales Director)*
Mrs Lucy Duckworth *(Director)*
Dominic Roter *(E-commerce)*

Antiques & Collecting; Architecture & Design; Biography & Autobiography; Crafts & Hobbies; Fashion & Costume; Fine Art & Art History; History & Antiquarian; Illustrated & Fine Editions; Military & War; Natural History; Nautical; Photography; Reference Books, Directories & Dictionaries; Travel & Topography

New Titles: 3 (2012) , 25 (2013)

Imprints, Series & ISBNs:
Unicorn Press Ltd: 978-0-906290, 978-1-906509
Uniform Press
Unity Press

Associated Companies:
Russia: Liki Rossii

Distributor for:
UK: Churchill Heritage Ltd

Overseas Representation:
Australia, New Zealand and Fiji: Inbooks Marketing, Frenchs Forest, Australia
EU, Scandinavia, Russia and the Middle East: Durnell Marketing, Tunbridge Wells, UK
India, Far East : The White Partnership, Tunbridge Wells, UK
South America, Latin America and the Caribbean: David Williams, London, UK
USA and Canada: Antique Collectors Club Ltd, Easthampton, MA, USA

2603 ▬▬▬▬▬

UNITED WRITERS PUBLICATIONS LTD
Ailsa, Castle Gate, Penzance, Cornwall
TR20 8BG
Telephone: 01736 365954
Fax: 01736 365954
Email: sales@unitedwriters.co.uk
Website: www.unitedwriters.co.uk

Personnel:
M. Sheppard *(Editorial & Sales)*
T. Sully *(Production)*
Jacob Sheppard *(Digital Editor)*

Biography & Autobiography; Children's Books; Cinema, Video, TV & Radio; Educational & Textbooks; Fiction; History & Antiquarian; Humour; Industry, Business & Management; Military & War; Nautical; Psychology & Psychiatry; Science Fiction; Sports & Games; Travel & Topography

New Titles: 6 (2012) , 6 (2013)

Imprints, Series & ISBNs:
United Writers Publications Ltd: 978-0-901976, 978-1-85200

2604 ▬▬▬▬▬

UNIVERSITY COLLEGE OF DUBLIN PRESS
Newman House, 86 St Stephen's Green,
Dublin 2, Republic of Ireland
Telephone: +353 (0)1 477 9812 & 9813
Fax: +353 (0)1 477 9821
Email: ucdpress@ucd.ie
Website: www.ucdpress.ie

Distribution (Republic of Ireland):
Irish Book Distribution, Unit 12, North Park,
North Road, Finglas, Dublin 11,
Republic of Ireland
Telephone: +353 (0)1 923 9580
Fax: +353 (0)1 823 9599
Email: sales@irishbookdistribution.ie

Representation (Republic of Ireland):
Hibernian Book Services,
93 Longwood Park, Rathfarnham,
Dublin 14, Republic of Ireland
Telephone: +353 (0)1 493 6043
Fax: +353 (0)1 493 7833

Distributor UK:
Central Books, 99 Wallis Road, London
E9 5LN
Telephone: 020 8986 4854
Fax: 020 8533 5821
Email: orders@centralbooks.com

Personnel:
Noelle Moran *(Executive Editor)*

Academic & Scholarly

Imprints, Series & ISBNs:
University College of Dublin Press: 978-1-900621, 978-1-904558, 978-1-906359

Overseas Representation:
Australia & New Zealand: Eleanor Brasch Enterprises, Artarmon, NSW, Australia
North America: Dufour Editions Inc, Chester Springs, PA, USA
Spain & Portugal: Iberian Book Services, Madrid, Spain
UK & Benelux: Theo Van de Bilt Sales and Marketing, Sawbridgeworth, UK
UK, Europe & all other countries (distribution): Central Books Ltd, London, UK

Book Trade Association Membership:
Publishing Ireland (Foilsiú Éireann)

2605 ▬▬▬▬▬

UNIVERSITY OF EXETER PRESS
Reed Hall, Streatham Drive, Exeter EX4 4QR
Telephone: 01392 263066
Fax: 01392 263064
Email: uep@exeter.ac.uk
Website: www.exeterpress.co.uk

Distribution:
NBN International, Estover Road, Plymouth
PL6 7PY
Telephone: 01752 202301
Fax: 01752 202331
Email: cservs@nbninternational.com
Website: www.nbninternational.com

Personnel:
Simon Baker *(Publisher)*

Academic & Scholarly; Archaeology; Cinema, Video, TV & Radio; History & Antiquarian; Literature & Criticism; Theatre, Drama & Dance

Imprints, Series & ISBNs:
Bristol Phoenix Press: 978-1-904675
The Exeter Press: 978-1-905816
University of Exeter Press: 978-0-85989

Parent Company:
UK: The Exeter Press Ltd

Overseas Representation:
Australia & New Zealand: Footprint Books Pty, Mona Vale, NSW, Australia
China, Hong Kong, Taiwan & South East Asia: Tony Poh, Singapore
Greece: Charles Gibbes Associates, Louslitges, France
India: Viva Books Pvt Ltd, New Delhi, India
Japan & Korea: United Publishers Services Ltd, Tokyo, Japan
Middle East: The Avicenna Partnership, Oxford, UK
Republic of Ireland: Quantum Publishing Solutions Ltd, Paisley, UK
Spain & Portugal: Iberian Book Services, Madrid, Spain
USA & Canada, Central & South America: University of Chicago Press, Chicago, IL, USA

Book Trade Association Membership:
Independent Publishers Guild

2606 ▬▬▬▬▬▬

UNIVERSITY OF HERTFORDSHIRE PRESS
College Lane, Hatfield, Hertfordshire AL10 9AB
Telephone: 01707 284654
Fax: 01707 284666
Email: UHPress@herts.ac.uk
Website: www.herts.ac.uk/UHPress

Trade Enquiries & Orders:
Central Books Ltd, 99 Wallis Road, London E9 5LN
Telephone: 0845 458 9911
Fax: 0845 458 9912
Email: info@centralbooks.com
Website: www.centralbooks.com

Personnel:
Jane Housham *(Press Manager)*
Gill Cook *(Administration Assistant)*
Sarah Elvins *(Production Editor)*

Academic & Scholarly; Educational & Textbooks; Environment & Development Studies; Geography & Geology; History & Antiquarian; Law; Magic & the Occult; Mathematics & Statistics; Psychology & Psychiatry; Sociology & Anthropology; Theatre, Drama & Dance

Imprints, Series & ISBNs:
Guidelines for Research in Parapsychology: 978-0-900458, 978-1-905313
Hertfordshire Publications: 978-0-9542189, 978-1-905313, 978-1-907396
The Interface Collection: 978-0-900458, 978-1-905313, 978-1-907396
Regional and Local History: 978-0-900458, 978-1-905313, 978-1-907396
University of Hertfordshire (Faculties): 978-1-898543, 978-1-905313, 978-1-907396
University of Hertfordshire Press: 978-1-902806, 978-1-905313, 978-1-907396

Parent Company:
UK: University of Hertfordshire

Overseas Representation:
Benelux: Netwerk Academic Book Agency, Rotterdam, Netherlands
Spain & Portugal: Iberian Book Services, Madrid, Spain
USA: Independent Publishers Group (IPG), Chicago, IL, USA

2607 ▬▬▬▬▬▬

UNIVERSITY OF OTTAWA PRESS
5 Victoria House, 138 Watling Street, Towcester NN12 6BT
Telephone: 01327 357770
Fax: 01327 359572
Website: www.press.uottawa.ca

Warehouse & Distribution:
Marston Book Services, 160 Milton Park, PO Box 169, Abingdon, Oxon OX14 4YN
Telephone: 01235 465521
Email: direct.orders@marston.co.uk
Website: www.marston.co.uk

Personnel:
Gary Hall *(Marketing Manager)*

Academic & Scholarly; Cinema, Video, TV & Radio; Economics; Educational & Textbooks; Gender Studies; Industry, Business & Management; Languages & Linguistics; Literature & Criticism; Politics & World Affairs; Reference Books, Directories & Dictionaries; Sociology & Anthropology; Theatre, Drama & Dance

Imprints, Series & ISBNs:
University of Ottawa Press: 978-0-8020, 978-1-4426

Parent Company:
Canada: University of Ottawa Press

2608 ▬▬▬▬▬▬

UNIVERSITY OF TORONTO PRESS
5 Victoria House, 138 Watling Street East, Towcester NN12 6BT
Telephone: 01327 357770
Fax: 01327 359572
Website: utppublishing.com

Warehouse & Distribution:
NBN International, 10 Thornbury Road, Plymouth PL6 7PP
Telephone: 01752 202301
Fax: 01752 202331
Email: orders@nbninternational.com
Website: www.nbninternational.com

Personnel:
Gary Hall *(Manager)*

Academic & Scholarly; Cinema, Video, TV & Radio; Economics; Gender Studies; History & Antiquarian; Law; Literature & Criticism; Medical (incl. Self-Help & Alternative Medicine); Military & War; Philosophy; Politics & World Affairs; Reference Books, Directories & Dictionaries; Sociology & Anthropology; Theatre, Drama & Dance

Imprints, Series & ISBNs:
University of Toronto Press: 978-0-8020, 978-1-4426

2609 ▬▬▬▬▬▬

UNIVERSITY OF WALES PRESS
10 Columbus Walk, Brigantine Place, Cardiff CF10 4UP
Telephone: 029 2049 6899
Fax: 029 2049 6108
Email: press@press.wales.ac.uk
Website: uwp.co.uk

Distribution (UK):
NBN International Ltd, Estover Road, Plymouth PL6 7PY
Telephone: 01752 202301
Fax: 01752 202333

Personnel:
Helgard Krause *(Head of the Press)*
Eleri Lloyd-Cresci *(Sales & Marketing Manager)*
Sarah Lewis *(Commissioning Editor)*
Catrin Harries *(Marketing Assistant)*
Sian Chapman *(Production Manager)*

Academic & Scholarly; Archaeology; Biography & Autobiography; Educational & Textbooks; Gender Studies; History & Antiquarian; Illustrated & Fine Editions; Languages & Linguistics; Literature & Criticism; Military & War; Music; Philosophy; Poetry; Politics & World Affairs; Reference Books, Directories &

Dictionaries; Religion & Theology; Sociology & Anthropology; Sports & Games

Imprints, Series & ISBNs:
GPC Books: 978-0-7083, 978-0-900768
Gwasg Prifysgol Cymru: 978-0-7083, 978-0-900768
University of Wales Press: 978-0-7083, 978-0-900768

Parent Company:
UK: University of Wales

Overseas Representation:
India: Cambridge University Press – India Pvt Ltd, New Delhi, India
Japan: United Publishers Services Ltd, Tokyo, Japan
North & South America, Australia & New Zealand: Chicago University Press, Chicago, IL, USA
South East Asia: STM Publisher Services Pte Ltd, Singapore
Wales: Welsh Books Council, Aberystwyth, UK

Book Trade Association Membership:
Independent Publishers Guild; Literary Publishers (Wales) Ltd

2610 ▬▬▬▬▬▬

MERLIN UNWIN BOOKS LTD
Palmers House, 7 Corve Street, Ludlow, Shropshire SY8 1DB
Telephone: 01584 877456
Fax: 01584 877457
Email: books@merlinunwin.co.uk
Website: www.merlinunwin.co.uk

Warehouse & Returns:
Merlin Unwin Books Warehouse, c/o Wow Distribution, The Yard, Woofferton Grange, Brimfield, Ludlow SY8 4NP

Personnel:
Merlin Unwin *(Design Director)*
Karen McCall *(Managing Director, Editorial)*
Joanne Potter *(Marketing & Production)*
Sue Bradley *(Finance)*

Animal Care & Breeding; Biography & Autobiography; Humour; Illustrated & Fine Editions; Medical (incl. Self-Help & Alternative Medicine); Natural History; Reference Books, Directories & Dictionaries; Sports & Games

New Titles: 12 (2012) , 10 (2013)
No of Employees: 4

Imprints, Series & ISBNs:
Merlin Unwin Books Ltd: 978-1-873674, 978-1-906122

Book Trade Association Membership:
Independent Publishers Guild

2611 ▬▬▬▬▬▬

USBORNE PUBLISHING LTD
Usborne House, 83–85 Saffron Hill, London EC1N 8RT
Telephone: 020 7430 2800
Fax: 020 7242 0974 & 7430 1562
Email: mail@usborne.co.uk
Website: www.usborne.com

Warehouse:
HarperCollins, Westerhill Road, Bishopsbriggs, Glasgow G64 2QT
Telephone: 0141 306 3100
Fax: 0141 306 3767
Email: uk.orders@harpercollins.co.uk

Personnel:
Peter Usborne *(Managing Director)*
Robert Jones *(General Manager)*
Jilly Black *(Foreign Editions Director)*
Jenny Tyler *(Editorial Director)*
David Harte *(Director)*

Keith Ball *(Company Secretary)*
Paula Ziedna *(Foreign Rights Director)*
Christian Herisson *(UK Sales & Marketing Director)*
Rebecca Hill *(Fiction Editorial Director)*
Anna Howorth *(UK Marketing & Publicity Manager)*
Garry Lewis *(Production)*
Grant Hartley *(Export Sales Director)*

Children's Books; Crafts & Hobbies; Fiction; Geography & Geology; Languages & Linguistics; Music; Natural History; Reference Books, Directories & Dictionaries; Scientific & Technical; Sports & Games

Imprints, Series & ISBNs:
Usborne Publishing Ltd: 978-0-7460, 978-0-86020, 978-1-4095

Book Trade Association Membership:
Independent Publishers Guild

2612 ▬▬▬▬▬▬

*V&A PUBLISHING
Victoria & Albert Museum, South Kensington, London SW7 2RL
Telephone: 020 7942 2966
Fax: 020 7942 2967
Email: vanda@vam.ac.uk
Website: www.vandabooks.com

Distribution:
Macmillan Distribution (MDL), Houndmills, Basingstoke RG21 6XS
Telephone: 01256 302692
Fax: 01256 812558 (UK orders) & 842084 (Export orders)
Email: mdl@macmillan.co.uk
Website: www.macmillandistribution.co.uk

Personnel:
Mark Eastment *(Head of Publishing)*
Anjali Bulley *(Managing Editor)*
Nina Jacobson *(Rights Manager)*
Julie Chan *(PR & Marketing Manager)*
Clare Davis *(Production Manager)*
Clare Faulkner *(Marketing Manager)*
Tom Windross *(Senior Editor)*

Academic & Scholarly; Antiques & Collecting; Architecture & Design; Biography & Autobiography; Children's Books; Crafts & Hobbies; Fashion & Costume; Fine Art & Art History; Guide Books; Photography; Theatre, Drama & Dance

Imprints, Series & ISBNs:
V&A Publishing: 978-0-905209, 978-0-948107, 978-1-85177

Parent Company:
UK: Victoria & Albert Museum

Overseas Representation:
Australia & New Zealand: Allen & Unwin Pty Ltd, Sydney, NSW, Australia
Central & Eastern Europe: Grazyna Soszynska, Poznan-Baranowo, Poland
France: Critiques Livres Distribution, Bagnolet, France
Germany & Austria: Penguin Books Deutschland GmbH, Frankfurt-am-Main, Germany
India: Maya Publishers Pvt Ltd, New Delhi, India
Italy: Penguin Italia srl, Milan, Italy
Netherlands, Belgium & Luxembourg: Penguin Books BV, Amsterdam, Netherlands
Singapore, Indonesia & Thailand: APD Singapore Pte Ltd, Singapore
South America & Central America: David Williams, InterMedia Americana (IMA) Ltd, London, UK
Southern Africa: Book Promotions Pty Ltd, Cape Town, South Africa
Spain & Portugal: Penguin Books SA, Madrid, Spain

Turkey, Africa, Middle East, Japan, Hong Kong, Taiwan, Korea, Scandinavia, Switzerland, Malta, Greece, Cyprus, Israel, China & Philippines: International Sales Department, Penguin Books Ltd, London, UK
USA: Harry N. Abrams Inc, New York, NY, USA

Book Trade Association Membership:
Independent Publishers Guild; International Association of Museum Publishers

2613 ▬▬

VALLENTINE MITCHELL PUBLISHERS
29–45 High Street, Edgware, Middx HA8 7UU
Telephone: 020 8952 9526
Fax: 020 8952 9242
Email: info@vmbooks.com
Website: www.vmbooks.com

Trade Distribution:
NBN International, 10 Thornbury Road, Plymouth PL6 7PP
Telephone: 01752 202301
Fax: 01752 202331
Email: orders@nbninternational.com
Website: www.nbninternational.com

Personnel:
Stewart Cass *(Managing Director)*
Jenni Tinson *(Production)*
Heather Marchant *(Editor)*
Deborah Mulqueen *(Accounts)*
Toby Harris *(Sales, Marketing, Publicity)*

Academic & Scholarly; Biography & Autobiography; History & Antiquarian; Literature & Criticism; Military & War; Politics & World Affairs; Religion & Theology

Imprints, Series & ISBNs:
Vallentine Mitchell Publishers: 978-0-85303

Overseas Representation:
North America: ISBS, Portland, OR, USA

Book Trade Association Membership:
Independent Publishers Guild

2614 ▬▬

VELOCE PUBLISHING LTD
Veloce House, Parkway Farm Business Park, Middle Farm Way, Poundbury, Dorchester DT1 3AR
Telephone: 01305 260068
Fax: 01305 268864
Email: veloce@veloce.co.uk
Website: www.veloce.co.uk

Personnel:
Rod Grainger *(Publisher)*
Judith Brooks *(Publisher)*
Kevin Quinn *(General Manager)*

Animal Care & Breeding; Biography & Autobiography; Crafts & Hobbies; Do-It-Yourself; History & Antiquarian; Illustrated & Fine Editions; Military & War; Reference Books, Directories & Dictionaries; Sports & Games; Transport; Travel & Topography; Veterinary Science

New Titles: 50 (2012) , 47 (2013)
No of Employees: 16

Imprints, Series & ISBNs:
Battle Cry!
Hubble & Hattie
Veloce Publishing Ltd: 978-1-84584, 978-1-874105, 978-1-901295, 978-1-903706, 978-1-904788

Overseas Representation:
Australia & New Zealand: Capricorn Link (Australia) Pty Ltd, Windsor, NSW, Australia

Central Europe: European Marketing Services, London, UK
China, Hong Kong, Taiwan: China Publisher's Marketing, Shanghai, China
France: Librairie du Collectionneur, Paris, France
Germany: Heel-Verlag, Konigswinter, Germany
Germany, Austria & Benelux: Anselm Robinson, London, UK
Japan: Shimada & Co Inc, Tokyo, Japan; Takahara Bookstore Co Ltd, Aichi-ken, Japan
Middle East: RCA Books & Software, Comberbach, UK
New Zealand: Octane Books, Auckland, New Zealand; South Pacific Books (Imports) Ltd, Auckland, New Zealand
North America: Quayside Distribuion Services, Minneapolis, MN, USA
Scandinavia: Angell Eurosales, Berwick-upon-Tweed, UK; MarGie Bookshop, Stockholm, Sweden
South Africa: Motor Books, Johannesburg, South Africa
South East Asia: Ashton International Marketing Services, Sevenoaks, UK; Ashton International Marketing Services, Sevenoaks, UK
Spain & Italy: Bookport Associates, Corsico (MI), Italy; Libro Motor SI, Madrid, Spain

2615 ▬▬

VERITAS PUBLICATIONS
Veritas House, 7–8 Lower Abbey Street, Dublin 1, Republic of Ireland
Telephone: +353 (0)1 878 8177
Fax: +353 (0)1 878 6507
Email: publications@veritas.ie
Website: www. veritas.ie

Send Orders to:
Veritas Warehouse, Veritas Distribution, 14 Rosemount Business Park, Ballycoolin, Dublin 11, Republic of Ireland
Email: warehouse@veritas.ie
Website: www. veritas.ie

Personnel:
Maura Hyland *(Director)*
Aidan Chester *(Business Manager)*
Caitriona Clarke *(Publications Manager)*
Cathy O'Toole *(Finance Manager)*
Donna Doherty *(Commissioning Editor)*
Derek Byrne *(Publicity & Marketing)*
Liam McCabe *(Sales Agent)*

Academic & Scholarly; Biography & Autobiography; Children's Books; Educational & Textbooks; Philosophy; Religion & Theology

Imprints, Series & ISBNs:
Veritas Publications: 978-0-85390, 978-0-86217, 978-1-84730, 978-1-85390

Parent Company:
Republic of Ireland: Veritas Communications

Distributor for:
USA: Abbey Press; Abingdon Press; ACTA; Augsburg Press; Ave Maria Press; Bantam Press; Baronius Press; Candle Books; Catholic Truth Society; Catholic Word; Crossroad Publishing; Darton, Longman and Todd; Doubleday; Eerdman; HarperCollins; HarperOne; Ignatius Press; Liturgy Training Publications; Orbis Books; Our Sunday Visitor / Oxford University Press / Piatkus / Sheldon Press / SPCK

Overseas Representation:
Australia: John Garrett Publishing, Mulgrave, Vic, Australia
Malta: Libreria Taghlim Nisrani, Sliema, Malta
New Zealand: Catholic Supplies (NZ) Ltd, Wellington, New Zealand
South Africa: The Catholic Bookshop, Cape

Town, South Africa; St Augustine's Catholic Bookshop, Port Elizabeth, South Africa
USA: Acta, Chicago, IL, USA; Dufour Editions Inc, Chester Springs, PA, USA; Ignatius Press, San Francisco, CA, USA

Book Trade Association Membership:
Publishing Ireland (Foilsiú Éireann)

2616 ▬▬

VERTICAL EDITIONS
Unit 4a, Snaygill Industrial Estate, Skipton, North Yorkshire BD23 2QR
Telephone: 01756 790362
Fax: 01756 798618
Email: custserv@verticaleditions.com
Website: www.verticaleditions.com

Personnel:
Karl Waddicor *(Publisher)*

Biography & Autobiography; Cinema, Video, TV & Radio; Crime; History & Antiquarian; Sports & Games

Imprints, Series & ISBNs:
Vertical Editions: 978-1-904091

Book Trade Association Membership:
Independent Publishers Guild

2617 ▬▬

WALKER BOOKS LTD
87 Vauxhall Walk, London SE11 5HH
Telephone: 020 7793 0909
Email: rights@walker.co.uk
Website: www.walker.co.uk

Book Trade Association Membership:
Publishers Association

2618 ▬▬

WARBURG INSTITUTE
University of London, Woburn Square, London WC1H 0AB
Telephone: 020 7862 8949
Fax: 020 7862 8955
Email: warburg.books@sas.ac.uk
Website: warburg.sas.ac.uk

Personnel:
Professor Peter Mack *(Director)*
Ms Catherine Charlton *(Institute Manager)*

Academic & Scholarly; Archaeology; Architecture & Design; Bibliography & Library Science; Biography & Autobiography; Fine Art & Art History; History & Antiquarian; Magic & the Occult; Philosophy; Religion & Theology

New Titles: 3 (2012) , 4 (2013)
No of Employees: 33
Annual Turnover: £2.4M

Imprints, Series & ISBNs:
Special Publications (Warburg): 978-0-85481
Studies of the Warburg Institute: 978-0-85481
Warburg Institute Colloquia: 978-0-85481
Warburg Institute Surveys and Texts: 978-0-85481
Warburg Studies and Texts: 978-0-85481

Overseas Representation:
Italy: Nino Aragno Editore, Savigliano, Italy

2619 ▬▬

*WARD LOCK EDUCATIONAL CO LTD
Bic Ling Kee House, 1 Christopher Road, East Grinstead, West Sussex RH19 3BT
Telephone: 01342 318980
Fax: 01342 410980
Website: www.wardlockeducational.com

Personnel:
Au Bak Ling *(Chairman – Hong Kong)*
Eileen Parsons *(Company Secretary & Sales, Rights & Permissions)*

Biology & Zoology; Chemistry; Educational & Textbooks; Geography & Geology; Mathematics & Statistics; Music; Physics; Religion & Theology

Imprints, Series & ISBNs:
Ward Lock Educational Co Ltd: 978-0-7062

Parent Company:
UK: Ling Kee (UK) Ltd

Associated Companies:
UK: BLA Publishing Ltd

Overseas Representation:
Australia (KMP only): Concept Mathematics Pty Ltd, Frankston, Vic, Australia
Canada: Bacon & Hughes Ltd, Ottawa, Ont, Canada
Republic of Ireland: International Educational Services, Leixlip, Republic of Ireland

2620 ▬▬

WATERSIDE PRESS
Sherfield Gables, Reading Road, Sherfield-on-Loddon, Hook, Hants RG27 0JG
Telephone: 01256 882250
Fax: 01256 883987
Email: enquiries@watersidepress.co.uk
Website: www.WatersidePress.co.uk

Personnel:
Bryan Gibson *(Proprietor)*

Academic & Scholarly; Biography & Autobiography; Crime; Educational & Textbooks; Electronic (Educational); Electronic (Professional & Academic); History & Antiquarian; Law; Reference Books, Directories & Dictionaries; Sociology & Anthropology

Imprints, Series & ISBNs:
Waterside Press: 978-1-872870, 978-1-904380, 978-1-906534, 978-1-908162

2621 ▬▬

PAUL WATKINS PUBLISHING
1 High Street, Donington, Lincs PE11 4TA
Telephone: 01775 821542
Email: pwatkins@ pwatkinspublishing.fsnet.co.uk

Personnel:
Dr Shaun Tyas *(Proprietor)*

Academic & Scholarly; Architecture & Design; Fine Art & Art History; History & Antiquarian; Languages & Linguistics; Nautical

New Titles: 11 (2012) , 12 (2013)

Imprints, Series & ISBNs:
Shaun Tyas: 978-1-900289
Paul Watkins: 978-1-871615

Distributor for:
UK: Caedmon of Whitby; English Place-Name Society; Richard III and Yorkist History Trust; Society for Name Studies in Britain and Ireland

Book Trade Association Membership:
Small Press Centre

2622 ▬▬

WAVERLEY BOOKS
144 Port Dundas Road, Glasgow G4 0HZ
Telephone: 0141 567 2830
Fax: 0141 567 2831
Email: liz@waverley-books.co.uk

Website: www.waverley-books.co.uk

Warehouse:
Booksource, 50 Cambuslang Road,
Glasgow G32 8NB
Telephone: 0845 370 0067
Fax: 0845 370 0068

Personnel:
Ron Grosset (Publisher)
Liz Small (Sales & Marketing)

Atlases & Maps; Children's Books; Cookery,
Wines & Spirits; History & Antiquarian;
Magic & the Occult; Medical (incl. Self-Help
& Alternative Medicine); Reference Books,
Directories & Dictionaries

Imprints, Series & ISBNs:
Waverley Books: 978-1-84934, 978-1-
85534, 978-1-902407

Parent Company:
UK: D. C. Thomson & Co Ltd

Overseas Representation:
Philippines: WS Pacific, Philippines
Russia: Alexander Korzhenevski, Alex
Agency, Moscow, Russia
South Africa: Peter Matthews, Zambia

Book Trade Association Membership:
Publishing Scotland

2623

WEIDENFELD & NICOLSON
[imprint of The Orion Publishing Group Ltd]
Orion House, 5 Upper St Martin's Lane,
London WC2H 9EA
Telephone: 020 7240 3444
Fax: 020 7240 4822

Trade Counter & Warehouse:
Littlehampton Book Services Ltd,
Faraday Close, Durrington, Worthing,
West Sussex BN13 3RB
Telephone: 01903 828500
Fax: 01903 828802

Personnel:
Lisa Milton (Managing Director)
Alan Samson (Publisher – Non-Fiction)
Kirsty Dunseath (Publishing Director –
Fiction)
Amanda Harris (Publishing Director – Non-
fiction)
Jane Sturrock (Editorial Director)
Bea Hemming (Editoria Director)
Lucinda McNeile (Editorial Director)

Biography & Autobiography; Fiction;
Humour; Illustrated & Fine Editions;
Industry, Business & Management; Law;
Philosophy; Photography; Politics & World
Affairs; Sports & Games; Travel &
Topography

Imprints, Series & ISBNs:
Weidenfeld & Nicolson: 978-0-297

Parent Company:
UK: The Orion Publishing Group Ltd

Overseas Representation:
see: The Orion Publishing Group Ltd,
London, UK

2624

JOSEF WEINBERGER LTD
12–14 Mortimer Street, London W1T 3JJ
Telephone: 020 7580 2827
Fax: 020 7436 9616
Email: general.info@jwmail.co.uk
Website: www.josef-weinberger.com

Personnel:
Sean Gray (Managing Director)
Robert Heath (Financial Director)
Michael Callahan (Head of Plays)

Music; Theatre, Drama & Dance

Imprints, Series & ISBNs:
Dramatists Play Service Inc: 978-0-8222,
978-0-85676
Josef Weinberger Plays: 978-0-85676

Distributor for:
USA: Dramatists Play Service Inc

Overseas Representation:
Australia: Hal Leonard (Australia),
Melbourne, Vic, Australia
New Zealand: Play Bureau of New Zealand
Ltd, New Plymouth, New Zealand
Republic of Ireland & Northern Ireland:
Drama League of Ireland, Dublin,
Republic of Ireland
South Africa: Dalro (Pty) Ltd, Braamfontein,
South Africa
USA: Dramatists Play Service Inc, New York,
NY, USA

2625

DAVID WEST CHILDREN'S BOOKS
7 Princeton Court, 55 Felsham Road,
London SW15 1AZ
Telephone: 020 8780 3836
Fax: 020 8780 9313
Email: dww@btinternet.com
Website:
www.davidwestchildrensbooks.com and
www.davidwestchildrensebooks.com

Head Office:
St Mary's Lodge, Kitson Road, London
DW13 9HJ
Telephone: 020 8741 2890
Email: (see above)
Website: (see above)

Personnel:
David West (Proprietor/Publisher)
Lynn Lockett (Publisher)

Aviation; Biography & Autobiography;
Biology & Zoology; Children's Books; Crafts
& Hobbies; Electronic (Educational);
Electronic (Entertainment); Fashion &
Costume; Fiction; Geography & Geology;
History & Antiquarian; Military & War;
Music; Natural History; Scientific &
Technical; Sports & Games; Transport

New Titles: 40 (2012) , 45 (2013)

Imprints, Series & ISBNs:
David West Children's Books: 978-1-
909089

2626

WHICH? LTD
2 Marylebone Road, London NW1 4DF
Telephone: 020 7770 7000
Fax: 020 7770 7600
Email: which@which.co.uk
Website: www.which.co.uk

Send orders to:
Littlehampton Book Services Ltd,
Faraday Close, Durrington, Worthing,
West Sussex BN13 3RB
Telephone: 01903 828500

Personnel:
Angela Newton (Head of Book Publishing)

Accountancy & Taxation; Computer
Science; Gardening; Law; Photography;
Reference Books, Directories &
Dictionaries; Vocational Training & Careers

Imprints, Series & ISBNs:
Which? Ltd: 978-1-84490

2627

WHITE ROW
159 Lower Braniel Road, Belfast BT5 7NN
Telephone: 028 9087 4861

Email: info@whiterowpress.com
Website: www.whiterowpress.com

Imprints, Series & ISBNs:
White Row: 978-1-870132

2628

WHITING & BIRCH LTD
90 Dartmouth Road, London SE23 3HZ
Telephone: 020 8244 2421
Fax: 020-7183-5996
Email: enquiries@whitingbirch.net
Website: www.whitingbirch.net

Personnel:
David Whiting (Director)
Diana Birch (Director)

Academic & Scholarly; Languages &
Linguistics; Medical (incl. Self-Help &
Alternative Medicine); Psychology &
Psychiatry; Sociology & Anthropology

Imprints, Series & ISBNs:
Whiting & Birch Ltd: 978-1-86177, 978-1-
871177

Overseas Representation:
Australia: Lightning Source AU Pty Ltd,
Scoresby, Vic, Australia
USA: Ingram Publisher Services Inc,
Chambersburg, PA, USA; Lightning
Source Inc (US), Lavergne, TN, USA

2629

WHITTET BOOKS LTD
1, St John's Lane, Stansted, Essex
CM24 8JU
Telephone: 01279 815871
Email: mail@whittetbooks.com
Website: www.whittetbooks.com

Sales Office:
Book Systems Plus (at HDM LTD),
Station Road, Linton, Cambs CB21 4UX
Telephone: 01223 893261
Fax: 01223 893852
Email: mail@booksystemsplus.com
Website: www.booksystemsplus.com

Personnel:
George Papa (Managing Director)
Shirley Greenall (Publisher)

Animal Care & Breeding; Biology &
Zoology; Gardening; Natural History;
Veterinary Science

Imprints, Series & ISBNs:
Whittet Books Ltd: 978-0-905483, 978-1-
873580

Parent Company:
UK: Book Systems Plus Ltd

Overseas Representation:
USA & Canada: Diamond Farm Book
Publishers, Brighton, Canada

2630

WHITTLES PUBLISHING
Dunbeath Mill, Dunbeath, Caithness
KW6 6EG
Telephone: 01593 731333
Fax: 01593 731400
Email: info@whittlespublishing.com
Website: www.whittlespublishing.com

Warehouse/Distributor:
BookSource, 50 Cambuslang Road,
Glasgow G32 8NB
Telephone: 0845 370 0063
Fax: 0845 370 0064
Email: customerservice@booksource.net
Website: www.booksource.net

Personnel:
Dr Keith Whittles (Publisher)

Mrs Sue Steven (Sales & Promotions
Manager)
Ms Shelley Teasdale (Production Editor)

Academic & Scholarly; Architecture &
Design; Biography & Autobiography;
Educational & Textbooks; Engineering;
Geography & Geology; Military & War;
Natural History; Nautical; Reference Books,
Directories & Dictionaries; Scientific &
Technical

New Titles: 25 (2012) , 30 (2013)
No of Employees: 5

Imprints, Series & ISBNs:
Whittles Publishing: 978-1-84995, 978-1-
870325, 978-1-904445

Overseas Representation:
Africa, Ethiopia, Eritrea, Ivory Coast &
Rwanda: Kelvin van Hesselt, UK
Germany, Austria & Switzerland: Missing
Link International Booksellers, Bremen,
Germany
Hong Kong, China, Taiwan & Korea: Asia
Publishers Services Ltd, Hong Kong
India: Sara Books Pvt Ltd, New Delhi, India
Latin America, Caribbean & Sub-Saharan
Africa: InterMedia Americana (IMA) Ltd,
London, UK
Pakistan, Indonesia, Japan, Malaysia and
Singapore: The White Partnership, UK
Philippines and Thailand: Edwin
Makabenta, Philippines

Book Trade Association Membership:
Publishing Scotland

2631

WILD GOOSE PUBLICATIONS
4th Floor, Savoy House,
140 Sauchiehall Street, Glasgow G2 3DH
Telephone: 0141 332 6292
Fax: 0141 332 1090
Email: admin@ionabooks.com
Website: www.ionabooks.com

Trade Orders:
BookSource, 50 Cambuslang Road,
Glasgow G32 8NB
Telephone: 0845 370 0067
Fax: 0845 370 0068
Email: orders@booksource.net
Website: www.booksource.net

Personnel:
Sandra Kramer (Publishing Manager)
Alex O'Neill (Assistant Publishing Manager
(Marketing))
Neil Paynter (Project Editor)
Jane Riley (Production)
Susie Hay (Administration Assistant)

Music; Religion & Theology

Imprints, Series & ISBNs:
Wild Goose Publications: 978-0-947988,
978-1-84952, 978-1-901557, 978-1-
905010

Parent Company:
UK: The Iona Community

Overseas Representation:
Australia & New Zealand: Willow
Connection Pty Ltd, Brookvale, NSW,
Australia
Canada: Novalis Inc, Toronto, Ont, Canada
New Zealand: Pleroma Christian Supplies,
Otane, Central Hawkes Bay, New Zealand

Book Trade Association Membership:
Independent Publishers Guild

2632

WILEY
The Atrium, Southern Gate, Chichester,
West Sussex PO19 8SQ
Telephone: 01243 779777

Fax: 01243 775878
Email: europe@wiley.co.uk
Website: www.wiley.com

Send Orders to:
Wiley, European Distribution Centre,
New Era Estate, Oldlands Way,
Bognor Regis, West Sussex PO22 9NQ
Telephone: 01243 779777
Fax: 01243 843123
Email: customer@wiley.com
Website: www.wiley.com

Also at:
Wiley, 9600 Garsington Road, Oxford
OX4 2DQ
Telephone: 01865 776868
Website: www.wiley.com

Personnel:
D. Bova (Vice-President & Director, HR,
Europe)
P. Carpenter (Vice-President & Managing
Director, Research Communications)
U. D'Arcy (Financial Director, Corporate
Finance)
M. Davis (Vice-President & Managing
Director, Research Innovations)
C. Hall (Vice-President & Director, Finance,
Global Research)
S. Joshua (Director of Legal Affairs, Europe)
P. Kisray (Vice-President, International
Development, Sales Management)
M. Leete (Director of Publishing Operations,
UK Professional Development)
C. Nobbs (Vice-President, Distribution &
Customer Service, EMEA & Asia)
A. Robinson (Vice-President & Managing
Director, Professional & Business
Innovations)
S. Stevens (Vice-President, Higher Education
Development, EMEA & Asia)
J. Walmsley (Vice-President & Managing
Director, Professional Practice & Learning)
K. Wootton (Vice-President & Sales Director,
EMEA)

Academic & Scholarly; Accountancy &
Taxation; Agriculture; Animal Care &
Breeding; Archaeology; Architecture &
Design; Atlases & Maps; Aviation;
Biography & Autobiography; Biology &
Zoology; Chemistry; Computer Science;
Crafts & Hobbies; Do-It-Yourself;
Economics; Educational & Textbooks;
Electronic (Educational); Electronic
(Professional & Academic); Engineering;
Environment & Development Studies;
Fashion & Costume; Gardening; Geography
& Geology; Guide Books; Health & Beauty;
History & Antiquarian; Industry, Business &
Management; Languages & Linguistics;
Literature & Criticism; Mathematics &
Statistics; Medical (incl. Self-Help &
Alternative Medicine); Military & War;
Music; Natural History; Nautical;
Philosophy; Photography; Physics; Poetry;
Politics & World Affairs; Psychology &
Psychiatry; Reference Books, Directories &
Dictionaries; Religion & Theology; Scientific
& Technical; Sociology & Anthropology;
Sports & Games; Veterinary Science

Imprints, Series & ISBNs:
John Wiley & Sons Ltd: 978-0-470, 978-0-
471

Parent Company:
USA: John Wiley & Sons Inc

Associated Companies:
Germany: Wiley-VCH Verlag GmbH
UK: John Wiley & Sons Ltd

Distributor for:
UK: Fernhurst Books Limited ; Polity Press
USA: Columbia University Press; Harvard
University Press; Johns Hopkins University
Press; LOEB Classical Library; The MIT
University Press; W. W. Norton & Co Ltd;
O'Reilly UK Ltd; Princeton University
Press; University of California Press; The

University of Chicago Press; Yale
University Press

Book Trade Association Membership:
Publishers Association; Booksellers
Association; Educational Publishers
Council; International Group of Scientific,
Medical & Technical Publishers

2633

WILLOW ISLAND EDITIONS
41 Water Lane, Middlestown, Wakefield,
West Yorkshire WF4 4PX
Telephone: 01924 270723
Email: richard@willowisland.co.uk
Website: www.willowisland.co.uk

Personnel:
Richard Bell (Contact)

Crafts & Hobbies; Gardening; Guide Books;
Natural History; Travel & Topography

Imprints, Series & ISBNs:
Willow Island Editions: 978-1-902467

2634

NEIL WILSON PUBLISHING LTD
226 King Street, Castle Douglas DG7 1DS
Telephone: 01556 504119
Fax: 01556 505065
Email: info@nwp.co.uk
Website: www.nwp.co.uk

**Distribution, Sales Ledger & Trade
Orders:**
BookSource, 50 Cambuslang Road,
Glasgow G32 5NB
Telephone: 0845 370 0067
Fax: 0845 370 0068
Email: orders@booksource.net
Website: www.booksource.net

Personnel:
Neil Wilson (Managing Director, Sales,
Rights & Permissions)

Biography & Autobiography; Cookery,
Wines & Spirits; Crime; Guide Books;
History & Antiquarian; Humour; Military &
War; Music; Nautical; Travel & Topography

New Titles: 41 (2012) , 32 (2013)
No of Employees: 1
Annual Turnover: £100,000

Imprints, Series & ISBNs:
11:9
The Angel's Share
The In Pinn
The Vital Spark
Neil Wilson Publishing Ltd: 978-1-897784,
978-1-903238, 978-1-906476

Overseas Representation:
London and Key Accounts: Simon Perks, UK
Republic of Ireland: Geoff Bryan, Dublin,
Republic of Ireland
Scotland: Don Morrison, UK
USA: Interlink Publishing Group Inc,
Northampton, MA, USA

Book Trade Association Membership:
Publishing Scotland

2635

PHILIP WILSON PUBLISHERS
6 Salem Road, London W2 4BU
Telephone: 020 7243 1225
Fax: 020 7243 1226
Email: sales@philip-wilson.co.uk
Website: www.philip-wilson.co.uk

Personnel:
Jonathan McDonnell (Managing Director)
Philip Wilson (Publisher)
Anne Jackson (Commissioning Editor)
Liz Stuckey (Company Secretary)

Academic & Scholarly; Antiques &
Collecting; Architecture & Design; Fine Art
& Art History; History & Antiquarian;
Illustrated & Fine Editions; Photography

Imprints, Series & ISBNs:
Philip Wilson Publishers: 978-0-85667

Parent Company:
UK: I. B. Tauris & Co Ltd

Overseas Representation:
USA: Palgrave Macmillan, New York, NY,
USA
Worldwide: I. B. Tauris & Co Ltd, London,
UK

2636

WINDHORSE PUBLICATIONS
169 Mill Road, Cambridge CB1 3AN
Telephone: 01223 213300
Email: info@windhorsepublications.com
Website:
www.windhorsepublications.com

UK Trade Orders:
BookSource, 50 Cambuslang Road,
Cambuslang, Glasgow G32 8NB
Telephone: 0845 370 0063
Fax: 0845 370 0064
Email: customerservice@booksource.net
Website: www.booksource.net

Personnel:
Peter Joseph (Publishing Director)
Michelle Bernard (Publishing Controller)
Lee Walford (Accountant)
Hannah Atkinson (Marketing Assistant)

Biography & Autobiography; Philosophy;
Religion & Theology

Imprints, Series & ISBNs:
Windhorse Publications: 978-0-904766,
978-1-899579, 978-1-907314, 978-1-
909314

Overseas Representation:
Asia: Horizon Books Pte Ltd, Singapore
Australia & New Zealand: Windhorse
Books, Newtown, NSW, Australia
South Africa: Stephan Phillips (Pty) Ltd,
Cape Town, South Africa
USA: Consortium Book Sales & Distribution
Inc, St Paul, MN, USA

2637

WIT PRESS
Ashurst Lodge, Ashurst, Southampton,
Hampshire SO40 7AA
Telephone: 023 8029 3223
Fax: 023 8029 2853
Email: witpress@witpress.com
Website: www.witpress.com

Personnel:
Prof C. A. Brebbia (Chairman)
David Anderson (Chief Executive Officer)
Ms Isabelle Rham (Production Editor)
Ms Lorraine Carter (Sales Co-ordinator)

Academic & Scholarly; Architecture &
Design; Biology & Zoology; Computer
Science; Electronic (Professional &
Academic); Engineering; Environment &
Development Studies; Geography &
Geology; Industry, Business &
Management; Mathematics & Statistics;
Medical (incl. Self-Help & Alternative
Medicine); Physics; Scientific & Technical;
Transport

Imprints, Series & ISBNs:
WIT Press: 978-0-90545, 978-0-905451,
978-1-84564, 978-1-85312

Associated Companies:
USA: Computational Mechanics
International Ltd

Book Trade Association Membership:
LAPSLD

2638

WORDSWORTH EDITIONS LTD
8b East Street, Ware, Herts SG12 9HJ
Telephone: 01920 465167
Fax: 01920 462267
Email: enquiries@wordsworth-
editions.com
Website: www.wordsworth-editions.com

Personnel:
Helen Trayler (Managing Director)
Derek Wright (Finance Director)

Children's Books; Crime; Fiction;
Philosophy; Poetry; Reference Books,
Directories & Dictionaries

Imprints, Series & ISBNs:
Wordsworth Editions Ltd: 978-1-84022,
978-1-85326

Overseas Representation:
Australia & Papua New Guinea: Peribo Pty
Ltd, Mount Kuring-Gai, NSW, Australia
India: OM Book Services, Delhi, India
New Zealand: Nationwide Book Distributors
Ltd, Oxford, New Zealand
USA: L. B. May & Associates, Knoxville, TN,
USA

Book Trade Association Membership:
Booksellers Association

2639

WORTH PRESS LTD
34 South End, Bassingbourn,
S Cambridgeshire SG8 5NJ
Telephone: 01763 248075
Fax: 01763 248155
Email: info@worthpress.co.uk
Website: www.worthpress.co.uk

Warehouse:
Antony Rowe Ltd, Units 3 & 4,
Pegasus Way, Bowerhill, Melksham
SN12 6TR
Telephone: 01225 703691
Fax: 01225 704518

Personnel:
Ken Webb (Chairman)
Rupert Webb (Managing Director)

Architecture & Design; Aviation; Crime;
Fiction; Illustrated & Fine Editions;
Literature & Criticism; Military & War;
Physics; Religion & Theology

Imprints, Series & ISBNs:
Worth Press Ltd: 978-1-84931, 978-1-
903025

Overseas Representation:
Europe: Cristina Galimberti, Bristol, UK

2640

Y LOLFA CYF
Hen Swyddfa'r Heddlu, Talybont,
Ceredigion SY24 5HE
Telephone: 01970 832304
Fax: 01970 832782
Email: ylolfa@ylolfa.com
Website: www.ylolfa.com

Personnel:
Garmon Gruffudd (Director)
Sonia Hughes (Administrator)
Lefi Gruffudd (Editor)
Branwen Huws (Marketing)
Paul Williams (Production)
Eirian Jones (English Language Editor)

Biography & Autobiography; Children's
Books; Cookery, Wines & Spirits; Crafts &

Hobbies; Fiction; Guide Books; Humour;
Languages & Linguistics; Music; Poetry;
Politics & World Affairs; Sports & Games;
Travel & Topography

Imprints, Series & ISBNs:
Dinas
Y Lolfa: 978-0-86243, 978-0-904864

Overseas Representation:
North America: Dufour Editions, USA

Book Trade Association Membership:
Union of Welsh Publishers & Booksellers

2641 ▬▬▬▬

YALE UNIVERSITY PRESS LONDON
47 Bedford Square, London WC1B 3DP
Telephone: 020 7079 4900
Fax: 020 7079 4901
Website: www.yalebooks.co.uk

Warehouse & Fulfilment:
John Wiley & Sons Ltd, Distribution Centre,
Shripney Road, Bognor Regis, West Sussex
PO22 9SA
Telephone: 01243 829121
Fax: 01243 820250

Personnel:
Robert Baldock (Managing Director)
Noel Murphy (Sales & Marketing Director)
Gillian Malpass (Art & Architecture
    Publisher)
Sally Salvesen (Decorative Arts Publisher)
Heather McCallum (Trade Books Publisher)
Phoebe Clapham (Politics, Economics &
    Current Affairs Editor)
Katie Harris (Publicity Manager)
Charlotte Stafford (Promotion & Direct Mail
    Manager)
Andrew Jarmain (Sales Manager)
Karen McTigue (International Sales
    Manager)
Anne Bihan (Head of Rights)
Stephen Kent (Production & Design
    Manager)
Emma Duncalf (Finance Director)

Academic & Scholarly; Archaeology;
Architecture & Design; Biography &
Autobiography; Economics; Fashion &
Costume; Fine Art & Art History; Gender
Studies; History & Antiquarian; Illustrated &
Fine Editions; Languages & Linguistics;
Military & War; Music; Natural History;
Philosophy; Photography; Politics & World
Affairs; Religion & Theology; Theatre,
Drama & Dance

New Titles: 400 (2012) , 410 (2013)
No of Employees: 45
Annual Turnover: £8M

Imprints, Series & ISBNs:
Yale University Press London: 978-0-300

Parent Company:
USA: Yale University Press

Associated Companies:
UK: Yale Representation Ltd

Overseas Representation:
Africa (excluding Southern Africa & Nigeria):
    Kelvin van Hasselt Publishing Services,
    Norfolk, UK
Australia, New Zealand, Fiji & Papua New
    Guinea: Inbooks, NSW, Australia
Austria, Germany, Italy, Switzerland, Spain
    & Portugal: Uwe Lüdemann, Berlin,
    Germany
Benelux, Denmark, Finland, France, Iceland,
    Norway & Sweden: Fred Hermans,
    Bovenkarspel, Netherlands
Central Europe: Ewa Ledóchowicz,
    Konstancin-Jeziorna, Poland
China, Hong Kong & Philippines: Ed
    Summerson, Asia Publishers Services Ltd,
    Hong Kong
India: S. Janakiraman, Book Marketing
    Services, Chennai, India
Iran: Farhad Maftoon, Tehran, Iran
Israel: International Publishers
    Representatives, Nicosia, Cyprus
Malaysia: APD Malaysia Pte Ltd, Malaysia
Middle East: Claire de Grucy & Bill Kennedy,
    Avicenna Partnership, Oxford, UK
Nigeria: Bounty Books, Ibadan, Nigeria
Pakistan: Anwer Iqbal, Book Bird Publishers
    Representatives, Lahore, Pakistan
Republic of Ireland & Northern Ireland:
    Robert Towers, Monkstown, Co Dublin,
    Republic of Ireland
Singapore, Thailand, Vietnam, Cambodia,
    Indonesia & Brunei: APD Singapore Pte
    Ltd, Singapore
Southern Africa: Book Promotions Pty Ltd,
    Diep River, South Africa
USA, Central & South America, Mexico,
    Canada, Japan, Korea & Taiwan: Yale
    University Press, New Haven, CT, USA

Book Trade Association Membership:
Independent Publishers Guild

2642 ▬▬▬▬

ZAMBEZI PUBLISHING LTD
22 Second Avenue, Camels Head,
Plymouth, Devon PL2 2EQ
Telephone: 01752 367300
Fax: 01752 350453
Email: info@zampub.com
Website: www.zampub.com

Business:
PO Box 221, Plymouth, Devon PL2 2YJ

Telephone: 01752 367300
Fax: 01752 350453
Email: (as above)
Website: (as above)

Personnel:
Mrs Sasha Fenton (Chief Executive Officer)
Jan Budkowski (Managing Director)

Industry, Business & Management; Magic &
the Occult; Medical (incl. Self-Help &
Alternative Medicine); Psychology &
Psychiatry

Imprints, Series & ISBNs:
Zambezi Publishing Ltd: 978-0-9533478,
    978-1-903065

Associated Companies:
UK: Stellium Ltd

Overseas Representation:
Europe: Deep Books Ltd, UK
USA & Rest of the World: Sterling
    Publishing Co Inc, New York, NY, USA

2643 ▬▬▬▬

ZED BOOKS LTD
7 Cynthia Street, London N1 9JF
Telephone: 020 7837 4014 & 8466
Fax: 020 7833 3960
Email: sales@zedbooks.net
Website: www.zedbooks.co.uk

Distribution:
NBN International Ltd, 10 Thornbury Road,
Plymouth PL6 7PP
Telephone: 01752 202301
Fax: 01752 202331
Email: orders@nbninternational.com

**Trade Representation – UK & Republic
of Ireland:**
Compass Academic
Telephone: 020 8994 6477
Email: ca@compass-academic.co.uk
Website: www.academic.compass-
    booksales.co.uk/academic

Personnel:
Ken Barlow (Senior Commissioning Editor)
Kim Walker (Commissioning Editor)
Kika Sroka-Miller (Assistant Commissioning
    Editor)
Anneberth Lux (Sales and Marketing
    Manager)
Peter Bennett (Finance Manager)
Dan Och (Production Manager)
Ruben Mootoosamy (Operations Manager)
Renata Kasprzak (Foreign Rights and
    Marketing Executive)
Federico Campagna (Rights Manager)
Kika Sroka-Miller (Editorial Assistant)

Academic & Scholarly; Economics;
Environment & Development Studies;
Gender Studies; Politics & World Affairs;
Sociology & Anthropology

Imprints, Series & ISBNs:
Zed Books Ltd: 978-0-86232, 978-0-
    905762, 978-1-78032, 978-1-84277,
    978-1-84813, 978-1-85649

Overseas Representation:
Australia & New Zealand: Inbooks, Frenchs
    Forest, NSW, Australia
Canada: Brunswick Books Ltd, Toronto, ON,
    Canada
Europe: Durnell Marketing, Tunbridge
    Wells, UK
India: Maya Publishers, New Delhi, India
Ireland: Geoff Bryan Publishers Agent,
    Dublin, Republic of Ireland
Middle East: Avicenna Partnership, Witney,
    UK
South Africa, Botswana, Namibia, Lesotho,
    Swaziland: Blue Weaver, Cape Town,
    South Africa
South America & Caribbean: David
    Williams, Intermedia Americana, London,
    UK
Sub-Saharan Africa (excluding South Africa,
    Botswana, Namibia, Lesotho, Swaziland):
    Tony Moggach, IntermediaAfricana,
    London, UK
USA: Palgrave Macmillan, New York, USA

Book Trade Association Membership:
Independent Publishers Guild

2644 ▬▬▬▬

ZYMURGY PUBLISHING
Hoults Estate, Walker Road,
Newcastle upon Tyne NE6 2HL
Telephone: 0191 276 2425
Fax: 0191 276 2425
Email:
ZymurgyPublishing@googlemail.com
Website: Zymurgypublishing.co.uk

Personnel:
Martin Ellis (Publisher)

Biography & Autobiography; Children's
Books; Fiction; Gardening; Health &
Beauty; Humour; Illustrated & Fine Editions;
Music; Natural History; Photography

Imprints, Series & ISBNs:
Zymurgy Publishing: 978-1-903506

Book Trade Association Membership:
Independent Publishers Guild; Publishers
Publicity Circle

3 Packagers

3001

ALBION PRESS LTD
Spring Hill, Idbury, Oxon OX7 6RU
Telephone: 01993 831094

Personnel:
Emma Bradford *(Managing Director)*
Neil Philip *(Editorial Director)*

Children's Books; Illustrated & Fine Editions

3002

AMOLIBROS
Loundshay Manor Cottage,
Preston Bowyer, Milverton, Taunton,
Somerset TA4 1QF
Telephone: 01823 401527
Fax: 01823 401527
Email: amolibros@aol.com
Website: www.amolibros.co.uk

Trade Enquiries & Orders:
Gardners Books, 1 Whittle Drive,
Eastbourne, East Sussex BN23 6QH
Telephone: 01323 521555
Fax: 01323 521666

Personnel:
Jane Tatam *(Managing Consultant)*

*Academic & Scholarly; Biography &
Autobiography; Biology & Zoology;
Chemistry; Children's Books; Cookery,
Wines & Spirits; Fiction; Fine Art & Art
History; Gardening; Geography & Geology;
Guide Books; History & Antiquarian; Magic
& the Occult; Medical (incl. Self-Help &
Alternative Medicine); Music; Nautical;
Philosophy; Poetry; Politics & World Affairs;
Religion & Theology; Scientific & Technical;
Sports & Games; Theatre, Drama & Dance;
Travel & Topography; Vocational Training &
Careers*

3003

NICOLA BAXTER LTD
The Brew House, Framingham Earl Road,
Yelverton, Norwich NR14 7PD
Telephone: 01508 491111
Email: nb@nicolabaxter.co.uk
Website: www.nicolabaxter.co.uk

Personnel:
Nicola Baxter *(Proprietor)*

Children's Books; Educational & Textbooks

3004

BENDER RICHARDSON WHITE
PO Box 266, Uxbridge UB9 5NX
Telephone: 01895 832444
Fax: 01895 835213

Email: brw@brw.co.uk
Website: www.brw.co.uk

Personnel:
Lionel Bender *(Editorial Director)*
Kim Richardson *(Sales & Production
Director)*
Ben White *(Art & Design Director)*

*Biology & Zoology; Children's Books;
Educational & Textbooks; Natural History;
Reference Books, Directories &
Dictionaries; Religion & Theology*

3005

*BLA PUBLISHING LTD
1 Christopher Road, East Grinstead,
West Sussex RH19 3BT
Telephone: 01342 318980
Fax: 01342 410980
Email: eileen@wleducat.freeserve.co.uk

Personnel:
Au Bak Ling *(Chairman)*
Eileen Parsons *(Company Secretary, Sales,
Rights & Permissions)*

*Antiques & Collecting; Aviation; Biology &
Zoology; Chemistry; Children's Books;
Computer Science; Gardening; Medical
(incl. Self-Help & Alternative Medicine);
Military & War; Music; Natural History;
Nautical; Physics; Reference Books,
Directories & Dictionaries; Religion &
Theology*

Imprints, Series & ISBNs:
Thames Head

Parent Company:
UK: Ling Kee (UK) Ltd

Associated Companies:
UK: Ward Lock Educational Co Ltd

3006

*BLUE BEYOND BOOKS
4 Paget Road, Ipswich IP1 3RP
Telephone: 01473 423247
Fax: 01473 214096
Email: martin.spettigue@virgin.net

Personnel:
Martin Spettigue *(Manager)*
Mark Thomas *(Sales Representative)*
Nelly Coudoa *(Sales Representative)*
Hita Hirons *(Sales Representative)*

*Magic & the Occult; Music; Philosophy;
Poetry; Religion & Theology*

Associated Companies:
USA: Aum Publications; McKeever
Publishing

Distributor for:
USA: Aum Publications; McKeever
Publishing

Overseas Representation:
Australia: Wisdom's Delight, Brisbane, Qld,
Australia
Canada: Peace Publishing, Ottawa, Ont,
Canada
France: Editions Sri Chinmey, Paris, France
Germany: The Golden Shore, Nurnberg,
Germany
USA: Heart-Light Distributors, Seattle, WA,
USA

3007

**CAMBRIDGE PUBLISHING
MANAGEMENT LTD**
Burr Elm Court, Main Street, Caldecote,
Cambs CB23 7NU
Telephone: 01954 214000
Fax: 01954 214002
Email: c.kanani@cambridgepm.co.uk
Website: www.cambridgepm.co.uk

Personnel:
Jackie Dobbyne *(Managing Director)*
Catherine Burch *(Editorial Manager)*
Claire Kanani *(Marketing/PA)*

*Academic & Scholarly; Archaeology;
Architecture & Design; Biography &
Autobiography; Cookery, Wines & Spirits;
Crafts & Hobbies; Economics; Educational &
Textbooks; English as a Foreign Language;
Fine Art & Art History; Gardening; Guide
Books; Illustrated & Fine Editions; Industry,
Business & Management; Law; Medical
(incl. Self-Help & Alternative Medicine);
Military & War; Natural History; Reference
Books, Directories & Dictionaries; Religion &
Theology; Scientific & Technical; Travel &
Topography; Vocational Training & Careers*

Imprints, Series & ISBNs:
Cambridge Editions
Cambridge Independent Press

Book Trade Association Membership:
Publishers Association; Independent
Publishers Guild

3008

**DIAGRAM VISUAL INFORMATION
LTD**
34 Elaine Grove, London NW5 4QH
Telephone: 020 7485 5941
Fax: 020 7485 5941
Email: info@diagramgroup.com
Website: www.diagramgroup.com

Personnel:
Bruce Robertson *(Managing Director)*
Patricia Robertson *(Director)*

*Children's Books; Educational & Textbooks;
Geography & Geology; Health & Beauty;
Reference Books, Directories &
Dictionaries; Sports & Games*

Overseas Representation:
Bulgaria: Nika Literary Agency, Sofia,
Bulgaria
Eastern Europe: DS Druck- und Verlags
Service, London, UK
Hungary: DS Budapest Kft, Budapest,
Hungary
Japan: Tuttle-Mori Agency Inc, Tokyo, Japan
Korea: KCC, Seoul, Republic of Korea
Lithuania: Musa Knyga, Vilnius, Lithuania
Netherlands & Scandinavia: Kolar Rights
and Translation, Feidamsee, Austria
Poland: DS Druck Warszawa, Warsaw,
Poland
Romania: Mast Publishing, Bucharest,
Romania
Russia: DS, Moscow, Russia
Thailand: Big Apple Tuttle-Mori Agency
(Thailand) Co Ltd, Bangkok, Thailand

3009

D & N PUBLISHING
8 Fiveways, Baydon, Wilts SN8 2LH
Telephone: 01672 540556
Email: d@dnpublishing.co.uk

Personnel:
David Price-Goodfellow *(Manager/Owner)*
Namrita Price-Goodfellow *(Designer/
Owner)*

*Animal Care & Breeding; Antiques &
Collecting; Aviation; Biology & Zoology;
Crafts & Hobbies; Do-It-Yourself; Fine Art &
Art History; Gardening; Guide Books;
History & Antiquarian; Medical (incl. Self-
Help & Alternative Medicine); Military &
War; Natural History; Photography;
Reference Books, Directories &
Dictionaries; Sports & Games; Theatre,
Drama & Dance; Transport; Travel &
Topography; Veterinary Science*

3010

EDDISON SADD EDITIONS LTD
St Chad's House, 148 King's Cross Road,
London WC1X 9DH
Telephone: 020 7837 1968
Fax: 020 7837 2025
Email: info@eddisonsadd.co.uk
Website: www.eddisonsadd.com

Accounts:
Facts & Figures
Telephone: 01280 813111
Fax: 01280 817229

Personnel:
Nick Eddison *(Managing Director)*

75

David Owen *(Financial Director)*
Sarah Rooney *(Production Director)*

Children's Books; Cookery, Wines & Spirits; Health & Beauty; Magic & the Occult; Medical (incl. Self-Help & Alternative Medicine)

Imprints, Series & ISBNs:
Bookinabox

Associated Companies:
UK: Connections Book Publishing

Overseas Representation:
Worldwide: Melia Publishing Services for Connections Book Services, UK

3011 ▬▬▬▬▬▬▬▬▬▬▬▬

ESSENTIAL WORKS LTD
The Green, 29 Clerkenwell Green, London EC1R 0DU
Telephone: 020 7017 0890
Email: info@essentialworks.co.uk
Website: www.essentialworks.co.uk

Personnel:
John Conway *(Managing Director)*
Mal Peachey *(Publishing Director)*

Biography & Autobiography; Cinema, Video, TV & Radio; Fashion & Costume; Humour; Illustrated & Fine Editions; Military & War; Music; Photography; Sports & Games; Transport

Imprints, Series & ISBNs:
Rocket 88 Books

3012 ▬▬▬▬▬▬▬▬▬▬▬▬

FREELANCE MARKET NEWS
8–10 Dutton Street, Manchester M3 1LE
Telephone: 0161 819 9919
Fax: 0161 819 2842
Email: fmn@writersbureau.com
Website: www.freelancemarketnews.com

Personnel:
Miss Angela Cox *(Editorial & Circulation)*

Educational & Textbooks; Fiction; Literature & Criticism; Photography; Poetry

Parent Company:
UK: The Writers Bureau Ltd

3013 ▬▬▬▬▬▬▬▬▬▬▬▬

GRAHAM-CAMERON PUBLISHING & ILLUSTRATION
The Studio, 23 Holt Road, Sheringham, Norfolk NR26 8NB
Telephone: 01263 821333
Fax: 01263 821334
Email: enquiry@gciforillustration.com
Website: www.gciforillustration.com

Marketing & Sales:
Duncan Graham-Cameron,
59 Hertford Road, Brighton BN1 7GG
Telephone: 01273 385890
Email: duncan@gciforillustration.com
Website: www.gciforillustration.com

Personnel:
Duncan Graham-Cameron *(Managing Director)*
Helen Graham-Cameron *(Art Director)*

Architecture & Design; Children's Books; Educational & Textbooks; English as a Foreign Language; Military & War; Natural History; Reference Books, Directories & Dictionaries; Religion & Theology

Imprints, Series & ISBNs:
Graham-Cameron Publishing & Illustration: 978-0-947672

Associated Companies:
UK: Graham-Cameron Illustration

Book Trade Association Membership:
Independent Publishers Guild; Cambridge Book Association; CAMPUS; The Paternosters

3014 ▬▬▬▬▬▬▬▬▬▬▬▬

HART McLEOD LTD
14A Greenside, Waterbeach, Cambridge CB25 9HP
Telephone: 01223 861495
Fax: 01223 862902
Email: jo@hartmcleod.co.uk
Website: www.hartmcleod.co.uk

Personnel:
Graham Hart *(Editorial Director)*
Joanne Barker *(Design Director)*

Academic & Scholarly; Educational & Textbooks; Electronic (Educational); Sports & Games

3015 ▬▬▬▬▬▬▬▬▬▬▬▬

THE IVY PRESS LTD
210 High Street, Lewes, East Sussex BN7 2NS
Telephone: 01273 487440
Fax: 01273 487441
Website: www.ivypress.co.uk

Personnel:
Stephen Paul *(Managing Director)*
Nikki Tilbury *(Associate Publisher)*
Peter Bridgewater *(Creative Director)*

Children's Books; Crafts & Hobbies; Fashion & Costume; Gardening; Illustrated & Fine Editions; Natural History

3016 ▬▬▬▬▬▬▬▬▬▬▬▬

LITTLE PEOPLE BOOKS
The Home of BookBod, Knighton, Radnorshire LD7 1UP
Telephone: 01547 520925
Email: littlepeoplebooks@thehobb.tv
Website: www.thehobb.tv/lpb

Personnel:
Grant Jessé *(Production Director, Managing Editor)*

Audio Books; Children's Books; Educational & Textbooks

Imprints, Series & ISBNs:
Little People Books: 978-1-899573

Parent Company:
UK: Grant Jessé

Book Trade Association Membership:
Independent Publishers Guild; Book Packagers Association

3017 ▬▬▬▬▬▬▬▬▬▬▬▬

MARKET HOUSE BOOKS LTD
Suite B, Elsinore House,
43 Buckingham Street, Aylesbury, Bucks HP20 2NQ
Telephone: 01296 484911
Fax: 01296 338934
Email: books@mhbref.com
Website: www.markethousebooks.com

Personnel:
Elizabeth Martin *(Chief Editor)*
Anne Stibbs/Kerr *(Director (Production))*
Jonathan Law *(Director (Editorial))*

Computer Science; Industry, Business & Management; Law; Medical (incl. Self-Help & Alternative Medicine); Music; Psychology & Psychiatry; Reference Books, Directories & Dictionaries; Scientific & Technical; Theatre, Drama & Dance

3018 ▬▬▬▬▬▬▬▬▬▬▬▬

METHODIST PUBLISHING
Methodist Church House, London NW1 5JR
Telephone: 020 7486 5502
Email: resources@methodistchurch.org.uk
Website:
www.methodistpublishing.org.uk

Personnel:
Ms Sarah Bennison *(Publishing & Fundraising Team Leader)*

Educational & Textbooks; Electronic (Educational); Reference Books, Directories & Dictionaries; Religion & Theology

Imprints, Series & ISBNs:
Methodist Publishing: 978-1-85852

Parent Company:
UK: The Methodist Church

3019 ▬▬▬▬▬▬▬▬▬▬▬▬

NEW CARAMEL LONDON LTD
[a division of Editions Caramel SA]
12–13 Ship Street, Brighton, East Sussex BN1 1AD
Website: www.caramel.be

Contact:
Jean-Luc Dubois, Otto de Mentockplein 19, 1853 Strombeek-Bever, Belgium
Telephone: +32 2 263 20 51
Fax: +32 2 263 20 50
Email: jeanluc.dubois@caramel.be
Website: www.caramel.be

Personnel:
Jean-Michel d'Oultremont *(Joint Managing Director)*
Jean-Luc Dubois *(Joint Managing Director)*

Children's Books

Parent Company:
Belgium: Editions Caramel SA

Book Trade Association Membership:
Publishers Association

3020 ▬▬▬▬▬▬▬▬▬▬▬▬

ORPHEUS BOOKS LTD
6 Church Green, Witney, Oxon OX28 4AW
Telephone: 01993 774949
Fax: 01993 700330
Email: info@orpheusbooks.com
Website: www.orpheusbooks.com

Personnel:
Nicholas Harris *(Director)*
Sarah Hartley *(Director)*

Children's Books

Imprints, Series & ISBNs:
Orpheus Books Ltd: 978-1-901323, 978-1-905473

3021 ▬▬▬▬▬▬▬▬▬▬▬▬

PARAGON PUBLISHING
4 North Street, Rothersthorpe, Northants NN7 3JB
Telephone: 01604 832149
Email: mark.webb@tesco.net
Website: www.intoprint.net

Personnel:
Mark Webb *(Proprietor)*

Academic & Scholarly; Archaeology; Architecture & Design; Bibliography & Library Science; Biography & Autobiography; Children's Books; Cinema, Video, TV & Radio; Computer Science; Cookery, Wines & Spirits; Crime; Educational & Textbooks; Electronic (Educational); Electronic (Professional &

Academic); English as a Foreign Language; Environment & Development Studies; Fashion & Costume; Fiction; Fine Art & Art History; Gay & Lesbian Studies; Geography & Geology; Guide Books; Humour; Industry, Business & Management; Languages & Linguistics; Literature & Criticism; Magic & the Occult; Medical (incl. Self-Help & Alternative Medicine); Military & War; Music; Natural History; Nautical; Philosophy; Photography; Physics; Poetry; Religion & Theology; Science Fiction; Scientific & Technical; Sports & Games; Theatre, Drama & Dance; Travel & Topography; Vocational Training & Careers

New Titles: 110 (2012) , 120 (2013)
No of Employees: 2

Imprints, Series & ISBNs:
KinderKlub
Paragon Publishing: 978-1-78222, 978-1-899820, 978-1-907611, 978-1-908341
Primary Modern Language
Stadium & Arena
Venue Safety and Security

Overseas Representation:
Australia: Ingram Lightning Source, Australia
Europe: Ingram Lightning Source, UK
USA, Canada: Ingram Lightning Source, UK

3022 ▬▬▬▬▬▬▬▬▬▬▬▬

*QUANTUM PUBLISHING
6 Blundell Street, London N7 9BH
Telephone: 020 7700 6700
Fax: 020 7700 4191
Email: sarah.bloxham@quarto.com
Website: www.quarto.com

Personnel:
Sarah Bloxham *(Publisher)*
Valerie Saint-Pierre *(Foreign Rights Director)*

Animal Care & Breeding; Antiques & Collecting; Architecture & Design; Atlases & Maps; Aviation; Children's Books; Cookery, Wines & Spirits; Crafts & Hobbies; Crime; Do-It-Yourself; Fashion & Costume; Fine Art & Art History; Gardening; Health & Beauty; History & Antiquarian; Humour; Industry, Business & Management; Magic & the Occult; Medical (incl. Self-Help & Alternative Medicine); Military & War; Music; Natural History; Nautical; Photography; Religion & Theology; Sports & Games; Transport

Imprints, Series & ISBNs:
Cartographica Press
Oceana
Quantum

Parent Company:
UK: Quarto Publishing Plc

3023 ▬▬▬▬▬▬▬▬▬▬▬▬

READER'S DIGEST CHILDREN'S PUBLISHING LTD
The Ice House, 124–126 Walcot Street, Bath BA1 5BG
Telephone: 01225 473200
Fax: 01225 460942

Personnel:
Paul E. Stuart *(Commercial Director)*
Jennifer Fifield *(International Sales Director)*

Children's Books

Imprints, Series & ISBNs:
Reader's Digest Children's Publishing Ltd: 978-1-84880, 978-1-85724

Parent Company:
USA: The Reader's Digest Association Inc

Associated Companies:
USA: Reader's Digest Children's Publishing
 Inc

3024 ■■■■■■■■■■■■■■■

TANGERINE DESIGNS LTD
Level 5, The Old Malthouse,
Clarence Street, Bath BA1 5NS
Telephone: 01225 720001
Email: enquiries@tangerinedesigns.co.uk

Website: www.tangerinedesigns.co.uk

Personnel:
Christine Swift *(Managing Director)*

Children's Books

Overseas Representation:
Worldwide: Tangerine Designs Ltd, UK

3025 ■■■■■■■■■■■■■■■

TOUCAN BOOKS LTD
The Old Fire Station, 140 Tabernacle St,
London EC2A 4SD
Telephone: 020 7250 3388
Email: ellen@toucanbooks.co.uk

Personnel:
Ellen Dupont *(Managing Director)*
Robert Sackville-West *(Director)*

*Animal Care & Breeding; Architecture &
Design; Atlases & Maps; Children's Books;
Cookery, Wines & Spirits; Crafts & Hobbies;
Fine Art & Art History; Gardening; History &
Antiquarian; Illustrated & Fine Editions;
Military & War; Natural History; Reference
Books, Directories & Dictionaries; Travel &
Topography*

Book Trade Association Membership:
Book Packagers Association

4 Authors' Agents

AITKEN ALEXANDER ASSOCIATES
18–21 Cavaye Place, London SW10 9PT
Telephone: 020 7373 8672
Fax: 020 7373 6002
Email: reception@aitkenalexander.co.uk
Website: www.aitkenalexander.co.uk

Personnel:
Gillon Aitken *(Chairman)*
Clare Alexander *(Director)*
Sally Riley *(Director/Foreign Rights)*
Andrew Kidd *(Managing Director)*
Lesley Thorne *(Director/Film & TV)*
Joaquim Fernandes *(Company Secretary)*

All MSS except plays, illustrated children's books, film & TV scripts, short stories & articles if not by existing clients.

Specialization: quality full-length fiction & non-fiction.

Rights Representative in UK for:
DeFiore and Company, USA; Paradigm, USA

Overseas Representation:
America: Aitken Alexander Associates LLC, New York, NY, USA
Indian Subcontinent: Aitken Alexander Associates Pvt Ltd, New Delhi, India

THE AMPERSAND AGENCY LTD
Ryman's Cottages, Little Tew, Oxon OX7 4JJ
Telephone: 01608 683677 & 683898
Fax: 01608 683449
Email: info@theampersandagency.co.uk
Website: www.theampersandagency.co.uk

Personnel:
Peter Buckman *(Managing Director)*
Peter Janson-Smith *(Consultant)*
Anne-Marie Doulton *(Editor & Director)*

All MSS except poetry, science fiction, horror, fantasy or illustrated children's books.

Specialization: literary and commercial fiction and non-fiction for all markets. A full range of services including foreign and media rights is offered. Member of the Association of Authors' Agents.

Overseas Representation:
Worldwide: The Buckman Agency, Oxfordshire, UK

DARLEY ANDERSON LITERARY, TV & FILM AGENCY
Estelle House, 11 Eustace Road, London SW6 1JB
Telephone: 020 7386 2674
Fax: 020 7386 5571
Email: enquiries@darleyanderson.com
Website: www.darleyanderson.com

Personnel:
Darley Anderson *(Sole Proprietor)*
Camilla Bolton *(Agent (crime, thrillers, suspense, general fiction, women's fiction and love stories))*
Steve Fisher *(Film & TV)*
Rosanna Bellingham *(Financial Controller)*
Andrea Messent *(Assistant to Darley Anderson)*
Clare Wallace *(Head of Rights and Associate Agent (general fiction, children's and illustrator's agent))*
Mary Darby *(Rights Executive)*
Vicki Le Feuvre *(Agency Editor)*

All MSS except short stories, academic or poetry.

Specialization: fiction: all types of thrillers & all types of fiction including contemporary, romantic comedy, bonkbusters, women in jeopardy, accessible literary, historical, exotic sagas, psychological suspense, paranormal, supernatural and cross-over fiction; also crime (cosy/hard-boiled/historical), horror, comedy & Irish novels; popular culture; children's, young adult and picture books; non-fiction: celebrity autobiographies, biographies, 'true life' women in jeopardy, popular psychology, self-improvement, diet, health, beauty & fashion, gardening, cookery, inspirational & religious.

Overseas Representation:
Bulgaria: Anthea Literary Agency, Sofia, Bulgaria
China & Taiwan: The Grayhawk Agency, Taipei, Taiwan
Czech & Slovak Republics: Andrew Nurnberg Associates, Prague, Czech Republic
Germany: Thomas Schlück Literary Agency, Garbsen, Germany
Greece: O A Literary Agency, Markopoulo, Athens, Greece
Hungary: Kàtai & Bolza Literary Agents, Budapest, Hungary
Israel: I. Pikarski Literary Agency, Tel Aviv, Israel
Italy: Natoli, Stefan & Oliva Agenzia Letteraria, Milan, Italy
Japan: Japan Uni Agency, Tokyo, Japan; Tuttle-Mori Agency Inc, Tokyo, Japan
Korea: Danny Hony Agency, Republic of Korea
Poland: Graal Ltd, Warsaw, Poland
Romania: International Copyright Agency, Bucharest, Romania
Russia: Synopsis Literary Agency, Moscow, Russia
Serbia: PLIMA Literary Agency, Belgrade, Serbia
Turkey: Akcali Copyright Agency, Istanbul, Turkey
USA: Darley Anderson Books, London, UK

ARTELLUS LTD
30 Dorset House, Gloucester Place, London NW1 5AD
Telephone: 020 7935 6972
Fax: 020 8609 0347
Website: www.artellusltd.co.uk

Personnel:
Leslie Gardner *(Director)*
Darryl Samaraweera *(Company Secretary)*
Gabriele Pantucci *(Chair)*
Angus MacDonald *(Research Assistant)*

All MSS except film scripts.

Specialization: fiction (commercial, speculative and literary), history, science, art history, politics, economics, self-help.

TASSY BARHAM ASSOCIATES
231 Westbourne Park Road, London W11 1EB
Telephone: 020 7792 5899
Email: tassy@tassybarham.com

Personnel:
Tassy Barham *(Agent)*

Specialization: Brazil. Representing European and American agencies and publishers in Brazil, and Portuguese-language writers into the UK. No unsolicited MSS.

LORELLA BELLI LITERARY AGENCY (LBLA)
54 Hartford House, 35 Tavistock Crescent, Notting Hill, London W11 1AY
Telephone: 020 7727 8547
Fax: 0870 787 4194
Email: info@lorellabelliagency.com
Website: www.lorellabelliagency.com

Personnel:
Lorella Belli *(Proprietor)*

All MSS except children's books, science fiction, fantasy, academic, poetry, original scripts. No reading fee. May suggest revision. Approach by query letter or email in the first instance.

Specialization: general fiction and non-fiction (particularly interested in first-time writers, commercial women's fiction, crime, thrillers, historical, international and multicultural writing, journalists with original book ideas, books on/about Italy, current affairs, pop history, pop science, pop music, lifestyle, memoirs, biography, autobiography, MBS, cookery, fashion, personal finance, business, travel). The agency represents a number of international bestselling and award-winning authors of fiction and non-fiction. Also represents leading American agencies in the UK and handles translation rights on behalf of UK publishers and literary agencies. Commission: 15% home; 20% overseas and dramatic rights. Works with co-agents abroad; film & TV rights handled by an associate agency. Member of the Association of Authors' Agents.

Rights Representative in UK for:
Folio Literary Management, New York, NY, USA; Park Literary Group, New York, NY, USA; Creative Culture Agency, New York, NY, USA; Fine Print Agency, New York, NY, USA; Mildred Marmur Associates, Larchmont, NY, USA; Paula Balzer Literary Agency, New York, NY, USA; Sarah Lazin Books, New York, NY, USA; Susan Schulman Agency, New York, NY, USA

BERLIN ASSOCIATES LTD
7 Tyers Gate, London SE1 3HX
Telephone: 020 7836 1112
Fax: 020 7632 5296
Email: agents@berlinassociates.com
Website: www.berlinassociates.com

All MSS except The majority of new clients are taken on through recommendation or invitation. However, if you would like your work to be considered for representation, please email your CV and the work you would like to submit for consideration, to: submissions@berlinassociates.com We represent writers of dramatic work only, we do not represent novelists.

Specialization: Berlin Associates is one of the UK's most respected boutique agencies, representing writers, directors, producers, designers, composers and below-the-line talent across the industry. We also handle the sale of film, theatre, television and radio rights in books, and advise producers on acquisitions.

4008 ▄▄▄▄▄▄

BLAKE FRIEDMANN LITERARY AGENCY LTD
122 Arlington Road, London NW1 7HP
Telephone: 020 7284 0408
Fax: 020 7691 9626
Email: info@blakefriedmann.co.uk
Website: www.blakefriedmann.co.uk

Personnel:
Carole Blake (Book Sales Director & Agent)
Julian Friedmann (Film & TV Director & Agent)
Isobel Dixon (Book Sales Director & Agent)
Conrad Williams (Film, TV & Radio Sales)
Adrian Clark (Accounts Manager)
Tom Witcomb (Book Sales Agent)
Christine Glover (Film & TV Agent)
Louise Brice (Rights Manager)
Juliet Pickering (Book Sales Agent)

All MSS except picture books, poetry & short stories.

Specialization: placing book rights internationally; film, television & radio rights.

Overseas Representation:
Bulgaria: Anthea Literary Agency, Sofia, Bulgaria
China: Andrew Nurnberg Associates, Beijing, China
Czech Republic: Kristin Olson Literary Agency, Prague, Czech Republic
France: La Nouvelle Agence, Paris, France
Germany: Liepman AG, Zurich, Switzerland
Hungary: Kàtai & Bolza, Literary Agents, Budapest, Hungary
Japan: The English Agency Japan Ltd, Tokyo, Japan
Korea: KCC International Ltd, Seoul, Republic of Korea
Poland: Graal Ltd, Warsaw, Poland
Romania: S. Kessler International Copyright Agency, Bucharest, Romania
Russia: Andrew Nurnberg Associates, Moscow, Russia
Scandinavia: Leonhardt & Hoier Literary Agency, Copenhagen, Denmark
Spain, Brazil & Portugal: The Foreign Office, Spain
Taiwan: Andrew Nurnberg Literary Agency, Taipei, Taiwan
Turkey: Amy Spangler, Anatolialit Agency, Turkey
USA, Canada, the Balkans & Greece: Blake Friedmann Literary Agency, London, UK

4009 ▄▄▄▄▄▄

LUIGI BONOMI ASSOCIATES LTD
91 Great Russell Street, London WC1B 3PS
Telephone: 020 7637 1234
Fax: 020 7637 2111
Email: info@bonomiassociates.co.uk
Website: www.bonomiassociates.co.uk

Personnel:
Luigi Bonomi (Director)
Amanda Preston (Director)
Ajda Vucicevic (Literary Agent)
Alison Bonomi (Accounts Director)

All MSS except poetry, children's stories or adult science fiction/fantasy.

Specialization: fiction: commercial and literary fiction, thrillers, crime, women's fiction. Non-fiction: history, science, parenting, lifestyle, diet, health, TV tie-ins. Keen to find new authors and help them develop their careers. Send preliminary letter, synopsis and first three chapters via email submission (check on website for full details). No reading fee. Will suggest revision. Works with foreign agencies and has links with TV presenters' agencies and production companies. Authors include Will Adams, James Barrington, Hannah

Beckerman, Amanda Brooke, Fern Britton, Jo Carnegie, Sam Christer, Gennaro Contaldo, Josephine Cox, Dean Crawford, Matthew Dunn, David Gibbins, Andrew Hammond, Richard Hammond, Matt Hilton, John Humphrys, Graham Joyce, Simon Kernick, John Lucas, Colin McDowell, Richard Madeley and Judy Finnigan, James May, Mike Morley, Sue Palmer, Andrew Pepper, Melanie Phillips, Gervase Phinn, Alice Roberts, Mike Rossiter, Catherine Sampson, Sarah Skye, Karen Swan, Prof Bryan Sykes, Alan Titchmarsh, Phil Vickery, Sir Terry Wogan. Founded 2005. Fiction and non-fiction (home 15%, overseas 20%).

Overseas Representation:
Trident: Trident Media Literary Agency, USA
USA: Inkwell Management, USA
USA : RWSG Agency, USA
Worldwide: Intercontinental Literary Agency, London, UK, UK

4010 ▄▄▄▄▄▄

JENNY BROWN ASSOCIATES
33 Argyle Place, Edinburgh EH9 1JT
Telephone: 0131 229 5334
Email: jenny@jennybrownassociates.com
Website: www.jennybrownassociates.com

Personnel:
Jenny Brown (Agent)
Mark Stanton (Agent)
Lucy Juckes (Children's Agent)
Allan Guthrie (Agent)
Kevin Pocklington (Agent & Foreign Rights)

All MSS except academic, poetry, science fiction, horror & fantasy. Submissions: see website for submission information.

Specialization: non-fiction (including sport & music), literary fiction (including crime & thrillers) and writing for children. Many of the agency's clients are based in Scotland, but the company represents writers from all over the UK, and sells their work worldwide.

4011 ▄▄▄▄▄▄

FELICITY BRYAN
2a North Parade, Banbury Road, Oxford OX2 6LX
Telephone: 01865 513816
Fax: 01865 310055
Email: agency@felicitybryan.com
Website: www.felicitybryan.com

All MSS except science fiction, fantasy, romance, gardening, memoirs, self-help, picture/illustrated books, film, TV and play scripts or poetry.

Specialization: adult fiction & general non-fiction, history & popular science, children's fiction aged 8+ and Young Adult

Overseas Representation:
Europe: Andrew Nurnberg Associates, London, UK
Greece: JLM, Greece
Israel: The Deborah Harris Agency, Israel
Japan: Japan Uni Agency, Tokyo, Japan; Tuttle-Mori Agency Inc, Tokyo, Japan
Korea: EYA, Seoul, Republic of Korea
Mainland China: Andrew Nurnberg Associates, Beijing, China
Taiwan, Hong Kong: Andrew Nurnberg Associates, Taiwan, Taiwan
Turkey: ONK Agency, Turkey

4012 ▄▄▄▄▄▄

THE BUCKMAN AGENCY
Ryman's Cottage, Little Tew, Oxford OX7 4JJ
Telephone: 01608 683677
Fax: 01608 683449
Email: r.buckman@talk21.com

Personnel:
Rosemarie Buckman (Partner)
Jessica Buckman (Partner)

Specialization: handling of translation rights in all foreign rights markets for fiction and non-fiction, working on behalf of UK and US agencies.

4013 ▄▄▄▄▄▄

BRIE BURKEMAN & SERAFINA CLARKE LTD
14 Neville Court, Abbey Road, London NW8 9DD
Telephone: 0870 199 5002
Fax: 0870 199 1029
Email: info@burkemanandclarke.com
Website: www.burkemanandclarke.com

Personnel:
Brie Burkeman (Proprietor)

All MSS except academic, text, poetry, short stories, musicals or short films. No reading fee but return postage essential. Unsolicited email attachments will be deleted without opening. Please see website for full submission guidelines and whether we are currently accepting submissions.

Specialization: adult commercial and literary full-length fiction and non-fiction books, children's books as well as full-length scripts for the theatre. Worldwide representation, works with sub-agents where necessary. Also independent film and TV consultant to literary agents and publishers. Commission: 15% home, 20% overseas. Member of AAA and PMA.

Overseas Representation:
Worldwide – contact: Brie Burkeman & Serafina Clarke Ltd, London, UK

4014 ▄▄▄▄▄▄

JULIET BURTON LITERARY AGENCY
2 Clifton Avenue, London W12 9DR
Telephone: 020 8762 0148
Fax: 020 8743 8765
Email: juliet.burton@btinternet.com

Personnel:
Juliet Burton (Director)

All MSS except poetry, children's, SF/fantasy, drama, film/television scripts.

Specialization: crime fiction and women's fiction.

4015 ▄▄▄▄▄▄

CASAROTTO RAMSAY & ASSOCIATES LTD
Waverley House, 7–12 Noel Street, London W1F 8GQ
Telephone: 020 7287 4450
Fax: 020 7287 9128
Email: info@casarotto.co.uk
Website: www.casarotto..co.uk

Personnel:
Giorgio Casarotto (Director)
Tom Erhardt (Director)
Jenne Casarotto (Director)
Mel Kenyon (Director)
Jodi Shields (Director)
Rachel Holroyd (Director)

Specialization: film scripts, TV scripts, play scripts, radio scripts only after preliminary letter. No books.

4016 ▄▄▄▄▄▄

CHAPMAN & VINCENT
7 Dilke Street, London SW3 4JE
Email: chapmanvincent@hotmail.co.uk

Personnel:
Jennifer Chapman (Director)
Gilly Vincent (Director)

All MSS except fiction of any kind, writing for children, poetry, scripts, domestic tragedies or academic work.

Specialization: non-fiction illustrated work in the areas of interiors, gardening, cookery, heritage and fashion. Write with two sample chapters and SAE. Email attachments will not be opened. A small agency whose clients come mainly from personal recommendation. The agency is not actively seeking clients but is happy to consider really original work. Clients include George Carter, Leslie Geddes-Brown, Lucinda Lambton, Rowley Leigh and Eve Pollard. Commission: Home 15%; US & Europe 20%. Member of the Association of Authors' Agents.

Overseas Representation:
USA: Elaine Markson Literary Agency, New York, NY, USA

4017 ▄▄▄▄▄▄

JANE CONWAY-GORDON LTD
38 Cromwell Grove, London W6 7RG
Telephone: 020 7371 6939
Email: jane@conway-gordon.co.uk
Website: www.janeconwaygordon.com

Personnel:
Jane Conway-Gordon (Company Director)

All MSS except science fiction, poetry, children's, short pieces; return postage essential.

Specialization: commercial and literary fiction, crime fiction, some biography.

Overseas Representation:
Europe (excluding Germany & France): Intercontinental Literary Agency, London, UK
Germany: Liepman AG, Zurich, Switzerland
USA: Lyons Literary LLC, New York, NY, USA

4018 ▄▄▄▄▄▄

COOMBS MOYLETT LITERARY AGENCY
120 New Kings Road, London SW6 4LZ
Telephone: 020 8740 0454
Fax: 020 7736 3500
Email: lisa@coombsmoylett.com
Website: www.coombsmoylett.com

Personnel:
Lisa Moylett (Proprietor)

All MSS except science fiction, poetry or children's.

Specialization: commercial and literary fiction. Special interests are thrillers, crime/mystery; women's literary and contemporary fiction and historical fiction. We are not interested in poetry, children's fiction or screenplays. The agency is particularly interested in finding and developing new talent. Services include the selling of subsidiary rights such as film & TV and translation. The agency has good relations with US publishers and is represented in both Japan by Tuttle Mori and in Germany by the Michael Meller Literary Agency. Guidelines for submission: first three chapters, a short synopsis and SAE (essential for the return of material). No email or disc submissions.

Overseas Representation:
Germany: Michael Meller Literary Agency, Munich, Germany
Japan: Tuttle-Mori Agency Inc, Tokyo, Japan

4019

RUPERT CREW LTD
[International Literary Representation]
6 Windsor Road, London N3 3SS
Telephone: 020 8346 3000
Fax: 020 8346 3009
Email: info@rupertcrew.co.uk
Website: www.rupertcrew.co.uk

Personnel:
Doreen Montgomery (Chairman & Joint
  Managing Director)
Caroline Montgomery (Company Secretary
  & Joint Managing Director)

All MSS except science fiction, fantasy, short
stories, poetry, film & TV scripts (although at
the present time we are unable to accept
unsolicited MSS of any kind).

Specialization: international business
management for authors desiring world
representation. Preliminary letter with SAE
required. Also acts as publishers'
consultants.

Overseas Representation:
China: Big Apple Agency Inc, Shanghai,
  China
Eastern Europe: Andrew Nurnberg
  Associates, London, UK
France: Eliane Benisti, Paris, France
Germany: Paul & Peter Fritz AG Literary
  Agency, Zurich, Switzerland
Hungary: Kàtai & Bolza Literary Agents,
  Budapest, Hungary
Israel: The Deborah Harris Agency, Israel
Italy: Agenzia Letteraria Internazionale SRL,
  Milan, Italy
Japan: The English Agency Japan Ltd, Tokyo,
  Japan; Tuttle-Mori Agency Inc, Tokyo,
  Japan
Taiwan: Big Apple Tuttle-Mori Associates,
  Shin-Juang, Taiwan
Turkey: The Kayi Literary Agency, Turkey
USA, Spain and Scandinavia: Maria White
  at Booklink, UK
Worldwide (Film/TV): The Ki Agency Ltd,
  London, UK

4020

CURTIS BROWN GROUP LTD
Haymarket House, 28–29 Haymarket,
London SW1Y 4SP
Telephone: 020 7393 4400
Fax: 020 7393 4401
Email: cb@curtisbrown.co.uk
Website: www.curtisbrown.co.uk

Personnel:
Jonathan Lloyd (Chairman)
Jonny Geller (CEO)
Nick Marston (Chair – Media (Director))
Vivienne Schuster (Literary Agent)
Ben Hall (CEO)
Jacquie Drewe (Chair – Presenters (Director))
Sarah Spear (Head of Actors' Dept
  (Director))
Emma Bailey (Operations Manager)
Felicity Blunt (Literary Agent)
Sheila Crowley (Literary Agent)
Karolina Sutton (Literary Agent)
Stephanie Thwaites (Literary Agent)
Kate Cooper (Joint Head of Foreign Rights)
Betsy Robbins (Joint Head of Foreign Rights)
Daisy Meyrick (Rights Agent)
Katie McGowan (Rights Agent)
Helen Manders (Rights Agent)
Alice Lutyens (Audio Manager)
Anna Davis (Literary Agent)
Melissa Pimentel (Rights Agent)

All MSS except short stories & poetry.

Specialization: negotiation in all publishing
markets; and television, film & dramatic
writing, directing, presenting & acting.

Rights Representative in UK for:
  Gelfman Schneider Literary Agents Inc,

New York, NY, USA; ICM, New York, NY,
USA

4021

THE ELISE DILLSWORTH AGENCY
9 Grosvenor Road, London N10 2DR
Telephone: 020 8351 3629
Email:
submissions@elisedillsworthagency.com
Website: www.elisedillsworthagency.com

All MSS except science fiction, fantasy and
children's books.

Specialization: literary and commercial
fiction and non-fiction, including
autobiography and memoir.

4022

ROBERT DUDLEY AGENCY
50 Rannoch Road, London W6 9SR
Telephone: 07879 426574
Email: info@robertdudleyagency.co.uk
Website: www.robertdudleyagency.co.uk

Personnel:
Robert Dudley (Agent)

All MSS except film scripts.

Specialization: Robert Dudley Agency is a
non-fiction agency specializing in
management, history, militaria, politics,
health and well-being, travel, biography,
film and archaeology.

Parent Company:
UK: Bowerdean Publishing Co Ltd

Associated Companies:
UK: Bowerdean Publishing Co Ltd

4023

EDWARDS FUGLEWICZ
49 Great Ormond Street, London
WC1N 3HZ
Telephone: 020 7405 6725
Fax: 020 7405 6726
Email: ros@efla.co.uk

Personnel:
Ros Edwards (Partner)
Helenka Fuglewicz (Partner)

All MSS except children's books, science
fiction or horror. No unsolicited MSS.

Specialization: literary and commercial
fiction including romance, crime, thrillers
and mystery; non-fiction: biography, history
and humorous animal stories.

Rights Representative in UK for:
  The Bodleian Library, Oxford, UK;
  Poolbeg Press, Dublin, Republic of Ireland

4024

FAITH EVANS ASSOCIATES
27 Park Avenue North, London N8 7RU
Telephone: 020 8340 9920
Email: faith@faith-evans.co.uk

Specialization: Small agency. No phone calls
or unsolicited MSS. Submissions will not be
acknowledged.

4025

FOX & HOWARD LITERARY AGENCY
39 Eland Road, London SW11 5JX
Telephone: 020 7223 9452 & 01824
790817
Fax: 01824 790745
Email: fandhagency@googlemail.com
Website: www.foxandhoward.co.uk

Personnel:
Chelsey Fox (Agent)
Charlotte Howard (Agent)

Specialization: general non-fiction:
biography, business, current affairs,
education and language, health and fitness,
history, hobbies and sport, interiors and
style, lifestyle, mind, body and spirit, natural
history, popular culture and reference,
popular science and maths, self-help (home
15%, overseas 20%). No reading fee, but
preliminary letter and synopsis with SAE
essential. Founded 1992.

4026

FOX MASON LTD
[Literary agency]
36-38 Glasshouse Street, London W1B 5DL
Telephone: 020 7287 0972
Email: info@foxmason.com
Website: http://www.foxmason.com

Personnel:
Ben Mason (Director)

All MSS except from children's authors,
poets, playwrights, screenwriters, or bog-
standard genre authors.

Specialization: non-fiction: memoir,
biography, travel & adventure, history,
popular culture, philosophy, psychology,
food writing; fiction: literary fiction, crime,
thrillers, mystery & suspense, science fiction,
fantasy, supernatural, horror.

4027

FRASER ROSS ASSOCIATES
6 Wellington Place, Edinburgh EH6 7EQ
Telephone: 0131 657 4412
Email: kjross@tiscali.co.uk
Website: www.fraserross.co.uk

Personnel:
Lindsey Fraser (Partner)
Kathryn Ross (Partner)

All MSS except poetry and short stories.

Specialization: representing writers and
illustrators for children's books, and writers
for adults (home 10–15%, overseas 20%).
Send – by post or email – the first three
chapters (or equivalent), a synopsis, CV and
covering letter. Return postage is essential.
Submissions from overseas will not be
returned – senders should include an email
contact address. Current clients include
Barry Hutchison, Ella Burfoot, Joan Lingard,
Tanya Landman, Vivian French, Lari Don,
Cate James and Jamie Rix.

4028

JÜRI GABRIEL
35 Camberwell Grove, London SE5 8JA
Telephone: 020 7703 6186
Email: Juri@JuriGabriel.com

Personnel:
Jüri Gabriel (Proprietor)

All MSS except screenplays, tele or radio
scripts (only handles performance rights in
existing works for existing clients); science
fantasy; children's books, poetry, short
stories or articles.

Specialization: literary fiction, popular
academic and anything that combines
intellect, originality and wit. In first instance
please send a two-page synopsis, three
sample chapters, a brief c.v. and return
postage if you want the material back. No
submissions by fax or email. Clients include
Jack Allen, Nick Bradbury, Tom Clempson,
Miriam Dunne, Matt Fox, Paul Genney, Pat
Gray, Mikka Haugaard, Robert Irwin,
Andrew Killeen, John Lucas, David Madsen,

Richard Mankiewicz, David Miller, John
Outram, Phil Roberts, Roger Storey, Dr
Stefan Szymanski, Jeremy Weingard, Dr
Terence White. Commission: home 10%, US
& translation 20%.

4029

DAVID GODWIN ASSOCIATES
55 Monmouth Street, London WC2H 9DG
Telephone: 020 7240 9992
Website:
www.davidgodwinassociates.co.uk

Personnel:
David Godwin (Literary Agent)
Heather Godwin (Company Secretary)
Kirsty McLachlan (Film & TV Rights
  Manager)
Anna Watkins (Foreign Rights Manager)
Caitlin Ingham (Assistant)

Specialization: UK, US and translation
rights, TV & film.

Overseas Representation:
China: Big Apple Agency Inc., China
Eastern Europe: Prava i Prevodi Literary
  Agency, Serbia
Hungary: Kàtai & Bolza Literary Agents,
  Hungary
Israel: The Deborah Harris Agency, Israel
Italy: Marco Vigevani & Associati Agenzia
  Letteraria, Italy
Japan: Japan Uni Agency, Japan
Korea: KCC (Korea Copyright Center, Inc.),
  Republic of Korea
Poland: Graal Ltd, Poland
Romania: I. Simona Kessler International
  Copyright Agency Ltd, Romania
Russia: Synopsis Literary Agency, Russia
Turkey: Akcali Copyright Agency , Turkey

4030

GRAHAM MAW CHRISTIE
19 Thornhill Crescent, London N1 1BJ
Telephone: 020 7609 1326
Email: enquiries@grahammawchristie.com
Website: www.grahammawchristie.com

Personnel:
Jane Graham Maw (Director)
Jennifer Christie (Director)

All MSS except fiction, children's or poetry.

Specialization: literary agents for general
non-fiction: autobiography/memoir,
humour and gift, business, history for the
general market, web-to-book, food and
drink, health, lifestyle, parenting, personal
development, popular culture, popular
science and popular philosophy, reference,
TV tie-in. No reading fee. Will suggest
revision. See website for guidance on
submissions.

Overseas Representation:
Foreign Rights: Rebecca Winfield, UK

4031

LOUISE GREENBERG BOOKS LTD
The End House, Church Crescent, London
N3 1BG
Telephone: 020 8349 1179
Fax: 020 8343 4559
Email: louisegreenberg@msn.com

All MSS except sport, leisure, poetry,
children's. No telephone approaches from
authors.

Specialization: full-length literary fiction and
serious non-fiction. Screen work for book
clients only.

4032

GREGORY AND CO
3 Barb Mews, London W6 7PA

Telephone: 020 7610 4676
Fax: 020 7610 4686
Email: info@gregoryandcompany.co.uk
Website: www.gregoryandcompany.co.uk

Personnel:
Jane Gregory (Proprietor)
Stephanie Glencross (Editorial)
Claire Morris (Rights)
Terry Bland (Accounts)
Linden Sherriff (Rights Assistant)
Mary Jones (Submissions)
Ruth Murray (General Assistant)

All MSS except children's, juvenile, academic & technical books, poetry & plays, TV & film scripts, science fiction, short stories. Preliminary letter with synopsis, in the first instance either to maryjones@gregoryandcompany.co.uk or to the company address above.

Specialization: fiction: commercial, crime, literary, suspense and thrillers. Editorial advice given to own authors. Film & TV rights for own published authors only, no original scripts.

Overseas Representation:
Brazil: Tassy Barham Associates, London, UK
Bulgaria: Interrights Literary & Translation Agency, Sofia, Bulgaria
China: Big Apple Associates, Zhonghe City, Taiwan
Czech Republic & Slovakia: Andrew Nurnberg Associates, Prague, Czech Republic
France: La Nouvelle Agence, Paris, France
Hungary: Lex Copyright, Budapest, Hungary
Israel: Pikarski Agency, Tel Aviv, Israel
Japan: Japan Uni Agency Inc, Tokyo, Japan; Tuttle-Mori Agency Inc, Tokyo, Japan
Korea: EYA, Seoul, Republic of Korea
Poland: Andrew Nurnberg Associates, Warsaw, Poland
Romania: Simona Kessler International Copyright Agency Ltd, Bucharest, Romania
Russia: Andrew Nurnberg Associates, Moscow, Russia
Scandinavia: Leonhardt & Hoier Literary Agency, Copenhagen, Denmark
Spain: Carmen Balcells Agencia Literaria SA, Barcelona, Spain
Thailand: Tuttle Mori Thailand, Bangkok, Thailand

4033 ▬▬▬▬

THE HANBURY AGENCY LTD
28 Moreton Street, London SW1V 2PE
Telephone: 020 7630 6768
Email: enquiries@hanburyagency.com
Website: www.hanburyagency.com

Personnel:
Margaret Hanbury (Managing Director)
Henry de Rougemont (Media Manager)

Specialization: commercial fiction and quality non-fiction (home 15%, overseas 20%). See website for submission details. Authors include George Alagiah, Simon Callow, Jimmy Connors, Imran Khan, Judith Lennox, Katie Price. Founded in 1983.

Overseas Representation:
All translation rights: Intercontinental Literary Agency, London, UK
USA: The Hanbury Agency Ltd, London, UK

4034 ▬▬▬▬

ANTONY HARWOOD LTD
103 Walton Street, Oxford OX2 6EB
Telephone: 01865 559615
Email: mail@antonyharwood.com
Website: www.antonyharwood.com

Personnel:
Antony Harwood (Agent)
James Macdonald Lockhart (Agent)

All MSS except screenwriting, poetry.

Specialization: fiction and non-fiction. Founded 2000.

4035 ▬▬▬▬

A. M. HEATH & CO LTD
6 Warwick Court, London WC1R 5DJ
Telephone: 020 7242 2811
Fax: 020 7242 2711
Website: www.amheath.com

Personnel:
Bill Hamilton (Managing Director)
Euan Thorneycroft (Director / Company Secretary)
Victoria Hobbs (Director)
Jennifer Custer (Foreign Rights Director)
Oli Munson (Agent)
Julia Churchill (Children's Agent)

All MSS except plays, scripts, poetry, scientific, technical for the layman only.

Rights Representative in UK for:
Anne Edelstein Literary Agency, New York, NY, USA; Brandt & Hochman Inc, New York, NY, USA; Gina Maccoby Literary Agency, New York, NY, USA; Jane Chelius Literary Agency, Brooklyn, NY, USA; Lescher & Lescher Ltd, New York, NY, USA; Miriam Altshuler Literary Agency, Red Hook, NY, USA

Overseas Representation:
Brazil: Tassy Barham, London, UK
Bulgaria & Serbia: Andrew Nurnberg Literary Agency, Sofia, Bulgaria
China & Taiwan: Andrew Nurnberg Literary Agency, Shanghai, China; Andrew Nurnberg Literary Agency, Taipei, Taiwan
Czech & Slovak Republics & Slovenia: Andrew Nurnberg Associates, Prague, Czech Republic
France, Italy, Israel, Greece, Indonesia, Portugal, Latvia, Lithuania, Estonia, Spain & Netherlands: A. M. Heath & Co Ltd, London, UK
Germany, Switzerland & Austria: Mohrbooks Literary Agency, Zurich, Switzerland
Hungary & Croatia: Andrew Nurnberg Ltd, Budapest, Hungary
Japan (fiction): The English Agency Japan Ltd, Tokyo, Japan
Japan (non-fiction): Tuttle-Mori Agency Inc, Tokyo, Japan
Korea: EYA, Seoul, Republic of Korea
Romania: Simona Kessler International Copyright Agency Ltd, Bucharest, Romania
Russia: Andrew Nurnberg Associates, Moscow, Russia
Scandinavia: Licht & Burr Literary Agency, Copenhagen, Denmark

4036 ▬▬▬▬

DAVID HIGHAM ASSOCIATES
5–8 Lower John Street, Golden Square, London W1F 9HA
Telephone: 020 7434 5900
Fax: 020 7437 1072
Email: dha@davidhigham.co.uk
Website: www.davidhigham.co.uk

Specialization: agents for the negotiation of all rights in fiction, general non-fiction, children's fiction and picture books, plays, film and TV scripts. Represented in all foreign markets. Please see website for submissions guidelines. No reading fee. Founded 1935.

4037 ▬▬▬▬

KATE HORDERN LITERARY AGENCY
18 Mortimer Road, Clifton, Bristol BS8 4EY
Telephone: 0117 923 9368

Email: katehordern@blueyonder.co.uk & annewilliamskhla@googlemail.com
Website: www.katehordern.co.uk

Personnel:
Kate Hordern (Proprietor)
Anne Williams (Associate Agent)

Specialization: Quality literary and commercial fiction, including women's fiction, crime and thrillers, and general non-fiction, and children's/YA. Clients include Lyn Andrews, Richard Bassett, Jeff Dawson, Kylie Fitzpatrick, Sven Hassel, Duncan Hewitt, Julian Lees, Will Randall, Dave Roberts, John Sadler.

4038 ▬▬▬▬

VALERIE HOSKINS ASSOCIATES LTD
20 Charlotte Street, London W1T 2NA
Telephone: 020 7637 4490
Fax: 020 7637 4493
Email: vha@vhassociates.co.uk

Personnel:
Valerie Hoskins (Managing Director)
Rebecca Watson (Associate)
Sara Moore (PA/ Manager)

Specialization: film & television rights for published work. The company is not a publishing agency.

4039 ▬▬▬▬

IMG UK LTD
McCormack House, Burlington Lane, London W4 2TH
Telephone: 020 8233 5300
Fax: 020 8233 5268
Email: sarah.wooldridge@img.com
Website: www.imgworld.com

Personnel:
Sarah Wooldridge (Consultant)
Sally Matthews (Accountant)

All MSS except science fiction, fiction, children's, short stories and poetry.

Specialization: non-fiction. No reading fee. Please send synopsis with sample chapter and SAE. Also handle IMG speakers. 20% commission.

4040 ▬▬▬▬

THE INSPIRA GROUP
5 Bradley Road, Enfield, Middx EN3 6ES
Telephone: 020 8292 5163
Fax: 0870 139 3057
Email: darin@theinspiragroup.com
Website: www.theinspiragroup.com

Personnel:
Darin Jewell (Managing Director)

Specialization: children's books, fantasy/sci-fi, and general fiction. Manuscripts in all genres are considered. Clients include Michael Tolkien, Simon Hall, Mark Leigh and Simon Brown. Authors should email their full MSS, synopsis and short literary CV (with their postal address and landline tel. no.) to darin@theinspiragroup.com

4041 ▬▬▬▬

INTERCONTINENTAL LITERARY AGENCY LTD
Centric House, 390 Strand, London WC2R 0LT
Telephone: 020 7379 6611
Fax: 020 7240 4724
Email: ila@ila-agency.co.uk
Website: www.ila-agency.co.uk

Personnel:
Nicki Kennedy (Managing Director)
Sam Edenborough (Agent)
Mary Esdaile (Agent)

Clementine Gaisman (Agent)
Katherine West (Agent)
Jenny Robson (Agent)

Specialization: translation rights exclusively.

Rights Representative in UK for:
Intercontinental Literary Agency, London, UK

4042 ▬▬▬▬

JANKLOW & NESBIT (UK) LTD
13a Hillgate Street, London W8 7SP
Telephone: 020 7243 2975
Fax: 020 7376 2915
Email: queries@janklow.co.uk
Website: www.janklowandnesbit.co.uk

Personnel:
Will Francis (Literary Agent)
Rebecca Folland (Foreign Rights Director)
Jessie Botterill (Office Manager)
Ms Rebecca Carter (Literary Agent)
Ms Hellie Ogden (Literary Agent)

All MSS except poetry, plays, film & TV scripts.

Specialization: fiction and non-fiction; commercial and literary. Send full outline (non-fiction), synopsis and first three sample chapters (fiction) plus informative covering letter by email to submissions@janklow.co.uk

Parent Company:
USA: Janklow & Nesbit Associates

Associated Companies:
USA: Janklow & Nesbit Associates

Overseas Representation:
USA: Janklow & Nesbit Associates, New York, NY, USA

4043 ▬▬▬▬

JANE JUDD LITERARY AGENCY
18 Belitha Villas, London N1 1PD
Telephone: 020 7607 0273
Fax: 020 7607 0623
Website: www.janejudd.com

Personnel:
Jane C. Judd (Proprietor)

All MSS except plays, film scripts, poetry and short stories.

Specialization: general non-fiction & fiction.

Rights Representative in UK for:
Marian Young, New York, NY, USA; Mercury House, San Francisco, CA, USA; Permanent Press, Sag Harbor, NY, USA; RLR Associates, New York, NY, USA

Overseas Representation:
Eastern Europe: Prava i Prevodi Agency, Belgrade, Serbia
France: La Nouvelle Agence, Paris, France
Germany: Thomas Schlück Literary Agency, Garbsen, Germany
Italy: Stefania Fietta ALI, Milan, Italy
Netherlands & Scandinavia: Jan Michael, Amsterdam, Netherlands
Spain & Portugal: Julio F. Yañez Literary Agency, Barcelona, Spain
USA: The Unter Agency, New York, NY, USA

4044 ▬▬▬▬

*MICHELLE KASS ASSOCIATES
85 Charing Cross Road, London WC2H 0AA
Telephone: 020 7439 1624
Fax: 020 7734 3394
Email: office@michellekass.co.uk

Personnel:
Michelle Kass (Agent)
Andrew Mills (Agent)

Specialization: an agency representing novelists, writers and directors for film, TV and theatre. No unsolicited MSS without preliminary phone call.

4045

THE FRANCES KELLY AGENCY
111 Clifton Road, Kingston-upon-Thames, Surrey KT2 6PL
Telephone: 020 8549 7830
Fax: 020 8547 0051

Personnel:
Frances Kelly (Proprietor)

Specialization: general non-fiction, all academic & professional disciplines; return postage & preliminary letter requested.

4046

*KNIGHT FEATURES LTD
20 Crescent Grove, London SW4 7AH
Telephone: 020 7622 1467
Fax: 020 7622 1522
Email: info@knightfeatures.co.uk
Website: www.knightfeatures.co.uk

Personnel:
Peter Knight (Proprietor)
Gaby Martin (Associate)
Andrew Knight (Associate)
Samantha Ferris (Associate)

All MSS except short stories, poetry & unsolicited MSS (reading fee). No e-mail submissions.

Specialization: worldwide selling of strip cartoons, major features and serializations. Exclusive syndication agent in UK & Irish Republic for United Feature Syndicate (Peanuts, Dilbert, etc.) & Newspaper Enterprise Association (Frank & Ernest, Born Loser, King Baloo, etc.), also Paws Inc (Garfield), Creators Syndicate (The Far Side).

Rights Representative in UK for:
Paws Inc, USA; The Puzzle Co, New Zealand; United Media Inc, New York, NY, USA

4047

FURNISS LAWTON
James Grant Group Ltd,
94 Strand on the Green, Chiswick, London W4 3NN
Telephone: 020 8987 6804
Email: info@furnisslawton.co.uk
Website: http://furnisslawton.co.uk/

Personnel:
Rowan Lawton (Agent)
Eugenie Furniss (Agent)

All MSS except We no longer accept physical submissions. Please note that we do not represent screenwriters for film or television. We're always pleased to hear from new writers. If you'd like us to consider your work, please send us up to 10,000 words of your manuscript, or the first three chapters, as either a word or pdf document along with a one page synopsis to: info@furnisslawton.co.uk. Please ensure that the word 'submission' is clearly marked in the subject line and that any attachments include the title of your work and your name.

Specialization: See website for more information.

Parent Company:
UK: James Grant Group Ltd.

Associated Companies:
UK: James Grant Group Ltd.

4048

LENZ-MULLIGAN RIGHTS & CO-EDITIONS
15 Sandbourne Avenue, London SW19 3EW
Telephone: 020 8544 0983
Email: lenzmulligan@btinternet.com

Personnel:
Gundhild Lenz-Mulligan (Rights Manager)

All MSS except poetry and film scripts.

Specialization: sale of co-editions and rights in the Nordic countries and Dutch, English and German-speaking markets. Particularly interested in children's books. Also offers proofreading and translation services of German-language material. Represents European, American and Australian publishers, packagers and authors.

Rights Representative in UK for:
Ars Edition, Germany; Best Publishing Ever, UK

4049

BARBARA LEVY LITERARY AGENCY
64 Greenhill, Hampstead High Street, London NW3 5TZ
Telephone: 020 7435 9046
Fax: 020 7431 2063
Email: blevysubmissions@gmail.com

Personnel:
John F. Selby (Solicitor Associate)

Specialization: general fiction & non-fiction, and TV presenters.

Rights Representative in UK for:
Arcadia, Danbury, CT, USA; Richard Parks, New York, NY, USA

Overseas Representation:
Foreign Language Markets: The Buckman Agency, London, UK
USA: Marshall Rights, London, UK

4050

LIMELIGHT CELEBRITY MANAGEMENT LTD
10 Filmer Mews, 75 Filmer Road, London SW6 7JF
Telephone: 020 7384 9950
Fax: 020 7384 9955
Email: mail@limelightmanagement.com
Website: www.limelightmanagement.com

Personnel:
Fiona Lindsay (Managing Director, Owner/Founder)
Maclean Lindsay (Operations Manager)
Alison Lindsay
Roz Ellman (Agents Assistant)

Specialization: full-length book MSS. Commercial fiction and non-fiction. Food, wine, health, crafts, gardening, history, biography/memoirs, popular culture, travel, women's interest (home 15%, overseas 20%), TV and radio rights (15–20%); will suggest revision where appropriate. No reading fee.

4051

CHRISTOPHER LITTLE LITERARY AGENCY LLP
[in association with Curtis Brown Group Ltd]
48 Walham Grove, London SW6 1QR
Telephone: 020 7736 4455
Email: info@christopherlittle.net
Website: www.christopherlittle.net

Personnel:
Christopher Little (Agent Proprietor)

All MSS except poetry, plays, science fiction, fantasy, textbooks, illustrated children's, short stories. Film scripts for established clients only.

Specialization: full-length commercial fiction. No reading fee. Please email covering letter, along with one-page synopsis and first three chapters to submissions@christopherlittle.net.

4052

LONDON INDEPENDENT BOOKS
26 Chalcot Crescent, London NW1 8YD
Telephone: 020 7706 0486
Fax: 020 7724 3122

Personnel:
Carolyn Whitaker (Literary Agent)

All MSS except computers & young children's.

Specialization: fiction & non-fiction, particularly travel & fantasy.

4053

ANDREW LOWNIE LITERARY AGENCY LTD
36 Great Smith Street, London SW1P 3BU
Telephone: 020 7222 7574
Fax: 020 7222 7576
Email: lownie@globalnet.co.uk
Website: www.andrew.lownie.co.uk

Personnel:
Andrew Lownie (Proprietor)
David Haviland (Fiction agent)

All MSS except poetry, short stories, self-help, women's fiction, religion.

Specialization: history, biography, packaging celebrities for book market and representing book projects for journalists. David Haviland is also developing a fiction list specialising in thrillers, crime and commercial fiction. Titles agented include Norma Major's books on Joan Sutherland and Chequers, Juliet Barker, Duncan Falconer, Laurence Gardner, Lawrence James, Christopher Lloyd, Sian Rees, David Stafford, Christian Wolmar, Sir John Mills, authorized lives of Sir Henry Cooper and Dick Emery, Desmond Seward, Daniel Tammet, Joyce Cary and Julian Maclaren – Ross Estates, numerous memoirs including Kerry Katona, various tv reality stars and inspirational memoirs by authors such as Cathy Glass and Casey Watson. Only accepts email submissions. No reading fee. Commission 15% worldwide or 20% if a sub-agent for film or translation

Overseas Representation:
Poland: Graal, Poland
Worldwide (excluding Poland, China, USA & Japan): The Marsh Agency, London, UK

4054

LUTYENS & RUBINSTEIN LITERARY AGENCY
21 Kensington Park Road, London W11 2EU
Telephone: 020 7792 4855
Fax: n/a
Email: info@lutyensrubinstein.co.uk
Website: www.lutyensrubinstein.co.uk

Personnel:
Felicity Rubinstein (Partner)
Sarah Lutyens (Partner)
Jane Finigan (Agent and Rights Manager)
Anna Steadman (General Assistant)

All MSS except poetry, screenplays, scripts for theatre and/or TV and radio.

Specialization: general adult non-fiction and fiction.

Overseas Representation:
France: La Nouvelle Agence, Paris, France
Germany: Eggers & Landwehr, Berlin, Germany
Italy: Grandi & Associates, Milan, Italy
USA: Inkwell Management, New York, NY, USA

4055

DUNCAN MCARA LITERARY AGENCY
28 Beresford Gardens, Edinburgh EH5 3ES
Telephone: 0131 552 1558
Email: duncanmcara@mac.com

All MSS except 'genre' fiction, educational & children's.

Specialization: literary fiction; non-fiction: art, architecture, archaeology, biography, history, military, Scottish. Home: 15%; Overseas: 20%. Preliminary email or letter with SAE essential. No reading fee. Also acts as editorial consultant on all aspects of general trade publishing. Editing, re-writing, copy-editing, proof correction for wide range of UK publishers.

4056

*THE MCKERNAN LITERARY AGENCY & CONSULTANCY
5 Gayfield Square, Edinburgh EH1 3NW
Telephone: 0131 557 1771
Email: maggie@mckernanagency.co.uk
Website: www.mckernanagency.co.uk

Personnel:
Maggie McKernan (Agent)

All MSS except film scripts, screenplays, picture books for children.

Specialization: assisting and developing writers, as well as representing their interests in their dealings with publishers, selling rights and handling negotiations of contracts. Handle fiction and non-fiction (commercial and literary novels of all kinds, including crime, historical, contemporary). Consideration will be given to novels for children over the age of 10, but not picture books.

Overseas Representation:
USA & Worldwide (translation rights):
Capel & Land Ltd, London, UK

4057

EUNICE MCMULLEN LTD
Low Ibbotsholme Cottage, off Bridge Lane, Troutbeck Bridge, Windermere, Cumbria LA23 1HU
Telephone: 01539 448551
Email: eunicemcmullen@totalise.co.uk
Website: www.eunicemcmullen.co.uk

Personnel:
Eunice McMullen (Director)

Specialization: Children's books (fiction only) for all ages – from picture books for toddlers to YA. No unsolicited MSS.

4058

ANDREW MANN LTD
39–41 North Road, London N7 9DP
Telephone: 020 7609 6218
Email: info@andrewmann.co.uk
Website: www.andrewmann.co.uk

Personnel:
Anne Dewe (Director)

Tina Betts *(Director)*
Louise Burns *(Agent)*

All MSS except poetry, spiritual / new age philosophy, short stories, misery memoirs, screenplays.

Specialization: commercial fiction, literary fiction and children's fiction, general non-fiction including current affairs, popular culture, and general history. No unsolicited manuscripts. Email submissions only. No reading fee.

Rights Representative in UK for:
Richard McDonough, Irvine, CA, USA

Overseas Representation:
All Translation, except Germany : Louisa Pritchard Associates (LPA), London, UK
Germany: Thomas Schlück Literary Agency, Garbsen, Germany
USA: Jonathan Lyons, Curtis Brown Ltd, New York, NY, USA

4059 ▬

MARJACQ SCRIPTS LTD
Box 412, 19/21 Crawford Street, London W1H 1PJ
Telephone: 020 7935 9499
Fax: 020 7935 9115
Email: enquiries@marjacq.com
Website: www.marjacq.com

Personnel:
Philip Patterson *(Literary Agent)*
Luke Speed *(Film Agent)*
Ms Isabella Floris *(Foreign Rights Agent)*
Guy Herbert *(Director)*

All MSS except poetry or stage plays.

Specialization: literary and commercial fiction, crime, thrillers, science fiction and women's fiction, and general non-fiction. Please submit three sample chapters and synopsis in first instance. SAE essential for return of MS.

Parent Company:
UK: Marjacq Micro Ltd

Associated Companies:
UK: Marjacq Micro Ltd

Overseas Representation:
Austria, Germany, Switzerland & parts of Eastern Europe: Transnet Contracts Ltd, Vienna, Austria
China: Big Apple Tuttle Mori, Taiwan
Hungary: Kátai & Bolza Literary Agents, Budapest, Hungary
Japan: The English Agency Japan Ltd, Tokyo, Japan
Korea: Eric Yang Agency, Republic of Korea
Poland: Graal Ltd, Warsaw, Poland
Scandinavia, Netherlands, Spain & Portugal: Lennart Sane Agency, Karlshamn, Sweden
Turkey: AnatoliaLit, Istanbul, Turkey

4060 ▬

THE MARSH AGENCY LTD
[incorporating Paterson Marsh Ltd and Campbell Thomson & McLaughlin Ltd]
50 Albemarle Street, London W1S 4BD
Telephone: 020 7493 4361
Fax: 020 7495 8961
Website: www.marsh-agency.co.uk

Personnel:
Camilla Ferrier *(Foreign Rights Director)*
Jessica Woollard *(English Language Agent)*
Stephanie Ebdon *(English Language Agent)*
Jemma McDonagh *(Foreign Rights Agent)*
Hannah Ferguson *(English Language Agent)*
Georgina Le Grice *(Foreign Rights Executive)*

All MSS except children's/picture books, poetry, drama, TV, film & radio scripts.

Specialization: The Marsh Agency offers international representation to a wide range of writers, agents and publishing companies. Traditionally known for specializing in selling translation rights, we also have an English language division offering worldwide represenatation for our clients.

4061 ▬

MBA LITERARY AGENTS
62 Grafton Way, London W1T 5DW
Telephone: 020 7387 2076
Website: www.mbalit.co.uk

Personnel:
Diana Tyler *(Joint Managing Director)*
Laura Longrigg *(Joint Managing Director)*
Timothy Webb *(Financial Director)*
David Riding *(Director)*
Susan Smith *(Director)*
Jean Kitson *(Director)*
Sophie Gorell Barnes *(Agent)*
Stella Kane *(Foreign Rights Manager)*

All MSS except poetry, short stories.

Specialization: fiction and non-fiction. Also scripts for film, TV, radio & theatre.

Rights Representative in UK for:
Harlequin, New York, USA

Overseas Representation:
Brazil: Tassy Barham, London, UK
Eastern Europe & Greece: Prava i Prevodi, Belgrade, Serbia
France: Anna Jarota Agency, Paris, France
Germany: Thomas Schlück Literary Agency, Garbsen, Germany
Italy: Vicki Satlow Literary Agency, Milan, Italy
Japan: Tuttle-Mori Agency Inc, Tokyo, Japan
Netherlands: Sebes & Van Gelderen Literary Agency, Amsterdam, Netherlands
Scandinavia: Licht & Burr Literary Agency, Denmark
Spain: Agencia Carmen Balcells, Barcelona, Spain

4062 ▬

MADELEINE MILBURN LITERARY, TV & FILM AGENCY
42A Great Percy Street, London WC1X 9QR
Telephone: 020 3602 6425
Email: submissions@madeleinemilburn.com
Website: www.mmla.co.uk

Personnel:
Mrs Madeleine Milburn *(Literary Agent)*

All MSS except film and TV scripts

Specialization: accessible literary 'reading club' fiction and bestselling genre fiction including crime, thrillers, mystery, historical, women's, romance, humour and New Adult. The Agency also handles YA and children's fiction for all ages.

4063 ▬

THE CATHY MILLER FOREIGN RIGHTS AGENCY
29A The Quadrangle, 49 Atalanta Street, London SW6 6TU
Telephone: 020 7386 5473
Fax: 020 7385 1774
Email: cathy@millerrightsagency.com

Personnel:
Mrs Cathy Miller *(Principal/Managing Director)*

All MSS except poetry & educational.

Specialization: foreign rights; acting as consultants to publishers on sales of foreign rights of non-fiction titles (psychoanalysis, medical, business & management, esoteric, health & general trade books); handling market research for lists or one-off projects; helping to set up rights departments; advising on all matters concerning translation rights and negotiations with foreign publishers.

Rights Representative in UK for:
Foulsham Publishers, UK; Free Association Books, UK; Karnac Books, UK; Mark Fisher, Canada; Shepheard-Walwyn, UK; Thorogood Publishing Ltd, UK

Overseas Representation:
China: Mei Yao, New York, NY, USA
Greece: Read n Right Agency, Cahlkida, Greece
Japan: The English Agency Japan Ltd, Tokyo, Japan
Korea: EYA, Seoul, Republic of Korea
Poland: Graal Ltd, Warsaw, Poland
Russia: Alexander Korzhenevski Literary Agency, Moscow, Russia
Spain: Julio F. Yañez Literary Agency, Barcelona, Spain

4064 ▬

NEW WRITING SOUTH
9 Jew Street, Brighton BN1 1UT
Telephone: 01273 735353
Email: admin@newwritingsouth.com
Website: www.newwritingsouth.com

Personnel:
Chris Taylor *(Director)*
Georgia Barrington *(Operations Manager)*
Anna Jefferson *(Deputy Director)*

Specialization: New Writing South is the new writing development agency for the south-east region. We find and enable new creative writing talent to flourish, support emerging and mid-career writers, bring the work of professional writers to new audiences and create new paid work for writers.

4065 ▬

*THE MAGGIE NOACH LITERARY AGENCY
7 Peacock Yard, Iliffe Street, London SE17 3LH
Telephone: 020 7708 3073
Email: info@mnla.co.uk

All MSS except short stories, poetry, plays, screenplays, cookery, gardening, mind/body/spirit, illustrated children's, scientific/academic/specialist non-fiction. Absolutely no illustrated books.

Specialization: fiction, general non-fiction and children's books. No unsolicited manuscripts – submissions by arrangements only. Home 15%, USA & translation 20%.

Overseas Representation:
Worldwide: Jill Hughes, Aubourn, Lincs, UK

4066 ▬

ANDREW NURNBERG ASSOCIATES LTD
20–23 Greville Street, London EC1N 8SS
Telephone: 020 3327 0400
Fax: 020 7430 0801
Email: contact@andrewnurnberg.com
Website: www.andrewnurnberg.com

Personnel:
Andrew Nurnberg *(Managing Director)*
Sarah Nundy *(Deputy Managing Director)*
Vicky Mark *(Director)*

Specialization: representing leading British & American agents & authors throughout the world.

4067 ▬

JOHN PAWSEY
8 Snowshill Court, Giffard Park, Milton Keynes, Bucks MK14 5QG
Telephone: 01908 611841
Email: john.pawsey@virgin.net

Personnel:
John Pawsey *(Sole Proprietor)*

All MSS except fiction, poetry, short stories, journalism, children's, original film & stage scripts. But please note we are not looking for new clients and will only take on work of exceptional potential.

Specialization: sport, popular culture.

Overseas Representation:
France: Lora Fountain Associates, Paris, France
Germany: Thomas Schlück Literary Agency, Garbsen, Germany
Hungary: Lex Copyright, Budapest, Hungary
Japan: The English Agency Japan Ltd, Tokyo, Japan
Korea: Korea Copyright Center, Seoul, Republic of Korea
Netherlands: International Literatur Bureau BV, Hilversum, Netherlands
Russia: Prava i Prevodi RAO, Moscow, Russia
Spain & South America: International Editors Co, Barcelona, Spain
USA: Alison J. Picard, Cotuit, MA, USA
Yugoslav States: Prava i Prevodi, Belgrade, Serbia

4068 ▬

POLLINGER LIMITED
9 Staple Inn, Holborn, London WC1V 7QH
Telephone: 020 7404 0342
Fax: 020 7242 5737
Email: info@pollingerltd.com
Website: www.pollingerltd.com

Personnel:
Lesley Pollinger *(Managing Director)*
Leigh Pollinger *(Director)*
Joanna Devereux *(Literary Agent)*
Tim Bates *(Literary Agent)*
Katherine Judge *(Rights Manager)*

All MSS except poetry & articles & screenplays – see website for submission details.

Specialization: adult fiction and non-fiction, children's and literary estates.

Rights Representative in UK for:
New Directions Publishing Corporation, New York, NY, USA; Summersdale, UK

Overseas Representation:
China: Big Apple Tuttle-Mori Agency, Taipei, Taiwan
Denmark, Finland, Norway & Sweden: Licht & Burr Literary Agency, Copenhagen, Denmark
Dutch language rights: Sebes & Van Gelderen Literary Agency, Netherlands
Eastern Europe & Russia: Prava i Prevodi, Belgrade, Serbia
France: Michelle Lapautre Agency, Paris, France
Germany & Switzerland: Mohrbooks Literary Agency, Zurich, Switzerland
Greece: Read n Right Agency, Cahlkida, Greece
Hungary: Lex Copyright, Budapest, Hungary
Israel: The Book Publishers Association of Israel, Tel Aviv, Israel
Japan: Tuttle-Mori Agency Inc, Tokyo, Japan
Korea: The Eric Yang Agency, Seoul, Republic of Korea

Portugal & Brazil: Ilidio da Fonseca Matos, Lisbon, Portugal
Spain & South America: Carmen Balcells Agencia Literaria SA, Barcelona, Spain
Turkey: ONK Agency Ltd, Istanbul, Turkey

4069

SHELLEY POWER LITERARY AGENCY LTD
35 Rutland Court, New Church Road, Hove BN3 4AF
Telephone: 01273 728730
Email: sp@shelleypower.co.uk

Personnel:
Shelley Power *(Director, Literary Agent)*

All MSS except children's books, poetry, plays or film/tv scripts. No horror, science fiction or fantasy.

Overseas Representation:
China: Big Apple Tuttle-Mori Agency Inc, Shanghai, China
Czech Republic: Transnet Contracts, Czech Republic
Germany: Liepman AG, Germany
Greece: JLM Literary Agency, Athens, Greece
Hungary: Kàtai & Bolza Literary Agents, Budapest, Hungary
Israel: Ilana Pikarski Literary Agency, Tel Aviv, Israel
Italy: Natoli, Stefan & Oliva Agenzia Letteraria, Milan, Italy
Japan: The English Agency Japan Ltd, Tokyo, Japan
Korea: The Eric Yang Agency, Seoul, Republic of Korea
Poland: Graal Ltd, Warsaw, Poland
Romania: Simona Kessler International Copyright Agency Ltd, Bucharest, Romania
Spain: Julio F. Yañez Literary Agency, Barcelona, Spain
Taiwan: Big Apple Tuttle-Mori Agency, Taipei, Taiwan

4070

PRENTICE BEAUMONT
1 Park Village East, London NW1 7PX
Telephone: 0207 387 8637
Email: info@prenticebeaumont.co.uk
Website: www.prenticebeaumont.co.uk

Personnel:
Kate Prentice *(Agent, Founder)*
Vanessa Beaumont *(Agent, Founder)*

All MSS except We are currently accepting submissions by email. Please send us a covering letter telling us about yourself and your work. For fiction, please provide a synopsis and ten pages. For non-fiction, please send a proposal and sample chapter.

Specialization: Prentice Beaumont specialises in literary and commercial fiction and quality non-fiction. We are acquiring a diverse list of clients, from debut authors at the beginning of their journey to established writers looking for a change in direction.

Overseas Representation:
Translation Rights: Andrew Nurnberg Associates, UK

4071

THE SAYLE LITERARY AGENCY
1 Petersfield, Cambridge CB1 1BB
Telephone: 01223 303035
Website: www.sayleliteraryagency.com

Personnel:
Rachel Calder *(Proprietor)*

All MSS except children's, poetry, technical, science fiction.

Specialization: fiction (literary & crime), biography, history, current affairs, travel, social issues.

Rights Representative in UK for:
The Naher Agency, Australia; Darhansoff Verrill Feldman Literary Agency, New York, NY, USA

Overseas Representation:
Europe & Rest of the World: The Marsh Agency, London, UK
USA: Dunow, Carlson & Lerner Agency, New York, NY, USA

4072

CAROLINE SHELDON LITERARY AGENCY LTD
71 Hillgate Place, London W8 7SS
Telephone: 020 7727 9102
Email:
carolinesheldon@carolinesheldon.co.uk & pennyholroyde@carolinesheldon.co.uk
Website: www.carolinesheldon.co.uk & www.carolinesheldonillustrators.co.uk

Personnel:
Caroline Sheldon *(Literary Agent)*
Penny Holroyde *(Literary Agent)*

All MSS except short stories.

Specialization: fiction, women's fiction & children's books, human interest non-fiction.

4073

DORIE SIMMONDS AGENCY LTD
Riverbank House,
1 Putney Bridge Approach, London SW6 3JD
Telephone: 020 7736 0002
Email: dorie@doriesimmonds.com

Personnel:
Dorie Simmonds *(Proprietor)*

All MSS except plays, poetry,short stories.

Specialization: commercial fiction and non-fiction in both the adult and children's markets.

4074

JEFFREY SIMMONS
15 Penn House, Mallory Street, London NW8 8SX
Telephone: 020 7224 8917
Email: jasimmons@unicombox.co.uk

All MSS except children's books, cookery, science fiction, romances & some specialist subjects.

Specialization: biography & memoirs; cinema, drama & the arts; general fiction; history; law & crime; literature; politics & world affairs.

Overseas Representation:
Japan: The English Agency Japan Ltd, Tokyo, Japan
Spain: Julio F Yañez Literary Agency, Barcelona, Spain

4075

*SINCLAIR-STEVENSON
3 South Terrace, London SW7 2TB
Telephone: 020 7581 2550
Fax: 020 7581 2550

Translation Rights:
c/o David Higham Associates Ltd,
5–8 Lower John Street, Golden Square, London W1F 9HA

All MSS except children's books, science fiction, science, fantasy, film or play scripts.

Specialization: non-fiction – biography and autobiography, the arts, politics and current affairs, travel, history; and fiction.

Rights Representative in UK for:
T. C. Wallace Ltd, New York, NY, USA

Overseas Representation:
USA: T. C. Wallace Ltd, New York, NY, USA

4076

ROBERT SMITH LITERARY AGENCY LTD
12 Bridge Wharf, 156 Caledonian Road, London N1 9UU
Telephone: 020 7278 2444
Fax: 020 7833 5680
Email:
robertsmith.literaryagency@virgin.net
Website:
www.robertsmithliteraryagency.com

Personnel:
Robert Smith *(Managing Director)*
Anne Smith *(Director)*

All MSS except fiction, poetry, children's books or reference. Writers may submit synopses but no unsolicited manuscripts.

Specialization: the agency sells books, series and articles to book publishers, newspapers and magazines across the world. It operates only in non-fiction. Main areas are autobiography and biography, show business, hot topics, history, health, lifestyle and true crime.

Overseas Representation:
All Foreign Language Markets: Louisa Pritchard Associates, London, UK
USA: Renee Zuckerbrot Literary Agency, New York, USA

4077

*SHIRLEY STEWART LITERARY AGENCY
3rd Floor, 4a Nelson Road, London SE10 9JB
Telephone: 020 8293 3000

Personnel:
Shirley Stewart *(Director)*

All MSS except children's books, poetry, plays, science fiction and fantasy.

Specialization: full-length MSS only. Fiction and non-fiction (home 10–15%, overseas 20%). No reading fee but preliminary letter and return postage essential.

Rights Representative in UK for:
Curtis Brown Ltd, New York, NY, USA

4078

THE SUSIJN AGENCY LTD
3rd Floor, 64 Great Titchfield Street, London W1W 7QH
Telephone: 020 7580 6341
Fax: 020 7580 8626
Email: info@thesusijnagency.com
Website: www.thesusijnagency.com

Personnel:
Laura Susijn *(Literary Agent)*
Priya Bora *(Literary Agent)*

All MSS except children's books, sci-fi, romantic fiction, fantasy, sagas, self-help, business, military and computer books.

Specialization: selling rights world-wide in literary fiction and non-fiction. Also represents non-English language publishers and authors for UK, US and translation rights world-wide. Deals direct, using sub-agent in Eastern Europe, Israel and the Far East. Preliminary letter, synopsis and first two chapters preferred. No reading fee.

4079

THE TENNYSON AGENCY
10 Cleveland Avenue, London SW20 9EW
Telephone: 020 8543 5939
Email: submissions@tenagy.co.uk
Website: www.tenagy.co.uk

Personnel:
Adam Sheldon *(Partner)*

All MSS except gameshow/reality television proposals, poetry, short stories, science fiction, popular romantic and historical fiction, children's books and non-fiction unrelated to the arts.

Specialization: original writing and adaptations for the theatre, television, radio and film. Intelligent fiction is considered on an ad hoc basis. Commission rates: literature: 12.5%, drama: 15%, overseas: 20%. Submissions by post, on invitation, following introductory letter. Full details on the agency's website.

4080

J. M. THURLEY MANAGEMENT
Archery House, 33 Archery Square, Walmer, Deal, Kent CT14 7JA
Telephone: 01304 371721
Email: JMThurley@aol.com
Website: www.thecuttingedge.biz

Personnel:
Jon Thurley *(Contact)*
Patricia Preece *(Contact)*

All MSS except short stories & poetry.

Specialization: will give editorial help by arrangement on all types of projects.

4081

LAVINIA TREVOR
29 Addison Place, London W11 4RJ
Telephone: 020 7603 5254
Fax: 0870 129 0838
Email: info@laviniatrevor.co.uk
Website: www.laviniatrevor.co.uk

Personnel:
Lavinia Trevor *(Agent)*

Specialization: fiction and non-fiction for the general trade market (see website). Sorry, no unsolicited material.

4082

*JANE TURNBULL AGENCY
58 Elgin Crescent, London W11 2JJ
Telephone: 020 7727 9409
Email: jane@janeturnbull.co.uk
Website: www.janeturnbull.co.uk

Mailing Address:
Barn Cottage, Veryan, Truro, Cornwall TR2 5QA
Telephone: 01872 501317

Personnel:
Jane Turnbull *(Proprietor)*

All MSS except science or romantic fiction, children's fiction, poetry or plays.

Specialization: literary fiction, current affairs, biography, design, lifestyle, health, TV tie-ins, humour, natural history. Initial letter essential; no unsolicited MSS. Commission 15% home sales, 20% US, 20% translation, 15% radio/TV/film. Founded 1986, member of the Association of Authors' Agents.

Overseas Representation:
Worldwide: Aitken Alexander Associates, London, UK

4083

*UNITED AGENTS LTD
12–26 Lexington Street, London W1F 0LE
Telephone: 020 3214 0800
Fax: 020 3214 0801
Website: www.unitedagents.co.uk

Personnel:
Simon Trewin *(Head, Books Department)*
Caroline Dawnay *(Agent)*
Sarah Ballard *(Agent)*
Carol MacArthur *(Agent)*
James Gill *(Agent)*
Robert Kirby *(Agent)*
Rosemary Scoular *(Agent)*
Charles Walker *(Agent)*
Anna Webber *(Agent)*
Jodie Marsh *(Agent)*

Specialization: literary and talent agency, operating across books, theatre, film, TV and commercials. Offers a full service to its client base and is always interested in new clients. Please consult website at www.unitedagents.co.uk for full submission guidelines.

4084

*ED VICTOR LTD
6 Bayley Street, Bedford Square, London WC1B 3HE
Telephone: 020 7304 4100
Fax: 020 7304 4111
Email: mary@edvictor.com

Personnel:
Ed Victor *(Executive Chairman)*
Margaret Phillips *(Joint Managing Director)*
Sophie Hicks *(Foreign Rights & Joint Managing Director)*
Leon Morgan *(Director)*
Carol Ryan *(Director)*
Graham Greene *(Director)*
Hitesh Shah *(Finance Director)*

All MSS except unsolicited manuscripts.

Specialization: fiction, non-fiction, biography, children's books.

4085

WADE & DOHERTY LITERARY AGENCY LTD
33 Cormorant Lodge, Thomas More Street, London E1W 1AU
Telephone: 020 7488 4171
Fax: 020 7488 4172
Email: rw@rwla.com
Website: www.rwla.com

Personnel:
Broo Doherty *(Partner)*

All MSS except scripts, poetry, plays, children's books including picture books or short stories.

Specialization: handles general fiction and non-fiction excluding children's books. Send detailed synopsis and first 10,000 words by e-mail. No reading fee. Commission: home 10%; film, TV and translation 20% (fees negotiable if a contract has already been offered). Founded 2001. Please see our website for detailed email submission guidelines.

4086

WATSON, LITTLE LTD
48–56 Bayham Place, London NW1 0EU
Telephone: 020 7388 7529
Fax: 020 7388 8501
Email: office@watsonlittle.com
Website: www.watsonlittle.com

Personnel:
Mandy Little *(Chairman)*
James Wills *(Managing Director)*
Sallyanne Sweeney *(Director)*

All MSS except short stories, plays and poetry.

Specialization: literary and commercial fiction, serious non-fiction, psychology, self-help, popular culture, health, sport, humour, children's.

Rights Representative in UK for:
The Chudney Agency, New York, NY, USA

Overseas Representation:
USA (adult): Howard Morhaim Literary Agency, New York, NY, USA
USA (children's): The Chudney Agency, New York, NY, USA
Worldwide: The Marsh Agency, London, UK
Worldwide (film & TV associates): The Ki Agency, London, UK; The Sharland Organisation, Raunds, Northants, UK

4087

*A. P. WATT LTD
20 John Street, London WC1N 2DR
Telephone: 020 7405 6774
Fax: 020 7831 2154
Email: apw@apwatt.co.uk
Website: www.apwatt.co.uk

Personnel:
Caradoc King *(Director)*
Linda Shaughnessy *(Director)*
Georgia Garrett *(Director)*

Derek Johns *(Director)*
Natasha Fairweather *(Director)*

All MSS except poetry.

Specialization: general fiction and non-fiction. No unsolicited manuscripts.

4088

JOSEF WEINBERGER PLAYS LTD
[formerly Warner/Chappell Plays Ltd]
12–14 Mortimer Street, London W1T 3JJ
Telephone: 020 7580 2827
Fax: 020 7436 9616
Email: general.info@jwmail.co.uk
Website: www.josef-weinberger.com

Personnel:
Michael Callahan *(Manager)*
Fiona Staples *(Licensing)*

Specialization: stage plays. Works in conjunction with overseas agents. No unsolicited manuscripts, preliminary letter essential.

Parent Company:
UK: Josef Weinberger Ltd

Associated Companies:
UK: Josef Weinberger Ltd

Rights Representative in UK for:
Dramatists Play Service Inc, New York, NY, USA

Overseas Representation:
Australia: Hal Leonard (Australia) Ltd, Melbourne, Vic, Australia
Canada & USA: Dramatists Play Service Inc, New York, NY, USA
New Zealand: Play Bureau (NZ) Ltd, New Plymouth, New Zealand
South Africa: Dalro (Pty) Ltd, Johannesburg, South Africa

4089

EVE WHITE LITERARY AGENT
54 Gloucester Street, London SW1V 4EG
Telephone: 020 7630 1155
Email: eve@evewhite.co.uk
Website: www.evewhite.co.uk

Personnel:
Eve White *(Director)*

All MSS except poetry, plays, screenplays.

Specialization: UK agency representing internationally published authors of commercial and literary fiction and non-fiction, children's fiction and picture books. Foreign rights handled in conjunction with Rebecca Winfield and Caroline Hill-Trevor. Film rights in conjunction with Knight Hall.

Clients include: Rae Earl, Saskia Sarginson, Jane Shemilt, Ruth Saberton, Fergus McNeill, Yvette Edwards, Susannah Corbett. Children's authors: Andy Stanton, Ivan Brett, Rae Earl, Ruth Warburton, Michaela Morgan, Kate Maryon, Tracey Corderoy & Abie Longstaff. Authors wishing to submit work must consult the submission page of our website.

Rights Representative in UK for:
Jennifer Unter, USA

Overseas Representation:
Commonwealth countries & USA: Eve White, London, UK
Worldwide (children's books): Caroline Hill-Trevor, Gloucestershire, UK
Worldwide (excluding Commonwealth countries & USA): Rebecca Winfield, London, UK

4090

DINAH WIENER LTD
12 Cornwall Grove, London W4 2LB
Telephone: 020 8994 6011
Fax: 020 8994 6044
Email: dinah@dwla.co.uk

Personnel:
Dinah Wiener *(Director)*
D. P. Wiener *(Director)*
B. M. Wiener *(Director)*

All MSS except juvenile, plays, film scripts, poetry & short stories.

Specialization: general fiction and non-fiction.

4091

JONATHAN WILLIAMS LITERARY AGENCY
Rosney Mews, Upper Glenageary Road, Glenageary, Co Dublin, Republic of Ireland
Telephone: +353 (0)1 280 3482
Fax: +353 (0)1 280 3482

Personnel:
Jonathan Williams *(Director)*

All MSS except plays or film scripts. Return postage and packing is appreciated. Irish postage stamps or international postal coupons, please.

Specialization: typescripts of Irish interest.

Overseas Representation:
Italy: Agenzia Piergiorgio Nicolazzini, Milan, Italy
Japan: Tuttle-Mori Agency Inc, Tokyo, Japan
Spain & Spanish-speaking Latin America: Antonia Kerrigan Literary Agency, Barcelona, Spain

5   Trade & Allied Associations

5.1   INTERNATIONAL

5001 ▬▬▬▬▬

EDITEUR LTD
United House, North Road, London N7 9DP
Telephone: 020 7503 6148
Fax: 020 7503 6418
Email: info@editeur.org
Website: www.editeur.org

Personnel:
Mark Bide (*Executive Director*)
Stella Griffiths (*Associate Director*)
Sarah Hilderley (*Accessibility Project Lead*)
Graham Bell (*Chief Data Architect*)
Tim Devenport (*Lead Consultant to ICEDIS*)
Nick Woods (*Operations Manager*)
Michael Hopwood (*Linked Heritage, Project Lead*)

EDItEUR is the international group co-ordinating development of the standards infrastructure for electronic commerce in the book and serials sectors.

EDItEUR provides its membership with research, standards and guidance in such diverse areas as:
• EDI and other e-commerce standards for book and serial transactions
• Bibliographic and product information
• The standards infrastructure for digital publishing
• Rights management and trading
• Radio frequency identification tags.

Established in 1991, EDItEUR is a truly international organization with 100 members from 20 countries, including Australia, Canada, Japan, South Africa, United States and most of the European countries.

A leader in global standards for the exchange of bibliographic information (particularly the ONIX for Books Product Information standard) and of e-commerce messages in the book and journal supply chains, EDItEUR is also engaged in shaping key national and international projects aimed at developing rights and permissions expressions.

5002 ▬▬▬▬▬

INTERNATIONAL BOARD ON BOOKS FOR YOUNG PEOPLE – IBBY
Nonnenweg 12, Postfach, 4003 Basel, Switzerland
Telephone: +41 (0)61 272 29 17
Fax: +41 (0)61 272 27 57
Email: luzmaria.stauffenegger@ibby.org
Website: www.ibby.org

Personnel:
Elizabeth Page (*Executive Director*)
Ahmad Redza Ahmad Khairuddin (*President of the Executive Committee*)
Luzmaria Stauffenegger (*Administrative Assistant*)

Promotion of children's books and reading worldwide.

5003 ▬▬▬▬▬

THE INTERNATIONAL ISBN AGENCY
United House, North Road, London N7 9DP
Telephone: 020 7503 6418
Fax: 020 7503 6418
Email: info@isbn-international.org
Website: www.isbn-international.org

Personnel:
Stella Griffiths (*Executive Director*)
Nick Woods (*Operations Manager*)

The International ISBN Agency is the registration authority for the ISBN system globally. The administration of the ISBN system is carried out on three levels:
• International agency
• Group agencies
• Publisher level.

The main functions of the International ISBN Agency are:
• To promote, co-ordinate and supervise the worldwide use of the ISBN system
• To approve the definition and structure of group agencies
• To allocate group identifiers to group agencies
• To advise on the establishment and functioning of group agencies
• To advise group agencies on the allocation of international publisher identifiers
• To publish the assigned group numbers and publishers' prefixes.

There are over 150 local ISBN agencies, covering 200 countries. Publishers apply to their local ISBN agency to obtain ISBNs.

5004 ▬▬▬▬▬

PRIVATE LIBRARIES ASSOCIATION
29 Eden Drive, Hull HU8 8JQ
Email: maslen@maslen.karoo.co.uk
Website: www.plabooks.org

Personnel:
Giles Mandelbrote (*Hon President*)
David Chambers (*Hon Chairman*)
Jim Maslen (*Hon Secretary*)
Robert Hirst (*Hon Treasurer*)

An international society of book collectors, run on a voluntary basis. Publications include a quarterly journal and *The Exchange List*, which circulate among member collectors throughout the world, an annual bibliography, and other books concerned with book collecting.

5.2   UNITED KINGDOM & REPUBLIC OF IRELAND

5005 ▬▬▬▬▬

THE ACADEMIC AND PROFESSIONAL DIVISION OF THE PUBLISHERS ASSOCIATION
29B Montague Street, London WC1B 5BW
Telephone: 020 7691 9191
Fax: 020 7691 9199
Email: mail@publishers.org.uk
Website: www.publishers.org.uk

Personnel:
Ms Emma House (*Director of Publisher Relations*)

Parent Company:
UK: The Publishers Association

The Academic and Professional Division of The Publishers Association represents the interests of publishers serving higher education, scholarly communication and the professional and commercial market. Collective activities are organized on their behalf. Membership is open to any publisher in membership of the Publishers Association, which produces books, journals or similar published material for these markets.

5006 ▬▬▬▬▬

ALLIANCE OF LITERARY SOCIETIES (ALS)
59 Bryony Road, Selly Oak, Birmingham B29 4BY
Telephone: 0121 475 1805
Email: l.j.curry@bham.ac.uk
Website: www.allianceofliterarysocieties.org.uk

Personnel:
Linda J. Curry (*Chair*)
Julie Shorland (*Hon Treasurer / Membership Secretary*)
Anita Fernandez-Young (*Secretary*)

The ALS is an umbrella organization for literary societies/groups within the UK. The AGM is hosted by different member societies each year, with accompanying talks etc covering a weekend (usually around the end of May/beginning of June). Members of affiliated societies are welcome to attend but only the delegate of the affiliated society may have a vote. Details are on the website – including subscription rates. An annual journal (*ALSo#*) is also produced. This is freely available to member societies but can be purchased by non-members.

5007 ▬▬▬▬▬

ARCHIVES AND RECORDS ASSOCIATION (UK & IRELAND)
Prioryfield House, 20 Canon Street, Taunton, Somerset TA1 1SW
Telephone: 01823 327030 & 327077
Fax: 01823 271719
Email: ara@archives.org.uk
Website: www.archives.org.uk

Personnel:
John Chambers (Chief Executive)
Lorraine Logan (Membership & Office Administrator)
Marie Owens (Head of Public Affairs)

Publication of texts/periodicals on archives and records management. Conferences and training courses.

5008

ASSOCIATION OF AUTHORS' AGENTS
Clerkenwell House, 45-47 Clerkenwell Green, London
EC1R 0HT
Website: www.agentsassoc.co.uk

Personnel:
Peter Straus (President)
Jodie Marsh (Treasurer)
Ed Wilson (Secretary)

Founded in 1974 to institute and maintain a code of professional behaviour, to discuss matters of common professional interest and to provide a vehicle for representing the view of authors' agents in discussions on matters of common interest with other professional bodies.

5009

ASSOCIATION OF FREELANCE EDITORS, PROOFREADERS & INDEXERS (IRELAND)
11 Clonard Road, Sandyford, Dublin 16, Republic of Ireland
Telephone: +353 (0)1 295 2194 & + 353 (0)1 440 4299
Email: Brenda@ohanlonmedia.com and
liz@littleredpen.com
Website: www.afepi.ie

Personnel:
Brenda O'Hanlon (Joint Chair)
Joint Chair Liz Hudson

The AFEPI was established to provide information to publishers on Irish freelancers working in this field, and to protect the interests of those freelancers. Membership is restricted to freelancers with experience and/or references, but skills of members are not tested or evaluated.

5010

ASSOCIATION OF ILLUSTRATORS
Somerset House, Strand, London WC2R 1LA
Telephone: 020 7759 1010
Email: info@theaoi.com
Website: www.theaoi.com

Personnel:
Heng Khoo (Managing Director)
Derek Brazell (Projects Manager)
Rasheed Musa (Finance Manager)
Helen Thomas (Events & Marketing Manager)
Matthew Shearer (Membership Co-ordinator)

Established in 1973 to advance and protect illustrators' rights, the AOI is a non-profit-making trade association dedicated to its members' professional interest and the promotion of illustration.

Corporate members (agents and clients) receive a free copy of the Illustration Awards catalogue, discounts on events, publications and our Awards competition entry, plus

Varoom – the illustration report, published four times per year.

5011

ASSOCIATION OF LEARNED & PROFESSIONAL SOCIETY PUBLISHERS (ALPSP)
51 Middletons Road, Yaxley, Peterborough PE7 3NU
Telephone: +44 (0)1733 247178
Fax: +44 (0)8707 626178
Email: admin@alpsp.org
Website: www.alpsp.org

Director of Marketing & Membership Services:
Suzanne Kavanagh, 157 South Croxted Road, London
SE21 8AX
Telephone: 020 8670 4244
Email: suzanne.kavanagh@alpsp.org
Website: www.alpsp.org

Personnel:
Audrey McCulloch (Chief Executive)
Suzanne Kavanagh (Director of Marketing & Membership Services)
Isabel Czech (Executive Director, North America)
Ian Hunter (Finance & Administration Manager)
Lesley Ogg (Events & Membership Manager)
Amanda Whiting (Training Manager)
Dee French (Administrator)
Melissa Marshall (Training & Admin Assistant)
Melanie Goinden (Events Administrator)
Alan Singleton (Editor-in-Chief, Learned Publishing Editor)

ALPSP is an international trade association for the community of not-for-profit publishers and those who work with them to disseminate academic and professional information. It was founded in 1972, and currently has over 320 members in 39 countries. ALPSP aims to connect, inform, develop and represent its members. It carries out research and other projects, monitors national and international issues and represents members' interests to the wider world. The Association provides co-operative services such as the ALPSP Learned Journals Collection. It also offers an extensive programme of courses and seminars, an informative website, a quarterly journal (Learned Publishing) and a monthly electronic newsletter (ALPSP Alert).

5012

ASSOCIATION OF SUBSCRIPTION AGENTS AND INTERMEDIARIES
5 Whitecroft Gardens, Woodford Halse, Northants
NN11 3PY
Telephone: +1 (773) 685 2007
Email: ASAOffice@subscription-agents.org
Website: www.subscription-agents.org

Personnel:
Dr. Nawin Gupta (Secretary General)
Peter Lawson (Chairman)
Tony Roche (Treasurer)

The ASA is the international trade association serving subscription agents and information services intermediaries providing products and services within the professional and scholarly information supply chain. The ASA exists to provide information to its members from all areas of the information industry, to create a forum for exchange amongst these groups and to represent members' common interests to publishers, customers, representative and governmental organizations and associations.

5013

AUTHORS' LICENSING & COLLECTING SOCIETY (ALCS)
The Writers' House, 13 Haydon Street, London EC3N 1DB
Telephone: 020 7264 5700
Fax: 020 7264 5755
Email: alcs@alcs.co.uk
Website: www.alcs.co.uk

Personnel:
Owen Atkinson (Chief Executive)
Barbara Hayes (Deputy Chief Executive)
Alison Baxter (Communications Manager)

The Authors' Licensing & Collecting Society is the UK collective rights management society for writers of all genres. Members grant to the Society the right to administer on their behalf those rights which an author is unable to exercise as an individual or which are best handled on a collective basis. These include photocopying, rental and lending right, off-air and private recording, electronic rights, cable retransmission and rights for the public reception of broadcasts. Membership costs a one-off lifetime fee of £25. Please contact the Society for further information. The ALCS administers these rights in the UK and Northern Ireland. Under reciprocal arrangements with foreign collecting societies other territories are also covered. Distributions to members are made bi-annually. For advice and further information please contact the ALCS office or click www.alcs.co.uk.

5014

BAPLA (BRITISH ASSOCIATION OF PICTURE LIBRARIES AND AGENCIES)
59 Tranquil Vale, Blackheath, London SE3 0BS
Email: enquiries@bapla.org.uk
Website: www.bapla.org.uk

Personnel:
Susanne Kittlinger (Membership & Communications Manager)

The British Association of Picture Libraries and Agencies, or BAPLA, is the trade association for picture libraries in the UK, and has been a trade body since 1975. Members include the major news, stock and production agencies as well as Sole Traders and cultural heritage onstitutions.

Please see our website for details.

5015

THE BIBLIOGRAPHICAL SOCIETY
c/o Institute of English Studies, Senate House, Malet Street, London WC1E 7HU
Telephone: 020 7862 8675
Fax: 020 7862 8720
Email: bibsoc@london.ac.uk
Website: www.bibsoc.org.uk

Personnel:
Margaret Ford (Hon Secretary)

The Bibliographical Society promotes the study of historical, analytical, descriptive and textual bibliography. It publishes its own journal, The Library, and supports a publishing programme of books and monographs on bibliographical subjects.

5016

BOOK AID INTERNATIONAL
39–41 Coldharbour Lane, Camberwell, London SE5 9NR
Telephone: 020 7733 3577
Fax: 020 7978 8006
Email: info@bookaid.org
Website: www.bookaid.org

Personnel:
HRH The Duke of Edinburgh KG, KT, OM (Patron)
Nigel Newton (President)
Philip Walters (Chair)
Alison Hubert (Director)

Every year, Book Aid International sends over half a million books to sub-Saharan Africa. Almost 90% of these are donated to us new by UK publishers from returned, obsolete or excess stock. These books reach public and community libraries, and libraries in schools, universities, slums, refugee centres and prisons.

We are always in need of suitable books, especially: children's; education; EFL; teacher training; vocational; medical; law; fiction; library and information management; computing.

Without the books we send, many of the libraries we support would have nothing on their shelves. Please get in touch if you can help.

5017

BOOK INDUSTRY COMMUNICATION LTD
7 Ridgmount Street, London WC1E 7AE
Telephone: 020 7255 0516
Email: info@bic.org.uk
Website: www.bic.org.uk

Personnel:
Karina Luke (Executive Director)

Book Industry Communication (BIC) is an independent organization set up and sponsored by the Publishers Association, Booksellers Association, the Chartered Institute of Library and Information Professionals and the British Library to promote supply chain efficiency in all sectors of the book world through e-commerce and the application of standard processes and procedures. Its subscribers include most of the UK's major publishers, booksellers and service providers.

5018

THE BOOK TRADE CHARITY (BTBS)
The Foyle Centre, The Retreat, Kings Langley, Herts
WD4 8LT
Telephone: 01923 263128
Fax: 01923 270732
Email: david@btbs.org
Website: www.booktradecharity.org

Personnel:
David Hicks *(Chief Executive)*
Nigel Batt *(Treasurer)*
Glenda Barnard *(Housing & Welfare Manager)*
Claire Walton *(Administration Manager)*

The welfare charity of the book trade, offering support to colleagues in difficult personal circumstances. The Book Trade Charity gives direct financial support, regular and one-off, to individuals, to help with a wide range of problems. Accommodation at The Retreat, Kings Langley, offers pre-retirement and retirement housing. The book trade Helpline (freephone 0808 100 2304) provides sympathetic, confidential help. Anyone who has worked in the book trade (publishing, distribution, bookselling, etc for more than one year, employed, self-employed or freelance) is eligible to apply for assistance.

5019

BOOKSELLERS ASSOCIATION OF THE UNITED KINGDOM & IRELAND LTD
6 Bell Yard, London WC2A 2JR
Telephone: 020 7421 4640
Fax: 020 7421 4641
Email: mail@booksellers.org.uk
Website: www.booksellers.org.uk

Personnel:
Patrick Neale *(President)*
Tim Godfray *(Chief Executive)*

Associated Companies:
UK: Batch.co.uk Ltd; Book Industry Communication Ltd; Book Tokens Ltd; Word Book Day Ltd

Founded in 1895. Represents over 4400 outlets. Promotes and looks after the interests of booksellers, helps them become more efficient and fights for better distribution in the trade. It also helps booksellers increase sales and reduce costs, and gives advice on opening and running a bookshop. Among other services, the Association produces catalogues for distribution throughout the retail trade at Christmas, and directories of members, publishers and services.

5020

BOOKTRUST
Book House, 45 East Hill, London SW18 2QZ
Telephone: 020 8516 2977
Fax: 020 8516 2978
Email: query@booktrust.org.uk
Website: www.booktrust.org.uk

Personnel:
Viv Bird *(Chief Executive)*

Booktrust is an independent reading and writing charity that makes a nationwide impact on individuals, families and communities, and culture in the UK. Booktrust's work supports children and young people, parents and carers, and indeed anyone who would benefit from the positive impact that books, reading and writing can have on their lives.

5021

BRITISH CENTRE FOR LITERARY TRANSLATION (BCLT)
University of East Anglia, Norwich NR4 7TJ
Telephone: 01603 592785
Fax: 01603 592737
Email: bclt@uea.ac.uk
Website: www.bclt.org.uk

Personnel:
Ms Kate Griffin *(International Programme Director)*
Daniel Hahn *(National Programme Director)*
Miss Catherine Fuller *(Co-ordinator)*

Parent Company:
UK: University of East Anglia

Raises the profile of literary translation and the professional development of literary translators. Organizes events, readings, workshops aimed at translators, professionals in arts and publishing, and the general public.

5022

THE BRITISH GUILD OF TRAVEL WRITERS
335 Lordship Road, London N16 5HG

Telephone: 020 8144 8713
Website: www.bgtw.org

Personnel:
Robert Ellison *(Secretariat)*

The Guild has a membership of around 270, all professional journalists, broadcasters and photographers who derive the majority of their earnings from travel writing, broadcasting or photography. Monthly meetings are devoted to discussion of travel topics, usually with outside speakers, and take place at a variety of venues. There is a monthly *Newsletter* for members. An annual yearbook giving full details of all members together with comprehensive lists of PRs and other contacts in the travel trade is available for purchase.

5023

CHARTERED INSTITUTE OF JOURNALISTS
2 Dock Offices, Surrey Quays Road, London SE16 2XU
Telephone: 020 7252 1187
Fax: 020 7232 2302
Email: memberservices@cioj.co.uk
Website: www.cioj.co.uk

Personnel:
Charlie Harris *(President)*
Michael Hardware *(Treasurer)*
Dominic Cooper *(General Secretary)*

The senior professional society of journalists worldwide. Incorporated by Royal Charter in 1890, it had its origin in the National Association of Journalists, which was founded in 1884 and converted into the Institute in 1889. Its primary object is 'the promotion by all reasonable means of the interests of journalists and journalism'. Representing the profession as a whole, it is a completely independent body free of political partiality. It gives equal rights of membership to all members of the profession, including radio and television journalists, press photographers and public relations officers with journalistic qualifications. Trade union representation is provided by the IOJ (TU), an independent certificated trade union.

5024

CHILDREN'S BOOKS IRELAND
17 North Great George's Street, Dublin 1, Republic of Ireland
Telephone: +353 (0)1 872 7475
Fax: +353 (0)1 872 7476
Email: info@childrensbooksireland.com
Website: www.childrensbooksireland.com

Personnel:
Mags Walsh *(Director)*
Aoife Murray *(Programme Officer)*
Jenny Murray *(Communications & Publications)*
Patricia Kennon *(Features Editor – Inis Magazine)*
Juliette Saumande *(Reviews Editor – Inis Magazine)*
Claire Marie Dunne *(Irish Language Editor – Inis Magazine)*
David Maybury *(Digital Editor – Inis Magazine)*

Associated Companies:
Republic of Ireland: Children's Book Festival; Inis Magazine; Laureate na nÓg – children's laureate

Children's Books Ireland is the national children's book organization of Ireland. The aim of Children's Books Ireland is to promote quality children's books and reading. CBI runs an annual nationwide Children's Book Festival, the CBI Book of the Year Awards, publishes *Inis* magazine, which carries a wide range of articles about children's books in Ireland and abroad as well as an extensive review section, and hosts an annual Children's Books conference.

CBI is a resource and support organization for teachers, pupils, writers, publishers, booksellers and librarians as well as an imaginative programmer of events for young readers.

Our mission is to make books a part of every child's life. We champion and celebrate the importance of authors and illustrators and we work in partnership with the people and organizations that enhance children's lives through books.

CBI, Making books part of every child's life.

5025

CHILDREN'S WRITERS & ILLUSTRATORS GROUP
The Society of Authors, 84 Drayton Gardens, London SW10 9SB

Telephone: 020 7373 6642
Fax: 020 7373 5768
Email: jmccrum@societyofauthors.org
Website: www.societyofauthors.org

Personnel:
Jo McCrum *(Secretary)*

Parent Company:
UK: The Society of Authors

The Children's Writers and Illustrators Group is an organization, founded in 1963, for writers and illustrators of children's books, who are members of The Society of Authors. Meetings are held regularly, with opportunities for members to meet each other, as well as to hear talks or discussions on various aspects of their work.

5026

COMHAIRLE NAN LEABHRAICHEAN / THE GAELIC BOOKS COUNCIL
32 Mansfield Street, Glasgow G11 5QP
Telephone: 0141 337 6211
Email: brath@gaelicbooks.org
Website: www.gaelicbooks.org

Personnel:
Donald-Ian Brown *(Chair)*
Rosemary Ward *(Manager)*

The Council was set up in 1968 to administer the Gaelic Books Grant awarded by the Scottish Education Department, and its purpose is to stimulate Gaelic publishing. It normally has about ten members as its board, and a paid staff of four. In April 1983 the Scottish Arts Council became its main funding body, and its Assessor attends meetings. The Council became a charitable company in July 1996.

It provides financial assistance in the form of publication grants (paid to the publisher) for individual Gaelic books, and also commission grants for authors. Editorial advice is available, and a word-processing and proofreading service.

In 2003 it launched the highly successful Ùr-Sgeul imprint for prose work in Gaelic, with the associated books, CDs and DVDs being issued by the publisher Clàr.

As a retailer, the Council stocks all Gaelic and Gaelic-related works in print, regular lists of these being published in its catalogue, and on its website. It has its own shop at the address above, and also does mail order and mobile selling at selected events, as well as running a book club (A' Chiste Leabhraichean).

5027

COPYRIGHT TRIBUNAL
4 Abbey Orchard Street, London SW1P 2HT
Telephone: 020 7034 2836
Fax: 020 7034 2826
Email: catherine.worley@ipo.gov.uk
Website: www.ipo.gov.uk/ctribunal.htm

Personnel:
Judge Birss QC *(Chairman)*
Catherine Worley *(Secretary/Head)*

The main function of the Tribunal is to decide, where the parties cannot agree between themselves, the terms and conditions of licences offered by, or licensing schemes operated by, collective licensing bodies in the copyright and related rights area. It has the statutory task of conclusively establishing the facts of a case and of coming to a decision that is reasonable in the light of those facts. Its decisions are appealable to the High Court only on points of law. (Appeals on a point of law against decisions of the Tribunal in Scotland are to the Court of Session.)

Broadly, the Tribunal's jurisdiction is such that anyone who has unreasonably been refused a licence by a collecting society or considers the terms of an offered licence to be unreasonable may refer the matter to the Tribunal. The Tribunal also has the power to decide some matters even though collecting societies are not involved. For example, it can settle disputes over the royalties payable by publishers of TV programme listings to broadcasting organizations.

5028

THE EDUCATIONAL PUBLISHERS COUNCIL
[Schools Division of The Publishers Association]

The Publishers Association, 29B Montague Street, London WC1B 5BW
Telephone: 020 7691 9191
Fax: 020 7691 9199
Email: mail@publishers.org.uk
Website: www.publishers.org.uk

Personnel:
Ms Emma House *(Director of Publisher Relations)*

Parent Company:
UK: The Publishers Association

The Educational Publishers Council is the division within the PA that looks after the interests of educational publishers. It promotes the nature and importance of educational publishers' work both to the educational system and to the general public, and organizes collective activities on their behalf. Membership is open to any publisher in membership of The Publishers Association which produces books or other published learning resources for use in schools.

5029

EDUCATIONAL WRITERS GROUP
The Society of Authors, 84 Drayton Gardens, London SW10 9SB
Telephone: 020 7373 6642
Fax: 020 7244 0743
Email: info@societyofauthors.org
Website: www.societyofauthors.org

Personnel:
Sarah Baxter *(Secretary)*

Parent Company:
UK: The Society of Authors

The Educational Writers Group is a subsidiary group of The Society of Authors. Its purpose is to advise members on their publishing problems etc, to study the conditions peculiar to the market at home and overseas, to watch developments in teaching as they affect the educational writer, and to hold meetings at which experience can be pooled and matters of mutual interest discussed.

5030

ENGLISH ASSOCIATION
University of Leicester, University Road, Leicester LE1 7RH
Telephone: 0116 229 7622
Fax: 0116 229 7623
Email: engassoc@le.ac.uk
Website: www.le.ac.uk/engassoc

Personnel:
Helen Lucas *(Chief Executive)*
Julia Hughes *(Assistant)*

Founded in 1906 to promote the knowledge, enjoyment and study of the English language and its literatures.

The Year's Work in English Studies is the annual qualitative narrative bibliographical overview of scholarly work on English language and literature written in English. Published annually in December.

The Year's Work in Critical and Cultural Theory, companion volume to YWES, provides a narrative bibliography of work in the field of critical and cultural theory.

Other journals also published. See website. Order from: email Julia Hughes (email above) or tel 0116 229 7622.

5031

FACET PUBLISHING
7 Ridgmount Street, London WC1E 7AE
Telephone: 020 7255 0590
Fax: 020 7255 0591
Email: info@facetpublishing.co.uk
Website: www.facetpublishing.co.uk

Facet Publishing, the commercial publishing and bookselling arm of CILIP: the Chartered Institute of Library and Information Professionals, is the leading publisher of books for library and information professionals worldwide.

Previously known as Library Association Publishing, Facet Publishing has an internationally established list of over 200 specialist titles in print.

Together these products cover all the major aspects of professional LIS activity.

Facet Publishing sells its books and e-books in virtually every country in the world. It has customers in the public and private sectors and publishes books for library, museum, archive, records management and publishing communities, as well as students on information, media, business and communications courses.

5032

THE FEDERATION OF CHILDREN'S BOOK GROUPS
Hampton Farm, Bowerhill, Melksham, Wiltshire SN12 6QZ
Telephone: 01225 353710
Email: info@fcbg.org.uk
Website: www.fcbg.org.uk

Personnel:
Mrs Julia Miller *(chair)*
Mrs Sarah Stuffins *(vice chair)*
Mrs Jane Etheridge *(treasurer)*

We are a national, voluntary organization concerned with bringing children and books together. The Federation's aim is to promote enjoyment and interest in children's books and reading, and to encourage the availability of a range of literature for all ages, from pre-school to teenage. The Federation supports its member book groups, and liaises with schools, playgroups, publishers, libraries and other official bodies.

National activities include:
• organizes, annually, The Red House Children's Book Award
• promotes National Share-a-Story Month in May and National Non-Fiction day in November
• organizes an annual Conference each spring.

Individual and Professional Members receive Federation publications, such as the *Federation Newsletter*, booklists for all age groups, as well as the annual *Red House Children's Book Award 'Pick of the Year' Top Fifty Booklet*. We send out information about National Share-a-Story Month and National Non-Fiction day, and a monthly email update, and members can take advantage of discounted delegate rates at Conference.

5033

GAY AUTHORS WORKSHOP
BM Box 5700, London WC1N 3XX
Email: eandk2@btinternet.com

Personnel:
Kathryn Bell *(Secretary)*

Associated Companies:
UK: Gay Authors Self-Publishing Society

Gay Authors Workshop is an association of lesbians, gay men and bisexuals who are creative writers – poets, dramatists, fiction writers. Its aim is to raise the standard of gay literature by providing opportunities for gay writers to meet, read, discuss and criticize their work in a constructive way. Monthly meetings are held at different places in the London area (and occasionally elsewhere) for that purpose, and to share information about publishing outlets and competitions. Although London-based, it is a national organization. The quarterly newsletter (print and tape) keeps members in touch with activities. Membership is open to all gay writers, beginners as well as published authors. We produce an in-house magazine, *Gazebo*, twice yearly, to which members contribute short stories and reviews. The subscription is £8 a year, £4 unwaged.

5034

GIBB MEMORIAL TRUST
2 Penarth Place, Cambridge CB3 9LU
Telephone: 01223 566630
Email: Secretary@gibbtrust.org
Website: www.gibbtrust.org

Book Distribution:
Oxbow Books Ltd, 10 Hythe Bridge Street, Oxford OX1 2EW
Telephone: 01865 241249
Fax: 01865 794449
Email: oxbow@oxbowbooks.com
Website: www.oxbowbooks.com

Personnel:
P. R. Bligh *(Secretary to the Trustees)*

The Trust is a registered charity whose aim is to support the publication of works of scholarly research within the areas of the history, literature, philosophy and religion of the Persians, Turks and Arabs. Its activities are in financing and organizing the production and publication of books, and in marketing the published works. The books are distributed by Oxbow Books in Oxford, UK, and Oakville, USA.

5035

GUILD OF FOOD WRITERS
255 Kent House Road, Beckenham, Kent BR3 1JQ
Telephone: 020 8659 0422
Email: guild@gfw.co.uk
Website: www.gfw.co.uk

Personnel:
Jonathan Woods *(Administrator)*

The Guild of Food Writers is the professional association of food writers and broadcasters in the UK. Established in 1984, it now has 450 authors, columnists, freelance journalists and broadcasters amongst its members.

The objectives of the Guild as set out in its constitution are as follows:
• To bring together professional food writers, to print and issue an annual list of members, to extend the range of members' knowledge and experience, and to encourage the development of new writers by every means, including competitions and awards.
• To contribute to the growth of public interest in, and knowledge of, the subject of food and to campaign for improvements in the quality of food.

The Guild is a self-supporting body that offers its members a busy calendar that includes annual awards, monthly workshops, AGM, an autumn event and occasional professional and social events. It also publishes a monthly newsletter and comprehensive and detailed directory of members.

The Guild offers professional support and guidance to its members.

5036

INDEPENDENT PUBLISHERS GUILD (IPG)
PO Box 12, Llain, Whitland SA34 0WU
Telephone: 01437 563335
Fax: 01437 562071
Email: info@ipg.uk.com
Website: www.ipg.uk.com

Personnel:
Bridget Shine *(Chief Executive)*

The Independent Publishers Guild (IPG) actively represents the interests of independent publishers in the UK and is represented on many committees and forums, which form the strategy for the UK book trade. The IPG helps publishers to do better business and is somewhere they can find advice, ideas and information.

With more than 560 members and steadily growing with combined revenues of more than £500M, the IPG provides a vibrant networking base. Members receive regular e-newsletters, training courses and seminars covering important areas. The IPG Conference is a must attend event in the publishing calendar.

The IPG runs a collective stand for members at leading international book fairs, including Frankfurt and London.

5037

INSTITUTE OF INTERNAL COMMUNICATION
Suite GA2, Oak House, Woodlands Business Park, Breckland, Milton Keynes MK14 6EY
Telephone: 01908 313755
Fax: 01908 313661
Email: enquiries@ioic.org.uk
Website: www.ioic.org.uk

Personnel:
Steve Doswell *(Chief Executive)*

The Institute of Internal Communication (IoIC) (formerly CiB) is the UK's professional body for internal communication, with members working in-house, agency or freelance roles in all sectors of the economy in the UK and Ireland.

Whatever your responsibility – strategy, planning and delivery, consultancy, change management, writing, design, online, print, measurement, brand management – if internal communication is your focus, the Institute exists to support you.

Major activities include the annual IoIC and Icon Awards competitions, annual conference and a regular programme of regional educational and training events as well as our ongoing professional qualifications in internal communications.

5038

MEDICAL WRITERS GROUP

The Society of Authors, 84 Drayton Gardens, London SW10 9SB
Telephone: 020 7373 6642
Fax: 020 7373 5768
Email: info@societyofauthors.org & sbaxter@societyofauthors.org
Website: www.societyofauthors.org

Personnel:
Sarah Baxter (Secretary)

The Medical Writers Group is a group within The Society of Authors. Its principal objects are to represent its members in all matters affecting their interests as medical writers; to hold meetings from time to time for the discussion of matters of common interest; and to provide, through the Society, advice to members on the special problems of medical authorship. Authors who have had a book accepted for publication, but not yet published, can join the Society and obtain advice.

5039

MUSIC PUBLISHERS ASSOCIATION

6th Floor, British Music House, 26 Berners Street, London W1T 3LR
Telephone: 020 7580 0126
Fax: 020 7637 3929
Email: info@mpaonline.org.uk
Website: www.mpaonline.org.uk

Associated Companies:
UK: MCPS Ltd; Printed Music Licensing Ltd

The Music Publishers Association (MPA) was established in 1881 and is governed by an elected Board. The MPA exists to safeguard the interests of music publishers and the writers signed to them. It provides them with a forum and a collective voice, and aims to inform and to educate the wider public in the importance and value of copyright.

The MPA offers a range of services and publications to those interested in music publishing (including training) and participates in education and information initiatives across the music industry.

5040

NATIONAL ACQUISITIONS GROUP

12–14 King Street, Wakefield WF1 2SQ
Telephone: 01924 383010
Fax: 01924 383010
Website: www.nag.org.uk

Personnel:
Karen Carden (Chair)
Susan Wills (Vice Chair)
Regina Ferguson (Hon. Treasurer)
Judith Rhodes (Administrator)

Established in 1986, NAG is a broadly based organization which stimulates, co-ordinates and publicizes developments in library acquisitions and the book trade. The membership includes individuals and organizations within publishing, bookselling and systems supply, as well as librarians responsible for choosing and buying books for academic, public, national, government and special institutions.

NAG has two main aims:
• to bring together all those in any way concerned with library acquisitions, to assist them in exchanging information

and comment, and to promote understanding and good practice between them;
• to seek to influence other organizations and individuals to adopt its opinions and standards.

NAG's objectives are to:
• provide a forum for discussion and the exchange of information;
• extend knowledge and understanding of technological developments;
• promote the dissemination of information about library acquisitions;
• develop the awareness of producers, suppliers and librarians;
• act as a channel of communication with Government and other bodies.

5041

NIELSEN BOOKDATA

3rd Floor, Midas House, 62 Goldsworth Road, Woking, Surrey GU21 6LQ
Telephone: 01483 712200
Fax: 01483 712201
Email: info.bookdata@nielsen.com
Website: www.nielsenbookdata.co.uk

Personnel:
Ann Betts (Commercial Director)
Simon Skinner (Sales Director)
Mo Siewcharran (Head of Marketing)
Paul Dibble (Head of Data Sales)
Vesna Nall (Publisher & Subscriptions Manager)
Lucy Huddlestone (Export Sales Manager)
Melanie Brassington (Export Sales Manager)
Helen Anderson (Key Account Manager)
Richard Merrick (Customer Services Manager)

Parent Company:
UK: Nielsen

Associated Companies:
UK: Nielsen BookNet; Nielsen BookScan; Nielsen Registration Agencies (ISBN, SAN & ISTC)

Nielsen BookData is an information provider worldwide. The company has a range of products and services which provide content-rich, accurate and timely book information for English-language titles published internationally. These services are sold to booksellers, libraries and publishers in over 100 countries, including the UK, Ireland, Europe, Australia, New Zealand, South Africa and the USA.

5042

NIELSEN ISBN AGENCY

3rd Floor, Midas House, 62 Goldsworth Road, Woking, Surrey GU21 6LQ
Telephone: 01483 712215
Fax: 01483 712214
Email: isbn.agency@nielsen.com
Website: www.isbn.nielsenbook.co.uk

Personnel:
Julian Sowa (Senior Manager)
Diana Williams (Manager)

Parent Company:
UK: Nielsen

Associated Companies:
UK: Nielsen BookData; Nielsen ISTC Agency; Nielsen SAN Agency

The UK International Standard Book Numbering Agency is responsible for assigning ISBN prefixes to publishers based in the UK or the Irish Republic. The UK ISBN Agency cannot assign ISBNs to publishers based in other countries.

The Agency:
• allocates ISBN publisher prefixes to eligible publishers based on the information provided by the publisher;
• advises publishers on the correct and proper implementation of the ISBN system;
• maintains a database of publishers and their prefixes for inclusion in the Publishers' International ISBN Directory;
• encourages and promotes the use of the Bookland EAN bar code format;
• encourages and promotes the importance of the ISBN for a proper listing of titles with bibliographical agencies;

• provides technical advice and assistance to publishers and the booktrade on all aspects of ISBN usage.

Any new publishers wishing to apply for an allocation of ISBNs should contact the ISBN Agency for an application pack. A registration fee is payable.

5043

NIELSEN ISTC AGENCY

3rd Floor, Midas House, 62 Goldsworth Road, Woking, Surrey GU21 6LQ
Telephone: 01483 712215
Fax: 01483 712714
Email: istc.agency@nielsen.com
Website: www.istc.nielsenbook.co.uk

Personnel:
Julian Sowa (Senior Manager)
Diana Williams (Manager)

Parent Company:
UK: Nielsen

Associated Companies:
UK: Nielsen BookData; Nielsen ISBN Agency; Nielsen SAN Agency

The International Standard Text Code (ISTC) is a global identification system for textual works, i.e. the content in text-based publications. Nielsen operates one of the first ISTC registration agencies, enabling authors, publishers and other authorized representatives to register textual works with an ISTC. It also provides advice and guidance on how to make the most of this important new system. Nielsen also runs the ISBN and SAN agencies.

5044

NIELSEN SAN AGENCY

3rd Floor, Midas House, 62 Goldsworth Road, Woking, Surrey GU21 6LQ
Telephone: 01483 712215
Fax: 01483 712214
Email: san.agency@nielsen.com
Website: www.san.nielsenbook.co.uk

Personnel:
Julian Sowa (Senior Manager)
Diana Williams (Manager)

Parent Company:
UK: Nielsen

Associated Companies:
UK: Nielsen BookData; Nielsen ISBN Agency; Nielsen ISTC Agency

SANs, Standard Address Numbers, are unique for geographical locations and can be assigned to the addresses of organizations involved in the bookselling and publishing industries. The SAN Agency is responsible for managing the scheme on behalf of Book Industry Communication in any country except the USA, Canada, Australia and New Zealand. Nielsen also runs the ISBN and ISTC agencies.

5045

PROFESSIONAL PUBLISHERS ASSOCIATION

Queens House, 28 Kingsway, London WC2B 6JR
Telephone: 020 7404 4166
Fax: 020 7404 4167
Email: info@ppa.co.uk
Website: www.ppa.co.uk

Personnel:
Barry McIlheney (Chief Executive)
Nicola Rowe (Director of Circulation & Members Services)
Helen Rosemier (Commercial Director)
James Papworth (PPA Marketing Director)

Associated Companies:
UK: Professional Publishers Association Scotland

PPA promotes and protects the interests of the UK's multi-platform consumer magazine and business information publishers. The PPA has around 200 publishing companies in its membership, which collectively produce more than 2500 consumer and business magazines and journals, as well as digital media, data products and events.

5046

PUBLIC LENDING RIGHT
Richard House, Sorbonne Close, Stockton-on-Tees
TS17 6DA
Telephone: 01642 604699
Fax: 01642 615641
Email: authorservices@plr.uk.com
Website: www.plr.uk.com

Personnel:
Dr Jim Parker *(Registrar)*

Public Lending Right (PLR) exists to make payments to
authors for the borrowing of their books from public libraries. PLR is funded by the Department for Culture, Media and
Sport, and is headed by a Registrar. To qualify, authors must
register their books with the PLR office. Payment calcula-
tions are based on book loans from a representative sample
of public libraries. Payments are made annually. No author
may receive more than £6600.

5047

THE PUBLISHERS ASSOCIATION
29B Montague Street, London WC1B 5BW
Telephone: 020 7691 9191
Fax: 020 7691 9199
Email: mail@publishers.org.uk
Website: www.publishers.org.uk

Personnel:
Richard Mollet *(Chief Executive)*
Emma House *(Trade & International Director)*
Mark Wharton *(Operations Director)*

The Publishers Association is a trade organization serving
book, journal and electronic publishers in the UK. It brings
publishers together to discuss the main issues facing the
industry and to define the practical policies that will take the
industry forward. The aim of The Publishers Association is to
serve and promote by all lawful means the interest of book,
journal and electronic publishers and to protect their interests.

5048

PUBLISHERS PUBLICITY CIRCLE
65 Airedale Avenue, London W4 2NN
Email: ppc@lineone.net
Website: www.publisherspublicitycircle.co.uk

Personnel:
Heather White *(Secretary/Treasurer)*

For over 50 years, the Publishers Publicity Circle has enabled
book publicists – both from publishing houses and freelance
PR agencies – to meet and share information regularly. Representatives of the media are invited to speak about the
ways in which they can feature authors and their books, and
how book publicists can provide most effectively the information and material needed.

Annual prizes are awarded for the best publicity campaigns
of the year.

A directory of the PPC membership is published each year
and distributed to over 2500 media contacts, providing the
names of publicity staff, their fax and telephone numbers,
and email addresses.

5049

PUBLISHING IRELAND (FOILSIÚ ÉIREANN)
25 Denzille Lane, Dublin 2, Republic of Ireland
Telephone: +353 (0)1 639 4868
Email: info@publishingireland.com
Website: www.publishingireland.com

Personnel:
Michael McLoughlin *(Acting President Publishing Ireland)*
Jolly Ronan *(Project Manager)*
Karen Kenny *(Administrator)*
Clara Schuessler *(Admin Assistant)*

Publishing Ireland promotes the publication, distribution,
sale and publicity of books at home and abroad. There are
over 100 members of the association. Publishing Ireland is a
member of the Federation of European Publishers and of the
International Publishers Association.

5050

PUBLISHING SCOTLAND
Scott House, 10 South St Andrew Street, Edinburgh
EH2 2AZ
Telephone: 0131 228 6866
Fax: 0131 524 8157
Email: enquiries@publishingscotland.org
Website: www.publishingscotland.org

Personnel:
Marion Sinclair *(Chief Executive)*
Lucy Feather *(Member Services Manager)*
Joan Lyle *(Training and Information Manager)*

Associated Companies:
UK: BookSource Ltd

Publishing Scotland is an organization with responsibility for
the support and development of the book publishing sector
in Scotland. The remit is to work with companies, organizations and individuals in the industry, and to co-ordinate joint
initiatives and partnerships.

Publishing Scotland represents its members' interests in a
number of capacities, in training, co-operative promotion
and marketing of their books, attendance at international
book fairs, joint catalogue mailings and export services.

Publishing Scotland has been in existence for 40 years, representing over 60 book publishers. It also offers network
membership to those individuals, organizations and
companies that work with or within the publishing industry.

5051

ROMANTIC NOVELISTS' ASSOCIATION
(contact by email only)
Email: RNAHonSec@o2.co.uk
Website: www.romanticnovelistsassociation.org

Personnel:
j Dixon *(Hon. Secretary)*

The Romantic Novelists' Association (RNA) was formed in
1960 to promote romantic fiction and to encourage good
writing, and now represents more than 700 writers, agents,
editors and other publishing professionals. The Romantic
Novel of the Year was launched in the same year, and recog-
nizes excellence in romantic novels, thereby enhancing the
standing of the genre. The RNA runs a critique scheme for
unpublished writers, who may join the Association under
the New Writers' Scheme (non-voting) members. The Joan
Hessayon Award is made annually for the best published
novel to have gone through the NWS critique scheme. The
RNA's annual residential conference takes place over a weekend in early July. Regional chapters, around the country,
organize their own meetings and events. In addition, there
are members' meetings in London, with guest speakers, and
summer and winter parties where published and unpublished writers network with agents, editors and publishers.
The RNA's magazine, *Romance Matters*, is published four
times a year and distributed free to members.

5052

ROYAL SOCIETY OF LITERATURE
Somerset House, Strand, London WC2R 1LA
Telephone: 020 7845 4676
Email: info@rslit.org
Website: www.rslit.org

Personnel:
Colin Thubron FRSL *(President)*
Anne Chisholm FRSL *(Chair)*
Maggie Fergusson FRSL *(Director)*

The Royal Society of Literature, founded by George IV in
1820, celebrates and nurtures all that is best in British literature, past and present. We organize roughly twenty-four
events a year; make awards and grants to established and
emerging writers; run regular Masterclasses with the Booker
Prize Foundation; and campaign on issues affecting writers,
such as the closure of local libraries or reductions in PLR payments; and manage a Schools Outreach Programme.

At the heart of the RSL is its Fellowship, which encompasses
the most distinguished authors working in the English language. One of our aims is to build bridges between our Fel-
lows and those who enjoy their work, so that their unique
talents are shared as widely as possible.

5053

SAN AGENCY
36 Mackenzie Road, Beckenham, Kent BR3 4RU
Email: ra@britishscbwi.org
Website: www.britishscbwi.org

Personnel:
Natascha Biebow *(Regional Advisor (Chair))*
Anne-Marie Perks *(Illustrator Co-ordinator)*
Anita Loughrey *(Membership Co-ordinator)*
Nick Cross *(Website Co-ordinator)*
Jan Carr *(Blog Magazine Editor)*

Parent Company:
USA: SCBWI

The SCBWI is an international professional organization for
writers and illustrators of children's books. It is a network for
the exchange of knowledge between writers, illustrators,
editors, publishers, agents, librarians, educators, booksellers
and others involved with literature for young people. There
are currently more than 18,000 members worldwide, in over
70 regions.

The SCBWI International sponsors three annual conferences
on writing and illustrating books and multimedia, one in
New York in February, one in Bologna, Italy, and one in Los
Angeles in August, as well as dozens of regional conferences
and events throughout the world. It also publishers a bi-
monthly newsletter, *The Bulletin*, awards grants for works in
progress, and provides many informational publications on
the art and business of writing and selling written, illustrated
and electronic material. The SCBWI also presents numerous
grants and awards, including the Golden Kite Award for the
best fiction and non-fiction books.

The SCBWI British Isles (SCBWI-BI) region meets bi-monthly,
usually in London, for a speaker or workshop event. It also
sponsors local critique groups, master classes and regional
networks events. Its innovative blog magazine, *Words and
Pictures*, includes entertaining and informative features on
industry issues, craft tips and marketing advice, interviews
and tips from editors, art directors, agents, librarians and
booksellers, profiles of established writers and illustrators,
booksellers and librarians, illustrator showcases and member competitions. It can be found at www.wordsand-
pics.org. SCBWI-BI runs a yearly Writers' and Illustrators'
Conference with hands-on seminars on improving your craft
and the opportunity to meet publishing professionals and
find out what they are looking for, a listserve and social networking site, where writers and illustrators can set up their
own promotional website.

SCBWI is open to both published and unpublished writers
and illustrators. Full membership is open to those whose
work for children's books, illustrations or photographs,
films, electronic media, articles, poems or stories has been
published or produced. Associate membership is open to all
those with an interest in children's literature or media,
whether or not they have published. To join, see our web site
www.britishscbwi.org.

5054

SCHOOL LIBRARY ASSOCIATION
1 Pine Court, Kembrey Park, Swindon SN2 8AD
Telephone: 01793 530166
Fax: 01793 481182
Email: info@SLA.org.uk
Website: www.SLA.org.uk

Personnel:
Steve Hird *(Editor)*
Chris Brown *(Review Editor)*
Richard Leveridge *(Production Editor)*

The School Library Association is an independent organization working to promote the development of school libraries, primary and secondary. Services to members include
advice and information, publications at reduced prices, *The
School Librarian*, a quarterly journal of articles and reviews,
training courses and a network of area branches. Membership includes schools, colleges, local education authorities,
public libraries, publishers and individuals in the United
Kingdom and overseas. Membership costs £85.00 p.a.

5055

SOCIETY FOR EDITORS & PROOFREADERS LTD
Apsley House, 176 Upper Richmond Road, London
SW15 2SH

Telephone: 020 8785 6155
Email: admin@sfep.org.uk
Website: www.sfep.org.uk

Personnel:
Wendy Toole (Chair)
Bridget Buckle (Company Secretary)

Founded in 1988 with the twin aims of promoting high editorial standards and achieving recognition of its members' professional status, the Society works to disseminate information and training, foster good relations between members and their clients, and combat the isolation often experienced by freelances. It supports recognized standards of training and accreditation for editors and proofreaders, and is establishing recognized standards for its own members. Membership in 2011 was approximately 1500.

One of the major aims of the Society for Editors and Proofreaders is to help editorial freelances and staff to improve and update their skills. It is gradually building up a wide range of one-day courses, from 'Introduction to Proofreading' to 'Project Management' and 'On-Screen Editing', as well as more specialized courses. Most of its courses are run in London. About twice a year, two or three courses are run in Edinburgh, York and Bristol. Discounts are offered to members of the SFEP and to SI and NUJ members. Current details can be found on the SFEP website.

5056

SOCIETY OF AUTHORS
84 Drayton Gardens, London SW10 9SB
Telephone: 020 7373 6642
Fax: 020 7373 5768
Email: info@societyofauthors.org
Website: www.societyofauthors.org

Personnel:
Anne Sebba (Chairman)
Nicola Solomon (Chief Executive)

An independent trade union for authors. Its purpose is to further the interests of its 8500 members through individual advice and general campaigning. It is controlled by an elected Committee of Management and administered by a staff with long experience in the business and legal aspects of authorship. Members have access to a comprehensive advisory service and may seek advice on all forms of contracts. The Society also serves the interests of specialist writers through a number of subsidiary groups – viz the Broadcasting Group, the Translators Association, Children's Writers and Illustrators, Educational Writers, Academic Writers and Medical Writers Groups. It makes representations to government departments and promotes campaigns on behalf of the profession as a whole (eg public lending right, tax concessions for authors, etc). It also administers literary estates, publishes a quarterly journal, The Author, issues numerous Quick Guides to its members and manages a variety of awards and trust funds for authors.

5057

SOCIETY OF EDITORS
University Centre, Granta Place, Cambridge CB2 1RU
Telephone: 01223 304080
Fax: 01223 304090
Email: office@societyofeditors.org
Website: www.societyofeditors.org

Personnel:
Bob Satchwell (Executive Director)

The Society of Editors has more than 400 members in national, regional and local newspapers, magazines, broadcasting and digital media, journalism, education and media law. It campaigns for media freedom, self-regulation, the public's right to know and the maintenance of standards in journalism.

5058

SOCIETY OF INDEXERS
Woodbourn Business Centre, 10 Jessell Street, Sheffield
S9 3HY
Telephone: 0114 244 9561
Email: admin@indexers.org.uk
Website: www.indexers.org.uk

Personnel:
John Silvester (Company Secretary)

Founded in 1957 as an autonomous professional body to promote greater awareness of indexing and raise standards in all forms of indexing. The Society's well-established distance learning course (with CILIP seal of recognition) now runs on a web-based platform and gives a thorough grounding in the principles (and pitfalls) of indexing. Workshops and an annual conference provide additional training opportunities. An online directory, Indexers Available, contains full details of qualified and experienced indexers with specialist subjects ranging from accountancy to zoology, together with advice on commissioning an indexer and guidelines on fees. The Society also publishes a quarterly international journal, The Indexer, plus occasional papers on specialized aspects of indexing and a newsletter for members. The Wheatley Medal is awarded annually for an outstanding index, conferring prestige on indexer, author and publisher. The Society wishes to impress on both publishers and authors the need for adequate and competent indexes in non-fiction works, whether in print or electronic format.

5059

SOCIETY OF MEDICAL WRITERS
Corner Croft, Lonsties, Keswick, Cumbria CA12 4TD
Telephone: 01768 774689
Email: dorothy@crowther.eu
Website: www.somw.org.uk

Personnel:
Dr Dorothy Crowther (Chairman)
Dr Richard Cutler (Finance Officer)
Dr Mary Anderson (Acting Editor)

Membership of the Society of Medical Writers is open to anyone who publishes or aspires to publish their work of whatever nature – medical or non-medical, fact or fiction, prose or poetry. It is intended that the association should be enjoyable, stimulating and educational so that writing from medical practice, including general practice, is improved and encouraged.

The aims of the Society are therefore to:
• improve standards of writing by medical practitioners;
• encourage literacy whether in scientific papers, review articles, or historical or anecdotal essays;
• provide meetings for practitioners interested in writing, for the exchange of views, skills and ideas;
• provide education on the preparation, presentation and submission of written material for publication;
• act as a means of introduction between practitioners and suitable publishers and editors;
• maintain a register of members of the SOMW, available to commissioning editors and others;
• advise on sources of assistance with regard to technical, legal and financial aspects of writing;
• consider questions of ethics relating to writing and publication;
• further developments in the art of writing and to facilitate access to educational opportunities for those motivated to become better writers.

5060

SOCIETY OF YOUNG PUBLISHERS
The Publishers Association, 29B Montague Street, London
WC1B 5BW
Email: membersec@thesyp.org.uk
Website: www.thesyp.org.uk

Personnel:
Ella Kahn (Chair)
Naomi Holt (Vice-Chair)
Alex Higson (Membership Secretary)
Alice Herbert (Treasurer and Secretary)
Lizzie Jones (Press and Publicity Officer)
Konstantinos Vasdekis (Marketing Officer)
Francesca Brazzorotto (Web Content Editor)
Lucia Sandin (Social Co-ordinator)
Bhav Mehta (Special Projects)
Laura Givans (InDigital Commissioning Editor)

Established in 1949, the Society of Young Publishers is open to anyone in publishing or a related trade (in any capacity) – or who is hoping to be soon. Its aim is to assist, inform and enthuse anyone trying to break into the publishing industry or progress within it.

It organizes monthly speaker meetings which discuss different topics of relevance to the publishing industry. Guest speakers are drawn from a variety of backgrounds. The society also organizes a highly successful annual conference.

Members receive approximately four issues per year of its magazine, InPrint, to keep them up-to-date with the Society and events and issues within the industry. The online magazine is available on the website. The SYP informs its members of jobs vacancies from across the UK through its weekly Jobs Bulletin.

Members are also entitled to discounts at Foyles bookshop and on several publishing and related training courses.

5061

TRANSLATORS ASSOCIATION
84 Drayton Gardens, London SW10 9SB
Telephone: 020 7373 6642
Fax: 020 7373 5768
Email: info@societyofauthors.org
Website: www.societyofauthors.org

Personnel:
Sarah Burton (Secretary)

The Translators Association is a subsidiary of the Society of Authors and advises literary translators on such matters as contracts and fees. Publishers seeking book translators can search the online database.

5062

WATCH (WRITERS ARTISTS & THEIR COPYRIGHT HOLDERS)
The Library, University of Reading, PO Box 223,
Whiteknights, Reading RG6 6AE
Telephone: 0118 378 8783
Fax: 0118 378 6636
Email: d.c.sutton@reading.ac.uk
Website: www.watch-file.com

Personnel:
Dr D. Sutton (Director)

WATCH provides a free online database of information about the copyright holders of literary authors, artists and prominent persons. The database is in the form of an open-access public website, jointly maintained by the Universities of Texas and Reading.

5063

WELSH BOOKS COUNCIL / CYNGOR LLYFRAU CYMRU
Castell Brychan, Aberystwyth, Ceredigion SY23 2JB
Telephone: 01970 624151
Fax: 01970 625385
Email: castellbrychan@cllc.org.uk
Website: www.cllc.org.uk & www.gwales.com

Personnel:
Elwyn Jones (Chief Executive)
Sion Ilar (Design)
Marian Beech Hughes (Editorial)
D. Philip Davies (Information Services)
Angharad Tomos (Children's Books)
Neville Evans (Distribution)
Arwyn Roderick (Finance)
Moelwen Gwyndaf (Administration)
Helena O'Sullivan (Sales & Marketing)
Richard Owen (Grants)

The Welsh Books Council is a national organization with charitable status funded by the Welsh Government. Established in 1961, it is responsible for promoting all sectors of the publishing industry in Wales, in both languages, in conjunction with publishers, booksellers, libraries and schools. The Council is also responsible for distributing publishing grants for Welsh-language publishing and Welsh writing in English. Its Wholesale Distribution Centre stocks the vast majority of Welsh-interest titles currently available. www.gwales.com, the Council's online information and ordering service, is a one-stop shop for titles of relevance to Wales.

5064

WORSHIPFUL COMPANY OF STATIONERS AND NEWSPAPER MAKERS
Stationers' Hall, Ave Maria Lane, London EC4M 7DD
Telephone: 020 7248 2934
Fax: 020 7489 1975
Email: admin@stationers.org
Website: www.stationers.org

Personnel:
T. Hempenstall *(Master)*
W. J. Alden MBE DL *(Clerk)*

The Worshipful Company of Stationers had its beginnings in a Guild dating back at least to 1403; the original Charter was granted in 1557. The Company was expanded in modern times (1933) to include the Newspaper Makers. For nearly four centuries it was essential for the protection of copyright to register books at Stationers' Hall; in 1924 an extensively used system of voluntary registration came into force. This was discontinued in February 2000.

The Company's object has always been to promote the interests of the printing and allied trades, among them publishing and bookbinding. Its activities at the present day include the binding of apprentices and the award of scholarships to young men and women in these trades and the provision of pensions and financial help for tradesmen and their widows. The Company also plays a full part in the life of the City of London.

The Stationers' Hall may be hired for functions.

6   Trade & Allied Services

6.1   EDITORIAL SERVICES

6001

AESOP (ALL EDITORIAL SERVICES ONLINE FOR PUBLISHERS & AUTHORS)
28 Abberbury Road, Iffley, Oxford OX4 4ES
Telephone: 01865 429563
Fax: 01865 389589
Email: mart@copyedit.co.uk
Website: www.copyedit.co.uk OR www.all-eds.com

Personnel:
Martin Noble (Owner/Editor)

AESOP provides the following editorial services to publishers, authors, academics and businesses: copy-editing; proofreading; structural editing; rewriting; co-writing; ghostwriting; thesis and dissertation editing and printing; improving use of English of non-native English writers of academic reports and books; indexing; editorial reports and reviews; advice to publishers, authors and literary agents; novelization; research; fact-checking; bibliographical research; CRC (camera ready copy) in Word format; text capture; scanning/OCR; e-book production on CD-ROM or online; keying in MSS; audio transcription; tagging. Specializes in fiction, literature, poetry, media, music, performing arts, humour, biography, memoirs, travel, education, economics, psychology, history, alternative health, new age, esoteric and spiritual subjects, special needs.

6002

BLUE ELEPHANT STORYSHAPING
36 Mackenzie Road, Beckenham BR3 4RU
Telephone: 07951 604097
Email: hello@blueelephantstoryshaping.com
Website: www.blueelephantstoryshaping.com

Personnel:
Natascha Biebow (Editor, Coach and Mentor)

Parent Company:
UK: Blue Elephant Storyshaping

Blue Elephant Storyshaping offers a range of creative services to children's book authors, illustrators, agents and publishers. It also runs workshops and seminars. For children's book authors and illustrators, it offers supportive editorial reviews, creative brainstorming sessions, portfolio advice, ongoing project development, and mentoring services to help you fine-tune work for submission. Blue Elephant Storyshaping specializes in picture books and young fiction up to 30,000 words. For publishers, it offers freelance editing, project management, storyshaping and creative brainstorming sessions. For agents, it offers manuscript reviews, fine-tunes projects for submission and scouts for new talent.

6003

FIRST EDITION TRANSLATIONS LTD
34a Fitzroy Street, Cambridge CB1 1EW
Telephone: 01223 356733
Fax: 01223 322601

Email: info@firstedit.co.uk
Website: www.firstedit.co.uk

Personnel:
Sheila Waller (Director)
Melanie Fitzgerald (Head of Editorial)

First Edition offers complete and specialized editorial and translation services, including all necessary liaison: translation, research, editing, Americanization, localization, proofreading, indexing, transcription, desktop publishing, print ready PDF or CD output. Assessment of foreign language books for the market.

6004

PETER B. J. GILL
18 Selwyn House, Selwyn Road, Eastbourne, East Sussex BN21 2LF
Telephone: 01323 646853
Fax: 01323 646853
Email: pbj.gill@btinternet.com

Personnel:
Peter B. J. Gill (Editorial Consultant)

With more than 25 years' experience as a senior editor and formerly Associate Editor at Encyclopaedia Britannica's London editorial office, where clarity of communication and attention to detail were paramount, Peter Gill can offer clients a top-notch UK-based service project-managing, fact-checking, copy-editing/proofreading business, STM and other non-fiction material to a high standard and within tight deadlines, at an economic rate. Clients include Blackwell Science, CUP, Elsevier, Jessica Kingsley, Kogan Page, Macmillan, OUP, Philips, Routledge, Royal College of Psychiatrists, Taylor & Francis and Wiley. Unsolicited testimonials from both publishers and authors can be provided.

6005

LIBRIOS LTD
20 Lochaline Street, London W6 9SH
Telephone: 020 3355 0200
Fax: 020 3355 0201
Email: info@librios.com
Website: www.librios.com

Personnel:
Hal Robinson (Managing Director)

Associated Companies:
UK: Book Creation Ltd

6006

CHRISTOPHER PICK
41 Chestnut Road, London SE27 9EZ
Telephone: 020 8761 2585
Email: christopher@the-picks.co.uk

Personnel:
Christopher Pick (Publications Consultant)

Research, writing, editing and producing information materials for public- and voluntary-sector agencies and for the

corporate sector. Specialist in corporate publications, e.g. organizational histories, from initial concept and planning through writing, editorial, design and on to printed books.

6007

DAVID PRICE
4 Harbidges Lane, Long Buckby, Northampton NN6 7QL
Telephone: 01327 844119
Email: david@d-price.co.uk
Website: www.d-price.co.uk

Personnel:
David Price (Contact)

Writing, rewriting, editing, proofreading.

Special interests:
• Fine Art (particularly Modern Art);
• Music (particularly operettas and musicals, pop and rock music);
• Travel Guides;
• Modern European History and Politics (particularly 19th Century France, Eastern Europe 1945–1989, and the former Soviet Union);
• Social and Cultural History.

6008

THE PUZZLE HOUSE
Ivy Cottage, Battlesea Green, Stradbroke, Suffolk IP21 5NE
Telephone: 01379 384656
Fax: 01379 384656
Email: puzzlehouse@btinternet.com
Website: www.the-puzzle-house.co.uk

Personnel:
Roy Preston (Partner)
Sue Preston (Partner)

The Puzzle House creates, designs and compiles crossword, quiz and puzzle material for books and magazines. A full editorial service is offered on all projects ranging from a one-off puzzle to a complete series of books. All subject areas and age ranges are catered for. We have a specialist interest and many years of experience in the children's activity market. Puzzles are available for syndication. The Puzzle House was established in 1988.

6009

RONNE RANDALL
26 Oak Tree Avenue, Radcliffe-on-Trent, Nottingham NG12 1AD
Telephone: 0115 933 5804
Email: ronnerandall@aol.com
Website: www.freelancersintheuk.co.uk/ronne-randall-i430.html

Personnel:
Ronne Randall (Proprietor)

Accurate Americanization by a native of the USA, as well as editorial services including editing, copy-editing, writing, rewriting/adapting, and proofreading. More than 30 years of experience on both sides of the Atlantic. Special interest and experience in children's books. Recent clients include Ladybird, Quarto/QED, Parragon, Hamlyn, Boxer Books.

6010 ▬▬▬▬

READING AND RIGHTING – ROBERT LAMBOLLE SERVICES
618b Finchley Road, London NW11 7RR
Telephone: 020 8455 4564
Email: lambhorn@gmail.com

Personnel:
Robert Lambolle *(Literary/Script Consultant & Managing Director)*

Established in 1987, Reading & Righting is an independent script consultancy providing evaluation and editing services, based on wide-ranging agency and publishing experience. Detailed assessment, analysis of prospects and next-step guidelines for fiction, non-fiction, screenplays, plays and poetry, plus full editing service, one-to-one tutorials, mentoring, lectures, creative writing courses, and research. Prospective clients can request an emailed or hard-copy leaflet outlining procedure and terms.

Specialist interests include cinema, the performing arts, popular culture, psychotherapy and current affairs.

6011 ▬▬▬▬

SANDHURST EDITORIAL
36 Albion Road, Sandhurst, Berks GU47 9BP
Telephone: 01252 877645
Email: lionel.browne@sfep.net

Personnel:
Lionel Browne *(Proprietor)*

Sandhurst Editorial provides a complete editorial service for clients inside and outside the UK, both private sector and public sector: academic and educational publishers, research associations, commercial clients, and government departments. The skills on offer include editorial development and consultancy, project management, writing, rewriting, copy-editing and proofreading.

We specialize in technology, management and education, but have handled projects as diverse as bibles, biography, travel and nature guides, and corporate reports.

6012 ▬▬▬▬

HANS ZELL PUBLISHING CONSULTANTS
Glais Bheinn, Lochcarron, Ross-shire IV54 8YB
Telephone: 01520 722951
Email: hanszell@hanszell.co.uk
Website: www.hanszell.co.uk/

Personnel:
Hans M. Zell *(Proprietor)*

Associated Companies:
UK: Hans Zell Publishing

Consultancy service to publishers and academic institutions, in particular providing advisory services and individual project management for publishers, research institutes, and the book community in Africa and in other developing countries.

Specialization:
• scholarly publishing, especially university press publishing, and publishing by research institutions and NGOs, including editorial and financial management, administration, marketing and promotion, pricing and distribution, general publishing management, and dealing with author and publisher contracts
• journals publishing management, including subscription management and fulfilment, financial control, journals promotion, and market assessments
• reference book publishing, particularly for reference resources focusing on Africa and the developing world, including research, project evaluations, editorial services, and market assessments
• training: in-house or through workshops and seminars: in editorial and production management, financial planning, and all areas of marketing
• marketing and distribution of books on African and development studies, and African literature and culture
• providing a range of specialist mailing list services in this area, full details available on request – Internet training for the book professions in developing countries.

Under the Hans Zell Publishing imprint we publish a number of reference resources (print and online) on Africa, African studies and African publishing.

6.2 DESIGN & PRODUCTION SERVICES

6013 ▬▬▬▬

BBR SOLUTIONS LTD
12 Cutthorpe Road, Chesterfield S42 7AE
Telephone: 01246 271662
Email: bbr@bbr-online.co.uk
Website: www.bbr-online.co.uk

Personnel:
Chris Reed *(Director)*
Amanda Thompson *(Director)*

BBR provides editorial, design, typesetting and project management services for publishers. With over 25 years'? experience in publishing, the company meticulously proofs and edits manuscripts for publication, and creates clean, typography-led designs for books and journals.

Please visit the company's website for more information and to view its portfolio.

6014 ▬▬▬▬

BOOK PRODUCTION CONSULTANTS
Willow End, Kings Mill Lane, Great Shelford, Cambridge CB22 5EN
Telephone: 01223 841748
Fax: 01223 841748
Email: cs_walsh@btinternet.com
Website: www.bpccam.co.uk

Personnel:
Colin Walsh *(Managing Director)*

A totally comprehensive publishing service including editing, sub-editing, designing, technical mark-up, illustrating, technical drawing, estimating, paper buying, typesetting and origination. BPC arranges the printing and binding of black-and-white or colour publications in the UK or overseas and supervises quality control and delivery schedules; also computer software packs including design of packaging and manufacture of boxes, tapes and discs. Other specialities include the design and production of illustrated books, music and foreign language setting projects, academic journals and institutional publications, producing company-sponsored books and company histories. Electronic publishing and CD-ROM origination, particularly as joint ventures, form part of current expansion. Specialist divisions include business histories (providing authors, archivists and picture researchers), contract magazine production and company literature.

Colin Walsh has now semi-retired to absorb decades of publishing lunches and Debbie Wayment, for 25 years with BPC, has taken over existing and new business at Wayment Print & Publishing Solutions (see BPC website for further information).

6015 ▬▬▬▬

BOOKCRAFT LTD
18 Kendrick Street, Stroud, Glos GL5 1AA
Telephone: 0870 1601900
Fax: 0870 1601901
Email: information@bookcraft.co.uk
Website: www.bookcraft.co.uk

Personnel:
John Button *(Publishing Director)*

Bookcraft provides publishers with a wide range of editorial, design, technical and training services.

Main areas of activity are:
• publishing consultancy
• publishing software training
• design services
• editorial and proofreading services
• project management.

6016 ▬▬▬▬

FOTOLIBRA
22 Mount View Road, London N4 4HX
Telephone: 020 8348 1234
Email: professionals@fotoLibra.com
Website: www.fotoLibra.com

Personnel:
Gwyn Headley *(Managing Director)*
Yvonne Seeley *(Marketing Director)*

Parent Company:
UK: VisConPro Ltd

Associated Companies:
USA: Idea Logical Company Inc

fotoLibra is a picture library set up by publishers for publishers. The company has 10,000+ photographers in over 150 countries ready and willing to take the required image if it is not already in the library – and there's no obligation to buy. Over 700,000 images online.

6017 ▬▬▬▬

GRAHAM-CAMERON ILLUSTRATION
The Studio, 23 Holt Road, Sheringham, Norfolk NR26 8NB
Telephone: 01263 821333
Email: enquiry@gciforillustration.com
Website: www.gciforillustration.com

Illustration commissions:
Duncan Graham-Cameron, 59 Hertford Road, Brighton BN1 7GG
Telephone: 01273 385890
Email: duncan@gciforillustration.com
Website: www.gciforillustration.com

Personnel:
Duncan Graham-Cameron *(Managing Director)*
Helen Graham-Cameron *(Art Director)*

Parent Company:
UK: Graham-Cameron Publishing

This agency represents some 37 qualified professional published illustrators who use a wide range of techniques and media. GCI specializes in supplying commissioned illustrations for educational and children's books, and for general information publications.

6018 ▬▬▬▬

HYBERT DESIGN LTD
52 High Street, Eton, Berkshire SL4 6BL
Telephone: 01753 206723
Email: info@hybertdesign.com
Website: www.hybertdesign.com

Also at:
Buterud P1 8722, 464 91 Dals Rostock, Sweden
Telephone: +46 (0)530 30084
Email: info@hybertdesign.com
Website: www.hybertdesign.com

Personnel:
Tom Hybert *(Director)*
Kate Hybert *(Company Secretary)*
Linda Elliott *(Senior Designer)*

We're a small, friendly, family-run studio with over 35 years experience. We design books, marketing, and corporate material for print and web. We specialize in design for publishers. We keep it simple, stylish, successful and speedy.

6019 ▬▬▬▬

IMAGO PUBLISHING LTD
Albury Court, Albury, Thame, Oxon OX9 2LP
Telephone: 01844 337000
Fax: 01844 339935
Email: debbiek@imago.co.uk
Website: www.imago.co.uk, www.ibiblios.co.uk

Personnel:
Colin Risk *(Managing Director)*
Jim Allpass *(Finance Director)*
Ms Cherry Jaquet *(Production Director)*
Ms Debbie Knight *(Marketing Director)*
Ms Angela Young *(Director)*
Simon Rosenheim *(Director of New Business Areas)*

Ms Martina Scheible *(European Sales Director)*
Ms Sarah O'Connor *(Director of Sales Development)*

Imago offers production services including print management, sourcing, training and consultancy to the publishing and creative industries. With offices in the UK, Paris, Hong Kong, China, Singapore, Malaysia, Sydney, New York and California, the group is able to locate and control sources of manufacture on a worldwide basis. The group works with a wide range of clients, offering its extensive expertise in many ways, from running all the production needs for small publishers/packagers, to sourcing and arranging for the manufacture of individual projects on a competitive broking basis. All types of work are handled, including the manufacture of children's books involving handwork, books plus, product sourcing, short- and long-run general books and packaging.

The Imago Training School was established in 2003 and offers bespoke training and scheduled courses in the UK on Book Production, Digital Marketing, eBook Publishing, Colour, Product Safety, Paper and InDesign.

In 2012 the company launched a new digital division, iBiblios, offering a range of digital services and app development using sophisticated visual recognition technology.

6020

ROYAL NATIONAL INSTITUTE OF BLIND PEOPLE (RNIB)
Bakewell Road, Orton Southgate, Peterborough PE2 6XU
Telephone: 0303 123 9999
Fax: 01733 375001
Email: helpline@rnib.org.uk
Website: rnib.org.uk

Royal National Institute of Blind People (RNIB) is one of the UK's leading charities offering information, support and advice to over two million people with sight loss.

It produces accessible format editions of publications so that blind and partially sighted people can read them in a format such as braille, large print or audio – from textbooks supporting children in education to a Mills and Boon romance, and everything in between. It offers transcription services for businesses and publishers.

It publishes a range of material about living with sight loss, such as eye condition leaflets and information on benefits.

6021

SMALL PRINT
The Old School House, 74 High Street, Swavesey,
Cambridge CB24 4QU
Telephone: 01954 231713
Email: info@smallprint.co.uk
Website: www.smallprint.co.uk

Personnel:
Naomi Laredo *(Proprietor)*

Flexible project management service specializing in multilingual and multimedia packages. Founded in 1986 and highly experienced in educational, vocational, academic and business publishing.

Specialists in translation from/into English and editing of translated and non-native texts. Also development editing, proofreading, design and layout (for web or print), multilingual audio production.

Clients include Association of Commonwealth Universities, Collins, Edco of Ireland, Historic Chapels Trust, Nelson Thornes, Palgrave Macmillan, Pearson Education, Teach Yourself (Hodder).

6.3　ELECTRONIC PUBLISHING SERVICES

6022

GLOBAL MAPPING
Unit 3, Glebe Farm, Turweston, Brackley, Northants
NN13 5JE
Telephone: 01280 840770
Fax: 01280 840816

Email: sales@globalmapping.uk.com
Website: www.globalmapping.uk.com

Personnel:
Alan Smith *(Managing Director)*

Publishes its own range of maps. Also creates bespoke map products for other publishers, including interactive map-based websites. Online retailer of map-based products such as wall maps, postcode maps, Ordnance Survey data, atlases, globes and guides. Global Mapping aims to be a one-stop shop for all map-based requirements.

6023

KOALA PUBLISHING LTD
Downend House, 112 North Street, Downend, Bristol
BS16 5SE
Telephone: 0117 910 9111
Fax: 0117 910 9222
Email: gordon.dennis@koalapub.co.uk
Website: www.koalapub.co.uk

Personnel:
Gordon Dennis *(Commercial Director)*
Vivienne Willoughby-Ellis *(Managing Director)*
Robin Shobbrook *(QA and Testing Manager)*

Koala provides software and systems for the creation, maintenance and electronic delivery of technical information and documentation. Our customers can:
 • create straightforward, easy-to-use documentation and get it to their customers in the most effective way possible, from PDAs to printed manuals;
 • efficiently organize, write and deliver their technical manuals, policies and procedures;
 • reduce the cost and time constraints on professional staff of providing information to their users, and reduce the long-term risks of litigation caused by faulty documentation.

Koala provides software products for publishing technical documentation, including manuals, training materials, catalogues, directories and listings. Services include project management and control, analysis and design, bespoke programming, data format conversion, and full training and support.

6024

LIGHTNING SOURCE UK LTD
Chapter House, Pitfield, Kiln Farm, Milton Keynes
MK11 3LW
Telephone: 0845 1244620
Fax: 0845 121 4594
Email: enquiries@lightningsource.co.uk
Website: www.ingramcontent.com

Personnel:
David Taylor *(Group Managing Director)*
Dave Piper *(Managing Director)*
Terry Gridley *(Operations Director)*
Frank Devine *(Finance Director)*
Bromley Andrew *(Group Marketing Manager)*

Parent Company:
USA: Ingram Content Group, Inc.

Associated Companies:
USA: Lightning Source, Inc.

Ingram Lightning Source is part of Ingram Content Group, the world's largest and most trusted distributor of physical and digital content. We provide books, music and media content to over 38,000 retailers, libraries, schools and distribution partners in 195 countries. More than 25,000 publishers use Ingram's fully integrated physical and digital solutions and programs to realize the full business potential of books.

6025

NIELSEN BOOKNET
3rd Floor, Midas House, 62 Goldsworth Road, Woking,
Surrey GU21 6LQ
Telephone: 01483 712200
Fax: 01483 712201
Email: sales.booknet@nielsen.com
Website: www.nielsenbooknet.co.uk

Personnel:
Ann Betts *(Commercial Director)*
Stephen Long *(Head of BookNet)*

Mo Siewcharran *(Head of Marketing)*
David Walter *(Business Development Manager)*
Paul Dibble *(Head of Data Sales)*
Lucy Huddlestone *(Export Sales Manager)*
Melanie Brassington *(Export Sales Manager)*
Richard Merrick *(Customer Services Manager)*

Parent Company:
UK: Nielsen

Associated Companies:
UK: Nielsen BookData; Nielsen BookScan; Nielsen Registration Agencies (ISBN, SAN & ISTC)

Nielsen BookNet provides a range of e-commerce services that allow electronic trading between booksellers, distributors, publishers, libraries and other suppliers, regardless of their size and location. Services include BookNet Transaction Services for booksellers and publishers/distributors, Tele-Ordering and EDI. Nielsen BookNet is uniquely placed in the book trade to be the trading hub for orders, invoices, delivery notes and other EDI messaging.

6026

TRILOGY GROUP
Aries House, 43 Selkirk Street, Cheltenham, Glos GL52 2HJ
Telephone: 01242 222132
Email: enquiries@trilogygroup.com
Website: www.trilogygroup.com

Personnel:
Alex Dare *(Managing Director)*
Simon Gough *(Technical Director)*
Mike Ribbins *(Group Chairman)*
Ms Laura Mackenzie *(Operations Director)*

The Trilogy Group specializes in software for the publisher/distributor, especially those requiring a totally integrated business solution to handle publishing management, administration, and direct and distribution sales, together with active marketing. Our software, which uses Microsoft SQL Server technology, offers:
 • title & metadata management
 • customer management with profiles and buying history
 • active marketing facilities
 • direct mail management with optional integration to MailSort
 • subscriptions management
 • rights & royalties management
 • integration to accounting systems
 • vast range of 'real-time' management reports
 • real-time stock management
 • warehouse and dispatch management
 • integrated online shopping facilities with web hosting
 • multi-site management
 • electronic points of sale (EPOS)
 • production control, scheduling and job costing.

6.4　TRANSLATION SERVICES

6027

FIRST EDITION TRANSLATIONS LTD
34a Fitzroy Street, Cambridge CB1 1EW
Telephone: 01223 356733
Fax: 01223 322601
Email: info@firstedit.co.uk
Website: www.firstedit.co.uk

Personnel:
Sheila Waller *(Director)*
Melanie Fitzgerald *(Head of Editorial)*
Ana Grilo *(Commercial Translations Manager)*

Translations – commercial, technical, academic and of any length – undertaken in any language according to publisher's requirements. Editing, proofreading, Americanization, localization, transcription, indexing, typesetting/desktop publishing.

Output to print-ready PDF or CD. Quotations given without obligation.

6028

SATRAP PUBLISHING & TRANSLATION
500 Chiswick High Road, London W4 5RG

Telephone: 020 8748 9397
Email: satrap@btconnect.com
Website: www.satrap.co.uk

Personnel:
Alex Vahdat *(Managing Director)*
Mrs Homa Lohrasb *(Technical Manager)*

Satrap Publishing is a UK-based international company, specializing in the fields of translation, typesetting and print services in Oriental and East European languages.

The company produces promotional literature, exhibition catalogues, information pamphlets, books, reports, manuals, business stationery, product labels, diaries, etc for Western European companies, trade centres and various organizations which have foreign language requirements for their overseas trade links.

The human resources and advanced technical facilities available are ideal for those clients who wish to target ethnic minorities for their social, cultural and educational programmes. Satrap Publishing offers a complete package of expert translation, typesetting, professional graphic design as well as printing. Production of exclusive greeting cards and wedding stationery in non-European languages are among other services from Satrap Publishing.

6029

SWEDISH-ENGLISH LITERARY TRANSLATORS ASSOCIATION (SELTA)
PO Box 7596, Bishop's Stortford, Herts CM23 2WF
Email: SELTAsecretary@gmail.com
Website: www.selta.org.uk &
www.swedishbookreview.com

Personnel:
Ruth Urbom *(Chair)*
Deborah Bragan-Turner *(Honorary Secretary)*
Sarah Death *(Editor, Swedish Book Review)*

SELTA aims to promote the publication of Swedish literature in English and to represent the interests of those involved in its translation. Publishes *Swedish Book Review* (ISSN: 0265 8119): biannual, £17 p.a.

6.5 SALES & MARKETING SERVICES

6030

BERTOLI MITCHELL LLP
53 Chandos Place, Covent Garden, London WC2N 4HS
Telephone: 020 7812 6416
Fax: 020 7812 6677
Email: nb@bertolimitchell.co.uk
Website: www.bertolimitchell.co.uk

Personnel:
Natalina Bertoli *(Managing Partner)*
William Mitchell *(Managing Partner)*
Paul Mitton *(Senior Associate)*
Philip Shaw *(Associate)*

Bertoli Mitchell LLP is a specialist mergers and acquisitions advisory firm in the publishing and information industries.

The partnership offers corporate finance services for mergers, acquisitions and divestitures including:
• sell-side advisory representation to sellers of privately held businesses and corporate clients seeking to divest business units or assets
• buy-side advisory services and representation
• commercial and contracts due diligence
• valuations.

Since Bertoli Mitchell was founded in 1994 it has advised successfully on over 100 transactions.

Bertoli Mitchell also undertakes strategic research and consultancy. Activities include:
• profiling, analysis, forecasting and recommendations for clients considering entry into specific markets or sectors
• benchmarking, cost audits and development of financial targets
• development of business plans.

Clients range from large fully-listed international companies to shareholders of small and medium-sized private businesses.

6031

BOOKLINK
42 Reigate Road, Ewell, Epsom, Surrey KT17 1PX
Telephone: 020 8394 1578
Email: info@booklink.co.uk
Website: www.booklink.co.uk

Also at:
15 Bd Ralli – 13008 Marseille, France
Telephone: +33 (0)4 91 77 76 38
Email: info@booklink.co.uk
Website: www.booklink.co.uk

Personnel:
Evelyne Duval *(Managing Director)*
Maria White *(Agent)*

An international connection for foreign rights sales and consultancy.

6032

BOOKS ON MUSIC
3 Kendal Green, Kendal, Cumbria LA9 5PN
Telephone: 01539 740049
Website: www.booksonmusic.co.uk

Personnel:
Rosemary Dooley *(owner)*

Books on Music runs collaborative publishers' exhibitions at academic music conferences. Specialization in music.

6033

BROOKSIDE PUBLISHING SERVICES LTD
2 Brookside, Dundrum Road, Dublin 14, Republic of Ireland
Telephone: +353 (0)1 298 3411
Fax: +353 (0)1 298 2783
Email: sales@brookside.ie

Personnel:
Edwin Higel *(Managing Director)*
Michael Darcy *(Sales & Marketing Manager)*

Agents for various imprints in Ireland including:
A & A Farmar; Bloomsbury Professional Publishing; Cambridge University Press; Chartered Accountants Ireland; Clarus Press; Jessica Kingsley Publishers; Jones & Bartlett; Lippincott Williams & Wilkins; Nick Hern Books; Pharmaceutical Press; Pluto Press; Radcliffe Medical; Taxation Advice Bureau Guide
Republic of Ireland: New Island

Represents both trade and academic publishers.

6034

BROOMFIELD BOOKS LTD
36 De La Warr Road, East Grinstead, West Sussex RH19 3BP
Telephone: 01342 313237
Fax: 01342 322525
Email: nic@broomfieldbooks.co.uk
Website: www.broomfieldbooks.co.uk

Personnel:
Nic Webb *(Director)*
Mrs Andrea Grant-Webb *(Director)*

Broomfield Books is a publishing consultancy and sales agency for small and medium publishers of non-fiction and fiction. The sales agency covers London and the south-east of England, together with UK key accounts and the export market. We also deal in quality overstocks and remainder books. We welcome contact from publisher's seeking sales representation and we can also offer consultancy services. We would request that publishers with overstocks to offer us details in the first instance.

6035

THE CENTRE FOR INTERFIRM COMPARISON
32 St Thomas Street, Winchester, Hants SO23 9HJ
Telephone: 01962 844144
Fax: 01962 843180
Email: mikebayliss@cifc.co.uk
Website: www.cifc.co.uk

Personnel:
M. J. Bayliss *(Director)*

An independent organization established in 1959 by the British Institute of Management and the British Productivity Council specifically to meet the demand for a neutral specialist body to conduct interfirm comparisons (IFCs) and benchmarking projects on a confidential basis as a service to management.

The Centre has run a series of confidential IFCs specifically designed for book publishers in conjunction with the Publishers Association. These provided participants with measures for assessing how their overall performance compared, where and why it differed, and lines of action for improvement. More recently the Centre carried out projects for learned journal and magazine publishers. It has become a specialist in conducting in-depth and carefully defined benchmarking projects for firms and organizations of all kinds, based on information supplied confidentially by participants.

6036

THE COLUMBA BOOKSERVICE
55A Spruce Avenue, Stillorgan Industrial Park, Blackrock, Co Dublin, Republic of Ireland
Telephone: +353 (0)1 294 2556
Fax: +353 (0)1 294 2564
Email: info@columba.ie
Website: www.columba.ie

Personnel:
Fearghal O Boyle *(Managing Director)*

UK distributor/representative for:
Canada: Novalis
Republic of Ireland: The Columba Press
USA: Michael Glazier Books; The Liturgical Press; Loyola Press; Paraclete Press; Paulist Press; Pueblo Books; Resource Publications; Twenty-third Publications

The Columba Bookservice provides trade representation, sales and marketing services for a number of religious publishers.

6037

COMPASS INDEPENDENT PUBLISHING SERVICES LIMITED
Swan Centre, Fishers Lane, Chiswick, London W4 1RX
Telephone: 020 8996 5766
Email: alan@compass-dsa.co.uk
Website: www.compass-dsa.co.uk

Personnel:
Alan Jessop *(Managing Director)*

Associated Companies:
UK: Compass Academic Ltd

Client publishers:
Republic of Ireland: Collins Press; New Island Books Ltd
Sweden: Max Strom
UK: Arcturus Publishing; Arena Books; BackPage Press; Benefactum; Birlinn Ltd; Biteback Publishing; Bluffer's Guides; Cargo ; Carnegie Publishing; Connections Limited; Countdown; Enitharmon Press; Freight Books; Gallic Books; Good Hotel Guide; Hay House Publishers; Heritage House; Hesperus Press; Hudsons Media; Little Books; Malavan Media; Myrmidon Books; Oldie Publications; Oxygen Books; Parthian; Peter Owen; Plexus; Polygon Ltd; Pomona Books; Radio Times; Robson Press; Splendid Books; Summersdale; Telegram; Thorogood; TMI; Westbourne Press; Which?; Wild Things

Compass Independent Publishing Services Limited are one of the leading independent sales companies, providing sales and marketing services for publishers to both the traditional and non-traditional markets across the UK and Ireland. We also have access to the academic market through our Compass Academic operation.

6038

DAVENPORT PUBLISHING SERVICES
11 Silbury Rise, Keynsham, Bristol BS31 1JP
Telephone: 0117 986 2914
Fax: 0117 986 2074
Email: anne@annedavenport.demon.co.uk

Personnel:
Anne Davenport *(Proprietor & Consultant)*

Davenport Publishing Services offers consultancy in marketing, promotion, sales and distribution for academic, STM and society publishers.

Projects successfully completed include marketing planning and market research, promotion planning, copywriting for print and electronic media, sales advice, sourcing of overseas agents, representatives and distributors, and lapsed subscriber chasing.

Davenport Publishing Services offers a full service from consultancy to implementation of marketing campaigns. Long-term or short-term projects are welcome.

Clients include society publishers, university presses and independent institutions with publishing interests.

6039

DURNELL MARKETING LTD
2 Linden Close, Tunbridge Wells, Kent TN4 8HH
Telephone: 01892 544272
Fax: 01892 511152
Email: admin@durnell.co.uk & orders@durnell.co.uk
Website: www.durnell.co.uk

Personnel:
Andrew Durnell *(Managing Proprietor/Director)*
Julia Lippiatt *(Finance Proprietor/Director)*

Durnell Marketing provides a solution for publishers wishing to maximize their sales – via a single sales force – to all of Central, Eastern and Western Europe's diverse markets, including Ireland (but excluding the UK). A team of multilingual sales representatives ensures maximum, effective and personal coverage of publishers' potential customers, be they library suppliers, general wholesalers, bookshop chains, specialist independents, campus bookshops, non-trade, museum or institutional accounts. Travelling representatives are supported by office-based multilingual sales specialists who provide extra sales backup by promoting trade books, potential textbooks and major reference works to the trade, individual academics and institutions. In addition, Durnell Marketing organizes specific promotions, exhibitions, mailings, author signings and more.

6040

FOUR COLMAN GETTY
20 St Thomas Street, London SE1 9BF
Telephone: 020 3697 4200
Fax: 020 3697 4201
Email: info@fourcolmangetty.com
Website: http://www.fourcommunications.com/

Personnel:
Dotti Irving *(Chief Executive)*
Liz Sich *(Managing Director)*
Amy Maclaren *(Associate Director)*
Truda Spruyt *(Associate Director)*
Jane Acton *(Associate Director)*
Ruth Cairns *(Associate Director)*
Iliana Taliotis *(Associate Director)*
Julia Wilde *(Marketing & Digital Director)*

Parent Company:
UK: Four Communications

Four Colman Getty is a leading arts, campaigning and events PR agency. We build profile through culture, causes and celebrity thanks to our unrivalled network of media contacts and influencers.

We offer:
• Senior consultancy and strategic planning
• A deep understanding of the news agenda and the rapidly changing market in which we work
• Creative thinking and attention to detail.

We have won PR Week's coveted Specialist Agency of the Year award and the PRCA (Public Relations Consultants Association) Media Relations Award for The Lost Man Booker Prize campaign. We were shortlisted in 2011 for our work with the Natural History Museum.

6041

GLOBAL BOOK MARKETING LTD
99b Wallis Road, London E9 5LN

Telephone: 020 8533 5800
Fax: 020 8533 5800
Email: info@globalbookmarketing.co.uk

Personnel:
A. Zurbrugg *(Managing Director)*
A. Howe *(Sales Manager)*
A. Hanson *(IT Manager)*

European agents for:
Canada: Between the Lines; Fernwood Publishing
France: Cacimbo Editions
Germany: Bayreuth African Studies; Barbara Budrich; LIT Verlag
Netherlands: International Books (Utrecht); Techne
Nigeria: Kachifo
South Africa: Blue Weaver Marketing; Briza Publications; Human & Rousseau; Jacana Education; Kwela Books; Pharos; David Philip / Spearhead / New Africa Books Consortium; Protea; Tafelberg
Switzerland: Basler Afrika Bibliografien
Tanzania: Blue Mango Publishing
UK: Battlebridge; Eastern Arts / Saffron; Horniman Museum Publications
USA: International Publishers (New York)

Agents and representatives. Many publishers are distributed by Central Books Ltd.

6042

HAWKINS PUBLISHING SERVICES
12 Parkview Cottages, Crowhurst Lane End, Oxted, Surrey RH8 9NT
Telephone: 01342 893029
Email: gill.hawkins@virgin.net

Personnel:
Gillian Hawkins *(Director)*

Distributor for:
UK: J. A. Allen; Arachne Press; Aves Press; Collector's Library; Digital Leaf; Firestep; Full Circle Editions; Robert Hale; Hopcyn Press; Lunicorn

Sales, marketing, publicity, rights and distribution.

6043

HUMPHRYS ROBERTS ASSOCIATES
5 Voluntary Place, Wanstead, London E11 2RP
Telephone: 020 8530 5028
Fax: 020 8530 7870
Email: humph4hra@aol.com

Personnel:
Christopher Humphrys *(Managing Director)*

Publishers' agents and representatives, representing UK and US publishers in Central America, Mexico, the Caribbean, Bermuda, Spain, Portugal and Gibraltar.

6044

JEM EDUCATION DIRECT
Staplehurst Road, Sittingbourne, Kent ME10 2NH
Telephone: 01795 415115
Fax: 01795 439551
Email: info@jem.co.uk
Website: www.jem.co.uk

Personnel:
Andre Kleinman *(Managing Director)*
David Edwards *(Sales and Client Services Director)*
Karen Neal *(Account Manager)*
Gemma Wyatt *(Account manager)*
Joanna Pope *(Account Manager)*
David Harman *(Resources4Schools Manager)*
Jack Schneider *(Account Manager)*
Matt Wellard *(Account Manager)*
Nick McKenna *(Account Manager)*

Parent Company:
UK: John Menzies Plc; Orbital Marketing Services Group

Fulfilment and Distribution Services:
UK: Canals & River Trust; English and Media Centre; Robert Powell Publications; Reading Force; Royal Mail

Jem Education Direct offers a most comprehensive range of data, marketing services and direct marketing solutions to a wide range of clients who market their products and services

to the UK education sector, enabling them to communicate with and promote to schools, colleges, universities and other educational establishments in the most effective, cost-efficient way.

We have an integrated project management service called project-ed which offers complete end-to-end delivery from resource content creation to design production and delivery. resources4schools.co.uk is a completely free portal for teachers to access free resources.

The company has production facilities in Sittingbourne, Kent, while our client services team operates from both Sittingbourne and the group's head office in Ashford, Kent.

Core services are complemented by additional services that are available either from within the Orbital Marketing Services Group or from carefully selected partners with whom we have developed close working relationships. These services include Education Market Research, Design & Print, Response & Fulfilment and Marketing Consultancy.

For more information call our Client Services Team on 01795 415115, or email us.

6045

KUPERARD PUBLISHERS
59 Hutton Grove, London N12 8DS
Telephone: 020 8446 2440
Fax: 020 8446 2441
Email: office@kuperard.co.uk
Website: www.kuperard.co.uk

Personnel:
Joshua Kuperard *(Chief Executive)*
Martin Kaye *(Sales & Marketing Manager)*
Linda Tenenbaum *(Special Sales Manager)*

Distributor for:
Israel: Koren Publishers; Maggid Books; Toby Press
UK: Cade's Camping Guides; Caravan Club of Great Britain; Culture Smart! Guides; Customs & Etiquette; Kuperard Books; Monjeune Publishers; Simple Guides
USA: Convergent (Random House); HarperCollins; Howard Books (Simon & Schuster); Lerner Books; Living Language (Random House); The Modern Library (Random House); Penguin US; Schocken Books / Random House; Smithsonian Institute

Kuperard, a division and imprint of Bravo Ltd, acts as publishers, co-publishers and distributors, handling marketing and representation. Kuperard handle over 30 UK and overseas publishers.

Travel subjects include leisure guides covering a wide variety of destinations. Kuperard publishes a series of cross-cultural guides (Culture Smart) offering expert advice, awareness and understanding of different cultures, to a broad spectrum of travellers, ranging from backpackers to businessmen. Religion subjects include Christianity in its broadest sense, a wide range of Bibles, biblical literature and commentary, the Holy Land and its jurisprudence. History of religion, language, mysticism, health & fitness, parenting, the Holocaust, faith, prayer, gender awareness and spirituality.

Stocklists, catalogues and brochures are available upon request.

6046

CHRIS LLOYD SALES & MARKETING SERVICES
50a Willis Way, Poole, Dorset BH15 3SY
Telephone: 01202 649930
Fax: 01202 649950
Email: chrlloyd@globalnet.co.uk
Website: www.chrislloydsales.co.uk

Representation/Distribution:
Orca Book Services
Telephone: 01202 665432

Personnel:
Christopher Lloyd *(Proprietor)*

Publishers & Imprints represented include:
Australia: Brolga Publishing; Jane Curry Publishing; Exisle Publishing
Belgium: Versant Sud
Canada: Annick Press; Boston Mills Press; Firefly Books; Master Point Press; Robert Rose

France: Herrisey Editions
New Zealand: Ventura Publications
Spain: Loft Publications
UK: Amateur Winemaker Books; Argus Books; Book Guild
Publishing; Bretwalda Books; Bromley Books; Centenar
Publishing; Clissold Books; CP Press; D & B Publishing;
Everyman Mindsports; Fighting High; Full Back Media;
Galago Books; Golden Guides Press; Herridge & Sons;
Jaguar Daimler Heritage Trust; Key Books; LDA (Learning
Development Aids); Mushroom Model Publications;
Panther Publishing; Plane Essentials; Ravette; Special
Interest Model Books (SIMB) *(formerly Nexus Special
Interests)*; Speedman Press; Step Beach Press; Veloce
Publishing
USA: David Bull Publishing; Cycle Publishing / van der Plas
Publications; Heliconia Press; Meadowbrook Press;
Mikaya

An independent sales and marketing agency for small and
medium-sized publishers.

6047

THE MANNING PARTNERSHIP LTD
7c Green Park Station, Green Park Road, Bath BA1 1JB
Telephone: 01225 478444
Fax: 01225 478440
Email: karen@manning-partnership.co.uk
Website: www.manning-partnership.co.uk

Personnel:
Garry Manning *(Joint Managing Director)*
Roger Hibbert *(Joint Managing Director)*
James Wheeler *(Sales Manager)*
Karen Twissell *(Office Manager)*

Associated Companies:
UK: Brown Dog Books; Nightingale Press

UK Distributor for:
UK: Accent; Anness Publishing; Arcturus; Armadillo; ATP;
Bookmart; Carroll & Brown; Hometown World; Humpty
Dumpty; Interpet Publishing; Junkcraft; Nestle; Oval
Books; Search Press; Selectabook; Source Books; Worth
Press; Xcite

The Manning Partnership Ltd offers a total sales, marketing
and distribution solution for publishers both in the UK and in
English-language export markets. Formed in March 1997.
Traditional and non-traditional markets are serviced.

6048

MARKETABILITY (UK) LTD
12 Sandy Lane, Teddington, Middx TW11 0DR
Telephone: 020 8977 2741
Email: rachel@marketability.info
Website: www.marketability.info

Personnel:
Rachel Maund *(Director)*

Current and recent clients include:
Australia: Australian Publishers Association
Canada: B. C. Decker
China: Elsevier; Higher Education Press
Mexico: CANIEM (Mexican Publishers Association)
Republic of Ireland: CLÉ (Irish Publishers Association); New
Island
Russia: Guild of Book Dealers
Singapore: National Book Development Council; Singapore
Book Publishers' Association; Taylor & Francis; Wiley Asia;
World Scientific
UK: ALPSP; Ashgate Publishing; Bradt Travel Guides;
Brilliant Publications; Cambridge University Press; Centre
for Alternative Technology; Dundee University Press;
Elsevier; European Database of Libraries; HarperCollins
Publishers; Hodder Education; Hymns Ancient and
Modern; Institute of Physics; Kogan Page Ltd; Little,
Brown Book Group; Lonely Planet; Macmillan; McGraw-
Hill; Natural History Museum Publications; NBN
International; NCVO (National Council for Voluntary
Organisations); Oxford University Press; Palgrave
Macmillan; Paperless Proofs; Pearson Education; Pen and
Sword Books; Pluto Press; ProQuest; Publishing Scotland;
Publishing Training Centre; Random House Group; Roots
for Churches; Royal Society; SAGE Publications; Specialist
Schools & Academies Trust; Taylor & Francis Group;
University College London; University of Wales Press;
John Wiley & Sons; World Scientific

Marketability is a group of experienced publishing consultants, all ex-publishers, providing complete support to publishers' marketing departments, from campaigns to
consultancy. It supplies resources when needed: to manage
catalogue or direct-marketing campaigns, devise and conduct market research, or provide consultancy and advice on
strategic and practical issues. Its experience is across all publishing sectors, and with both small and large organizations.

Also provides in-company and external training courses –
see our separate entry under Training.

6049

MIDAS PUBLIC RELATIONS LTD
10 Old Court Place, Kensington, London W8 4PL
Telephone: 020 7361 7860
Fax: 020 7398 1268
Email: info@midaspr.co.uk
Website: www.midaspr.co.uk

Personnel:
Tony Mulliken *(Chairman)*
Steven Williams *(Chief Executive Officer)*
Penny Clifton *(Executive Managing Director)*
Fiona Marsh *(Executive Director, New Business)*

Midas Public Relations is the country's leading PR agency for
the publishing industry, with a reputation for delivering
award-winning and cost-effective campaigns for authors,
publishers and suppliers alike.

Midas has worked with many of the top publishing houses
and high-profile authors over the past two
decades. Originally formed to service the publishing industry, Midas PR's areas of expertise now span related sectors,
including magazines, the arts, awards, events, media, entertainment, music and children's products. Named in The
Bookseller Magazine's Top 100 'most influential in publishing', Midas Public Relations has an excellent reputation for
its contacts in the industry, its expertise in the digital and
online sphere, and for understanding the commercial reality
of the arts and publishing world.

Midas is a PR Week Top 50 consumer agency and a fully
accredited member of the Public Relations Consultants
Association.

6050

NIELSEN BOOKSCAN
3rd Floor, Midas House, 62 Goldsworth Road, Woking,
Surrey GU21 6LQ
Telephone: 01483 712222
Fax: 01483 712201
Email: sales.bookscan@nielsen.com
Website: www.nielsenbookscan.co.uk

Personnel:
Mo Siewcharran *(Head of Marketing)*
Ann Betts *(Commercial Director)*
Reeta Windsor *(Business Development Manager)*
Carol Brownlee *(Deputy Director)*
Paul Dibble *(Head of Data Services)*
Andre Breedt *(Head of Publisher Account Management)*
Lucy Huddlestone *(Export Sales Manager)*
Melanie Brassington *(Export Sales Manager)*

Parent Company:
UK: Nielsen

Associated Companies:
UK: Nielsen BookData; Nielsen BookNet; Nielsen
Registration Agencies (ISBN, SAN & ISTC)

Nielsen BookScan is a continuous book sales tracking service
operating in the UK, Ireland, Australia, the USA, South
Africa, Italy, New Zealand, Denmark, Spain and India. Book-
Scan collects total transaction data at the point of sale
directly from tills and dispatch systems of all major book
retailers. This ensures that detailed and highly accurate sales
information on what books are selling, and at what price, is
available to the book trade. LibScan measures book borrow-
ings in public libraries.

6051

THE OXFORD PUBLICITY PARTNERSHIP LTD
2 Lucas Bridge Business Park, Old Greens Norton Road,
Towcester NN12 8AX
Telephone: 01327 357770

Email: info@oppuk.co.uk
Website: www.oppuk.co.uk

Personnel:
Gary Hall *(Director)*

Founded in 1989, The Oxford Publicity Partnership Ltd (OPP)
successfully manages sales, marketing and publicity for publishers in the UK and Europe. OPP works for some highly rec-
ognizable names in North American, British and European
publishing – from internationally renowned university
presses to some of the best-known commercial publishers as
well as small, niche publishing companies, and other organizations for which publishing is just part of their remit.

Providing a range of solutions for a variety of clients, in serious non-fiction, academic and professional markets, OPP
has a reputation for garnering attention for publishing
projects, a knack for defining what is right for sales growth,
while ensuring author retention and the development of
publisher name and brand recognition.

OPP provides sales and key-account management, publicity
and marketing services to publishers, either combined with
full service distribution or as standalone services.

6052

STAR BOOK SALES
PO Box 20, Whimple, Exeter EX5 2WY
Telephone: 01404 515050
Fax: 01404 823820
Email: enquiries@starbooksales.com
Website: www.starbooksales.com

Personnel:
Dennis Buckingham *(Managing Director)*
Geoff Cowen *(Chairman)*

UK distributor for:
Australia: Rockpool Publishing
Belgium: Marc Sluszny Books; Nova Vista Books
Canada: UCM Publishing
CHINA: Earnshaw Books; Make-Do Publishing
France: Editions Esmod
GERMANY: EditorailRM; Heel Verlag; Meyer & Meyer Sports
UK; Tushita Verlag
Italy: Archidios Libri; Edit Vallard; Giorgio Nada; Renzo Piano
Foundation
MALTA: Portfolio Curtains
Switzerland: Bergli Books
UK: Angela Patchell Books; Artists Bookworks; Ashgrove
Press; Choc Lit; Coastal Publishing; Dynasty Press;
Earlswood Press; Earlswood Press; Envisage Books; Evans
Mitchell Books; Guinea Pig Education; John Beaufoy
Publishing; Last Passage; Rickshaw Publishing; Troubador
Publishing
USA: Changing Lives Press; Dalton Watson Fine Books;
Fastdates Publishing; Octane Press; Parker House
Publishing; Power Hiking; Red Rock Publishing

Star Book Sales provides sales and distribution for publishers
thoughout the UK & Europe.

6053

THE UNIVERSITY PRESS GROUP (US) LTD
LEC 1 New Era Estate, Oldlands Way, Bognor Regis
PO22 9QN
Telephone: 01243 842165
Fax: 01243 842167
Email: lois@upguk.com

Personnel:
Andrew Brewer *(Managing Director)*
Lois Edwards *(Business Manager)*

6054

UNIVERSITY PRESSES MARKETING
The Tobacco Factory, Raleigh Road, Southville, Bristol
BS3 1TF
Telephone: 0117 902 0275
Fax: 0117 902 0294
Email: sales@universitypressesmarketing.co.uk
Website: www.universitypressesmarketing.co.uk

Personnel:
Andrew Gilman *(Managing Director)*
Paul Skinner *(Office Manager)*
Helena Svojsikova *(Area Manager)*

Sales agent for (mainly) American university presses in the UK and Europe.

6.6 DISTRIBUTORS

6055

AFRICAN BOOKS COLLECTIVE
PO Box 721, Oxford OX1 9EN
Telephone: 01865 589756
Fax: 01865 412341
Email: orders@africanbookscollective.com
Website: www.africanbookscollective.com

Personnel:
Justin Cox *(Chief Executive Officer)*
Mary Jay *(Consultant)*
David Brooks *(Director)*

Participating publishers include:
Benin: Centre Panafricain de Prospective Sociale / Pan-African Social Prospects Centre
Botswana: Foundation for Education with Production; Lightbooks Publishers; Pyramid Publishing
Cameroon: Dept of Women & Gender Studies,University of Buea; Langaa Research & Publishing Common Initiative Group
Eritrea: Hdri Publishers
Ethiopia: Addis Ababa University Press; Development Policy Management Forum (DPMF); Forum for Social Studies; Organisation for Social Science Research in Eastern and Southern Africa (OSSREA)
Gambia: Educational Services
Ghana: Afram Publications (Ghana) Ltd; Africa Christian Press; Association of African Universities Press; Blackmask; Freedom Publishers; Ghana Universities Press; Sankofa Educational Publishers; Sedco Publishing; SEM Financial Training Centre Ltd; Sub-Saharan Publishers; Third World Network Africa; Woeli Publishing Services; Women's Health Action Research Centre
Kenya: Academy Science Publishers; African Research & Resource Forum; Chrisley Ltd.; East African Educational Publishers; Focus Books; Kwani Trust; LawAfrica; LawAfrica; Longhorn Publishers; P-J Kenya; Solidarity for African Women's Rights coation; Storymoja; Twaweza Communications; University of Nairobi Press; Zand Graphics; Zapf Chancery
Lesotho: Institute of Southern African Studies, National University of Lesotho
Liberia: Cotton Tree Press
Malawi: Central Africana; Chancellor College Publishers; E&V Publications; Imabili Idigenous Knowledge Publications; Kachere Series; WASI
Mali: Editions Yeelen
Mauritius: Editions Vivazi
Morocco: Editions du Sirocco; Senso Unico Editions
Namibia: Brookridge Publishing; Reader in Namibian Sociology; University of Namibia Press; Wordweaver Publishing House
Nigeria: African Heritage Press; Apex Books; Books and Gavel; College Press Publishers; Compumetrics Solutions; Concept Publishers; CSS Ltd; Dokun Publishing House; Enicrownfit Publishers; Fourth Dimension Publishing Co Ltd; Frontpage Media; Handel Books; HEBN Books; Humanities Publishers; Ibadan Cultural Studies Group; Ibadan University Press; Kemuela Publications; Kraft Books; Maiyati Chambers; Malthouse Press Ltd; Manila Publishers; New Horn Press Ltd; Niyi Osundare; Obafemi Awolowo University Press; Onyoma Research Publications; Opon ifa Readers; Progress Publishing Company; Safari Books; Saros International Publishers; SCRIBO Publications; Spectrum Books Ltd; Statco Publishers; The Book Company; University of Lagos Press; University Press Ltd; Urhobo Historical Society; West African Book Publishers; Women's Health & Action Research; Yintab Books
Senegal: African Renaissance; Council for the Development of Social Science Research in Africa (CODESRIA); Union for African Population Studies
Sierra Leone: PenPoint Publishers
South Africa: Africa Institute of South Africa; African Minds Publishers; African Perspectives; Brenthurst Collection / Frank Horley Books; Idasa; Ikhwezi Afrika Publishers; Johnson & KingJames Books; Mail and Guardian Books; Modjaji Books; Umsinsi Books; UNISA Press
Swaziland: Academic Publishers; JAN Publishing Centre; TTI Publishing
Tanzania: Centre for Energy, Environment, Science & Technology (CEEST); Dar es Salaam University Press; E &

D Ltd; Mkuki na Nyota Publishers; Tanzania Publishing House
Uganda: Femrite (Uganda Women Writers' Association); Fountain Publishers; Pelican Publishers
Zambia: Bookworld Publishers; Image Publishers; Lembani Trust; Multimedia Zambia; University of Zambia; Zambia Women Writers' Association
Zimbabwe: Africa Community Publishing & Development Trust; amabooks; Amaguge Publishers; Baobab Books; Booklove Publishers; GALZ; Kimaathi Publishing House; Mambo Press; Southern African Printing and Publishing House / SAPES Trust; Southern African Research and Documentation Centre; Southern and Eastern Africa Trade, Information and Negotiations Institute; University of Zimbabwe Publications; Weaver Press Ltd; Women and Law in South Africa Research Trust; Zimbabwe International Book Fair Trust; Zimbabwe Publishing House Ltd

African Books Collective is a major initiative to promote African-published books in Europe, North America, and in Commonwealth countries outside Africa. It is owned by the founding publishers, and is non-profit making on its own behalf. Centralized billing and shipping is provided from Oxford. Over 2000 titles are available, from 147 publishers in 25 African countries.

The greater part of the list is available print-on-demand, supplied from within the US for North America; from Australia for Australia and New Zealand; and from the UK for the rest of the world. Joint catalogues are available, and on the website for download. New title information is sent monthly to the e-subscriber list; RSS feeds are also available.

English-language material is stocked, with an emphasis on scholarly, literature and children's titles. A small number of titles in French and Portugues are stocked. Titles are also available in African languages: Swahili, Shona, Ndebele, and Igbo. Standing order / blanket order plans are available and can be geared to meet libraries' specific requirements or acquisitions profiles.

Trading started in May 1990.

6056

ANGLO AMERICAN BOOKS
Crown Buildings, Bancyfelin, Carmarthen SA33 5ND
Telephone: 01267 211880
Fax: 01267 211882
Email: books@anglo-american.co.uk
Website: www.anglo-american.co.uk

Personnel:
D. Bowman *(Managing Director)*
Mrs C. Lenton *(Marketing Director)*

Parent Company:
UK: Crown House Publishing Ltd

UK Distributor/Representative for:
USA: Center Press; Milton H. Erickson Foundation Press; Free Spirit Publishing; Genesis II; Great River Publishing; International Society of Neuro-Semantics; Kagan ; Kendall/Hunt; Leading Edge Communications; Meta Publications; Network 3000 Publishing; NLP Comprehensive; Science and Behavior Books; Success Strategies; Teacher Created Materials; Transforming Press; Westwood Publishing

Anglo-American Books is a stockholding distributor of British and American books with particular expertise in the NLP, personal growth, hypnotherapy, accelerated learning and psychotherapy fields. Stock book orders received by 2.30 pm are dispatched the same day.

Order Department opening times: 9–5 Monday to Friday.

6057

BEBC DISTRIBUTION
4 Albion Close, Parkstone, Poole, Dorset BH12 3LL
Telephone: 01202 715555
Fax: 01202 715556
Website: www.bebc.co.uk

Personnel:
John Walsh *(Managing Director)*
Rosy Jones *(Operations Manager)*
Charles Kipping *(Marketing Manager)*
Karen Bickers *(Client Services Manager)*

Parent Company:
UK: The Bournemouth English Book Centre Ltd

UK Distributor/Representative for:
Australia: Academic English Press; Actual Enterprises; Adams & Austen Press; Boyer Education; Insearch Publications; One-Sided Paper (CELUSA)
Austria: Helbling Languages
Germany: Ernst Klett *(ELT Titles only)*; Executive English
Netherlands: John Benjamins bv
New Zealand: Catt Education
UK: Academic Book Collection; Bath Publishing; The British Council; Brookemead ELT; Coat Meur Press; Ferard-Reeve Publishing; First Press ELT; FunSongs Ltd; Gem Publishing; Global ELT; The Language Factory; Listen & Speak Publications; Richmond ; Roslin Publishing; Three Vee; TP Publications; York Associates

Distributors for educational publishers specializing in Business, Law, English Language Teaching, ICT books, Human Rights and Conservation. For further information or to order, please telephone 01202 715555.

6058

THE BOOK SERVICE LTD
Colchester Road, Frating Green, Colchester, Essex CO7 7DW
Telephone: 01206 256000 (orders: 255678)
Fax: 01206 255929 (orders: 255930)
Email: sales@tbs-ltd.co.uk
Website: www.TheBookService.co.uk

Personnel:
Mark Williams *(Managing Director)*
Colin James *(Deputy Managing Director)*
Samantha Blackwell *(Head of Business Development)*
Andy Willis *(Business Development Director)*

Parent Company:
UK: Penguin Random House Group

Associated Companies:
UK: Grantham Book Services

Distributors for::
Andersen Press; Atlantic Books; Canongate Books; Constable & Robinson; Faber & Faber; Granta Books; Harlequin UK D2C; Icon Books; Kogan Page; Mainstream Publishing; Methuen Publishing; Nicholas Brealey; Profile Books; Quercus; Random House Group; Sort of Books; Transworld; Walker Books

The Book Service (TBS) is the UK's leading distributor. Distributing over 100 million books per year, TBS has high-tech fully-automated handling systems and offers full electronic ordering and e-Commerce capabilities. TBS operates a full sales ledger, offers cash collection, debt and stock insurance policies, telesales, royalties and sub-rights services. Ancillary work such as mailing, shrink-wrapping, re-pricing, dump-bin and counter pack make-up is also offered.

6059

BOOK SYSTEMS PLUS LTD
Book Systems Plus, (at HDM LTD), Station Road, Linton, Cambs. CB21 4UX
Telephone: 01223 893261
Fax: 01223 893852
Email: bsp2b@aol.com
Website: www.booksystemsplus.com

Personnel:
George J. Papa *(Managing Director)*
Shirley Greenall *(Marketing & New Business)*

Parent Company:
UK: Whittet Books Ltd

Publishers represented:
Australia: A & B Publishers Pty Ltd; Bookbiz International
Canada: The Althouse Press; The Charlton Press; Detselig Enterprises Ltd; Greatest Escapes.com
Germany: Chateaux & Manoirs
Netherlands: Mo' Media
South Africa: Dreams 4 Africa
UK: Aardvark Publishing; Alice & Fred Books; Caister Academic Press; Chakula Press Ltd; Classic Locations; Cobwebs Brentwood; Cracking It; Delfryn Publications; EFL Ltd; Euro Impala; Fitzwarren Publishing; Focus Publications Ltd; Gudrun Publishing / Edda UK; Hiller Airguns; Hoopoe Books; Idlewild Publishers; Institute for

Psychophysical Research; Oxford Forum; Pathfinder Audio; Porpoise Books; Raleo Publishing Ltd; RevengeInk Ltd; Tricorn; UK International Ceramics; Vista Consulting Team Ltd; Whittet Books Ltd; Wild Boar Trading
USA: John F. Blair, Publisher

Book Systems Plus provides full distribution, invoicing and customer services to publishers from the UK and overseas. It also offers bookshop representation and marketing support. It has particular marketing expertise with travel guides and books on antiques and collectables. It acts as the UK sole agent for publishers in North America, Australia, South Africa and Europe.

6060

BOOKPOINT LTD
Park Drive,130 Milton Park, Abingdon, Oxon OX14 4SB
Telephone: 01235 400400
Fax: 01235 832068
Website: www.bookpoint.co.uk

Personnel:
Chris Emerson *(Chief Operating Officer)*
Martyn Burchall *(Head of Operations)*
Ray Webb *(Head of Customer Services)*
Graham Money *(General Manager & Director)*
Lesley Morgan *(Group IT Director)*
Jon Swan *(Head of Credit Control)*
Matt Wright *(Managing Director Distribution)*

Parent Company:
UK: Hachette UK

Distributor for:
UK: Ashgate/Gower Publishing; Debretts; Facet Publishing *(formerly Library Association)*; Hachette Children's; Headline Book Publishing; Hodder & Stoughton; Hodder Education; Hodder Gibson; Hodder Religious; In Easy Steps; John Murray; Plexus Publishing; Souvenir Press; Taylor & Francis

Bookpoint services encompass a number of industry-leading initiatives, plus a full suite of EDI applications, order processing, accounting, royalty maintenance, management reporting, warehousing, dispatch and ancillary functions. Bookpoint also operate a Premier Next Day Service, and offer PUBEASY to booksellers.

6061

BOOKSOURCE
50 Cambuslang Road, Cambuslang, Glasgow G32 8NB
Telephone: 0845 370 0063
Fax: 0845 370 0064
Email: info@booksource.net
Website: www.booksource.net

Personnel:
Davinder Bedi *(Managing Director)*
Lorraine Fannin *(Director)*
Mike Miller *(Director)*
Christian Maclean *(Director)*
Dr Keith Whittles *(Director)*
Marion Sinclair *(Director)*
Philip Walters *(Director)*
Kirsty O'Connor *(Credit Control Manager)*
Louise Morris *(Customer Service Director)*
Jim O'Donnell *(Operations Director)*
David Warnock *(Systems Manager)*

Parent Company:
UK: Publishing Scotland

Distribution on behalf of:
UK: Acair Ltd; Appletree Press; APS *(for the Scottish Executive)*; Argyll Publishing; Association for Scottish Literary Studies; Atelier Books; Backpage Press; BILD Publications; Birlinn Ltd; Books Noir; Cargo Publishing; Carnegie Publishing; Catkin Press; Cicerone Press; Clairview Books; Clan Publishers; Coolcanals Guide; John Donald; Richard Drew Ltd; Dundee University Press; Fledgling Press; Floris Books; Fort Publishing; Freight Books; Grey Tiger Publishing; Hallewell Publications; Handspring Publishing; Hawthorn Press; Islands Book Trust; Kitchen Press; Kohl Publishing; Legend Press; Librario Publishing; Lunicorn Press; Macdonald Media Publishing; Mercat Press; Moonlight Publishing; Glen Murray Publishing; My Little Big Town; Myhobbystore.com; NMS Enterprises Ltd Publishing; Phoenix Yard Books; Polygon; Publishing Scotland; Real

Reads; Really Decent Books; Rider French Publications; Ringwood Publishing; Roving Press; Royal Commission on the Ancient and Historical Monuments of Scotland; Rucksack Readers; Steve Savage Publishing; Scottish Society for Northern Studies; Scottish Text Society; Sparkling Books; Starlet; Rudolf Steiner Press; Stone Country Press; Strident Publishing; Sunday Herald Books; Temple Lodge Publishing; Tuckwell Press; Two Ravens Press; Waverley Press; Whittles Publishing; Wild Goose Publications; Neil Wilson Publishing; Windhorse Publications

Established in 1995, BookSource offers warehousing and worldwide distribution services to book trade publishers, charities and funded institutions, and other commercial enterprises.

6062

BUSHWOOD BOOKS LTD
6 Marksbury Avenue, Kew Gardens, Surrey TW9 4JF
Telephone: 020 8392 8585
Fax: 020 8392 9876
Email: info@bushwoodbooks.co.uk
Website: www.bushwoodbooks.co.uk

Personnel:
Richard Hansen *(Director)*
Victoria Hansen *(PA)*
Ian McLellan *(Sales)*

Exclusive distributor for:
USA: Schiffer *(Mind, Body, Spirit titles)*; Schiffer Collectibles Arts & Crafts; Schiffer Publishing Ltd *(Military Aviation)*

The company also carries in stock hundreds of titles on antiques and collectibles, predominantly horology, jewellery, ceramics and glass. It specializes in providing a service for UK customers to purchase from North American publishers.

Bushwood Books is one of the leading UK distributors of German World War II titles in English, and also carries the Schiffer Mind, Body, Spirit list.

6063

CENGAGE LEARNING EMEA
[a division of Cengage Learning]
Cheriton House, North Way, Andover, Hants SP10 5BE
Telephone: 01264 332424
Fax: 01264 342732
Website: www.cengage.co.uk

Personnel:
Julian Drinkall *(Chief Executive Officer)*
Chad Bonney *(CFO & COO)*
Carrie Willicome *(Operations Director)*

Parent Company:
USA: Cengage Learning Inc

Distributors for:
UK: Cengage Learning *(selected imprints)*; Evans Publishing Group; Janes

6064

COMBINED ACADEMIC PUBLISHERS LTD
Windsor House, Cornwall Road, Harrogate, N Yorks HG1 2PW
Telephone: 01423 562232
Email: enquiries@combinedacademic.co.uk
Website: www.combinedacademic.co.uk

Personnel:
Nicholas Esson *(Managing Director)*
Ms Julia Monk *(Marketing Director)*
David Pickering *(Sales Director)*
Ms Denise Martin *(Accounts Manager)*
Emma Williams *(Sales Manager)*

UK & European distributor for:
Canada: McGill-Queen's University Press
USA: Duke University Press; Fordham University Press; Indiana University Press; New York University Press; Ohio University Press; Temple University Press; University of Illinois Press; University of Nebraska Press; University of Washington Press; Univresity of Texas Press

Combined Academic Publishers, in association with Marston Book Services, is a professional representation and distribution agency for academic and university presses.

UK and Republic of Ireland field sales are handled by our own representative and a team of experienced commisson agents, while agents are active in five continental European territories – Scandinavia; the Netherlands and Belgium; Southern Europe; Germany, Austria and Switzerland; Central and Eastern Europe – as well as the Middle East and Africa.

CAP has a proactive marketing department offering direct mail campaigns, space advertising and review copy distribution.

6065

COMBINED BOOK SERVICES LTD
Unit D, Paddock Wood Distribution Centre, Paddock Wood, Tonbridge, Kent TN12 6UU
Telephone: 01892 837171
Fax: 01892 837272
Email: info@combook.co.uk
Website: www.combook.co.uk

Personnel:
Keith Neale *(Joint Managing Director)*
Allan Smith *(Joint Managing Director)*

Associated Companies:
UK: Eddington Hook

Distributors for:
Finland: Habakuk Books
Germany: earBOOKS (edel)
India: Roman Books
Italy: Istituto Fotocromo Italiano
New Zealand: Burke Publishing
Singapore: Black Sheep Guides
UK: A Jot Publishing; J. A. Allen *(Equestrian)*; Andrews UK; Animated Books; Anshan Publishers; Arachne Press; Balloon View Ltd; Bene Factum Publishing; Cambridge House; Chandos Publishing; Claerhout Publishing; Classical Comics; Digital Leaf; Discovery Books; Encyclopaedia Britannica; Graffito Books; Greenvale Books; Greenwich Book Company; Robert Hale; Hammersmith Health Books; Hammersmith Press; Hawkins Publishing Services; Hide Stationery; Hoberman Collection; Imagier Publishing; Jonescat Publishing; Kiosk Publishing; Korero Books; Lotus Publishing; Management Books 2000; NAG Publishers; Northcote House Publishers; Park Lane Books; Phoenix Publishers; Pocket Issue; Splendid Books; Thomas Telford Ltd *(Institute of Civil Engineers)*; teneues Publishing UK; Trevelyan Publishers ; Woodhead Publishing
USA: Ahmadiyya Anjuman Isha'at Islam Lahore

Combined Book Services provides worldwide distribution for UK and International publishers, distributing a wide range of books, calendars, diaries, stationery products and DVDs. CBS is BIC accredited for Supply Chain Excellence, a PubEasy affiliate as well as a Batch Payments and Batch Returns supplier.

6066

CONTOUR MANAGEMENT SERVICES (CMS)
PO Box 3042, New Milton, Hants BH25 7XG
Telephone: 01425 620532
Fax: 01425 620532
Email: mikecms@btinternet.com
Website: www.contourmanagementservices.com

Personnel:
Mike Cranidge *(Managing Partner)*
Sue Cranidge *(Partner)*

Agent and distributor for:
Australia: Meridian Maps
Portugal: Turinta
USA: Hedberg Maps Inc; Map Link

Importers and distributors of maps with a difference.

6067

CORNERHOUSE PUBLICATIONS
70 Oxford Street, Manchester M1 5NH
Telephone: 0161 200 1503
Fax: 0161 200 1504
Email: Publications@Cornerhouse.org
Website: www.Cornerhouse.org/books

Personnel:
Paul Daniels *(Publications Director)*

Debbie Fielding *(Administrator)*
Suzanne Davies *(Publications Officer)*
James Brady *(Publications Officer)*

Clients include:
Germany: DuMont Buchverlag; Kerber Verlag; Richter
Verlag; Verlag für moderne Kunst Nurnberg; Walther
König
Switzerland: JRPRingier
UK: British Council Visual Arts & Design; Haunch of
Venison; Hayward Gallery; ICA; Ikon; Modern Art Oxford;
Henry Moore Institute; Photoworks; Ridinghouse

Distributor of contemporary visual arts and photography
books for publishers, museums and galleries worldwide. A
full list of publishers to which we distribute is available in our
catalogue or at our website: www.Cornerhouse.org/books.

6068

DEEP BOOKS LTD
Unit 3, Goose Green Trading Estate, 47 East Dulwich Road,
London SE22 9BN
Telephone: 020 8693 0234
Fax: 020 8693 1400
Email: sales@deep-books.co.uk
Website: www.deep-books.co.uk

Personnel:
Chris Custance *(Managing Director)*
Alan Ritchie *(Marketing Manager)*
Paul Woodfield *(Sales Manager)*

Client Publishers include:
Australia: Michelle Anderson Publishing *(formerly Hill of
Content Publishing)*; Finch Publishing; Barry Long Books
(Australia); Milne Books
Austria: Ennsthaler Publishing House
Italy: Lo Scarabeo
Monaco: Alpen Editions
Netherlands: Gottmer Publishing Group
UK: Camino Guides; Earthdancer; Findhorn Press; Gothic
Image Publications; Khaniqahi Nimatullahi Publications
(KNP); Barry Long Books (Britain); Polair Publishing
USA: Alpha Books / Penguin USA; Amber Lotus; ARE Press;
Avery/Penguin USA; Basic Health Publications; Bear & Co;
Bear Cub Books; Berkley Publishing Group; Best Life
Media; Bindu Books; Blue Dolphin Publishing Inc;
Bluestar Communications; Boys Town Press; Career Press;
Celebra; Chamberlain Bros / Penguin USA; Chiron
Publications; Crystal Clarity Publishers; Dawn
Publications; Dawnhorse Publications; De Vorss & Co;
Destiny Audio Books; Destiny Books; Destiny Recordings;
Dragonhawk Publishing; Dutton / Penguin USA; Earth
Magic Productions Inc; Freedom Press; Glorian
Publishing; Golden Sufi Center; Gotham Books / Penguin
USA; Hampton Roads Publishing; Nicolas Hays; Healing
Arts Press; Himalayan Institute Press; Hologram Books;
Hudson Street / Penguin USA; Hunter House Inc; Ibis
Press; Inner Traditions International; Inner Travel Books;
Integral Yoga Publications; Jewish Light Publishing; JZK
Publishing; Veronica Lane Books; Lantern Books; Music
Design; New American Library; New Page Books;
Original Publications; Park St Press; Penguin Group USA
(selected imprints); Perigee/Penguin; Plume; Polair
Publishing; Power Press; Red Wheel Weiser *(selected
imprints)*; Self-Realization Fellowship; Skylight Paths;
Square One Publishing *(Vital Health Publishing)*;
Synergetic Press; Timeless Books; Veronica Lane Books;
Witches Almanac; World Wisdom Books

Specialist mind body spirit distributors. Deep Books handles
publishers lists from the UK, the USA and Australia. It provides sales and distribution for these publishers throughout
the UK, Republic of Ireland, mainland Europe and Scandinavia and acts as their exclusive agents in those territories.

6069

EUROPEAN SCHOOLBOOKS LTD
Ashville Trading Estate, The Runnings, Cheltenham
GL51 9PQ
Telephone: 01242 245252
Fax: 01242 224137
Email: direct@esb.co.uk
Website: www.eurobooks.co.uk

Personnel:
Frank Preiss *(Managing Director)*
Ruth Trippett *(Marketing)*

Associated Companies:
UK: The European Bookshop; The Italian Bookshop

Distributor for:
Brazil: Pontes Editores
Denmark: Grafisk Forlag
France: 10/18; Assimil; Bordas; Casterman; CLE
International; Armand Colin; Didier; École des loisirs;
Editions du Fallois; Editions du Seuil; Flammarion; Folio;
Foucher; Gallimard; Garnier Flammarion; Gault Millau;
Hachette; Hatier; J'ai lu; Larousse; Livres de poche;
Minuit; Nathan; Presses de la cité; Presses Pocket; Presses
Universitaires de France; Presses Universitaires de
Grenoble; Le Robert
Germany: Arena; Bibliographisches Institut Mannheim;
Brockhaus; Carlsen; Cornelsen; Deutscher Taschenbuch
Verlag; Diogenes; Duden; Fischer; Gilde Buchhandlung;
Goldmann; Heyne; Max Hueber Verlag; Insel;
Kiepenheuer & Witsch; Knaur; Langenscheidt;
Luchterhand; Reclam; Rowohlt; Suhrkamp; Ullstein;
Verlag Dürr & Kessler; Verlag für Deutsch; Verlag Moritz
Diesterweg
Italy: Alma Edizioni; Bonacci Editore; Edilingua; Einaudi;
European Language Institute; Fabbri-Bompiani;
Feltrinelli; Garzanti; Giunti; Guerra; Mondadori; Le
Monnier; Oscar; Piemme; Rizzoli; Rux; La Spiga;
Zanichelli
Netherlands: Intertaal
Portugal: Dinapress; Lidel Edições Técnicas; Porto Editora
Lda; Public. Europa-America
Spain: Alfaguara; Alianza; Anaya; Anaya ELE; Austral;
Catedra; Colegio de España; Destino; Difusión; EDELSA;
Ediciones Edhasa

Distributors of some 120,000 titles in the main European
languages on behalf of over 100 publishers. Large-scale promotion in all sectors of the foreign languages educational
market. Suppliers of foreign-published stock to academic
and general bookshops. General wholesale service for non-
stock titles.

6070

FREELANCE MARKET NEWS
8–10 Dutton Street, Manchester M3 1LE
Telephone: 0161 819 9919
Fax: 0161 819 2842
Email: fmn@writersbureau.com
Website: www.freelancemarketnews.com

Personnel:
Miss Angela Cox *(Managing Editor)*

Parent Company:
UK: The Writers Bureau Ltd

Distributor for:
USA: Writer's Digest Books *(books on writing)*

6071

GAZELLE BOOK SERVICES LTD
White Cross Mills, Hightown, Lancaster LA1 4XS
Telephone: 01524 68765
Fax: 01524 63232
Email: sales@gazellebooks.co.uk
Website: www.gazellebookservices.co.uk

Personnel:
Brian Haywood *(Company Secretary & Finance Director)*
Mark Trotter *(Distribution & Sales Director)*
Kevin Dixon *(Warehouse Manager)*
Lee Hodgkiss *(Marketing & Exhibitions Manager)*
Gareth Hindson *(Customer Service Manager)*
Melanie Warren *(Sales & Marketing Manager)*
Analyn Dixon *(Book-keeper)*

Gazelle Book Services handles both trade and academic lists
and covers the whole of the UK and Europe. It provides:
• fast order turn-round
• comprehensive stock and regular stock replenishment
• efficient reporting and information service to customers
• regular sales calling and regular liaison with booksellers in
connection with promotion, exhibitions, special events, etc
• following through
• friendly, helpful service
• regular and adaptable reporting to publishers
• flexibility and co-operation.

Complete list of client publishers is available on request.

GRANTHAM BOOK SERVICES
Trent Road, Grantham, Lincs NG31 7XQ
Telephone: 01476 541000 (541080)
Fax: 01476 541060 (541061)
Email: orders@gbs.tbs-ltd.co.uk
Website: www.granthambookservices.co.uk

Personnel:
Mark Williams *(Managing Director)*
Colin James *(Deputy Managing Director)*
Andy Willis *(Business Development Director)*
Samantha Blackwell *(Head of Business Development)*
Colleen McMorran *(Client Services Manager)*

Parent Company:
UK: Penguin Random House Group

Associated Companies:
UK: The Book Service

Clients include::
Bonnier Publishing; Crimson; Hometown World; Marco
Polo; Panini Stickers; Punk; Watkins
UK: Barrington Stoke; Bounce Sales & Marketing; Compass
Maps; Crombie Jardine; Crown House; The Crowood
Press; Footprint Handbooks; FW Media; Hay House; Nick
Hern Books; Hesperus Press; How To Books; Lerner;
Lonely Planet; Manchester United; Manning Partnership;
Melia Publishing Services; New Holland; Nosy Crow;
Oneworld Publications; Osprey Publishing; Oval; Perseus
Books; PGUK; Piccadilly Press; Prestel; Quiller Publishing;
Reaktion Books; Running Press; Severn House Publishers;
Templar Publishing; Timber Press; Titan Books
USA: Everyman; MBI; Workman Publishing

Grantham Book Services (GBS) is the UK's Independent's
Specialist.

Distributing over 26 million books per year, GBS offers a
bespoke book distribution service with full electronic ordering and e-Commerce capabilities. GBS operates a full sales
ledger, cash collection service, telesales, royalties / sub-rights
and digital distribution services.

Ancillary work such as mailing, shrink-wrapping, re-pricing,
dump-bin and counter pack make-up is also offered.

LITTLEHAMPTON BOOK SERVICES LTD
Faraday Close, Durrington, Worthing, West Sussex
BN13 3RB
Telephone: 01903 828500
Fax: 01903 828625
Email: enquiries@lbsltd.co.uk
Website: www.lbsltd.co.uk

Personnel:
Chris Emerson *(Chief Operating Officer)*
Matt Wright *(Finance Director)*
Lesley Morgan *(Group IT Director)*
Bridget Radnedge *(Publishing Services Director)*
Alan Rakes *(Inventory Director)*

Parent Company:
UK: Hachette UK Publishing Group

Clients include:
Abrams & Chronicle; Ian Allan; Aurum Press, Apple, QED,
Quayside & Rotovision; Automobile Association;
Barefoot Books; Best Ever Publishing; Cardoo; John Blake
Publishing; DAAB; Everyman Chess; Express Newspapers;
Eye Books Ltd; Grub Street; Halban Publishers; Infinite
Ideas Co; Kyle Books; Little Brown Book
Group; Myrmidon Books; Michael O'Mara Books;
Octopus Publishing Group; Old Steet Publishing; Oldie
Publications; Orion Group; Pitch Publishing Ltd; Private
Eye; Raceform Ltd; Radio Times; Stripe Publishing;
Summersdale; Taschen; Thames & Hudson, Thames &
Hudson Distributed; Which? The Consumer Association

Littlehampton Book Services provides publishers with full
warehouse management and distribution services that
include credit control and trust accounting, sophisticated
management reporting, telesales, customer service and royalty accounting.

6074

B. McCALL BARBOUR

28 George IV Bridge, Edinburgh EH1 1ES
Telephone: 0131 225 4816
Fax: 0131 225 4816
Website: www.mccallbarbour.co.uk

Personnel:
Rev Dr T. C. Danson-Smith *(Managing Partner)*
Miss G. A. Danson-Smith *(Dispatch Manager)*

USA companies represented:
USA: AMG Publishers; Chick Publications; Dake Bible Sales; Discovery House; Harvest-House; Kirkbride Bible Co; Kregel Publishers; Living Stories Inc; Thomas Nelson & Sons; Oxford University Press *(Bibles)*; John Peterson Music; Rainbow Study Bibles; Schoette Publishing House; Singspiration Inc; Sword of the Lord Publishers; Zondervan Corporation

Distributor of Bibles, Christian books and greeting cards, also videos, DVDs, gifts.

6075

MACMILLAN DISTRIBUTION (MDL)

Brunel Road, Houndmills, Basingstoke, Hants RG21 6XS
Telephone: 01256 302840
Fax: 01256 841426
Email: www-mdl@macmillan.co.uk
Website: www.macmillandistribution.co.uk

Personnel:
Andrew Weber *(Chairman)*
David Smith *(Managing Director)*
Matthew Hogg *(Commercial Director)*
Guy Browning *(Distribution Director)*
Michael Grimes *(Credit Services Director)*
Mark Walker *(Head of IT)*

Parent Company:
UK: Macmillan Ltd

Distributor for:
Accent Press Ltd; Acumen Publishing; Allegra Publications; Alma Books; And Other Stories; Arcadia; Arcturus Publishing Ltd; Arden Shakespeare; Berg Publishers; A. & C. Black; Black and White; Bloodaxe Books; Bloomsbury Academic; Bloomsbury Continuum; Bloomsbury Information; Bloomsbury Publishing Plc; Boxtree; Camra; Cico Books; Clarus Press; Class Publishing (London) Ltd; CRW Publishing Ltd; Dennis Publishing; Domino; Gerald Duckworth & Co Ltd; Edinburgh University Press; Elliott & Thompson Ltd; Fairchild; Featherstone; First Second Editions; Fonthill Media; W. Foulsham & Co Ltd; W. H. Freeman & Worth Publishers; Gallic Books; Gibson Square; Guinness World Records Ltd; Head of Zeus; C. Hurst; Jones & Bartlett; Kingfisher; Jessica Kingsley Publishers; Little Tiger Press (Magi); Macmillan Children's Books; Macmillan Compass; Macmillan Digital Audio; Macmillan Education; Macmillan English Campus; Macmillan New Writing; Mantle; MARG; Methuen Drama; Murdoch Books (UK) Ltd; Nature Publishing Group; Office for National Statistics (ONS); One World Classics; Ovolo; Palgrave; Pan Macmillan; Pharmaceutical Press; Picador; Pinter and Martin; Priddy Books; Pushkin Press; Quadrille Publishing Ltd; Raintree; Rodale; Alan Rogers; Ryland Peters & Small; Sandstone Press; Saraband; Scribe; Sidgwick & Jackson; Sinauer Associates; SPCK; Tagman Press; I. B. Tauris; Unbound; John Wisden & Co Ltd

Macmillan Distribution (MDL) offers a full book distribution service for Macmillan publishers and a wide range of third-party clients. It provides order fulfilment, physical and digital invoicing, cash collection and information provision through its sophisticated sales analysis system, MIDAS, which has been short-listed for a supply chain innovation award. It recently invested in separate units of 120,000 sq feet and 60,000 sq feet of new state-of-the-art warehousing. MDL was one of the first publisher's distribution companies to obtain ISO9000 certification, the internationally recognized standard for quality systems, and is fully accredited under BIC's 'Supply Chain Excellence' programme. It consciously looks for ways to expand and improve the services it offers, which now include a client portal for a simple way to transfer data and orders and links with reps using PDAs for order transfer and title and price availability. MDL hosts an open day for its clients in London and at the Swansea warehouse and also an annual compliance conference. MDL recently announced a strategic partner-

ship with Faber Factory to provide digital distribution for its clients. In May 2013 MDL won the CILT Wales award for supply chain and logistics best practice for Project Apple, which provides faster service to export customers with E-invoices and consolidated delivery for the freight forwarders.

6076

MARSTON BOOK SERVICES LTD

160 Eastern Avenue, Milton Park, Abingdon OX14 4SD
Telephone: 01235 465604
Fax: 01235 465655
Email: monica.harding@marston.co.uk
Website: www.marston.co.uk

Marston Digital Print:
Omega 2, Southmead Industrial Estate, Didcot, Oxon OX11 7WB
Telephone: 01235 515700
Website: www.marston.co.uk

Personnel:
John Holloran *(Chairman)*
Ross Clayton *(Managing Director)*
Graham Cooper *(Financial Director)*
Melanie Khosla *(Customer Service Manager)*
Donna Green *(Assistant Customer Service & Trade Manager)*
Monica Harding *(Client Development & Service Manager)*
Annemarie Cuddon *(Assistant Client Development & Service Manager)*
Simon Clayton *(Marston Print Client Service Manager)*

Associated Companies:
UK: Orca Book Services

Clients represented:
NIACE (National Institute of Adult Continuing Education); Pluto Journals; Robin House Books; The Robson Press; The White Review
Belgium: Brepols Publishing; Harvey Miller Publishers
Denmark: Copenhagen Business School Press
Germany: Actar Birkhauser Dist; Boerm Bruckmeier Verlag GmbH; Fraunhofer Verlag; Hogrefe Publishing
Republic of Ireland: Cork University Press / Attic Press
Singapore: World Scientific Publishing
UK: Adamson Publishing; Alban Books; Alpha International; Alpha Science International Ltd; Anthem Press; Artifice; Assouline Publishing Inc; The Barbirolli Society; Bennett & Bloom; Bibles for Children; Biteback Publishing Ltd; Black Dog Publishing Ltd; Bloomsbury Professional; Burke Publishing; CIPAC; Claritax Books; Clarity Press ; Clinical Publishing; Combined Academic Publishers Ltd; Edward Elgar Publishing Ltd; Enzo Arts & Publsihing ; Flame Tree Publishing; Gestalten UK; Goodfellow Publishing ; Hann Barton; Harriman House Ltd; The History Press; ICSA; Imaginative Minds; Island Press; John Libbey Publishing; Karnac ; Knox Robinson Publishing ; Peter Lang Ltd; Legal Action Group; LID Publishing; Lion Hudson Plc; Manticore Books Ltd; Marshall Cavendish; Merrell Publishers Ltd; Morel Books; Multilingual Matters Ltd / Channel View Publications; NGT Publishing; NIAS; Nova Law & Finance; Now Publishing; Oberon; Orthodox Logos; Oxford Publicity Partnership; Permillion; Pluto Press; The Policy Press; Royal Botanic Gardens Kew; The Royal Society of Medicine Press Ltd; John Rule Sales & Marketing; Saqi Books; Scottish Council for Law Reporting; Scripture Union for England & Wales; Third Millennium Publishing; Thorogood Publishing; Turning Point; Unicorn Press; University of Buckingham; Vagabond Voices; Verso; The Voltaire Foundation; WARC
USA: ABC-CLIO; Enisen Publishing; National Academies Press; Rizzoli International Publications; University of Pennsylvania Press

Provides fulfilment services to the publishing world.

Services available include: order processing; customer service; credit control; management reporting; production of royalty statements; pick, pack and dispatch (automated warehouse management system); digital print facility; journal fulfilment; ancillary work; exhibition services; EDI; IT support and development.

6077

MELIA PUBLISHING SERVICES LTD

ONE, St Peter's Road, Maidenhead, Berkshire SL6 7QU
Telephone: 01628 633673
Fax: 01628 635562
Email: melia@melia.co.uk
Website: www.melia.co.uk

Personnel:
Terry Melia *(Managing Director)*
Joanna Melia *(Deputy MD)*
Rob Richardson *(Key Accounts)*
Vikki Klonowicz *(Sales Administrator)*
Linda West *(Accounts/ Payroll Manager)*

Distributor for:
The Experiment; Oxmoor House
UK: Belly Kids; Paperwasp
USA: Algonquin; Artisan; Farrar, Straus & Giroux; Forge; Griffin; Harcourt Trade Books; Harvard Common Press; Henry Holt; Houghton Mifflin Harcourt; Kensington Publishing Corporation; Minotaur; Papercutz; Picador; Rodale; Seven Seas; St Martins Press; Storey Books; Time Inc Home Entertainment; Tor; Workman Publishing; Zest Books

Sales and distribution for English language publishers.

6078

METANOIA BOOK SERVICE

[Book service of the London Mennonite Trust]
PO Box 68073, London N22 9HS
Telephone: 0845 4500 214
Fax: 0845 4500 214
Email: administrator@menno.org.uk
Website: www.menno.org.uk

Personnel:
Will Newcomb *(Manager)*

Parent Company:
UK: London Mennonite Centre

To raise awareness of Mennonite and Anabaptist distinctives through the selling of Mennonite/Anabaptist and radical discipleship literature/publications.

6079

MK BOOK SERVICE

7 East Street, Hartford Road, Huntingdon PE29 1WZ
Telephone: 01480 353710
Fax: 01480 431703
Email: mkbooks@tiscali.co.uk

Personnel:
M. R. King *(Owner)*

UK distributor/representative for clients including:
Argentina: Del Nuevo Extremo; Lola
Australia: Academic English Press; Art Media; Ausmed; Australian Medical Publications; Blue Cat Books; Boolarong Press ; Coffee School Melbourne; Corkwood Press; Crossing Press; Eagles Nest Golf Guides; East Street Publications; Golden Point Press; Haese Mathematics Pty Ltd ; Hobby Investment; IBID Press; Indo Lingo Surf; JB Books; Ken Duncan Panographs; Linford; Melting Pot Press; Mitchell Wordsmith; Parrot Books; Perfect Potion; Simone Braverman; Slouch Hat Publications; Soul to Sole NSW; Wizard Study Guides; Woodmore
Bangladesh: University Press Dhaka
Canada: Creative Newfoundland; Empty Mirror Press; Fitzhenry & Whiteside; St James Publishing BC
Estonia: Periodika
Germany: ADAC
Iceland: Forglaid; Mimir
India: Abhjeet Publications ; Aditya Prakashan; Allied Publications; Anmol; Asa; Ashish/APH; Asia Bookclub; Atlantic Publishing; Authors Press; Best Books Kolkata; Biotech; Book Enclave; Concord Press; Daya; Deep & Deep; Diamond Pocket Books; DK Printworld Pty Ltd; Galaxy; Gene-Tech Books; India Research Press; Indus; Intellectual Book Corner; ISPCK; Kaushal; Kaveri books ; Low Price Publications; Mahaveer & Sons; Minerva Associates; Modern Publishers; Munishram Manoharial; National Book Trust; Nest and Wings ; New Royal Publishing Lucknow; Oxford Book Company Jaipur ; Papyrus; Prestige; Rajesh; Regency; South Asian Publications
Israel: Ben Zvi Press; Bible Lands Museum; Carta; Francisian Printing Press; Gefen; Israel Academy of Sciences; Israel Exploration Society; Magnes Press; Rubin Mass Publishing Jerusalem; Yad Vaschem
Italy: Biblico Pontificio
Latvia: Avots
Malaysia: Islamic Book trust
New Zealand: Craigs prints Invercargill; Edge Press; Hyndmans; Nationwide books ; Photo Image Blenheim ; Tucker Media

Pakistan: Sang e Meel Lahore ; Vanguard Books
South Africa: Tortoise Press
Taiwan: SMC Publishing
Thailand: Fast track Publishing; White Lotus
UK: John Bell Local History; Popular Publications; Sole to Soul Refexology Books; SIAS Somerset Industrial Archeological Society ; Trevor A Bevis ; Williangham Press
USA: Eisenbrauns; Kendall Hunt

Distributor for overseas publishers; importer from overseas, for when we are not agents; distributor for selected UK publishers; library supply; booksearch for out-of-print UK books.

6080

MOTILAL (UK) – BOOKS OF INDIA
367 High Street, London Colney, St Albans, Herts AL2 1EA
Telephone: 01727 761677
Fax: 01727 761357
Email: barbara@motilalbooks.com
Website: www.motilalbooks.com

Personnel:
R. J. McLennan *(Managing Director)*
Ms Ann Moister *(Finance)*
Barbara Doffman *(Customer Service Manager)*
Mrs Nancy Willingham *(Assistant Customer Service)*
Mrs Arcana Smith *(Key Accounts)*
Mrs Ken Riley *(Key Accounts)*

Parent Company:
UK: Moneysavers (Ldn) Ltd

Indian publishers represented include:
India: Abhinav Publications; Amexfel Publishers; Anmol Publications; Aravali Books International; Aryan Books International; Asian Educational Services; Asiatic Publishing House; Banjara Academy; Bihar School of Yoga; Bookwell Publications; Brijbasi Art Press; Centre for Studies in Civilizations; Commonwealth Youth Programme; Cosmo Publications; Crest Publishing House; Deep & Deep Publications; DK Printworld; Excel Books; Foundation Books; Full Circle Publishing Ltd; Gemini Books; Gulshan Publishers; Gyan Publishing House; HarperCollins India; Hind Pocket Books; Indian Book Centre; Indiana Publishing House; Indica Books; Indus Publishing; Institute for Human Development; Jaico Publishing House; Jaya Books; Jaypee Brothers Medical Publishers; Kalpaz Publications; Katha; Kitab Bhavan; Laxmi Publications; Low Price Publications; Malhotra Publishing; Manas Publications; Manohar Publishers; Motilal Banarsidass; New Age Books; Orient Paperbacks; Paljor Publications; Pentagon Press; Pragati Publications; Sandeep Prakashan; Prentice-Hall of India Pvt Ltd; Pustak Mahal; Rawat; Readworthy Publications Pvt Ltd; Sahasrara Publications; Sanskrit Religious Institute; Sanskriti; Shubhi Publications; Spectrum Publications; Sura Books; Torchlight Publishing; Unisun Publications; Universal Law Publishing; Vanity Books International; Wordspeak; Worldview Publications; Zubaan

Distributor of books and other materials dealing with the philosophies, religions and cultures of India.

In November 1998 the company took over Motilal Books, which is the European distributor for Motilal Banarsidass Ltd (MLBD) of New Delhi. MLBD are the foremost publishers for the academic market on the topics of Hinduism, Buddhism, Jainism and all subjects unique to India. We supply all markets with titles in all fields, books from India in general, representing all major Indian publishers.

The company now represents over 300 Indian publishers as their UK distributor, with over 35,000 English titles listed on Nielsen BookData.

6081

NMD TRADING CO
[trading as Mayfield Books & Gifts]
9 Orgreave Close, Sheffield S13 9NP
Telephone: 0114 288 9522
Fax: 0114 269 1499
Email: sales@mayfield-books.co.uk
Website: www.mayfieldgifts.co.uk

Personnel:
Andrew Smith *(Managing Director)*
David N. Smith *(Director)*
Bill Noakes *(Sales Director)*

Supply bookshops, heritage outlets, Tourist Info centres, supermarkets, outdoor shops and other trade outlets through the UK with maps, guides and local book product. Specialize in walking and outdoor activity books. Four representatives call regularly throughout the year. Main suppliers are Ordnance Survey, History Press, Amberley, AA Publishing and Geographers A–Z Map Co. Provide a service for small publishers into the multiple chains, e.g. W. H. Smith, Waterstone's. Distributor for Myriad Books and a growing range of nostalgia products from the Frith Collection. Distibute Bradwell Books to all outlets.

Sole supplier of LAM-fold maps. Also supply laminated flat maps and other special product, such as library supply.

6082

OHL INTERNATIONAL
Action Court, Ashford Road, Ashford, Middx TW15 1XS
Telephone: 01784 890005
Fax: 01784 890013
Email: pbarrett@ohl.com
Website: www.ohl.com

Oceanfreight Division:
OHL International, Watkins Close,
Burnt Mills Industrial Estate, Basildon, Essex SS13 1TL
Telephone: 01268 724400
Fax: 01268 728226
Email: mcaines@ohl.com
Website: www.ohl.com

Personnel:
Paul Barrett *(International Sales Director)*
Martin Caines *(Oceanfreight Director)*
Chris Packwood *(Managing Director)*

Parent Company:
USA: OHL Inc

Freight forwarder to the publishing industry, providing efficient cost-effective services specifically designed for the worldwide movement of trade and academic books. Services offered are by air, sea and road between publisher's warehouse and bookshop door.

6083

ORCA BOOK SERVICES LTD
Unit A3, Fleets Corner, Poole, Dorset BH17 0HL
Telephone: 01235 465521
Fax: 01235 465555
Email: tradeorders@orcabookservices.co.uk
Website: www.orcabookservices.co.uk

Orders to:
Orca Book Services, 160 Milton Park, Abingdon, Oxon OX14 4SD

Personnel:
Martyn Chapman *(Commercial Director)*
Denise Shonfeld *(Publisher Services Manager)*
Ian Whyte *(Logistics Director)*
Trish Clapp *(Publisher Services Development Manager)*

Parent Company:
UK: Marston Book Services Ltd

UK distributor for:
Amberley Publishing; Blue Ibex; Book Foundation; Book Guild; Casemate UK; College of Law Publishing; De Agostini; Dynasty Press; English Heritage; Evans Mitchell Books; Family Doctor Publications; Firefly Books; Global Oriental; Guild of Master Craftsmen Publications; Haus Publishing; Heni Publishing; Hirmer Verlag; Industrial Press; Islamic Texts; JB Publishing; John Hunt Publishing; Kuperard Publishers; Lark Books; Learning Development Aids; Management Briefs; Maverick Arts; Metro Publications; O Books; Oxbow Books; Palazzo Editions; Parkstone Press; Pepin Press; Potomac Books; Ransom Publishing; Ravette Publishing; Redcliffe Press; Roundhouse Publishing; Special Interest Model Books; Sterling Publishing; T & G Publishing; Taunton Press; Tonto; Trolley Books; Troubador; Ullmann; Veloce Publishing; Vine House

Orca Book Services provides a full distribution service to general, academic and specialist publishers. A comprehensive package of management reports comes as standard, via Vista. Royalty accounting is also available as well as representation through the various sales agencies with which we have arrangements.

6084

SCANDINAVIA CONNECTION
26 Woodsford Square, London W14 8DP
Telephone: 020 7602 0657
Email: books@scandinavia-connection.co.uk
Website: www.scandinavia-connection.co.uk

Personnel:
Max Morgan-Witts *(Chairman)*

Parent Company:
UK: Max Morgan-Witts Productions Ltd

UK distributor for:
Norway: Cappelen; KOM; Normann's

Sole UK supplier for various Norwegian publishers of non-fiction English edition Norwegian books.

6085

TRADE COUNTER DISTRIBUTION LTD
Mendlesham Industrial Estate, Norwich Road, Mendlesham, Norfolk IP14 5ND
Telephone: 01449 766629
Fax: 01449 767122
Email: patrick.curran@tradecounter.co.uk
Website: www.tradecounter.co.uk

Personnel:
Patrick Curran *(Managing Director)*
Martin Leigh *(General Manager)*
Alan Wagstaff *(Chairman)*

Distributor:
Laburnum Press; Meg & Lucy Books; Mogzilla Books; Readzone
UK: Brilliant Publishing; Capital Transport; Miles Kelly; Rising Stars Publishing

Storage, packing and distribution of books for publishers.

Order processing and credit control. Operates both full service and fulfilment.

6086

TURNAROUND PUBLISHER SERVICES LTD
Unit 3, Olympia Trading Estate, Coburg Road, London N22 6TZ
Telephone: 020 8829 3000
Fax: 020 8881 5088
Email: sales@turnaround-uk.com
Website: www.turnaround-uk.com

Personnel:
Bill Godber *(Managing Director)*
Claire Thompson *(Marketing Director & Company Secretary)*
Sue Gregg *(Finance Director)*
Andy Webb *(Sales Director)*

Clients include:
Australia: Etram Publishing; Ocean Press; Outre Gallery & Publishing; Power Publications (Australia)
Canada: McClelland & Stewart; Random House Canada; Tradewind
China: Better Link
France: MonaGallery SARL
Germany: From Here to Fame Publishing; Bruno Gmunder Verlag; Kehrer Verlag; Konkursbuch Verlag; Mix of Pix
Italy: Europa Editions
Jamaica: LMH Publishing Ltd
Japan: Kumon Publishing Group
Philippines: Paddleless Press
Republic of Ireland: Maverick House; Mount Eagle Publications
Sweden: Dokument Press; Nicotext; Premium Publishing
Thailand: Creation / Oneiros Books; Creation / Solar Books; Creation / Wet Angel; Sun Vision Press
UK: Adelita Ltd; AK Press; Allison & Busby; Anorak Press; The Aquarium; Artists' & Photographers' Press Ltd; Ayebia Clarke Publishing Ltd; Black Spring; Blackamber Books; Bookmarks; Borderline Publications; Cinebook; Creative Essentials; Crocus Books; Cutting Edge Press; Dalen Books; Dexter Haven Publishing; Education Now Books; Emerald Publishing; Erotic Review Books; Eurocrime; Facts, Figures & Fun; Fanfare; Galley Beggar Press; Guerilla Books; Hansib Publications; Helter Skelter Publishing; High Stakes Publishing; Honno Welsh

Women's Press; Hoxton Mini Press; Jacaranda Books; Kamera; Kodansha Europe; Dewi Lewis Publishing; London Books; Monday Books; Myriad Editions; New Internationalist; Noir Publishing; Oldcastle Books; Probe; Rankin Photography Ltd; Reel Art Press; Salt Publishing; Satchel; Southbank Publishing; Sportsbooks; Straightforward Publishing; Strange Attractor; Suitcase Press; Tripwire; True Crime Library; Vice UK; Vision Sports Publishing; Zidane Press; Ziji Publishing

USA: Africa World Press; Angel City Press; Arcata Arts; Atria Books; Barricade Books; Blood Moon Productions; Bywater Books; Catbird Press; Checker Publishing; Cleis Press; Demo; DGN Productions Inc; Disinformation Co Ltd; Dominion Press; Drag City; Exact Change; Fantagraphics; Ferine Books; Fulcrum; Green Candy Press; Green Integer; Haymarket Books; IG Publishing; Last Gasp; Leyland Publications; Majority Press; Manic D Press; Microcosm Publishing; NBM; The New Press; Penny Ante Editions; Process; The Red Sea Press; Santa Monica Press; Speck Press; Starbooks; Steerforth Press; Testify Books; Turtle Point Press; Van Patten; Varnish Fine Art

Turnaround provides a sales, marketing and distribution service for a range of UK, US and Irish publishers in the UK and Europe. The above list is only a selection: contact Turnaround for a complete list.

6087

TURPIN DISTRIBUTION SERVICES LTD
Pegasus Drive, Stratton Business Park, Biggleswade, Beds SG18 8TQ
Telephone: 01767 604868
Fax: 01767 604949
Email: neil.castle@turpin-distribution.com
Website: www.turpin-distribution.com

Also at:
Turpin North America, The Bleachery, 143 West Street, New Milford, CT 06778, USA
Telephone: +1 (860) 350 0041
Fax: +1 (860) 350 0039
Email: turpinna@turpin-distribution.com
Website: www.turpin-distribution.com

Personnel:
Lorna Summers *(Managing Director)*
Neil Castle *(Operations Director)*
Julie Barnes *(Director of HR & Business Performance)*
Richard Stroud *(Group Financial Controller)*
Alan Medd *(Head of IT)*
Robert Rooney *(VP Publisher Relations)*

Parent Company:
UK: Eurospan Group

Clients include:
France: Organisation for Economic Co-operation and Development (OECD)
Greece: Adcotec
Japan: Japanese Society for Analytical Chemistry
Netherlands: Brill Academic Publishers; Hes en de Graaf; Kluwer Law International
Switzerland: World Trade Organisation (WTO)
UK: Adcotec; Advanced Materials; The Association of Learned and Professional Society Publishers (ALPSP); The Association of Project Managers; Beech Tree Publishing; Berg Publishing; Biohealthcare; Callan Method Organisation; Dunedin Academic Press; Euromoney PLC; Eurospan Group; Fiscal Publications; Greenleaf Publishing; Hodder Education; Intellect Journals; Internet Archaeology; IP Publishing; John Harper Publishing; Journal of Transport & Economic Policy; Liverpool University Press; Modern Humanities Research Association; Pickering & Chatto; Pion Publishers; Royal College of Psychiatrists; Spiramus; The Way; White Horse Press; Zophorus Books
USA: American Association Cancer Research; American School of Classical Studies; Aspen Publishers Inc; Berghahn Journals; The Freer Gallery of Art; United Nations

Turpin Distribution is an international fulfilment and distribution company providing services to the academic, scholarly and professional publishing industry. We provide solutions for book, journal and digital distribution that includes:
• Global fulfilment and distribution
• eBook distribution
• UK and US offices with multilingual customer care advisors

• Order and renewals processing
• Billing and account collection
• Comprehensive warehouse services with global distribution for books and journals
• Full subscription management for print and online journals with e-commerce ordering
• Online sales reporting with data manipulation for analysis and customer management.

Turpin can accommodate any business model and pricing policy, enabling publishers to retain control of their products, develop collections, set multiple pricing options, use a variety of routes to market; and manage its customers successfully.

6088

VINE HOUSE DISTRIBUTION LTD
The Old Mill House, Mill Lane, Uckfield, East Sussex TN22 5AA
Telephone: 01825 767396
Fax: 01825 765649
Email: sales@vinehouseuk.co.uk
Website: www.vinehouseuk.co.uk

Personnel:
Sarah Squibb *(Managing Director)*
Pauline Gosden *(Client & Customer Services Manager)*
Julie McCarron *(Sales & Marketing Manager)*
Tara Horwood *(Research & Marketing Manager)*

Book Publishers:
Australia: Hedgebury; Inn Australia
Estonia: Unitas Foundation
Finland: Fine Publishing
France: ETAI; Vinipresse
India: Spenta Multimedia
Netherlands: Crossbill Guides; Kavino Book Publishing
New Zealand: Wooden Dragon Press
South Africa: Cheviot Publishing; Medspice
Spain: Editorial Moll
Sweden: MagDig Media
Switzerland: Valais Guides
UK: Action in Rural Sussex; Aha Press UK; Andrew Martin International; Bearmondsey Publishing; Bed & Breakfast Nationwide; Bill Hill Family Ltd; Brighton & Hove Libraries; Calder Walker Associates; Dance Books; Dove Publishing; Easy on the Eye; Fitzjames Press; Focalpoint Press; Foresight Preconception; Function Books; Grenadine Publishing; Haldane Mason; Honeyglen Publishing; Horse's Mouth Publications; The International Institute for Islamic Thought; Jaspal Jandu Photography; Julian Richer Publishing; Philip Kaplan; Leonard Hedges; Martin Holmes Rallying; J. W. McKenzie; Motor Racing Publications; Muze Media; Oval Publishing; Oxbridge Applications; Park Lane Books; Picnic Publishing; Puck Books; Red Kite Books; Royal Academy of Dance; Saxon Books; R. D. & A. S. Shepherd Partnership; Silent But Deadly Publications; Superbrands; Tiger Books; Touchstone Books; Turn End Charitable Trust; Umbria Press; Windrush Publishing; WSG Media
USA: Dance Horizons; Princeton Book Co; Wanderlearn Inc; Wine Appreciation Guild

Vine House Distribution provides a comprehensive range of services for small and medium-sized book publishers, including representation, distribution, marketing, publicity and promotion, and mail order fulfilment.

6089

WINDSOR BOOKS
31 Furze Platt Road, Maidenhead, Berkshire SL6 7NE
Telephone: 01628 770542
Fax: 01628 770546
Email: geoffcowen@windsorbooks.co.uk
Website: www.windsorbooks.co.uk

Personnel:
Geoff Cowen *(Managing Director)*
Angela Prysor-Jones *(Publicity Manager)*

Associated Companies:
UK: Meyer & Meyer Sport (UK); Star Book Sales

UK Distributor/Representative for:
Germany: Meyer & Meyer Verlag

Windsor Books provides full representation and distribution in the UK and Ireland for the English language division of the sports book publisher Meyer & Meyer. Its associated company, Star Book Sales, also provides sales representation, dis-

tribution and marketing in the UK and European markets for publishers, linked to order fulfillment by Orca Distribution Services Ltd.

6.7 REMAINDER MERCHANTS

6090

BOOKMARK REMAINDERS LTD
Rivendell, Illand, Launceston, Cornwall PL15 7LS
Telephone: 01566 782728
Fax: 01566 782059
Email: andrew.rattray@book-bargains.co.uk
Website: www.book-bargains.co.uk

Personnel:
Andrew Rattray *(Director)*
Carol Rattray *(Director)*

A wide range of genuine remainders and bargain books. Prompt payment to publishers, authors for surplus stocks.

6091

FANSHAW BOOKS LTD
Unit 7, Lysander Mews, Lysander Grove, London N19 3QP
Telephone: 020 7281 9387
Fax: 020 7561 3502
Email: info@roybloom.com
Website: www.roybloom.com

Personnel:
Adam Bloom *(Managing Director)*
Paul White *(Sales)*

Remainder company specializing in real UK publishers' books, mainly non-fiction, art, military, history, etc. It also has a number of retail stores, so customers can buy from one to 50,000 copies of a book.

6092

OCTAGON BOOKS (WHOLESALE) LTD
The Old Exchange, New Pond Road, Holmer Green, High Wycombe, Bucks HP15 6SU
Telephone: 01494 711717 (mobile: 07718 364857)
Fax: 01494 711176

Personnel:
Ron Ive *(Director)*
Bernard McDonnell *(Commercial Director)*

All types of remainders and promotional reprints.

6093

SANDPIPER BOOKS LTD
6 Battle Road, Heathfield Estate, Newton Abbot, Devon TQ12 6RY
Telephone: 01626 897090
Fax: 01626 897129
Email: enquiries@sandpiper.co.uk
Website: www.sandpiper.co.uk & www.psbooks.co.uk

Distribution:
Alton Logistics Ltd, Unit 4 Heathfield Industrial Estate, Battle Road, Heathfield, Newton Abbot, Devon TQ12 6RY
Telephone: 01626 897097
Fax: 01626 832398
Email: enquiries@altonlogistics.co.uk

Personnel:
Robert Collie *(Managing Director)*
Simon Lang *(Mail Order (Postscript))*

Primarily a mail order company of remainders and overstocks, trading with a monthly catalogue and online sales, Sandpiper also wholesales to an extensive network of trade and non-trade outlets both in the UK and overseas. We buy from major publishers as well as university presses and small trade publishers. Subjects range across the visual arts, history, philosophy, reference, travel, STM and literature, and from general interest publications to scholarly works. We have been trading for almost 35 years, and moved our offices to Devon where our distribution is in September 2011.

6.8 MAIN WHOLESALERS

6094

ARGOSY LIBRARIES LTD
Unit 12, North Park, North Road, Finglas, Dublin 11,
Republic of Ireland
Telephone: +353 (0)1 823 9500
Fax: +353 (0)1 823 9599
Email: info@argosybooks.ie
Website: www.argosybooks.ie

Personnel:
Larry MacHale *(Managing Director)*
Ronan Richmond *(Sales Manager)*
Mary Healy *(Buyer)*
Fergal Stanley *(Executive Chairman)*

Trade book wholesaler specializing in books of Irish interest
and maps and guides to Ireland. Export service available.

6095

*BERTRAMS
1 Broadland Business Park, Norwich NR7 0WF
Telephone: 0871 803 6666
Fax: 0871 803 6709 (customer services)
Email: sales@bertrams.com
Website: www.bertrams.com

Personnel:
Graeme Underhill *(Managing Director)*
Ian Hendrie *(Finance Director)*
Chris Rushby *(Sales & Marketing Director)*
Roger Miah *(Buying Director)*

Parent Company:
UK: Smiths News PLC

Bertrams is wholly owned by Smiths News PLC, the UK's
leading wholesaler of newspapers and magazines. Bertrams
celebrated 40 years of trading in 2008 and has a stockholding of over 220,000 titles from over 18,000 publishers and
can source over 5 million English language titles from both
the UK and USA. With a customer base of over 5,000 it supplies books and other related products into independent
booksellers, online retailers, chain booksellers, library suppliers and other multinationals/non-book trade outlets worldwide. Customers can access availability of stock, product
information, ordering and shipping details in real time
through www.bertrambooks.com, Bertrams' own stock
management system as well as its Customer Services department. A proactive marketing program enables publishers to
market their titles effectively and efficiently through all sales
channels, both business to business and to the end consumer. The warehouse works at 24/7 at peak season and
provides a market leading customer service.

Bertram Library Services business provides stock and selection advice for public libraries throughout the country. Bertram Publisher Services, the distribution arm of the group,
provides distribution facilities for a range of publishers and
retailers.

Bertrams is a key industry player with membership of the BA
and BIC, working towards improving the supply chain
throughout the book industry.

6096

BOOKSPEED
16 Salamander Yards, Edinburgh EH6 7DD
Telephone: 0131 467 8100
Fax: 0131 467 8008
Email: sales@bookspeed.com
Website: www.bookspeed.com

Personnel:
Kingsley Dawson *(Chairman)*
Fiona Stout *(Sales Director)*
Matthew Perren *(Operations Director)*
Lewis Dawson *(Commercial Director)*
Shona Rowan *(Marketing & Bibliographic Manager)*
Dean Rougvie *(Sales Manager)*

Parent Company:
UK: Rhodawn Ltd

The company provides a wholesale bookselling and consultancy service to non-bookshop outlets in the UK and Republic of Ireland, most of which operate in the Gift, Heritage
and Tourist sectors. For publishers we provide an easy route
to this difficult-to-reach market.

6097

BOOKWORLD WHOLESALE LTD
Unit 10, Hodfar Road, Sandy Lane Industrial Estate,
Stourport-on-Severn, Worcs DY13 9QB
Telephone: 01299 823330
Fax: 01299 829970
Email: info@bookworldws.co.uk
Website: www.bookworldws.co.uk

Personnel:
Justin Gainham *(Sales Director)*
Andrea Gainham *(Director)*

Transport, military, aviation and modelling book wholesaler
and distributor. Mail order department worldwide. Mini-
mum order one book, full trade terms given but postage
added to orders under £50 in value. Teleordering mnemonic
BK WORLD. Range of distribution whole of UK. Number of
publishers for whom we distribute is in excess of 70.

6098

GARDNERS BOOKS LTD
1 Whittle Drive, Eastbourne, East Sussex BN23 6QH
Telephone: 01323 521555
Fax: 01323 521666
Email: sales@gardners.com
Website: www.gardners.com

Personnel:
Alan Little *(Chairman)*
Jonathan Little *(Managing Director)*
Andrew Little *(Technical Director)*
Nicky Little *(Finance Director)*
Bob Jackson *(Commercial Director)*
Simon Morley *(Buying Director)*
Garry Elwood *(Sales Director)*
David O'Reilly *(Warehouse Director)*
Phil Edwards *(Senior Buying Manager)*
David Brewster *(Customer Care Manager)*

Gardners is Britain's leading independent book and DVD
wholesale distributor, offering the largest in-stock catalogue
in the UK with 500,000+ titles, books, DVD's, music CDs and
associated gift lines. Additional services include e-commerce
solutions, including 400,000+ ebooks, drop-ship fulfilment,
Gardlink EPoS System, publisher distribution services and
Print on demand

Orders can be placed 24 hours a day via its account holders'
website, Gardlink electronic ordering system, Gardcall automated telephone enquiry service, fax and EDI. Gardners
experienced customer care team is available from Monday
to Saturday between 9am and 6pm to take orders and assist
customers.

Gardners' trade website, www.gardners.com, is free to
account holders and features real-time stock figures,
invoices, backorders and promotional offers. Information on
additional services Gardners offers, such as B2B and B2C
home delivery fulfilment, marketing materials and initiatives,
including the Independent Booksellers Affiliate Programme,
can also be found on the site.

6.9 MAIN LIBRARY SUPPLIERS

6099

ROY YATES BOOKS
Smallfields Cottage, Cox Green, Rudgwick, Horsham,
West Sussex RH12 3DE
Telephone: 01403 822299
Fax: 01403 823012
Email: royyatesbooks@btconnect.com

Personnel:
Roy Yates *(Managing Director)*

Specialist supplier of children's books to schools and libraries; distributes multilingual books; distributes foreign-lan-
guage books, especially bilingual dictionaries.

6.10 BOOK CLUBS

6100

BIBLIOPHILE BOOKS
Unit 5 Datapoint Business Centre, 6 South Crescent,
London E16 4TL
Telephone: 020 7474 2474
Fax: 020 7474 8589
Email: orders@bibliophilebooks.com
Website: www.bibliophilebooks.com

Personnel:
Anne Quigley *(Director)*
Jackie McDaid *(General Manager)*
Martyn Daniels *(Director)*
Steven Lee *(Distribution)*

Produces 10 catalogues a year, offering books at bargain
prices to private buyers.

Range: general, eg biography, history, travel, handicrafts,
humour, literature.

6101

LETTERBOX LIBRARY
Unit 151 Stratford Wkshops, Burford Road, Stratford,
London E15 2SP
Telephone: 020 7503 4801
Fax: 020 7503 4800
Email: info@letterboxlibrary.com
Website: www.letterboxlibrary.com

Personnel:
Kerry Mason *(Contact)*
Fen Coles *(Contact)*

Letterbox Library is a children's bookseller specializing in children's books which celebrate inclusion, equality and diver-
sity. Book can be bought via an annual catalogue, highlights
leaflets and website. Books are multicultural and non-sexist
and also show groups of people traditionally under-repre-
sented in children's books, e.g. different faith groups, dis-
abled children, refugees. All books are approved by an independent team of volunteer reviewers. Letterbox Library also
provides book displays for schools and libraries, attends
exhibitions and administers the Little Rebels Children's Book
Award for radical children's fiction on behalf of the ARB.

Subscription is £5 a year and entitles members to discounts.
Non-members can buy books at the retail price. Letterbox
Library is a not-for-profit social enterprise.

6102

POETRY BOOK SOCIETY
Dutch House, 307–308 High Holborn, London WC1V 7LL
Telephone: 020 7831 7468
Fax: 020 7833 5990
Email: info@poetrybooks.co.uk
Website: www.poetrybooks.co.uk &
www.poetrybookshoponline.com

Personnel:
Chris Holifield *(Director)*

Charity, membership organization and mail order book club
promoting contemporary poetry titles to an international
readership. Quarterly publication of *Bulletin* magazine new
poetry titles selected by our Poet Selectors. The Society also
acts as distributor for The Poetry Archive CDs, and runs and
awards the annual T. S. Eliot Prize for Poetry, with its Shad-
owing and Reading Group schemes.

Membership from £16 p.a., full membership with the quarterly Choice is £10.

Also runs www.poetrybookshoponline.com, selling 90,000
poetry titles.

6.11 LITERARY & TRADE EVENTS

6103

BOOKSELLERS ASSOCIATION ANNUAL CONFERENCE
6 Bell Yard, London WC2A 2JR
Telephone: 020 7421 4640
Fax: 020 7421 4641
Email: mail@booksellers.org.uk
Website: www.booksellers.org.uk

Personnel:
Tim Godfray *(Chief Executive)*
Naomi Gane *(Conference Organizer)*
Alan Staton *(Head of Marketing & Communications)*
Meryl Halls *(Head of Membership Services)*

Major UK book trade event. The Booksellers Association Annual Conference provides an opportunity for all those working in the book trade to meet and discuss the issues facing them. Details from: above address.

6104

THE TIMES CHELTENHAM LITERATURE FESTIVAL
Cheltenham Festivals Ltd, 109 Bath Road, Cheltenham, Glos GL53 7LS
Telephone: 01242 537282
Fax: 01242 256457
Email: rose.stuart@cheltenhamfestivals.com
Website: www.cheltenhamfestivals.com

Personnel:
Donna Renney *(Chief Executive)*
Jane Furze *(Festival Director)*
Sarah Smyth *(Artistic Director)*

Annual in October. Promoted by Cheltenham Festivals Ltd. Performances, poetry readings, talks and discussions by literary personalities. Includes Book It! Festival for Children, and Write Away creative writing workshops.

Details from: Artistic Director: Sarah Smyth or Festival Director: Jane Furze.

6105

CHILDREN'S BOOK WEEK
Booktrust, Book House, 45 East Hill, Wandsworth, London SW18 2QZ
Telephone: 020 8516 2976
Fax: 020 8516 2992
Email: cbw@booktrust.org.uk
Website: www.booktrust.org.uk

Personnel:
HRH The Duchess of Cornwall *(Patron)*
Viv Bird *(Chief Executive)*
Alistair Burtenshaw *(Chair of Board)*

Children's Book Week is a national celebration of reading for pleasure for children of primary school age, which takes place each year in the first full week of October. During the week, a range of book-related events and activities take place in schools and libraries across England.

6106

CIANA LTD
Rockholt, Ellimore Road, Lustleigh, Newton Abbot TQ13 9TF
Telephone: 01626 897106
Email: enquiries@ciana.co.uk
Website: www.ciana.co.uk

Personnel:
Robert Collie *(Director)*
Sarah Weedon *(Director)*

Organizers of two annual trade fairs for the remainder, overstock and promotional book market. Over 100,000 discounted books, stationery items, CDs and DVDs.

The September Fair is held in Islington, London. The January Fair is in the Barbican in the City of London.

6107

EDINBURGH INTERNATIONAL BOOK FESTIVAL
5A Charlotte Square, Edinburgh EH2 4DR
Telephone: 0131 718 5666
Email: admin@edbookfest.co.uk
Website: www.edbookfest.co.uk

Personnel:
Nick Barley *(Director)*
Janet Smyth *(Children & Education Programme Director)*
Sarah Loveday *(Administrative Director)*
Amanda Barry *(Head of Marketing & PR)*
Sadie McKinlay *(Head of Sponsorship & Development)*
James Shaw *(Head of Booksales & Retail)*

The Edinburgh International Book Festival is a public celebration of the written word and takes place every August. Over 800 events feature writers from across the globe, bringing authors together with their readers to talk about books, discuss ideas and share the latest thinking on a range of subjects from the environment to poetry.

The festival runs its own independent book sales operation on the site – a tented village in Edinburgh's Charlotte Square Gardens – offering three large retail outlets, including a bookshop dedicated to children's books.

6108

FRANKFURT BOOK FAIR
Braubachstr. 16, 60311 Frankfurt am Main, Germany
Telephone: +49 (0)69 2102 0
Fax: +49 (0)69 2102 227 & 277
Email: info@book-fair.com
Website: www.book-fair.com

Personnel:
Juergen Boos *(Chief Executive Officer)*
Katja Böhne *(Director, Marketing & Communication)*

Parent Company:
Germany: Börsenverein des Deutschen Buchhandels

The Frankfurt Book Fair is the biggest book and media fair in the world – with around 7300 exhibitors from around 100 countries. It also organizes the participation of German publishers at around 20 international book fairs. It maintains the most visited website worldwide for the publishing industry and its directory of decision-makers in the book and media industries features around 40,000 contacts. The Frankfurt Academy – the new conference brand of the Frankfurt Book Fair in co-operation with the German Publishers & Booksellers Association – organizes international conferences and trade events all year long. The Frankfurt Book Fair is a subsidiary of the German Publishers & Booksellers Association.

6109

THE LONDON BOOK FAIR
Gateway House, 28 The Quadrant, Richmond, Surrey TW9 1DN
Telephone: 020 8271 2124
Email: lbf.helpline@reedexpo.co.uk
Website: www.londonbookfair.co.uk

Personnel:
Jacks Thomas *(Director)*
Sam D'Elia *(Sales Coordinator)*

Parent Company:
UK: Reed Exhibitions

The London Book Fair is the global marketplace for rights negotiation and the sale and distribution of content across print, audio, TV, film and digital channels. Taking place every spring in the world's premier publishing and cultural capital, it is a unique opportunity to explore, understand and capitalize on the innovations shaping the publishing world of the future. The London Book Fair brings you direct access to customers, content and emerging markets.

The London Book Fair 2014, the 43rd Fair, will take place from Tuesday 8 to Thursday 10 April 2014, at Earls Court, London.

6110

WORLD BOOK DAY
c/o Booksellers' Association, 6 Bell Yard, London WC2A 2JR
Telephone: 020 7421 4640

Email: kirsten.grant@btinternet.com
Website: www.worldbookday.com

Personnel:
Kirsten Grant *(Director, World Book Day)*

One of the UK's biggest celebrations of books and reading, held on the first Thursday in March. It is a partnership of publishers, booksellers and interested parties who work together to promote books and reading for the personal enrichment and enjoyment of all. One of the main aims of World Book Day is to encourage children to explore the pleasures of reading by providing them with the opportunity to have a book of their own. Thanks to the generosity of National Book Tokens and participating booksellers, school-children are entitled to receive a World Book Day £1 book token, which can be exchanged for one of the specially published £1 books or is redeemable against a book or audiobook of their choice.

6.12 PUBLISHING REFERENCE BOOKS & PERIODICALS

6111

BOOKS FOR KEEPS
Unit 1, Brampton Park Road, London N22 6BG
Telephone: 020 8889 1292
Email: enquiries@booksforkeeps.co.uk
Website: www.booksforkeeps.co.uk

Personnel:
Andrea Reece *(Managing Director)*

ISSN: 0143-909X

Available to all via website.

Reviews all children's books and carries articles/features about authors, publishing, education, etc. Main readership – teachers, librarians and parents.

6112

THE BOOKSELLER
Ground Floor, Crowne House, 56-58 Southwark Street, London SE1 1UN
Telephone: 020 3358 0387
Fax: 020 7836 4081
Email: firstname.surname@bookseller.co.uk
Website: www.theBookseller.com

Personnel:
Nigel Roby *(Managing Director)*
Nicola Chin *(Advertising Manager)*
Samantha Missingham *(Head of Audience Marketing)*
Neill Denny *(Editor-in-Chief)*
Marzia Ghiselli *(Business Development Director)*

Parent Company:
UK: Bookseller Media Group Ltd

ISSN: 0006-7539

Weekly £4.40. Annual subscription: £177 (UK: public libraries), £186 (UK: all other businesses), £192 (Europe – airmail), £264 (rest of world – airmail).

The weekly newspaper of the book trade, offering in the course of a year over 7000 pages of news, analysis, features, letters, advertising and lists of books published in the UK. Major national and international events reported, regular authoritative articles on matters of trade, special features, book features and rights, stock market, legal and financial pages. Twice a year a six-month special issue of over 700 pages provides the best reference source for British publishers' publishing plans. Regular supplements in specialist areas.

6113

BRITISH COPYRIGHT COUNCIL
Copyright House, 29–33 Berners Street, London W1T 3AB
Telephone: 01986 788122
Email: info@britishcopyright.org
Website: www.britishcopyright.org

The BCC was founded in 1965 and incorporated in 2007. It is a national consultative and advisory body representing those who create, hold interests in or manage rights in literary, dramatic, musical and artistic works, films, sound recordings, broadcasts and other material in which there are rights of copyright or related rights; and those who perform such works.

6114

PUBLISHING, BOOKS & READING IN SUB-SAHARAN AFRICA: A CRITICAL BIBLIOGRAPHY
Hans Zell Publishing, Glais Bheinn, Lochcarron, Ross-shire IV54 8YB
Telephone: 01520 722951
Email: hanszell@hanszell.co.uk
Website: www.hanszell.co.uk/pbrssa/index.shtml

Personnel:
Hans Zell (Editor & Publisher)

ISBN: 978 0 9541029 5 1

Published October 2008, 762 pp, cased, £130/€195/$260. Print and online (online access bundled with print). Online only £65/€97.50/$130.

This much acclaimed reference resource charts the growth of publishing and book development in the countries of Africa south of the Sahara, as well as containing a very large number of entries on many other topics as they relate to books and reading in Africa, including digital media and electronic publishing.

To provide maximum currency the online version continues to be frequently updated and expanded with numerous new entries – all with abstracts, or critically annotated – of books, articles, studies, reports, and Internet documents that have been published since the cut-off date of the 2008 print edition, thus offering a continuing resource in the field. Currently containing almost 2900 fully annotated records, it is now the most comprehensive database, and ongoing analysis, of the state of publishing and the book sector in Africa. Select blog postings, as well as video recordings and radio/TV broadcasts are now also included on a regular basis. Additionally, frequent updates are made to the extensive listings of organizations and African book professional associations, as well as agencies, networks, NGO's, and book charities supporting the book and information sector in Africa.

6115

SHEPPARD'S WORLD
Richard Joseph Publishers Ltd, PO Box 15, Torrington, Devon EX38 8ZJ
Telephone: 01805 625750
Email: office@sheppardsworld.com
Website: www.sheppardsworld.com

Personnel:
Richard Joseph (Managing Director)

Sheppard's World is a central reference source for businesses in the secondhand and antiquarian book trades, and includes dealers in antique maps, prints and ephemera. Subscribers can search on line (and in printed directories as and when published) covering all the details previously found in our printed directories – full contact details, opening hours, size of stock, major subjects stocked, credit cards accepted, and membership of trade associations. Details are posted to www.sheppardsworld.co.uk

Dealers, collectors and members of the trade can receive our free trade newsletter Sheppard's Confidential, which carries the latest trade news, news about forthcoming fairs and auctions – and reviews of fairs and auctions. The website www.sheppardsconfidential.com includes dealers' catalogues, calendar of fairs and auctions, and books wanted.

6116

THE TIMES LITERARY SUPPLEMENT
3 Thomas More Square, London E98 1BS
Telephone: 020 7782 5000
Fax: 020 7782 4966
Email: editor@the-tls.co.uk
Website: www.the-tls.co.uk

Personnel:
Sir Peter Stothard (Editor)

Alan Jenkins (Deputy Editor)
Robert Potts (Managing Editor)

The TLS is a weekly literary publication, featuring reviews by leading authorities on up to 3000 books a year, covering literature and language, history, politics, philosophy, the arts and music, social studies, economics, natural history and many other subjects. It reviews exhibitions and performing arts; features new writing and research on a wide range of topics in the 'Commentary' section; publishes new poetry; and has a letters page, which is the principal forum for literary debate. It is essential reading for anyone with a passion for literature and the arts.

6117

WRITERS' FORUM
[owned by Select Publisher Services Ltd]
PO Box 6337, Bournemouth BH1 9EH
Telephone: 01202 586848
Website: www.selectps.com & www.writers-forum.com

Advertisement & PR Manager:
Wendy Kearns, 6 Wallace Avenue, Exeter EX4 8DB
Telephone: 01392 466099
Email: advertising@writers-forum.com

Personnel:
Tim Harris (Publisher)
Carl Styants (Editor)
Wendy Kearns (Advertising & PR Manager)
Chris Wigg (Subscriptions Manager)

Parent Company:
UK: Select Publisher Services

Associated Companies:
UK: The Flower Press; Tailormade Publishing

12 issues a year. Subscription: UK £38; Europe £49; Rest of World £56.

Writers' Forum is a major resource for writers of books, short stories, freelance articles and poetry, covering the who, why, where, what and how on the craft and business of writing; it runs monthly story and poetry competitions featuring cash prizes and publication of the winning entries in the magazine.

The editor welcomes queries by email for articles on any aspect of the craft and business of writing. Length: by arrangement. Payment: by arrangement. Founded 1993.

6.13 TRAINING

6118

CITY UNIVERSITY LONDON
Department of Creative Practice and Enterprise, Northampton Square, London EC1V 0HB
Telephone: 020 7040 8266
Fax: 020 7040 8594
Email: maryann.kernan.1@city.ac.uk
Website: http://www.city.ac.uk/courses/postgraduate/publishing-studies

Personnel:
Mary Ann Kernan (Programme Director)
Dr Casey Brienza (Lecturer in Publishing and Digital Media)
Max Adam (Visiting Lecturer)
Stephen Mesquita (Visiting Lecturer)
Brenda Stones (Visiting Lecturer)

The City MA publishing programme offers two Master's degrees, an MA in Publishing Studies and an MA in International Publishing Studies, both of which can be studied full time or part time in the heart of London. They aim to both deliver excellent Masters-level analytical education and enhance the students' career prospects within the industry.

The MAs offer eight taught modules (including the choice of a 5–week placement or an International Publishing Case Study module) and a dissertation. Modules are led by City's top-rated research staff, and the teaching is actively supported by a range of lecturers and visitors, who share experience from across the industry, including project supporters, industry visits and presentations, and dissertation support. The programmes have a strong track record of student satisfaction, and of supporting our graduates to gain transferable publishing skills which support them to gain

employment in the industry. Our graduates have also been awarded the UK MA dissertation prize more often than any other programme.

In addition to gaining informal publishing placements in London through the teaching year, students who opt for the MA in International Publishing are encouraged to work directly with publishers in other countries to develop their market awareness and enhance their skills in business analysis.

The MSc in Electronic Publishing, run within City's School of Informatics, offers a practical introduction to digital media, information management and multi-media production. Please contact Dr Neil Thurman in the Department of Journalism: 020 7040 8222 or n.j.thurman@city.ac.uk.

6119

GERMAN TUITION – BARBARA CLASSEN
255 Temple Chambers, 3–7 Temple Avenue, London EC4Y 0DT
Telephone: 020 7583 9337
Email: barbara@germantuition.com
Website: www.germantuition.com

Personnel:
Barbara Classen (Director/Tutor)
Nicole Nagel (Co-Tutor)
Marina de Quay (Co-Tutor)
Itamar Groisman (Co-Tutor)
Matina Grebener (Co-Tutor)
Andrea Reinacher (Co-Tutor)
Theresa Weisensee (Co-Tutor)

Associated Companies:
Germany: Deutsch in Freiburg

The company offers lively German tuition at all levels and specializes in German for the book trade. Students can choose between one-to-one tuition or small groups of 4–6. German Tuition also offers short-term tailor-made intensive courses.

Tutors are professional, experienced native speakers and offer free consultations with trial lesson. Students may work towards one of many recognized exams. Clients include publishers, booksellers, journalists and other professionals. Classes are held in the central London German Tuition office or in client's office/home 7 days a week.

German Tuition London has a small branch in Freiburg, Germany, offering tailor-made German language holidays and Business German courses for the book trade, usually over one week.

6120

MARKETABILITY (UK) LTD
12 Sandy Lane, Teddington, Middx TW11 0DR
Telephone: 020 8977 2741
Email: rachel@marketability.info
Website: www.marketability.info

Personnel:
Rachel Maund (Director)

Marketability provides practical training to publishers, both through its small-group open workshop programme and through tailored in-house training. These flexible courses can be devised to cover a wide range of publishing issues. All tutors are actively working for publishers in the areas in which they are training. Our clients represent all areas of publishing, from large academic, STM and university presses, to small institutes, to large and small trade publishers. We devise and deliver training programmes for publishers' associations internationally as well as in the UK. (See our client list in our other entry under section 6.5 of this directory for more details.)

The open course programme includes: academic marketing, e-marketing, social media marketing, email marketing, copywriting, SEO marketing, schools marketing, marketing planning, marketing digital products, introduction to marketing in publishing, publicity, essential editorial skills, and profitable commissioning. There are numerous in-house course options, including market research, direct mail, working with authors, grammar and proofreading.

Also provides marketing support and consultancy. See separate entry under 6.5 Sales and Marketing Services.

6121

OXFORD INTERNATIONAL CENTRE FOR PUBLISHING STUDIES

Oxford Brookes University, Buckley Building, Gipsy Lane, Headington, Oxford OX3 0BP
Telephone: 01865 484967
Fax: 01865 484082
Email: angus.phillips@brookes.ac.uk
Website: http://publishing.brookes.ac.uk/

Personnel:
Angus Phillips (Director)

The Oxford International Centre for Publishing Studies, at Oxford Brookes University, is renowned for its degree programmes at both undergraduate and postgraduate level. Our students come from all over the world to study for both the BA and MA in Publishing in the largest department in Europe. Ranked first in the 2013 Sunday Times University Guide league table, Publishing at Oxford Brookes is the market leader.

The Centre is also active in the areas of research, consultancy and professional development. It has excellent contacts throughout the industry and works closely with industry and other organizations such as the Publishers Association, Arts Council, and the London Book Fair.

Staff have published widely on the history and future of publishing. Its website has podcasts, the latest news about the Centre, and listings of job vacancies and work experience opportunities.

6122

THE PUBLISHING TRAINING CENTRE

45 East Hill, Wandsworth, London SW18 2QZ
Telephone: 020 8874 2718
Fax: 020 8870 8985
Email: publishing.training@bookhouse.co.uk
Website: www.train4publishing.co.uk

Personnel:
Peter McKay (Chief Executive)
Becky Hunter (Course Manager)
Edelweiss Arnold (Marketing Manager)

The Publishing Training Centre was set up in 1979 as an educational charity for book and journal publishers.

It offers over 40 different courses, most of which are run several times a year. Courses are between one and four days long and cover a wide range of publishing and management skills.

Courses are held at The Publishing Training Centre's London premises, and other regional centres.

In addition, The Publishing Training Centre offers:
• in-company courses in the UK and overseas;
• distance learning courses in proofreading, editing, editorial project management, grammar, freelancing;
• consultancy service;
• training needs analysis;
• books.

The Publishing Training Centre is responsible for the development and updating of the industry-agreed standards for each job function specific to publishing.

6123

STIRLING CENTRE FOR INTERNATIONAL PUBLISHING & COMMUNICATION

School of Arts and Humanities, Pathfoot Building, University of Stirling, Stirling FK9 4LA
Telephone: 01786 467510
Fax: 01786 466210
Email: alison.scott@stir.ac.uk
Website: www.publishing.stir.ac.uk

Personnel:
Jane Gregory (Owner)
Claire Morris (Rights Manager)
Mary Jones (Submissions Editor)
Stephanie Glencross (Editor)

The Stirling Centre for International Publishing and Communication at the University of Stirling was established in 1982, and has since developed a global reputation for its postgraduate degrees in publishing, its research activities, and its industry links. Focusing on book, magazine, journal and digital publishing, the Centre trains the publishers of the future, provides opportunities for those currently working in the industry to reflect on their professional practice and, through its research, critically analyses the past, present and future of publishing.

The Centre offers an Mlitt in Publishing Studies and an MRes in Publishing Studies (one year full time or two years part time), as well as facilities for research at PhD level.

7   Appendices

7.1   PUBLISHERS CLASSIFIED BY FIELDS OF ACTIVITY

The categories shown below are those in which the publishers listed have declared their interest. The list is intended to be neither exclusive nor comprehensive.

Packagers are shown in *italic* print.

ACADEMIC & SCHOLARLY

Acumen Publishing Ltd
Adam Matthew Digital Ltd
Alban Books Ltd
Alpha Science International Ltd
American Psychiatric Publishing
Amolibros
Anglo-Saxon Books
Anshan Ltd
Anthem Press
Arena Books (Publishers)
Ashgate Publishing Ltd
Association for Learning Technology
Association for Scottish Literary Studies
Aurora Metro Publications Ltd
Authentic Media
Authorhouse UK LLC
Ayebia Clarke Publishing Ltd
Berghahn Books
Joseph Biddulph Publisher
Bloomsbury Academic & Professional
Blue Ocean Publishing
Blueberry Press Ltd
Bodleian Library Publishing
Borthwick Publications
Bowker Market Research (formerly BML)
Bowker (UK) Ltd
Boydell & Brewer Ltd
British Association for Adoption & Fostering
British Library
British Museum Press
CABI
Calypso Publications
Cambridge Publishing Management Ltd
Cambridge University Press
Capuchin Classics
Carnegie Publishing Ltd
Cengage Learning EMEA Ltd
Centre for Economic Policy Research
Centre for Policy on Ageing
CfBT Education Trust
Chalksoft
Channel View Publications Ltd
Chartered Institute of Personnel & Development
Chartridge Books Oxford
Christian Education
James Clarke & Co

Clear Answer Medical Publishing Ltd
Cois Life
Columba
Commonwealth Secretariat
Cork University Press
Countyvise Ltd
Crown House Publishing Ltd
Dance Books Ltd
The Davenant Press
Richard Dennis Publications
Denor Press Ltd
J. M. Dent
Ashley Drake Publishing Ltd
Dunedin Academic Press
Edinburgh University Press
Edward Elgar Publishing Ltd
Elsevier Ltd
Encyclopaedia Britannica (UK) Ltd
Energy Institute
English Heritage
Equinox Publishing Ltd
The Erskine Press
Ethics International Press Ltd
Everyman's Library
A. & A. Farmar
Filament Publishing Ltd
First & Best in Education
Five Leaves Publications
Four Courts Press
Friends of the Earth
Geography Publications
The Geological Society
Gill & Macmillan
Gracewing Publishing
Greenleaf Publishing
Guildhall Press
John Harper Publishing Ltd
HarperCollins Publishers Ltd
Hart McLeod Ltd
Hart Publishing
Harvard University Press
Hawthorn Press
Roger Heavens
Helion & Co Ltd
Historical Publications Ltd
Hobnob Press
Hodder Education
Hodder Gibson
Holo Books
Human Kinetics Europe Ltd
C. Hurst & Co (Publishers) Ltd
Hymns Ancient & Modern Ltd
Hypatia Publications
Imperial College Press
Imprint Academic Ltd
Institute for Employment Studies
Institute of Acoustics
Institute of Education Press
Institute of Employment Rights
Institution of Engineering and Technology (IET)
Intellect Ltd
Inter-Varsity Press
International Medical Press

Irish Academic Press
The Islamic Texts Society
Ithaca Press
IWA Publishing
James & James (Publishers) Ltd
Janus Publishing Co Ltd
Jarndyce Booksellers
S. Karger AG
Kew Publishing
Jessica Kingsley Publishers
Sean Kingston Publishing
Kogan Page Ltd
Kube Publishing Ltd
Peter Lang Ltd
Learning Matters
The Lilliput Press Ltd
The Littman Library of Jewish Civilization
Liverpool University Press
Londubh Books
Lund Humphries
The Lutterworth Press
McGraw-Hill Education
Manchester University Press
Maney Publishing
Melisende UK Ltd
Mercier Press Ltd
The Merlin Press Ltd
Merton Priory Press Ltd
Microform Academic Publishers
The MIT Press Ltd
Myriad Editions
The National Academies Press
National Children's Bureau
National Galleries of Scotland
National Housing Federation
National Portrait Gallery Publications
National Records of Scotland
The National Trust
Natural History Museum Publishing
NMS Enterprises Limited - Publishing
Northcote House Publishers Ltd
W. W. Norton & Company Ltd
Oak Tree Press
Open University Worldwide
Optimus Education
Optimus Professional Publishing
Orpen Press
Oxfam Publishing
Oxford University Press
Packard Publishing Ltd
Pagoda Tree Press
Palgrave Macmillan
Paragon Publishing
Paupers' Press
PCCS Books Ltd
Penguin Random House UK Ltd
Phaidon Press Ltd
Pickering & Chatto (Publishers) Ltd
Policy Press
PP Publishing
Princeton University Press

The Professional and Higher Partnership Ltd
ProQuest
The Radcliffe Press
Round Hall
Joseph Rowntree Foundation
Royal Collection Trust
Royal College of General Practitioners
The Royal College of Psychiatrists
Royal Geographical Society
Royal Irish Academy
Royal Society of Chemistry
Saint Albert's Press
St Jerome Publishing Ltd
Sandstone Press Ltd
Saqi Books
Schott Music Ltd
Scion Publishing Ltd
Scottish Text Society
Shepheard-Walwyn (Publishers) Ltd
Shire Publications Ltd
Sigel Press
Slightly Foxed
Smith Settle Printing & Bookbinding Ltd
Colin Smythe Ltd
Social Affairs Unit
The Society for Promoting Christian Knowledge (SPCK)
The Society of Metaphysicians Ltd
Souvenir Press Ltd
Stainer & Bell Ltd
Sussex Academic Press
The Swedenborg Society
Symposium Publications Literary & Art
Tate Publishing
I. B. Tauris & Co Ltd
Taylor & Francis
tfm publishing Ltd
Thames & Hudson Ltd
Trentham Books
Troubador Publishing Ltd
UCAS
University College of Dublin Press
University of Exeter Press
University of Hertfordshire Press
University of Ottawa Press
University of Toronto Press
University of Wales Press
V&A Publishing
Vallentine Mitchell Publishers
Veritas Publications
Warburg Institute
Waterside Press
Paul Watkins Publishing
Whiting & Birch Ltd
Whittles Publishing
Wiley
Philip Wilson Publishers
WIT Press
Yale University Press London
Zed Books Ltd

ACCOUNTANCY & TAXATION

Bloomsbury Academic & Professional
Cengage Learning EMEA Ltd
The Chartered Institute of Public Finance & Accountancy
Filament Publishing Ltd
Gower Publishing Co Ltd
Harriman House
HB Publications
Hodder Education
In Easy Steps Limited
Jordan Publishing Ltd
Kogan Page Ltd
McGraw-Hill Education
Nelson Thornes Ltd
Oak Tree Press
Orpen Press
Palgrave Macmillan
PP Publishing
ProQuest
Round Hall
Sigel Press
Thorogood Publishing Ltd
Trog Associates Ltd
Troubador Publishing Ltd
Which? Ltd
Wiley

AGRICULTURE

Alpha Science International Ltd
CABI
Clairview Books Ltd
The Crowood Press Ltd
Eco-logic Books
Edward Elgar Publishing Ltd
Elsevier Ltd
Food Trade Press Ltd
The National Academies Press
The National Trust
Oxfam Publishing
Packard Publishing Ltd
ProQuest
Smith Settle Printing & Bookbinding Ltd
Wiley

ANIMAL CARE & BREEDING

J. A. Allen
Alpha Science International Ltd
CABI
Calypso Publications
Capall Bann Publishing Ltd
Carroll & Brown Ltd
Chalksoft
The Crowood Press Ltd
D & N Publishing
Findhorn Press Ltd
Robert Hale Ltd
HarperCollins Publishers Ltd
Haynes Publishing
How To Books Ltd
Lavender and White Publishing

The National Academies Press
Octopus Publishing Group
Quantum Publishing
Quiller Publishing Ltd
Roundhouse Publishing Ltd
Souvenir Press Ltd
Toucan Books Ltd
Merlin Unwin Books Ltd
Veloce Publishing Ltd
Whittet Books Ltd
Wiley

ANTIQUES & COLLECTING

Antique Collectors' Club Ltd
Bene Factum Publishing Ltd
BLA Publishing Ltd
Bodleian Library Publishing
Bowker Market Research
 (formerly BML)
British Museum Press
The Crowood Press Ltd
D & N Publishing
Richard Dennis Publications
W. Foulsham & Co Ltd
Robert Hale Ltd
HarperCollins Publishers Ltd
How To Books Ltd
Icon Books Ltd.
Lund Humphries
The Lutterworth Press
Melisende UK Ltd
Milestone Publications
Miller's
Mitchell Beazley
The National Trust
NMS Enterprises Limited -
 Publishing
Octopus Publishing Group
The Orion Publishing Group Ltd
Penguin Random House UK Ltd
Quantum Publishing
Quiller Publishing Ltd
Royal Collection Trust
Scala Arts & Heritage Publishers
 Ltd
Shire Publications Ltd
Souvenir Press Ltd
Thames & Hudson Ltd
Third Millennium Publishing Ltd
Unicorn Press Ltd
V&A Publishing
Philip Wilson Publishers

ARCHAEOLOGY

Acumen Publishing Ltd
Archaeopress Ltd
The Armchair Traveller at the
 bookHaus Ltd
Batsford
Bloomsbury Academic &
 Professional
Bloomsbury Publishing PLC
Borthwick Publications
Bowker Market Research
 (formerly BML)
Boydell & Brewer Ltd
British Museum Press
*Cambridge Publishing
 Management Ltd*
Cambridge University Press
Capall Bann Publishing Ltd
Capuchin Classics
Carnegie Publishing Ltd
Caxton Publishing Group Ltd
Colour Heroes Ltd
Cork University Press
Cornwall Editions Ltd
Council for British Archaeology
The Davenant Press
The Dovecote Press
English Heritage
Equinox Publishing Ltd
Ex Libris Press
Four Courts Press
Geography Publications
Gibson Square
Heart of Albion Press
Hobnob Press
Holo Books
The King's England Press

Sean Kingston Publishing
Logaston Press
Maney Publishing
Melisende UK Ltd
Merton Priory Press Ltd
Mitchell Beazley
The National Trust
NMS Enterprises Limited -
 Publishing
North York Moors National Park
 Authority
The Orion Publishing Group Ltd
Paragon Publishing
Penguin Random House UK Ltd
Prestel Publishing Ltd
Roundhouse Publishing Ltd
Royal Irish Academy
Shire Publications Ltd
Smith Settle Printing &
 Bookbinding Ltd
Souvenir Press Ltd
Stacey Publishing Limited
Stobart Davies Ltd
Sussex Academic Press
I. B. Tauris & Co Ltd
Taylor & Francis
Thames & Hudson Ltd
Twelveheads Press
Tyne Bridge Publishing
University of Exeter Press
University of Wales Press
Warburg Institute
Wiley
Yale University Press London

ARCHITECTURE & DESIGN

Antique Collectors' Club Ltd
Architectural Association
 Publications
Ashgate Publishing Ltd
Batsford
Joseph Biddulph Publisher
Black Dog Publishing Ltd
Bloomsbury Academic &
 Professional
Bloomsbury Publishing PLC
Bodleian Library Publishing
Bowker Market Research
 (formerly BML)
Boydell & Brewer Ltd
*Cambridge Publishing
 Management Ltd*
Cambridge University Press
Colour Heroes Ltd
Conran Octopus
Cork University Press
Countryside Books
The Crowood Press Ltd
Richard Dennis Publications
Gerald Duckworth & Co Ltd
Eco-logic Books
English Heritage
Fircone Books Ltd
Garnet Publishing Ltd
Gibson Square
Gower Publishing Co Ltd
Gracewing Publishing
Graffeg Limited
*Graham-Cameron Publishing &
 Illustration*
HarperCollins Publishers Ltd
Haynes Publishing
Hayward Publishing
Historical Publications Ltd
John Hunt Publishing Ltd
The Ilex Press Ltd
Intellect Ltd
Ithaca Press
Laurence King Publishing Ltd
Dewi Lewis Publishing
Liberties Press
The Lilliput Press Ltd
Liverpool University Press
Logaston Press
Lund Humphries
The Lutterworth Press
McGraw-Hill Education
Manchester University Press
Maney Publishing
Melisende UK Ltd
Merrell Publishers Ltd

The MIT Press Ltd
Mitchell Beazley
National Galleries of Scotland
The National Trust
NMS Enterprises Limited -
 Publishing
W. W. Norton & Company Ltd
The O'Brien Press Ltd
Octopus Publishing Group
Open University Worldwide
Oxford University Press
Packard Publishing Ltd
Palazzo Editions Ltd
Papadakis Publisher
Paragon Publishing
Penguin Random House UK Ltd
Phaidon Press Ltd
Prestel Publishing Ltd
ProQuest
Quadrille Publishing Ltd
Quantum Publishing
Redcliffe Press Ltd
RotoVision SA
Roundhouse Publishing Ltd
Joseph Rowntree Foundation
Royal Collection Trust
Sansom & Co Ltd
Saqi Books
Scala Arts & Heritage Publishers
 Ltd
Sheldrake Press
Shire Publications Ltd
Tate Publishing
I. B. Tauris & Co Ltd
Taylor & Francis
teNeues Publishing UK Ltd
Thames & Hudson Ltd
Toucan Books Ltd
Unicorn Press Ltd
V&A Publishing
Warburg Institute
Paul Watkins Publishing
Whittles Publishing
Wiley
Philip Wilson Publishers
WIT Press
Worth Press Ltd
Yale University Press London

ATLASES & MAPS

AA Publishing
Ian Allan Publishing Ltd
Amber Books Ltd
Anthem Press
The Belmont Press
Bowker Market Research
 (formerly BML)
Bradwell Books
British Geological Survey
Carel Press Ltd
Caxton Publishing Group Ltd
Collins Geo
Cork University Press
Crimson Publishing
G. L. Crowther
Discovery Walking Guides Ltd
The Geographical Association
Geography Publications
Alan Godfrey Maps
HarperCollins Publishers Ltd
Harvey Map Services Ltd
Haynes Publishing
Hodder Education
The Ilex Press Ltd
Instant-Books UK Ltd
Macmillan Science and Education
Maney Publishing
Michelin Travel Partner
Myriad Editions
Octopus Publishing Group
Pagoda Tree Press
Penguin Random House UK Ltd
Philip's
Quantum Publishing
Roundhouse Publishing Ltd
Royal Irish Academy
Shire Publications Ltd
Tarquin Publications
Toucan Books Ltd
Waverley Books
Wiley

AUDIO BOOKS

Ashgrove Publishing
AudioGO Ltd
Barefoot Books
John Blake Publishing Ltd
Bowker Market Research
 (formerly BML)
Canongate Books
Cois Life
Creative Content Ltd
Filament Publishing Ltd
Gatehouse Media Ltd
H & S Media
Hachette Children's Books
HarperCollins Publishers Ltd
Headline Book Publishing Ltd
Hodder Education
Hodder & Stoughton
ISIS Publishing Ltd
Kube Publishing Ltd
Little, Brown Book Group
Little People Books
Macmillan Children's Books Ltd
Magna Large Print Books
The Orion Publishing Group Ltd
Pan Macmillan
Penguin Random House UK Ltd
Porter House of Publishing Ltd
Ransom Publishing Ltd
Sigel Press
Simon & Schuster (UK) Ltd
Rudolf Steiner Press Ltd
Stillwater Publishing Ltd
Summersdale Publishers Ltd
Thorogood Publishing Ltd
Topical Resources
Transworld Publishers Ltd

AVIATION

Air-Britain (Historians) Ltd
Ian Allan Publishing Ltd
Amber Books Ltd
Ashgate Publishing Ltd
Atlantic Books
Bene Factum Publishing Ltd
BLA Publishing Ltd
Bridge Books
Countryside Books
Crécy Publishing Ltd
The Crowood Press Ltd
D & N Publishing
Energy Institute
Greenhill Books / Lionel Leventhal
 Ltd
Grub Street
Haynes Publishing
McGraw-Hill Education
The Nostalgia Collection
Osprey Publishing Ltd
Quantum Publishing
Souvenir Press Ltd
Special Interest Model Books Ltd
Stenlake Publishing Ltd
David West Children's Books
Wiley
Worth Press Ltd

BIBLIOGRAPHY & LIBRARY
SCIENCE

Ashgate Publishing Ltd
Bowker (UK) Ltd
British Library
James Clarke & Co
Galactic Central Publications
Hypatia Publications
Jarndyce Booksellers
LISU
Maney Publishing
The MIT Press Ltd
Nielsen
Paragon Publishing
ProQuest
Sussex Academic Press
Warburg Institute

BIOGRAPHY &
AUTOBIOGRAPHY

Acumen Publishing Ltd

Allison & Busby
Alma Books Ltd
Amolibros
Anshan Ltd
Arcadia Books Ltd
Arena Books (Publishers)
Ashgrove Publishing
Atlantic Books
Attic Press
Authentic Media
Authorhouse UK LLC
Barny Books
Bene Factum Publishing Ltd
Berghahn Books
Black Spring Press Ltd
John Blake Publishing Ltd
Bloomsbury Publishing PLC
Bodleian Library Publishing
Bowker Market Research
 (formerly BML)
Marion Boyars Publishers Ltd
Nicholas Brealey Publishing
Brewin Books Ltd
British Library
*Cambridge Publishing
 Management Ltd*
Camra Books
Canongate Books
Capuchin Classics
The Catholic Truth Society
Christian Focus Publications
James Clarke & Co
Constable & Robinson Ltd
David C. Cook (UK)
Cork University Press
Countyvise Ltd
The Davenant Press
Richard Dennis Publications
Denor Press Ltd
J. M. Dent
The Dovecote Press
Ashley Drake Publishing Ltd
Gerald Duckworth & Co Ltd
Dynasty Press
Elliott & Thompson
Equinox Publishing Ltd
The Erskine Press
Essential Works Ltd
Ex Libris Press
Faber & Faber Ltd
Filament Publishing Ltd
Geography Publications
Gibson Square
Gill & Macmillan
Gomer
Gothic Image Publications
Gracewing Publishing
Granta Books
Guildhall Press
Gwasg Gwynedd
Halban Publishers
Robert Hale Ltd
HarperCollins Publishers Ltd
Harvard University Press
Haus Publishing Ltd
Haynes Publishing
Headline Book Publishing Ltd
Highland Books
Hodder Faith
Hodder & Stoughton
Alison Hodge Publishers
Holo Books
Honno (Welsh Women's Press)
House of Stratus
Hymns Ancient & Modern Ltd
Hypatia Publications
Icon Books Ltd.
Independent Music Press
Indepenpress Publishing Ltd
Indigo Dreams Publishing Ltd
Inter-Varsity Press
Irish Academic Press
ISIS Publishing Ltd
Janus Publishing Co Ltd
The King's England Press
The Lilliput Press Ltd
Lion Hudson Plc
Little, Brown Book Group
The Littman Library of Jewish
 Civilization
Londubh Books
Luath Press Ltd

The Lutterworth Press
McNidder & Grace
Mainstream Publishing Co
 (Edinburgh) Ltd
Maney Publishing
Mercier Press Ltd
The Merlin Press Ltd
Merton Priory Press Ltd
Microform Academic Publishers
The MIT Press Ltd
Motor Racing Publications Ltd
Murdoch Books
John Murray Publishers
The Myrtle Press
National Portrait Gallery
 Publications
The National Trust
New Island Books Ltd
NMS Enterprises Limited -
 Publishing
The O'Brien Press Ltd
The Old Stile Press
Omnibus Press
Orion Books Ltd
The Orion Publishing Group Ltd
Pan Macmillan
Paragon Publishing
Penguin Random House UK Ltd
Piatkus Books
Polperro Heritage Press
Profile Books
Quadrille Publishing Ltd
Quartet Books
Quiller Publishing Ltd
The Radcliffe Press
Roundhouse Publishing Ltd
Royal Collection Trust
Sandstone Press Ltd
Saqi Books
Seren
Shepheard-Walwyn (Publishers)
 Ltd
The Shetland Times Ltd
Shire Publications Ltd
Short Books Ltd
Simon & Schuster (UK) Ltd
Slightly Foxed
Smith Settle Printing &
 Bookbinding Ltd
Colin Smythe Ltd
Souvenir Press Ltd
Stacey Publishing Limited
Stainer & Bell Ltd
Rudolf Steiner Press Ltd
Summersdale Publishers Ltd
Sussex Academic Press
Tabb House
I. B. Tauris & Co Ltd
Thames & Hudson Ltd
Thorogood Publishing Ltd
F. A. Thorpe Publishing
Thoth Publications
Transworld Publishers Ltd
Troubador Publishing Ltd
Tyne Bridge Publishing
Unicorn Press Ltd
United Writers Publications Ltd
University of Wales Press
Merlin Unwin Books Ltd
V&A Publishing
Vallentine Mitchell Publishers
Veloce Publishing Ltd
Veritas Publications
Vertical Editions
Warburg Institute
Waterside Press
Weidenfeld & Nicolson
David West Children's Books
Whittles Publishing
Wiley
Neil Wilson Publishing Ltd
Windhorse Publications
Y Lolfa Cyf
Yale University Press London
Zymurgy Publishing

BIOLOGY & ZOOLOGY

Alpha Science International Ltd
Amolibros
Bender Richardson White
BLA Publishing Ltd

Bloomsbury Publishing PLC
CABI
Calypso Publications
Cambridge University Press
Cengage Learning EMEA Ltd
Class Professional
Clear Answer Medical Publishing
 Ltd
D & N Publishing
Elsevier Ltd
HarperCollins Publishers Ltd
Harvard University Press
Hodder Education
Icon Books Ltd.
Imperial College Press
Kew Publishing
McGraw-Hill Education
Macmillan Science and Education
The MIT Press Ltd
The National Academies Press
Natural History Museum
 Publishing
Nelson Thornes Ltd
NMS Enterprises Limited -
 Publishing
North York Moors National Park
 Authority
W. W. Norton & Company Ltd
Open University Worldwide
Oxford University Press
Palgrave Macmillan
Princeton University Press
ProQuest
Royal Irish Academy
Scion Publishing Ltd
Taylor & Francis
Ward Lock Educational Co Ltd
David West Children's Books
Whittet Books Ltd
Wiley
WIT Press

CHEMISTRY

Alpha Science International Ltd
Amolibros
Anshan Ltd
Anthem Press
Atlantic Europe Publishing Co Ltd
BLA Publishing Ltd
Cambridge University Press
Cengage Learning EMEA Ltd
Chartridge Books Oxford
Class Professional
Elsevier Ltd
Energy Institute
Food Trade Press Ltd
HarperCollins Publishers Ltd
Hodder Education
Icon Books Ltd.
Imperial College Press
S. Karger AG
McGraw-Hill Education
Macmillan Science and Education
The National Academies Press
Nelson Thornes Ltd
W. W. Norton & Company Ltd
Open University Worldwide
Oxford University Press
Palgrave Macmillan
Royal Society of Chemistry
Scion Publishing Ltd
Taylor & Francis
Ward Lock Educational Co Ltd
Wiley

CHILDREN'S BOOKS

Acair Ltd
Alanna Books
Alban Books Ltd
Albion Press Ltd
Allison & Busby
Amber Books Ltd
Amolibros
Andersen Press Ltd
Antique Collectors' Club Ltd
Archive Publishing
Atlantic Europe Publishing Co Ltd
Aurora Metro Publications Ltd
Authentic Media
Authorhouse UK LLC

Award Publications Ltd
Ayebia Clarke Publishing Ltd
b small publishing ltd
Badger Publishing Ltd
Barefoot Books
Barny Books
Nicola Baxter Ltd
The Belmont Press
Bender Richardson White
Bene Factum Publishing Ltd
Bible Reading Fellowship
Birlinn Ltd
BLA Publishing Ltd
Bloomsbury Publishing PLC
Blue Ocean Publishing
Blueberry Press Ltd
Bodleian Library Publishing
Marion Boyars Publishers Ltd
Bradwell Books
British Association for Adoption &
 Fostering
British Museum Press
Brown Dog Books
Capuchin Classics
The Catholic Truth Society
Caxton Publishing Group Ltd
Chalksoft
Chicken House Publishing Ltd
Child's Play (International) Ltd
Christian Education
Christian Focus Publications
Cois Life
Cornwall Editions Ltd
Countyvise Ltd
CRW Publishing Ltd
Cyhoeddiadau'r Gair
Delancey Press Ltd
Denor Press Ltd
J. M. Dent
Diagram Visual Information Ltd
Ashley Drake Publishing Ltd
Dramatic Lines
Gerald Duckworth & Co Ltd
Eddison Sadd Editions Ltd
Everyman's Library
Faber & Faber Ltd
Fircone Books Ltd
Five Leaves Publications
Floris Books Trust Ltd
Galore Park Publishing Ltd
Glowworm Books & Gifts Ltd
Gomer
*Graham-Cameron Publishing &
 Illustration*
Guildhall Press
Gwasg Gwynedd
Hachette Children's Books
Haldane Mason Ltd
HarperCollins Publishers Ltd
Hawthorn Press
Haynes Publishing
Highland Books
John Hunt Publishing Ltd
Indepenpress Publishing Ltd
The Ivy Press Ltd
Janus Publishing Co Ltd
Kew Publishing
The King's England Press
Jessica Kingsley Publishers
Kube Publishing Ltd
The Lettermen
Lexus Ltd
Lion Hudson Plc
Little People Books
Little Tiger Press
Lomond Books Ltd
Luath Press Ltd
The Lutterworth Press
McCrimmon Publishing Co Ltd
Macmillan Children's Books Ltd
Macmillan Science and Education
Mandrake of Oxford
Meadowside Children's Books &
 Gullane Children's Books
Mercier Press Ltd
Michelin Travel Partner
mPowr Ltd
MW Educational
The National Autistic Society
 (NAS)
The National Trust

Natural History Museum
 Publishing
Nelson Thornes Ltd
New Caramel London Ltd
New Caramel London Ltd
New Island Books Ltd
NMS Enterprises Limited -
 Publishing
North York Moors National Park
 Authority
Nosy Crow
The O'Brien Press Ltd
Orion Books Ltd
The Orion Publishing Group Ltd
Orpheus Books Ltd
Oxford University Press
Palazzo Editions Ltd
Pan Macmillan
Paragon Publishing
Penguin Random House UK Ltd
Percy Publishing
Phaidon Press Ltd
Phoenix Yard Books
Piccadilly Press
Porter House of Publishing Ltd
Prestel Publishing Ltd
Prospera Publishing
Pushkin Press
Quantum Publishing
Ransom Publishing Ltd
Raven's Quill Ltd
Ravette Publishing Ltd
*Reader's Digest Children's
 Publishing Ltd*
Ripley Publishing Ltd
Vanessa Robertson
Robinswood Press Ltd
Roundhouse Publishing Ltd
Royal Collection Trust
Scholastic UK Ltd
Scripture Union Publishing
Sheldrake Press
Short Books Ltd
Sigel Press
Simon & Schuster (UK) Ltd
Slightly Foxed
Smallfish Books
Snowflake Books Ltd
Stacey Publishing Limited
Sweet Cherry Publishing
Symposium Publications Literary &
 Art
Ta Ha Publishers Ltd
Tabb House
Tangerine Designs Ltd
Tango Books Ltd
Tarquin Publications
Tate Publishing
Templar Publishing
Thames & Hudson Ltd
Tiny Island Press
Top That! Publishing Ltd
Topical Resources
Toucan Books Ltd
Troubador Publishing Ltd
United Writers Publications Ltd
Usborne Publishing Ltd
V&A Publishing
Veritas Publications
Waverley Books
David West Children's Books
Wordsworth Editions Ltd
Y Lolfa Cyf
Zymurgy Publishing

CINEMA, VIDEO, TV & RADIO

Anthem Press
Arena Books (Publishers)
Aurora Metro Publications Ltd
Berghahn Books
Black Dog Publishing Ltd
Black Spring Press Ltd
Bloomsbury Publishing PLC
Bowker Market Research
 (formerly BML)
Marion Boyars Publishers Ltd
Canongate Books
Cork University Press
Gerald Duckworth & Co Ltd
Essential Works Ltd
Faber & Faber Ltd

Gibson Square
Robert Hale Ltd
HarperCollins Publishers Ltd
Harvard University Press
Hodder & Stoughton
The Ilex Press Ltd
Intellect Ltd
Luath Press Ltd
Mainstream Publishing Co
 (Edinburgh) Ltd
Manchester University Press
W. W. Norton & Company Ltd
The Orion Publishing Group Ltd
Palazzo Editions Ltd
Pan Macmillan
Paragon Publishing
Penguin Random House UK Ltd
Phaidon Press Ltd
Polperro Heritage Press
ProQuest
RotoVision SA
Roundhouse Publishing Ltd
Simon & Schuster (UK) Ltd
Charles Skilton Ltd
Souvenir Press Ltd
I. B. Tauris & Co Ltd
Telos Publishing Ltd
Transworld Publishers Ltd
United Writers Publications Ltd
University of Exeter Press
University of Ottawa Press
University of Toronto Press
Vertical Editions

COMPUTER SCIENCE

Alpha Science International Ltd
Anshan Ltd
Bernard Babani (Publishing) Ltd
BLA Publishing Ltd
Cambridge University Press
Class Professional
Elsevier Ltd
Haynes Publishing
Hodder Education
The Ilex Press Ltd
Imperial College Press
In Easy Steps Limited
Institution of Engineering and
 Technology (IET)
Intellect Ltd
McGraw-Hill Education
Market House Books Ltd
The MIT Press Ltd
Nelson Thornes Ltd
W. W. Norton & Company Ltd
Open University Worldwide
O'Reilly UK Ltd
Palgrave Macmillan
Paragon Publishing
ProQuest
Stillwater Publishing Ltd
Which? Ltd
Wiley
WIT Press

COOKERY, WINES & SPIRITS

Amolibros
Antique Collectors' Club Ltd
Appletree Press Ltd
Ashgrove Publishing
Attic Press
Aurora Metro Publications Ltd
Barny Books
Bene Factum Publishing Ltd
Birlinn Ltd
John Blake Publishing Ltd
Bloomsbury Publishing PLC
Blue Ocean Publishing
Bossiney Books Ltd
Bowker Market Research
 (formerly BML)
Brown Dog Books
*Cambridge Publishing
 Management Ltd*
Camra Books
Capall Bann Publishing Ltd
Capuchin Classics
Carnegie Publishing Ltd
Jon Carpenter Publishing
Carroll & Brown Ltd

Caxton Publishing Group Ltd
Clairview Books Ltd
Conran Octopus
Constable & Robinson Ltd
Copper Beech Publishing Ltd
Cork University Press
Eddison Sadd Editions Ltd
Equinox Publishing Ltd
Ex Libris Press
Faber & Faber Ltd
W. Foulsham & Co Ltd
F&W Media International Ltd
Garnet Publishing Ltd
Gill & Macmillan
Graffeg Limited
Grub Street
Haldane Mason Ltd
HarperCollins Publishers Ltd
Haynes Publishing
Ian Henry Publications Ltd
Hodder Education
Hodder & Stoughton
Alison Hodge Publishers
How To Books Ltd
Icon Books Ltd.
Indepenpress Publishing Ltd
Ithaca Press
Kyle Books
Liberties Press
Lomond Books Ltd
Londubh Books
Luath Press Ltd
McNidder & Grace
Mainstream Publishing Co
  (Edinburgh) Ltd
Mercier Press Ltd
Merrell Publishers Ltd
Mitchell Beazley
Murdoch Books
The National Trust
NMS Enterprises Limited -
  Publishing
W. W. Norton & Company Ltd
The O'Brien Press Ltd
Octopus Publishing Group
The Orion Publishing Group Ltd
Paragon Publishing
Penguin Random House UK Ltd
Phaidon Press Ltd
Piatkus Books
Prospect Books
Quadrille Publishing Ltd
Quantum Publishing
Quiller Publishing Ltd
RotoVision SA
Roundhouse Publishing Ltd
Saqi Books
Sheldrake Press
Shire Publications Ltd
Sigma Press
Simon & Schuster (UK) Ltd
Charles Skilton Ltd
Souvenir Press Ltd
Special Interest Model Books Ltd
Stacey Publishing Limited
Stillwater Publishing Ltd
Stobart Davies Ltd
Summersdale Publishers Ltd
Toucan Books Ltd
Transworld Publishers Ltd
Troubador Publishing Ltd
Waverley Books
Neil Wilson Publishing Ltd
Y Lolfa Cyf

CRAFTS & HOBBIES

Amber Books Ltd
b small publishing ltd
Bernard Babani (Publishing) Ltd
Batsford
Black Dog Publishing Ltd
Bloomsbury Publishing PLC
Blue Ocean Publishing
Bowker Market Research
  (formerly BML)
Calypso Publications
*Cambridge Publishing
  Management Ltd*
Capall Bann Publishing Ltd
Carroll & Brown Ltd
Conran Octopus

Constable & Robinson Ltd
Crimson Publishing
The Crowood Press Ltd
D & N Publishing
Eco-logic Books
Filament Publishing Ltd
Floris Books Trust Ltd
W. Foulsham & Co Ltd
F&W Media International Ltd
Stanley Gibbons
Haldane Mason Ltd
Robert Hale Ltd
HarperCollins Publishers Ltd
Hawthorn Press
Haynes Publishing
The Ilex Press Ltd
In Easy Steps Limited
Indepenpress Publishing Ltd
Instant-Books UK Ltd
The Ivy Press Ltd
Kyle Books
Liberties Press
Lomond Books Ltd
The Lutterworth Press
Melisende UK Ltd
Mercier Press Ltd
Merrell Publishers Ltd
Mitchell Beazley
Murdoch Books
The Nostalgia Collection
Octopus Publishing Group
The Orion Publishing Group Ltd
Penguin Random House UK Ltd
Quadrille Publishing Ltd
Quantum Publishing
Quiller Publishing Ltd
RotoVision SA
Roundhouse Publishing Ltd
Shire Publications Ltd
Sigma Press
Souvenir Press Ltd
Special Interest Model Books Ltd
Stenlake Publishing Ltd
Stillwater Publishing Ltd
Stobart Davies Ltd
Summersdale Publishers Ltd
Tarquin Publications
Thames & Hudson Ltd
Top That! Publishing Ltd
Toucan Books Ltd
Unicorn Press Ltd
Usborne Publishing Ltd
V&A Publishing
Veloce Publishing Ltd
David West Children's Books
Wiley
Willow Island Editions
Y Lolfa Cyf

CRIME

Allison & Busby
Alma Books Ltd
Amber Books Ltd
Arcadia Books Ltd
Atlantic Books
Authorhouse UK LLC
Bitter Lemon Press
John Blake Publishing Ltd
Bloomsbury Publishing PLC
Bowker Market Research
  (formerly BML)
Canongate Books
CBD Research Ltd
Constable & Robinson Ltd
Countyvise Ltd
Creative Content Ltd
Gerald Duckworth & Co Ltd
Dynasty Press
The Erskine Press
Five Leaves Publications
Garnet Publishing Ltd
Gibson Square
Guildhall Press
Robert Hale Ltd
HarperCollins Publishers Ltd
Haus Publishing Ltd
Haynes Publishing
Headline Book Publishing Ltd
Hodder & Stoughton
Honno (Welsh Women's Press)
House of Stratus

Indepenpress Publishing Ltd
Indigo Dreams Publishing Ltd
ISIS Publishing Ltd
Janus Publishing Co Ltd
Jordan Publishing Ltd
Liberties Press
Librario Publishers Ltd
Little, Brown Book Group
Luath Press Ltd
Mainstream Publishing Co
  (Edinburgh) Ltd
Mandrake of Oxford
Mercier Press Ltd
Myriad Editions
The O'Brien Press Ltd
Open University Worldwide
The Orion Publishing Group Ltd
Pan Macmillan
Paragon Publishing
Penguin Random House UK Ltd
Percy Publishing
Piatkus Books
Profile Books
Pushkin Press
Quantum Publishing
Sandstone Press Ltd
Silver Moon Books
Simon & Schuster (UK) Ltd
Social Affairs Unit
Stillwater Publishing Ltd
Summersdale Publishers Ltd
Telos Publishing Ltd
Thorogood Publishing Ltd
F. A. Thorpe Publishing
Transworld Publishers Ltd
Troubador Publishing Ltd
Vertical Editions
Waterside Press
Neil Wilson Publishing Ltd
Wordsworth Editions Ltd
Worth Press Ltd

DO-IT-YOURSELF

The Crowood Press Ltd
D & N Publishing
W. Foulsham & Co Ltd
HarperCollins Publishers Ltd
Haynes Publishing
How To Books Ltd
Indepenpress Publishing Ltd
Janus Publishing Co Ltd
Murdoch Books
Octopus Publishing Group
Penguin Random House UK Ltd
Quadrille Publishing Ltd
Quantum Publishing
Stobart Davies Ltd
Veloce Publishing Ltd
Wiley

ECONOMICS

Anthem Press
Arena Books (Publishers)
Ashgate Publishing Ltd
Atlantic Books
Berghahn Books
Birlinn Ltd
Bowker Market Research
  (formerly BML)
Nicholas Brealey Publishing
*Cambridge Publishing
  Management Ltd*
Cambridge University Press
Jon Carpenter Publishing
Cengage Learning EMEA Ltd
Centre for Economic Policy
  Research
The Chartered Institute of Public
  Finance & Accountancy
Commonwealth Secretariat
Cork University Press
Delta Alpha Publishing Ltd
J. M. Dent
DJØF
Gerald Duckworth & Co Ltd
Edward Elgar Publishing Ltd
Elliott & Thompson
Elsevier Ltd
Fabian Society
Gibson Square

Gill & Macmillan
Gower Publishing Co Ltd
HarperCollins Publishers Ltd
Harriman House
Harvard University Press
Hodder Education
Icon Books Ltd.
Imperial College Press
Institute of Employment Rights
Ithaca Press
Janus Publishing Co Ltd
Jarndyce Booksellers
Kube Publishing Ltd
Liberties Press
Luath Press Ltd
McGraw-Hill Education
Manchester University Press
The Merlin Press Ltd
Microform Academic Publishers
The MIT Press Ltd
Nelson Thornes Ltd
W. W. Norton & Company Ltd
Oak Tree Press
Open University Worldwide
Orpen Press
Oxfam Publishing
Oxford University Press
Palgrave Macmillan
Penguin Random House UK Ltd
Pickering & Chatto (Publishers) Ltd
Princeton University Press
Profile Books
ProQuest
Joseph Rowntree Foundation
Saqi Books
Shepheard-Walwyn (Publishers)
  Ltd
Social Affairs Unit
Spokesman
Sussex Academic Press
Taylor & Francis
Troubador Publishing Ltd
University of Ottawa Press
University of Toronto Press
Wiley
Yale University Press London
Zed Books Ltd

EDUCATIONAL & TEXTBOOKS

Acair Ltd
Acumen Publishing Ltd
Adamson Publishing Ltd
Advance Materials Ltd
Alban Books Ltd
Alpha Science International Ltd
AMS Educational
Anglo-Saxon Books
Anshan Ltd
Anthem Press
Ashgate Publishing Ltd
Association for Scottish Literary
  Studies
Atlantic Europe Publishing Co Ltd
Aurora Metro Publications Ltd
Ayebia Clarke Publishing Ltd
Bernard Babani (Publishing) Ltd
Badger Publishing Ltd
Balberry Publishing
Barefoot Books
Nicola Baxter Ltd
Bender Richardson White
Bible Reading Fellowship
Bloomsbury Academic &
  Professional
Bloomsbury Publishing PLC
Blue Ocean Publishing
Blueberry Press Ltd
Borthwick Publications
Brilliant Publications
Butterfingers Books
Calypso Publications
*Cambridge Publishing
  Management Ltd*
Cambridge University Press
Capall Bann Publishing Ltd
Carel Press Ltd
Cengage Learning EMEA Ltd
CfBT Education Trust
Chalksoft
Channel View Publications Ltd

Chartered Institute of Personnel &
  Development
Chemcord Ltd
Christian Education
Christian Focus Publications
City & Guilds
Claire Publications
Class Professional
Clear Answer Medical Publishing
  Ltd
Cois Life
Collins Geo
Colour Heroes Ltd
Coordination Group Publications
  Ltd (CGP Ltd)
Crimson Publishing
The Davenant Press
Delta ELT Publishing Ltd
Denor Press Ltd
Diagram Visual Information Ltd
Ashley Drake Publishing Ltd
Dramatic Lines
Edinburgh University Press
Edward Elgar Publishing Ltd
Egon Publishers Ltd
Elsevier Ltd
English Heritage
Equinox Publishing Ltd
Espresso Education
Ethics International Press Ltd
Filament Publishing Ltd
First & Best in Education
The Fostering Network
W. Foulsham & Co Ltd
Freelance Market News
Friends of the Earth
Galore Park Publishing Ltd
Gatehouse Media Ltd
The Geographical Association
Geography Publications
Gill & Macmillan
Gower Publishing Co Ltd
*Graham-Cameron Publishing &
  Illustration*
Greenleaf Publishing
Gresham Books Ltd
Guildhall Press
Hachette Children's Books
Haldane Mason Ltd
John Harper Publishing Ltd
HarperCollins Publishers Ltd
Hart McLeod Ltd
Hawthorn Press
HB Publications
Ian Henry Publications Ltd
Hinton House Publishers Ltd
Hodder Education
Hodder Gibson
Hopscotch
How To Books Ltd
Human Kinetics Europe Ltd
Hymns Ancient & Modern Ltd
Hypatia Publications
Icon Books Ltd.
ICSA Information & Training Ltd
The Ilex Press Ltd
In Easy Steps Limited
Indepenpress Publishing Ltd
Institute of Education Press
Institution of Engineering and
  Technology (IET)
Intellect Ltd
IPS Educational Publishing
Janus Publishing Co Ltd
Jolly Learning Ltd
Jessica Kingsley Publishers
Kogan Page Ltd
Kube Publishing Ltd
Learning Matters
Learning Together
Lexus Ltd
Lion Hudson Plc
Little People Books
The Littman Library of Jewish
  Civilization
Liverpool University Press
The Lutterworth Press
McCrimmon Publishing Co Ltd
McGraw-Hill Education
Macmillan Science and Education
Manchester University Press
Methodist Publishing

The MIT Press Ltd
MW Educational
The National Academies Press
The National Autistic Society
(NAS)
National Children's Bureau
National Housing Federation
Natural History Museum
Publishing
Nelson Thornes Ltd
NMS Enterprises Limited -
Publishing
North York Moors National Park
Authority
Northcote House Publishers Ltd
W. W. Norton & Company Ltd
Oak Tree Press
Open University Worldwide
Optimus Education
Optimus Professional Publishing
Oxford University Press
Packard Publishing Ltd
Palgrave Macmillan
Paragon Publishing
Philip's
Policy Press
Practical Pre-School Books
Princeton University Press
Ransom Publishing Ltd
Robinswood Press Ltd
Round Hall
Roundhouse Publishing Ltd
Royal Society of Chemistry
St Jerome Publishing Ltd
Saqi Books
Scholastic UK Ltd
SchoolPlay Productions Ltd
Scripture Union Publishing
Sigel Press
SLP Education
Social Affairs Unit
The Society of Metaphysicians Ltd
Southgate Publishers
Stacey Publishing Limited
Rudolf Steiner Press Ltd
Sussex Academic Press
Symposium Publications Literary &
Art
Tango Books Ltd
Tarquin Publications
Taylor & Francis
Teachit (UK) Ltd
Thames & Hudson Ltd
Third Millennium Publishing Ltd
THRASS (UK) Ltd
Topical Resources
Trentham Books
Trotman Publishing
UCAS
United Writers Publications Ltd
University of Hertfordshire Press
University of Ottawa Press
University of Wales Press
Veritas Publications
Ward Lock Educational Co Ltd
Waterside Press
Whittles Publishing
Wiley

ELECTRONIC (EDUCATIONAL)

Adam Matthew Digital Ltd
Adamson Publishing Ltd
Alpha Science International Ltd
Anthem Press
Atlantic Europe Publishing Co Ltd
Bernard Babani (Publishing) Ltd
Badger Publishing Ltd
Bloomsbury Publishing PLC
Bowker (UK) Ltd
Cambridge University Press
Carel Press Ltd
Chalksoft
City & Guilds
Claire Publications
Collins Geo
Crimson Publishing
Encyclopaedia Britannica (UK) Ltd
Espresso Education
Ethics International Press Ltd
First & Best in Education
Galore Park Publishing Ltd

The Geographical Association
Gower Publishing Co Ltd
HarperCollins Publishers Ltd
Hart McLeod Ltd
Hodder Education
Hodder Gibson
Hopscotch
Human Kinetics Europe Ltd
Imperial College Press
In Easy Steps Limited
Intellect Ltd
Jolly Learning Ltd
Jessica Kingsley Publishers
Kogan Page Ltd
McCrimmon Publishing Co Ltd
McGraw-Hill Education
Methodist Publishing
Nelson Thornes Ltd
Open University Worldwide
Optimus Professional Publishing
Palgrave Macmillan
Paragon Publishing
ProQuest
Ripley Publishing Ltd
Robinswood Press Ltd
Royal Geographical Society
Royal Society of Chemistry
SchoolPlay Productions Ltd
The Society of Metaphysicians Ltd
Souvenir Press Ltd
Summersdale Publishers Ltd
Tate Publishing
Teachit (UK) Ltd
THRASS (UK) Ltd
Waterside Press
David West Children's Books
Wiley

**ELECTRONIC
(ENTERTAINMENT)**

Amber Books Ltd
Bernard Babani (Publishing) Ltd
Bowker Market Research
(formerly BML)
Carroll & Brown Ltd
Constable & Robinson Ltd
Robert Hale Ltd
HarperCollins Publishers Ltd
Haynes Publishing
The Ilex Press Ltd
Penguin Random House UK Ltd
Ripley Publishing Ltd
SchoolPlay Productions Ltd
Souvenir Press Ltd
Summersdale Publishers Ltd
Thorogood Publishing Ltd
David West Children's Books

**ELECTRONIC (PROFESSIONAL &
ACADEMIC)**

Adam Matthew Digital Ltd
Alpha Science International Ltd
Anthem Press
Ashgate Publishing Ltd
Bernard Babani (Publishing) Ltd
Berghahn Books
Bloomsbury Academic &
Professional
Bowker Market Research
(formerly BML)
Bowker (UK) Ltd
Cambridge University Press
Centre for Policy on Ageing
Christian Education
Edward Elgar Publishing Ltd
Elsevier Ltd
Energy Institute
Equinox Publishing Ltd
Ethics International Press Ltd
Filament Publishing Ltd
Gower Publishing Co Ltd
HarperCollins Publishers Ltd
Haynes Publishing
Human Kinetics Europe Ltd
Imperial College Press
In Easy Steps Limited
Institution of Engineering and
Technology (IET)
Intellect Ltd
International Medical Press

IT Governance Publishing
IWA Publishing
Jordan Publishing Ltd
Jessica Kingsley Publishers
Kogan Page Ltd
Learning Matters
McGraw-Hill Education
Maney Publishing
Microform Academic Publishers
The MIT Press Ltd
Myriad Editions
National Children's Bureau
National Records of Scotland
Oak Tree Press
Oxford University Press
Paragon Publishing
Princeton University Press
The Professional and Higher
Partnership Ltd
ProQuest
Round Hall
The Royal College of Psychiatrists
Royal Geographical Society
Royal Society of Chemistry
St Jerome Publishing Ltd
Stillwater Publishing Ltd
Summersdale Publishers Ltd
Tate Publishing
Taylor & Francis
Teachit (UK) Ltd
Thorogood Publishing Ltd
Waterside Press
Wiley
WIT Press

ENGINEERING

Alpha Science International Ltd
Anshan Ltd
Anthem Press
Bernard Babani (Publishing) Ltd
Cambridge University Press
Cengage Learning EMEA Ltd
Elsevier Ltd
Energy Institute
The Geological Society
Gower Publishing Co Ltd
Hemming Information Services
Imperial College Press
Institute of Acoustics
Institute of Physics & Engineering
in Medicine
Institution of Engineering and
Technology (IET)
IWA Publishing
McGraw-Hill Education
Maney Publishing
The MIT Press Ltd
The National Academies Press
Nelson Thornes Ltd
Open University Worldwide
Palgrave Macmillan
The Professional and Higher
Partnership Ltd
ProQuest
Sigel Press
Special Interest Model Books Ltd
Stillwater Publishing Ltd
Taylor & Francis
Tee Publishing Ltd
Whittles Publishing
Wiley
WIT Press

**ENGLISH AS A FOREIGN
LANGUAGE**

b small publishing ltd
Balberry Publishing
*Cambridge Publishing
Management Ltd*
Cambridge University Press
Cengage Learning EMEA Ltd
Delta ELT Publishing Ltd
Gatehouse Media Ltd
*Graham-Cameron Publishing &
Illustration*
HarperCollins Publishers Ltd
Hodder Education
McGraw-Hill Education
Macmillan Science and Education
MW Educational

New Island Books Ltd
Open University Worldwide
Oxford University Press
Paragon Publishing
Robinswood Press Ltd
Sandstone Press Ltd
SLP Education
Symposium Publications Literary &
Art

**ENVIRONMENT &
DEVELOPMENT STUDIES**

Alpha Science International Ltd
Anshan Ltd
Anthem Press
Arena Books (Publishers)
Ashgate Publishing Ltd
Atlantic Europe Publishing Co Ltd
Berghahn Books
Black Dog Publishing Ltd
Bloomsbury Academic &
Professional
CABI
Cambridge University Press
Capall Bann Publishing Ltd
Channel View Publications Ltd
Clairview Books Ltd
Collins Geo
Commonwealth Secretariat
Cork University Press
Eco-logic Books
Edward Elgar Publishing Ltd
Energy Institute
Ethics International Press Ltd
Fabian Society
Friends of the Earth
The Geological Society
Greenleaf Publishing
HarperCollins Publishers Ltd
Haus Publishing Ltd
Hodder Education
Imperial College Press
Instant-Books UK Ltd
Intellect Ltd
Macmillan Science and Education
Maney Publishing
The MIT Press Ltd
Myriad Editions
The National Academies Press
Nelson Thornes Ltd
North York Moors National Park
Authority
Open University Worldwide
Oxfam Publishing
Palgrave Macmillan
Paragon Publishing
Princeton University Press
Royal Geographical Society
Sandstone Press Ltd
Saqi Books
Sigel Press
Social Affairs Unit
The Society of Metaphysicians Ltd
Southgate Publishers
Stacey Publishing Limited
Sussex Academic Press
Tango Books Ltd
Taylor & Francis
Thames & Hudson Ltd
University of Hertfordshire Press
Wiley
WIT Press
Zed Books Ltd

FASHION & COSTUME

Amber Books Ltd
Antique Collectors' Club Ltd
Arena Books (Publishers)
Batsford
Bene Factum Publishing Ltd
Black Dog Publishing Ltd
Bloomsbury Academic &
Professional
Bloomsbury Publishing PLC
Copper Beech Publishing Ltd
Gerald Duckworth & Co Ltd
Dynasty Press
Essential Works Ltd
W. Foulsham & Co Ltd
The Ilex Press Ltd

Intellect Ltd
The Ivy Press Ltd
Laurence King Publishing Ltd
Maney Publishing
Merrell Publishers Ltd
Mitchell Beazley
National Portrait Gallery
Publications
The National Trust
Nelson Thornes Ltd
The Orion Publishing Group Ltd
Papadakis Publisher
Paragon Publishing
Penguin Random House UK Ltd
Phaidon Press Ltd
Prestel Publishing Ltd
ProQuest
Quadrille Publishing Ltd
Quantum Publishing
Quartet Books
RotoVision SA
Royal Collection Trust
Saqi Books
Scala Arts & Heritage Publishers
Ltd
Shire Publications Ltd
Charles Skilton Ltd
teNeues Publishing UK Ltd
Thames & Hudson Ltd
Unicorn Press Ltd
V&A Publishing
David West Children's Books
Wiley
Yale University Press London

FICTION

Acair Ltd
Alban Books Ltd
Albyn Press
Allison & Busby
Alma Books Ltd
Alma Classics
Amolibros
Arcadia Books Ltd
Archive Publishing
Arena Books (Publishers)
Ashgrove Publishing
Association for Scottish Literary
Studies
Atlantic Books
Aurora Metro Publications Ltd
Authorhouse UK LLC
Ayebia Clarke Publishing Ltd
Barny Books
Birlinn Ltd
Bitter Lemon Press
Black Spring Press Ltd
Bloomsbury Publishing PLC
Blue Sky Press
Blueberry Press Ltd
Bowker Market Research
(formerly BML)
Marion Boyars Publishers Ltd
Brewin Books Ltd
Canongate Books
Capuchin Classics
Cois Life
Colour Heroes Ltd
Constable & Robinson Ltd
Cornwall Editions Ltd
Countyvise Ltd
Creative Content Ltd
CRW Publishing Ltd
Delancey Press Ltd
Denor Press Ltd
J. M. Dent
Gerald Duckworth & Co Ltd
Enitharmon Press
Everyman's Library
Faber & Faber Ltd
Five Leaves Publications
Freelance Market News
Garnet Publishing Ltd
Victor Gollancz Ltd
Gothic Image Publications
Granta Books
Guildhall Press
Hachette Children's Books
Halban Publishers
Robert Hale Ltd
Harlequin Mills & Boon Ltd

HarperCollins Publishers Ltd
Haus Publishing Ltd
Headline Book Publishing Ltd
Ian Henry Publications Ltd
Highland Books
Hodder Faith
Hodder & Stoughton
Honno (Welsh Women's Press)
House of Stratus
John Hunt Publishing Ltd
Indepenpress Publishing Ltd
Indigo Dreams Publishing Ltd
ISIS Publishing Ltd
Ithaca Press
Janus Publishing Co Ltd
Jarndyce Booksellers
The King's England Press
Kube Publishing Ltd
Lavender and White Publishing
Liberties Press
Librario Publishers Ltd
The Lilliput Press Ltd
Lion Hudson Plc
Little, Brown Book Group
Luath Press Ltd
McNidder & Grace
Magna Large Print Books
Mandrake of Oxford
Mercier Press Ltd
John Murray Publishers
Myriad Editions
Myrmidon Books Ltd
New Island Books Ltd
W. W. Norton & Company Ltd
The O'Brien Press Ltd
Orion Books Ltd
The Orion Publishing Group Ltd
Pan Macmillan
Paragon Publishing
Penguin Random House UK Ltd
Percy Publishing
Piatkus Books
Profile Books
Prospera Publishing
Pushkin Press
Quartet Books
Raven's Quill Ltd
Revenge Ink
Ripley Publishing Ltd
Robinswood Press Ltd
Sandstone Press Ltd
Saqi Books
Seren
Short Books Ltd
Sigel Press
Silver Moon Books
Simon & Schuster (UK) Ltd
Charles Skilton Ltd
Slightly Foxed
Snowflake Books Ltd
Souvenir Press Ltd
Spokesman
Sportsbooks Ltd
Stacey Publishing Limited
Stellium Ltd
Sweet Cherry Publishing
Tabb House
Telegram Books
Telos Publishing Ltd
Templar Publishing
Thorogood Publishing Ltd
F. A. Thorpe Publishing
Top That! Publishing Ltd
Total-E-Ntwined Ltd
Transworld Publishers Ltd
Troubador Publishing Ltd
United Writers Publications Ltd
Usborne Publishing Ltd
Weidenfeld & Nicolson
David West Children's Books
Wordsworth Editions Ltd
Worth Press Ltd
Y Lolfa Cyf
Zymurgy Publishing

FINE ART & ART HISTORY

Albyn Press
Amolibros
Antique Collectors' Club Ltd
Arena Books (Publishers)
Ashgate Publishing Ltd

Bene Factum Publishing Ltd
Black Dog Publishing Ltd
Blackthorn Press
Bloomsbury Publishing PLC
Bodleian Library Publishing
Bowker Market Research
   (formerly BML)
British Library
British Museum Press
Cambridge Publishing
   Management Ltd
Cambridge University Press
Canongate Books
Colour Heroes Ltd
Cork University Press
D & N Publishing
Richard Dennis Publications
Gerald Duckworth & Co Ltd
Fircone Books Ltd
Four Courts Press
Garnet Publishing Ltd
Gibson Square
Gothic Image Publications
Graffeg Limited
H & S Media
Hachette Children's Books
Robert Hale Ltd
HarperCollins Publishers Ltd
Harvard University Press
Hayward Publishing
Alison Hodge Publishers
John Hunt Publishing Ltd
Hypatia Publications
The Ilex Press Ltd
Ithaca Press
Janus Publishing Co Ltd
Kew Publishing
Laurence King Publishing Ltd
Sean Kingston Publishing
Dewi Lewis Publishing
Liberties Press
The Lilliput Press Ltd
The Littman Library of Jewish
   Civilization
Liverpool University Press
Logaston Press
Lund Humphries
The Lutterworth Press
McNidder & Grace
Mainstream Publishing Co
   (Edinburgh) Ltd
Mandrake of Oxford
Maney Publishing
Melisende UK Ltd
Merrell Publishers Ltd
The MIT Press Ltd
Mitchell Beazley
John Murray Publishers
National Galleries of Scotland
National Portrait Gallery
   Publications
The National Trust
Natural History Museum
   Publishing
NMS Enterprises Limited -
   Publishing
W. W. Norton & Company Ltd
Octopus Publishing Group
Open University Worldwide
The Orion Publishing Group Ltd
Oxford University Press
Papadakis Publisher
Paragon Publishing
Penguin Random House UK Ltd
Phaidon Press Ltd
Prestel Publishing Ltd
ProQuest
Quantum Publishing
Quartet Books
Quiller Publishing Ltd
Redcliffe Press Ltd
RotoVision SA
Roundhouse Publishing Ltd
Royal Collection Trust
Sansom & Co Ltd
Saqi Books
Scala Arts & Heritage Publishers
   Ltd
Seren
Charles Skilton Ltd
Stacey Publishing Limited
Rudolf Steiner Press Ltd

Sussex Academic Press
Symposium Publications Literary &
   Art
Tate Publishing
I. B. Tauris & Co Ltd
Thames & Hudson Ltd
Third Millennium Publishing Ltd
Toucan Books Ltd
Unicorn Press Ltd
V&A Publishing
Warburg Institute
Paul Watkins Publishing
Philip Wilson Publishers
Yale University Press London

GARDENING

Amolibros
Antique Collectors' Club Ltd
Barny Books
Batsford
Bene Factum Publishing Ltd
BLA Publishing Ltd
Black Dog Publishing Ltd
Bloomsbury Publishing PLC
Cambridge Publishing
   Management Ltd
Capall Bann Publishing Ltd
Capuchin Classics
Caxton Publishing Group Ltd
Chalksoft
Conran Octopus
Constable & Robinson Ltd
Copper Beech Publishing Ltd
Cork University Press
The Crowood Press Ltd
D & N Publishing
J. M. Dent
Eco-logic Books
Ex Libris Press
Floris Books Trust Ltd
W. Foulsham & Co Ltd
Friends of the Earth
Graffeg Limited
Robert Hale Ltd
HarperCollins Publishers Ltd
Hawthorn Press
Haynes Publishing
Alison Hodge Publishers
How To Books Ltd
The Ivy Press Ltd
Kew Publishing
Kyle Books
Liberties Press
Luath Press Ltd
Merrell Publishers Ltd
Mitchell Beazley
Murdoch Books
The National Trust
W. W. Norton & Company Ltd
The O'Brien Press Ltd
Octopus Publishing Group
The Orion Publishing Group Ltd
Packard Publishing Ltd
Pan Macmillan
Penguin Random House UK Ltd
Quadrille Publishing Ltd
Quantum Publishing
Quiller Publishing Ltd
The Shetland Times Ltd
Shire Publications Ltd
Simon & Schuster (UK) Ltd
Slightly Foxed
Souvenir Press Ltd
Stacey Publishing Limited
Thames & Hudson Ltd
Toucan Books Ltd
Transworld Publishers Ltd
Which? Ltd
Whittet Books Ltd
Wiley
Willow Island Editions
Zymurgy Publishing

GAY & LESBIAN STUDIES

Arcadia Books Ltd
Aurora Metro Publications Ltd
Bloomsbury Academic &
   Professional
Cork University Press
Dynasty Press

Gibson Square
Guildhall Press
John Hunt Publishing Ltd
Indepenpress Publishing Ltd
Manchester University Press
The MIT Press Ltd
Paragon Publishing
St Jerome Publishing Ltd
Saqi Books
Silver Moon Books
Charles Skilton Ltd
Souvenir Press Ltd
Taylor & Francis
Thames & Hudson Ltd

GENDER STUDIES

Adam Matthew Digital Ltd
Anthem Press
Arcadia Books Ltd
Ashgate Publishing Ltd
Attic Press
Aurora Metro Publications Ltd
Berghahn Books
Bloomsbury Academic &
   Professional
Cambridge University Press
Capall Bann Publishing Ltd
Commonwealth Secretariat
Cork University Press
Dynasty Press
Edward Elgar Publishing Ltd
Equinox Publishing Ltd
W. Foulsham & Co Ltd
HarperCollins Publishers Ltd
Harvard University Press
Hawthorn Press
Holo Books
C. Hurst & Co (Publishers) Ltd
Icon Books Ltd.
Intellect Ltd
Irish Academic Press
Ithaca Press
Manchester University Press
The Merlin Press Ltd
The MIT Press Ltd
Myriad Editions
New Island Books Ltd
W. W. Norton & Company Ltd
Oxfam Publishing
Palgrave Macmillan
PCCS Books Ltd
Piatkus Books
Policy Press
St Jerome Publishing Ltd
Saqi Books
Sheldon Press
Souvenir Press Ltd
Sussex Academic Press
I. B. Tauris & Co Ltd
Taylor & Francis
Trentham Books
University of Ottawa Press
University of Toronto Press
University of Wales Press
Yale University Press London
Zed Books Ltd

GEOGRAPHY & GEOLOGY

Albyn Press
Amolibros
Anthem Press
Ashgate Publishing Ltd
Atlantic Europe Publishing Co Ltd
Bloomsbury Publishing PLC
British Geological Survey
Cambridge University Press
Caxton Publishing Group Ltd
Chalksoft
Class Professional
Coastal Publishing Ltd
Collins Geo
Colour Heroes Ltd
Cork University Press
G. L. Crowther
Diagram Visual Information Ltd
The Dovecote Press
Dunedin Academic Press
Ex Libris Press
The Geographical Association
Geography Publications

The Geological Society
Graffeg Limited
HarperCollins Publishers Ltd
Hodder Education
Alison Hodge Publishers
Icon Books Ltd.
Imray Laurie Norie & Wilson Ltd
Logaston Press
Luath Press Ltd
McGraw-Hill Education
Macmillan Science and Education
Maney Publishing
The National Academies Press
Natural History Museum
   Publishing
Nelson Thornes Ltd
NMS Enterprises Limited -
   Publishing
North York Moors National Park
   Authority
W. W. Norton & Company Ltd
Open University Worldwide
Optimus Professional Publishing
Oxford University Press
Packard Publishing Ltd
Pagoda Tree Press
Palgrave Macmillan
Paragon Publishing
Roadmaster Publishing
Royal Geographical Society
SLP Education
Stacey Publishing Limited
Sussex Academic Press
I. B. Tauris & Co Ltd
Taylor & Francis
University of Hertfordshire Press
Usborne Publishing Ltd
Ward Lock Educational Co Ltd
David West Children's Books
Whittles Publishing
Wiley
WIT Press

GUIDE BOOKS

AA Publishing
Albyn Press
Amolibros
Appletree Press Ltd
The Armchair Traveller at the
   bookHaus Ltd
Authorhouse UK LLC
Birlinn Ltd
Bossiney Books Ltd
Bowker Market Research
   (formerly BML)
Bradt Travel Guides Ltd
Bradwell Books
British Geological Survey
Cambridge Publishing
   Management Ltd
Camra Books
Capall Bann Publishing Ltd
Capuchin Classics
The Catholic Truth Society
Caxton Publishing Group Ltd
Cicerone Press Ltd
Coastal Publishing Ltd
Collins Geo
Colour Heroes Ltd
Countryside Books
Crimson Publishing
D & N Publishing
Discovery Walking Guides Ltd
The Dovecote Press
English Heritage
Everyman's Library
Ex Libris Press
Findhorn Press Ltd
Fircone Books Ltd
Footprint Travel Guides
W. Foulsham & Co Ltd
Garnet Publishing Ltd
The Geographical Association
Gill & Macmillan
Gothic Image Publications
Gracewing Publishing
Graffeg Limited
Guildhall Press
HarperCollins Publishers Ltd
Haynes Publishing
Heart of Albion Press

Hobnob Press
Alison Hodge Publishers
Holo Books
How To Books Ltd
Indigo Dreams Publishing Ltd
Instant-Books UK Ltd
Liberties Press
Logaston Press
Lomond Books Ltd
Londubh Books
Luath Press Ltd
McNidder & Grace
Mainstream Publishing Co
 (Edinburgh) Ltd
Michelin Travel Partner
National Galleries of Scotland
National Portrait Gallery
 Publications
The National Trust
New Island Books Ltd
NMS Enterprises Limited -
 Publishing
North York Moors National Park
 Authority
The Nostalgia Collection
The O'Brien Press Ltd
The Orion Publishing Group Ltd
Pagoda Tree Press
Paragon Publishing
Penguin Random House UK Ltd
Quiller Publishing Ltd
Roadmaster Publishing
Roundhouse Publishing Ltd
Royal Collection Trust
S. B. Publications
Scala Arts & Heritage Publishers
 Ltd
Sheldrake Press
The Shetland Times Ltd
Shire Publications Ltd
Sigma Press
Simon & Schuster (UK) Ltd
Charles Skilton Ltd
Stillwater Publishing Ltd
Stobart Davies Ltd
Summersdale Publishers Ltd
Tate Publishing
I. B. Tauris & Co Ltd
Thames & Hudson Ltd
Third Millennium Publishing Ltd
Troubador Publishing Ltd
Twelveheads Press
V&A Publishing
Wiley
Willow Island Editions
Neil Wilson Publishing Ltd
Y Lolfa Cyf

HEALTH & BEAUTY

Amber Books Ltd
Anshan Ltd
Ashgrove Publishing
Bloomsbury Publishing PLC
Bowker Market Research
 (formerly BML)
Capall Bann Publishing Ltd
Carroll & Brown Ltd
Caxton Publishing Group Ltd
Cengage Learning EMEA Ltd
Clairview Books Ltd
Constable & Robinson Ltd
Crimson Publishing
Diagram Visual Information Ltd
Eddison Sadd Editions Ltd
The Erskine Press
Findhorn Press Ltd
Floris Books Trust Ltd
W. Foulsham & Co Ltd
Gibson Square
Haldane Mason Ltd
HarperCollins Publishers Ltd
Harvard University Press
Hawker Publications
Haynes Publishing
Hodder Education
How To Books Ltd
Human Kinetics Europe Ltd
Icon Books Ltd.
Indepenpress Publishing Ltd
Jessica Kingsley Publishers
Kyle Books

Liberties Press
Londubh Books
Mainstream Publishing Co
 (Edinburgh) Ltd
Mitchell Beazley
Murdoch Books
Nelson Thornes Ltd
Octopus Publishing Group
The Orion Publishing Group Ltd
Pan Macmillan
Penguin Random House UK Ltd
Piatkus Books
Quadrille Publishing Ltd
Quantum Publishing
RotoVision SA
Roundhouse Publishing Ltd
Sheldon Press
Short Books Ltd
Simon & Schuster (UK) Ltd
Southgate Publishers
Souvenir Press Ltd
Summersdale Publishers Ltd
Temple Lodge Publishing
Trog Associates Ltd
Wiley
Zymurgy Publishing

HISTORY & ANTIQUARIAN

Acair Ltd
Acumen Publishing Ltd
Adam Matthew Digital Ltd
Albyn Press
Ian Allan Publishing Ltd
Amber Books Ltd
Amolibros
Anglo-Saxon Books
Appletree Press Ltd
Arena Books (Publishers)
Ashgate Publishing Ltd
Atlantic Books
Atlantic Europe Publishing Co Ltd
Authorhouse UK LLC
Barny Books
Batsford
BBH Publishing Ltd
The Belmont Press
Bene Factum Publishing Ltd
Berghahn Books
Birlinn Ltd
Blackthorn Press
Bloomsbury Academic &
 Professional
Bloomsbury Publishing PLC
Blue Ocean Publishing
Bodleian Library Publishing
Borthwick Publications
Bossiney Books Ltd
Bowker Market Research
 (formerly BML)
Boydell & Brewer Ltd
Brewin Books Ltd
Bridge Books
British Library
British Museum Press
Cambridge University Press
Canongate Books
Capall Bann Publishing Ltd
Capuchin Classics
Carnegie Publishing Ltd
Jon Carpenter Publishing
The Catholic Truth Society
Caxton Publishing Group Ltd
Christian Focus Publications
James Clarke & Co
Colour Heroes Ltd
Columba
Copper Beech Publishing Ltd
Cork University Press
Cornwall Editions Ltd
Countryside Books
Countyvise Ltd
Crécy Publishing Ltd
D & N Publishing
The Davenant Press
Richard Dennis Publications
J. M. Dent
The Dovecote Press
Ashley Drake Publishing Ltd
Dramatic Lines
Gerald Duckworth & Co Ltd
Dunedin Academic Press

Dynasty Press
Edinburgh University Press
Elliott & Thompson
English Heritage
Equinox Publishing Ltd
The Erskine Press
Ex Libris Press
A. & A. Farmar
Five Leaves Publications
Four Courts Press
F&W Media International Ltd
Garnet Publishing Ltd
Geography Publications
Gibson Square
Gill & Macmillan
Alan Godfrey Maps
Gomer
Gracewing Publishing
Greenhill Books / Lionel Leventhal
 Ltd
Gresham Books Ltd
Guildhall Press
Halban Publishers
Robert Hale Ltd
HarperCollins Publishers Ltd
Harvard University Press
Haus Publishing Ltd
Haynes Publishing
Heart of Albion Press
Helion & Co Ltd
Ian Henry Publications Ltd
Historical Publications Ltd
Hobnob Press
Hodder Education
Hodder Faith
Hodder & Stoughton
Alison Hodge Publishers
Holo Books
Hypatia Publications
Icon Books Ltd.
Intellect Ltd
Irish Academic Press
Ithaca Press
James & James (Publishers) Ltd
Janus Publishing Co Ltd
The King's England Press
Liberties Press
Librario Publishers Ltd
The Lilliput Press Ltd
Little, Brown Book Group
The Littman Library of Jewish
 Civilization
Liverpool University Press
Logaston Press
Lomond Books Ltd
Londubh Books
Luath Press Ltd
The Lutterworth Press
Macmillan Science and Education
McNidder & Grace
Mainstream Publishing Co
 (Edinburgh) Ltd
Manchester University Press
Maney Publishing
Melisende UK Ltd
Mercier Press Ltd
The Merlin Press Ltd
Merrell Publishers Ltd
Merton Priory Press Ltd
Microform Academic Publishers
Mitchell Beazley
Moorley's Print & Publishing Ltd
Murdoch Books
John Murray Publishers
National Portrait Gallery
 Publications
National Records of Scotland
The National Trust
Nelson Thornes Ltd
New Island Books Ltd
NMS Enterprises Limited -
 Publishing
North York Moors National Park
 Authority
W. W. Norton & Company Ltd
The Nostalgia Collection
Octopus Publishing Group
Open University Worldwide
The Orion Publishing Group Ltd
Osprey Publishing Ltd
Oxford University Press
Palgrave Macmillan

Pan Macmillan
Penguin Random House UK Ltd
Piatkus Books
Pickering & Chatto (Publishers) Ltd
Polperro Heritage Press
Princeton University Press
Profile Books
ProQuest
Pushkin Press
Quantum Publishing
Quartet Books
The Radcliffe Press
Redcliffe Press Ltd
Reflections of a Bygone Age
Roundhouse Publishing Ltd
Royal Collection Trust
Royal Irish Academy
S. B. Publications
Saint Albert's Press
Saqi Books
Scala Arts & Heritage Publishers
 Ltd
Scottish Text Society
Sheldrake Press
Shepheard-Walwyn (Publishers)
 Ltd
The Shetland Times Ltd
Shire Publications Ltd
Short Books Ltd
Slightly Foxed
SLP Education
Smith Settle Printing &
 Bookbinding Ltd
Society of Genealogists
 Enterprises Ltd
Spokesman
Sportsbooks Ltd
Stacey Publishing Limited
Stainer & Bell Ltd
Stenlake Publishing Ltd
Summersdale Publishers Ltd
Sussex Academic Press
I. B. Tauris & Co Ltd
Taylor & Francis
Thames & Hudson Ltd
Toucan Books Ltd
Transworld Publishers Ltd
Troubador Publishing Ltd
Twelveheads Press
Tyne Bridge Publishing
Unicorn Press Ltd
United Writers Publications Ltd
University of Exeter Press
University of Hertfordshire Press
University of Toronto Press
University of Wales Press
Vallentine Mitchell Publishers
Veloce Publishing Ltd
Vertical Editions
Warburg Institute
Waterside Press
Paul Watkins Publishing
Waverley Books
David West Children's Books
Wiley
Philip Wilson Publishers
Neil Wilson Publishing Ltd
Yale University Press London

HUMOUR

Allison & Busby
Alma Books Ltd
Ammonite Press
Antique Collectors' Club Ltd
Appletree Press Ltd
Atlantic Books
Aurora Metro Publications Ltd
Authorhouse UK LLC
Barny Books
Bene Factum Publishing Ltd
Birlinn Ltd
John Blake Publishing Ltd
Bloomsbury Publishing PLC
Bodleian Library Publishing
Bowker Market Research
 (formerly BML)
Bradwell Books
Brown Dog Books
Canongate Books
Constable & Robinson Ltd
Countryside Books

Countyvise Ltd
CRW Publishing Ltd
Delancey Press Ltd
Gerald Duckworth & Co Ltd
Dynasty Press
Essential Works Ltd
W. Foulsham & Co Ltd
F&W Media International Ltd
Gibson Square
Gill & Macmillan
Gothic Image Publications
Guildhall Press
Robert Hale Ltd
HarperCollins Publishers Ltd
Haynes Publishing
Headline Book Publishing Ltd
Ian Henry Publications Ltd
Hodder & Stoughton
Holo Books
House of Stratus
Icon Books Ltd.
Indepenpress Publishing Ltd
Indigo Dreams Publishing Ltd
ISIS Publishing Ltd
Janus Publishing Co Ltd
The King's England Press
Liberties Press
Little, Brown Book Group
Lomond Books Ltd
Luath Press Ltd
Mainstream Publishing Co
 (Edinburgh) Ltd
Mercier Press Ltd
John Murray Publishers
The National Trust
New Island Books Ltd
The O'Brien Press Ltd
The Orion Publishing Group Ltd
Paragon Publishing
Penguin Random House UK Ltd
Percy Publishing
Piatkus Books
Quadrille Publishing Ltd
Quantum Publishing
Quiller Publishing Ltd
Ravette Publishing Ltd
Sandstone Press Ltd
Saqi Books
Sheldrake Press
Shire Publications Ltd
Short Books Ltd
Simon & Schuster (UK) Ltd
SLP Education
Souvenir Press Ltd
Summersdale Publishers Ltd
Top That! Publishing Ltd
Transworld Publishers Ltd
Troubador Publishing Ltd
United Writers Publications Ltd
Merlin Unwin Books Ltd
Weidenfeld & Nicolson
Neil Wilson Publishing Ltd
Y Lolfa Cyf
Zymurgy Publishing

ILLUSTRATED & FINE EDITIONS

Albion Press Ltd
Albyn Press
Amber Books Ltd
Ashgate Publishing Ltd
Bene Factum Publishing Ltd
Birlinn Ltd
Black Dog Publishing Ltd
British Library
Cambridge Publishing
 Management Ltd
Canongate Books
Colour Heroes Ltd
Constable & Robinson Ltd
Richard Dennis Publications
Gerald Duckworth & Co Ltd
Enitharmon Press
The Erskine Press
Essential Works Ltd
Everyman's Library
HarperCollins Publishers Ltd
Hayward Publishing
The Ivy Press Ltd
Dewi Lewis Publishing
Liberties Press
The Lilliput Press Ltd

Lomond Books Ltd
Lund Humphries
The Lutterworth Press
Mainstream Publishing Co
    (Edinburgh) Ltd
Manchester University Press
Maney Publishing
Melisende UK Ltd
Merrell Publishers Ltd
Mitchell Beazley
National Galleries of Scotland
National Portrait Gallery
    Publications
Natural History Museum
    Publishing
The Old Stile Press
The Orion Publishing Group Ltd
Palazzo Editions Ltd
Papadakis Publisher
Penguin Random House UK Ltd
Phaidon Press Ltd
Quartet Books
Quiller Publishing Ltd
Royal Collection Trust
Sandstone Press Ltd
Saqi Books
Scala Arts & Heritage Publishers
    Ltd
Shepheard-Walwyn (Publishers)
    Ltd
Shire Publications Ltd
Charles Skilton Ltd
Slightly Foxed
Smith Settle Printing &
    Bookbinding Ltd
Stacey Publishing Limited
Tate Publishing
teNeues Publishing UK Ltd
Thames & Hudson Ltd
Third Millennium Publishing Ltd
Toucan Books Ltd
Unicorn Press Ltd
University of Wales Press
Merlin Unwin Books Ltd
Veloce Publishing Ltd
Weidenfeld & Nicolson
Philip Wilson Publishers
Worth Press Ltd
Yale University Press London
Zymurgy Publishing

INDUSTRY, BUSINESS & MANAGEMENT

Alpha Science International Ltd
Anthem Press
Arena Books (Publishers)
Ashgate Publishing Ltd
Atlantic Books
Aurelian Information Ltd
Barny Books
Bene Factum Publishing Ltd
Bloomsbury Academic &
    Professional
Bloomsbury Publishing PLC
Blue Ocean Publishing
Blueberry Press Ltd
Bowker Market Research
    (formerly BML)
Nicholas Brealey Publishing
*Cambridge Publishing
    Management Ltd*
Cambridge University Press
Carnegie Publishing Ltd
Cengage Learning EMEA Ltd
Centre for Economic Policy
    Research
Chartered Institute of Personnel &
    Development
Chartridge Books Oxford
Commonwealth Secretariat
Crimson Publishing
DJØF
Ashley Drake Publishing Ltd
Edward Elgar Publishing Ltd
Elliott & Thompson
Elsevier Ltd
Energy Institute
Ethics International Press Ltd
Executive Grapevine International
    Ltd
Filament Publishing Ltd

W. Foulsham & Co Ltd
Gower Publishing Co Ltd
Greenleaf Publishing
HarperCollins Publishers Ltd
Harriman House
Hawthorn Press
HB Publications
Hodder Education
How To Books Ltd
John Hunt Publishing Ltd
ICSA Information & Training Ltd
Imperial College Press
In Easy Steps Limited
Indepenpress Publishing Ltd
Institute for Employment Studies
Institution of Engineering and
    Technology (IET)
IT Governance Publishing
IWA Publishing
James & James (Publishers) Ltd
Jordan Publishing Ltd
Kogan Page Ltd
McGraw-Hill Education
Market House Books Ltd
The MIT Press Ltd
The National Academies Press
National Housing Federation
Nelson Thornes Ltd
Oak Tree Press
Open University Worldwide
Orpen Press
Oxford University Press
Palgrave Macmillan
Paragon Publishing
Penguin Random House UK Ltd
Piatkus Books
PP Publishing
Princeton University Press
Profile Books
ProQuest
Quantum Publishing
Round Hall
Roundhouse Publishing Ltd
Sherwood Publishing
Sigel Press
Simon & Schuster (UK) Ltd
Social Affairs Unit
Souvenir Press Ltd
Stillwater Publishing Ltd
Sussex Academic Press
Taylor & Francis
Thorogood Publishing Ltd
Trog Associates Ltd
Trotman Publishing
Troubador Publishing Ltd
United Writers Publications Ltd
University of Ottawa Press
Weidenfeld & Nicolson
Wiley
WIT Press
Zambezi Publishing Ltd

LANGUAGES & LINGUISTICS

Advance Materials Ltd
Anglo-Saxon Books
Association for Scottish Literary
    Studies
Ayebia Clarke Publishing Ltd
b small publishing ltd
Berghahn Books
Joseph Biddulph Publisher
Bloomsbury Academic &
    Professional
Bloomsbury Publishing PLC
Bowker Market Research
    (formerly BML)
Brilliant Publications
Cambridge University Press
Carel Press Ltd
CfBT Education Trust
Channel View Publications Ltd
Claire Publications
Cois Life
Creative Content Ltd
Delta ELT Publishing Ltd
Edinburgh University Press
Elsevier Ltd
Equinox Publishing Ltd
Geography Publications
Gomer
HarperCollins Publishers Ltd

Hinton House Publishers Ltd
Hodder Education
Icon Books Ltd.
Intellect Ltd
Ithaca Press
Jarndyce Booksellers
Lexus Ltd
Liverpool University Press
Luath Press Ltd
Macmillan Science and Education
Manchester University Press
Maney Publishing
The MIT Press Ltd
John Murray Publishers
Nelson Thornes Ltd
Open University Worldwide
Oxford University Press
Packard Publishing Ltd
Palgrave Macmillan
Paragon Publishing
Royal Irish Academy
St Jerome Publishing Ltd
Saqi Books
Stacey Publishing Limited
Ta Ha Publishers Ltd
Taigh na Teud Music Publishers
Taylor & Francis
Troubador Publishing Ltd
University of Ottawa Press
University of Wales Press
Usborne Publishing Ltd
Paul Watkins Publishing
Whiting & Birch Ltd
Wiley
Y Lolfa Cyf
Yale University Press London

LAW

Anthem Press
Ashgate Publishing Ltd
Atlantic Books
Bene Factum Publishing Ltd
Bloomsbury Academic &
    Professional
Borthwick Publications
Bowker Market Research
    (formerly BML)
*Cambridge Publishing
    Management Ltd*
Cambridge University Press
Class Professional
Commonwealth Secretariat
Delta Alpha Publishing Ltd
J. M. Dent
DJØF
Dynasty Press
Edinburgh University Press
Edward Elgar Publishing Ltd
Ethics International Press Ltd
Four Courts Press
W. Green The Scottish Law
    Publisher
Hart Publishing
Harvard University Press
Hodder Education
Holo Books
Incorporated Council of Law
    Reporting for England and
    Wales
Institute of Employment Rights
The Islamic Texts Society
Ithaca Press
Jordan Publishing Ltd
Jessica Kingsley Publishers
Kube Publishing Ltd
Law Reports International Ltd
Law Society Publishing
Legal Action Group
McGraw-Hill Education
Manchester University Press
Market House Books Ltd
Nelson Thornes Ltd
Oak Tree Press
Orpen Press
Oxford University Press
Palgrave Macmillan
PP Publishing
Princeton University Press
Round Hall
Saqi Books
Sussex Academic Press

Taylor & Francis
Third Millennium Publishing Ltd
Thomson Reuters – Professional
    Division
Thorogood Publishing Ltd
Trentham Books
University of Hertfordshire Press
University of Toronto Press
Waterside Press
Weidenfeld & Nicolson
Which? Ltd

LITERATURE & CRITICISM

Adam Matthew Digital Ltd
Albyn Press
Alma Classics
Anthem Press
Arena Books (Publishers)
Ashgate Publishing Ltd
Ashgrove Publishing
Association for Scottish Literary
    Studies
Atlantic Books
Ayebia Clarke Publishing Ltd
Berghahn Books
Bloodaxe Books Ltd
Bloomsbury Academic &
    Professional
Bloomsbury Publishing PLC
Blue Ocean Publishing
Bodleian Library Publishing
Marion Boyars Publishers Ltd
Boydell & Brewer Ltd
Cambridge University Press
Canongate Books
Carel Press Ltd
Caxton Publishing Group Ltd
James Clarke & Co
Cois Life
Cork University Press
The Davenant Press
J. M. Dent
Ashley Drake Publishing Ltd
Gerald Duckworth & Co Ltd
Edinburgh University Press
Enitharmon Press
Everyman's Library
Faber & Faber Ltd
Four Courts Press
Freelance Market News
Garnet Publishing Ltd
Gomer
Guildhall Press
H & S Media
Halban Publishers
HarperCollins Publishers Ltd
Harvard University Press
Haus Publishing Ltd
Hippopotamus Press
Hobnob Press
Hodder Education
House of Stratus
How To Books Ltd
John Hunt Publishing Ltd
Icon Books Ltd.
Indepenpress Publishing Ltd
Intellect Ltd
Irish Academic Press
Ithaca Press
Janus Publishing Co Ltd
Jarndyce Booksellers
Liberties Press
The Lilliput Press Ltd
Little, Brown Book Group
The Littman Library of Jewish
    Civilization
Liverpool University Press
Luath Press Ltd
The Lutterworth Press
Mainstream Publishing Co
    (Edinburgh) Ltd
Manchester University Press
Mandrake of Oxford
Maney Publishing
Mercier Press Ltd
Microform Academic Publishers
Nelson Thornes Ltd
New Island Books Ltd
Northcote House Publishers Ltd
W. W. Norton & Company Ltd
The Old Stile Press

Open University Worldwide
Oxford University Press
Palgrave Macmillan
Pan Macmillan
Paragon Publishing
Paupers' Press
Penguin Random House UK Ltd
Pickering & Chatto (Publishers) Ltd
ProQuest
Pushkin Press
Quartet Books
Redcliffe Press Ltd
Roundhouse Publishing Ltd
Sandstone Press Ltd
Sansom & Co Ltd
Saqi Books
Scottish Text Society
Seren
Charles Skilton Ltd
Colin Smythe Ltd
Souvenir Press Ltd
Stenlake Publishing Ltd
Sussex Academic Press
The Swedenborg Society
Symposium Publications Literary &
    Art
Tabb House
Taylor & Francis
Thames & Hudson Ltd
Trog Associates Ltd
Troubador Publishing Ltd
University of Exeter Press
University of Ottawa Press
University of Toronto Press
University of Wales Press
Vallentine Mitchell Publishers
Wiley
Worth Press Ltd

MAGIC & THE OCCULT

Aeon Books
Amolibros
Anglo-Saxon Books
Archive Publishing
Blue Beyond Books
Bowker Market Research
    (formerly BML)
Capall Bann Publishing Ltd
Carnegie Publishing Ltd
Gerald Duckworth & Co Ltd
Eddison Sadd Editions Ltd
W. Foulsham & Co Ltd
Godsfield Press Ltd
Gothic Image Publications
Robert Hale Ltd
HarperCollins Publishers Ltd
Heart of Albion Press
John Hunt Publishing Ltd
Indepenpress Publishing Ltd
Janus Publishing Co Ltd
Luath Press Ltd
Mandrake of Oxford
Paragon Publishing
Piatkus Books
Quadrille Publishing Ltd
Quantum Publishing
The Society of Metaphysicians Ltd
Souvenir Press Ltd
Rudolf Steiner Press Ltd
Temple Lodge Publishing
Thames & Hudson Ltd
Thoth Publications
Troubador Publishing Ltd
University of Hertfordshire Press
Warburg Institute
Waverley Books
Zambezi Publishing Ltd

MATHEMATICS & STATISTICS

Alpha Science International Ltd
Anshan Ltd
Anthem Press
Atlantic Books
Atlantic Europe Publishing Co Ltd
Bernard Babani (Publishing) Ltd
Cambridge University Press
Carel Press Ltd
Cengage Learning EMEA Ltd
Chalksoft
Claire Publications

Class Professional
Elsevier Ltd
W. Foulsham & Co Ltd
HB Publications
Hodder Education
Icon Books Ltd.
Imperial College Press
Institute of Mathematics and its
  Applications
McGraw-Hill Education
Macmillan Science and Education
MW Educational
The National Academies Press
National Records of Scotland
Nelson Thornes Ltd
W. W. Norton & Company Ltd
Open University Worldwide
Oxford University Press
Palgrave Macmillan
Princeton University Press
ProQuest
Royal Irish Academy
Saqi Books
SLP Education
Souvenir Press Ltd
Tarquin Publications
Taylor & Francis
University of Hertfordshire Press
Ward Lock Educational Co Ltd
Wiley
WIT Press

MEDICAL (INCL. SELF-HELP & ALTERNATIVE MEDICINE)

Alpha Science International Ltd
American Psychiatric Publishing
Amolibros
Anshan Ltd
Anthem Press
Archive Publishing
Ashgrove Publishing
Barny Books
Bene Factum Publishing Ltd
BLA Publishing Ltd
CABI
Cambridge Publishing
  Management Ltd
Cambridge University Press
Capall Bann Publishing Ltd
Carroll & Brown Ltd
Chartridge Books Oxford
Clairview Books Ltd
Class Professional
Clear Answer Medical Publishing
  Ltd
Constable & Robinson Ltd
Crown House Publishing Ltd
D & N Publishing
Denor Press Ltd
Dunedin Academic Press
Eddison Sadd Editions Ltd
Elsevier Ltd
The Erskine Press
Filament Publishing Ltd
Findhorn Press Ltd
Floris Books Trust Ltd
W. Foulsham & Co Ltd
Gibson Square
Godsfield Press Ltd
Haldane Mason Ltd
HarperCollins Publishers Ltd
Hawker Publications
Hawthorn Press
Haynes Publishing
Ian Henry Publications Ltd
Hinton House Publishers Ltd
How To Books Ltd
Human Kinetics Europe Ltd
John Hunt Publishing Ltd
Imperial College Press
Indepenpress Publishing Ltd
Institute of Physics & Engineering
  in Medicine
International Medical Press
Janus Publishing Co Ltd
S. Karger AG
Jessica Kingsley Publishers
Librario Publishers Ltd
Londubh Books
Luath Press Ltd
McGraw-Hill Education

Mainstream Publishing Co
  (Edinburgh) Ltd
Mandrake of Oxford
Maney Publishing
Market House Books Ltd
Mitchell Beazley
The National Academies Press
Nelson Thornes Ltd
Open University Worldwide
Orpen Press
Oxford University Press
Palgrave Macmillan
Paragon Publishing
PCCS Books Ltd
Penguin Random House UK Ltd
Piatkus Books
PP Publishing
ProQuest
Quadrille Publishing Ltd
Quantum Publishing
Round Hall
Roundhouse Publishing Ltd
Royal College of General
  Practitioners
The Royal College of Psychiatrists
Scion Publishing Ltd
Sheldon Press
Simon & Schuster (UK) Ltd
Social Affairs Unit
The Society of Metaphysicians Ltd
Souvenir Press Ltd
Rudolf Steiner Press Ltd
Tabb House
Taylor & Francis
Temple Lodge Publishing
tfm publishing Ltd
Troubador Publishing Ltd
University of Toronto Press
Merlin Unwin Books Ltd
Waverley Books
Whiting & Birch Ltd
Wiley
WIT Press
Zambezi Publishing Ltd

MILITARY & WAR

Adam Matthew Digital Ltd
Air-Britain (Historians) Ltd
Ian Allan Publishing Ltd
Amber Books Ltd
Anglo-Saxon Books
Arena Books (Publishers)
Ashgate Publishing Ltd
Ashgrove Publishing
Atlantic Books
Barny Books
Bene Factum Publishing Ltd
Berghahn Books
Birlinn Ltd
BLA Publishing Ltd
John Blake Publishing Ltd
Bloomsbury Academic &
  Professional
Bloomsbury Publishing PLC
Bodleian Library Publishing
Bowker Market Research
  (formerly BML)
Boydell & Brewer Ltd
Brewin Books Ltd
Bridge Books
Cambridge Publishing
  Management Ltd
Carnegie Publishing Group Ltd
Caxton Publishing Group Ltd
Chatham Publishing
Clairview Books Ltd
Colour Heroes Ltd
Constable & Robinson Ltd
Cork University Press
Countryside Books
Countyvise Ltd
Creative Content Ltd
Crécy Publishing Ltd
The Crowood Press Ltd
D & N Publishing
The Dovecote Press
Ashley Drake Publishing Ltd
Gerald Duckworth & Co Ltd
Elliott & Thompson
English Heritage
The Erskine Press

Essential Works Ltd
Filament Publishing Ltd
W. Foulsham & Co Ltd
Four Courts Press
Graham-Cameron Publishing &
  Illustration
Greenhill Books / Lionel Leventhal
  Ltd
Grub Street
Robert Hale Ltd
HarperCollins Publishers Ltd
Harvard University Press
Haus Publishing Ltd
Haynes Publishing
Helion & Co Ltd
Hodder & Stoughton
C. Hurst & Co (Publishers) Ltd
Icon Books Ltd.
Indepenpress Publishing Ltd
Irish Academic Press
ISIS Publishing Ltd
Janus Publishing Co Ltd
The King's England Press
Librario Publishers Ltd
Little, Brown Book Group
Luath Press Ltd
Lund Humphries
The Lutterworth Press
Mainstream Publishing Co
  (Edinburgh) Ltd
Maney Publishing
Maritime Books
Mercier Press Ltd
Microform Academic Publishers
Middleton Press
John Murray Publishers
Myriad Editions
NMS Enterprises Limited -
  Publishing
W. W. Norton & Company Ltd
The Nostalgia Collection
The Orion Publishing Group Ltd
Osprey Publishing Ltd
Oxford University Press
Paragon Publishing
Penguin Random House UK Ltd
Percy Publishing
Piatkus Books
Polperro Heritage Press
Quantum Publishing
Quiller Publishing Ltd
The Radcliffe Press
Roundhouse Publishing Ltd
Shire Publications Ltd
Sigel Press
Simon & Schuster (UK) Ltd
Charles Skilton Ltd
Souvenir Press Ltd
Spokesman
Stacey Publishing Limited
Sussex Academic Press
I. B. Tauris & Co Ltd
Taylor & Francis
Thames & Hudson Ltd
Third Millennium Publishing Ltd
Thorogood Publishing Ltd
Toucan Books Ltd
Transworld Publishers Ltd
Troubador Publishing Ltd
Unicorn Press Ltd
United Writers Publications Ltd
University of Toronto Press
University of Wales Press
Vallentine Mitchell Publishers
Veloce Publishing Ltd
David West Children's Books
Whittles Publishing
Wiley
Neil Wilson Publishing Ltd
Worth Press Ltd
Yale University Press London

MUSIC

Amolibros
Archive Publishing
Ashgate Publishing Ltd
Atlantic Books
Attic Press
Birlinn Ltd
BLA Publishing Ltd
Black Dog Publishing Ltd

Black Spring Press Ltd
John Blake Publishing Ltd
Bloomsbury Academic &
  Professional
Bloomsbury Publishing PLC
Blue Beyond Books
Blue Sky Press
Bowker Market Research
  (formerly BML)
Marion Boyars Publishers Ltd
Boydell & Brewer Ltd
Cambridge University Press
Canongate Books
Capall Bann Publishing Ltd
Chalksoft
Cork University Press
Dance Books Ltd
Denor Press Ltd
J. M. Dent
Gerald Duckworth & Co Ltd
Elliott & Thompson
Equinox Publishing Ltd
Essential Works Ltd
Faber & Faber Ltd
Four Courts Press
Gresham Books Ltd
Guildhall Press
H & S Media
Robert Hale Ltd
HarperCollins Publishers Ltd
Harvard University Press
Hawthorn Press
Haynes Publishing
Helter Skelter Publishing Ltd
Hymns Ancient & Modern Ltd
Icon Books Ltd.
Independent Music Press
Indepenpress Publishing Ltd
Indigo Dreams Publishing Ltd
Liberties Press
The Lilliput Press Ltd
Little, Brown Book Group
The Littman Library of Jewish
  Civilization
Luath Press Ltd
McCrimmon Publishing Co Ltd
McNidder & Grace
Mainstream Publishing Co
  (Edinburgh) Ltd
Market House Books Ltd
The MIT Press Ltd
Mitchell Beazley
Moorley's Print & Publishing Ltd
Nelson Thornes Ltd
W. W. Norton & Company Ltd
Omnibus Press
Oxford University Press
Palazzo Editions Ltd
Paragon Publishing
Penguin Random House UK Ltd
Phaidon Press Ltd
Piatkus Books
Porter House of Publishing Ltd
ProQuest
Quantum Publishing
Quartet Books
Saqi Books
SchoolPlay Productions Ltd
Schott Music Ltd
Scripture Union Publishing
Sheldrake Press
The Shetland Times Ltd
Simon & Schuster (UK) Ltd
Souvenir Press Ltd
Spartan Press Music Publishers Ltd
Stainer & Bell Ltd
Rudolf Steiner Press Ltd
Sussex Academic Press
Taigh na Teud Music Publishers
Taylor & Francis
Thames & Hudson Ltd
Transworld Publishers Ltd
Troubador Publishing Ltd
University of Wales Press
Usborne Publishing Ltd
Ward Lock Educational Co Ltd
Josef Weinberger Ltd
David West Children's Books
Wild Goose Publications
Wiley
Neil Wilson Publishing Ltd
Y Lolfa Cyf

Yale University Press London
Zymurgy Publishing

NATURAL HISTORY

AA Publishing
Amber Books Ltd
Antique Collectors' Club Ltd
Atlantic Books
Bender Richardson White
BLA Publishing Ltd
Bloomsbury Publishing PLC
Bodleian Library Publishing
Bowker Market Research
  (formerly BML)
Calypso Publications
Cambridge Publishing
  Management Ltd
Cambridge University Press
Capall Bann Publishing Ltd
Capuchin Classics
Carnegie Publishing Ltd
Chalksoft
Colour Heroes Ltd
Cork University Press
Cornwall Editions Ltd
Countyvise Ltd
The Crowood Press Ltd
D & N Publishing
The Dovecote Press
Gerald Duckworth & Co Ltd
Elliott & Thompson
The Erskine Press
Ex Libris Press
Graffeg Limited
Graham-Cameron Publishing &
  Illustration
Haldane Mason Ltd
Robert Hale Ltd
HarperCollins Publishers Ltd
Harvard University Press
Hodder Education
Alison Hodge Publishers
Icon Books Ltd.
The Ivy Press Ltd
Kew Publishing
Librario Publishers Ltd
Logaston Press
Lomond Books Ltd
Luath Press Ltd
The Lutterworth Press
Merrell Publishers Ltd
The MIT Press Ltd
Mitchell Beazley
The National Academies Press
The National Trust
Natural History Museum
  Publishing
NMS Enterprises Limited -
  Publishing
North York Moors National Park
  Authority
W. W. Norton & Company Ltd
Octopus Publishing Group
Open University Worldwide
The Orion Publishing Group Ltd
Papadakis Publisher
Paragon Publishing
Penguin Random House UK Ltd
Philip's
Polperro Heritage Press
Princeton University Press
ProQuest
Quantum Publishing
Quiller Publishing Ltd
Royal Collection Trust
S. B. Publications
Sheldrake Press
The Shetland Times Ltd
Shire Publications Ltd
Short Books Ltd
Souvenir Press Ltd
Stacey Publishing Limited
Stobart Davies Ltd
Subbuteo Natural History Books
Tango Books Ltd
Thames & Hudson Ltd
Top That! Publishing Ltd
Toucan Books Ltd
Troubador Publishing Ltd
Unicorn Press Ltd
Merlin Unwin Books Ltd

Usborne Publishing Ltd
David West Children's Books
Whittet Books Ltd
Whittles Publishing
Wiley
Willow Island Editions
Yale University Press London
Zymurgy Publishing

NAUTICAL

Ian Allan Publishing Ltd
Amber Books Ltd
Amolibros
The Belmont Press
BLA Publishing Ltd
Bloomsbury Publishing PLC
Brown, Son & Ferguson, Ltd
Chatham Publishing
Countyvise Ltd
Crécy Publishing Ltd
The Crowood Press Ltd
Delancey Press Ltd
Ex Libris Press
W. Foulsham & Co Ltd
Haynes Publishing
Imray Laurie Norie & Wilson Ltd
Janus Publishing Co Ltd
Librario Publishers Ltd
Middleton Press
The National Academies Press
W. W. Norton & Company Ltd
The Nostalgia Collection
The Orion Publishing Group Ltd
Paragon Publishing
Polperro Heritage Press
Quantum Publishing
Quiller Publishing Ltd
Roadmaster Publishing
Souvenir Press Ltd
Special Interest Model Books Ltd
Stenlake Publishing Ltd
Twelveheads Press
Unicorn Press Ltd
United Writers Publications Ltd
Paul Watkins Publishing
Whittles Publishing
Wiley
Neil Wilson Publishing Ltd

PHILOSOPHY

Acumen Publishing Ltd
Alban Books Ltd
Amolibros
Anthem Press
Arena Books (Publishers)
Ashgate Publishing Ltd
Atlantic Books
Ayebia Clarke Publishing Ltd
Bloomsbury Academic &
  Professional
Bloomsbury Publishing PLC
Blue Beyond Books
Bowker Market Research
  (formerly BML)
Marion Boyars Publishers Ltd
Boydell & Brewer Ltd
Cambridge University Press
Canongate Books
Capall Bann Publishing Ltd
James Clarke & Co
Cork University Press
Gerald Duckworth & Co Ltd
Dynasty Press
Edinburgh University Press
Everyman's Library
Fabian Society
Filament Publishing Ltd
Floris Books Trust Ltd
Four Courts Press
Gibson Square
Gothic Image Publications
Gracewing Publishing
Halban Publishers
Harvard University Press
Heart of Albion Press
Hodder Education
Hodder Faith
House of Stratus
John Hunt Publishing Ltd
Hymns Ancient & Modern Ltd

Icon Books Ltd.
Imprint Academic Ltd
Indepenpress Publishing Ltd
Intellect Ltd
Janus Publishing Co Ltd
The Littman Library of Jewish
  Civilization
The Lutterworth Press
McGraw-Hill Education
Mandrake of Oxford
Maney Publishing
The MIT Press Ltd
Nelson Thornes Ltd
W. W. Norton & Company Ltd
The Orion Publishing Group Ltd
Oxford University Press
Palgrave Macmillan
Paragon Publishing
Paupers' Press
Penguin Random House UK Ltd
Pickering & Chatto (Publishers) Ltd
Princeton University Press
Roundhouse Publishing Ltd
Saqi Books
Shepheard-Walwyn (Publishers)
  Ltd
Short Books Ltd
The Society of Metaphysicians Ltd
Souvenir Press Ltd
Spokesman
Rudolf Steiner Press Ltd
Stillwater Publishing Ltd
Sussex Academic Press
I. B. Tauris & Co Ltd
Taylor & Francis
Temple Lodge Publishing
Thames & Hudson Ltd
Tharpa Publications
Troubador Publishing Ltd
University of Toronto Press
University of Wales Press
Veritas Publications
Warburg Institute
Weidenfeld & Nicolson
Wiley
Windhorse Publications
Wordsworth Editions Ltd
Yale University Press London

PHOTOGRAPHY

AA Publishing
Acair Ltd
Ammonite Press
Antique Collectors' Club Ltd
Arcadia Books Ltd
BBH Publishing Ltd
Birlinn Ltd
Black Dog Publishing Ltd
Bowker Market Research
  (formerly BML)
Bradwell Books
Coastal Publishing Ltd
Cork University Press
D & N Publishing
Delta Alpha Publishing Ltd
Essential Works Ltd
Freelance Market News
F&W Media International Ltd
Garnet Publishing Ltd
Gomer
Graffeg Limited
Guildhall Press
Robert Hale Ltd
HarperCollins Publishers Ltd
Haynes Publishing
Hayward Publishing
Alison Hodge Publishers
The Ilex Press Ltd
In Easy Steps Limited
Dewi Lewis Publishing
The Lilliput Press Ltd
Luath Press Ltd
Lund Humphries
McNidder & Grace
Mainstream Publishing Co
  (Edinburgh) Ltd
Merrell Publishers Ltd
The MIT Press Ltd
Mitchell Beazley
National Galleries of Scotland

National Portrait Gallery
  Publications
The O'Brien Press Ltd
Pagoda Tree Press
Palazzo Editions Ltd
Papadakis Publisher
Paragon Publishing
Penguin Random House UK Ltd
Phaidon Press Ltd
Polperro Heritage Press
Prestel Publishing Ltd
Quadrille Publishing Ltd
Quantum Publishing
RotoVision SA
Roundhouse Publishing Ltd
Royal Collection Trust
Saqi Books
Seren
Sheldrake Press
Sigel Press
Stacey Publishing Limited
Tate Publishing
Taylor & Francis
teNeues Publishing UK Ltd
Thames & Hudson Ltd
Third Millennium Publishing Ltd
Unicorn Press Ltd
V&A Publishing
Weidenfeld & Nicolson
Which? Ltd
Wiley
Philip Wilson Publishers
Yale University Press London
Zymurgy Publishing

PHYSICS

Alpha Science International Ltd
Anshan Ltd
Anthem Press
Atlantic Europe Publishing Co Ltd
BLA Publishing Ltd
Cambridge University Press
Cengage Learning EMEA Ltd
Class Professional
Gerald Duckworth & Co Ltd
Elsevier Ltd
HarperCollins Publishers Ltd
Hodder Education
Icon Books Ltd.
Imperial College Press
Institute of Physics & Engineering
  in Medicine
McGraw-Hill Education
Macmillan Science and Education
The National Academies Press
Nelson Thornes Ltd
W. W. Norton & Company Ltd
Open University Worldwide
Oxford University Press
Palgrave Macmillan
Paragon Publishing
ProQuest
Taylor & Francis
Ward Lock Educational Co Ltd
Wiley
WIT Press
Worth Press Ltd

POETRY

Acair Ltd
Albyn Press
Alma Books Ltd
Alma Classics
Amolibros
Anglo-Saxon Books
Anthem Press
Anvil Press Poetry Ltd
Association for Scottish Literary
  Studies
Atlantic Books
Authorhouse UK LLC
Barny Books
Batsford
Bene Factum Publishing Ltd
Joseph Biddulph Publisher
Birlinn Ltd
Bloodaxe Books Ltd
Blue Beyond Books
Blue Ocean Publishing
Blue Sky Press

Bonacia Ltd
Bowker Market Research
  (formerly BML)
Canongate Books
Cois Life
Countyvise Ltd
Enitharmon Press
Everyman's Library
Ex Libris Press
Faber & Faber Ltd
Five Leaves Publications
W. Foulsham & Co Ltd
Freelance Market News
The Gallery Press
Gomer
Guildhall Press
H & S Media
Hachette Children's Books
HarperCollins Publishers Ltd
Hippopotamus Press
Indepenpress Publishing Ltd
Indigo Dreams Publishing Ltd
ISIS Publishing Ltd
Ithaca Press
Janus Publishing Co Ltd
Jarndyce Booksellers
The King's England Press
Lapwing Publications
Liberties Press
Liverpool University Press
Luath Press Ltd
Macmillan Children's Books Ltd
Mandrake of Oxford
Mercier Press Ltd
Moorley's Print & Publishing Ltd
Nelson Thornes Ltd
New Island Books Ltd
NMS Enterprises Limited -
  Publishing
W. W. Norton & Company Ltd
The Old Stile Press
Pan Macmillan
Paragon Publishing
Penguin Random House UK Ltd
Porter House of Publishing Ltd
ProQuest
Redcliffe Press Ltd
Robinswood Press Ltd
Saint Albert's Press
Saqi Books
Scottish Text Society
Seren
Charles Skilton Ltd
Smith Settle Printing &
  Bookbinding Ltd
Spokesman
Stellium Ltd
Stenlake Publishing Ltd
Symposium Publications Literary &
  Art
Tabb House
Troubador Publishing Ltd
University of Wales Press
Wiley
Wordsworth Editions Ltd
Y Lolfa Cyf

POLITICS & WORLD AFFAIRS

Acumen Publishing Ltd
Amolibros
Anthem Press
Arcadia Books Ltd
Arena Books (Publishers)
Ashgate Publishing Ltd
Atlantic Books
Attic Press
Ayebia Clarke Publishing Ltd
Berghahn Books
Birlinn Ltd
Bloomsbury Academic &
  Professional
Bloomsbury Publishing PLC
Bodleian Library Publishing
Bowker Market Research
  (formerly BML)
Cambridge University Press
Canongate Books
Capuchin Classics
Centre for Economic Policy
  Research
Clairview Books Ltd

Commonwealth Secretariat
Constable & Robinson Ltd
The Davenant Press
Ashley Drake Publishing Ltd
Gerald Duckworth & Co Ltd
Dynasty Press
Eco-logic Books
Edinburgh University Press
Edward Elgar Publishing Ltd
Elliott & Thompson
Ethics International Press Ltd
Faber & Faber Ltd
Fabian Society
Five Leaves Publications
Garnet Publishing Ltd
Gibson Square
Gill & Macmillan
Gothic Image Publications
Granta Books
Guildhall Press
H & S Media
Halban Publishers
Robert Hale Ltd
John Harper Publishing Ltd
HarperCollins Publishers Ltd
Harvard University Press
Haus Publishing Ltd
Hawthorn Press
Hemming Information Services
Hodder Education
Hodder & Stoughton
House of Stratus
John Hunt Publishing Ltd
C. Hurst & Co (Publishers) Ltd
Icon Books Ltd.
Imprint Academic Ltd
Indepenpress Publishing Ltd
Institute of Employment Rights
Irish Academic Press
Ithaca Press
Janus Publishing Co Ltd
Liberties Press
Little, Brown Book Group
The Littman Library of Jewish
  Civilization
Liverpool University Press
Luath Press Ltd
The Lutterworth Press
McGraw-Hill Education
McNidder & Grace
Mainstream Publishing Co
  (Edinburgh) Ltd
Manchester University Press
Melisende UK Ltd
Mercier Press Ltd
The Merlin Press Ltd
Microform Academic Publishers
The MIT Press Ltd
Myriad Editions
Nelson Thornes Ltd
New Island Books Ltd
W. W. Norton & Company Ltd
The O'Brien Press Ltd
Open University Worldwide
The Orion Publishing Group Ltd
Orpen Press
Oxfam Publishing
Oxford University Press
Pagoda Tree Press
Palgrave Macmillan
Penguin Random House UK Ltd
Policy Press
Princeton University Press
Profile Books
ProQuest
Quartet Books
The Radcliffe Press
Roundhouse Publishing Ltd
Joseph Rowntree Foundation
Royal Irish Academy
Sandstone Press Ltd
Saqi Books
Shepheard-Walwyn (Publishers)
  Ltd
Simon & Schuster (UK) Ltd
Social Affairs Unit
Spokesman
Stacey Publishing Limited
Rudolf Steiner Press Ltd
Sussex Academic Press
I. B. Tauris & Co Ltd
Taylor & Francis

Temple Lodge Publishing
Transworld Publishers Ltd
Trentham Books
Troubador Publishing Ltd
University of Ottawa Press
University of Toronto Press
University of Wales Press
Vallentine Mitchell Publishers
Weidenfeld & Nicolson
Wiley
Y Lolfa Cyf
Yale University Press London
Zed Books Ltd

PSYCHOLOGY & PSYCHIATRY

American Psychiatric Publishing
Anshan Ltd
Archive Publishing
Ashgrove Publishing
Atlantic Books
Bloomsbury Publishing PLC
Bowker Market Research
  (formerly BML)
Nicholas Brealey Publishing
British Association for Adoption &
  Fostering
Cambridge University Press
Canongate Books
Capall Bann Publishing Ltd
Cengage Learning EMEA Ltd
Channel View Publications Ltd
Class Professional
Constable & Robinson Ltd
Cork University Press
Crown House Publishing Ltd
Delancey Press Ltd
Dynasty Press
Elsevier Ltd
The Fostering Network
W. Foulsham & Co Ltd
Gibson Square
Gill & Macmillan
Gothic Image Publications
HarperCollins Publishers Ltd
Harvard University Press
Hawthorn Press
Heart of Albion Press
Hinton House Publishers Ltd
Hodder Education
Human Kinetics Europe Ltd
John Hunt Publishing Ltd
Icon Books Ltd.
Imprint Academic Ltd
S. Karger AG
Karnac Books Ltd
Jessica Kingsley Publishers
Learning Matters
Liberties Press
Little, Brown Book Group
Londubh Books
McGraw-Hill Education
Mainstream Publishing Co
  (Edinburgh) Ltd
Market House Books Ltd
The MIT Press Ltd
The National Academies Press
The National Autistic Society
  (NAS)
Nelson Thornes Ltd
W. W. Norton & Company Ltd
Open University Worldwide
Orpen Press
Oxford University Press
Palgrave Macmillan
PCCS Books Ltd
Penguin Random House UK Ltd
Piatkus Books
ProQuest
Roundhouse Publishing Ltd
The Royal College of Psychiatrists
Sheldon Press
Sherwood Publishing
Sigel Press
Souvenir Press Ltd
Stillwater Publishing Ltd
Sussex Academic Press
Taylor & Francis
Troubador Publishing Ltd
United Writers Publications Ltd
University of Hertfordshire Press
Whiting & Birch Ltd

Wiley
Zambezi Publishing Ltd

REFERENCE BOOKS,
DIRECTORIES & DICTIONARIES

Acumen Publishing Ltd
Adamson Publishing Ltd
Alban Books Ltd
Albyn Press
Ian Allan Publishing Ltd
Alpha Science International Ltd
Amber Books Ltd
American Psychiatric Publishing
Ammonite Press
Anglo-Saxon Books
Anshan Ltd
Anthem Press
Antique Collectors' Club Ltd
Appletree Press Ltd
Ashgate Publishing Ltd
Atlantic Books
Atlantic Europe Publishing Co Ltd
Aurelian Information Ltd
Aurora Metro Publications Ltd
Award Publications Ltd
Bender Richardson White
Bene Factum Publishing Ltd
Joseph Biddulph Publisher
BLA Publishing Ltd
Bloomsbury Academic &
  Professional
Bloomsbury Publishing PLC
Bodleian Library Publishing
Bowker Market Research
  (formerly BML)
Boydell & Brewer Ltd
Bradwell Books
British Association for Adoption &
  Fostering
British Museum Press
Calypso Publications
*Cambridge Publishing
  Management Ltd*
Cambridge University Press
Camra Books
Capuchin Classics
Carel Press Ltd
The Catholic Truth Society
Caxton Publishing Group Ltd
CBD Research Ltd
Cengage Learning EMEA Ltd
Church House Publishing
James Clarke & Co
Commonwealth Secretariat
Constable & Robinson Ltd
Countryside Books
D & N Publishing
Delta Alpha Publishing Ltd
J. M. Dent
Diagram Visual Information Ltd
Gerald Duckworth & Co Ltd
Edward Elgar Publishing Ltd
Encyclopaedia Britannica (UK) Ltd
Energy Institute
Equinox Publishing Ltd
Executive Grapevine International
  Ltd
Food Trade Press Ltd
W. Foulsham & Co Ltd
Four Courts Press
Friends of the Earth
Geography Publications
Stanley Gibbons
Gill & Macmillan
Gomer
*Graham-Cameron Publishing &
  Illustration*
Hachette Children's Books
Robert Hale Ltd
HarperCollins Publishers Ltd
Harvard University Press
Haynes Publishing
Hemming Information Services
Hodder Education
How To Books Ltd
Hymns Ancient & Modern Ltd
Hypatia Publications
Icon Books Ltd.
The Ilex Press Ltd
In Easy Steps Limited
Indepenpress Publishing Ltd

Inter-Varsity Press
IWA Publishing
Jarndyce Booksellers
Richard Joseph Publishers Ltd
Kew Publishing
Kogan Page Ltd
Kyle Books
Dewi Lewis Publishing
Lexus Ltd
The Lilliput Press Ltd
LISU
Logaston Press
Lomond Books Ltd
The Lutterworth Press
McGraw-Hill Education
Macmillan Science and Education
McNidder & Grace
Manchester University Press
Market House Books Ltd
Methodist Publishing
The MIT Press Ltd
Mitchell Beazley
National Housing Federation
National Portrait Gallery
  Publications
The National Trust
The Orion Publishing Group Ltd
Oxford University Press
Pagoda Tree Press
Palgrave Macmillan
Penguin Random House UK Ltd
Philip's
Princeton University Press
ProQuest
Ripley Publishing Ltd
RotoVision SA
Round Hall
Roundhouse Publishing Ltd
Royal Irish Academy
Royal Society of Chemistry
St Jerome Publishing Ltd
Social Affairs Unit
Stainer & Bell Ltd
I. B. Tauris & Co Ltd
Taylor & Francis
Thames & Hudson Ltd
Top That! Publishing Ltd
Toucan Books Ltd
Trotman Publishing
UCAS
Unicorn Press Ltd
University of Ottawa Press
University of Toronto Press
University of Wales Press
Merlin Unwin Books Ltd
Usborne Publishing Ltd
Veloce Publishing Ltd
Waterside Press
Waverley Books
Which? Ltd
Whittles Publishing
Wiley
Wordsworth Editions Ltd

RELIGION & THEOLOGY

Acumen Publishing Ltd
Alban Books Ltd
Amolibros
Arena Books (Publishers)
Ashgate Publishing Ltd
Ashgrove Publishing
Atlantic Books
Atlantic Europe Publishing Co Ltd
Authentic Media
Authorhouse UK LLC
The Banner of Truth Trust
Bender Richardson White
Berghahn Books
Bible Reading Fellowship
Joseph Biddulph Publisher
BLA Publishing Ltd
Bloomsbury Academic &
  Professional
Bloomsbury Publishing PLC
Blue Beyond Books
Blue Ocean Publishing
Borthwick Publications
Bowker Market Research
  (formerly BML)
Bryntirion Press

*Cambridge Publishing
  Management Ltd*
Cambridge University Press
Canongate Books
Capall Bann Publishing Ltd
Capuchin Classics
The Catholic Truth Society
Christian Education
Christian Focus Publications
Church House Publishing
Clairview Books Ltd
James Clarke & Co
Colour Heroes Ltd
Columba
David C. Cook (UK)
Countyvise Ltd
Cyhoeddiadau'r Gair
The Davenant Press
Ashley Drake Publishing Ltd
Gerald Duckworth & Co Ltd
Dynasty Press
Edinburgh University Press
Equinox Publishing Ltd
Filament Publishing Ltd
Findhorn Press Ltd
Floris Books Trust Ltd
Four Courts Press
Garnet Publishing Ltd
Godsfield Press Ltd
Gothic Image Publications
Gracewing Publishing
*Graham-Cameron Publishing &
  Illustration*
Gresham Books Ltd
H & S Media
Halban Publishers
HarperCollins Publishers Ltd
Harvard University Press
Hawthorn Press
Heart of Albion Press
Highland Books
Hodder Education
Hodder Faith
John Hunt Publishing Ltd
C. Hurst & Co (Publishers) Ltd
Hymns Ancient & Modern Ltd
Icon Books Ltd.
Imprint Academic Ltd
Indepenpress Publishing Ltd
Inter-Varsity Press
Irish Academic Press
The Islamic Texts Society
Ithaca Press
Janus Publishing Co Ltd
Jessica Kingsley Publishers
Kube Publishing Ltd
Liberties Press
Lion Hudson Plc
The Littman Library of Jewish
  Civilization
The Lutterworth Press
McCrimmon Publishing Co Ltd
Mandrake of Oxford
Maney Publishing
Melisende UK Ltd
Mercier Press Ltd
Methodist Publishing
Microform Academic Publishers
Moorley's Print & Publishing Ltd
Nelson Thornes Ltd
W. W. Norton & Company Ltd
The Open Bible Trust
Open University Worldwide
Oxford University Press
Palgrave Macmillan
Paragon Publishing
PCCS Books Ltd
Penguin Random House UK Ltd
Pickering & Chatto (Publishers) Ltd
Porter House of Publishing Ltd
ProQuest
Quantum Publishing
Redemptorist Publications
Roundhouse Publishing Ltd
Saint Albert's Press
Saqi Books
Scripture Union Publishing
Shepheard-Walwyn (Publishers)
  Ltd
Simon & Schuster (UK) Ltd
The Society for Promoting
  Christian Knowledge (SPCK)

Souvenir Press Ltd
Stainer & Bell Ltd
Rudolf Steiner Press Ltd
Stillwater Publishing Ltd
Sussex Academic Press
The Swedenborg Society
Ta Ha Publishers Ltd
Tabb House
I. B. Tauris & Co Ltd
Taylor & Francis
Temple Lodge Publishing
Thames & Hudson Ltd
Tharpa Publications
Thoth Publications
Trinitarian Bible Society
University of Wales Press
Vallentine Mitchell Publishers
Veritas Publications
Warburg Institute
Ward Lock Educational Co Ltd
Wild Goose Publications
Wiley
Windhorse Publications
Worth Press Ltd
Yale University Press London

SCIENCE FICTION

Allison & Busby
Arena Books (Publishers)
Atlantic Books
Authorhouse UK LLC
Bowker Market Research
  (formerly BML)
Constable & Robinson Ltd
Gerald Duckworth & Co Ltd
Everyman's Library
Victor Gollancz Ltd
HarperCollins Publishers Ltd
Headline Book Publishing Ltd
Hodder & Stoughton
House of Stratus
Icon Books Ltd.
Indepenpress Publishing Ltd
ISIS Publishing Ltd
Janus Publishing Co Ltd
Little, Brown Book Group
Liverpool University Press
Orion Books Ltd
The Orion Publishing Group Ltd
Pan Macmillan
Paragon Publishing
Penguin Random House UK Ltd
Percy Publishing
Sandstone Press Ltd
Sigel Press
Simon & Schuster (UK) Ltd
Transworld Publishers Ltd
Troubador Publishing Ltd
United Writers Publications Ltd

SCIENTIFIC & TECHNICAL

Alpha Science International Ltd
Amolibros
Anshan Ltd
Anthem Press
Atlantic Europe Publishing Co Ltd
Bernard Babani (Publishing) Ltd
Bowker Market Research
  (formerly BML)
British Geological Survey
CABI
Calypso Publications
*Cambridge Publishing
  Management Ltd*
Cambridge University Press
Chalksoft
Chartridge Books Oxford
Class Professional
Colour Heroes Ltd
Commonwealth Secretariat
J. M. Dent
Elsevier Ltd
Energy Institute
Food Trade Press Ltd
Forensic Science Society
The Geological Society
Greenleaf Publishing
HarperCollins Publishers Ltd
Haynes Publishing
Hemming Information Services

Hodder Education
Human Kinetics Europe Ltd
Icon Books Ltd.
Imperial College Press
Imprint Academic Ltd
In Easy Steps Limited
Institute of Acoustics
Institute of Food Science & Technology
Institute of Physics & Engineering in Medicine
Institution of Engineering and Technology (IET)
Intellect Ltd
IT Governance Publishing
IWA Publishing
Kew Publishing
McGraw-Hill Education
Maney Publishing
Market House Books Ltd
The MIT Press Ltd
The National Academies Press
Nelson Thornes Ltd
NMS Enterprises Limited - Publishing
Open University Worldwide
Oxford University Press
Packard Publishing Ltd
Palgrave Macmillan
Papadakis Publisher
Paragon Publishing
Pickering & Chatto (Publishers) Ltd
Princeton University Press
The Professional and Higher Partnership Ltd
ProQuest
Royal Society of Chemistry
Scion Publishing Ltd
Sigel Press
The Society of Metaphysicians Ltd
Stillwater Publishing Ltd
Stobart Davies Ltd
Tarquin Publications
Taylor & Francis
Trog Associates Ltd
Usborne Publishing Ltd
David West Children's Books
Whittles Publishing
Wiley
WIT Press

SOCIOLOGY & ANTHROPOLOGY

Acumen Publishing Ltd
Anthem Press
Arena Books (Publishers)
Ashgate Publishing Ltd
Berghahn Books
Bloomsbury Academic & Professional
Bowker Market Research (formerly BML)
British Association for Adoption & Fostering
British Museum Press
Cambridge University Press
Centre for Policy on Ageing
Channel View Publications Ltd
Countryside Books
Dunedin Academic Press
Equinox Publishing Ltd
Garnet Publishing Ltd
Gibson Square
Harvard University Press
Hawthorn Press
Heart of Albion Press
Hodder Education
John Hunt Publishing Ltd
C. Hurst & Co (Publishers) Ltd
Icon Books Ltd.
Imperial College Press
Imprint Academic Ltd
Institute of Education Press
Intellect Ltd
Irish Academic Press
Ithaca Press
Janus Publishing Co Ltd
Jarndyce Booksellers
Jessica Kingsley Publishers
Sean Kingston Publishing
Learning Matters

The Littman Library of Jewish Civilization
Liverpool University Press
McGraw-Hill Education
Manchester University Press
Mandrake of Oxford
The Merlin Press Ltd
Microform Academic Publishers
Nelson Thornes Ltd
NMS Enterprises Limited - Publishing
W. W. Norton & Company Ltd
Open University Worldwide
Orpen Press
Palgrave Macmillan
Piatkus Books
Policy Press
Princeton University Press
ProQuest
Joseph Rowntree Foundation
Saqi Books
Shire Publications Ltd
Social Affairs Unit
Souvenir Press Ltd
Spokesman
Rudolf Steiner Press Ltd
Stillwater Publishing Ltd
Sussex Academic Press
I. B. Tauris & Co Ltd
Taylor & Francis
Thames & Hudson Ltd
Troubador Publishing Ltd
University of Hertfordshire Press
University of Ottawa Press
University of Toronto Press
University of Wales Press
Waterside Press
Whiting & Birch Ltd
Wiley
Zed Books Ltd

SPORTS & GAMES

Ian Allan Publishing Ltd
J. A. Allen
Amber Books Ltd
Amolibros
Appletree Press Ltd
Atlantic Books
John Blake Publishing Ltd
Bloomsbury Publishing PLC
Bodleian Library Publishing
Bowker Market Research (formerly BML)
Brown Dog Books
Butterfingers Books
Carel Press Ltd
Christian Focus Publications
Cicerone Press Ltd
Class Professional
Colour Heroes Ltd
Constable & Robinson Ltd
Copper Beech Publishing Ltd
Cork University Press
Countyvise Ltd
The Crowood Press Ltd
D & N Publishing
Diagram Visual Information Ltd
Ashley Drake Publishing Ltd
Gerald Duckworth & Co Ltd
Elliott & Thompson
Essential Works Ltd
Filament Publishing Ltd
First & Best in Education
Footprint Travel Guides
W. Foulsham & Co Ltd
Gomer
Graffeg Limited
Haldane Mason Ltd
Robert Hale Ltd
HarperCollins Publishers Ltd
Hart McLeod Ltd
Harvey Map Services Ltd
Haynes Publishing
Roger Heavens
Hodder Education
Hodder & Stoughton
Alison Hodge Publishers
Human Kinetics Europe Ltd
Icon Books Ltd.
Imray Laurie Norie & Wilson Ltd
Indepenpress Publishing Ltd

Janus Publishing Co Ltd
Jessica Kingsley Publishers
Kyle Books
Lavender and White Publishing
Dewi Lewis Publishing
Liberties Press
Little, Brown Book Group
Lomond Books Ltd
Luath Press Ltd
The Lutterworth Press
Mainstream Publishing Co (Edinburgh) Ltd
Mercier Press Ltd
Mitchell Beazley
Motor Racing Publications Ltd
The Myrtle Press
Nelson Thornes Ltd
W. W. Norton & Company Ltd
The O'Brien Press Ltd
Octopus Publishing Group
The Orion Publishing Group Ltd
Pan Macmillan
Paragon Publishing
Penguin Random House UK Ltd
Quantum Publishing
Quiller Publishing Ltd
Reflections of a Bygone Age
Sandstone Press Ltd
Shire Publications Ltd
Short Books Ltd
Sigma Press
Simon & Schuster (UK) Ltd
SLP Education
Smith Settle Printing & Bookbinding Ltd
Soccer Books Ltd
Souvenir Press Ltd
Sportsbooks Ltd
Summersdale Publishers Ltd
Sussex Academic Press
Taylor & Francis
Top That! Publishing Ltd
Transworld Publishers Ltd
Troubador Publishing Ltd
United Writers Publications Ltd
University of Wales Press
Merlin Unwin Books Ltd
Usborne Publishing Ltd
Veloce Publishing Ltd
Vertical Editions
Weidenfeld & Nicolson
David West Children's Books
Wiley
Y Lolfa Cyf

THEATRE, DRAMA & DANCE

Amolibros
Ashgate Publishing Ltd
Association for Scottish Literary Studies
Aurora Metro Publications Ltd
Berghahn Books
Bloomsbury Academic & Professional
Bloomsbury Publishing PLC
Blue Ocean Publishing
Marion Boyars Publishers Ltd
Brown, Son & Ferguson, Ltd
Cambridge University Press
Capall Bann Publishing Ltd
Carel Press Ltd
Cois Life
Cork University Press
Cressrelles Publishing Co Ltd
The Crowood Press Ltd
D & N Publishing
Dance Books Ltd
Dramatic Lines
Gerald Duckworth & Co Ltd
Faber & Faber Ltd
Filament Publishing Ltd
Samuel French Ltd
The Gallery Press
Gibson Square
Guildhall Press
H & S Media
Ian Henry Publications Ltd
Nick Hern Books
Hinton House Publishers Ltd
Human Kinetics Europe Ltd
Indepenpress Publishing Ltd

Intellect Ltd
Irish Academic Press
Janus Publishing Co Ltd
Kenyon-Deane
The Littman Library of Jewish Civilization
Luath Press Ltd
McNidder & Grace
Manchester University Press
Market House Books Ltd
Mercier Press Ltd
J. Garnet Miller
Moorley's Print & Publishing Ltd
Nelson Thornes Ltd
New Island Books Ltd
New Playwrights' Network
Northcote House Publishers Ltd
W. W. Norton & Company Ltd
The Old Stile Press
Open University Worldwide
Oxford University Press
Palgrave Macmillan
Paragon Publishing
The Playwrights Publishing Co
ProQuest
Quartet Books
RotoVision SA
SchoolPlay Productions Ltd
Charles Skilton Ltd
SLP Education
Colin Smythe Ltd
Souvenir Press Ltd
Spokesman
Stainer & Bell Ltd
Rudolf Steiner Press Ltd
Sussex Academic Press
Taylor & Francis
Thames & Hudson Ltd
Trentham Books
Troubador Publishing Ltd
University of Exeter Press
University of Hertfordshire Press
University of Ottawa Press
University of Toronto Press
V&A Publishing
Josef Weinberger Ltd
Yale University Press London

TRANSPORT

AA Publishing
Albyn Press
Ian Allan Publishing Ltd
Amber Books Ltd
Ashgate Publishing Ltd
Atlantic Books
Barny Books
The Belmont Press
Brewin Books Ltd
Chatham Publishing
Copper Beech Publishing Ltd
Countryside Books
Countyvise Ltd
Crécy Publishing Ltd
The Crowood Press Ltd
G. L. Crowther
D & N Publishing
The Dovecote Press
Edward Elgar Publishing Ltd
Essential Works Ltd
Ex Libris Press
Friends of the Earth
F&W Media International Ltd
Gomer
Robert Hale Ltd
HarperCollins Publishers Ltd
Haynes Publishing
Hemming Information Services
Ian Henry Publications Ltd
Imray Laurie Norie & Wilson Ltd
Irwell Press Ltd
The King's England Press
Kogan Page Ltd
McGraw-Hill Education
Manchester University Press
Maney Publishing
Maritime Books
Merrell Publishers Ltd
Merton Priory Press Ltd
Middleton Press
Motor Racing Publications Ltd

NMS Enterprises Limited - Publishing
The Nostalgia Collection
Penguin Random House UK Ltd
Quantum Publishing
Reflections of a Bygone Age
Roadmaster Publishing
Sheldrake Press
Shire Publications Ltd
Charles Skilton Ltd
Soccer Books Ltd
Special Interest Model Books Ltd
Stenlake Publishing Ltd
Troubador Publishing Ltd
Twelveheads Press
Veloce Publishing Ltd
David West Children's Books
WIT Press

TRAVEL & TOPOGRAPHY

AA Publishing
Amolibros
Chris Andrews Publications Ltd
Antique Collectors' Club Ltd
Appletree Press Ltd
Arcadia Books Ltd
Arena Books (Publishers)
The Armchair Traveller at the bookHaus Ltd
Aurora Metro Publications Ltd
BBH Publishing Ltd
The Belmont Press
Bene Factum Publishing Ltd
Berghahn Books
Black Dog Publishing Ltd
Bossiney Books Ltd
Bowker Market Research (formerly BML)
Boydell & Brewer Ltd
Bradt Travel Guides Ltd
Bradwell Books
Nicholas Brealey Publishing
Bridge Books
Calypso Publications
Cambridge Publishing Management Ltd
Camra Books
Canongate Books
Capuchin Classics
Channel View Publications Ltd
Cicerone Press Ltd
Coastal Publishing Ltd
Collins Geo
Countryside Books
Crimson Publishing
D & N Publishing
Discovery Walking Guides Ltd
The Dovecote Press
Ashley Drake Publishing Ltd
Gerald Duckworth & Co Ltd
Eland Publishing Ltd
English Heritage
The Erskine Press
Everyman's Library
Ex Libris Press
Footprint Travel Guides
W. Foulsham & Co Ltd
Garnet Publishing Ltd
The Geographical Association
Gibson Square
Gomer
Gothic Image Publications
Graffeg Limited
Granta Books
Robert Hale Ltd
HarperCollins Publishers Ltd
Harvey Map Services Ltd
Haynes Publishing
Historical Publications Ltd
Hobnob Press
Alison Hodge Publishers
Holo Books
How To Books Ltd
Imray Laurie Norie & Wilson Ltd
Indepenpress Publishing Ltd
Indigo Dreams Publishing Ltd
Instant-Books UK Ltd
The King's England Press
Little, Brown Book Group
Londubh Books
Luath Press Ltd

Mainstream Publishing Co
(Edinburgh) Ltd
Maney Publishing
Melisende UK Ltd
Michelin Travel Partner
Mitchell Beazley
Murdoch Books
John Murray Publishers
The National Trust
North York Moors National Park
Authority
The O'Brien Press Ltd
The Orion Publishing Group Ltd
Pagoda Tree Press
Pan Macmillan
Paragon Publishing
Penguin Random House UK Ltd
Prestel Publishing Ltd
Prospera Publishing
Quadrille Publishing Ltd
The Radcliffe Press
Roadmaster Publishing

Alan Rogers Guides Ltd
Roundhouse Publishing Ltd
S. B. Publications
Sheldrake Press
Shire Publications Ltd
Sigma Press
Simon & Schuster (UK) Ltd
Charles Skilton Ltd
Slightly Foxed
Smith Settle Printing &
Bookbinding Ltd
Souvenir Press Ltd
Stacey Publishing Limited
Stobart Davies Ltd
Summersdale Publishers Ltd
I. B. Tauris & Co Ltd
teNeues Publishing UK Ltd
Thames & Hudson Ltd
Thorogood Publishing Ltd
F. A. Thorpe Publishing
Toucan Books Ltd
Transworld Publishers Ltd

Troubador Publishing Ltd
Unicorn Press Ltd
United Writers Publications Ltd
Veloce Publishing Ltd
Weidenfeld & Nicolson
Willow Island Editions
Neil Wilson Publishing Ltd
Y Lolfa Cyf

VETERINARY SCIENCE

J. A. Allen
Alpha Science International Ltd
CABI
Calypso Publications
D & N Publishing
Elsevier Ltd
Luath Press Ltd
The National Academies Press
Quiller Publishing Ltd
Souvenir Press Ltd
Taylor & Francis

Veloce Publishing Ltd
Whittet Books Ltd
Wiley

**VOCATIONAL TRAINING &
CAREERS**

Amolibros
Bene Factum Publishing Ltd
Nicholas Brealey Publishing
*Cambridge Publishing
Management Ltd*
Cengage Learning EMEA Ltd
CfBT Education Trust
City & Guilds
Class Professional
Creative Content Ltd
Crimson Publishing
Ethics International Press Ltd
Filament Publishing Ltd
The Fostering Network
Gower Publishing Co Ltd

Hawker Publications
Hodder Education
How To Books Ltd
In Easy Steps Limited
Institute of Education Press
Jessica Kingsley Publishers
Kogan Page Ltd
Learning Matters
McGraw-Hill Education
Macmillan Science and Education
National Children's Bureau
National Housing Federation
Nelson Thornes Ltd
Optimus Professional Publishing
Palgrave Macmillan
Paragon Publishing
Practical Pre-School Books
Souvenir Press Ltd
Stillwater Publishing Ltd
Trotman Publishing
UCAS
Which? Ltd

7.2 INDEX OF ISBN PREFIXES

7.3 INDEX OF PERSONAL NAMES

7.4   INDEX OF COMPANIES & IMPRINTS

7.5 UK PUBLISHERS BY POSTCODE

LONDON & SOUTH-EAST ENGLAND

Brighton
BN1 1AD **2417, 3019**
BN1 1UJ **2309**
BN2 1AH **2497**
BN2 1GJ **2306**
BN3 1DD **2495**
BN3 1FL **2403**
BN7 1XU **2020**
BN7 2NS **2299, 3015**
BN23 6NT **2148**
BN24 9BP **2560**
BN25 2UB **2511**
Bromley
BR3 5JS **2116**
BR7 6LH **2588**
Canterbury
CT11 9DA **2451**
CT54JD **2279**
Croydon
CR0 4PA **2204**
CR2 6NZ **2595**
CR9 5YP **2398**
Guildford
GU5 9SW **2169**
GU7 2EP **2276**
GU9 7PT **2036, 2238, 2370, 2437**
GU21 6LQ **2420**
GU29 9AZ **2391**
GU32 2EW **2258**
GU34 3HQ **2486**
GU34 4PH **2165**
Harrow
HA3 8RU **2062**
HA8 7UU **2613**
Hemel Hempstead
HP4 3BL **2475**
HP19 8TE **2320**
HP20 2NQ **3017**
Ilford
IG7 6DL **2331**
Kingston-upon-Thames
KT12 4RG **2012**
KT17 1QS **2210**
London
E1 6NW **2178**
E1W 3AB **2359**
E9 5LN **2386**
EC1A 9DD **2134**
EC1M 5QL **2328, 2582**
EC1M 7BA **2543**
EC1N 8RT **2611**
EC1N 8SB **2114**
EC1N 8TS **2094**
EC1R 0DU **3011**
EC1R 0HT **2013, 2254**
EC1R 0JH **2472, 2527**
EC1R 4QB **2090**
EC1R 4QL **2185**
EC1V 0AT **2196**
EC1V 0BB **2435, 2436**
EC1V 1LR **2338**
EC1V 1NG **2410**

EC1V 2TT **2479**
EC1V 3PZ **2118**
EC1V 3RS **2342**
EC1V 4PY **2399**
EC1V 7QE **2407**
EC1Y 0TG **2295**
EC1Y 1SP **2350**
EC2A 3AR **2070**
EC2A 3DU **2584**
EC2A 4SD **3025**
EC3R 5AT **2119**
EC3R 5DD **2319**
EC4A 2HS **2383**
EC4A 3AG **2084, 2085**
EC4Y 0DY **2362, 2460**
N1 2LZ **2168**
N1 6PB **2533**
N1 7JQ **2217**
N1 9BE **2340**
N1 9JF **2643**
N1 9PA **2457**
N1 9PF **2018**
N1 9RR **2374, 2448**
N1 9UN **2352**
N1 9XW **2375**
N3 1DZ **2552**
N7 9BH **3022**
N7 9DP **2297**
N12 8EY **2171**
N19 4PT **2103**
N22 7BW **2256**
NW1 1DB **2514**
NW1 2DB **2096**
NW1 2FB **2500**
NW1 3BH **2221, 2250, 2251, 2268, 2282, 2283, 2284, 2401**
NW1 4DF **2626**
NW1 5JR **3018**
NW1 5RA **2112**
NW3 3PF **2583**
NW3 5HT **2335**
NW5 4QH **3008**
NW6 1LU **2046**
NW6 3HR **2530**
NW10 3YB **2253**
SE1 0HX **2387**
SE1 1QR **2426**
SE1 2BH **2188**
SE1 8HA **2026, 2213**
SE1 8XX **2266**
SE1 9PX **2414**
SE10 8RF **2028**
SE10 9NA **2535**
SE11 4AQ **2180**
SE11 5AY **2113**
SE11 5HH **2617**
SE23 3HZ **2628**
SE24 0PB **2288, 2468**
SE27 9NT **2564**
SW1A 1JR **2499**
SW1H 0QS **2327**
SW1H 9BU **2512**
SW1H 9EU **2201**
SW1P 3AZ **2132**
SW1P 4RG **2569**

SW1P 4ST **2521, 2542**
SW1V 2SA **2022, 2454**
SW1V 2SS **2273**
SW1X 8PG **2501**
SW1X 9AH **2035, 2262**
SW1Y 5HX **2145**
SW3 4AH **2011, 2532**
SW5 9JH **2056**
SW6 1RU **2334**
SW6 6AW **2363**
SW7 2AR **2502**
SW7 2RL **2612**
SW7 5BD **2415**
SW8 5WZ **2063**
SW11 5DH **2263**
SW11 6SS **2246**
SW12 0DA **2522**
SW13 9NG **2086**
SW14 8LS **2523**
SW15 1AZ **2625**
SW15 2TG **2400**
SW16 1WJ **2267**
SW19 1JQ **2123**
SW19 3NN **2594**
W1B 1AH **2298**
W1B 5SA **2541**
W1B2HA **2156**
W1F 7BB **2516**
W1F 9JW **2252**
W1G 7AR **2189**
W1J 6HE **2167**
W1T 2LD **2478**
W1T 3JJ **2624**
W1T 3LJ **2432**
W1T 3PD **2469**
W1T 3QT **2424**
W1T 4HF **2344**
W1T 4QE **2602**
W1T 5JR **2216**
W1T 6DW **2014**
W1U 6BY **2329**
W1W 6AN **2395**
W2 4BU **2481, 2570, 2635**
W2 4QS **2139**
W2 5RH **2510, 2574**
W4 5TF **2230**
W4 5YD **2567**
W5 4YX **2007**
W5 5SA **2592**
W6 7NF **2054**
W6 7NJ **2313**
W6 7NL **2194**
W6 8JB **2257**
W8 4BH **2108, 2551**
W8 9FA **2272**
W10 6PH **2030**
W11 2LW **2068**
W11 4QR **2241**
W12 8QP **2275**
W14 0RA **2060**
W14 9PB **2072**
WC1A 2JL **2191**
WC1A 2QS **2260**
WC1A 2TH **2462, 2561**
WC1B 3DA **2200**

WC1B 3DP **2074, 2075, 2641**
WC1B 3ES **2032**
WC1B 3JH **2115**
WC1B 3PA **2330**
WC1B 3PD **2546**
WC1B 3PL **2294**
WC1B 3QQ **2097**
WC1B 4HP **2147**
WC1H 0AB **2618**
WC1H 0AL **2311, 2593**
WC1H 9NE **2490**
WC1N 2BX **2037, 2186**
WC1N 3JZ **2041**
WC1V 6NY **2408**
WC1V 7QX **2580**
WC1X 8HB **2531**
WC1X 9DH **3010**
WC1X 9LW **2459**
WC1X 9NG **2069**
WC2A 1PL **2349**
WC2A 1PP **2304**
WC2H 0HE **2412**
WC2H 0LS **2477**
WC2H 8JY **2146, 2234, 2394, 2396, 2430, 2458**
WC2H 9EA **2172, 2235, 2438, 2439, 2623**
WC2H 9HE **2300**
WC2H 9JQ **2476**
WC2N 6RL **2124**
WC2R 0LX **2227**
Luton
LU6 2ES **2093**
Medway
ME1 1JS **2491**
Portsmouth
PO8 9JL **2392**
PO14 1BU **2076**
PO19 1RP **2559**
PO19 7DN **2444**
PO19 8SQ **2632**
PO20 7EQ **2081, 2536**
Reading
RG1 4BS **2120**
RG1 4QS **2222, 2326**
RG8 0NR **2042**
RG8 8LU **2433**
RG14 5DS **2154**
RG19 6HW **2199**
RG20 8AN **2449**
RG21 4EA **2001**
RG21 6XS **2447**
RG27 0JG **2620**
Redhill
RH5 4AT **2461, 2576**
RH12 9GH **2484**
RH14 9QP **2483**
RH18 5ES **2553, 2577**
RH19 3BT **2619, 3005**
RH19 4FS **2150**
RH19 4QQ **2136**
Romford
RM1 4LH **2274**

Slough
SL1 2LR **2009**
SL3 3UF **2214**
SL6 2QL **2373**
SL9 8BA **2538**
SL9 9RZ **2088**
Southall
UB9 5NX **3004**
Southampton
SO24 9JH **2293**
SO40 7AA **2637**
Southend
SS1 1EF **2314**
SS3 0EQ **2372**
SS9 2SA **2402**
St Albans
AL1 1DT **2467, 2568**
AL1 3WZ **2310**
AL1 4LW **2105**
AL8 6HG **2198**
AL10 9AB **2606**
Tonbridge
TN4 9AT **2025**
TN11 8HL **2008**
TN12 6UU **2578**
TN17 1HE **2494**
TN30 6BW **2245**
TN35 4PG **2544**
Twickenham
TW1 4HX **2047**
TW2 5RQ **2177**
TW8 0BX **2291**
TW9 1SR **2255**
TW9 2LL **2015, 2016**
TW9 2ND **2159, 2596**
TW9 3AE **2337**
TW9 3HA **2053**
Watford
WD6 3PW **2126, 2243**
WD17 1JA **2389**

SOUTH-WEST ENGLAND

Bath
BA1 1HA **2450**
BA1 1JB **2098**
BA1 2JQ **2446**
BA1 2NE **2572**
BA1 3JN **2226**
BA1 5BG **3023**
BA1 5NS **3024**
BA1 6JX **2445**
BA2 3AF **2181**
BA2 3BH **2044**
BA2 3DZ **2211**
BA6 8AF **2101**
BA6 9DP **2237**
BA11 1DS **2128**
BA11 4EL **2278**
BA12 7BZ **2280**
BA15 1ED **2197**
BA22 7JJ **2265**
Bournemouth
BH15 2QS **2548**
BH20 6AE **2140**
BH21 4JD **2175**

Bristol
BS1 2AW **2122**
BS1 6JS **2332**
BS8 1SD **2464**
BS8 3EA **2485, 2509**
BS16 3JG **2317**
Dorchester
DT1 3AR **2614**
Exeter
EX4 4QR **2605**
EX5 5HY **2301**
EX17 4LW **2545**
EX21 5UU **2307**
EX38 8ZJ **2333**
Plymouth
PL2 2EQ **2554, 2642**
PL13 1AD **2289**
PL14 4EL **2382**
PL19 9NQ **2423**
PL23 1EQ **2152**
PL28 8BG **2565**
Salisbury
SP3 5EU **2061**
SP10 5BE **2117**
Swindon
SN2 2EH **2190**
SN2 2NA **2409**
SN4 0AA **2045**
SN5 7YD **2129**
SN8 1RF **2269**
SN8 2AG **2004**
SN8 2HR **2161**
SN8 2LJ **3009**
Taunton
TA4 1NE **2107**
TA4 1QF **3002**
TA6 4RR **2138**
TA19 0JT **2170**
Torquay
TQ9 7DL **2474**
TQ12 4PU **2218**
Truro
TR4 8ZJ **2598**
TR20 8BG **2603**
TR20 8XA **2285**
TR20 8XN **2296**
TR20 9AX **2347**

MIDLANDS

Birmingham
B24 9FE **2038**
B29 6LB **2130**
B60 3HS **2456**
B80 7LG **2091**
B91 1UE **2271**
Coventry
CV31 1XN **2573**
CV32 4LY **2303**
Derby
DE7 5DA **2397**
Dudley
DY8 3XY **2493**
DY8 4AZ **2078**
Gloucester
GL5 1BJ **2264**

GL7 3QB **2163**
GL50 2JA **2183**
GL50 2JR **2550**
GL52 3LZ **2600**
GL53 7TH **2416**
Hereford
HR3 6QH **2366**
HR4 8NN **2341**
HR6 0QF **2239**
HR9 5LA **2453**
Leicester
LE5 3EB **2562**
LE7 7FU **2585**
LE8 0RX **2597**
LE11 3TU **2361**
LE11 5DN **2586**
LE67 9SY **2343**
Milton Keynes
MK2 2EB **2519**
MK7 6AA **2434**
MK8 0ES **2048**
MK18 1NT **2277**
MK45 4BE **2322**
Northampton
NN5 7HJ **2173, 2308**
NN7 1NH **2405**
NN7 3JB **3021**
NN12 6BT **2174, 2406, 2607, 2608**
NN12 8AX **2019**
NN14 4BW **2425**
NN17 4HH **2207**
Nottingham
NG1 9AW **2208**
NG2 3BP **2452**
NG6 0BT **2549**
NG7 2RD **2518**
NG7 3HR **2318**
NG12 5GG **2095**
NG12 5HT **2487**
NG14 5AL **2463**
NG32 3HG **2059**
Oxford
OX1 1AP **2380**
OX1 1BN **2348**
OX1 2JW **2259**
OX1 3HJ **2286**
OX1 3LU **2345**
OX2 0ES **2323**
OX2 0EW **2079**
OX2 0LX **2023**
OX2 0PH **2441**
OX2 0UJ **2364**

OX2 6DP **2443**
OX2 7DR **2360**
OX2 7ED **2031, 2058**
OX2 9PH **2526**
OX3 0BP **2039**
OX3 0JP **2539**
OX4 1RE **2064**
OX4 2JY **2442**
OX4 2JZ **2017**
OX5 1GB **2187**
OX5 1RX **2290**
OX7 3PH **2111**
OX7 6RU **3001**
OX10 8DE **2102**
OX14 3FE **2065**
OX14 4RN **2571**
OX15 4FF **2556**
OX16 1FR **2052**
OX16 9UX **2517**
OX17 3RR **2206**
OX18 4SG **2166**
OX20 1TR **2470**
OX28 4AW **3020**
OX28 4BN **2125**
Shrewsbury
SY1 3TE **2051**
SY4 1JA **2480**
SY4 4UR **2558**
SY5 6LX **2579**
SY6 6WZ **2305**
SY8 1DB **2610**
Wolverhampton
WV2 4NL **2203**
Worcester
WR6 6EN **2465**
WR13 6RN **2158, 2336, 2393, 2419**

EAST ANGLIA

Cambridge
CB1 2NT **2137, 2371**
CB1 3AN **2636**
CB2 8RU **2104**
CB4 0WF **2504**
CB4 0WS **2077**
CB4 1GQ **2601**
CB4 3BW **2528**
CB5 8SW **2473**
CB6 2UA **2024**
CB7 4EH **2325**
CB8 0TG **2471**
CB22 5EN **2324**

CB23 7NU **3007**
CB25 9HP **3014**
Chelmsford
CM16 7LS **2455**
CM21 9JX **2384**
CM23 2EJ **2489**
CM24 8JU **2629**
Colchester
CO3 3HU **2515**
CO6 1JE **2135**
Ipswich
IP1 3RP **3006**
IP12 1AP **2589**
IP12 3DF **2087**
IP12 4SD **2027**
IP33 2BL **2034**
IP33 3PH **2195**
Lincoln
LN6 7FL **2591**
LN9 5HZ **2466**
LN11 0BL **2270**
Norwich
NR3 3AX **2005**
NR14 7PD **3003**
NR16 2PB **2193**
NR26 8NB **3013**
NR27 0AX **2507**
Peterborough
PE2 9BF **2080**
PE11 1NZ **2121**
PE11 4TA **2621**
PE27 5BT **2302**
Stevenage
SG1 2AY **2316**
SG1 2DX **2055**
SG8 5NJ **2624**
SG12 9HJ **2638**
SG14 2JA **2524**
SG19 3JA **2006**

NORTH-EAST ENGLAND

Bradford
BD23 2QR **2616**
BD23 4ND **2377**
Darlington
DL7 8SL **2353**
Doncaster
DN35 8HU **2540**
Durham
DH1 3NP **2003**
DH8 7PW **2233**
DH11 9HN **2033**

Harrogate
HG1 1BX **2212**
Huddersfield
HD4 7BG **2339**
HD8 0NQ **2513**
Leeds
LS3 1AB **2381**
LS8 2SP **2219**
LS19 7XY **2537**
LS28 6AT **2292**
LS29 9QW **2083**
Newcastle-upon-Tyne
NE1 3DY **2404**
NE6 2HL **2644**
NE48 1RP **2073**
NE99 1DX **2599**
Sheffield
S1 4BF **2224**
S3 8AF **2192**
S3 8GG **2244**
S13 9NP **2089**
S023 9HX **2482**
S41 0FR **2388**
S80 3LR **2050**
Wakefield
WF1 2LT **2184**
WF3 2AP **2390**
WF4 4PX **2633**
York
YO10 5DD **2082**
YO10 5DX **2505**
YO18 8AL **2071**
YO24 1ES **2315**
YO30 6WP **2498**
YO30 7BZ **2153**
YO61 3FE **2143**
YO62 5BP **2422**

NORTH-WEST ENGLAND

Carlisle
CA2 5AU **2109**
Chester
CH2 2PD **2587**
CH41 9HH **2155**
Crewe
CW10 0HS **2021**
Lancaster
LA1 4SL **2110**
LA7 7PY **2133**
LA12 9QQ **2581**
LA20 6BN **2149**

Liverpool
L3 8EG **2312**
L69 7ZU **2365**
Manchester
M3 1LE **3012**
M4 6DE **2428**
M9 4LY **2563**
M13 9NR **2379**
M22 5LH **2157**
M23 9HH **2506**
M50 3UB **2232**
Preston
PR1 8JP **2162**
PR3 5LT **2590**
Stockport
SK4 4ND **2354**
SK7 5DA **2488**
Warrington
WA4 9DE **2223**

WALES

Cardiff
CF10 4UP **2609**
CF14 7ZY **2176**
CF24 5PJ **2240**
CF31 3AE **2520**
CF31 4DX **2100**
CF37 5PB **2066**
Llandrindod Wells
LD7 1UP **3016**
SY23 3GL **2287**
SY24 5HE **2640**
Llandudno
LL12 7AW **2092**
LL14 5HL **2534**
LL19 9SH **2575**
LL53 5YE **2249**
LL53 6SH **2164**
Newport (Gwent)
NP25 4TN **2431**
Swansea
SA18 3HP **2529, 2557**
SA33 5ND **2160**
SA44 4JL **2236**
SA72 6UN **2376**

SCOTLAND

Dumfries
DG7 1DS **2634**
Edinburgh
EH1 1JF **2421**

EH1 1TE **2106**
EH1 2ND **2369**
EH1 3QB **2179**
EH1 3UG **2378**
EH1 3YY **2413**
EH2 4PS **2242**
EH3 5HT **2492**
EH4 3BL **2010**
EH4 3DR **2411**
EH8 9LF **2182**
EH9 1QS **2067**
EH11 1SH **2209**
EH12 6EL **2057**
EH52 5LY **2231**
EH52 5NF **2367**
Falkirk
FK16 6BJ **2261**
Glasgow
G2 3DH **2631**
G4 0HZ **2622**
G12 8QH **2040**
G40 2AB **2355**
G41 2SD **2099**
G64 2QT **2142**
G74 2JZ **2127**
Inverness
IV15 9WJ **2508**
IV20 1TW **2131**
IV36 2TF **2205**
IV36 2UA **2357**
IV42 8PY **2566**
Kilmarnock
KA5 6RD **2555**
Orkney
KW6 6EG **2630**
Paisley & Isles
HS1 2QN **2002**
PA1 1NB **2281**
Perth
PH20 1BU **2547**
Shetland
ZE1 0PX **2525**

NORTHERN IRELAND

Belfast
BT5 6NW **2351**
BT5 7NN **2627**
BT9 5LL **2029**
BT14 8HQ **2346**
BT48 0LZ **2247**